*Intellectual Life
in Antebellum
Charleston*

Intellectual Life in Antebellum Charleston

Edited by
MICHAEL O'BRIEN
and
DAVID MOLTKE-HANSEN

THE UNIVERSITY OF TENNESSEE PRESS
Knoxville

FRONTISPIECE: *The Circular Congregational Church and the South Carolina Institute Hall, where the
Ordinance of Secession was signed. From* Premium List of the South Carolina Institute . . . *(Charleston, S.C., 1870), opposite p. 42, a variation of an engraving that appeared on p. 253 of the 21 April
1860 issue of* Harper's Weekly. *Courtesy of the South Carolina Historical Society.*

Library of Congress Cataloging in Publication Data

Main entry under title:
Intellectual life in antebellum Charleston.

Includes index.
1. Charleston (S.C.)—Intellectual life—Addresses,
essays, lectures. 2. Southern States—Civilization—
1775–1865—Addresses, essays, lectures. 3. Charleston
(S.C.)—History—1775–1865—Addresses, essays, lectures.
4. Charleston (S.C.)—Biography—Addresses, essays,
lectures. I. O'Brien, Michael, 1948–   . II. Moltke-
Hansen, David.
F279.C45158   1986   975.7'91503   85-15022
ISBN 0-87049-484-8 (alk. paper)

Contents

Preface: MICHAEL O'BRIEN, ix

I: STRUCTURES

1. *The Expansion of Intellectual Life: A Prospectus*
   DAVID MOLTKE-HANSEN, 3

II: LUMINARIES

2. *David Ramsay and the Limits of Revolutionary Nationalism*
   ARTHUR H. SHAFFER, 47

3. *Charles Pinckney and the American Republican Tradition*
   MARK D. KAPLANOFF, 85

4. *Politics, Romanticism, and Hugh Legaré: "The Fondness of Disappointed Love"*
   MICHAEL O'BRIEN, 123

5. *James Louis Petigru: The Last South Carolina Federalist*
   LACY FORD, 152

6. *Poetry and the Practical: William Gilmore Simms*
   JOHN MCCARDELL, 186

7. *Schemes of Usefulness: Christopher Gustavus Memminger*
   LAYLON W. JORDAN, 211

III: SENSIBILITIES

8. *Intellectual Life in the 1830s: The Institutional Framework and the Charleston Style*
   JANE H. PEASE *and* WILLIAM H. PEASE, 233

9. *"If You Ain't Got Education"*: Slave Language and Slave Thought in Antebellum Charleston
CHARLES JOYNER, 255

10. The Southern Agriculturist *in an Age of Reform*
THEODORE ROSENGARTEN, 279

11. *City, Country, and the Feminine Voice*
STEVEN M. STOWE, 295

12. Ludibria Rerum Mortalium: *Charlestonian Intellectuals and Their Classics*
RICHARD LOUNSBURY, 325

Abbreviations, 373
Notes, 375
Acknowledgments, 453
The Contributors, 455
Index, 457

Illustrations

Meeting Street, Charleston, ca. 1860, *ii*

Charleston, S.C., and Its Vicinity, 1863, *1*

Charleston, 1851, *3*

States Rights & Union Ticket, *45*

David Ramsay (1749–1815), *47*

Charles Pinckney III (1757–1824), *85*

Hugh Swinton Legaré (1797–1843), *123*

James Louis Petigru (1789–1863), *152*

William Gilmore Simms (1806–1870), *186*

Christopher Gustavus Memminger (1803–1888), *211*

Townhouse of Charles Pinckney III, *231*

Friends and Amateurs in Musik, ca. 1827, *233*

Slave Cottages West of Charleston, 1828, *255*

Southern Agriculturist, March 1841, *279*

Elizabeth Washington Burnet Rhett (d.1852) and
  Daughter (b.1841), *295*

Louisa Cheves McCord (1810–1879), *325*

John C. Calhoun (1782–1850), *349*

General M'Gowan in Front of the Charleston Hotel,
  1861, *371*

Preface

MICHAEL O'BRIEN

CHARLESTON offers intellectual historians an opportunity. A zealous population has not only restored the most beautiful of antebellum American cities; it has busied itself with generations of antiquarian and historical inquiry. The prominence of Charleston in the political and social history of South Carolina and the South has meant much research and reflection by outsiders. Historians of the South are rewriting the region's intellectual history; to this reassessment Charleston, a publishing center, a molder of literary and political ideology, must be central. Social historians have been looking to Charleston as the home of a planting elite, of free blacks and slaves, of women and the Irish. Urban historians are suspecting that the influence of cities upon Southern culture, even before the twentieth century, has been underestimated, and Charleston, one of the region's most important entrepôts, is proving worth an examination. Literary historians, weary of the dog-eared pages of Emerson and restless with the narrative prescriptions of the novel, have widened their definition of texts worthy of scrutiny, and Charleston, possessed of an abundance of gratefully miscellaneous literature, offers opportunities of explication. Political historians have rediscovered ideology and the legacy of civic humanism, and Charleston, the city state, is drawing their eye.[1] So it is natural that a volume of essays upon the intellectual culture of Charleston should have been commissioned and is hazarded, to survey and to sample.

A preface should not anticipate the discrete arguments of the essayists, who are capable of speaking for themselves and properly wary of letting anyone else speak for them, but it is useful to establish a few perspectives and indicate a few limitations of this book.

It is assumed that it makes sense to focus an intellectual history upon a city. As Thomas Bender has persuasively argued, after the decline

of monasteries and medieval universities, with the shrinking of aristocratic patronage, and before the rise of the academic professions, the
city was "the place of intellect," the object of patriotism and the occasion for effort.[2] That tradition was much alive in early nineteenth-
century America, nurtured by those who reflected upon Athens and
admired Edinburgh. Few places were more anxiously civic than Charleston, the minds of whose citizens were delicately implicated in the social condition and fortunes of the city. William Gilmore Simms once
observed, "To account for the successes of individual minds, will go
far to account for those of the community; and the history of a community, will, in turn, measurably illustrate the progress of its individual
minds."[3] That dialectic has ceased to have much meaning for the modern alienated intellectual, whose city is a profession or university, but
between the early eighteenth and mid-nineteenth century this inter-
mingling of self and city had great force.

It can be concluded that Charleston's antebellum economic crisis
offers the surest clue to the city's evolution, just as slavery is the firmest
explanation of its nature. At the heart of the city's social life and mind
was a change in fortune. In 1790, Charleston was one of the new republic's great cities, ambitious for yet more wealth and power, confident of achieving it and, for a full decade and more, rewarded in that
optimism. But the early nineteenth century brought difficulties. The
city went into relative though not absolute decline, its population growth
drained away westward, its wealth dwarfed by the prosperities of New
York and Boston. Yet the fact that decline was only relative added confusion, subtlety, and ambivalence to Charleston's perspective. Matters
before 1860 were fluctuating, not yet irrevocably dismal, and the city
had not become that place of shy misfortune and faded pretension,
defended by the same "ancient shallow crones who guard the locked
portals and the fallen pride of provincial palazzini," visited by Henry
James in 1905.[4] The guess of declension was balanced by the vigors
of hope and, between the two, emerged a special Charlestonian voice.
"What is hope itself but a happy sort of discontent?" Simms once asked
in a spirit, characteristic of his place and time, that the revolutionaries
of 1776, whom he delighted to celebrate, would have found unintelligible.[5] Yet, it is crucial to observe, the city did grow and acquire institutions of Victorian solidity. Its eighteenth century was, by the civic
standards of 1860, almost formless, shifting, expedient. Later Charles-

ton gained more churches, schools, newspapers, periodicals, societies —more public things. Since the population did not grow at the same pace, it might be said that the city not only expanded but differentiated itself. Organization offered hope of stability and recovery but, more significantly for this volume, encouraged articulation. David Ramsay's generation published very little or composed for the moment of fugitive influence. By the 1850s Charlestonians, like other Americans, were a more systematic, if still doggedly amateur, scribbling people. Indeed the weakness of the city's intellectual life lay less in barrenness of thought or self-awareness than in an excess of producers over consumers. In intellectuality, as in politics, the city and the state encouraged ambition and promised reward, but too many entered the race, and there were insufficient prizes to go around.

It is apparent that slavery, the great fact of Charleston's life, is not omnicompetent as an explanation of the city's intellectual life. The institution did constrict communication with the outside world, even as it strengthened links with the South. It was not that Charleston was less open to new influences, suitably inspected, for her citizens were no less travelers and readers in 1860 than they had been in 1790. The increasing privateness of the city's discourse lay not just in a recoiling from an antislavery world. In the eighteenth century the colonial, and then lately colonial, city had thought that intellectual prestige was earned abroad, in London or Edinburgh, and brought back like a trophy. Cosmopolitanism was a function of dependent provincialism. David Ramsay saw Charleston as the world in microcosm, the two analytically indistinguishable. But by 1860 the city had consolidated its own cultural institutions. To be heard, the Charlestonian no longer needed to travel to Edinburgh or send his botanical specimens to Linnaeus; he could stroll down the street to be published. Being more robust and developed, Charleston became idiosyncratic and focused more resolutely upon itself, by a reasoning familiar and natural to cultural nationalists everywhere. The later writers of the city grew sociological, determined to know themselves and to preserve themselves. Charlestonians, once other-directed, grew Burkean. They might have chosen, in an instantly rational world, a different Charleston, but they came to realize they were stuck with the one they had, knew more closely than in 1790 what it was they had, and were outraged that outsiders should be so intellectually infirm as to defy the logic of historicism for the paltry consideration of a Haitian morality. The city did not, as George Rogers has elegantly suggested, become closed so much as it undertook the characteristic intellectual venture of the romantic Victorian, the consolidation of the local within the rectitudes of the universal.[6] It has always been an awkward business, even without the ramifications of slavery.

It is evident that the estrangement of Charleston and the non-Southern world did not extinguish argument and alienation. Charlestonians came to understand the strategic virtue of solidarity in an ominous world; they preferred that their talent for polemic not be construed as an ethic; they chose "rounded edges." An equal constraint on contention lay in the social amenities of a small city, which suggested indirection and tact. But still they argued with one another, the more so for impoverishment. The city's American Revolution had been a civil war, the most brutal of debates. Nullification was a controversy in Charleston before it was a contention with the nation. Charlestonians disputed over racial anthropology, over religion, over politics, over art, over constitutional theory, over the necessity of the classics, over agricultural policy. Much of the interest of this volume lies in its recovery and contemplation of these debates. As slavery was a consensus, it is a direction-finder for the historian because a tautology, since "consensus extends only to the principles about which there is agreement, and deep disagreement may be concealed by different readings of the same sacred texts."[7] Here, as with much Southern history, a desire to define the shared should not blind historians to things unshared that generated a need for community.

It may be speculated that by its compensating relevance to the slave-holding South, Charleston became an ideological entrepôt, rather like New York in the 1920s. The city imported foreign ideas, redefined and domesticated them, to reexport them westward. The *Southern Review* found its way to Alabama. J.D.B. DeBow of the College of Charleston migrated to New Orleans. William Gilmore Simms became a regional luminary. Charles Pinckney articulated a vision of domestic social harmony being threatened by external forces that, generalized to the South, later secessionists were to find resonant. Hugh Swinton Legaré transmitted sentiments of loss that were to mutate into the themes of the Lost Cause. The Victorian boosters and reformers of Charleston expressed mythic ambitions that a New South could adopt. Much of this influence was accidental. Charleston had the fate of anticipating in its antebellum years the strategic problem of the whole South after 1865: how to cope ideologically with past wealth, present dearth, and anticipated prosperity. But a transition was necessary. Ideas shaped for a civic culture had to be translated into concepts for a region, that vaguer, more metaphysical, more flexible construct. Within the origins of the modern Southern idea was the memory of an older form, the city, a real place.

These are a few perspectives. A few limitations need to be sketched. It is not to be expected of an exploratory volume that synthesis be instant or complete, for contributors are properly truculent. Synthesis has difficulty, both in coping with the lines that Charlestonians themselves drew—between black and white, men and women—and in reconciling the differing methodologies of urban historians, literary students, political historians, classical scholars, social historians. The reader will find much omitted. While care has been taken to consider the three major figures of Charleston's formal intellectual life—Ramsay, Legaré, Simms—many are scanted, though most are mentioned. With a plethora of subjects available for analysis, there are gaps—science, artisans, theology, historiography, art, economics—due to lack of space or of historians. In general, the editors preferred to find interesting writers, rather than to plan the perfect volume only to see it executed very unevenly. We are conscious that a city, though a serviceable category, is not a tidy one, so it has seemed right to deal with the interaction of city and country, and occasionally to permit scrutiny of someone like Louisa McCord who, though she was born, published, and died in Charleston, might have placed her *pretium affectionis* elsewhere. Nor can this volume deal only with the distinctive qualities of Charleston, for the city shared much with elsewhere. A history that excluded the characteristic, because it is not peculiar, would distort. Even sharing themes with New York or Edinburgh, Charleston embodied them in particular individuals and a specific location, a room with a view. While it is hoped that this book will help to comprehend the intellectual life of the city, it does not disdain intellectual activity in the city. Thus the reader will discern two strands of historiographical preoccupation, the traditional history of ideas and that intellectual history which wishes to effect a rapprochement with the "new" social history. Both have their place and utility. While this volume is obdurate in finding serviceable the study of individuals, it is happy to see intellectual history broadened by anthropology to encompass community. It is in community that one can scrutinize the interpenetrations of ideas and social structure, the leading and vexatious task of this generation of intellectual historians.

Charleston, S.C., and Its Vicinity, by J. Wells (New York, 1863). Courtesy of the South Carolina Historical Society.

I: Structures

Charleston, 1851: View from the Ashley River at White Point Gardens, by William Hill. Courtesy of the South Carolina Historical Society.

The Expansion of Intellectual Life:
A Prospectus

DAVID MOLTKE-HANSEN

In 1868 an ill and tired William Gilmore Simms started jotting notes on literary life before the Civil War. "Well nigh [as] desperate as destitute," he hoped to sell his "personal anecdotes" to a magazine. They appeared in the *XIX Century* over the next two years under titles such as "Intellectual Growth in the Southern States" and "Intellectual Progress in the South." The regional scope suggested by the titles notwithstanding, each essay focused on Charleston, the city where Simms had been born sixty-two years earlier and where he had established himself as the late antebellum South's preeminent man of letters. All were intended to illustrate the same thesis, that Charleston's intellectual life had expanded throughout the antebellum period.[1]

In reminiscing before the Conversation Club fifteen years earlier, in the halcyon days before war had salted Charleston's literary soil, septuagenarian artist Charles Fraser had come to the same conclusion. Like Simms, he had had good reason. The development of education at every level, expansion of the periodical press, multiplication of learned organizations and institutions, and increase in the number of professionals over the first half of the nineteenth century had been dramatic. So had the extension in range, recognition, and influence and the increase in volume of Charlestonians' writings. By these measures, Charleston clearly was a much bigger, richer, more important intellectual community in 1850 or 1860 than sixty years earlier.[2]

That Charleston had displayed such signs of growth should not surprise, as they had appeared concurrently in cities all along the North Atlantic littoral and were at the heart of the Victorian justification for belief in progress. Yet outside the circle of Southern apologists and ancestor worshippers, historians have turned a blind eye to these signs in Charleston. Their reason: Charleston had failed to keep pace with Boston, New York, and Philadelphia, the only cities bigger than she at the birth of the nation. In addition to having fallen to twenty-second in population among American cities by 1860, she had not fostered a Harvard, Columbia, or American Philosophical Society; had not become the base for a Ticknor & Fields, Carey & Hart, or Harper Brothers publishing house; and would not garner the acclaim given to the writers of Knickerbocker New York and Transcendentalist Boston. Perhaps even more importantly, Charlestonians had not followed Bostonians, New Yorkers, and Philadelphians from use to abolition of slavery. As a result, it has been easy to conclude that Charleston not only had failed to experience the moral and intellectual progress of her Northern sisters, but actually had become a center of resistance to progress.[3]

Yet recent studies have shown that even ardent abolitionists could be ambivalent or hostile towards industrialization and other aspects of "progress," while slavery's most vehement defenders were often concerned to modernize and improve their society.[4] Despite the polarities in their views, then, pro- and antislavery writers shared a range of responses to the social and economic changes transforming their world. And as is reflected in the similar contents of their intellectual journals, in their intellectual and personal friendships, and in common efforts for a variety of causes from temperance to the restoration of George Washington's home as a national monument, the sharing did not stop there.[5]

It is such connections and correspondences which were to make the evolving differences between the cotton-growing and cotton-manufacturing sections important and bitter. Had South Carolina and Massachusetts not been united by ideology and interest, blood and business, they could not have been divided. Bonds between them grew strained as they tightened; differences became momentous. In the process, Charleston and Boston became centers of growing sectional feeling.

It is this Charleston, the Southern cultural and ideological center, that has attracted the most historiographical attention. Yet the city became a regional center only well into the nineteenth century. In 1800 her intellectuals still had more ties and affinities with Philadelphia and New York, Edinburgh and London than with the Chesapeake or even the South Carolina backcountry. A provincial center of metropolitan society and culture, Charleston could not become a focus and symbol of sectionalism until several things had happened. The rise to dominance in national political life of North-South over East-West divisions is perhaps the factor that has most concerned historians since the days of Frederick Jackson Turner. However, recently there has been increasing interest in the development of regional cultural identity and self-consciousness under the impact of romantic nationalism. The simultaneous building of sectionally concentrated social, economic, and communication networks also deserves further study.[6]

These were necessary, not sufficient, causes of Charleston's development as a regional cultural center. The city also had to expand her intellectual production sufficiently to meet at least some of the South's growing consumer demands, and in so doing, she had to attract enough diversity and depth of talent to give her journals and books wide appeal. That Charleston finally did these things more or less successfully is clear;[7] *why* and *how* are not. Charlestonians' motives for expanding their intellectual life have yet to be determined; the influence of a changing demographic, social, economic, political, and cultural environment still has to be assessed; the sequence or stages of intellectual expansion have to be established, and the place of individuals and institutions within this sequence has to be fixed. This essay offers a prospectus.

* * *

Motivating expansion in Charleston's intellectual life were a strong tradition of scientific observation and collection and such preoccupations as national, sectional, and civic development, the advance and preservation of democracy and religion, and the cultivation of gentility and professionalism.

At the end of the colonial period, South Carolina's natural history was better known than that of any other British mainland colony— even before an explosion in knowledge about the state in the last two decades of the eighteenth and the first decades of the nineteenth century. Charlestonian Thomas Walter's *Flora Caroliniana* (1788) and Pennsylvanian William Bartram's *Travels through North and South Carolina . . .* (1791) were early manifestations. Following in quick succession were surveys of the state by Charlestonians David Ramsay (1796) and John Drayton (1802), Dr. J.L.E.W. Shecut's *Flora Carolinaensis* (1806), Ramsay's and Shecut's studies of fevers in Charleston (issued by the former between 1797 and 1808, by the latter between 1817 and 1819), Stephen Elliott's two-volume *Sketch of the Botany of South Carolina and Georgia* (1811 and 1824), and Robert Mills' *Atlas* and *Statistics* of South Carolina (1825 and 1826). At the same time, Charleston physicians such as Ramsay, Shecut, Philip Tidyman, and Joseph Johnson were following the example of earlier practitioners by contributing to professional journals. However, it is the work of these men's successors in Charleston's scientific circles that looms largest in retrospect and shows most clearly the community's expanding scientific ambition and competence. John Bachman and John James Audubon's *Viviparous Quadrupeds of North America* (1845–49), John Holbrook's *North American Herpetology* (1836–42) and *Ichthyology of South Carolina* (1855 and 1860), Edmund Ravenel's *Echinidae, Recent and Fossil of South Carolina* (1848), Henry William Ravenel's *Fungi Caroliniani Exsiccati* (1853–60), and Michael Tuomey and Francis S. Holmes' *Pleiocene Fossils of South Carolina* (1857) are particularly notable examples.[8]

Illustrating at once international recognition and Charleston's pride is the 1836 report on the "Contributions of Charleston to Natural Science" in the *Southern Literary Journal*. Consisting of an "encomium upon two natives" quoted "from a work of the loftiest reputation in Europe,"

Cuvier and Valenciennes' *Histoire Naturelle des Poissons*, it reads: "M. M. Holbroock [*sic!*] et Ravenel, de Charleston, nous ont addressé deux envois, qui nous ont mis à meme d'enricher et d'[é]claircir, l'histoire des lomotis et des genres voisins, seulement ébauchée, si l'on peut s'exprimer ainsi, dans notre troisième volume." In conclusion, the report notes that Holbrook's and Ravenel's "zeal and qualifications promise [to add] not a little to the literary name of Charleston."[9] That conclusion points to the preoccupation with and pursuit of intellectual reputation and progress in Charleston, both stemming from community cultural values and ambitions.

These values and ambitions were colored by Charlestonians' belief that ethnicity, geography, and history together should define culture. An element in the perceptions and heritage of most Westerners in the nineteenth century, what this cultural nationalism meant to Charlestonians yet was distinctive. Local experience gave special meaning to the common ideal. As South Carolinians frequently noted, they had fought and suffered more in the Revolution than the people of any other state. Moreover, they lived in the only state that had been predominantly black (and slave) for generations. The juxtaposition of these two facts made liberty and civil order peculiarly precious to white Carolinians. It also fortified the equation both of slavery with community interests and of the maintenance of those interests with the community's hard-won liberty.[10]

These equations were coupled with another. "The highest glory of a nation," College of Charleston students argued in 1830, "is oftener the result of its intellectual culture and of the splendor, dignity and learning of its writers, than of its warlike achievements." In a piece commissioned by the American Lyceum and published in the *American Monthly Magazine*, Charles Fraser agreed. "The patriot and the philanthropist," he observed, take the "existence and success" of the arts "as the evidence of social improvement and national prosperity." Another supporter of the South Carolina Academy of Fine Arts, Joel Roberts Poinsett, made a related point in an address six years later, on the occasion of the first anniversary of the National Institute, which he had helped to create in 1840. "The literature of a country," he maintained, "is the vehicle of science, and upon its character the dignity and reputation of a nation depend." William Gilmore Simms would have added—in fact, would repeat tirelessly—that a national literature also helps a country to define itself to itself and to the rest of the world, and that lack

7

of a national literature is an indication of a nation's as yet unformed character. Political independence, he argued, was just America's first step towards national—that is, cultural—maturity; only with the flowering of American letters would the United States achieve complete nationhood.[11]

Charleston intellectuals, then, not only saw themselves reaping—and preserving—the rewards of slavery and the Revolution but, in addition, were committed to advancing culturally the nation their ancestors had helped create. With time, they also became convinced of and committed to their own region's cultural character and future. As New England–reared Daniel K. Whitaker reasoned in the inaugural issue of his *Southern Quarterly Review*, "The North . . . has acted *as* the North," so it behooves the South to contribute to "our country's literature . . . as the South." Whitaker believed, as did Simms, that sectionalism reflected nationalism, as it was based on the same combination of distinguishing ethnic, geographic, and historical factors. With this premise, it followed that sectionalism, like nationalism, should be expressed in and developed through literature and the arts. Charlestonians increasingly sought to do so as their sectional awareness grew in the years following the nullification controversy.[12]

Even on the eve of the Civil War, however, Charlestonians had energy for other concerns. The work of extending education and disseminating publications to ever larger segments of the population received increased attention with each passing decade. One sign was the dramatic expansion of public schooling in the 1850s, when renewed economic growth gave Charlestonians as well as other Southerners reason to plan again for an optimistic corporate future. This beginning was at once a commitment to that future and a culmination of long-term trends. As early as 1712, when the colonial legislature had ordered "the printing of one copy of the laws of South Carolina for every third or fourth white man in the colony," it had been widely assumed that books and knowledge should be generally accessible to those men. A century later, the assumption was being extended to include white women. "In nothing is the advancement of civilization in our country more strikingly exhibited," Charles Fraser wrote in 1854, than in "the enlarged means of female education."[13]

This expansion of women's education was only one of many signs of growth: the opening of Fraser's alma mater, the College of Charleston, in 1790, the same year the Charleston Orphan House was estab-

8

lished; the passage of a state free school act in 1811; the establishment of the South Carolina Academy of Fine Arts, a medical school, the South Carolina Society Academy, and the Apprentices Library Society in the 1820s; the addition of a children's library and magazine in the 1830s; the establishment of both the Military College of South Carolina and the South Carolina Institute in the 1840s; and the organization of the Elliott Natural History and South Carolina Historical Societies in the 1850s.[14] There was also development of black education. Despite laws and prejudices to the contrary, missionaries to blacks in the city taught their flocks to read the Bible. At the same time, free blacks joined together to employ white teachers for their children, and so Francis Asbury Mood and his older brothers were able to work their way through the College of Charleston.[15]

Aside from employment or profit, there were five principal motives behind these developments: democratic or republican ideals, religious beliefs, and ambitions for community development, a genteel culture, and professional growth. "The 'people of the United States,' Charles Pinckney approvingly told the delegates to the Federal Convention in Philadelphia in June 1787, were 'more equal in their circumstances than the people of any other Country.'" Eleven and a half years later, in the last days of his third term as governor of South Carolina, the Charleston planter and lawyer drew one of the corollaries of this belief: the state should establish public schools, because "general information is the only solid foundation upon which true republicanism can ever rest." Agreeing, and at the same time extending this analysis, a writer in the Charleston *City Gazette* for 1812 commended the passage in the previous year of the free school act. Knowledge, he argued, puts a

> shield of defence and weapons of punishment into the hands of the people, where they ought to be. They [the people] feel that they stand in the erect posture of freemen, when they have the *capacity* of judging of the correctness of the conduct of the stewards with whom they have entrusted the management of the estate, as well as the *power* of displacing them from their posts, if they abuse their trusts. It binds all citizens by a lasting tie to their country, by the supervision they are enabled thus to exercise over the public functionaries.[16]

To this democratic hope, other Charlestonians added a conservative caution: the popular mind needs to be led. This was part of the reasoning behind much support of Charleston periodicals. As College of Charleston students put it in 1830: "Reviews constitute a large portion of the standing literature of the day and, as most of them are regarded as of some authority, they will have weight in directing public opinion." Simms also hoped that reviews would serve to elevate public taste and discourse. Though at times he doubted the common man's interest in being elevated, in 1858 he professed excitement at the "local signs . . . in *belles lettres*" of a "general stir of the popular, as well as the individual intellect," and he urged Charleston's encouragement of the ferment by subscriptions to *Russell's Magazine*.[17]

An earlier writer gave a different reason to encourage and hope for popular awakening. His argument was religious: "A person must wear the armour that fits him as may be seen from the example of David and Saul; the offspring of Southern climes need the reins of reason strengthened with arithmetic and geometry, history and laws of God and man, and with the study of true philosophy; the education of Washington was of this kind." A more immediate point in the eyes of many religious leaders was the old Protestant one that had led the Society for the Propagation of the Gospel in Foreign Parts to establish schools and libraries in South Carolina as early as the beginning of the eighteenth century. Literacy is the first step to Biblical knowledge and by the 1820s was a basis for participation in religious community through the growing number of denominational newspapers and journals.[18]

Education and publications had other uses. They helped disseminate practical knowledge and encourage both individual and community development. Urging this point on an audience of local apprentices, Charleston lawyer and legislator William D. Porter reasoned: "You have before you every motive for exertion. . . . Respectability, fortune, influence—all the prizes of the social state, lie within the reach of your well directed efforts." However, he continued, "you must first serve an apprenticeship to books as well as tools, to science as well as art. It was thus that Watt, the humble mathematical instrument maker, became one of the greatest benefactors of his country and the world." Believing what he preached, Porter, like other Charleston leaders, supported the Apprentices Library Society, the exhibitions of fine and applied arts there in 1842, 1843, and 1845, and the annual South Carolina Institute fairs in 1849-52 and 1855-59. Similarly, Charlestonians began the *Southern Agriculturist* in 1828, the *Commercial Review of the South and Southwest* in 1846, and the *Self-Instructor* in 1853 to do for agriculture and commerce what the Apprentices Library was designed to do for mechanical arts: spread knowledge and encourage advancement.[19]

One rationale for these efforts in an aristocratically toned society (however democratic in principle) was noblesse oblige. Others were the almost universal assumptions among intellectuals that their learning should have practical uses, and that mercantile, industrial, and agricultural growth would make possible a more cultured and so more satisfying life than the community could otherwise afford. As Samuel Henry Dickson maintained, quoting German historian Arnold Heeren, "Exchange of merchandise led to exchange of ideas; and by this mutual friction was kindled the sacred flame of humanity."[20]

The corollary belief, fed by images of the life led by European cosmopolitans, by local aristocratic and intellectual ambitions, and by Enlightenment traditions, was that "civilization is PROGRESSIVE INTELLECTUAL DEVELOPMENT." It followed that intellectual activities should be fostered and placed at the center of the civilized man's life. Even leisure should be devoted to pleasures of the mind; even avocations should be intellectual or artistic. As Dickson put it, "The progress of man in civilization, his advancement in knowledge, will be found as distinctly impressed upon the character of his recreations, his favorite amusements, as upon his occupations and serious pursuits."[21] He and fellow Charlestonians, then, were fortifying images of themselves and the good life while pursuing intellectual avocations. This gave added keenness—and meaning—to the pursuit.

The same keenness fed professional development. Charleston's doctors, lawyers, and ministers as well as teachers, architects, and artists identified themselves in terms not only of their social and cultural milieu but of their professions, and they worked hard to expand their professional opportunities, facilities, standing, and numbers as the nineteenth century advanced. Thus medical and law schools and journals began to appear (albeit often to fail) in the 1820s; seminaries and denominational journals were established or supported by Charleston clergy from the decade before; the number of schools and students expanded at a faster rate than the population; the standards of teachers, according to various observers, improved; several professional architects came to compete in the 1840s and 1850s where, at the beginning of the century, only amateurs, carpenters, and visitors had worked; local artists had increasing opportunities to exhibit their work and began to receive recognition and commissions from over the entire East Coast.[22]

11

These and other signs—for instance, the number of works by Charlestonians receiving reviews in national and international journals, and the participation of Charlestonians in national and international learned societies—suggest both the extent to which and the ways in which Charleston's intellectual life expanded throughout the first half of the nineteenth century.[23]

However impressive, these achievements did not satisfy Charlestonians, aware of the even more rapid expansion of Philadelphia, New York, and Boston. In their eyes, Charleston, despite her extraordinary per capita wealth (three and a half times the northern mean in 1860), did not offer as favorable an environment for intellectual growth as did these Northern cities.

Abolitionists blamed slavery's influence, as have later historians. Sometime Charleston residents such as Mary Boykin Chesnut and Helena Wells, South Carolina's first novelist, also thought that the peculiar institution corrupted morals, while lowcountry planters such as William Elliott and Frederick Porcher decried the sloth—intellectual as well as moral and physical—of many slaveowners. The great majority of slaveowners in antebellum Charleston's sphere of influence, however, even those agreeing with such criticisms, considered slavery the very foundation of their culture. In their eyes it allowed those who profited from it the necessary income and leisure for genteel pursuits. If it also let some people sink into mindless and irresponsible self-indulgence, that seemed to them a small enough price. As the argument went, the necessary evil produced (and so became) the positive good.[24]

This favorable evaluation of slavery did not mean that Charlestonians were uncritical either of their society or of themselves. Indeed, their criticism was often pointed. A particularly sore point was a shortage of contributors and subscribers to local journals and books. In hindsight, the most obvious reason is not that the area's population growth rate slowed after 1830 but that Charleston society was substantially illiterate. Throughout the century before 1860, half or more of the city's and three-quarters or more of the lowcountry's population was made up of unschooled slaves. Subtract from the population slaves, young children, the poor, white illiterates, immigrants unable to read English well, and the intellectually uninterested, and it becomes clear that Charleston's writers had to find local audiences and contributors among just a few thousand people.[25]

In the city itself, the number may never have gone much over a thousand. Among 3,777 white males of twenty-one years or older in Charleston in 1830, less than a fifth (689) have been identified as politically active in that year's heated campaign. Almost every resident adult male who has been identified as a contributor to local publications or a participant in local cultural organizations for that year and the decades immediately before and after was among these activists. So were the great majority of planters resident in the city and approximately half of the city's professional men, governmental officeholders, and large merchants and factors, the pool from which came almost all of the city's adult male periodical contributors and supporters of cultural organizations. Add to this pool the women with the education, money, and inclination for buying, reading, and contributing to local publications independently of adult males in their households, and one still comes up shy of a thousand people. Assuming a comparable ratio (one culturally active person in every fifteen to twenty white inhabitants), the 1861 total would still have been well under two thousand, although the city's white population had more than doubled since 1830.[26]

Developing pools of contributors and readers was still harder because the population to which Charleston periodicals catered and on which they drew was largely rural and widely scattered. In 1790 only 8,089 (just over a quarter) of the 28,644 white people in the coastal districts lived in Charleston. In 1830 the story was much the same: 12,828 of the seven lowcountry counties' 47,433 whites lived in the city. The rest were sprinkled less than four to a square mile over an area larger than the state of Massachusetts (which, by comparison, had over fifty rural inhabitants per square mile). There were no other centers of substantial white population. The largest towns outside of Charleston — Beaufort and Georgetown — were scarcely more than villages and after about 1830 "remarkable," according to William Grayson, "for the conservative property of standing still." Observing that the rhythms and demands of country life are different from those of city life, Simms concluded: "Country Life [is] Incompatible with Literary Labor"; "Reflection comes from provocation rather than repose," and "literature . . . is the growth of the city." As he had noted before, the corollary was that planters, like most men of affairs everywhere, did not find much time for literature and other intellectual pursuits.[27]

Frederick Porcher concurred. His memory was that his fellow planters, though college educated almost to a man, "seemed desirous of forgetting and of having it forgotten that [they might have] ever been greedy of academic honours." In his neighborhood there were only "two exceptions, perhaps . . . three, to this general rule; instances of men cultivating their intellectual powers without at the same time neglecting their material interests." Bearing out this analysis is the 1832 census of Pineville, where Porcher summered. Though a number of people in the village took two, four, or more newspapers, and all but one household in eight took at least one, over half the households failed to subscribe to any periodicals or journals, and only two took more than two. One of these, the household of Charles Stevens (singled out by Porcher as that rara avis, a planter-intellectual), was among the 30 percent in the village that collectively accounted for over three-quarters of all periodical and over half of all newspaper subscriptions (but under two-fifths of all slaves and not even one-third of the carriages and livestock). Stevens was, then, distinctly in the minority. According to Porcher, the majority were preoccupied with "field sports" and how "to make a pound more of cotton . . . or to get half a cent a pound more for . . . cotton."[28]

Charleston-reared planter William Henry Trescot was defining his priorities very differently when he argued that to write while on his plantation helped him both "avoid being idle . . . and avoid the reputation of idleness." His values—which he shared with Simms, Porcher, and others—were not those of his planter neighbors, who saw themselves as country gentry; rather, they were those of cosmopolitan literati. Therefore, it was inevitable that, despite his pleasure in his plantation study, Trescot also found the isolation of rural life debilitating and longed for "the intense throbbing life of a great capital—the grace of that exquisite refinement which belongs only to the combination of culture, wealth and power . . . the conversation of all that is famous in the world of men and fascinating in the world of women—the unrivalled opportunity for observation which is . . . the great pleasure of life."[29]

To this complaint, Simms added another: politics took too much of the time and attention of Charlestonians. "The attractions of what is called public life," he wrote in 1842, "have perverted many a fine intellect in our Southern country, from its true design." Poet-editor Paul Hamilton Hayne agreed. "One great danger which has threatened our country, from the beginning," he wrote in the inaugural issue of *Russell's Magazine*, "lies in the ardent, inconsiderate haste with which our

14

young men of talent rush into *politics*." The fault stemmed from the rule of a "despotic custom," under which "every youth of independent fortune who . . . possessed . . . cleverness, thought it his duty—his *mission*—to adopt some party badge."[30]

In this planter-dominated and politicized atmosphere, Simms observed, authorship was slighted as "the work of the amateur, a labor of stealth or recreation, employed as a relief from other tasks and duties." This attitude, he continued, inhibited support of and participation in literary activity and accomplishment. Poet Henry Timrod was harsher. In the twilight days of *Russell's Magazine*, he wrote that "in no country in which literature has ever flourished has an author obtained so limited an audience. . . . It would scarcely be too extravagant to entitle the Southern author the Pariah of modern literature."[31]

Such debilitating feelings of isolation and frustration were compounded by popular romantic notions of the artist's lonely genius, by the social isolation periodically experienced by many Charlestonians on their plantations, and by the geographic isolation of Charleston herself.[32] Though located, according to the old conceit, where the Ashley and Cooper Rivers join to form the Atlantic Ocean, Charleston had no rivers giving her access deep into the hinterland. The Santee Canal, the longest in America when it was completed in 1800, and the Hamburg Railroad, the longest in the world when it was completed in 1833, extended Charleston's reach only to the South Carolina piedmont. Southern rivals such as Memphis, New Orleans, Mobile, and Savannah all developed longer reaches, as did such Northern cities as New York, putting Charleston at a considerable disadvantage in the competition for trade and influence in the American interior. As a result, the city's trade declined—absolutely in the short term and relatively in the long term—rather than growing with the opening of trans-Appalachia.[32]

Cut off to a great degree from the burgeoning West, Charleston was also substantially isolated even from the interior of South Carolina by sparsely peopled pine barrens, miasmic swamps, and the peculiar demands and regimen of rice and long-staple, or sea-island, cotton culture. Such agriculture, too, made for economic and political interests distinct from those of every other Southern (and American) city except Savannah, with whom Charleston was in intense rivalry.

In many ways then, Charleston was a city state inside, but separated from, the larger state of South Carolina and the South beyond.

15

Her closest ties outside her service area, the lower part of South Carolina, were outside of her region; Charleston found herself more and more a satellite of New York and other Northern cities. The fact galled, yet Charleston merchants could not raise the money "to invest in projects to establish trade between Charleston and European firms, or in packet services to foreign ports." Neither were they able to finish the Louisville, Cincinnati, and Charleston Railroad, which started with great expectations in 1835 only to fold in 1843. The Blueridge Railroad Company, begun nine years later, also collapsed, as did the Northeastern Railroad.[33]

Local industry fared no better. Only 2.5 percent of Charleston's population were engaged in industry in 1840, compared with 13.8 percent of New York's, 8.3 percent of Baltimore's, and 5.7 percent of Boston's populations. Furthermore, Charleston's industrial population remained roughly static, even though the total grew. Thus, "in 1860, Charleston ranked twenty-second among American cities in population and eighty-fifth in manufacturing (as determined from a composite measurement of capital invested, number of employees, and value of product), and was surpassed by New York and Philadelphia (respectively first and second in both categories), Boston (fifth in population and fourth in manufacturing), and Mobile, Richmond, and New Orleans." The consequence was that Charleston had to buy Northern goods, as well as import and export through Northern commercial centers.[34]

This satellite status directly impinged upon intellectual activity. As Hayne bitterly noted in an 1859 letter to a fellow poet in New York:

> The position of a literary man at the *South* is anomalous, & by no means agreeable. . . . [the] condition of things amongst us . . . is *such*, as to *compel* a poet (for example), to publish *abroad* [that is, outside the South], if he desires his *vol* to receive the *slightest* degree of attention. . . . In 1857, (of course, at my *own* expense), I published a small book (chiefly Sonnets). . . . *Three hundred copies*, were issued by Messr. *Harper & Calvo* of this city, *more* than 100 of which, now burden the shelves of my library.[35]

Poetry, as a rule, sells badly, but Simms had an additional explanation for Hayne's and others' failure: there was "not a single publisher in the whole South!" Rather, he argued, there were "booksellers and printers, who occasionally issue[d] books" which they could not market, as did Philadelphia, New York, and Boston publishing houses.[36]

The sad corollary for Southern authors, Simms concluded, was that

> all persons, even when most eminently endowed for letters, were com-
> pelled to turn to *quasi* mechanical professions rather than those, how-
> ever native to their special faculties, which promised neither distinc-
> tion nor aggrandisement; nay, which were allowed no opportunity for
> utterance, since in literature there was no publisher, and in art, no acad-
> emy; and the very publication of a book (which might hardly sell) could
> not be undertaken save at the expense of the author, himself, or by
> a humiliating subscription of the funds of unwilling friends.[37]

All the more trying for Simms was his exaggerated notion that friends
in the North were earning their livelihoods by writing and, moreover,
were being read in the thousands of copies. Timrod and Hayne saw
the same disparity; so did Whitaker. Yet there was no need for them
to dwell solely on this question of money and readers. Any number
of other reasons for finding Charleston's intellectual life comparatively
limited and limiting suggested themselves. Boston, New York, Philadelphia, Edinburgh, London, and Paris had colleges and universities
that attracted students from everywhere, but the College of Charleston served principally as a school for those local boys who could not
afford to go to Harvard, Yale, and the like. Rather than import students, Charleston exported them. In this, too, she was a satellite city,
not a center. Likewise, writers and artists living in Philadelphia, New
York, Edinburgh, Paris, and Rome found themselves in the midst of
high concentrations of college, professional, and intellectual friends,
whereas Charleston literati and artists often had many of their most
rewarding college friendships and professional contacts outside of
Charleston. As a consequence, Charlestonians frequently felt the lack
of the density of intellectual relationships available to their Northern
and European counterparts.[38]

That deficiency meant both a relative lack of intellectual stimulation and a heightened sense among Charlestonians of living on the
fringe, in the midst of provincial complacency and stolidity. "We are
a provincial, and not a highly cultivated people," Timrod wrote in 1859
(though he and many of his closest friends obviously belied, or limited
the validity of, the remark):

> There is scarcely a city of any size in the South which has not its clique
> of amateur critics, poets and philosophers, the regular business of whom

is to demonstrate truisms, settle questions which nobody else would think of discussing, to confirm themselves in opinions which have been picked up from the rubbish of seventy years agone, and above all to persuade each other that together they constitute a society not much inferior to that in which figured Burke and Johnson, Goldsmith and Sir Joshua [Reynolds].[39]

The portrait is much the same as that painted by New York journalist and actor Louis Tasistro in 1842. His conclusion then was that Charleston's "literary class differed from every learned body since the days of Noah, though possibly not without some antediluvian prototype." The satire had bite. Indeed, Timrod saw satire as "the best weapon, because against vanity it is the only effective one."[40]

The irritating vanity of Charleston's amateur belletrists dampened aspiring professionals. In Timrod's analysis, members of the amateur cliques were "unwilling to acknowledge the claims of a professional writer, lest in doing so they should disparage their own authority." By definition, too, the cliques were exclusive. As Simms complained in an 1858 letter to his friend James Henry Hammond, newly elected U.S. senator from South Carolina, "A Lecturer, or orator, or mountebank, foreign count, or foreign fiddler all require to be introduced by Mess'rs. Petigru, King, Dixon, Pringle *et id omne genus*," all born in the eighteenth century, all attorneys, and all prominent figures in the Literary and Philosophical Society or Conversation Club.[41]

Ironically, Simms, Timrod, and Hayne, although younger, had also read law and also were joined together in a clique. They dined in one another's houses and met informally with members of the Literary and Philosophical Society in "Lord" John Russell's bookstore. There, in the avuncular guise of "Father Abbot," Simms held forth as benign dictator, dispensing praise, encouragement, criticism, and an endless stream of rotund opinions from an armchair by the fire in the shop's back room. Hayne figured as the organizing spirit of the group's publication, *Russell's Magazine*.[42]

Other circles or groups formed and reformed throughout the antebellum years. Writing in 1866, octogenarian Jacob Cardozo recalled pleasantly the Philomathean Society in which he, journalist Isaac Harby, attorneys Langdon Cheves, William Lowndes, and Charles Fraser, the Rev. Mr. Charles Snowden and the Rev. Dr. Gallagher, merchant Christopher Gadsden, and physician David Ramsay had joined in weekly debate. Fraser and Simms remembered numerous additional clubs.[43]

Whether fond like Cardozo's or jaundiced like Timrod's and Tasistro's, memories and portraits make the same points: antebellum Charleston was conservative, sharply divided socially, and yet very intimate in tone and conduct. These were the principal, intellectually limiting characteristics of the society. All three derived from Charleston's relative smallness, her geographic isolation, and her plantation culture.

As eager for and open to intellectual discourse and new fashions in art, society, and thought as individual Charlestonians were, collectively they were conservative. Their pleasure in modern ideas and developments was offset by concern for the stability and integrity of their small city and its supporting plantation culture. Illustrating the point, a British traveler repeated an observation he had heard in Charleston in 1816: Charlestonians who had celebrated the French Revolution's outbreak in a democratic frenzy had, after the Terror, suddenly increased their church attendance and construction in "very serious alarm at the danger to which religion and social order were exposed."[44]

Social order was a constant preoccupation of Charleston. It seemed threatened on every hand—not just by ideas of class upheaval and racial equality but by the wild allure of the frontier, severe economic and demographic shifts, and the heat of politics. When Simms spoke of *The Social Principle* in 1842, he was voicing a common concern, not only by defining the principle in terms of domesticity and deference but by assuming that this ideal of order was continually being undermined by America's pell-mell rush westward. While a national phenomenon, the rush was felt particularly acutely in South Carolina. Free South Carolinians were nearly 80 percent more likely than the average American to have left their native state in the first half of the nineteenth century. By 1850, when 12,653 people from other states were living in South Carolina, 186,479 free South Carolinians—41 percent—were living outside of their state at the same time. In reviewing this "moving off *en masse* to the West," Charleston attorney, diplomat, and politician Hugh Swinton Legaré wrote in 1835: "Not only is it truly afflicting, for one so much under the influence of *local* attachment as I am, to think of the old families of the State leaving their homes in it forever, but . . . [I]t shews, what I have always *felt*, how terribly *uncertain* our whole existence in the South is." Becoming apocalyptic, he predicted that "society must be supplanted by complete anarchy." Then, with a rhetorical flourish, he asked: "And is it wonderful that we, the haughtiest of the free,—the most enthusiastic lovers of the blessed order of things under which we were born and educated, — that we should feel our hearts breaking as we survey the appalling prospect around us?" Legaré was writing to Charleston postmaster Alfred Huger, but all his Charleston friends shared the same heartbreak and were fearful for the same "blessed order" and the liberties it protected.[45]

The shared fear heightened the community's sense of itself, fostered suspicions of outside influences, and encouraged attachment to local traditions and associations, thus giving added force to convention. Remembering fellow planters in St. John's, Berkeley, Parish, not far from Charleston, Frederick Porcher commented: "Society had formed all nearly on the same model, and the description of one would answer very nearly for another."[46]

Giving further strength to conventions were class distinctions. Charleston's was a hierarchical society, the hierarchy defining the channels of intercourse, the conventions of discourse, and, to a great degree, cultural expectations and values. "Talents, education, morals, with the adventitious advantages of fortune," Charles Fraser explained, "formed the true basis of social distinction." Even those who did not enjoy the distinction were obligated to it. Not only were the hierarchs in Charleston the chief patrons of publications, schools, cultural organizations, and learned societies in the community, but they had many times more money and a considerably larger share of local wealth per capita than other urban elites in the United States. While they did not rub shoulders with hoi polloi (except at stump meetings, fire fights, and militia musters), their ranks were open to all whites who combined talent, education, and morals; partly from noblesse oblige and partly out of democratic principles, talent from below was often co-opted and cultivated. This process so strengthened the hold of hierarchy on community culture that few visitors noticed the diversity of ethnic subcultures in the city. At most they recognized that poet William Henry Timrod and naturalist-theologian John Bachman were of German Lutheran extraction; dramatist and critic Isaac Harby and poet Penina Moise were Jews; and theologian-philosopher Bishop John England was an Irish Catholic. For community culture, however, this diversity mattered less than that such people participated actively in a literary society dominated by Episcopalians and Presbyterians of British and Huguenot extraction, plantation heritage, cosmopolitan education and prejudice.[47]

That dominance extended to (and so delimited the range of) values

20

and their rhetorical expression. Even outlanders who lived in Charleston came to speak and think in terms that were comfortable to the city's hierarchy. Habitual association was one reason: Charleston was an intimate society. Built on an interlocking network of families, it became extraordinarily homogeneous despite the diverse ethnic heritages and cosmopolitan education of its members. Lying behind that homogeneity was a shared set of values. Frederick Porcher's observation upon the Literary and Philosophical Society has general applicability: "The Club," Porcher wrote, "did not require learned men, or eloquent men, but it did require genial men, social men, men who would take an interest in it." This dampened intellectual ardor and cooled, as well as controlled, debate. While Simms and Hayne might resent the fact, they and their Saturday night club were equally participant. Intellectual discourse in Charleston was preeminently and inevitably a social occasion: everyone knew everyone; as a result, ideas often assumed the personalities of their propagators, and debates were conducted according to the rules of social intercourse. To criticize or disagree was permissible; to attack directly or disparage (though done often enough) was not. In attacking ideas, it was understood, one could not help attacking their spokesmen—often one's friends or one's friends' friends. This being the case, decorum, grace, delicacy, and diplomacy often were valued more highly than directness, rigor, forcefulness, and cogency. While originality was permitted, it was not applauded.[48]

Under such constraints some Charlestonians gave up literary pursuits. Simms' "old friend" Joseph Dukes is a case in point: "a fine gentleman, of fine ability, a young man of excellent Charleston family," he abandoned poetry for "more lucrative employments"—in this instance, the law. Another example is planter William Soranzo Hasell, in Charles Fraser's opinion "a very worthy and excellent fellow"; he lived for forty-five years after writing his one noted poem, "Alfred," which he delivered upon graduating from Yale in 1799.[49]

Other Charlestonians did not outgrow their intellectual interests and identities. Yet to assert and maintain them in the face of Charleston's ruling ethos, some became rebellious, others eccentric. The Grimké family illustrates the two processes. Sarah and Angelina Grimké went North in the 1820s, becoming Quakers and advocates of women's rights and abolition. Their brother Thomas remained in Charleston and the Episcopal Church, becoming a successful lawyer but also an ardent promoter of temperance, educational reforms, and world peace. At his death in 1834, the Charleston bar wore mourning for thirty days, while his eulogists explained how peculiar were his ideas. To Grimké, this perception might not have mattered or, what is more likely, might have been a source of pride. However, a Ramsay, Simms, Trescot, or Hayne had a very different attitude. Not one of these men was willing either to see himself or to be seen as marginal because eccentric; they wanted to formulate community thought, not stand outside it. Their dilemma was to combine their personal intellectual ambitions with this public one. None ever felt himself entirely successful.[50]

The antebellum years saw numerous other Charlestonians either give up or not try. Rather than turn their backs on their intellectual and artistic ambitions or accept status as eccentrics, however, they left the city. Art collector Joseph Allen Smith was never more than a seasonal visitor in Charleston after his fourteen years in Europe; classical archaeologist John Izard Middleton deserted Charleston for Rome and Paris, and artist Washington Allston for London, then Boston. Journalist J.D.B. DeBow sought opportunity in New Orleans, as had editor D.K. Whitaker, while journalists Isaac Harby and James Wright Simmons went to New York. Even Hugh Swinton Legaré, who anguished so over the decline of the Charleston he loved, spent his last years largely in Brussels, then Washington, where architect Robert Mills had gone before him.[51]

Unlike the Grimké sisters, such men were not rebels, and their loss was felt keenly in Charleston. Nothing spoke more forcefully of the community's limitations or made clearer the dilemma of those Charlestonians who were ambitious for both personal and community intellectual development.

*   *   *

Ambition for intellectual development was shared by Charleston's Revolutionary and secession generations and by the generations in between. Yet to the extent that there was development, different generations necessarily led different intellectual lives. Not only did new men and women come to the fore, but new institutions at once multiplied and divided, restructuring and refocusing the community's intellectual activity. Complicating the plotting and the evaluation of these changes is the fact that there were concurrent changes in people's beliefs and values, attitudes and aspirations — changes often, though not always, influencing Bostonians and Parisians as well as Charlestonians. Then,

22

too, there were local as well as national and international political and economic developments with profound consequences for Charleston's intellectual life.

One fact dominated the intellectual careers of the Revolutionary generation, "those men young enough in 1776 to have been deeply influenced by the crisis and old enough to have taken some part in it."[52] That fact was the serious disruption of the old intellectual order in the city signaled by 1776. As loyalists, many of Charleston's leading prewar intellectuals—many of them also physicians—fled: Dr. Alexander Garden (the correspondent of Linnaeus), poet George Ogilvie, bookseller-poet-publisher Robert Wells, Robert's son William Charles (another physician and a future member of the Royal Society), Dr. James Clitheral, Dr. George Milligen, Dr. Hugh Rose, the Rev. Alexander Hewat, Lt. Gov. William Bull, and the Crown's cosmopolitan placemen. Never again would British-reared people play the large part in Charleston culture that these mostly Scottish- and English-born men had played. Neither would Charleston ever again give the same relative importance to intellectual correspondence and connections with Britain.[53]

The Revolution also directed intellectual energy towards politics and away from science and literature. Not until after the ratification of both the state and national constitutions did Charlestonians write or publish as much in natural history, medicine, law, and poetry as before the war. Individual lives illustrate the pattern. Both patriot David Ramsay and loyalist William Charles Wells neglected science for politics during and immediately after the Revolution; both later returned to medicine, the subject in which each had been trained.[54]

Despite such disruptions, there also were continuities. The Charleston Library Society still functioned as the chief intellectual institution in the city. Men still met informally at one another's houses, in private tavern rooms, and at bookshops to discuss recent issues and publications and to play music. Religious and political meetings were still the principal occasions for public discourse. Music was still a principal staple of public culture. Aside from memorial and patriotic addresses, religion and politics were still the mainstays of the pamphlet press. Few people were ambitious enough to write whole books, and few volumes were published. London books and booksellers still dominated library collecting.[55]

These continuities do not in any sense imply stasis. The Methodist Church was beginning to challenge the recently disestablished Episcopal Church. The new Agricultural Society of South Carolina was organized in 1785. Four years later the Medical Society of South Carolina began to meet and to publish papers. The College of Charleston finally opened its doors in the following year. Then, in January 1793, a new theater opened, proving "quite an event in the history of Charleston. Theatricals had been so long discontinued . . . that the rising generation [Charles Fraser among them] were strangers to the fascinations of the stage."[56]

Emerging with these new organizations and institutions was a new generation of intellectual and political leaders filling places that loyalists had left vacant and that older men—the fathers of the Revolution, such as Henry Laurens—were relinquishing. These new men were approximately thirteen to thirty-five years old when the Revolution began, twenty to forty-two when the Treaty of Paris was signed. Among their number were lawyer-politicians Charles Pinckney, Charles Cotesworth Pinckney, and Thomas Pinckney, Thomas Bee, Richard Beresford, Major Alexander Garden (son of the loyalist doctor), Ralph Izard, Francis Kinloch, William Loughton Smith, and Robert Tharin; amateur architect Gabriel Manigault; jurists John Faucheraud Grimké, Elihu Hall Bay, and John Julius Pringle; printer-publishers Peter Freneau, William Primrose Harrison, and Henry Jackson; clerics George Buist, Richard Furman, William Hollinshead, Isaac Keith, and William Percy; physicians Alexander Baron, Peter Fayssoux, Tucker Harris, Matthew Irvine, George Logan, David Ramsay, and Thomas Tudor Tucker; and planterbotanist Thomas Walter. Most were British educated; were comfortable with the religious thought of James Harvey and John Tillotson; recognized echoes from Shakespeare, Milton, the Augustans, Vergil, and Horace; went for definitions to Nathan Bailey's and Abel Boyer's as well as Samuel Johnson's dictionaries; and kept up with recent ideas, fashions, and events through such London journals as the *Universal Magazine*, the *London Magazine*, and the *Gentleman's Magazine*. Though American-born for the most part, these young Revolutionaries still lived in Britain's intellectual sphere. As before the war, newspapers gave many of their columns to news of European—especially British—personages and events; only gradually did a more American emphasis in news selection emerge.[57]

The first generation to have its education influenced by this emerging Americanism was that born between the end of the French and

Indian Wars and the British occupation of Charleston in 1780 – the children of the Revolution. By the time the older members of this cohort were ready to start university and professional studies, the Revolution was well underway. In the circumstances, few could – or would – go to Britain for their educations. Furthermore, with the war's end, there was no point for prospective lawyers in going to the Inns of Court to read law; neither, in the immediate postwar economy, was there as much money for European education. As a result, some Charlestonians had their educations cut short or delayed; many others, instead of going abroad, when north to Princeton, Yale, Harvard, and, for medicine, the College of Pennsylvania. Those preparing for the bar stayed at home, reading law with Charles Cotesworth Pinckney or John Julius Pringle.

Because of this Americanization of Charlestonians' education, new patterns in intellectual relationships started to form. Where ties with London and Edinburgh had once dominated, Boston and – above all – Philadelphia connections began to gain in importance. With this shift and the dramatic takeoff of the New York and Philadelphia presses at the turn of the century, Charlestonians also began buying and contributing to more American, and so relatively fewer British, books and magazines. Trade, too, started funneling through these Northern centers instead of running directly between Charleston and Britain.

While not instant, these transitions did cluster at about the turn of the century. Symbolizing the passing of the Revolutionary generation and the emergence to intellectual prominence and political power of the next generation in South Carolina were the deaths of Edward and John Rutledge and the succession of John Drayton to the governorship in 1800. The transition in trade followed after 1801, the peak year for antebellum Charleston's direct shipping to Europe, and was hastened by the embargo of 1807. Other transitions came in the decade before 1800 – for instance, the emergence of large-scale cotton culture, the completion of the shift from inland to tidal rice farming, and the final demise of indigo as a major crop.[58]

In the decade before 1800, too, the children of the Revolutionary era began to enter adult life and a world of novel uncertainties and unprecedented prosperity. The turmoil of Revolutionary childhoods and the economic and political instability of the period of reconstruction were followed by both the portentous era of the French Revolution and a boom in cotton and rice production (and in profits). The latter fostered optimism about South Carolina's and the nation's future. The former encouraged increasing political and social caution, particularly with regard to slavery and mobocracy.

The new wealth ushered in an era of more conspicuous (because more ostentatious) consumption. Dozens of homes of unprecedented splendor were contructed on the ruins of houses destroyed in the great fire of 1796, on fill land, and on the still unbuilt portions of the Charleston Neck. Specialty merchants began to cater to a growing desire to indulge. Leisure became a more pronounced pursuit. Planters and merchants began to build summer homes on Sullivan's Island and at Pineville. Local magazines of "entertainment and intelligence" appeared. Newspapers multiplied, as did theatrical and musical productions. Cabinetmakers, silversmiths, and portraitists flourished as they never had (and never would again). With the opening of the Washington race course in February 1793, the long popular sport gave rise to a new social season, race week. New ornamental gardens began to bloom —not only Vaux Hall, the public pleasure ground in Charleston, but the elaborate walks around "the rural retreats" that "dotted the Neck above the city . . . lined the Ashley River, and . . . were sprinkled over the neighboring sea islands."[59]

In these new gardens at the beginning of a new century, new books were being read. Swift, Fielding, and Smollett were making room for Walter Scott; Pope and Gray for Byron, Coleridge, Southey, and Wordsworth; Voltaire for Goethe. Moreover, the *Edinburgh Review* and, in its wake, the *North American Review* were beginning to suggest new possibilities for, and kinds of, intellectual discourse. Forms of logic and expression and topics of discussion inherited from Addison and Steele were gradually being supplanted. In the process, Charlestonians were coming to define intellectual life not as private conversation or *Spectator* sport, but as organized, extended, and public debate: witness the growth in the number and popularity of debating clubs.[60]

The Pinckneys and Rutledges, David Ramsay, and others from the Revolutionary generation were active in the founding of these clubs, but it was the children of the Revolution who dominated the rolls almost from the outset: physician-naturalist-banker Stephen Elliott, a founder of the Literary and Philosophical Society in 1813; physician-cleric-editor Frederick Dalcho; U.S. Supreme Court Justice William Johnson and his physician-brother Joseph. Then there were physicians

J.L.E.W. Shecut, Joseph Glover, Stubbins Ffirth, George Logan, and Philip Prioleau, all of whom studied at the medical school of the College of Pennsylvania and wrote on scientific and medical topics. Physician Philip Tidyman, after several years at Edinburgh, became the first of a long line of Charlestonians to study in Germany and the first American to take a degree at Göttingen. Samuel and Robert Wilson and Benjamin Bonneau Simons also went to Edinburgh, as most earlier university-trained physicians in Charleston had done. Other authors of this generation in Charleston's medical community included poet Joseph Brown Ladd, mathematician John Mackey, and playwright William Ioor.

Joining these physicians in debate were their contemporaries at the bar and pulpit. In addition to William Johnson, there were Langdon Cheves (who eventually became president of the Bank of the United States), Chancellor Henry William DeSaussure and his partner Timothy Ford, John Drayton, John Geddes, Daniel Elliott Huger, Keating Simons, and Robert Turnbull among publishing lawyers; Nathaniel Bowen, Andrew Flinn, and Theodore Dehon among intellectual clerics. Add to these Charles Cotesworth Pinckney's politically minded daughter Maria, and journalists Stephen Carpenter and Thomas R. Sheppard. The days when Charleston's intellectuals could all meet in the rooms of the Charleston Library Society were over; so were the days when one institution could serve as the central focus of intellectual life in the city. Not only had the intellectually engaged population burgeoned, but its needs and activities had multiplied.

Charlestonians were taking more time for intellectual pursuits. Having more money, they could afford to spend more on the life of the mind. A case in point is that of Joseph Allen Smith, wealthy scion of a planter family, who spent his adulthood in travel and art collecting and was rewarded by election as an honorary member (and, later, director) of the Pennsylvania Academy of Fine Arts. Joel Roberts Poinsett—though he had training in medicine, law, and military science as well as a brilliant, if episodic, career in diplomacy and politics—similarly devoted years to travel and art patronage. Neither he nor Smith, however, went to the extreme of William Brisbane and Washington Allston, who actually sold much of their estates to fund European travels and art studies.[61]

Not many Charlestonians would be as single-minded in their devotion to the arts and travel, though there were some. Of the last generation born in the eighteenth century—the cohort born in the twenty years after the British occupation of Charleston—artist-classicist John Izard Middleton spent his adult life in the salons of Paris and among the classical ruins of Italy; Robert Mills managed a professional architectural career but, like Allston, left Charleston to study his craft and pursue his ambition; Charles Fraser made enough at the bar to retire to his painting. Most of their contemporaries, however, found it necessary or desirable to have a more mundane profession as a source of income and social identity. Thus painter Henry Bounetheau, once a banker, later became an accountant; sculptor John Stevens Cogdell and artist-dramatist John Blake White practiced law. Other intellectual lawyers of the same generation included poets William Crafts and William Grayson; John Lyde Wilson, editor, duelist, and translator of *Cupid and Psyche: from the Golden Ass of Apuleius* (1842); political essayists and orators William Harper, Robert Y. Hayne, Henry Laurens Pinckney, and James Hamilton, Jr.; Hugh Swinton Legaré, coeditor of the *Southern Review* (1828–32); reformer Thomas Smith Grimké; and James Louis Petigru, who revived the Literary and Philosophical Society after Stephen Elliott's death. Attorney William Lowndes was reputed both to have "one of the best" libraries "in the Southern States" and to delight "in the pursuit of letters and general knowledge." Fellow attorney Benjamin Elliott was another "ever curious and diligent in research upon literary and scientific subjects, and always endeavoring, by every means in his power, to add to his stock, not only of useful information, but of mental embellishment"; he was a frequent speaker before local organizations, author of pamphlets and articles, and a student of the classics. Like Legaré and Lowndes, attorney Isaac Holmes served as a congressman, but he first gained local renown for *Recreations of George Taletell* (1822), an imitation of Washington Irving's *Sketch Book* (1819).[62]

Edward McCrady vividly sketched this legal community in a memorial address: "the sonorous voice, the graceful fancy, the beautiful language, and the deep pathos of Crafts"; the "smooth sentences" and "smoother propositions" of Hayne; Grimké's mingling of "the treasures of our ancient legal lore . . . with figures and imagery . . . poured forth in one continuous stream of rapid elocution"; King, who was unexcelled in "drawing from the fountains of the Civil Law, and presenting illustrations from its principles"; Petigru, who "could . . . rouse and attract the flagging attention with sprightly wit, pungent satire, or trenchant sarcasm" and was preeminent "in his scientific explorations of our common law from which to derive his arguments"; Legaré, who knew best where and how "to delve into the rich deposits of other ages and languages, and bring forth thoughts to be clothed and arrayed in gorgeous words and sentences . . . when he prepared himself for some great occasion, as for some literary and intellectual tournament, in which, if his argument shivered against his adversary's proof, his glittering array dazzled the lookers on"; Benjamin Faneuil Hunt, who, "gifted with the power of stirring the passions — arousing the anger and provoking the indignation — and without nice discrimination between law and right and justice — combining common sense, common sentiment, and too often common prejudice — all together in strong and pointed and burning utterances, [could] take the common heart and mould it to his purpose"; and finally, his kinsman, Benjamin Faneuil Dunkin, who "had too clear a perception of what law was" to imitate Hunt and, so, in W.D. Porter's estimate, "approved himself one of the noblest Romans of them all."[63]

The medical and religious communities also boasted savants and literati. Worth noting among the physicians are Jacob De La Motte, Samuel Henry Dickson, Henry Tudor Farmer, Henry Rutledge Frost, Eli Geddings, and John Holbrook, as well as James McBride, James Moultrie, Jr., Thomas Grimball Prioleau, Edmund Ravenel, William Hayne Simmons, Thomas Y. Simons, John Wagner, and Joshua Whitridge. All wrote on science and medicine. Dickson, Farmer, and Simmons also achieved recognition as poets. So did clerics Samuel Gilman and Albert Muller, though other ministers tended to prose. Lutheran minister John Bachman's writings in science and theology have already been mentioned. The Rev. Jasper Adams presided at the College of Charleston and wrote on education. Fellow Episcopalian Christian Hanckel taught at South Carolina College before coming to St. Paul's (the so-called planters') Church in Charleston. The Rev. Christopher Gadsden, longtime editor of *The Gospel Messenger*, became a bishop in 1840. Gadsden's counterparts among religious editors in the Presbyterian community were Benjamin Palmer of the *Southern Christian Intelligencer* and Benjamin Gildersleeve of the *Charleston Observer*. For much the same period (1822–42), South Carolina's first Roman Catholic Bishop, John England, edited the *United States Catholic Miscellany*. Methodist William Capers started first the *Wesleyan Journal* (1825–26) and then the *Southern Christian Advocate* (1837–), before becoming the founding bishop of the Methodist Episcopal Church South in 1846. Basil Manly, Sr., went in 1837 from the pastorship of the First Baptist Church to the presidency of the University of Alabama after having declined a similar post at South Carolina College two years earlier. His successor in Charleston was his former teacher at Beaufort College, William T. Brantly, Sr., who became president of the College of Charleston in 1838, following the example of an earlier pastor of the First (Scots) Presbyterian Church, George Buist, and Episcopalian clerics Robert Smith and Nathaniel Bowen, former rectors of St. Philip's and St. Michael's, respectively. Brantly also assisted in editing the *Southern Baptist* from its founding in 1839 through 1847.

There were numerous other editors. Caroline Gilman edited the *Rose Bud*, a children's magazine, during the 1830s. A decade earlier, Isaac Harby, though a layman, pioneered Reform Judaism in the midst of a career in journalism and drama criticism, and fellow newspaper editor Henry Laurens Pinckney edited a selection of Harby's writings while successfully gaining the speakership of the state House of Representatives. In turn, James Wright Simmons, brother of William Hayne Simmons, wrote more than twenty volumes of poetry, essays, and travel accounts while managing stints as an editor, journalist, and politician in Charleston, New York, and Texas. John D. Legaré founded and edited the *Southern Agriculturist* between episodes as a failed businessman. Edwin C. Holland was an editor of the paper founded by Thomas R. Sheppard, the *Times*, and wrote for the *Courier*. Bookbinder-poet William Henry Timrod reportedly edited the *Evening Spy*, a weekly, while bookseller Ebenezer Smith Thomas succeeded Peter Freneau & Co. as editor-publisher of the *Carolina Gazette* in 1810, to be succeeded in 1816 by Samuel Skinner and Joseph Whilden. Four years later, Skinner became editor of the *Times*. In 1822, Edmund Morford founded the *Mercury*, which Henry Laurens Pinckney took over the next year. Jacob Cardozo edited Harby's old paper, the *Southern Patriot*, from 1817 to 1845, when he established the *Evening News*; through these he first developed the free trade principles also propagated in his *Notes on Political Economy* (1826) and subsequent articles in the *Southern Review* and *Southern Quarterly Review*. "Goggles, Spectacles, & Co." edited the *Charleston Spectator and Ladies' Literary Portfolio* in 1806, ostensibly for an audience of women like Elizabeth Poyas, later author of numerous local histories; Eliza Murden, author of *Poems by a Young Lady of Charles-*

ton (1808) and *Miscellaneous Poems* (1827); and young Penina Moise, later poet and hymn writer for the new Reform Jewish synagogue.

Factor William Christopher Dukes also was a poet. Planter William Elliott advised his son against a career in poetry yet himself wrote plays, stories of *Carolina Sports by Land and Water*, pieces on agriculture and, occasionally, on politics. Fellow planters Joseph E. Jenkins, Francis D. Quash, and John Townsend had less time for letters but, like Elliott, wrote on agriculture in the midst of managing their hundred or more slaves each.[64]

These planters belonged to the first generation to be educated in an independent United States, and the last before World War II to grow up in an era of sustained prosperity. Starting school after the post-Revolutionary reconstruction of South Carolina's economy and society, the generation's members either had entered or were nearing adulthood by the time of the dislocations of the War of 1812. Against the background of such prosperity, ambitions were formed, career choices made, and hopes assumed.

Ambitions, careers, and hopes would all be frustrated by changes in Charleston's fortunes in the 1820s. However, first this generation added dramatically to Charleston's cultural landscape and, in the process, further changed intellectual life in the city. Starting to appear in print about 1800, they were the first cohort in Charleston to write and publish poetry, fiction, and drama in profusion; the first to publish medical, legal, agricultural, children's, women's, and religious journals and critical reviews; and the first to establish medical and law schools, institutes for applied arts, and academies for fine arts in the city. Given these accomplishments, it was an all the more bitter irony that the generation's intellectual life was just coming to full bloom when economic drought and political storms arose.

This drastic change in the intellectual climate had contradictory consequences. Intellectual activity and production actually increased as Charlestonians sought to reform and to modernize their city, to make it more competitive, and to restore growth. On the other hand, many aspects of intellectual life suffered attenuation or politicization in the highly charged air of the nullification controversy; intellectuals saw their horizons darkened and constricted by that controversy and recession, and social relations were strained by political partisanship. People began to feel embattled, thwarted. Optimism began to sour into bitter-

31

ness and even despair; expectations of a bright future gradually gave way in many minds to longing for a golden past. Art for art's sake began to lose ground to pursuit of the practical. Ways of making a living began to preoccupy many who had once deemed leisure the crown of life. Planters began to place their sons in merchant houses again, as they had in the days before the Revolution.[65]

These shifts in attitudes and behavior were only part of the legacy of the next generation, the first born in the nineteenth century. Awareness of slavery and sectionalism was heightened. New Southern colleges reduced the relative number of students going north to school.[66] The West loomed. Many Charlestonians were moving there; most had family emigrating; and all saw the production of new cotton lands in Alabama and Mississippi cutting into Carolina markets and forcing down prices under the weight of a growing oversupply. In a literal sense that took on symbolic significance, the childhoods of such youths were the most auspicious days of their lives. Never again in the antebellum years would Charleston provide either the aura or the reality of continually expanding opportunities on the same scale as between 1790 and the 1820s.

While having nothing to do with local conditions per se, another change would leave as great a legacy. Rooted in the late eighteenth century, the change yet was—and is—identified with the sense of propriety of Queen Victoria. Because of it, the eighteenth-century custom of wealthy men drinking each other under the table on good madeira and port gave way to more decorous dining, and the language of gentlemen was gradually pruned of the oaths freely used by the Revolutionary generation. Thus chastened, gentlemen became more suitable company for ladies. A salon society emerged. Ideas and books entered the drawing room, and lectures became suitable entertainment for both men and women. The sexes went together to Samuel Hart's fashionable circulating library on King Street, and publications aimed specifically at women (although edited by men) appeared.

Simultaneously, society developed reform impulses. Temperance and penal reform grew in popularity and influence, and again women played a new and prominent role in these and in forming aid societies for the deserving poor. Those born in the late eighteenth century were early leaders. John Blake White and Robert Mills pioneered in penal reform; White, Mills, and Crafts pursued care for the insane. White, along with Thomas Smith Grimké and Samuel Henry Dickson, also was an early proponent of temperance; Caroline Gilman was a founder of women's aid societies.[67]

It was not this generation, however, but the next, born in the first decades of the nineteenth century, that grew up with such reform ideas and organizations. Its older members entered adulthood just as the crises of the 1820s broke: the depression of 1819, the 1822 Denmark Vesey slave rebellion, the Missouri and tariff fights in Congress, the 1824 and 1827 depressions, and finally, the nullification question, which dominated the years 1828–34. As for the youngest of this generation, they were entering adulthood ten years later, between the depression of 1837 and the Mexican War. Under the impact of these crises and increasing Western competition, Charleston stopped growing in many sectors; indeed, by some measures, it began to decline. Opportunities for wealth, power, and influence diminished; pastures looked greener in areas of the North and West that were still expanding at the pace of Charleston before the 1820s. Furthermore, there leadership positions were open, and there younger men could rise more rapidly than in Charleston.

Yet Charleston's intellectual life continued to expand and change. New journals, cast in the more modern mold of a *Blackwood's Magazine*, competed with those modeled on the *Edinburgh Review*. A surge of building, following the terrible fires of 1835 and 1838, capitalized on new styles and materials. Artists emulated the recent successes of the German romanticism flourishing in Leutze's Düsseldorf studios. Hegel and Mill became staples of philosophical discussion, succeeding Kant, Hume, and Sismondi. Guizot, Ranke, and Macaulay were the new models of historicism. Cooper, Irving, Scott, and Wordsworth, as well as Byron, Goethe, Schiller, and the Schlegels, were increasingly being treated as precursors, not contemporaries. Bancroft, Emerson, and Hawthorne in America; Europeans Manzoni, Lamartine, Michelet, and Sue; Englishmen Thomas Arnold, Robert Browning, Carlyle, Dickens, Tennyson, and Trollope were the contemporaries. Charlestonians read, translated, imitated them, quarreled with their ideas, and in the process learned the realism and pudency shaping the aesthetics of midcentury. Current ideas of the role of the arts, race and ethnicity, the dynamics of civilization, social order, psychology, and political economy were absorbed in the same way. Phrenology became a fashion. Sir Charles Lyell, Louis Agassiz, and Thackeray found acute audiences in Charleston, as did an actor like Edwin Forrest.[68]

These audiences had all ages, but the majority by 1840 were from

33

the generation born between 1800 and 1820. This was Simms' generation. Its artists included Solomon Carvalho, James DeVeaux, and George Whiting Flagg; its architects and engineers Abbot Hall Brisbane, Edward C. Jones, and Edward Brickell White. Brisbane also was author of a political novel, *Ralphten, or the Young Carolinian in 1776*. Other fiction writers included Simms, lawyer Charles Carroll and his teacher brother Bartholomew, planter William Wragg Smith, newspaper editor John A. Stuart, and Mary Elizabeth Lee. Poets were legion, not only Simms, Smith and Lee but lawyers George S. Bryan, Joseph H. Dukes, and Stephen Augustus Hurlbut, Episcopal minister Edward Phillips, essayist and newspaper editor Maynard Davis Richardson, Edward Young, Mary Dana, and Anna Dinnies. Much of their poetry appeared in literary journals edited by local contemporaries: Simms, the Carroll brothers, journalist John Milton Clapp, Dr. John Beaufain Irving, and Daniel K. Whitaker. Simms, the Carrolls, Irving, Lee, Catherine Poyas, and planters David Flavel Jamison, Frederick A. Porcher, and Plowden Weston also wrote or edited historical works. In addition, Simms was a frequent public speaker, as were Citadel professor F.W. Capers, College of Charleston professor Nathaniel Russell Middleton, and lawyers Christopher Memminger and William Dennison Porter. They and many others availed themselves of the bookshops of two other contemporaries, Samuel Hart, Sr., and John Russell.[69]

Irving and Capers also belong on lists of the generation's scientists and medical writers, as do D.J.C. Cain, Henry W. DeSaussure, Sr., Elias Horry Deas, Lewis R. Gibbes, P.C. Gaillard, and Francis Glover; also Andrew Hasell, Francis S. Holmes, James Postell Jervey, J. Lawrence Smith, Benjamin R. Strobel, Charles Upham Shephard, and J.G.F. Wurdeman. Like Porcher and Carvalho, Wurdeman wrote travel accounts. Like Brisbane, Charles Carroll, and Porcher, many physicians taught intermittently. In addition, several edited professional journals, and Albert Mackey edited a masonic journal and newspapers.

The generation's clergy included teachers and editors as well. For instance, William Wightman edited the *Southern Christian Advocate* from 1840 until after the Civil War, and W.C. Dana the *Southern Christian Sentinel*; James Warley Miles taught at the College of Charleston; Miles, Dana, and John B. Adger were all philologists. Other intellectual ministers included Thomas Frederick Davis, Richard Fuller, Gustavus Poznanski, James L. Reynolds, Thomas Smyth, William Daniel Strobel, and Paul and Richard Trapier.[70]

Simms did not dominate these contemporaries as he has subsequent scholarship on the generation. However, his reputation as antebellum Charleston's—and the South's—man of letters *par excellence et sans pareil* does come from his contemporaries, and despite his singularity he reflects his generation well. Like other members of it, he spent considerable energy trying to establish and legitimate letters as a profession.[71] The ambition was not new: Isaac Harby had had it, and his contemporary, James W. Simmons, may have helped foster it in Simms when they edited the first *Southern Literary Gazette* in 1828. However, the ambition, a leitmotif to Harby's generation, became a major theme only in the next. The paying successes of Cooper and Irving in America, of Scott and Byron in Britain, and of Northern and British journals had fed expectations and provided models.

This expansion of literary ambitions in Charleston led to greater demands on the community for support of local writers and their writing. One literary journal after another appeared: while not properly a journal, the *Cosmopolitan* was issued occasionally in 1833; the monthly *Southern Literary Journal* began in 1835; the monthly *Magnolia* in 1840; the *Southern Quarterly Review*, the weekly *Chicora*, and the monthly *Orion* in 1842; the tri-weekly *Rambler* in 1843; the bi-weekly *Interpreter* and the monthly *Floral Wreath* in 1844; the monthly *Southern and Western* in 1845; the weekly *Southern Literary Gazette* (the second journal by this name) in 1849; the monthly *Whitaker's Magazine* in 1850. As these journals proliferated, the gap between expectation and realization also grew. Charleston was not expanding as fast as her press. Yet no sooner would one editor decide that his "attempt at reviving the dying energies of Southern Literature" was "the last" than another editor would step forward, determined to make Charleston a literary center to rival Boston or New York.[72]

The frustrating effort fueled both a growing criticism of Charleston's deficiencies and an aggressive modernism. It is no surprise that Columbian Edwin De Leon's 1845 call for a Young America movement was picked up and repeated by many of his Charleston contemporaries. After the 1820s, Hugh Legaré's generation often harked back to the golden past in the face of a diminished future, but Simms' did not. Under its leadership, improvements in public facilities, local government, police, fire protection, and public education followed quickly after each other.[73]

These efforts did less for Charleston's situation than did improved international market conditions, which halted Charleston's downward slide and turned her economy around; the city began to grow again. Coincidentally, a new generation was reaching maturity, and the conclusion of the Mexican War resulted in the country's adding large amounts of territory for the first time since the Louisiana Purchase. With this new land came renewed strife over the extension of slavery. Emboldened by growing prosperity—as, ironically, their nullifying predecessors had been made rash by mounting economic problems— the new generation often spoke and wrote of secession as a foregone conclusion. Though Simms' and Legaré's generations had begun to see secession as inevitable, they were more reluctant to act on their vision, having spent many years to preserve the union. The new generation lacked such a history but saw an opportunity to reenact and so preserve the Revolution. That vision and the realization of a comity with an increasing number of fellow Southerners were exciting.[74]

No longer was Charleston isolated, as she had been in nullification. Then, Alabama and Mississippi had been sparsely settled Western states, at war off and on with native Indians. Twenty years later, they supported maturing plantation cultures. By 1850, too, Virginia, Georgia, Alabama, Louisiana, and Tennessee all had urban centers nearly as big as or larger than Charleston; twenty years before they had not. These centers served as foci for new commercial and cultural connections which helped bond a region that in 1830 had, quite rightly, seen urban Charleston as eccentric. Furthermore, by 1850 large minorities in Alabama and other recently established Southern states were from South Carolina. In fact, nearly as many free persons of South Carolina birth were outside as inside their native state, and for every two South Carolinians in their own state legislature, there was one in another Southern state legislature.[75]

These bonds of blood, business, and power helped to establish a sense of and growing commitment to a regional culture. Heightening sectionalism in turn increased the urgency with which Charlestonians sought to make their city a center, to support and encourage regional cultural life independently of the North. Legaré's generation had acquired this sense in maturity; the next generation—Simms'—was schooled in it; the one after that—Hayne's—was born into it. No wonder that secession came to seem natural and inevitable to this last, as to their brothers and cousins scattered across the lower South.

While preoccupation with regional development gave purpose and direction to the new generation's collective life, it was not definitive of that life. A characteristic scientism also touched every aspect of culture, from poetry to theology. Young poets advocated a new rigor in literary criticism and attention to prosody. Science students clamored more and more loudly for a change in orientation from natural history to experimental laboratory work; medical students similarly sought increased clinical training. In turn, students of the classics were aspiring to scientific precision, not just the acquisition of culture. In the same spirit, theological students addressed issues being raised by Renan and others about the significant relationship of history to myth and belief, and young historians used comparable critical techniques in the acquisition and treatment of documentary evidence for political and diplomatic studies.[76]

In retrospect, this generation saw itself, and has since been portrayed, as coming to maturity in the twilight hours of the Old South. Its members spent the last part of their lives memorializing the old order and explaining, excusing, or condemning the weaknesses that had resulted in defeat, while constructing new lives out of the rubble of history. Yet the youth of this generation was not passed in twilight; indeed, the period was one of growth and promise. Whatever shadows darkened intellectual Charlestonians' collective life on the eve of the Civil War were not those of a culture thought to be entering its senectitude but those looming over intellectuals of the same generation throughout Western cultures generally. It was the age of Darwin, Ruskin, Marx, Wagner, Verdi, Baudelaire, and Dostoevski. Whitman and various boosters to the contrary notwithstanding, dark visions of the world were pandemic and popular. Henry Adams, Henry James, Jr., Charles Eliot Norton, Mark Twain, Theodore Mommsen, Nietzsche, Ibsen, Tchaikovsky, and Tolstoi were coming of age. Like them, young Charlestonians saw the Christian world changing at an accelerating pace.

The perception had contradictory results in Charleston, as elsewhere. It fueled anomie, a sense that the world was coming apart, to be transformed into something alien. It fed a desire among many to keep pace with progress and a concomitant anxiety about being left behind. Indeed, Charleston was not keeping up. Though her prospects were brighter by the 1850s than they had been for a generation, she was being outpaced by Southern as well as Northern rivals. In 1845, when John C. Calhoun and Joel Roberts Poinsett urged J.D.B. DeBow to establish a commercial review, they suggested he move to New Orleans from his native Charleston, where he had recently graduated from the College of Charleston and been assisting in the editing of the *Southern Quarterly Review*. DeBow took the advice. Shortly thereafter, Daniel Whitaker, who had started the *Review* in New Orleans, transferred his new journal, *Whitaker's*, to Columbia from Charleston.[77]

National political developments provided additional evidence that Charleston was losing ground. The days were over when the South had nearly equaled the North in Congress, and Charleston representatives such as the Pinckneys, Cheves, Robert Y. Hayne, and Legaré had been preeminent among Southern delegates. Charleston was failing to keep pace, not only in population but in political influence. Secession temporarily reversed the trend, putting the city and the state again at the center of national and regional affairs and laying anomie and anxiety to rest, for by taking action, Charlestonians were at once satisfying the desire to change and the desire to maintain the old order. The city's feeling—however temporarily—was one of relief, joy, and confidence. British journalist William Howard Russell called it "elation." Though apprehending a "black cloud ahead," Mary Boykin Chesnut described the atmosphere as "phospherescent" and added several days later: "I did not know that one could live such days of excitement."[78]

Her husband James, U.S. senator from South Carolina on the eve of secession, was of Simms' generation, but Mrs. Chesnut belonged to the next, which largely filled the ranks of the Confederate military and so lost many of its most productive members and year to war and defeat. Despite the brevity of its antebellum career, however, it produced nineteenth-century Charleston's most acclaimed poets, most scintillating women writers, most important historians since Ramsay, and, in *Russell's Magazine*, most celebrated literary journal. Joining older writers and journals in the 1850s, they made the decade the most brilliant in Charleston's intellectual life since the ten years preceding nullification.

The poets of Mrs. Chesnut's generation included, most notably, Timrod, Hayne, and James M. Legaré, but also lawyer-planter Joseph Blyth Allston, Dr. John Dickson Bruns, Caroline Augusta Rutledge Ball, teachers Joseph Brownlee Brown and William James Rivers, and Mary (wife of Daniel K.) Whitaker. Brown, in addition, was a classicist, a translator of Homer. Fellow classicists included William Porcher Miles and Basil Lanneau Gildersleeve, the greatest American classical scholar of his day. Both Miles and Gildersleeve also wrote essays on historical and literary subjects for the intellectual journals. Other writers on these subjects included John Peyre Thomas, teacher Gabriel E. Manigault, mathematician-teacher John McCrady, bookman-politician-industrialist William Ashmead Courtenay, the Rev. Henry Allen Tupper, the Rev. Ellison Capers, the Rev. John Johnson, and lawyers Wilmot Gibbes DeSaussure, Thomas Middleton Hanckel, Arthur Mazyck, and James Johnston Pettigrew. However, it was William Henry Trescot, pioneering historian of American diplomacy; Edward McCrady and William James Rivers, historians of colonial and Revolutionary South Carolina; and Harriott Horry Ravenel, biographer and historian of Charleston, whose historical works would receive the widest acclaim.[79]

Mrs. Ravenel was also a fictionist and in this typical of her contemporaries: Mary Chesnut, Essie Cheesborough, Susan Petigru King, Caroline Howard Gilman Jervey, and Ada (McElhenney) Clare, the actress. Economist-editor J.D.B. DeBow, too, belonged to this generation, as did theologians and educators James P. Boyce, C.P. Gadsden, John L. Girardeau, A. Toomer Porter, and Edwin T. Winkler; artists John Beaufain Irving, Jr. and William Aiken Walker; architects and engineers Louis Barbot, Edward Benjamin Bryan, and Francis D. Lee; student editor and later diplomat Julian Mitchell, and lawyers Thomas Caute Reynolds and Henry Laurens Pinckney, Jr. Joining them were a score or more of physicians, the more prominent medical writers and editors among them including Bruns, Simon Baruch, John Somers Buist, Julian John Chisolm, Christopher Happoldt, Alexander Kinloch, Samuel Logan, Thomas Jefferson McKie, Joseph Hinson Mellichamp, and Richard and William Michel; also Francis Turquand Miles, Francis LeJau Parker, Francis Peyre Porcher, Jacob Ford Prioleau, Theodore Thomas, and Octavius Augustus White. Mellichamp, William Michel, and Porcher in addition made contributions to botany—which, with allied fields in natural history, was almost the only area where Charleston-based scientists could still make their mark, given the city's lack of facilities for the physical sciences.[80]

Many of these physicians did postgraduate work in Europe, especially in France. Others of their contemporaries studied art, law, and philology in Germany. Many without European education had the grand tour or diplomatic posting in Europe. In the wake of the failed revolutions of 1848, this cosmopolitan experience gave Charlestonians reason to be at once grateful and apprehensive for their own Revolutionary heritage. In the midst of the subsequent nationalist struggles, they also had reason to pause and consider where and how to place their own allegiance. Charlestonians, like other Southerners, began to concentrate those attachments more narrowly and specifically, restricting them increasingly to their own region and culture. Their cosmopolitan experiences thus encouraged them to elevate this provincial identity to the central place it had for them at the outbreak of the Civil War. By this elevation, they became provincial in a way that their colonial ancestors could not have imagined.

*   *   *

Ardent to maintain the Revolution as well as develop a Southern nation, the Civil War generation in Charleston yet was intellectually far removed from the Founding Fathers. Not only had intellectual life expanded, but its content and structure had changed. The Revolutionary generation had treated their community as an intellectual outpost of London and Edinburgh. Eighty years later, she had more business ties with Liverpool, more collegiate ones with Boston and Columbia, and more subscriptions to New York and Philadelphia journals; moreover, her intellectuals were now mostly native—not immigrant, as formerly. Perforce, then, Charleston's intellectual population by 1860 was substantially less diverse, less cosmopolitan than in 1760. It was also less representative of the United States: while many of the most prominent Charleston intellectuals of Legaré's generation—Bachman and the Gilmans, for instance—were from the North, most of Hayne's intellectual contemporaries in the city were Charlestonians by birth; indeed, this generation did not even have the same infusions from the South Carolina upcountry as Legaré's generation. Instead of following Langdon Cheves and James Louis Petigru to Charleston, ambitious countrymen were moving west or to Columbia.

Yet while Charleston's intellectual population was increasingly parochial and homogeneous in its origins, with each passing generation its members had more cultural enterprises in which to participate. The result was that a Charlestonian of 1860 could share more specialized, focused, and varied interests and activities than could his Revolutionary ancestors and could do so at more levels. Yet he had more competition and, as knowledge expanded, his contributions declined in relative value. It followed that one had to master more knowledge, spend more time, become more specialized to contribute at all. While in 1760, or even 1820, the gap between amateur and professional was relatively small in many fields, by 1860 it was becoming a rift. But Charleston was not large enough to support a substantial community of specialized intellectuals. The infrastructure of universities, art academies, laboratories, seminaries, and publishing houses was not there. To function within Charleston, intellectuals could specialize more than their ancestors, but not as much as their contemporaries in Boston and New York. The city's intellectual life had expanded, but at a slower rate: hence historians' and literary scholars' persistent, if misleading, perception of antebellum Charleston's intellectual decline.

This perception notwithstanding, the city was regionally a much more influential intellectual center in 1860 than in 1760 or 1830. On the eve of the Revolution, Charleston was a remote and isolated outpost: the periodicals received or published over any month could be read easily in a day; her largest library was as easily housed in a private residence; the nearest college was four hundred miles away and the nearest medical school almost twice as far.[81] By the time of the nullification crisis, the situation had improved dramatically. Charleston had both a college (of sorts) and a medical school. The Charleston Library Society's quarters had expanded, as had its holdings. There were corresponding schools and learned institutions in piedmont South Carolina as well as neighboring North Carolina and Georgia, so Charleston intellectuals had nearby counterparts with whom to share interests and activities. This, in turn, made subscription publications such as Elliott and Legaré's *Southern Review* appear possible.[82]

Gradually the intellectual outpost had become a productive center. By the 1840s, Simms and other Charlestonians were being invited to address colleges and learned societies in the Southwest as well as the East. Charleston periodicals were circulating beyond the Mississippi and were receiving contributions from St. Louis and New Orleans as well as Baltimore and New York, and Charlestonians were helping to found national professional and cultural institutions.[83]

Until recently, these aspects of the city's intellectual expansion have been neglected by scholarship because of Charleston's role in the elaboration of Southern cultural identity. Most leading Southern nationalists were not Charlestonians, but no other community devoted as much print and talent over as long a time to the idea of a Southern culture. Consequently, North and South alike would think it fitting that the first secession ordinance was signed in Charleston and that the first shots of the Civil War were fired there. The city's press and writers had made her the region's symbolic as well as actual cultural center, the "capital of Southern Civilization."[84]

But this development hid paradoxes. By almost any standard, Charleston was not typical of the South. Throughout colonial history, she was the only relatively populous urban center in her region. After independence she still based her economy on crops that were raised nowhere else in the South. The percentage of slaves in her hinterland's population was greater than in most comparable areas within the region, and the average size of slaveholdings was correspondingly higher. As Michael Johnson has observed, in 1860 "the wealth of the Charleston planters put them in the top 2 percent of the adult male population" in the South, "which contained by far the largest share of the nation's economic elite."[85]

In these respects, Charleston represented an extreme — not the norm — even within the plantation South, and so is deemed the epitome of plantation culture. But Charleston not only steadily lost economic and political power to the Southwest; she also saw a shrinking of plantation production and slave population in her immediate hinterland. Moreover, planters never dominated the city, whether intellectually, economically, or politically; in 1860 as in 1760, the richest men were principally merchants and factors, and there were as many wealthy lawyers as planters. Most people who contributed to Charleston periodicals defined themselves as lawyers, doctors, ministers, teachers, journalists, editors — not planters, although many owned plantations. Similarly, the professional classes held the great majority of Charleston's political offices.[86]

This anomaly of urban professionals representing the plantocracy cannot be explained entirely by genealogy. Many Charleston intellectuals came from or became allied with planter families, but others did not. Nor, as the nullification controversy showed, did the mere social dominance of the planter class explain the anomaly. Planters, like others, were divided in their perceptions of their interests.[87]

A now classic essay by Robert Redfield and Milton Singer, "The Cultural Role of Cities," suggests a resolution of this paradox. Cities, the essay argues, have had two cultural roles, serving either as centers of local culture or as foci of metropolitan culture. In the former case, urban intellectuals have sought to elaborate and codify the local traditions and norms shared with a city's hinterland. In the latter case, the urban intellectual has cast himself as a bearer of foreign or ecumenical standards and often acted as "the reformer, the agitator . . . the missionary and the imported school teacher."[88]

Antebellum Charleston saw many such actors, but their relative number and influence declined over time, as did the volume and importance of Charleston's international trade. Following independence, and spurred by emerging romantic notions of culture and community, Charleston consciously turned her back on her colonial, metropolitan heritage and sought to develop as a center of indigenous civilization. Impelled thus by the nationalist and sectionalist ambitions of her citizens and aided by demographic and economic changes, the once heterodox imperial enclave became a center, and perhaps the principal focus, of regional culture and orthodoxy.

From this perspective, Simms appears justified in having given such titles as "Intellectual Growth in the Southern States" and "Intellectual Progress in the South" to his reminiscences of antebellum Charleston's literary life. Expansion in this sector had made possible, as it had reflected, his and others' belief in Southern civilization. Progress towards realizing that belief, in turn, had fundamentally altered Charleston's intellectual life and significance. Ironically, by codifying and elaborating their culture, Charlestonians had transformed it. To the extent that they had given voice to the plantation South, they had urbanized— civilized—the planter regime. To the same extent, however, they had also become provincial in their own and others' eyes.

There was a further tradeoff. As the city came to see herself and be seen as a sectional intellectual center, her intellectuals gained in local and regional recognition, but at a price. Intent on reaching the developing Southern audiences, they emphasized Southern interests, adopted a more consciously Southern point of view, thus reducing their appeal to national and international audiences.[89] This was not because Charlestonians did not care about these more distant audiences. Rather their first priority was to escape colonial dependence on distant metropolises for intellectual succor. They wanted to develop a full intellectual life of their own and, faced with negotiating the rising tide of antislavery sentiment, thought they had found in sectionalism an appropriate vessel.

Had the vessel not foundered, Charleston's intellectuals might not have sunk into virtual oblivion. As it is, however, historians often want to know little more of them than why it was they were intent on such a misguided voyage in such an unseaworthy craft. So long as the presuppositions behind this question shape scholars' interests, the Charleston of the essays in this volume will remain submerged. To change metaphors, the city's sectionalism will continue to upstage her other interests, and so the majority of the preoccupations of antebellum Charleston's intellectuals will continue to be ignored or disparaged.

From James Petigru Carson, *Life, Letters and Speeches of James Louis Petigru . . .*
(Washington, D.C., 1920), opposite p. 96. Courtesy
of the South Carolina Historical Society.

II: Luminaries

David Ramsay and the Limits of Revolutionary Nationalism

ARTHUR H. SHAFFER

I T was early Saturday afternoon, 6 May 1815. Dr. David Ramsay, born in Lancaster County, Pennsylvania, but long a resident of Charleston, was strolling down Broad Street. Within sight of his residence, he was passed by William Linnen, a tailor who nursed grudges against lawyers, judges, and juries in his unsuccessful lawsuits and against Drs. Ramsay and Benjamin Simons for having declared him legally insane. As Ramsay passed, Linnen took "a large horseman's pistol out of a handkerchief . . . [and] shot the doctor in the back." Friends carried the wounded man home where he declared that he was "not afraid to die;

but should that be my fate, I call on all here present to bear witness, that I consider the unfortunate perpetrator of this deed a lunatic, and free from guilt." After lingering two days, on Monday the 8th at about seven in the morning, David Ramsay, aged sixty-six, died. The societies of which he was a member resolved "to wear mourning for thirty days; a funeral sermon was preached by the Rev. Mr. Palmer; and a public eulogium was delivered by Robert Y. Hayne, Esq. by appointment of The Literary and Philosophical Society of South Carolina."[1]

Best known as historian, Ramsay can be said without exaggeration to have created American history. Among his contemporaries he stands out, singular not only for his productivity — six major and several minor historical works — but for having been the first to compose histories designed to "rub off asperities and mould us into a homogeneous people."[2] If any one work marked the beginnings of American national historiography, it was Ramsay's *History of the American Revolution* (1789), the major event in the development of a distinctly national historical consciousness. It stood as a prototype for scholars of his generation, and he quickly became the nation's most respected historian. "America has produced a Ramsay," exulted James K. Polk, who read Ramsay's history as a student at the University of North Carolina. He is "the Tacitus of this western hemisphere to transmit to posterity in the unpolished language of truth, the spirit of liberty which actuated the first founders of our republic."[3]

By the day of his death Ramsay was loved and respected, the grand old man of Charleston's cultural life, the recognized leader of the town's intellectual elite, a proud symbol of the community's achievements and ambitions. A newer, younger group stood ready to fill the void left by his death and that of many of his colleagues. Their world was rapidly changing and would be very different from his: romanticism and sectionalism were replacing Enlightenment ideals and the nationalism of his generation. Ramsay's death, then, marked not only the passing of a generation, but the end of an era. Perhaps he understood. In his own time he had symbolized the birth of a new era. The Revolution had virtually shattered the old intellectual order. There was, to be sure, much continuity with the past in both ideas and personnel, but independence necessitated a new political and intellectual agenda: to define an American identity, culture, political ideology, and institutions within the framework of something entirely new — an American nation-state. Entering the cosmopolitan world of Charleston on the eve of independence, Ramsay was well suited by background, education, experience, and philosophical commitment to embody that new man of the Revolution, a nationalist. Eager to promote a sense of common cultural and political identity out of thirteen disparate colonies, it was Ramsay the ardent nationalist who became a leading American and the chief Charleston spokesman for his generation of intellectuals.

The brave new world of cultural and political unity that Ramsay labored to create would elude him. Increasingly he would feel the strictures imposed by reality on his revolutionary vision. Despite real strides toward creating a national life, particularism would remain a stumbling block. Paradoxically, as the next generation would discover, sectional and national sentiment seemed to grow proportionately. Seen in this perspective, Ramsay's assassin may have done him a favor. Although Ramsay already had come to terms with the ethic of particularism—indeed, had attempted to absorb it within a nationalist framework—he still would have been deeply disturbed by the Missouri controversy and the nullification crisis. Undoubtedly he would have despaired over the demise of his revolutionary nationalist dream.

At his death, then, Ramsay's intellectual world was past. Yet the development and transformation of his ideas exemplify the patterns of thought common to less prolific but no less thoughtful contemporaries in Charleston. Ramsay's life spanned three of the five antebellum generations defined by David Moltke-Hansen in the foregoing essay.[4] A scholar of national and international renown from the 1780s until 1815, he was the town's most respected intellectual during the second and third. This is not to say that he is that elusive representative man, or that all educated Charlestonians can be conveniently categorized. But within the boundaries of his individual creativity and personality, he closely approximated the most salient characteristics of the Charleston intellectual community that he came to lead.

*   *   *

The David Ramsay who arrived in Charleston in 1774 was a Princeton graduate (1765), fresh from medical school at the College of Philadelphia, eager to succeed professionally and to make his mark in the world of intellect. Apparently he was pleased with the prospects; within a few months he reported to Benjamin Rush, "I am disposed to be thankful both to God & man for settling me in Charleston where I hope I shall be able to be of some good to the public, & especially

49

myself."[5] He was "of some good" to both in a city as cosmopolitan as the Philadelphia he had just left. While Charleston could not boast a Franklin or a Rush, the intellectually active there included a higher percentage of British-born and European- and British-educated than in any other American city. That statistic and the nature of the Carolina economy set the tone for the cultural life of pre-independence Charleston. An important provincial center and an integral part of a larger imperial economy, the city had ties throughout the empire—in England and Scotland, in North America and the West Indies.

Charleston's most intellectually dynamic element was the medical profession. Few among them became wealthy, and the state of medicine in the eighteenth century offered little satisfaction or sense of achievement to practitioners, who were therefore eager to pursue a more stimulating career in science and letters. Fortifying this zeal, at least for the privileged who had studied at Leyden or Edinburgh, was training in natural history. Since the more talented and educated among physicians sought the stimulation of intellectual achievement, they looked for recognition from the intellectual centers of Great Britain and the North.[6] Consequently, some kept up their contacts with European and American medical centers and joined what Brooke Hindle has called "an international circle devoted to the cultivation of natural History, which was one of the most dynamic intellectual forces in Europe and America."[7]

From the days of Mark Catesby to André Michaux, South Carolinians corresponded with those in England, Scotland, Holland, Sweden, Germany, France, Philadelphia, and New York who were interested in natural history. Dr. John Lining, a pupil of the legendary Boerhaave at Leyden, conducted experiments to establish the connection between weather conditions and diseases. Dr. Lionel Chalmers of St. Andrews University, who worked closely with Lining, wrote *An Account of the Weather and Diseases of South Carolina.* Chalmers' best known work, *Essay on Fevers,* was published in Charleston in 1767, in London in 1768, and in Riga in 1773. In 1774 the town's most renowned scientist was Dr. Alexander Garden, a botanist trained in Aberdeen and at Edinburgh and a member of the Royal Society of London. Otranto, his plantation at Goose Creek, was a botanical laboratory whose results were published in the proceedings of the Royal Society. Garden regularly corresponded as well with the Royal Society of Arts in London and such individuals as Cadwallader Colden of New York, Peter

Collinson of London, and Carolus Linnaeus of Sweden, the most celebrated naturalist of the eighteenth century.[8]

This was the world Ramsay entered and helped change through his native ability, learning, energy, and zeal. The change says as much about Charleston's Revolutionary generation and the circumstances of intellectual life in Revolutionary America as it does about Ramsay's considerable talent. Independence took its toll. Many of the community's intellectuals, especially physicians, were loyalists, who departed. Among the Whigs who remained, most had been educated abroad. The sons of Carolina merchants and planters formed the largest group of American students abroad on the eve of the Revolution. Though American-born for the most part, the Revolutionaries still resided in Britain's intellectual sphere.[9] Yet never again would the British-oriented predominate as they had before the Revolution, and in time their influence would virtually disappear. As the political focus shifted from Britain to America, so did the cultural center of gravity. Ramsay was ideally suited to exploit that shift, to help reorient Charleston to a new cosmopolitanism. That this cosmopolitanism encouraged a nationalistic bias in a community still wedded to the universal ideal of the Enlightenment is one of the paradoxes of the early national period.

Ramsay was neither educated in nor personally tied to Britain and Europe. Schooled in Radical Whig ideology, revolutionary republicanism, and reformist idealism at Princeton, in Philadelphia, and at the side of his friend and medical mentor, Dr. Benjamin Rush, he developed an enthusiasm for independence, dreams of liberating the creative energies of a republican society, and an almost mystical conviction that events in America were a turning point in world history. It was during those formative years that the seeds of his nationalism were planted. The founders of the College of New Jersey had envisioned and partially succeeded in creating a broadly based institution that would draw students from throughout North America. The philosophical basis of the curriculum reflected a desire to produce selfless rulers for a reformed colonial society. While they had no precise political program to fulfill their vision, they did promote a sense of a common American destiny. These ideals and the experience of fellowship with young men from all over the continent laid the foundation for Ramsay's sense of national identity.[10]

What had been largely visionary at Princeton took on more concrete reality during Ramsay's years in Philadelphia as a medical student (1770–73), later as a visitor (1781–82, 1789), and as a member of the Continental Congress (1782–83, 1785–86). Philadelphia came close to being an American intellectual capital where something akin to a provincial American culture was already emerging. It provided him with a model for an American republic of letters. There he associated with medical students from throughout the colonies whose intellectual interests and ties of professional identity transcended territorial boundaries. There he also formed friendships with political nationalists and men who joined in a campaign to foster an American culture. Even before independence, Ramsay predicted that "America will eventually prove the asylum for liberty learning religion & et [sic]. . . . A case to fight for–to bleed for–to die for."[11]

With his American orientation and his ardent Whiggism, Ramsay was well placed to help fill the vacuum created by the departure of the loyalist intellectuals, to assume Garden's role as an intellectual go-between with the outside world. But where Garden had served mainly to tie Charleston to Europe, Ramsay served to tie her to the North. Not that he was the only Charlestonian with extensive contacts: the Revolution had broadened Charleston's economic and political ties with the North; moreover, Ramsay's own church, the Independent or Congregational (probably more consequential to the town's intellectual life than the Established Church), consisted mainly of Northerners–especially New Englanders–and a handful of Princeton graduates, many of whom actively continued their connections with the North. But no other Charlestonian had so many contacts in the world of intellect as Ramsay; neither could anyone else equal the influence he achieved by his writing. His extensive network included individuals with wide-ranging interests from every part of the union: Thomas Jefferson of Virginia, John Jay of New York, and Hugh Williamson of North Carolina were only a few of the more prominent individuals. Ramsay also had ties with whole intellectual communities. Princeton was his spiritual home; he kept in touch with alumni and faculty, especially John Witherspoon, its internationally renowned president (to whom he was related by marriage), and Samuel Stanhope Smith, a close friend.[12] Ramsay's connections with New England, especially Boston, began ironically through his church in Charleston; they were extended by friendships formed in Philadelphia during the 1780s with Noah Webster and John Eliot, and by correspondence resulting from his scholarly reputation. The historian Jeremy Belknap and the geographer-historian Jedidiah Morse became particularly close friends, as did some other members of the Massachusetts Historical Society, of which Ramsay was a corresponding member.[13] Most important were his intimate associations in Philadelphia. His closest friends there were the painter Charles Willson Peale, the publisher Mathew Carey, and the physician Benjamin Rush, leaders in the several interlocking cultural communities of medicine, literature, and science in which Ramsay participated—becoming, for instance, a member of the American Philosophical Society.[14]

Most of Ramsay's intellectual friends were also cultural nationalists exhilarated by the prospect that political independence would result in cultural independence. They were equally convinced, too, that the latter was essential to secure the former—sentiments that were well expressed in 1787 by the Society for Political Inquiries, a group dedicated to freeing the country from the "intellectual imperialism of Europe."

> In having effected a separate government, we have as yet accomplished but a partial independence. The revolution can only be said to be compleat, when we shall have freed ourselves, no less from the influence of foreign prejudices than from the letters of foreign powers. When breaking through the bounds, in which a dependent people have been accustomed to think, and act, we shall properly comprehend the character we have assumed and adopt those maxims of policy, which are suited to our new situation.

Sensitive to the claims of many English and European writers that the United States had not been nor was likely to be the scene of important cultural achievements, these nationalist intellectuals were anxious to expound their country's virtues, "to ascertain what there is peculiar and distinguishing in the state of society in the federal union." "It is now full time," wrote James Sullivan, "that we should assume a national character, and opinions of our own; and convince the world, that we have some true philosophy on this side of the globe."[15] Dreams of a cultural renaissance were one reason why Ramsay joined others around the nation in a self-conscious effort to create a national culture. What Peale attempted for painting, Hugh Henry Brackenridge for the novel, William Dunlap for the theater, Webster for language, and Rush for medicine, Ramsay did for history.[16]

In Charleston, Ramsay aggressively promoted a national intellectual life—in public orations, in discussions at the Library Society and other intellectual wateringholes, and by serving as a conduit and dispenser of the ideas, scientific experiments, medical theories, and writings of American intellectuals. When Jeremy Belknap published his

History of New Hampshire, Ramsay acted as his agent in Charleston; he did the same for other authors. As a disciple of Rush, he helped spread his friend's unitary theory of disease and therapy, which both men regarded as particularly suited to a republican society.[17] He regularly informed his correspondents about the history, politics, social conditions, health, and economy of South Carolina. Conversely, he attempted to explain Northern perspectives to Charlestonians and introduced South Carolinians to his Northern friends and contacts. He aided in redirecting the flow of young men from British and European to Northern colleges, especially Princeton, and he encouraged numerous Charlestonians to study medicine with Rush at the University of Pennsylvania.[18]

This is not to suggest that Charleston was divided into intellectual camps: one American (consisting of Ramsay and such allies as his fellow Princetonians at the city's Congregational Church—Richard Hutson, James Hampden Thomson, and the Rev. William Tennent III), the other British oriented. Ramsay's influence was broad precisely because Charlestonians perceived that with independence his way represented the future. Nor would they have joined him if they had identified him with a narrow provincialism. His goal was to replace an imperial with an American cosmopolitanism without wholly rejecting British culture or withdrawing into a national shell. The patterns of Enlightenment and religious thought in Britain and the United States, North and South, created areas of compatibility and a sense of shared heritage. The curriculum at colonial colleges differed little from that at British institutions. Ramsay was a man of learning, a product of the Enlightenment who was connected with and committed to a transatlantic European culture and who proclaimed that "learned men of every clime constitute but one republic."[19] His veneration for British cultural achievements, if not British society, is evident from his writings. At Princeton he received a British education and his medical mentors were British-trained physicians teaching at an institution designed to replicate the University of Edinburgh. He was not rejecting Britain or Europe. It was his outlook and experience that were American, his passionate commitment to fostering an American culture that would take its place in the unfolding tapestry of Western civilization. In Ramsay's dream, and that of other cultural nationalists, London and Edinburgh would be replaced as the intellectual capitals of America by the new nation's own cities, and Americans would no longer regard Britain as the source of new ideas and fashions and as the arbiter of what was worthy.

Whatever services Ramsay performed as a go-between with the North, his contacts, like Garden's before him and those of Hugh Swinton Legaré and William Gilmore Simms in succeeding generations, were principally a consequence of his literary activities and reputation. In this respect he differed markedly from his generation of Charleston intellectuals. They eschewed science and literature for politics. The choice was understandable; the disruptions of revolution and war had redirected energies and made politics paramount. What Charlestonians did publish was usually devoted to immediate and concrete public issues. Not until 1790, with the ratification of both the state and national constitutions, did Charlestonians write or publish as much natural history, medicine, law, and poetry as they had done before the war.[20] Even then the output was not prodigious; the town's intellectuals were more consumers than producers of knowledge. Much of the intellectual community consisted of lawyers, physicians, merchants, and planters who were deeply involved in politics. While they took great pleasure in learning, they were also committed to the social usefulness of knowledge. The South Carolina members of the American Philosophical Society during the eighteenth century were almost all learned but practical men of affairs. Henry Laurens, Thomas and Charles Cotesworth Pinckney, and John Deas, for instance, were public figures whose intellectual activities—however personally satisfying—were invariably directed at some perceived public need. The Country Whig ideology so popular in South Carolina demanded vows of civic virtue that made it difficult for Charlestonians to appreciate the intellectual who sought only private moments of creativity unrelated to a communal purpose. The "proper channel" for ambition, wrote John Laurens, should lead to "the advancement of public good."[21]

The modern division between intellectual and practical men of affairs was hardly evident in the early national period. To a remarkable degree the nation's leading intellectuals were also its leading political figures, as the careers of Franklin, Jefferson, John Adams, and Madison so eloquently testify. What was true of the republic as a whole was also true of Charleston, as Moltke-Hansen's list of the town's leading intellectuals illustrates.[22] Charles Pinckney, Charles Cotesworth Pinckney, Thomas Pinckney, Ralph Izard, and William Loughton Smith were important not only to the politics of South Carolina, but to the nation: Charles as the leader of the state's Republicans and later as governor and congressman, Charles Cotesworth as a Federalist candidate for President, and Thomas as a diplomat; Izard as a U.S. senator, and Smith as a Federalist congressman. The physician Thomas Tudor Tucker served as a congressman; John Faucheraud Grimké, Elihu Hall Bay, and John Julius Pringle were prominent jurists, and Thomas Bee a Charleston intendant (or mayor). The list could also have included Henry Laurens and Christopher Gadsden, the town's Revolutionary leaders, the intendant Richard Hutson, or the wartime governor and later Supreme Court justice, John Rutledge. Ramsay belonged in this group of influential political figures, especially in the 1780s. Like his colleagues, he was preoccupied with politics and did not publish scientific treatises until the 1790s. History, which in his conception had direct bearing on politics, was another matter; between 1785 and 1789 he published two major studies of the Revolution. Yet Ramsay had not taken a divergent path. He had, to be sure, an almost obsessive personal commitment to scholarship, but its purpose and content flowed naturally from his political and civic preoccupations; he made no clear distinction between his private and public goals. His writings—whether historical, political, or medical—were designed as instruments of public policy.

In the 1780s the public goal that absorbed Ramsay was strengthening the national state; as early as 1778 he had advocated an even stronger federal government than the one that emerged in 1788.[23] Charleston's leading political figures were also nationalists; indeed, until the 1820s South Carolina was noted for its political nationalism. The South Carolina delegation to the federal convention was convinced that the state's interests would be served best within the framework of a stronger national government, and the Charleston delegates to the state ratifying convention unanimously endorsed the result.[24] Ramsay's loose coalition of cultural nationalists intersected with a network of political unionists, often the same people. His activities, then, were the literary counterpart of the campaign of such South Carolinians as the three Pinckneys (Charles, Charles Cotesworth, and Thomas), William Loughton Smith, and John Rutledge to strengthen union. That the campaign to promote a national culture had political as well as literary purposes is evident from the writings of the cultural nationalists. "Every engine should be employed to render the people of the country national," wrote Noah Webster, "to call their attachment home to their country; and

56

to inspire them with the pride of national character." Ramsay, Jeremy Belknap, Mercy Otis Warren, and John Marshall fashioned histories that would "promote the union and harmony of the different states." Though he had completed his *History of the American Revolution* by late 1787, Ramsay delayed its publication in order to include an account of the new federal constitution. "The Revolution," he declared, "cannot be said to be completed" until the federal constitution "or something equivalent is established."[25]

There is no question that Ramsay's histories were popular in Charleston. He stood on common ground with the community's political and intellectual leadership. He knew these men well from family ties, professional service, the legislature, the Library Society (the hub of the town's intellectual life), and the taverns and coffeehouses where Charlestonians read newspapers and magazines. He discussed his work with them; indeed, his manuscripts became a kind of community project, with the participants in the Revolution and other events being consulted.[26] One attractive quality of his histories is that they convey a sense of personal involvement and the judgment of the insider. No doubt Charlestonians were pleased that Ramsay had assured the state's place in the national past with his *History of the Revolution of South Carolina* (1785), the first major study of the Revolution. The national and international acclaim from that work and the later *History of the American Revolution* were a source of pride.

Beyond the satisfactions of local pride, the intellectual premises inherent in Ramsay's writings found easy acceptance. True, Ramsay and other cultural nationalists preached a brand of revolutionary nationalism that went beyond what most Charlestonians envisioned: even amidst the furor of the Revolutionary War, Ramsay proposed a national university and a uniform system of criminal laws, hoping that both measures would unify the states and encourage national loyalties. Charleston's nationalists were too preoccupied with such practical difficulties as national defense, trade, debt, and disorder to be impressed by the prospect of a national legal system (which in any event did not appear in Ramsay's histories), but they could be moved by appeals to national pride and a historic sense of the importance of the Revolution, the heart of the histories. Although the various strands of Ramsay's intellectual personality and nationalism preceded and transcended his connection with Charleston, he did live there for most of his adult life, and all his publications were composed there; it was there, too, that he experienced the most profound events of his public existence — revolution, independence, and war. Much of what he perceived as "American" was influenced by his having lived there; South Carolina and Charleston served as laboratories for many of his assumptions about American society and republicanism.

This said, it is also true that Ramsay's paradigm for a national history made few concessions to local differences. Anxious to use the national past to establish the existence of a common identity, Ramsay did not deny so much as he deliberately glossed over local and sectional variety, almost to the point of losing sight altogether of the diversity of American life. Social and economic differences, whether in farming methods, commerce, urbanization, or political and social structure, received little attention. In this, too, Ramsay was in agreement with other Charlestonians, although they and he recognized the one special difference most important to the city: slavery. With allowances for individual ability, personal idiosyncrasies, and experience, however, Ramsay's picture of American society, past and present, could have been presented by any number of his political and intellectual colleagues in Charleston.

The difficulty lay in finding a basis for nationality. Nineteenth-century European nationalists would proclaim national independence by referring to their old or unique civilizations, common religion and descent, or ancestral soil. No such traditions could unite Americans or differentiate them from other people; they had no roots in a semimythical past, common descent, or mystical attachment to an ancestral soil. While Protestantism imparted a certain uniformity in values, it was too diverse to provide unity. Independence had discredited the self-image of Americans as Englishmen, but language, law, culture, even sentiment still tied Charlestonians and Bostonians alike to the mother country. Publicly, Ramsay proclaimed the existence of an American nationality and the expectation that the Revolution would trigger "a vast expansion of the human mind" to produce a national culture. Privately, the nagging problem remained that among the few genuine cultural achievements, there were none that reflected a uniquely American society, and Ramsay had to concede the obvious: "We are too widely disseminated over an extensive country & too much diversified by different customs & forms of government to feel as one people." Even so, he insisted publicly and privately that "we really are" one people.[27]

But if being "one people" did not mean ethnic, cultural, or even political homogeneity, what did it mean? Ramsay embraced a practical alternative: he defined national identity in abstract terms, as the interplay of two basic ideas: the republicanism of the national character, and the nation's special destiny "to enlarge the happiness of mankind, by regenerating the principles of government in every quarter of the world." In this light, the term "America" meant more than geography, a territorial state, or nationality. "America" represented a way of life, an ideology, a new society less bound by the customs and values of the past than other nations. The interaction between the environment and the ideas brought to the New World by the first settlers had led to the development of the "short but substantial" political "creed of an American Colonist":

> He believed that God made all mankind originally equal: that he endowed them with the rights of life, property, and as much liberty as was consistent with the rights of others. That he had bestowed on his vast family of the human race, the earth for their support, and that all government was a political institution between men naturally equal, not for the aggrandizement of one, or a few, but for the general happiness of the whole community.[28]

If the nation lacked cultural and ethnic uniformity, Americans were one people by virtue of their loyalty to a common set of ideals and values. With American society itself as the standard of achievement, Ramsay could abandon the premises of high culture. If the nation had yet to produce outstanding literary artists, scientists, or philosophers, ordinary men had constructed the kind of society of which British and European philosophers could only dream. Yet the debt of Ramsay's generation to British culture and to the Enlightenment made it imperative that he express American distinctiveness without repudiating either. Convinced of the universality of human experience, he was not quite comfortable as a cultural chauvinist. "I am a citizen of the world, & therefore despise national reflections," he wrote apologetically. But, he continued, I "hope I am not inconsistent, when I express my ardent wish" that America be independent in "Law, Physic & Divinity."[29] His solution was to broaden America's British heritage and tradition of liberty beyond the confines of its historical-territorial limitations. By proclaiming America's purpose "to enlarge the happiness of mankind" by her example, he transformed an English ideal of liberty into a supranational ideology. But being an example to the world can be a narrow as well as a cosmopolitan concept. Ramsay was basing the essentially parochial ideal of nationalism upon values presumed to be nonparochial. The nation's special destiny "to prove the virtues of republicanism" was the one area of genuine national achievement. Emphasizing the point, he nationalized, even jingoized, the eighteenth-century idea of universal progress.

With his goals clearly in mind, Ramsay began the *History of the American Revolution* with an analytical account of the colonial period, for it was during those years that "the seeds of the revolution were sown." What followed was an example of Ramsay's environmentalism, which is a key to understanding his interpretation of history and society. The idea lacked rigor; it was, in fact, a hodgepodge of disparate civil and physical factors that never quite meshed or whose relative importance was never quite clear. There are echoes of a number of British and European writers, some with quite different points of view—particularly Montesquieu, Locke, and such Scottish scholars as David Hume, William Robertson, Francis Hutcheson, Lord Kames, Thomas Reid, and Adam Ferguson. Yet the overall impression is strikingly effective. The weight and, surprisingly, the logic of argument made quite believable Ramsay's simple but eloquent thesis that "from the first settlement of this country everything concurred to inspire its inhabitants with the love of liberty."[30]

First came the natural world: "The natural seat of freedom is among high mountains and pathless deserts, such as abound in the wilds of America." Then there was geography:

> The distance of America from Great-Britain generated ideas in the minds of Colonists favourable to liberty. Three thousand miles of ocean separated them from the mother country. Seas rolled, and months passed, between orders and their execution. In large governments the circulation of power is enfeebled at the extremities. This results from the nature of things, and is the eternal law of extensive or detached empire. Colonists, growing up to maturity, at such an immense distance from the seat of government, perceived the obligation of dependence much more feebly, than the inhabitants of the parent isle, who not only saw, but daily felt, the fangs of power.

But Ramsay was at his best when discussing civil and social matters. The crucial factor in his paradigm was always the actions of men. The significance of the physical environment lay more in the scope afforded than in the limits given a society's character. Above all, it was the English heritage that had enabled colonials to take advantage of circumstances uniquely suited to a republican society. "The English Colonists were from the first settlement in America, devoted to liberty, on English ideas, and English principles. They not only conceived themselves to inherit the privileges of Englishmen, but though in a colonial situation, actually possessed them." If Englishmen in the New World came with attitudes particularly favorable to liberty, that predisposition was strengthened by the historical experience and doctrines common to the period in which the colonies were founded.

> The first emigrants from England . . . left the Mother Country at a time when the dread of arbitrary power was the predominant passion of the nation. Except the very modern charter of Georgia, in the year 1732, all the English Colonies obtained their charters and their greatest number of European settlers between the years 1603 and 1688. In this period a remarkable struggle between prerogative and privilege commenced, and was carried on till it terminated in a revolution highly favourable to the liberties of the people. . . . It is remarkable that the same period is exactly co-incident with the settlement of the English Colonies.[31]

Finally, this physical environment and the English heritage of the colonists had facilitated the development of a republican political and social system.

> The Colonies were communities of separate independent individuals, under no general influence, but that of their personal feelings and opinions. They were not led by powerful families, nor by great officers in church or state. Residing chiefly on lands of their own, and employed in the wholesome labours of the field, they were in a great measure strangers to luxury. Their wants were few, and among the great bulk of the people, for the most part, supplied from their own grounds. . . . Unacquainted with ideal wants, they delighted in personal independence. . . . The great bulk of the British Colonists were farmers, or planters, who were also proprietors of the soil. The merchants, mechanics, and manufacturers, taken collectively, did not amount to one fifteenth of the whole number of inhabitants.[32]

Here, then, was an ideal milieu: a society of small farmers, uncorrupted by the temptations of wealth, dependent on no one but themselves, free from the controlling influences of great families, church, and state.

Thus, the American environment had acted as a prophylaxis against the depravity of man.

In Ramsay's analysis of the causes and consequences of the Anglo-American conflict, it becomes apparent that the colonial period, in his view, served as a backdrop for the Revolution. The Revolution is represented as neither a break with the past nor a radical departure from the basic fabric of American life. As the colonists perceived the danger to their liberties, they resisted because of "the high notions of liberty and independence, which were nurtured in the Colonies, by their local situation, and the state of society in the new world."[33] Existing forms and loyalties had been altered; independence, new state constitutions, and the successful implementation of a federal union were hardly inconsequential. But rather than being a radical departure, the Revolution served as a process of self-discovery, an opportunity to perfect and systematize what had already been true in practice, and to open the way to future improvements. Having provided American history with a unity that made the Revolution and nationhood appear as the logical fulfillment of a common national history, Ramsay then incorporated the culminating act of nationhood. He deliberately minimized, though he did not ignore, internal conflict, portraying the Constitution as the expression of a united people.

None of this conveys the full flavor or the brilliance of Ramsay's account, especially of the Revolution—his subtle analysis of the growing divergence on both sides of the Atlantic and the role played by revolutionary organizations, the churches, and the press; or his unusually sensitive treatment of the loyalists. Aside from being a first-rate piece of historical writing, Ramsay's study also contains a formula for an American nationality that stands as an intellectual tour de force, providing the seemingly unprovidable: a well-reasoned and plausible paradigm for a national historical identity. By clearly enunciating an interpretation of the national experience that stressed natural bonds of unity while deemphasizing internal conflict and cultural differences, Ramsay gave to American history a coherence it otherwise lacked. Like his "simple creed of an American," his overall interpretation was similarly straightforward: a sturdy, cohesive, freedom-loving American character arose from the unique conditions of the New World, was articulated and reinforced by the Revolution, and institutionalized by the Federal Constitution.

Ramsay's historical views were inseparable from his perception of the American present and his vision of the future. An assumption fundamental to both his historical and his social philosophy was the belief that the biological, social, psychological, and moral relations of humanity to its environment were so interlocked that they were all one. Disease, political institutions, cultural life, and economic organization were so interrelated that any general social change produced changes in every aspect of human endeavor. It was self-evident that the Revolution was such a general change. One such effect, particularly novel and exciting to the Revolutionary generation, was axiomatic to republican theory: the "emancipation from British tyranny" would liberate the creative energies of American society and open "an illustrious area in the history of the world." The removal of artificial restraints and regulations, which American nationalists identified with the British monarchy and empire, would result not in chaos but in harmony; religious and political health, scientific achievement, economic and cultural productivity would increase dramatically. In short, a republican environment would be "favourable to purity of morals, and better calculated to promote all our important interests"; the "arts and sciences . . . [would] now raise their drooping heads, and spread far and wide"; population would grow by immigration and natural increase; and the economy would flourish as never before.[34]

The idea that a republican political system would liberate human potential was not new. It had been a common refrain in Whig literature on both sides of the Atlantic at least since the early eighteenth century. Ramsay's Charleston audience understood his premise. For more than fifty years the writings of John Trenchard and Thomas Gordon enjoyed remarkable popularity in South Carolina. Many of their *Cato's Letters* were reprinted in the *South Carolina Gazette*, while individuals as well as the Library Society purchased collected editions. According to "Cato," "Polite Arts and Learning [are] naturally produced in Free States, and marred by such as are not free."[35] With the Revolution the concept took on new possibilities; for Ramsay it was what made the Revolution revolutionary.

Ramsay's vision of an American apotheosis was not limited to arts and letters. He first expressed these views in a speech, delivered on 4 July 1778, which was published and widely distributed. The oration was dedicated to Charleston's famed revolutionary leader Christopher Gadsden, Ramsay's friend and political mentor and a wealthy merchant. In defending the boycotts raised against Britain in 1769 and 1774,

Gadsden had argued for immediate sacrifices in return for future economic and political gains.[36] He and Ramsay contended that British trade regulations impeded commerce, and they presumed a link between economic growth and a climate of liberty. Gadsden must have nodded approvingly when Ramsay predicted that "our change of government" would smile "upon our commerce with an aspect peculiarly benign and favourable" and then went on to detail the disadvantages of British trade policy. It required "but a moment's recollection," Ramsay observed, to realize "that as we now have a free trade with all the world, we shall obtain a more generous price for our produce, and foreign goods on easier terms, than we could, while we were subject to a British monopoly." Then he tied the issue of economic and cultural liberation to Whig political theory and politics by characterizing the Navigation Acts as "a glaring monument of the all-grasping nature of unlimited power."[37] It is doubtful whether Ramsay had given more than passing attention to commercial policy before emigrating to South Carolina. But under the tutelage of Gadsden and then with the experience of representing a commercial constituency, he became an expert.[38]

That Ramsay interpreted the Revolution as a process of liberation was not just a matter of ideology. Personal experience reinforced ideology. "The times in which we live," he proclaimed with obvious enthusiasm, "and the governments we have lately adopted, all conspire to fan the spark of genius in every breast, and kindle them into a flame."[39] He was describing his own circumstances; his exultation at the advent of the Revolution was unmistakable. Independence created new possibilities for men like himself—zealous in the cause, talented, well-educated but without the traditional credentials of inherited wealth and prestigious family connections, intense in their private ambition yet genuinely craving to channel their creative energies into public service.[40] The volatile landscape of revolutionary Charleston smoothed Ramsay's access to political office. With his uncompromising Whiggism, he was chosen in 1775, only one year after his arrival, for the Committee of Public Safety, then in 1776 for the legislature, and in 1780 for the powerful and prestigious state council. All told, he served twenty-two years in the legislature and two terms in the Confederation Congress.

While at first glance Ramsay's celebration of a liberated economic, social, and political order could appear as a radical critique of privilege and the class structure, his views were acceptable to the well-to-do,

Whiggish lawyers, merchants, and planters he served as legislator and physician and to the intellectual community that closely mirrored the town's political and economic structure. Ramsay was not a leveler. Equality was not directly conceived of by most Americans—including devout republicans like Samuel Adams, Gadsden, Rush, and Ramsay—as social leveling. Certainly most Revolutionaries had no intention of destroying the gradations of social hierarchy by the introduction of republicanism.[41] Ramsay was content with the modest reforms of the South Carolina Constitution of 1778; he had been one of its most active advocates in the legislature. In a republican system, he maintained, "no one can command the suffrages of the people, unless by his superior merit and capacity." It was now possible, he exulted, that "the reins of state may be held by the son of the poorest man, if possessed of abilities equal to the important station."[42] As long as what he termed "artificial barriers and distinctions" were removed, he was satisfied. Even though he lived in a society where the extremes of wealth were at least as great as in any other place in the nation, Ramsay identified South Carolina, and by implication all of America, as a place of opportunity. His own career offered a telling example.

Not all of this is readily discernible from the *History of the American Revolution* or the later histories. Ramsay's purpose there, after all, was to foster a consensus, not partisan discussion of contemporary issues. While his specific views were more easily accessible in public debate and speeches, legislative forums, and correspondence, his political philosophy, while masked by generalities in the *History*, is inherent in its structure. The strong emphasis on continuity with the past—a central theme of the *History*—blunts a more radical interpretation of the Revolution. The liberation he so eloquently articulated was less a call to restructure society than an expected fulfillment, a culminating and orderly process that naturally grew out of the past. The ingredients were already there; what hindered American energies was not so much internal barriers or divisions as external forces: the British monarchy and empire. The sheer weight of evidence implied that while some internal changes such as disestablishment were required to complete the process, the structure of society was essentially sound.

If in colonial America the form was often less than republican, in practice there was a unity of interests between elected officials and the people. Ramsay strongly disapproved of the Pennsylvania Constitution of 1776, with its unicameral legislature and other unprecedented features, as a radical departuré. But those frames of government that legitimized and built on past practices, that in his judgment evolved naturally from the American character, he celebrated as truly republican. He took great pains, for example, to argue and demonstrate that the South Carolina constitutions of 1776 and 1778, while incorporating some innovations, especially disestablishment, were a natural product of the past. The results were such that the people and their government became one: "The far famed social compact between the people and their rulers did not apply to the United States," for in America "the sovereignty was in the people," who "deputed certain individuals as their agents to serve them in public stations agreeably to constitutions, which they prescribed for their conduct." Ramsay's political friends with political views close to his own, men such as Charles Cotesworth Pinckney and John Rutledge, wanted a republic, but an elitist or aristocratic one. Opposed to special privileges and the trappings of monarchy, they accepted talented individuals into their ranks while rejecting fundamental alterations in the distribution of political power and wealth.[43]

Just as the politics of the *History* generally mirrored that of the town's political and intellectual elite, so did its basic philosophy. Revolutionary Charleston was still an outpost of the Enlightenment, and Ramsay's writings reflect that fact, but it was a brand of Enlightenment thought that suited modest Whig revolutionary sentiments. There were, of course, sharply different Enlightenment thinkers, and each had his partisans among educated, intellectually articulate Charlestonians. But the Moderate Enlightenment, which preached balance, order, moderation, religious compromise, and the importance of intelligent, well-educated leadership—and which so nicely complemented Country Whig political ideology—was and would remain dominant into the nineteenth century.[44]

There are hints of a more revolutionary view of the Enlightenment in Ramsay's thought, especially in his environmentalism. At the same time, however, Ramsay often expressed a fear of that "corruption of human nature which wishes to exalt self at the expence & over the rights of others."[45] Believing that the love of liberty could triumph over depravity, he still disliked the Enlightenment's more revolutionary proponents: he was highly critical of the Pennsylvania Constitution of 1776, turned against the French Revolution, denounced Paine's *Age of Reason*, and disapproved of those radical republicans of the Charleston

Democratic Club who petitioned to be officially adopted by the Jacobin Club of Paris.[46] Most of the social reforms he advocated—antislavery, medical care for the poor, an end to capital punishment, promotion of education—were familiar Moderate Enlightenment causes. Indeed, Ramsay's campaigns against dueling and, especially, drinking, and his general distaste for social amusements make him seem more like a nineteenth-century evangelist than a radical revolutionary. Most important, if he sometimes used the language of revolution, by personal inclination and by legislative experience, he was most comfortable with the Moderate Enlightenment's emphasis on compromise and reform from the top.

As portrayed by Ramsay, the Revolution reads like a textbook for the Moderate Enlightenment and Country Whig ideology: rational, but militant in defense of liberty; men transformed more by ideas than emotions; political institutions easily adapted to independence; and all achieved through respect for and the efforts of intelligent leaders. Above all, the achievement most typical of Moderate Enlightenment principles was the disestablishment of the Anglican Church and the tolerant environment of Charleston's religious life. What is apparent is that fervent Protestants from George Whitefield on found the region lukewarm and apathetic in religion. By midcentury, relations between the easygoing Establishment and the powerful Dissenting churches, once hostile, were cordial. The emphasis was on compromise; when the issue of disestablishment came to a head in 1778, it was accomplished with a minimum of discord. The motives were strongly political—to win the loyalty of the Dissenting upcountry—but it was still a victory for the Moderate Enlightenment. Moreover, the Anglican Church tolerated, perhaps encouraged, a variety of religious views; there were fashionable conforming freethinkers of the English type, strictly observant churchmen like Henry Laurens, and pious ladies like the diarist Eliza Pinckney. Acceptable deists and quasi-deists were read.[47]

Looking back, Ramsay recalled that "among the carolinians deism was never common."[48] Perhaps it was not common, but there were prominent deists. Charles Cotesworth Pinckney was probably a deist. Francis Kinloch, scion and heir of a leading Carolina family, was deeply influenced by the two great British skeptics, Hume and Gibbon. Likewise, Thomas Tudor Tucker, who came from Bermuda to settle in Charleston, pursue a medical career, and later become a member of Congress, exemplified the deism of the Skeptical Enlightenment.[49] If there was only a handful of genuine deists in Charleston, most intellectuals were liberal Christians who saw nature as designed by a wise creator for the use and edification of man. True science, they would have agreed, and scripture could never be in disagreement. In Ramsay's words, Charlestonians "generally believed that a Christian church was the best temple of reason."[50]

Ramsay was representative. He drew an apparent though unstated distinction between his private religious feelings and his scholarship. It was possible throughout the eighteenth century, indeed common, for thoughtful persons to accept the ruling assumptions of the Enlightenment—its scientism, spirit of criticism, and humanism—and still remain attached to traditional religious precepts.[51] Ramsay's Enlightenment views and Christian faith existed side by side, as they did in individuals like Henry Laurens and Christopher Gadsden. In his histories, Ramsay presented naturalistic interpretations interspersed with an occasional acknowledgment of the role of Providence. The naturalistic version included lengthy and sometimes intricate cause-and-effect relationships; the Providential views were only statements. He never attempted to reconcile the two. What he undoubtedly had in mind was God as the ultimate initiator of human events but working through secondary causes. Even when Ramsay wrote specifically about religion, he did so in terms typical of the Moderate Enlightenment, describing the churches as useful vehicles for social control and cohesion. "Public preaching . . . seldom fails of rendering essential service to society, by civilizing the multitude and forming them to union."[52]

The publication of the *History of the American Revolution* in 1789 represents a kind of symbolic rite of passage for Charleston's post-independence intellectual community and for Ramsay. Its great achievement was to find the common ground and limits of nationalistic thought. Sensitive to opinion north and south, Ramsay defined a brand of revolutionary nationalism that was broadly acceptable throughout the nation and that comfortably fit into the acceptable parameters of social and political thought among Charleston's upper-class Whig revolutionaries. It was vaguely abstract and appealed to patriotic pride, was pro-American yet did not reject the British heritage or culture, made a case for American uniqueness while still holding to the Enlightenment ideal of the universality of human experience, represented the Revolution as the beginning of a new era and yet stressed continuity with the past and its essentially conservative character.

*   *   *

The care with which the *History* was constructed serves to illustrate that its publication was as much a political as a literary event. A product of that era in Charleston of nearly exclusive interest in politics, it appeared just as the intellectual community was about to change its focus. Moltke-Hansen has already described that community's activities and interests during the several decades after 1790, when, with the ratifications of the federal and state constitutions, the pace of intellectual life quickened and the range of intellectual discourse broadened. Ramsay was experiencing similar changes during this period. Like his colleagues, he showed much less interest in politics.[53] Like them, he devoted considerable energy to expanding and fostering local cultural life. But the most fundamental aspect of that change was his movement from the stark nationalism of the *History of the American Revolution*, with its nearly complete disregard for local differences, to an acknowledgement of an ethic of particularism. It was, of course, only a step, not a radical departure. Ramsay never retreated from his nationalistic political and cultural persuasion or his faith in the universal significance of the American Revolution. At the time of his death he had nearly completed two ambitious projects that confirmed those convictions: a *History of the United States* (1816–17) and a *Universal History Americanized* (1819). When he wrote his *History of South Carolina* (1809), he placed the state's past within the paradigm established in his national history, justifying his efforts with the hope that there would be "a history of every state." "We do not know half enough of each other," he explained to Jeremy Belknap. "Every man who is acquainted with the people of the neighboring state is I observe for the most part federal: narrow politics are generally the offspring of insulated local views."[54] But if the rhetoric was the same and the general framework remained intact, there was an unmistakable shift of emphasis that represented a transformation in Ramsay's thinking.

The reasons for Ramsay's shift were complex and cannot be charted with precision; they were related to a conjunction of circumstances and influences that coalesced at roughly the same time: the changing interests of the town's intellectual community, his growing disillusionment with the prospects for a national cultural renaissance, the trauma of a personal political defeat in 1788, and his acculturation to Charleston society. In the 4th of July oration of 1778, Ramsay confidently predicted a prosperous future for the new republic. In the more thoughtfully complex *History of The American Revolution*, he incorporated those upbeat predictions. Yet below the surface there was also an ambiguous but unmistakable gloom: the *History* is as much a clarion call to fulfill the promise of the Revolution as an account of its achievements. During the Revolutionary War, Ramsay had grumbled over a lack of sustained commitment, but in his *History* he depicts the war as a time when Americans were more unselfish, more disciplined, more devoted to the cause than during the postwar years. "The sober discretion of the present age will more readily censure than admire, but can more easily admire than imitate the fervid zeal of the patriots of 1775, who in an idea sacrificed property in the cause of liberty, with the ease that they now sacrifice almost every other consideration for the acquisition of property."[55] Here were the beginnings of a national myth, to be sure, but also rhetorical strategems calculated to shame the postwar generation.

The Charleston that Ramsay had found so promising, he now complained, was degenerating into frenzied pursuit of private wealth, declining cultural life, and provincialism. Nor were his complaints limited to Charleston. The realities of the 1780s were an inexplicable refutation of the best calculations of philosophy and political economy. "Liberty," he told John Eliot, "which ought to produce every generous principle has not in our republics been attended with its usual concomitants. Pride Luxury dissipation & a long train of unsuitable vices have overwhelmed our coun[try]." Writers and artists were finding it difficult to attract large audiences, and many, like Ramsay, had lost money on their publications. "I long to see the day," he wrote despairingly, "when an author will at least be on an equal footing with a taylor [sic] or shoemaker in getting his living."[56] The national scholarly network faced severe limitations—poor travel conditions, erratic postal service, political turbulence, economic uncertainty, divisions within as well as between states.

A number of political and economic issues were proving frustratingly intractable, as the correspondence and writings of Ramsay and his intellectual comrades reveals. One notable example of an issue dividing the states and individuals, one particularly affecting Ramsay, was the question of slavery. No issue better illustrates the threat to Ramsay's dreams of a republic of letters and of a cultural and political nationalism that would transcend local interests.

70

Ironically, Ramsay's well-known doubts about slavery and his connections with Northern antislavery circles did not prove a political liability until after his position had undergone revision. In the fall of 1788, Ramsay ran a poor third in a race for a seat in the United States House of Representatives: the victor, William Loughton Smith, had accused him of being "*principled against* the true political interests of this country" for "it is well known that he is *principled against slavery.*"[57] Whether or not Ramsay would have won if his views on slavery and the slave trade had not become an issue, he firmly believed that his ideals had led to his defeat. "I was a candidate and lost my election on two grounds. One was that I was a northward man and the other that I was represented as favoring the abolition of slavery."[58] Only a few months earlier the ratification of the federal constitution had, in unanticipated ways, exposed a weakness in his position within South Carolina's political society. Precisely because it was an effective instrument of federal power, it had kindled a distrust of Northerners, especially the fear of commercial domination and of the new government's power to threaten slavery. It is hardly surprising that Ramsay, as a man who had forcefully expressed sympathy for Northern interests during the ratification debate and who had a reputation as an abolitionist, would be rejected for national office.[59]

Charleston in the 1780s and 1790s was not a closed society on the question of slavery. Ramsay did not become a political or social pariah; not in his bitterest moments did he even hint at such a possibility. What he faced was the discomfort of standing against the cherished beliefs of friends and neighbors. His suitability for office, even his loyalty, was being questioned. The community pressure was irresistible. Never again would he directly or indirectly oppose slavery or even refer to it in his private correspondence. Twenty years later, when he published his *History of South Carolina* (1809), Ramsay began with a detailed mosaic of the state's population but ignored the African. The omission could not have been accidental. Perhaps his studious silence on race and slavery was an early example of that Charleston style of intellectual discourse described by Jane and William Pease as "rounded edges." The Peases are referring to the 1830s, but one reason for the emergence of that style was a fear about racial balance that dated back to the 1780s. By then, with black chattels in some parishes outnumbering whites by as many as seven to one and with the removal of British authority, the Africans' presence tended to unify whites and promote the beginning of a communal conformity on the issue of slavery.[60] Ramsay was not intimidated, but having become a Charlestonian, he began to empathize with his neighbors' yearning for solidarity on so fundamental a question. If he could not positively endorse it, he could remain silent.

Chagrined as he was by his chastisement at the polls, Ramsay did not interpret his defeat as merely a personal repudiation. He equated his own circumstances with the fate of the republic; it focused for him in a personal fashion the fears he had been expressing about the nation throughout the 1780s. The shock was that, unexpectedly, the fulfillment of the political side of the nationalist program — the acceptance of a new federal constitution — had, in his opinion, aroused fears and reinforced provincial perspectives that poisoned the political process. If men like himself — patriots, nationalists, devoted public servants, transplants from one section to another — were disqualified for federal office for parochial reasons, what hope was there for forging a cohesive, national society? His resulting pessimism led him to concede the persistence of local loyalties and distinctions.

His grudging admission that political nationalism could not be easily translated into a cohesive sense of common nationality did not necessarily mean that Ramsay himself had to adapt to particularism. A more positive and more enduring reason for his tilt in that direction predated the election of 1788. Before his arrival in Charleston, he had apparently not regarded any one place as "home." Evidently he had retained little contact with family and childhood friends. Friendships with Philadelphians such as Rush and Peale and an admiration for the city's cultural tradition seemed to constitute the extent of his personal interest in his native state. No doubt the absence of an emotional homeland explains why he came closer than any of his contemporaries to writing a national history relatively free of local or sectional bias. The problem for other historians was that despite an intellectual commitment to an American nationality, emotionally they were Virginians, New Yorkers, or New Englanders. Yet for reasons that cannot be charted exactly, just as he was composing his national history during the decade of the 1780s, the rootless Ramsay was gradually transformed into a Charlestonian. In the beginning he referred to Carolinians as "them"; in time, they became "us."[61]

Again, no issue better illustrates Ramsay's encounter with Charleston society and his transformation from transplanted Northerner to Charlestonian than his changing views on slavery. Ramsay brought to South Carolina a genuine moral anguish over slavery. "Oh that it had been my lot to have spent my days where slavery was unknown," he complained shortly after his arrival. "To speak as a Christian, I really fear some heavy judgement awaits us on that very score." To the abolitionist Rush, his friend and teacher, he wrote, "I think with you in respect of our enslaving the Africans and have a firm belief that there will not be a slave in these states fifty years hence." It is clear from their correspondence that they agreed on basics, understood each other's views, and thought of themselves as compatriots in the struggle against slavery. When Ramsay announced that he was contemplating marriage to a young Charleston heiress, he assured Rush that "her fortune does not consist in negroes, but is reducible to an annuity from the rent of houses and interest of money."[62]

Publicly Ramsay first faced the issue as one of the few state legislators to support John Laurens' scheme to enlist slaves in the Continental army. Though he had little faith in the military value of the plan, he regarded it as a step toward emancipation. At the same time, he championed a South Carolina ban on further importation of slaves and later defended the provision in the federal constitution abolishing the trade. Opposition to the slave trade was not necessarily antislavery; there were good economic reasons for opposition. But given his well-known ties to Northern antislavery elements who shared the conviction that destruction of the trade was a step towards abolition, it is not surprising that Ramsay's critics distinguished between his and a merchant's or planter's advocacy of prohibition.[63]

Yet even as Ramsay championed these causes, his attitude towards black freedom was changing under the impact of life in a slaveholding society. Personal experience had alerted him to the complexities of emancipation and the dilemma of the slaveowner, especially after he had become a slaveowner himself. Through marriage to Martha Laurens in 1787, domestic slaves came into his household, a dozen or more within a few years, and her lands in South Carolina and Georgia were worked by slave labor. The responsibility of owning slaves and of using the income derived from their labor must have been sobering. Perhaps Ramsay's conscience was eased by the fact that his father-in-law, Henry Laurens, had found no way to dispense with the slave system. These personal circumstances must have affected his social vision. Most of the men he knew and admired, who had befriended him and engaged his professional services, were slaveowners.

The metamorphosis was also a consequence of the complexities of slavery itself. Ramsay was grappling with the tension between an abstract conviction that all men were equal and therefore entitled to equal rights, and prejudices undoubtedly dating from his earliest years but augmented in South Carolina. Even when supporting the plan to arm slaves, he had believed that "abject submission, which is inculcated on slaves . . . tends to destroy every spark of courage in their breast. . . . From persons so educated no military service in the way of fighting is to be expected."[64] Though blamed on the environment, this conclusion was still damning. To a republican, an indispensable mark of citizenship was a willingness and capacity to bear arms. The African flavor of South Carolina, more like that of a West Indian island than of continental North America, was at first alien to Ramsay's experience. It did not reduce his opposition to slavery, since his environmental ideology was premised on the equality of mankind and the potential for human improvement, but this puzzling milieu sharpened the conflict between his ideology and experience, leading to doubts about the advisability of abolition. It was difficult for him to imagine these Africans as citizens. The result was not just a calculated reaction to diverse pressures but a genuine ambivalence about slavery which is reflected in his *History of the American Revolution.*

Ramsay affirmed his opposition to the institution and belief that all mankind "are originally the same"; attributed the low state of blacks to the environment of slavery, not an inherent inferiority; and bemoaned "its unhappy influence on the general state of society." Yet his attitude toward slavery and race had been transformed. First, he virtually absolved slaveowners from responsibility for the introduction of the institution or from any immediate obligation to terminate it. "The principal ground of difference . . . between the northern and southern provinces, arose, less from religious principles, than from climate, and local circumstances." His slaveholding friends (and his own conscience) must have been gratified by his contention that "interest concurs with the finer feelings of human nature, to induce slaveholders to treat with humanity and kindness those who are subject to their will and power . . . and life is often more pleasantly enjoyed by slave than master." Most revealing, the environmentalism that Ramsay had

74

used to attack slavery now became a vehicle to justify its existence. "Such is the force of habit, and the pliancy of human nature, that . . . negroes who have been born and bred in habits of slavery, are so well satisfied with their condition, that several have been known to reject proffered freedom, and . . . emancipation does not appear to be the wish of the generality of them." Moreover, his reputation for experience with infectious diseases gave a scientific legitimacy to his assertion that the Southern colonies used black labor because "there is a physical difference in the constitution of these varieties of the human species." Ironically, in 1780 he used the argument that the lowcountry "cannot be cultivated by white men" to promote the idea that the area should be farmed by communities of free blacks. Now, the same argument was used to justify "domesticated slavery."[65]

Ramsay had come a long way from his 1779 complaint that "White Pride and Avarice are great obstacles in the way of Black liberty." Now, the determining causes were the impersonal forces of climate, geography, African and European physiology, and historical circumstance — factors beyond the control of individuals. Just as he explained the existence and the necessity of slavery as the consequence of an impersonal physical environment, he rested his case for the Africans' unsuitability on the happenstance of the social environment.[66] In correspondence, in public orations, and in his histories he spoke eloquently of the transforming effect of a republican environment. Logically, then, he could have maintained that liberty would have a positive effect on blacks as well; presumably that was why he could denigrate their martial spirit in 1779 and still support arming them. But after that time he had revised his views. His implicit assumption was that a republican system could thrive only amongst a population conditioned by the right physical, social, and civic environment. Ramsay's Africans were so degraded that they had not acquired the qualities of character to benefit from and contribute to a free society.

What Ramsay could not bring himself to state explicitly in so visible a publication — that slavery was ineradicable and the African unsuited for citizenship — he said privately in a letter to his Boston friend John Eliot: "You speak feelingly for the poor negroes. I have long considered their situation, but such is our hard case here to the Southward that we cannot do without them." He now conceded that "our land cannot be cultivated by white men," only by black men bound by the discipline of slavery. Once he arrived at that conclusion, the abandonment of his antislavery stance was irresistible. "The negroes are here and in a state of slavery. Experience proves that they are incapable of the blessings of freedom."[67] The point is worth repeating: Ramsay's acculturation involved much more than his adapting to slavery. It involved the merging of a rootless man into the life of a close-knit community where neither his religion nor social origin was a barrier to professional, political, or financial success, where he could even marry into one of the state's most distinguished families. Though important in itself, the slavery question is also a convenient index of how and why that change took place. Ramsay had, in fact, changed his mind before November 1788, not because of coercion or intimidation, but because he was being molded by a social environment.

So the paradigmatic national history, with its implications of a malleable civil environment that had melded Americans into one people, contained a little noted but important caveat: the environment of the slave and the economy of the Southern states were distinguished by impersonal forces of climate, geography, and even physiology beyond the control of individuals. Originally, Ramsay formulated this understanding to explain what he regarded as an exception to a general rule. In the end, however, he came to see the exception as a rule: localism was a more intractable force than he had anticipated. Having arrived at this conclusion, Ramsay began to examine his surroundings with a new urgency. The result was a shift in emphasis toward the physical and away from civil or cultural factors in his environmental ideology.

If personal factors nudged Ramsay in the direction of a greater appreciation of the local environment, the agenda of issues he discussed within that framework reflected the concerns of the Charleston intellectual community. Having lived through the economic and political instability of the Revolution and the period of reconstruction, Charlestonians were now experiencing both the portentous era of the French Revolution and an economic boom.[68] The latter encouraged optimism about the future, which Ramsay would eventually share, although his initial reaction was to bemoan what he regarded as a mad pursuit of luxury. The former encouraged political and social caution, which he endorsed. So there is a unifying theme in Ramsay's post-1790 writings that is consistent with these concerns: the problem of social control in a republic and how men can be induced to obey both informal and formal law.

South Carolina became Ramsay's test case in a new book. As in the *History of the American Revolution*, he spoke with pride of the Americans' (now the South Carolinians') "love of liberty." But experience had tempered optimism, and he now drew a more sober, ambiguous picture. Once he had tipped the scales from civil to physical causes as prime determinants of social behavior, the result was a more fatalistic view of human possibilities. After all, civil factors lend themselves more to human engineering than the seemingly intractable elements of weather and geography. Not that Ramsay denied the good effects of religion, government, and moral leadership; indeed, he emphasized them. But he attributed many of South Carolina's problems to climate. "Drunkenness," for example, "may be called an endemic vice of Carolina. The climate disposes to it, and the combined influence of religion and education, too often fail to restrain it."[69]

What Ramsay had once praised as wholly admirable, then, took on a different hue: the instinctive "love of liberty" is at once desirable and dangerous. "Though this disposition nourishes freedom, and is highly deserving of praise, yet it has sometimes been carried too far; especially since the revolution, and by the younger part of the community." While a "repugnance to subjection . . . affords a guarantee to republican institution," it "too often transcends the temperate medium which as cheerfully submits to proper authority as it manfully opposes what is improper and degrading." To ensure the maximum dramatic effect, Ramsay used the practice of dueling in South Carolina to illustrate his point. A signator to a legislative petition opposing the practice, he still characterized that strong sense of honor, general in all classes of Carolinians, as exemplifying both the virtues and the liabilities of Carolinian (or national) character. Demands for satisfaction, even for trifling affronts, he noted, resulted in "a respectful behavior of the citizens reciprocally to each other. The licentiousness of the tongue and press is seldom indulged in Carolina. . . . There is such a general respect for propriety of behavior, that rude attacks on the character of individuals meet with no countenance." This was a trait essential to republican stability: namely, restraint in the conduct of public and private business. But that sense of honor "carried to extremes," as in South Carolina, "degenerates into a vice odious in its motive, mischievous in its consequences. . . . Mistaken views of honor give rise to duels."[70]

The challenge was to achieve a proper balance between individual initiative and the needs of society. Right behavior in a republic should be the consequence of internal compulsion with little external control. In this country, Ramsay declared, "the blessings of society are enjoyed with the least possible relinquishment of personal liberty."[71] Too much control would undermine republicanism. He hoped to bridge the gap between public and private virtue, to have a citizenry with a built-in warning system that was as effective against public transgression as it was against private misconduct. In short, a citizen would judge his public acts by an internalized code of moral behavior and would seek to reform society just as the individual was expected to reform himself. The need, then, was for public and private institutions that would function like a family—to teach the citizen to perform his duties voluntarily and with an inner compulsion to serve the best interests of society. It is no coincidence that Ramsay was an ardent advocate of and contributor to the many private organizations—educational, charitable, medical, and religious—that played such a prominent part in Charleston's public life.

Living in a society where a heavy concentration of slaves kept the necessity of maintaining order constantly on people's minds was reason enough for a preoccupation with social order and cohesion. But Ramsay was also echoing the sentiments of Federalists like Hamilton, who feared that a too ardent zeal for liberty would destroy the people's capacity for government.[72] Ramsay was himself a Federalist, but of a moderate, independent variety. His loyalty was based on the belief that the party's program would promote national unity and a respect for contracts that he thought essential to republican virtue. But he never joined in the more extreme forms of Federalism, and he counted among his friends such Republicans as Rush, Jefferson, and Charles Pinckney. He could write of the parties with detachment and concluded that "both did injustice to the other."[73] America in the 1790s was still a deferential society, and these men believed that the people should, in the words of Pinckney, look to leaders "of merits and talents" for guidance.[74] For all his rhetoric about the American's "love of liberty," his more sober political philosophy was premised on the assumption "that all men have hearts to feel, but few have heads to reason." So Ramsay emphasized the educative example of natural leaders. He blended the principle of virtuous exertion, learned from his New Side teachers at Princeton, with South Carolina's Country Whig ideology. He wrote sketches of prominent men such as Christopher Gadsden and Henry Laurens as public spirited and self-sacrificing. Cast as moral homilies, they read like the sermons of Finley and Davies at Princeton and appeared to describe the "virtuous citizen" of Radical Whig literature.[75]

The best example of Ramsay's post-1790 perspective can be seen in his medical writing, which provided not only an outlet for his renewed interest in natural history, and his growing preoccupation with climate and geography as determinants of social behavior, but a vehicle for integrating his interest in the particular with more universal concerns. Moreover, it illustrated his belief in the interconnectedness of human experience. Troubled by other aspects of national life—the failure to achieve a strong sense of national identity or to create a national culture—he at least retained with colleagues around the country, such as Rush and John Warren, the hope that freedom and independence would bring a revolution in medicine.[76] He genuinely believed that there was reason to be optimistic: America had produced such outstanding theorists as Rush and William Shippen, had trained practitioners in its own medical schools, had curtailed the incidence of smallpox with inoculation (a process to which Ramsay had been a major contributor), and curbed cholera and "autumnal fevers."[77]

Reflecting new pride in his local identity, Ramsay proclaimed Charleston a leader in medical progress: a "change has taken place much for the better," and as proof he calculated "a great reformation" in infant mortality rates between 1750 and 1800. The reason, he concluded, was that mothers now knew how to care better for their infants, and he estimated that the average number of living children per family had advanced from the four to five of colonial days to seven or eight by 1800.

> Bilious, remitting autumnal fevers have, for some years past, evidently decreased. The small-pox is now a trifling disorder, compared with what it was in 1760 and 1763. Pleurisies, which were formerly common and dangerous, are now comparatively rare, and so easily cured, as often to require no medical aid. The dry belly-ache has, in a great measure, disappeared . . . the diseases, which thirty years ago occasioned great mortality among children in the spring, have, for some years past, been less frequent and less mortal. Charleston is now more healthy than formerly, and likely to be more so.[78]

Like Jefferson, Rush, and other republican theorists, Ramsay assumed that health was a logical consequence of good government. But the introduction of the federal and reformed state constitutions had still not eradicated yellow fever, "more or less epidemic almost every year in nearly all the seaports of the United States." Strangers were more susceptible than longtime residents, though Ramsay did not know why. Stagnant water and putrefaction of vegetable matters seemed to be related, but he could demonstrate no correlation between urban "filth" and yellow fever epidemics: "In '98 we had none of it, in '99 we lost 269 strangers in four sickly months, and no obvious reason has been discovered why we should escape in the first year and suffer so much in the last."[79]

Puzzled by conflicting evidence and unaware that it was an acute infectious disease caused by a filterable virus transmitted by the female *Aëdes aegypti* mosquito, by the late 1790s Ramsay had dismissed yellow fever's contagious qualities. That decision may have been a medical determination, but no issue—medical, political, or social—was separable from his general philosophy. During the Philadelphia yellow fever epidemic of 1793, an acriminous debate had raged over its origins. Federalist physicians and politicians agreed that the disease had been imported by refugees from the Haitian revolution, while Republicans led by Rush insisted that "miasmata" from local swamps and "effluvia" from unsanitary docks bred the fever.[80] The moderate Federalist Ramsay sided with the Republican Rush. The local-cause thesis fit comfortably into his doctrine of localism and cultural voluntarism. The cure would be communal, local, and individual discipline.

The direction of Ramsay's thought was strongly influenced by his respect for Rush, whose general theory of the oneness of all disease was given definite form by the epidemic of 1793. Rush announced that yellow fever fed on the strength and vigor of the body; therefore, the disease could be curbed only by robbing the body of its vigor through intense bleeding, purges induced by mercurous chloride, and a nutrient-free diet. Ramsay adopted the cure and reported its success (somehow there were patients who survived both the disease and the treatment), yet yellow fever outbreaks continued.

So Ramsay turned to cultural voluntarism; the Charleston answer could also be the nation's. Rush had argued that to avert fever, people would have to curtail its "predisposing" causes: "effluvia" in the air from exposed refuse and sewage. Once contagion was present in the body, the "exciting" causes that induced sickness—overexertion and aroused passions—must also be avoided.[81]

To combat the predisposing causes, community action was required.

Ramsay urged the medical society and city officials to instruct and, if necessary, pressure local residents to keep their houses, yards, streets, and harbor clean. They should be induced to burn or at least remove "all offensive and putrifying substances." Only if the town's inhabitants drained bogs, filled ponds, widened streets, improved drainage, cleaned stables and yards, and eliminated "effluvia" could they prevent future outbreaks. But to secure support, Ramsay realized that the leading citizens and the major civic and religious associations would have to apply moral and legal pressures. Only through the leadership and example of their "betters" would citizens voluntarily join the crusade against "effluvia." Unless "an active, energetic policy pervades every part of our city, the inhabitants as well as strangers have reason to fear the summer and autumn," Ramsay warned. "Whoever builds a house, fills a pond, or drains a bog deserves well of his country."[82]

The "exciting" causes of yellow fever could be restrained by self-discipline. Even in the presence of "predisposing" causes, a citizen could avoid the disease by self-compulsion and a virtuous personal life: shunning excessive drinking and eating; living prudently in clean, airy rooms; avoiding night air, "depressing passions, hard ciders, long walks, a great fatigue, and excesses of all kinds."[83]

Moderation induced by inner compulsion, then, was the key to individual health even if collective action failed—and if yellow fever raged on despite these doctrines, Ramsay had an explanation: there had been insufficient pressure on citizens to behave properly. Yellow fever would continue to threaten the land until citizens policed their own behavior.

Ramsay's struggle with yellow fever illustrates his subordination of occupational to ideological considerations. The battle against the yellow scourge fitted well the mold of his unitary thought; it was the medical counterpart of his political and historical ideology. An epidemic was a test of many things that influenced community life: the physical environment, prevailing customs, and lifestyle. What Rush in Philadelphia and Ramsay in Charleston were calling for was reform of certain aspects of community life to fight disease, a program that closely resembled Ramsay's concept of cultural voluntarism to cure the political and social ills of the individual and the community. In short, Ramsay's doctrine of cultural voluntarism is similar in both instances and can be seen as part of the same struggle. As physician, he insisted that both "predisposing" and "exciting" causes of disease could be eradicated if citizens were voluntarily induced to police their behavior in the inter-

81

ests of community health. As a politician, he tried to frame city ordinances and medical society proclamations to put pressure on people voluntarily to behave "rightly." And as a historian, he ascribed the persistence of yellow fever outbreaks to the fact that cultural voluntarism had not yet become ascendant in national life.

Ramsay's discussions of these issues, though set in South Carolina, were not inconsistent with his nationalist ideology. For years he had been encouraging the publication of state histories as a way of illuminating the national past. Yet his *History of South Carolina* (1809) goes beyond defining the state as a piece of the whole; there is an intrinsic interest in place that is wholly absent from his earlier work. Meticulously, he gathered and presented in loving detail innumerable facts and figures about the state's past and present: its ethnic and religious composition, its geography, its medical practices and traditions, social customs, lists of its organizations, names of its towns. The portrait is not always flattering but, even when he used the state as representative, evidences pride of personal identification and hope for the future of the republic. Ramsay's South Carolina was a microcosm of America's geographic, religious, economic, and ethnic diversity. As intractable as those divisions were, the state and, by implication, the nation were beginning to work, to become more unified. In South Carolina the religious settlements of 1778 and 1790 had all but eliminated sectarian antagonisms; a diverse population was becoming socially integrated; and the spread of cotton and slavery was creating a unity of economic interests. These achievements had eased political tensions between low- and upcountry, symbolized by the moving of the state capital to Columbia and the creation of a college there to train a responsible upcountry leadership.[84] "Them" had certainly become "us."

*   *   *

David Ramsay's career was in some senses paradigmatic. His experience as a Northerner in Charleston anticipated that of others, John Bachman and Samuel and Caroline Gilman being perhaps the most notable examples. These Northerners, too, would serve to bond Charleston to the North through school ties and intellectual contacts and, so, to foster nationalism in the face of particularism. At the same time, they also adopted the point of view of native Charlestonians on slavery and many other issues, and spent a great part of their energy creating and participating in local culture.

Ramsay's achievement was to define a revolutionary nationalism within a historical context. It made him famous in America and abroad; the *History of the American Revolution* went through numerous editions and translations, although it brought him little monetary reward, and his dream of a national culture proved illusory. Of course, he understood the limits of cultural nationalism, so he defined what is American vaguely in a set of abstract ideals. But that very vagueness, which had the virtue of encompassing the mass of people who called themselves republican and who had been partisans of the Revolution, was politically sensible precisely because the bonds of nationality were so weak. Ramsay accepted the limits of American cultural nationalism, and that realization, combined with his personal acculturation, led him to chart Charleston's particularities and promote its culture—without, of course, repudiating the ideal of a national culture.

Still, Ramsay's shift of focus marked the beginnings of an ethic of particularism that would flower in the next generation. By the 1820s, former nationalists like Ramsay's contemporary Charles Pinckney would turn to a political particularism. The republicanism that Ramsay had defined in the *History of the American Revolution* was broad enough to include Pinckney, although the two had important differences.[85] What separated Ramsay and Pinckney was motivation. Pinckney's overriding commitment was to South Carolina; Ramsay's was to the nation. When circumstances changed, Pinckney's republicanism could be adapted to protect local interests. Ramsay did not live through the Missouri controversy or nullification, but it is difficult to imagine a similar response on his part. His nationalism, although it had been tempered by his acculturation to Charleston, was fundamental. His nod to an ethic of particularism was personal and cultural, not political. Like so many in the generations to follow, Ramsay's turn inward was influenced but not determined by slavery. As Michael O'Brien and David Moltke-Hansen have shown, having developed a more indigenous understanding of itself and having acquired a more various institutional structure, Charleston could define a more peculiar culture.[86] Perhaps this was inevitable. There was no countervailing influence from an American London or Paris, a national center rooted in a long-established, centralized court culture.

What the decentralization of American life fostered and the expansion of Charleston society promoted was given more precise form by romanticism. If Ramsay took pride in Charleston's achievements, it was for him a world in microcosm, not something entirely unique. It would take the perspective of the romantic to reveal the city's unique qualities; a preoccupation with the rare attributes of locality was part of the romantic temperament. The basic doctrine of the romantic school was a belief in the gradual development of a distinct and unique spirit, a unified and organic development of traditions, customs, laws, and culture that formed the peculiar essence (or *Zeitgeist*) of a people.[87] Although he was an Enlightenment man, initially more concerned with the unity than the variety of nature and history, Ramsay contributed to this particularism. His writings provided material and perhaps inspiration for historical and dramatic representation of South Carolina's past. His greatest achievement was to lay the groundwork for a new kind of history, one preoccupied with a distinctly national experience. From the notion that only the fundamental passions are uniform and universal, he went on to a definition of the distinctive character of American society. Romantic historians like George Bancroft built on these perceptions, adopting Ramsay's ardent nationalism but employing a different style.[88] It was only a few short steps from the provincialism of nationalism to that of sectionalism. Ramsay himself had gone part of the way; the romantic's fascination with the unique and the particular would do the rest.

If Ramsay could have been present to hear Hugh Swinton Legaré's 1823 4th of July oration, he would not have felt entirely out of place. The language was often different, and even when it was the same, the meaning could differ; the two men were products of disparate eras and intellectual training. Yet the message was remarkably similar. Ramsay would have agreed with Legaré that "the Revolution was altogether the work of principle," that it was a "striking peculiarity . . . that it occurred in a New World," that it was appropriate to contrast the despotism of Europe with the freedom of America, and that "our institutions have sprung up naturally in the progress of society."[89]

3

Charles Pinckney. An etching by Albert Rosenthal made in Philadelphia in 1888 after an original painting in the possession of Dr. Thomas Addis Emmett. Courtesy of Historical Pictures Service, Chicago.

Charles Pinckney and the American Republican Tradition

MARK D. KAPLANOFF

It was a striking performance. Speaking in 1821 at the height of the congressional debate on the Missouri question, Congressman Charles Pinckney of South Carolina held forth for over an hour in a forceful defense of Southern rights. With relentless eloquence, he attacked Northern political aggression; he defended slavery by appeals to the Bible and to experience; and he argued that the Constitution forbade any interference with slaveholders' rights. Continued agitation on the subject might well lead to "the division of this Union, and a civil war."[1] So impressive were his arguments that his speech was one of three published by the authoritative national journal *Niles' Weekly Register* to illustrate the Southern position in the debate.[2] When the issue came up once more a year later, Pinckney spoke again, making an even more powerful defense of slavery and attack upon the North.[3] There was no turning back; South Carolina's congressmen were committed to a stance of extreme Southern sectionalism which Carolinians would maintain until the Civil War. Pinckney was one of the first to articulate their arguments.

While contemporaries listening to the Missouri debates were surprised (and sometimes horrified) by South Carolina's aggressiveness, historians have seen it as a part of three important, long-term changes. Most obviously, South Carolina was assuming a new role in national politics. Previously the state had taken a strongly nationalist line; now it was committed to a new and vigorous defense of Southern rights.[4] Internally the state had changed as well, and its new stance in national politics reflected its own internal development as the spread of the cotton economy and a process of political accommodation had brought about internal harmony and self-confidence.[5] Finally, the relationship between South Carolina and the rest of the South was beginning to alter. At the time of the Missouri controversy, Carolinians went further than most Southerners cared to, but over the years the Carolinian argument linking the defense of slavery with Southern rights gained adherents and allowed the state to assume a new prominence within the South as a whole.[6] As one historian has put it, the Missouri debates "marked the dividing line between the Virginia-oriented conservatism of the Old Republicans and the development of Southern sectionalism under the leadership of South Carolina in the 1820s."[7]

Charles Pinckney himself was an important actor in all these changes.[8] He came to his nationalism early. Born in 1757, he served as a young officer in the Revolution. He sat in the Continental Congress and the Constitutional Convention at Philadelphia in 1787, and fought consistently for a stronger national government. In the late 1790s as a U.S. senator he led South Carolina's Jeffersonian Republican movement, yet in the next decade there was an estrangement between him and the Jefferson administration; by 1821 he enunciated an extreme suspicion of federal interference and made a strong defense of Southern rights. His career within South Carolina was equally important. Born into one of the state's wealthiest families, he was among the first men of the old rice-planting oligarchy of the seacoast to diversify into the new cotton economy of the interior. Pinckney served as governor of South Carolina from 1789 to 1791, 1796 to 1798, and 1806 to 1808;

he was elected twelve times to the state legislature; and he was a consistent and effective reformer in state politics. Finally, even after his death in 1824, he continued to have an important place in South Carolinian thought, and Carolinians remembered him with proprietorial pride. His obituary claimed that he illustrated the best of "what can be effected by a Charleston education"; forty years later it was recalled that "no man of his generation surpassed Charles Pinckney in all those elegant and courtly accomplishments which so much adorned the Carolina gentleman. Few, certainly, from this State, if any, have filled with distinction so many public offices; none floated longer on the people's praise, or sank deeper into the people's heart."[9]

Nor were his ideas forgotten; Carolinians constantly returned to them at times of crisis. During nullification they insisted that they still contended for the Jeffersonian principles of '98—principles preeminently enunciated within the state by Charles Pinckney—and even during the Civil War, he was remembered as one of the founders and exemplars of the Carolinian political tradition.[10] Charles Pinckney acted as South Carolina's spokesman at a turning point and, in a sense, continued to act as a spokesman for her afterwards. By studying his career and the formation of his thought, it is possible to see not only how he came to say what he said, but also where South Carolina was going, and even why the state would have such a disruptive impact.

Pinckney's speeches on Missouri contained a strikingly full elaboration of Southern sectionalist arguments to which his successors would have little to add. He began with allegations of blatant Northern aggression. The attempt to interfere with slavery in Missouri was a violation of states' rights, which, if permitted, would be a precedent for Congress to dictate all local laws; sarcastically, he asked, "If you say there shall be no slavery, may you not say there shall be no marriage?"[11] So clear to him was the constitutional position and so worthwhile the institution of slavery that Pinckney could only conclude that Northerners hid behind pretended motives "of religion, humanity, and love of liberty" while actually launching a sinister plot against the South.[12] The Northern and Eastern states, "who are always much more alive to their interests than the Southern," had gained an unfair advantage by insisting upon the three-fifths clause in the Constitution and now sought the means of "regaining an ascendancy on both the floors of Congress; of regaining the possession of the honors and offices of our Government, and of, through this measure, laying the foundation of forever securing their ascendancy, and the powers of the Government."[13] Nor was the threat merely a question of lust for political office; in an anticipation of later Carolinian arguments, Pinckney declared that once Northern power was assured, "we shall soon see a system established which, if it did not even go the length gradually to mould our republican institutions into forms much less democratic than the present, would at any rate soon make the interest of the South subservient on all occasions to the North, by protecting duties."[14]

But the crux of the matter was slavery, a question that Congress had no right to touch and a property that the Constitution guaranteed "was to be as sacredly preserved . . . as that of land, or any other kind of property in the Eastern states."[15] He had no doubt that slavery was a positive good. There was not "a single line in the Old or New Testament, either censuring it or forbidding it . . . but there are hundreds speaking of and recognising it."[16] Slavery had been known throughout the ages, but American slavery was a particularly beneficent kind. One had but to consider the condition of the laborers of the Old World: "Let those acquainted with the situation of the people of Asia and Africa, where not one man in ten can be called a freeman, or whose situation can be compared with the comforts of our slaves, throw their eyes over them. . . . Let him then go to England; the comforts, if they have any, of the lower classes of whose inhabitants are far inferior to those of our slaves."[17] The racial inferiority of blacks was recognized throughout the world: "The African man is still as savage as ever—he is as unchanged as the lion or tiger which roams in the same forests with himself."[18] In freedom, even in the New World, he sank into degradation; only in slavery was he productive (the labor of two or three slaves, Pinckney maintained, was more valuable than that of five inhabitants in the free states) and contented.[19]

In other ways, too, Pinckney anticipated later issues and events. He argued that Congress had no power to restrict slavery even in the territories, that there was no such thing as a black or colored citizen, and indeed that differences about slavery constituted "the only question which might produce a dissolution of the Union, as it was the only one on which ambitious and artful men might play, not only upon the bigotry and fanaticism, but the honest feelings and prejudices of their unsuspecting countrymen . . . to create new parties, and to give them dangerous directions and irritating names."[20] These speeches in 1820 and 1821 contained a remarkably complete enumeration of the argument that Southerners would use right up to the Civil War.

Yet Pinckney himself constantly looked backwards; drawing on his own extensive experience of public affairs, he reviewed American history to show how the North and South had joined together in a portentous and mutually beneficial experiment in republican government. During the Revolution the two sections "nobly toiled and bled together, really like brethren."[21] The Constitution was a work of disinterested compromise.[22] With its valuable production of staples, the South was proud to contribute to the revenues of government, to help to pay for Western expansion, to finance America's balance of trade, and to offer employment for Northern shipping.[23] Repeatedly, Pinckney emphasized the South's participation in America's formative experiences and allegiance to Americans' most fundamental shared principles. Southerners had distinguished themselves by their valor, wisdom, and patriotism during the Revolution.[24] It was the South that insisted, "On the subject of the Constitution, no compromise ought ever to be made."[25] Above all, the South was committed to republicanism. The allegation that slavery made Southerners "less manly and republican" was so base that it hardly bore repetition.[26] The South had disproved that charge by its patriotism; now—in a threat he took so seriously that he repeated it three times—agitation about slavery threatened to undermine the government of "the only free Republic . . . in existence" and to destroy thereby the hopes of all mankind.[27]

Republicanism was the hinge of Pinckney's thought. It allowed him to square his fervent nationalism with his aggressive sectionalism. It allowed him to connect his allegiance to the union and his loyalty to his state. It allowed him to speak about Missouri in 1821 as if he were saying the same things that he had said as a Federalist in the 1780s or a Jeffersonian Republican in the 1790s. Of course, that was not entirely true, but it was by no means entirely false. Moreover, although his speech on Missouri seemed shocking and new, the actual things he said about slavery and sectionalism, about economics and economic policy, and about politics in general all reiterated claims that he had been making for years. What had happened was that he had shaped his thought by considering conventional problems in unconventional circumstances. In the 1780s his concerns and their application allowed him to reach conclusions like those of a great many nationalists North and South. He continued to ask the same questions, but over the years his own experience and that of South Carolina allowed him to reach conclusions particular to a statesman from that state.

Yet he continued to present his conclusions in the common language of American republicanism, and that is a clue to solving another important historical problem. Historians have long recognized South Carolina's leadership in developing Southern sectionalism throughout the antebellum period, but they have also noted South Carolina's political oddities and isolation, even within the South.[28] How, then, did South Carolina lead? The answer lies in the ideas that Carolinians upheld. Politics within the state remained stable, and from Pinckney's time, Carolinians continued to proclaim a variety of republicanism integrated with a defense of slavery, an assertion of Southern rights, and a presentation of their own harmonious political system as a republican ideal. In other Southern states there were partisan political battles, and party conflicts ultimately built up unresolvable tensions. As the stress increased, Southerners responded more and more to Carolinian ideals, to the republican argument fashioned by Carolinians like Pinckney. It did not seem that they were betraying their patriotic traditions — the Carolinian argument was phrased in terms of common American words and symbols — but the argument spoke to specific Southern self-interest and presented an ideal to which Southerners particularly could respond. It was South Carolina that led the other Southern states out of the union in the winter of 1860–61, but as they left, Southerners maintained that they alone preserved the principles of the American Revolution and American republicanism in their pure form. Ultimately, differing interpretations of the common American republican tradition led — as Pinckney had foretold — to disunion and Civil War.

*   *   *

From the time of the Revolution, the Founders disagreed about the appropriate economy and economic policy for a republic. Traditional political theory assumed that republics had to be simple, precommercial societies. A few American thinkers clung to this view, but it was generally abandoned during the 1780s. By 1787 most of the framers of the new Constitution agreed that some economic development was necessary lest the people sink into indolence and savagery. They could not, however, agree on the sort of development they wanted. One group, for whom James Madison acted as able spokesman, advocated a trade policy to open markets for American agricultural exports so that Americans could afford to purchase foreign manufactures, while avoiding the avarice, luxury, and dangerous inequalities among men consequent upon the development of manufactures at home. Another group, led by Alexander Hamilton, sought an aggressive government policy to encourage precisely the sort of advanced, nonagricultural development that Madison sought to avoid, advocating it on the grounds that this was the surest way to national wealth and power.[29] The quarrel over policy continued into the early years of the nineteenth century, but the result was ironic. Hamilton failed to effect the specific transformations he envisioned but fostered a prosperity that began other broad-ranging economic transformations. Madison's defense of American exports led finally to a war that demonstrated federal weakness, sparked intense internal divisions, and encouraged manufactures. At the end of the War of 1812, America was a much more complicated country than it had been in 1788—its economy more developed and diverse, sectionalism more intense, and the demands on its government contradictory and confused. Again politicians divided. At one extreme a group led by Henry Clay advocated the enactment of the American System, a bold scheme of federal action to foster advanced economic development, strengthen the government, and knit the union together. Another group, of whom Virginians were the most prominent spokesmen, saw both the program and the forms of economic development it was designed to foster as threats. Linking suspicions of such new organizations of economic activity as banks and corporations with fears of encroaching federal power, they saw in events a concerted attack upon individual liberty, state and sectional rights, and republican government itself.[30]

Throughout his long career Pinckney participated fully in these debates, yet his thought developed in unusual ways. He worried about the economic base for a republic; he discoursed upon the necessity of advanced economic development; he thought about the limits of government intervention in the economy; and he discussed the nature and dangers of economic sectionalism. His conclusions on individual questions were shared by other national politicians, but ultimately, the way he put them together was his own. Partly, this was a matter of how his thought developed. In the 1780s Pinckney worked well within the parameters of national debate, moving from a position close to Hamilton's to one closer to, although not exactly like, Madison's. By 1821 he shared neither the Virginians' defensive agrarianism nor the nationalist vision of Clay and his followers. What set Pinckney off from the contemporary debate about economics was his optimism; he did not feel that advanced economic change was a danger, nor did he feel that it depended upon extraordinary exertions by the government. For other national politicians, economic development was a problem. To some it was a process to be feared and resisted; to others it was something America had to struggle for. To Pinckney, economic development was natural, easy, and unthreatening, and the reasons for his optimism were peculiarly Carolinian.

Pinckney's commitment to economic development was apparent early, and most of his subsequent concerns were already present during the 1780s. In his first pamphlet, published in 1783, he scorned conventional fears about advanced economic development and advocated an aggressive national policy to foster it. "Placed along the banks of an immense ocean," the United States was compelled to become a maritime power: "We can grow great only by commerce." Instead of worrying about the corrupting effects of luxury, he saw it as a spur to useful industry. He was also eager to encourage industry in other ways. Higher taxes would foster productive labor and could support a stronger national government, which would protect foreign trade and even impose tariffs to encourage manufactures.[31] Soon, however, he learned the dangers of government economic policy perverted by narrow, sectional interests. In the abortive Jay-Gardoqui treaty of 1786, Americans' rights of navigation on the Mississippi were to be sacrificed for concessions for American shipping to Spanish ports. To Pinckney this was a clear example of sacrificing national (and Southern and Western) interests for trifling benefits for a handful of selfish Eastern merchants, and he spoke bitterly against the treaty in the Continental Congress.[32]

By 1787 and 1788 his wholehearted advocacy of government support for advanced economic development had been qualified somewhat, but in drafting the Constitution at Philadelphia and in the South Carolina ratifying convention, he still spoke up as an economic nationalist. At Philadelphia he recognized that there were five distinct commercial interests in the United States, as well as "the two great divisions of Northern & Southern interests," and proposed that any act regulating foreign commerce should require a two-thirds majority in each house of Congress.[33] In recognition of South Carolina's particular interests, he insisted upon the primary importance of agriculture among economic activities and fought against any restrictions on the slave trade.[34] On the other hand, he cheerfully accepted the Constitution as finally drafted, argued that commerce and agriculture were inextricably linked, and even admitted that some kinds of commerce ought to be encouraged by the government.[35] Moreover, in a famous exchange with Madison at Philadelphia, he denied the dangers of economic growth in general and maintained that in America's situation development would sustain equality rather than foster dependence.[36] By the end of the 1780s, Pinckney had addressed all the questions of economics and economic policy that would concern him over his lifetime; although his emphases would shift in important ways, most of his basic ideas were formed—as was his overriding optimism.

If anything, Pinckney's enthusiastic support for economic development became even more pronounced over the years. Occasionally he made statements that appeared to take a narrowly agrarian position. In the South Carolina convention to ratify the U.S. Constitution, for example, he warned, "Foreign trade is one of the enemies against which we must be extremely guarded," and declared that "all the great objects of government should be subservient to the increase of agriculture and the support of the landed interest, and that commerce should only be so far attended to, as it may serve to improve and strengthen them: that the object of a republic is to render its citizens virtuous and happy; and that an unlimited foreign commerce can seldom fail to have a contrary tendency."[37] Periodically, he continued to make ritual affirmations of the importance of agriculture, but they gradually became less common while his support for other developments became more noticeable.[38]

He had always recognized that agricultural progress depended upon access to markets, including export markets. He realized that farmers needed ships and sailors to transport their crops, and traders to buy their produce; indeed, he argued, merchants "are of such consequence to our commerce and revenue, that it is impossible to separate their interests from that of the *owners of the soil*, or indeed *from the government itself.*"[39] After the 1780s he no longer expressed general doubts about commerce; his few reservations seem to have been restricted to the "trifling, insecure, and unprofitable" re-export trade in which Americans acted merely as middlemen, shipping foreign produce from one foreign country to another.[40] This he saw as an activity of limited use in fostering America's own economic development, a trade involving the government in great exertions favoring only a few selfish traders, and one that ultimately threatened to entangle America in foreign quarrels.

Still, this was the only small cloud Pinckney perceived on the horizon; unlike some of his Virginian contemporaries, he was not suspicious of the manifestations and forms of advanced economic growth or even of government policies that fostered it. Pinckney never expressed the slightest hesitation about banking or the system of funding the national debt; his complaints about fiscal policy were limited to specific grievances about heavy and unequal taxes on land from 1798 to 1800.[41] He applauded the growth of cities and rejoiced in America's attraction for immigrants—and not just immigrant farmers: "All foreigners of industrious habits should be welcome; and none more so than men of science, and such as may bring to us arts with which we are unacquainted; or the means of perfecting those in which we are not sufficiently skilled—capitalists whose wealth may add to our commerce or domestic improvements."[42] He supported the development of manufactures without hesitation, and he was even willing to accept a moderate protective tariff to foster infant industries.[43] Pinckney witnessed little economic development during his lifetime that he did not welcome.

Pinckney did, however, recognize that economic diversity and development might lead to sectional problems within the United States, but he was able to treat the dangers of sectionalism with equanimity. Even in his most nationalist period during the 1780s, he acknowledged the importance of separate regional commercial interests as well as the great division between North and South. By the 1820s things had grown more complex with the rise of a new interest in manufacturing and a new section in the West. Men like Henry Clay also recognized America's growth and growing diversity and sought to erect the American System, a scheme for federally sponsored economic development to knit the union closer together. Pinckney, however, reached precisely the opposite conclusion: the crucial thing was to limit federal activity in the economy. The real danger he saw was not in sectionalism per se but in the interaction of sectionalism and government policy. The model to which he constantly referred was the Jay-Gardoqui treaty in which, according to Pinckney, New England sought selfish gain at the expense of national interests.[44] Pinckney saw the same sort of threatening folly in the Jay Treaty, in the commercial measures taken by the Adams administration against France, and in New England opposition to the Embargo of 1807.[45] Yet though the threat was constant, Pinckney thought it containable. For one thing, although he did recognize the need of a federal government with the necessary powers to keep open world markets, he did not see much necessity for government action to encourage internal economic development. America was in a strong position in international trade: "Countries possessing within themselves the means of a growing and extensive commerce, particularly where they consisted of articles of the first necessity, such as provisions and raw materials necessary to the support and manufactures of other nations, ought not, except in very particular cases, to form treaties of commerce."[46] America need not engage in the sordid commercial bargaining of Old World nations. With some firmness (and Pinckney was willing even to contemplate force), America could capitalize upon her advantageous economic position to break through once and for all into a world of free trade in which the American economy would develop naturally.[47]

Finally, with the danger of partial government policy minimized, Pinckney found a natural complementarity in sectional economic diversity. Even during the Missouri debates, when his sense of sectional antagonism was at its highest, he outlined the mutually beneficial relations between regions. The West provided new land and new opportunities as Eastern areas became crowded. The South, with its economy based upon agricultural exports, provided work for Northern shippers, merchants, and manufacturers as well as more than her share of the revenue for the national treasury.[48] For Pinckney, an American system of linked economic development depended not upon aggressive government action but upon government inaction, which would allow the natural development of America's advantages in world trade and of the complementary interchanges within her domestic economy.

If Pinckney's faith in natural economic development set him off from economic interventionists like Hamilton and Clay, it also set him off from the Virginians, who were the most prominent critics of federal schemes for economic management.[49] The ultimate worry of these men was that advanced economic development within America would lead to enervating luxury, avaricious behavior, and dangerous economic dependencies that would undermine the social order necessary to sustain a republic. At the end of the 1780s, men like Madison had hoped that the new Constitution, the open lands to the west, and a mutually beneficial trade with Europe might avert these dangers, but problems continued to arise. In the 1790s, Jeffersonian Republicans worried that

95

Hamilton's fiscal measures would distort America's natural economic growth by diverting resources from agriculture and creating dangerous parasitical groups of stockjobbers and placemen. The Republican ascendancy after 1800 calmed these fears briefly, but by the end of the War of 1812 it was clear that the economy had changed in ways that many Virginian leaders found threatening. Even Jefferson and Madison became more pessimistic and joined with more narrowly agrarian figures like John Randolph and John Taylor of Caroline to attack the developments of the day. Some saw corporations as a form of threatening aristocracy, the illegitimate usurpation of public power for private purposes. Many warned about the corruption and constitutional laxity attendant upon federal support for economic development. Others worried that limited world demand for agricultural products and the pressure of a growing population on land within America would force Americans to turn to manufacturing and other dangerous economic activities that would introduce ominous social inequalities and conflicts into the United States. All agreed that advanced economic development was threatening to undermine republican government and a republican social order.

Pinckney shared neither these fears of the 1820s nor the anxieties that had anticipated them earlier. In the 1780s, for example, many had worried that a taste for luxury was undermining the austere manners necessary to support a republic. Pinckney saw things differently; as he put it in discussing the impost: "Taxes upon imported, manufactured articles generally fall upon the rich, who can afford to purchase luxuries, and it encourages the poor to learn useful arts, and supply by ingenuity, and industry, what they have not money to purchase. It would compel idle and dissolute people to labour, and introduce into all ranks a desire for gain, which luxury never fails to inspire, and which is ever proportioned to it."[50] In 1787, in a major speech at the Philadelphia convention, Pinckney described the situation of the Americans, among whom "there are fewer distinctions of fortune & less of rank, than among the inhabitants of any other nation." He contrasted American equality with the social divisions in England and the peculiar situation of the nobility, and declared "that such a body cannot exist in this Country for ages."[51] His speech provoked an acerbic reply from James Madison, who insisted that America was already a fairly complex, stratified society and that the growth of population would rapidly make divisions and dangers more acute.[52] But Pinckney remained unpersuaded;

96

to the end of his career he insisted that American equality could be preserved without difficulty.[53]

One reason for Pinckney's lack of apprehension was his faith that America's abundant supply of open land guaranteed economic opportunity and the possibility of economic independence for ordinary Americans. As he put it in 1787: "That vast extent of unpeopled territory which opens to the frugal & industrious a sure road to competency & independence will effectually prevent for a considerable time the increase of the poor or discontented, and be the means of preserving that equality of condition which so eminently distinguishes us."[54] This was a conventional idea, and one shared by Madison and Jefferson, but it developed differently in Pinckney's thinking. The Virginians had emphasized this argument during the 1780s and 1790s, but by 1820 they were beginning to have their doubts about the efficacy of open lands in maintaining American innocence. Pinckney's thought developed in the reverse direction. In the 1780s, in fact, he believed that it would be some time before the West was surveyed and settled, and his own vision was an Atlantic one: "placed along the banks of an immense ocean," the United States must grow great by commerce.[55] His real concentration on Western expansion developed only in the early years of the nineteenth century after the Louisiana Purchase. By 1816, however, he had found peculiar virtues in the West:

> The rapid and unexampled rise in population in the southern, and particularly the western States (while the eastern stand still) will give an overwhelming majority in the House of Representatives . . . and this increase, it is to be recollected, comes from quarters which have never known any form of government but the Republican. . . . The mind is almost lost in calculating the prodigious nation of freemen that must soon occupy them. A nation, whose mountain air, and Republican habits, will equally nerve their bodies and their minds, and whose remoteness from the seats of commerce and luxury, will always keep them untainted by the vices they produce.[56]

When he spoke in the Missouri debates at the end of his career about protecting the "rising empire of free men" in the West, it was not a rhetorical flourish; Pinckney had come to see Western expansion as deeply connected with the preservation of American freedom.

Ironically, the other thing that preserved freedom was slavery, and on this point Pinckney's thought never changed. Here too he was unlike the Virginians. While they hesitated about slavery, cursed history for saddling them with it, and hoped that westward diffusion might ameliorate or even end it, Pinckney always defended it.[57] As governor of South Carolina in 1798, he recommended a tightening of the slave code in the following terms:

> As most of us are planters, and deeply concerned in giving all the secu-
> rity and protection in our power to this species of property, I am sure
> you will excuse the anxiety I feel in recommending the subject to your
> early and correct attention. As they are the instruments of our cultiva-
> tion, and of the first importance to our wealth and commercial conse-
> quence . . . there can be no subject which calls more powerfully on you
> for attention, nor none I think to which you will more promptly reply.[58]

Nor was this message reserved for Carolinian audiences. At the Philadelphia convention, where he was an ardent nationalist, Pinckney was
quick to oppose any potential threat that the new federal government
might interfere with the slave system, and to defend slavery itself: "If
slavery be wrong, it is justified by the example of all the world. He
cited the case of Greece Rome & other antient [sic] States; the sanc-
tion given by France England, Holland & other modern States. In all
ages one half mankind have been slaves."[59]

In an abbreviated form, that speech outlined one argument behind
a moral defense of slavery—that it did not bear heavily on the blacks.
But there was another argument as well—that slavery was good because it preserved equality among whites. In order to make sense of
Pinckney's position, it is necessary to understand two things about his
concept of equality. First of all, what mattered most was equality of
opportunity rather than equality of result. It was vital that advancement be open to the industrious; there was no expectation that all men
would seize upon it or even that the industrious would all win the same
rewards. Second, the condition opposite to equality was not so much
inequality as dependence; the danger was that unequal wealth would
allow some men unfair power over others. But it was precisely this danger that slavery obviated. At the Philadelphia convention, a few days
after his exchange with Madison about the prospects of American equality, Pinckney made a revealing remark when he observed that "the blacks
are the labourers, the peasants of the Southern States."[60] Others worried about the prospect of the formation of a landless, dependent group
of laborers in America; Pinckney lived in a society where this role was
already filled by men who could never be citizens and whom God, in

Pinckney's opinion, had made little better than brutes. On this point, that slavery supported independence and republicanism, Pinckney would brook no criticism. In his first speech on Missouri, some of his most vitriolic comments were reserved to refute the proposition "that one of the evils of slavery is, the lessening and depreciating the character of the whites in the slaveholding States, and rendering it less manly and republican."[61] For Pinckney, the slaveholders were *more* republican, and he had no difficulty in talking about a "rising empire of free men" while fighting to keep Missouri open for slaves. Just like Western expansion, slavery was one of the guarantees of equality and republicanism.

Clearly, Pinckney's perspective on economics changed over his lifetime. By the early 1820s he had witnessed and applauded varieties of economic development that he had thought unlikely in the 1780s. Over the same period he generally abandoned his early idea that federal help might be necessary to promote economic growth, and his own gaze shifted from the Atlantic to the West. Yet at the same time his eye remained firmly fixed on South Carolina, and the particular experience of his own state did much to account for the shifts in his thinking and for his enduring optimism.

Between the early 1780s and the early 1820s, South Carolina was a remarkable economic success story.[62] At the end of the Revolution, the state's prospects had looked doubtful. Coastal planters like Pinckney found their produce excluded from familiar markets: one of their two traditional crops, indigo, was now valueless; the other, rice, was dependent upon expensive new capital investment for continued production. Inland, new settlers poured into the state, but they moved into a separate and markedly poorer area with little commercial development, no staple crop, and little commitment to slavery. Over the next decades all this changed. Coastal planters successfully switched to new forms of rice production and a new crop, sea-island cotton, which provided them with fabulous profits and lasting prosperity until the Civil War. The invention of the cotton gin allowed the interior to develop a staple crop, short-staple cotton, and men like Pinckney were quick to diversify from the coastal planting economy into this new inland one as well. By the first decade of the nineteenth century, the state was knit together by prosperity, investment, and a wholehearted commitment to plantation slavery. Nor did development stop at the state border. In 1803 the Louisiana Purchase gave the United States a vast amount of prime cotton land. If Pinckney himself did not actively in-

99

vest in the new Western territories, many of his friends and associates did. This became South Carolina's new frontier: Carolinians rushed west; cotton cultivation pushed all before it; and the United States witnessed an enormous geographical expansion of plantation slavery in a very short period of time. As it turned out, Western competition would undercut Carolinian cotton planters, but the signs were not apparent to observers at the time of the Missouri crisis. Instead, South Carolina seemed to be riding the crest of an economic wave.

Pinckney's own pride in Carolinian achievements was obvious. In his speeches on Missouri, he carefully reminded his listeners of South Carolina's success, noting that outsiders were always surprised at "the richness, order, and soil" of the state.[63] Pinckney boasted that he represented one of the leading commercial cities in the country, that South Carolina produced more domestic exports than any other state, and that the agriculture of the slave plantation was more efficient than that of the Northern free farm.[64] Taunting Northerners who complained about the three-fifths rule in federal representation, Pinckney proclaimed: "By this, I suppose, Mr. Chairman, is meant, that they would have had no idea that the Western and Southern States would have grown with the rapidity they have, and filled so many seats in the House."[65]

His perception of South Carolina's success also allowed him to take an aggressive and unusual position in national debate, and this was not limited to the question of Missouri. Others worried about America's economic prospects; Pinckney rejoiced. South Carolina had experienced growth without pain, and an abundant supply of open land to the west along with apparently limitless world demand for her crops appeared to promise the same in the future. Moreover, slavery was what made the system beneficent. It was good for the slaves; it was the basis of efficient production; and it shielded white men from the possible dangers of economic growth. In other states men worried about the growth of a dependent proletariat; in South Carolina that role was filled by slaves, and all white men were independent. Far from fostering a narrow agrarianism, the success of plantation agriculture in South Carolina allowed a planter like Pinckney to treat economic development of all kinds with a tolerant and expansive attitude.

*   *   *

In politics, too, Pinckney was pleased with South Carolina's experience and optimistic about the lessons to be drawn from it, but he was never able to be as relaxed in his political thought as he was in his economics. Like his contemporaries, he was always concerned with conventional problems of republican theory—how to maintain a well-directed and effective government without allowing governmental power to corrupt the rulers or to impinge upon popular liberty—and Pinckney thought that it would take a sustained effort to cope with these problems.[66] In the 1780s he worried about the weakness of government and the selfishness of the people; like many others, Pinckney sought the answer to these worries in the creation of the new federal government. Soon, however, he became alienated by what he saw as the high-handed and partial administration of the new government, and during the 1790s he began to advocate strict limits on federal power, increased popular participation in politics, and most important, the preservation of states' rights. For the rest of his life he argued that these were the safeguards necessary to defend republicanism. He was not obsessed by them, but he never forgot them or the dangers that they alone could forestall, and his extreme stance in the Missouri debates showed the depth of his fears and the lengths to which he would go if those fears were aroused.

The development of Pinckney's thought was similar to that of many of his contemporaries who moved from Federalism in 1787–88 to Jeffersonian Republicanism in the 1790s, and his individual principles were like those of many other Republicans, yet the overall cast of Pinckney's thought differed from that of many contemporaries. For one thing, most Americans in the early nineteenth century who strongly espoused states' rights also advocated limited government, but Pinckney did not agree;[67] he consistently advocated extensive governmental activity along with the preservation of states' rights. For another thing, some of the more active democratic politicians at the time were beginning to argue that party competition—previously considered a sign of danger and decay—was a necessary mechanism for full popular involvement in representative government.[68] Pinckney disagreed passionately. Although he took an advanced democratic position about popular participation in politics, he saw party development as a dangerous and corrupting influence.

The particular development of Pinckney's political thought can be explained by examining how he drew upon his own political experience. Throughout his life Pinckney believed that it was possible to achieve a specific vision of republican government—a government in which popular participation was consistent with internal harmony,

101

which was led by men of distinction and wisdom, and which was energetic and progressive in its policies. This is what he hoped to secure from the national government in the 1780s, but thereafter his attention was primarily directed elsewhere. After 1787 he held national office only briefly,[69] he was much more involved in government and politics within South Carolina, where he was able to find practical satisfaction as a popular leader and progressive reformer without resorting to party development. His experiences in national politics were much less positive. It would be wrong to depict him as alienated from the federal government or obsessed with its supposed errors; as the leader of the Jeffersonian Republican movement in an important state, Pinckney always had ties with national leaders and a role in national politics. Still, he maintained a certain distance; he quarreled with important Republican leaders; and most significantly, on the two occasions when national politics did become the focus of his attention—in the late 1790s and at the time of the Missouri debate—he did not like what he saw. Within South Carolina, Pinckney and his associates fashioned a political system very close to his ideal; in national politics, on the other hand, he perceived disharmony, corruption, and obvious mistakes in policy. Moreover, in the end he saw a distinct danger that national politics might begin to threaten what had been achieved in South Carolina. There is little difficulty, then, in explaining the development of Pinckney's political thought. His ideals did not change, but his conception of how and where to achieve them did. In the 1780s he sought to pursue his ideal of republicanism by linking the states closely into a new system of federal government; by 1821 he sought to preserve the same vision by insulating South Carolina from the dangers of national politics.

In the 1780s Pinckney took quite an extreme Federalist position and consistently fought for a stronger national government. His first pamphlet, published in 1783, argued in favor of granting customs revenues to the Continental Congress, maintained that the revolutionary debt must be paid off in full at face value, and suggested that Congress be given the power to place an interdict on the trade of any state that did not pay its share of national financial requisitions.[70] In Congress, Pinckney kept up the fight for sounder national finances.[71] In the Philadelphia convention he even proposed that Congress be given a veto on state laws![72] Behind these positions lay a body of high Federalist theory justifying a powerful central government under able leadership and insulated from popular pressure. Like other Federalists, Pinckney inverted traditional maxims of republicanism and argued that a virtuous people, small area, and strictly limited government were precisely *not* the conditions that could sustain an American republic. It was foolish, he claimed, to confide too much in the virtue of the people. Americans had already seen their government paralyzed by selfish sectional jealousies. Political leadership had fallen into disrepute. But a solution was at hand in the new government, and Pinckney carefully went through the structure, showing how it would subordinate conflicting interests to the national good. He defended the powers of the proposed government and—going further than most Federalists—argued that republican government must be particularly strong government: "In a system founded upon republican principles, where the powers of government are properly distributed . . . a greater degree of force and energy will always be found necessary than even in a monarchy." In a monarchy, the king provided a natural focus of national unity; in a republic, unity came naturally only from a popular commitment to the general welfare at the expense of sacrificing private interest—"and it will only prevail in moments of enthusiasm." The answer was power: "With respect to the Union, this can only be remedied by a strong government, which, while it collects its powers to a point, will prevent that spirit of disunion from which the most serious consequences are to be apprehended."[73] In his early years Pinckney was clearly something of a Federalist hotspur.

Pinckney never abandoned his commitment to vigorous government —he developed it over his life and accommodated it to much more relaxed notions about popular participation in politics—but he developed it almost entirely within South Carolina. During his several terms as governor of the state, he made continual proposals for government action, advocating the creation of a public school system, the foundation of a state board of agriculture, the construction of better roads and lighthouses, the improvement of inland navigation, judicial reform, and the erection of a penitentiary.[74] Not only were these specific proposals depicted as practical and useful, but they were part of a larger process. "The object of a republic," he said, "is to render its citizens virtuous and happy"; by the power of its laws and the force of its example, government could literally shape the manners of the people.[75] Public support for education was one means to this end, and Pinckney consistently campaigned for public schools in South Carolina. As he put it in his 1797 governor's message to the South Carolina legislature:

In governments, truly formed for the happiness and freedom of their Citizens, springing from their authority and depending upon their opinions, it is of the highest importance, that the means of knowledge and information should be generally diffused. However favourable republican governments certainly are to equal liberty, justice and order, no real stability can be expected, unless the minds of their citizens are enlightened, and sufficiently impressed with the importance of the principles from whence the blessings proceed. . . . It is among the beauties of Republics that they are founded in the affections and knowledge of their Citizens.[76]

Nor did learning stop after men left school. Politics itself was a form of education; conducted properly, it could lead to remarkable progress and enlightenment.

Indeed, this was what Pinckney thought was happening. Abandoning his doubts of the 1780s, he soon rediscovered the virtue of the people. The comparison with benighted Europeans raised under monarchical government was particularly revealing: Americans were "the most immaculate, and easily governed, and at the same time the best intentioned people in the world."[77] With these presuppositions, Pinckney had no hesitation about popular participation in politics. Representation was the fundamental basis of republicanism, and Pinckney emphasized the importance of free elections, of freely selected juries (which he conceived of as part of popular representation in government), and of the directly representative branches of government.[78] Within South Carolina he urged on the successful movement to repeal property qualifications for suffrage.[79] In national politics he saw the struggle against the Federalists in 1800 as a struggle against a selfish clique who sought "to prevent the *officious and giddy multitude,*' as a ministerial hireling has impudently called them, from presuming to interfere with questions of state."[80] Yet popular participation in politics was not inconsistent with an exalted conception of political leadership; Pinckney always insisted that leaders should be men "of merits and talents," and he assumed that the selection of selfish and undistinguished leaders was a sign of too little popular involvement in politics rather than too much.[81] To the end of his career, Pinckney maintained a remarkably harmonious vision of what was possible in politics—a virtuous people would elect wise leaders to carry out progressive policies. It was a vision containing the best of Federalism, ideas of the progressive potential of government and the possibility of disinterested leadership, along with a new commitment to popular participation in politics. But in another way, Pinckney's thought diverged dramatically from his initial Federalism. In the 1780s he had concentrated on reforming national government, but it was remarkable how his perspective changed afterwards. The positive developments he saw and advocated came in state politics; the national connection seemed increasingly threatening to internal state harmony.

Pinckney attached increasing importance to the role of the states in American government. Originally he saw the states as an answer to the problem of how government could work in a large territory (interestingly, Pinckney turned the conventional problem of the large republic upside down: instead of worrying how such a government could be responsive to the people, he was interested in how such a government could be effective),[82] and was eager to refute the conventional argument:

> that in a democratic constitution, the mechanism is too complicated, the motions too slow, for the operations of a great empire, whose defence and government require execution and despatch in proportion to the magnitude, extent, and variety of its concerns. . . . Much of the objection, he thought would be done away by the continuance of a federal republic, which, distributing the country into districts, or states, of a commodious extent, and leaving to each state its internal legislation, reserves unto a superintending government the adjustment of their general claims, the complete direction of the common force and treasure of the empire.[83]

As Americans pushed ever farther west, Pinckney argued that state governments were necessary to encourage and regulate expansion.[84]

Moreover, he had always been ready to concede that states had broad powers. In 1783, in his first published pamphlet, Pinckney declared: "There are two distinct sovereignties in the United States—That which is for the purpose of public safety, and that which is calculated more particularly to promote private happiness." The central government, he wrote, should deal with "the conduct of war, treaties, politics, and the necessary revenue"; state legislatures should decide upon "laws, police, order, justice, the cultivation and improvement of the social virtues."[85] Pinckney reiterated several times this particular scheme of a division between state and federal competence, and he seems to have maintained it consistently.[86] He was not opposed to the exercise of power

105

by the national government when it was operating within its proper sphere. Pinckney did not fear federal power in the way that many Jeffersonians did: he never complained about the fiscal system; he always recognized the need for an effective army and navy, and was even rather eager to go to war in the troubled days before 1812.[87] But it is notable how limited a conception he held of the sphere of federal competence and the action necessary within that sphere. Meanwhile, his estimation of the importance of state governments was steadily increasing. Not only did he advocate that states undertake new activities on their own; he saw a new role for them within national politics as peculiarly able to perceive and represent the view of their people, to judge the limits of constitutionality, and ultimately to set the federal government right when it overstepped its bounds.

One danger in federal government of which Pinckney was always aware was, of course, sectionalism—one region taking an unfair advantage of the others. He thought it an avoidable danger in economic policy, but as a broader political problem, it was one that would not go away. During the Missouri debates, when he remarked that "the Northern and Eastern States . . . are always much more alive to their interests than the Southern," his charge was based on the grievances of a lifetime.[88] For Pinckney, the threats came always from New England, which to him was the odd, isolated, and dangerous region that constantly sought a moral and political domination over the union.[89] Continually, it threatened to undermine American democracy: by sponsoring Alien and Sedition laws, instituting religious establishments, succumbing to foreign blandishments during the Embargo crisis, or seeking unfair political advantage by antislavery agitation.[90] Fortunately, state governments could check sectionalism in two ways. For one, they could remove a great deal of controversy from national politics: "By the individual States exercising, as they do, all the powers necessary for municipal or individual purposes . . . it eases them [the federal government] of a vast quantity of business that would very much disturb the exercise of their general powers."[91] Moreover, the number of states and their varying interests made it difficult for any one narrow interest to control the government. As Pinckney put it in one of his rare lapses from prescience, "With twenty or twenty-two governments, we shall be much more secure from disunion than with twelve, and ten times more so than if we were a single or consolidated one."[92]

The other dangers Pinckney saw in national politics were more insidious. Sectionalism was visible, difficult to justify, and pitted each region against the others. Other threatening developments were less obvious. They could be justified on principled grounds. Moreover, they could spread from national politics to affect and corrupt the internal affairs of the states. Nonetheless, Pinckney still thought that the states were the best defense and maintained that they could triumph.

One fear that Pinckney developed about national government was a fear of corruption—a fear that some selfish group would gain power, evade constitutional checks, cause the government to overstep its bounds, and pervert the whole American experiment. These were conventional ideas, of course, going back to the pre-Revolutionary radical tradition; they were at the heart of Jeffersonian opposition to Hamilton and his followers in the 1790s.[93] For some Southern Jeffersonians, particularly in Virginia, these fears became the basis of a deeply rooted and profoundly frightened view of politics: they saw never-ending conspiracies to give illegitimate powers to the national government; they became suspicious of political power in general; and they worried that political corruption could pervert economic and social development as well.[94]

It took Pinckney some time to learn these fears, and he learned them only in the specific context of the federal government; but when the time came, he learned his lesson well. During the 1780s he several times dismissed conventional warnings about these threats as "childish chimeras." Americans need not worry, because "we have no hereditary monarchy or nobles, with all their train of influence or corruption to contend with; nor is it possible to form a Federal Aristocracy."[95] Indeed, at the Philadelphia convention he argued against the proposal to make congressmen ineligible for other offices of profit under the new government.[96] It was not until the days of the Adams administration that Pinckney saw any danger—but what dangers he then saw. Speaking in the Senate in February 1800, on a measure to delegate power to the President to suspend trade with France if the necessity arose while Congress was in recess, Pinckney declared:

> I consider it as springing from the same source with most of the measures which have been agitated for the last two years, particularly the provisional army, and as going to establish the precedent of granting to the executive, powers, in my judgment, unwarranted by the constitution —of paving the way to that *executive and ministerial influence* in the affairs of our government, which may hereafter render the *representative part* of it . . . more a name than anything else.[97]

At that time Pinckney perceived a great many threats to liberty, and in all these warnings he cited the dangers of influence and corruption time and time again.[98] The President had undermined the independence of the judiciary, attacked freedom of the press, assumed despotic power over aliens, and now threatened even to tamper with elections.[99] The President was also guilty of political corruption in the modern sense; he had handed out offices with "no view but to enrich family connection, or reward the sycophants and supporters of particular interests."[100]

Pinckney had seen what could happen when the federal government was abused. It did not destroy his faith in government in general, nor did he share the Virginians' continuing fears about federal activity. But when the time came, he was ready to apply the lessons he had learned in 1799 and 1800.[101] What finally reawakened his fears was the threat of federal interference with slavery in Missouri. All at once the old worries about corruption were back in their most extreme form, along with a strengthened conviction that federal corruption might spill over and destroy much of what ordinary Americans held dear. He saw the whole affair as a Northern plot to gain "a fixed ascendancy" in the representation in Congress.[102] The motives were clear—"the love of power, and the never-ceasing wish to regain the honors and offices of the Government"—and so was an ultimate tendency "to mould our republican institutions into forms much less democratic than at present."[103] Fortunately, the remedy was apparent as well: state governments were the proper organs through which the people could express their disapproval of improper actions by the federal government.[104] The wisdom and alertness of state legislatures could guard against any attempts to violate the Constitution; the proliferation of states mitigated against faction in national government.[105] Pinckney expressed his final position in his first speech on Missouri:

> It is well known that faction is always much more easy and dangerous in small than large countries; and when we consider that, to the security afforded by the extent of our territory are to be added, the guards of the State legislatures, which being selected as they are, and always the most proper organs of their citizens' opinions as to the measures of the General Government, stand as alert and faithful sentinels to disprove . . . such acts as appear impolitic or unconstitutional. . . . With such guards it is impossible for any serious opposition to be made to the Federal Government on slight or trivial grounds; nor, through such

an extent of territory or number of States, would any but the most tyrannical or corrupt acts claim serious attention.[106]

It was up to the states to save the nation. This was a classic statement of the states' rights position that Southerners would maintain right to the Civil War.

In addition to sectional combinations in Congress, however, faction also took the form of party organization generally, and this was the final danger that Pinckney saw in national politics. The question whether sustained party organization and competition were legitimate was, of course, a common one among Pinckney's contemporaries, and it is possible to trace a gradual shift in opinion from a complete rejection of party to a gradual and grudging theoretical acceptance.[107] Pinckney, on the other hand, moved the opposite way: early on, he was relatively tolerant of party; by the end of his career he was much more dogmatically opposed. His few comments on the subject during the 1780s expressed a conventional dislike of party in a perfunctory way, but during the debate over the ratification of the Constitution, he declared, "The only remedy against despotism [is] to form a party against those who are obnoxious, and turn them out."[108] This was, of course, exactly what happened in the 1790s; when the Federalists seemed intent upon introducing despotic measures, Pinckney and the other Jeffersonian Republicans gradually built up a national movement to turn them out of power. Nor was Pinckney shy to admit what was going on; as he said in the Senate in 1800, "No man can say . . . that strong contending parties do not divide our councils and citizens, as well with respect to foreign politics, as to him who is hereafter to fill the executive department."[109]

Pinckney never altogether abandoned his notion of the utility of party, because he continued to consider the Federalists as a threat to republican government, but he increasingly began to emphasize the dangers of party politics generally.[110] He did this most vividly in 1800 when he spoke about the necessity of combatting any form of executive influence over the courts; unless things were changed, Pinckney declared, people had reason to fear "that faction or corruption may mount your bench of justice, fill the seats of your jurors, or stain the annals of your judiciary with innocent blood, sacrificed at the shrine of party or ambition."[111] Over the years his fears about party became less lurid but more precise. "The conduct of a few violent partisans" sabotaged American policy at the time of the Embargo and threatened national honor.[112] Party impugned leaders of talents and decision.[113] Party could bring "not only the name of an American, but what is worse of a republican, into contempt."[114]

Pinckney's vision of the dangers of party soon spread beyond the national government. In his final speech on the Missouri question, he examined state politics throughout the union and catalogued the baneful affects of party in state after state. In Maryland, a state "as equally torn by the near division of parties as any other," there was "a scene of perpetual hostility . . . adverse to the harmony which is always so essential to good government."[115] In Pennsylvania, in an astonishing "departure from the democratic principles which ought to prevail in the constitution of every State," the governor could appoint officers—including judges—without restriction, "just as his own unchecked will, or the influence of his partisans may please."[116] But worst of all was New York (where local Republicans were incidentally developing the first fully elaborated defense of party competition): there the legislature was elected annually and "as in this State parties are nearly equally balanced, the inconvenience, confusion, and injury arising to the public by this annual struggle, are inconceivable."[117] The legislature, moreover, had an indirect but effective power to remove men from office and to appoint the successors whom they pleased; the result was disgraceful: "Who of us belonging to other States can witness the complete and general removal of every officer in their government . . . without rejoicing that in our own State we are at least exempt from the effect of so wavering and fickle a system."[118] When Pinckney finally condemned party as the means whereby slavery agitation might destroy the union, he was not talking about an imaginary danger; he was talking about something he had observed himself.[119]

As Pinckney grew older, he witnessed many political changes that he found distasteful and some that he found profoundly alarming, but this did not mean that he was becoming an alienated old man, opposed to change and hankering for an idealized past. He remained an active and successful politician until a few years before his death, still optimistic about what politics could accomplish, and—in spite of a growing dislike for national and northern politics—satisfied with things in South Carolina. This is not surprising, for politics within the state had evolved very much in accordance with Pinckney's ideals and indeed to a considerable extent under Pinckney's direction. In order to understand the optimism in Pinckney's political thought, it is necessary finally to consider South Carolina's development and Pinckney's role in it.

* * *

At first glance, it is somewhat surprising to speak of the development of Carolinian politics at all; many have assumed that it was a state in which time stood still, which preserved idiosyncratic and archaic political practices until the end of the Civil War.[120] Behind those political arrangements lay the reality of planter power; as one historian has put it: "Throughout the pre–Civil War era, South Carolina's political order reflected the high-toned conservation of an entrenched landed aristocracy. . . . Nowhere else in America did the wealthy class so successfully conspire to keep power away from the common man."[121] As a result many historians have mistakenly concluded that there was simply a continuity in the Carolinian political system from the colonial period to secession.[122] The fact is, though, that the later stability of Carolinian politics was secured only as a result of important changes at the beginning of the nineteenth century. Nationally, the Federalists of the 1780s sought to fashion political arrangements that would endure relatively unchanged, despite America's growing complexity. In most places they failed; at the national capital and in most states, political practices changed continually. Within South Carolina, however, a settlement was achieved, not by the Federalists in the 1780s but a few years later by Charles Pinckney and the Jeffersonian Republicans.

As in most states, the changes in politics in South Carolina started in the last years of the eighteenth century when an established local elite began to be challenged by political outsiders.[123] The first signs of a conflict appeared in the 1780s when a shifting coalition of Charleston artisans, backcountry farmers, and idealistic radicals challenged the power of the "nabob phalanx" in the state legislature, but the nabobs held on.[124] At the beginning of the 1790s, South Carolinian politics was dominated by a small, tightly knit group of well-to-do planters, merchants, and professional men (the South Carolina Federalists) from the coastal areas near Charleston—probably the most wealthy and assertive such group in any state. They monopolized political offices and did not hesitate to profit from them, legally or otherwise; they were, as an opponent later remembered, among "the greediest of the 'Treasury Squad.'"[125] They treated outsiders with contempt; they derided Westerners in the legislature as "yahoos" and "a parcel of illiterate second rate fellows"; when they went to public meetings in their own beloved city of Charleston, they encountered "demagogues & block-heads."[126] Indeed, explicit elitism and fear of social upheaval lay at the heart of Federalist electioneering in South Carolina during the 1790s. Federalists dismissed their political opponents as "little petty insurgents, the mere journeymen of sedition" who used "the pretended factitious rights of man" to assert "the rights of a few noisy demagogues over the rights of the people."[127] Constantly they termed their opponents Jacobins; for an illustration of the horrors of Jacobinism, they turned not to France but to an example closer at hand and nearer to white Carolinians' worst fears—they turned to Saint Domingue.[128]

To their disgusted opponents, the assertion of the South Carolina Federalists was an arrant and arrogant example of aristocracy and oligarchy.[129] Arguments for freedom and free speech took on urgency in a situation where "a man becomes the subject of obloquy and ridicule who only pronounces the name of liberty. Utter it, and you are immediately denounced as an anarchist, a jacobin, a disorganizer, an atheist."[130] Many different Carolinians took offense. Some were prominent men with connections to the Federalist elite who quarreled with their friends and kinsmen, sometimes simply over personal affairs.[131] More, however, were complete outsiders. Charleston artisans chafed against the economic power and political pretensions of their planter patrons.[132] Westerners agitated against a system of unchanging representation in the legislature which unfairly preserved an eastern stranglehold on power.[133] Ordinary men throughout the state resented arrogance and corruption in political office.[134] Linking their internal grievances to the cause of national Jeffersonian Republicanism, they put together a coalition that finally defeated the Federalist planter oligarchy in 1800.[135]

On the face of it, Charles Pinckney was an improbable leader for this reform-minded coalition of outsiders, but lead it he did, and his leadership revealed much about the nature and limits of Jeffersonian Republicanism in South Carolina. Pinckney himself had been born in the heart of the coastal planter elite. His wealth was fabled: "he was the fortunate owner of seven plantations, and near two thousand negroes, with an income annually of about eighty thousand dollars."[136] His lifestyle was luxurious. His farm outside Charleston "was a villa in such as which Hortensius or Cicero would have felt at home, with its cellars of highly-flavored Madeira, its fountains, its shrubbery, its artificial lake, and its fish-ponds"; his magnificent townhouse in Charleston boasted elegant furnishings, the finest European paintings, and a library of nearly 20,000 of the rarest and choicest books.[137] But behind this ornate facade there were always hints of scandal. Pinckney was prodigal with his money; he borrowed heavily; he had difficulty paying his debts at times; and there were persistent reports that he took improper advantage of public monies and private trusts committed to his care. [138] After his wife died in 1794, he openly flaunted his affairs with women.[139] He was known for his personal vanity and his persistent political ambition.[140] Pinckney's initial alienation from the local Federalists resulted from their denying him – perhaps because they despised him for his loose moral standards – the political preferment he thought he deserved.[141]

Yet there was more to it than that. There were other members of the Carolinian establishment known for their vanity, ambition, and questionable personal lives who were not treated with such contempt and public vituperation.[142] Pinckney's own cousins would not speak to him, and he was held in such "universal abhorrance [sic] and contempt," one of his opponents remarked, that "nothing from him could produce much effect."[143] His personal life was paraded in the Charleston press, and he was parodied as "Charley, the Speech-writer."[144] In that parody lay hidden the real reasons for the intense resentment, for Pinckney had committed the unpardonable crime of taking his grievances to the people and trying to create a new style of popular politics. He was seen as a traitor to his class, Blackguard Charlie, driving around town in his old chariot "to receive the grateful tribute of bows from the sans culotte & other low fellows."[145]

Pinckney would have been amused by this distaste; he would have accepted their charges and gloried in them. There was no doubt that he was a tireless campaigner and that he enjoyed electioneering; at the height of the campaign in 1800, when he later boasted that he had been on his feet for two whole days, he found time to write, "I always loved Politics and I find as I grow older I become more fond of them."[146] But his appeal went deeper than his dedication to politicking. In his personal career as well as his public rhetoric, he exhibited an enthusiasm for popular politics, a demand for more open access to political office, an aggressive pursuit of economic opportunity, and a reckless desire for freedom from social constraint. It was an attractive message, and the people of South Carolina responded. The Federalists were decisively defeated in 1800 and effectively eliminated from state politics thereafter; Pinckney himself continued his long political career without losing an election.

The South Carolina Federalists were quite right to realize that their defeat entailed more than a simple transfer of power; fundamental changes were taking place in Carolinian life. Most of the old elite chose to drop out of politics altogether.[147] The victorious Jeffersonian Republicans made constitutional changes that settled sectional quarrels about representation in the state legislature and eliminated property requirements for the franchise. Moreover, although planter power remained a reality in Carolinian life, both the composition of the planter class and the nature of its power were changing. No longer was it simply a small group of interrelated families around Charleston; it broadened to include planters throughout the state and men who had achieved wealth from more humble beginnings.[148] No longer did wealthy planters maintain such a stranglehold on political office or exploit it so selfishly.[149] Some Carolinian leaders continued to express an arrogant political elitism, but they did so privately. No longer was elitism part of public electioneering as it had been for the Federalists.[150] Few whites were economically dependent on their richer neighbors; indeed, rich and poor appear to have had few dealings.[151] In ordinary social life the planters did not demand visible signs of deference from their poorer neighbors; if anything, social life emphasized the equality and neighborliness of all white men.[152] In other words, elite rule persisted but became in many ways less overt and less manipulative. Beneath the high-level leadership of the planters, ordinary white Carolinians had won personal and political independence.

Clearly the Federalists' fears of complete social and political upheaval were exaggerated. Pinckney's own role in the Republican victory indicated that there was still a place for gentlemen in Carolinian politics, and it turned out that Republican ascendancy secured a conservative political settlement. By themselves popular groups seeking power appeared selfish and self-interested; popular leaders seemed unskilled and presumptuous. Pinckney gave the people vital assistance. His sophisticated use of republican rhetoric offered a coherence and legitimacy to the aims of diverse, unsophisticated groups; his personal standing furnished them with a sort of legitimate leadership that they could not find among themselves. But he wanted to go only so far; Pinckney never approved of the process of democratization in the Northern states with its raucous quarrels and new-style political managers. His vision of politics was one of broad but harmonious participation, independent leadership, and principled discussion; the development of South Carolina's internal politics showed how successful Pinckney and his associates were at fixing the long-term contours of the state's political life.

Pinckney advocated popular participation but condemned political parties, and this was how things developed within South Carolina. The people began turning out to vote in record numbers.[153] But Pinckney and his allies explicitly sought to avoid the formation of institutionalized parties and, with the major local grievances being attended to and the principal opposition group withdrawing from politics, were able to do so. [154] Indeed, over the years it was the lack of party that most visibly separated Carolinian political life from that in other states, and the difference had profound implications.[155] In states where party politics provided the means and legitimacy for all sorts of groups to pursue self-interest, conflict persisted and became the norm. Without parties, these things did not happen in South Carolina. The periodic outbursts of popular excitement were not translated into independent, sustained, and articulated political demands.[156] South Carolina's antebellum harmony was a political construct. There were real divisions within the state, even among the whites, but as they did not lead to lasting political conflict, the state appeared to enjoy an unparalleled unity.

South Carolina also enjoyed a unique style of political leadership, and here too the influence of Pinckney was felt. Contemptuous of mere politicians, Carolinian leaders sought to conform to more elevated standards of statesmanship, emphasizing personal gentility, political independence, and principle.[157] For this Pinckney provided both a justification and an important example. He constantly emphasized the importance of filling offices with men of talent and respectability.[158] He proudly asserted his own gentility in the heat of congressional debate, and he exemplified a particular style of gentlemanly leadership with his wealth, his learning, his political independence, and his extraordinary personal assurance.[159] Elsewhere this old-fashioned style gradually disappeared as new-style political managers arose; within South Carolina it survived and blossomed, and Pinckney continued to be remembered as one of its leading exemplars. Moreover, Pinckney and his contemporaries had also done practical things that allowed the ideal of the Carolinian statesman to flourish. To begin with, their discouragement of political parties meant that there did not exist in South Carolina the mechanism which elsewhere worked to promote and legitimate a new kind of leader. Likewise, they worked out justifications for political leadership unlike those advanced before or those developed elsewhere. The Federalists had claimed that rule by the wise and well born was necessary to avert ever-threatening anarchy and social disorder. During the early nineteenth century this sort of arrogant elitism died out throughout the United States, most often to be replaced by new ideas about the nature of representative leadership: politicians boasted of their humble origins; they appealed to specific elements within the electorate; and they sought to further the interests of specific interest groups. In South Carolina, leadership was conceived of in very different terms. Denying the existence of divisions within the state, Carolinian thinkers like Pinckney advanced an ideal of political leadership in which men of talent and independence exercised their own superior judgment to defend the liberty and shared principles of all white Carolinians.

This brings up a final point about the idiosyncratic nature of South Carolina's antebellum politics—the importance of ideas; here too Pinckney's efforts bore lasting fruit.[160] Without parties, without the competition of interest groups, and with an elevated conception of political leadership, politics continued to be about principles. In no other state did political debate continue at such an elevated level of discourse; in no other state were abstract theories so important in practical politics. And in ideas as well as practice, it was those fashioned by Pinckney and his generation that continued to dominate Carolinian politics up to the Civil War; it was remarkable how Carolinians clung to them even in changed circumstances and with changed leaders after Pinckney's death. Pinckney's ideas certainly anticipated Calhoun's. Calhoun also worked in an old-fashioned republican tradition in which he depicted Carolinian politics as an ideal, worried about degeneration in the federal government, and warned that national corruption might spread into South Carolina.[161] Calhoun acknowledged his debt to the earlier Jeffersonians, of whom Pinckney had been the principal Carolinian spokesman. At the height of the nullification crisis, he insisted, "Mine are the opinions of the Republican party of '98, beyond which I do not go an inch."[162] In fact, Calhoun went considerably further, but even within South Carolina, few followed; his novel doctrines of nullification and the concurrent majority were forgotten after his death in 1850. Carolinians had listened to Calhoun, but they might as well have been hearing Pinckney. Indeed, the rhetoric of the 1850s in the state returned to old-fashioned republican arguments in their classical form, and it was by these that Carolinians justified secession in 1860.[163] At the height of the Civil War, it was appropriate that a leading Charleston magazine recalled Charles Pinckney as the first to formulate the state's political theories.[164]

The relationship between Pinckney's thought and Carolinian practice worked in two ways; Pinckney's optimistic view of what was possible in politics evolved from his experience and achievements in South Carolina, and later Carolinians continued to draw upon his ideals. Elsewhere in America, men worried that economic development would lead to dependency and social antagonisms, which could undermine republican government; in South Carolina, open land, world demand for cotton, and black slavery apparently guaranteed independence and opportunity for white Carolinians. In other states, political parties encouraged group conflict and provided opportunities for a new sort of political leader; within South Carolina, popular participation was supportive of respectable leadership and inimical to interest group politics. Pinckney's optimistic vision was an attractive way of depicting Carolinian reality, and Carolinians continued to picture themselves as he had done. Also like him, however, they tempered their optimism with a sense of separation and even threat from the outside; at a time of crisis, this theory would justify cutting the ties that bound South Carolina to the Union. Despite its overall optimism, Pinckney's thought contained the seeds of the outcome he feared most—"the division of this Union, and civil war."[165]

*   *   *

In the end, though, South Carolina did not secede alone; her ideals had a broader impact, and an explanation must begin by remembering how men like Pinckney had fashioned them. Although Pinckney was a Carolinian through and through, he worked in a common American tradition of republican thought. Some historians have seen this tradition as a straitjacket, a fully worked-out, inflexible world view that gave men little chance to develop or to express their individuality. The opposite was true in Pinckney's case, at least: working within this tradition gave his thought its flexibility and its ability to meet changing circumstances. For Pinckney, republicanism connected things that might appear unbridgeable. His thought did change over his lifetime, most notably from nationalism to sectionalism, but he did not see any inconsistency. The point is that republicanism connected his initial ideals and his later career; early on, he formulated a body of questions and continued consistently to test them against his experience. Likewise, republicanism bridged Pinckney's loyalty to the nation and to his state. He asked the same fundamental question in national and state politics — how to perfect and preserve republicanism — and if he finally found the answer in South Carolina, he continued to present it in a national language. This is the clue to how one final gap was bridged, for Pinckney's Carolinian ideology ulitmately commanded a considerable audience outside South Carolina. It did so because Pinckney addressed common American problems and paid allegiance to common American symbols. The example he worked from was unique and his conclusions his own, but because the words and worries were widely recognizable, Carolinian thought achieved a broader audience.

Pinckney and the South Carolinians were not the only Americans who drew upon the republican tradition to suit their particular needs. During Pinckney's lifetime Northern Republicans were slowly working out a theory of the legitimacy of party organization and continuing party contests.[166] In the North many local Republicans took the traditional opposition to an aristocracy of special legal privilege, and developed it into an attack on social and economic privilege as well.[167] Others began to abandon the traditional Republican aversion to federal power and to advocate projects involving great increases in federal activity.[168] There were continuing quarrels in the North, and these ideas did not develop unchallenged, but they ultimately triumphed. In 1860 a majority of the voters in the free states supported a new Republican party, proudly partisan, egalitarian and even populistic, and committed to a struggle against aristocracy. Moreover, it was in the South, in slavery and consequent Southern political arrangements, that the new party saw the source of the threat of aristocracy, and it was in the struggle against the South that the Republicans were finally willing to extend the powers of the federal government in unprecedented ways.[169]

This anti-Southernism, of course, worked to unite the South in 1860–61, but it is important to realize that the South had not always been united. Although most Southerners had always agreed on positions such as opposition to increasing federal power, the republican tradition developed differently in different Southern areas. From the time of the Missouri crisis, Virginians had shared a perception of the threat, articulated by Pinckney, that encroaching federal government would initiate economic and political changes, which would damage the pure republicanism of the Southern states.[170] But they were also anxious about internal developments and uneasy about slavery.[171] They worried that commercial expansion and greedy acquisitiveness would undermine republican virtue and simplicity within the Old Dominion.[172] They hesitated about political reform and popular politics, and used republican political theory to defend an existing state political system under attack for perceived inequalities in suffrage and legislative apportionment.[173] In the newer states of the cotton South, on the other hand, people did not share Virginians' hesitations. In these areas men were agreed in their defense of slavery, their pursuit of economic development, and their assertive democracy.[174] Like other Southerners they were keenly aware of any threat by the federal government to interfere with local rights, but they were more worried about threats from within. In these states lively two-party systems developed, with both parties attacking aristocracy and dependence, and vying to defend equality and freedom from various perceived threats within the workings of state political systems.[175] But South Carolina was different from both the Old Dominion and the New South. She combined the optimism of the newer states with the developed republicanism of the Old Dominion, but what South Carolinians did not share with other Southerners was a sense of internal threat. As far as they were concerned, their own political and social arrangements were stable and ideal; they were free to concentrate their worries on external threats. Over the years this set South Carolina off from the rest of the South; there were many times when Carolinians urged action against federal encroachments while other Southerners held back. Yet in 1860–61 it was these traditional Carolinian arguments that enabled South Carolina to lead the rest of the Southern states out of the union.

The opportunity arose because of the ultimate instability of Southern politics. Beneath the apparently successful development of well-established party politics, there were unresolved tensions; when they provoked a crisis, the Carolinians were able to offer a way to resolve them. During the 1830s and 1840s, party contests in Southern states appeared very much like those in Northern states. Party machinery was fully developed, and there were high turnouts in elections, fixed party loyalties over time, and close contests.[176] Local Whig and Democratic parties fought not only over national issues but also over local ones. The Democrats sought to preserve freedom by using government to curb any prospect of reducing men to economic dependence; the Whigs sought to use government to promote economic development so that men would have opportunities to amass sufficient wealth for economic independence.[177] But even at the height of these contests, there was evidence of a long-term instability in Southern politics. Historians have been unable to find marked economic or social divisions, like the ethnocultural divisions in the North, to account for mass voter loyalties.[178] The one division they have perceived—a division, broadly, between more and less commercially developed areas—is difficult to pinpoint precisely, and meant that men of fixed party loyalties would find their social and economic circumstances changing as commercial development advanced.[179] Moreover, this division does not explain the persistence of party loyalties over time, for party allegiance remained fixed even in areas where economic circumstances changed. Southerners continually attacked aristocracy, but planters and well-to-do men held office much more in the South than in the North.[180] Tensions between leaders and voters and between different elements in party constituencies meant that it was difficult for parties to come up with concrete local programs.[181] Government activities were underfinanced and often badly managed.[182] With these problems in local affairs, Southern electioneering tended to concentrate much more on national issues than did Northern, and it particularly emphasized issues of slavery and sectionalism.[183]

Moreover, things got markedly worse in the 1850s. Sectional antagonism became more bitter in national politics. In the lower South the Whig party collapsed, and no new party arose to continue the contest.[184] Within the South generally, more and more planters came into public office despite the reiteration of democratic rhetoric.[185] Southern governments embarked on elaborate schemes of economic development that seemed only to favor special interests and often proved to be costly failures.[186] The consequent popular alienation from politics was compounded by a sense of social and economic malaise; it seemed that the prosperity of the 1850s offered few opportunities for the small men, while forcing unwelcome economic changes upon them.[187] One result was the growth of populist movements, but they lacked the skill or staying power effectively to challenge existing political arrangements.[188] Instead, the crisis was resolved by changes within the Democratic party.

120

The situation was one that Southern extremists were able brilliantly to exploit, and to do so, they used the arguments that Pinckney and his successors in South Carolina had long articulated.

These showed Southerners a way out of their difficulties; they explained and justified things that had seemed troublesome within the South and offered a course of action that would remove other threats. Ordinary Southerners were worried about economic development; the radicals argued that expansion and keeping new territories open for slavery was the best way to defuse social tensions and to maintain independence and equality.[189] Southerners were worried about aristocracy and impending government activity; the radicals presented a vision of a harmonious society, of respectable leadership, and of vigorous government.[190] The threat they saw came not from within the South but from outside, from an avaricious and despotic North. That region had betrayed the ideals of the American nation; the South alone upheld the principles of the American Revolution and American republicanism.[191] The radicals were able to invoke familiar arguments about the defense of Southern rights and to fuse them with deeper beliefs about American principles and ideals. Chained to the North, the South was doomed to corruption and decay; by itself, the South could be an ideal republic. These were the arguments used by the Breckinridge Democrats in the election of 1860 and by the secessionists in the winter of 1860–61.[192]

Significantly, South Carolina was in the vanguard, and the dramatic first decision for secession was taken in Charles Pinckney's own city of Charleston. Moreover, Southerners did not forget Pinckney himself at the time of the final crisis. *DeBow's Review*, which claimed to speak for all the South, published a eulogistic piece on Pinckney in 1864, remembering him as a Carolinian but also as a Southerner, a pioneer defender of Southern rights who had fought to maintain a pure interpretation of the Constitution untainted by "Yankee notions." He had been one of the most eminent founders "of the true patriarchal Republican party."[193] There could have been no more eloquent testimony to the importance of Pinckney's republicanism and where it led.

This, then, was the final importance of Charles Pinckney's thought. It was more than the thought of one man at one time, although it was clear that he shaped his thinking in a brilliant response to his own experience and his own circumstances. It became the thought of one state for a long time, and ultimately of the whole South at a crucial time. Pinckney's republicanism can be seen as a bridge between the eighteenth century and the nineteenth, between South Carolina and the other Southern states, but also something that destroyed other bridges. Pinckney and those who followed him used common American symbols in a way that would ultimately justify leading the South out of the Union.

4

Hugh Swinton Legaré, by John Mix Stanley (1858), after Edward Marchant. Courtesy of the U.S. Department of Justice.

Politics, Romanticism, and Hugh Legaré: "The Fondness of Disappointed Love"

MICHAEL O'BRIEN

A VOLUME that addresses the echo chamber of social and intellectual life in the history of Charleston has a special responsibility: to consider the bonds connecting Charleston to the imagination of its citizens. Rootedness is a vexatious and prominent issue in the eschatology of Southern history. In the legend of Southern place, Charleston has loomed large, oddly for a city in a myth so agrarian. In that same legend Hugh Swinton Legaré has held a small but strategic place. He is a prime witness for the debilitations of excessive and unreflecting loyalty, "the great cham of Charleston literature,"[1] planted in a brocaded drawing room with a full glass of Old Carolina Madeira in one hand, a volume of Dryden in the other, declaiming pompously and obscurely to unreflecting admirers, a bar to younger doubting voices.

For the plausibility of this Augustan nightmare, one assumption has been vital, the loyalty of Legaré to Charleston and Charleston to Legaré. And there is evidence to the effect. Almost the first critical assessment of Legaré, that by William Campbell Preston less than five months after Legaré's death in 1843, declares it: "Though his bosom was inspired by a real love of country, in the broadest sense of patriotism, yet it was warmed with a more genial glow for his own State, and cherished a romantic passion for his native city of Charleston. It was to him a dear and beloved impersonation, of which he never spoke but with a sort of filial devotion. All its inanimate objects had a living interest to him. He felt its rebukes as those of a parent, and cherished its manifold kindnesses with the most grateful affection."[2] The impression was strengthened by Legaré's own letters, printed by his sister Mary in the collected *Writings* of 1846, where he could be found to observe Charleston as "a happy state of things – a society so charming and so accomplished," even though ravaged by the divisions of nullification, that he had to pray, "I ask of heaven only that the little circle I am intimate with in Charleston should be kept together while I live, – in health, harmony and competence; and that, on my return [he was writing from Brussels], I may myself be enabled to enjoy the same happiness, in my intercourse with it, with which I have been hitherto blessed."[3]

Legaré's first postbellum biographer, Paul Hamilton Hayne, intensified this belief in the complicity of Legaré and Charleston. He remarked, for example, that Legaré, upon leaving the South Carolina College in 1814, "repaired without delay to his mother's home in Charleston, then, as always, both to his eyes and to his heart, the brightest spot on earth. About the city itself his deepest affections were entwined. Wherever the needs or duties of his subsequent career carried him, he would watch from afar its progress, and the progress of the State, with an almost painful solicitude." But it was William P. Trent, in his 1892 biography of William Gilmore Simms, who most fully articulated Charleston's reciprocal reverence. "The death of Crafts," he observed, "had left an especially good opening [for a new Southern writer] .... But in the opinion of the Charlestonians, this opening could be filled by one man only, – Hugh Swinton Legaré, whose prodigious performances at the new state college were still remembered."[4]

124

The evidence seems solid: from the man himself, from his friend, from his heirs, from scholarship. Yet look more closely. Preston spoke in the final paragraph of a eulogy, commissioned by and delivered to the city of Charleston. Was it not fitting that, in honoring a son of the city, Preston should link the two in amity, and where better or more inescapably than in a peroration? Legaré's own letters seem an unimpeachable source. Yet note that his *Writings* contain a bare and bizarre sampling of his correspondence, edited watchfully by a sister, eager to memorialize her adored brother and excise passages inconvenient to his reputation in Charleston. As for Hayne, he wrote of Legaré in filiopietistic vein, when Hayne himself had been driven by war, illness, and penury to rusticate in the nether regions of Georgia, there to mislay his prewar discontent with Charleston and invent a vanished Eden with Legaré at its center. "A brief half century ago," Hayne had imagined, "and culture, refinement, hospitality, wit, genius, and social virtue, seemed to have taken up their lasting abode therein. A constellation of distinguished men—writers, politicians, lawyers, and divines gave tone to the whole society, brightened and elevated the general discourse of men with men, and threw over the dull routine of professional and commercial labor, the lustre of art, and the graces of a fastidious scholarship."[5] And William Trent, as is well known, was intent upon proving the rejection of Simms by a snobbish and Ciceronian Charleston.[6] Legaré, a snob and a student of Cicero, was more than convenient to the thesis.

So there are circumstantial doubts, attachable to the case for Legaré's rootedness, which turn to certainty of a contrary thesis for anyone surveying the whole corpus of his letters and essays. In fact, Legaré was alienated from his birthplace, the more so the older he grew.[7] The character of that alienation is especially illuminating, not only of Legaré himself but of the social dynamics of the city's intellectual life in his generation, which came of age during the crisis of nullification, and of the legacy of those years.

As a young man, he had been close to the city and the city to him. He came from a good, if not splendid, Huguenot family, impoverished by his father's early death and aided by the beneficence of his grandfather, Thomas Legaré. He was educated first at the College of Charleston, then upcountry at the Willington Academy and the South Carolina College, last at the University of Edinburgh. His social position in Charleston was solid, without being brilliant, sufficient to gain access to the best circles without effort. His prominence came chiefly from his intellectual eminence, first at college, later as a lawyer, eventually as the most prolific and accomplished contributor to the *Southern Review*. This was matched by political advancement: a term in the state legislature from St. John's, Colleton, from 1820 to 1822; removal to Charleston that led to three terms for St. Philip's and St. Michael's Parish from 1824 to 1830; a prominent place upon legislative committees, first as an ally of George McDuffie, later as a spokesman for the William Smith faction, catalyst for budging South Carolina politics from nationalism to states' rights criticism of the American system; election as attorney-general of the state in 1830. All this was almost by acclamation. With this rise came a deepening engagement with the city's affairs: as attorney for Stephen Elliott's Bank of South Carolina, as a member of the City Council for the Fourth Ward in 1825, as a lecturer before the Charleston Forensic Club, as a member of the Book Committee of the Charleston Library Society, as a lawyer upon Broad Street.[8] Born in the city's upper class, he had made himself one of its elite.[9]

All this was satisfactory, especially as he seemed to move in sympathy with his times, nationalist turning sectional. He had always been ambitious for fame and influence. "I have been as deliberate, in embracing my pursuits in life," he had told Francis Walker Gilmer in 1816, when just nineteen, "as if it were really a matter of consequence to the public."[10] It was the more satisfactory because he labored under physical disadvantages. As a child he had been inoculated for smallpox; the virus had turned virulent and confluent, nearly killing him. Recovering, he grew very little between the ages of five and twelve, then shot up suddenly but chiefly in the torso and head, less in the legs and arms. Benjamin F. Perry was to remember: "His bust was a noble one, and he appeared to a great advantage seated in his chair in the House of Representatives, but when he rose to speak, his legs were so short that he seemed dwarfed. . . . His head and face were very fine and striking. But in walking he was ungainly, and I noticed that he seldom walked to or from the State House in company with any one. He never married. He was very sensitive and morbid on the subject of his personal appearance. I have understood that he said he would give all his learning and talents for the manly and graceful form of Preston."[11] Thus sensitive, he warmed at the applause of his estate. While it was never quite enough to satisfy him, it came closest in the crescent years of his early manhood, honors sanctifying honor.

Turn to the mid-1830s, and one finds a very different Legaré. Removed to Brussels, where he was American chargé d'affaires between 1832 and 1836, he was advising his mother to sell her South Carolina property and himself toyed with abandoning the state permanently.[12] He developed a lament: Charleston was going to the dogs, its manners were deranged, its weather sultry and detestable, its streets dirty, its harvests unreliable, its cotton prices unremunerative.[13] By the late 1830s the lament was become a dirge. "My home [is] untenable," he observed in 1838. "I am disgusted with this place & must try my adverse fortunes elsewhere," he said in 1840. Charleston had become but "this hot & out of the way spot."[14] Seeing malaise, friends advised him variously. James Louis Petigru cautiously suggested the wisdom of leaving South Carolina. The younger Stephen Elliott tried to woo his staying with flattering offers of an undemanding professorship at the South Carolina College and the editorship of a revived *Southern Review*, defunct since 1832, while noting that Legaré was but "lingering upon the threshold of . . . [his] Fathers."[15]

For the last eleven years of his life, Legaré was—more often than not, and by design—a nonresident of Charleston. Going to Brussels, he had intended to stay only eighteen months to two years. Yet he remained for four years, perplexed about his probable fortunes in Charleston. "What should I do in Charleston, for heaven's sake?" he asked in 1833.[16] The answer, when he did return in 1836, was an unsolicited election to the House of Representatives. Duty in Washington neatly served his ambivalence, as he stood formally for the city yet was obliged to be much out of it. He traveled incessantly, in the winters to Washington, in the summers to Boston and New York and spas like Saratoga and White Sulphur Springs. Indeed, he was defeated for Congress in 1838 partly because he had spent so little time in his constituency. His friends were discouraged by a candidate who dallied irritatingly in New England and Virginia, reading *Manfred* to ladies, when he should have been upon the hustings.[17] Defeat returned him to the bar and Charleston between 1839 and 1841, but he stayed away from society, rusticating on a John's Island plantation and still traveling, both for private amusement and to further the political ambitions of the Whigs and his own splinter Conservative party. When he received news of his appointment by John Tyler as Attorney-General in 1841 he was not in Charleston but in Newport, Rhode Island.[18]

Cabinet office, in the insecure tented camp of Washington, implied but did not mandate removal from home. Unlike many federal officials, however, Legaré made his residence permanently in the District, even moving his mother and sister to a house there in the spring of 1842. He looked, it might be inferred, to a life as a well-remunerated Washington and Baltimore lawyer, with a practice based upon his deserved reputation in cases before the Supreme Court; a life dotted with further spells of federal office, in perhaps the Paris or London embassy, upon which he had long had an eye. It is a rhythm not unknown today along the Beltway and in Georgetown, though less common before the Civil War.

As with his political life, so with his intellectual. Writing in the last decade of his life, the old mainstay of the *Southern Review* wrote not for Charleston or Southern periodicals — offers from which he spurned — but for the *New York Review*.[19] Even in death, he was migrant and expatriate. Dying in Boston, he was buried in Mount Auburn Cemetery. Not until 1858 were his remains exhumed and transferred to Charleston, where they were placed in Magnolia Cemetery beneath a white marble monument that proclaims his Unionism. When Preston declaimed his eulogy in Charleston in 1843, testifying to the amity of city and son, Legaré was a thousand miles absent.

What had propelled Legaré away? What had happened to a man who once had dubbed himself a "thorough-faced Charlestonian"?[20] There were a variety of reasons, a few idiosyncratic, many characteristic of his generation.

There was economics. The crisis of the South Carolina economy, apparent since the 1820s, had made many expatriate and left a deep impression upon Legaré, not assuaged by the improvement of the 1830s. His essays for the *Southern Review* referred to Charleston as a city "mouldering away, in silence, amidst the unavailing fertility of nature," and were consistently gloomy about the intrinsic unprofitability of a slave economy.[21] His own financial situation, though never desperate, required constant effort and vigilance. He had a small estate from his grandfathers, but by no means equal to Legaré's needs and wants, and paltry beside the fortunes of many of the friends with whom he shared power but not magnificence. Apart from himself, he was obliged to sustain his mother, his unmarried sister Mary, and his elder sister Eliza — who required subvention, though married, but to a man as unsound financially as he was otherwise energetic, giving her twenty-one children and an early grave. Financial exigencies drove Legaré to the bar, a business he found tiresome, and to a "dusty, abominable" Broad Street office.[22] While he took pleasure in the rhetorical challenge of the courtroom, much of being a lawyer was tedious minutiae, and Legaré's passion for the law was philosophical, the contemplation of the elegance of the civil law or the devious sociology of the common law. As for the bench, promotion to which was often suggested, economics again forbade. Money lay in the fees of advocacy and conveyance; judges earned nothing exorbitant but dignity.[23] And Legaré practiced law most when politics drove him from office. Thus the Charleston bar grew into a melancholy symbol, of political defeat and the vulgar pursuit of money for its own sake. To flee Charleston was to embrace success and advancement, in Brussels or Washington or New York, where such things had been his.

There were intimate concerns and tastes. Legaré was never to marry, which might have bound him irrevocably into Charleston society. The reasons are only partly clear. His sensitivity about a smallpox-distorted body and constant ill health were significant factors. Equally, his very suspension between Charleston and the world beyond made marriage problematical. If he married a Northern girl, could he take her to Charleston? If he married a Charleston girl, could he take her north?[24] Whatever the cause of his bachelorhood, the consequence was the freedom to travel, restrained only by the call of sisters and mother, pressing but not sovereign. And he did love to travel. As early as 1819, in Edinburgh, he spoke of his "restless disposition". In 1832 he confessed himself a "great rambler."[25] He was to see much of the United States east of the Appalachians, England, Scotland, France, Holland, Belgium, the Austrian Empire, Prussia, Bavaria, and many of the lesser German states. He traveled for edification and amusement, but also for his health, to watering places like Aix-la-Chapelle, Saratoga Springs, and Spa itself, to imbibe sulphurous liquids and placate the ravaged bowels that were eventually to kill him. One of his chief delights in a modernizing world was the increased ease of communications. He would praise Macadam for leveling roads that, in youth, had battered his weakened frame. He would dwell fondly upon the steam engine, which rushed him so astonishingly from Charleston to Columbia, or from Washington to New York.[26]

There was the matter of friends. He had written to Isaac Holmes of his "little circle," whose survival he craved. By the late 1830s so many had died or become estranged. He had, no doubt, as a prodigy mingled with men his senior, and their deaths were to be expected: Stephen Elliott, whom Legaré revered, found dead with an unfinished contribution of the *Southern Review* on his desk; Samuel Prioleau, who had written so engagingly upon the ravages of dyspepsia; Edward Rutledge, who beguiled the holidays of a sickly and half-orphaned child; Thomas Pinckney, who had introduced Legaré to the intricacies and cadences of Greek.[27] But others, Legaré's contemporaries, went prematurely, as he himself was to go: Henry Junius Nott, Edward Pringle, Elizabeth Pringle, all drowned at sea; Thomas Grimké, intellectual opponent, eccentric and much loved; Joshua Toomer, who took his own life with unnerving deliberation and rationality; John Gadsden; Jennings Waring; Robert Hayne. By 1840, amid this wreckage, Legaré observed, "Another of *my* best friends gone! Charleston is becoming a dismal solitude to me."[28] To friends dead, he had to add friends lost: William Drayton, who left South Carolina in the wake of nullification; William Campbell Preston, the companion of Legaré's student days in Paris and Edinburgh, estranged by the politics of the 1830s,[29] whom Mary Legaré was offended to see her brother's eulogist;[30] above all, most poignantly, Isaac Holmes, the very man to whom Legaré had spoken in 1833 of his "little circle" and the closest of friends, to whom Legaré had addressed letters of unwonted gaiety and intimacy: dear dim "Ikey" Holmes, enlisted at the last moment by the improbable coalition of Calhoun, Poinsett, and Van Buren to defeat Legaré in 1838, poor Holmes who thought it might be nice to have a political standing equal to his wealth, poor Holmes who lisped that the Sub-Treasury was "wital," poor Holmes the foot soldier—who crushed Legaré at the polls. "He has been," Legaré explained to his Virginian political ally, William Cabell Rives, "for twenty years one of my most confidential & devoted friends, and contributed very much to place me where I am. I should have regarded his opposing me, under any circumstances, as a *moral impossibility*—but is there in this sinful world, any such thing? . . . I have *felt* this opposition very much. I am a being, you know, of exclusive habits & so condemned to few intimates at best, on whom I very much depend for sympathy & support. A cruel death—a double shipwreck—deprived me in poor Nott & Pringle of two of these, men who had grown up with me in perfect intimacy from childhood. Holmes was one of the survivors on whom I most counted, & here he is lending himself to my capital enemies. . . . You see that my griefs are not merely those of a politician."[31]

130

To friends lost in Charleston, he could add friends gained elsewhere, the harvest of his travels. George Ticknor, whom Legaré had known since Edinburgh, urged that he come to Boston, "our Western Florence," where nothing would be easier than to make his fortune at the bar or in the lecture hall, nothing more congenial than dinner with William Prescott and Jared Sparks, no summers less sultry than those upon Cape Cod.[32] Joseph Cogswell, also known from Edinburgh, pleaded the opportunities of New York, and certainly Legaré had there many friends, up and down the Hudson, so many rich and getting richer.[33] Legaré, the economist, the friend of Nassau Senior, knew that New York was crescent and Charleston faltering. He had seen it for twenty years, at least since he had urged his mother in 1820 to buy property in New York or Philadelphia. And then Baltimore was pleasant, with friends like John Pendleton Kennedy and the baronial Carrolls, the city's bar prosperous and inviting.[34] Legaré would visit them all, complain of the vexations of Charleston, and they would smile and say, come to us. And he would be very tempted, when he picked up a copy of the Charleston *Mercury* and saw himself damned at home. The Charleston press, in the heat of polemic, accused him of overrefinement, of too much learning, of being an overelaborate jurist, of dallying in the salons of Europe during the crisis of his times, of anything that came to hand, and Legaré would find himself saying that Charleston "never loved me," that his own class had proscribed him in 1838, that "they" had once chained him to the *Southern Review*. "You know how many nights & days of laborious thought I have given gratuitously to what *they* represented to me as a work necessary to the interests & honor of So. Carolina," he grumbled. "My sight was & is seriously impaired by those thankless vigils—& now they ask me tauntingly with what useful undertaking my name has ever been associated."[35] It was very hard, when he received a letter from Cogswell that spoke of Legaré's "glowing pen" and flattered with, "If we could secure the aid of such men as yourself, if there are any more such in our country, we would make the New York Review every way equal to the London Quarterly & I think a good deal better," and offered, what was more than Charleston ever did, a handsome stipend per page. Little wonder that Legaré would complain, not with entire accuracy, "I have found my *studies in Europe* impede me at every step of my progress. They have hung round my neck like a dead weight,—and do so to this very day. Our people have a fixed aversion to every thing that looks like foreign

131

education. They never give credit to any one for being *one of them*, who does not take his post in life early, and do and live as they do."[36]

Lastly, most importantly, there was politics. The political world of Legaré in 1830, of Legaré the acclaimed and rising man, was broken by the crisis of nullification. From the ideologue of a consensus, he became the orator of a Unionist party, badly organized, harassed from power, futile. From the tidy world that had advanced him so evenly, so pleasantly, he passed into another, slippery, ominous, apocalyptic. Friends split from friends, houses from houses. Conversations grew strained and divisive. The elite of Charleston, to which as politician and lawyer he belonged, found itself diminished of influence by mobilizing nullifier voters and politicians. Legaré, opposing Calhoun, commended himself thereby to a Jackson administration eager to patronize the opponents of an erring former Vice-President, and found himself offered the mission to Belgium. Seeing little prospect of advancement in a nullifying state, Legaré accepted exile. State politics became progressively closed to him. He would not go back to a state legislature he despised as a pandemonium. He had already been state attorney-general, a position good enough for a rising man, but not one risen. Governor was unlikely and uninviting. He could not afford to be a judge. No Unionist could expect to be senator in Calhoun's South Carolina. For much of Legaré's political course was plotted in reaction to the mysterious ways of Calhoun, who helped to drive Legaré out in 1832, assisted his election in 1836 to chastise Henry Pinckney for straying on the abolition petition issue, struck him down in 1838 when Legaré orchestrated opposition to the Sub-Treasury scheme and displeased the fleeting alliance of Calhoun and Van Buren. Calhoun's firm grip upon state politics, combined with erratic and whirling political schemes, bred a high mortality rate among the state's many ambitious politicians, created a centrifugal disillusionment that drove many, among them Legaré, to seek a political constituency beyond Calhoun's depredations. In Legaré's case, the refuge lay in federal officeholding. After 1838 a sanctuary was contrived by a venture into national presidential politics, by an alliance with William Cabell Rives of Virginia in support of the small but not unimportant Conservative party and, eventually, into the Tyler Cabinet, that refuge of the political misfit.

For a man so dedicated to public affairs, Legaré labored under the disadvantage of being an indifferent politician. He had received preferment when it was convenient for others that he be preferred. He never commanded events. He understood, in the abstract, how politics worked, and few Carolinians analyzed it more acutely or better understood how it could be deflected by unreasoning accident and angular passion. But Legaré could not bring himself to labor day in and day out, to ferret out information, to influence, to cajole, to intimate patronage, to use the propaganda of the press, to set loose plug-uglies and bullyboys. He had been genteelly appalled in 1831 when his brother-in-law had boasted of keeping gentlemen drunk for days in order to ensure their votes. Studying oratory, excited by its tense achievement, he conflated the power of words with the power of politics. Meeting opposition, he bridled and delivered a long, erudite, grand and subtle speech, which annihilated his opponents intellectually but changed little politically. Seeing this, witnessing intellectual superiority untranslated into advancement, he limped back to his solitary learning, wrote acid letters, and waited in discontent until events, at the will of others, turned smiling upon him again. Gouverneur Kemble of New York, a real politician in a Jacksonian age that perfected the American craft, was to remember Legaré to Joel Poinsett and deliver the professional's verdict: "But for his inordinate vanity, he would have been a very useful man, but this rendered him continually the dupe of others."[37] He was the victim of nullification's transformation of South Carolina politics, and he knew it. He wrote in 1839, "The South Carolina in which & for which I was educated has some how or other disappeared, & left a *simulacrum* behind of a very different kind—which I don't understand, neither am I understood by it."[38]

Such was his alienation, deeper because incomplete. Legaré did, after all, love Charleston and never ceased to do so. Preston was intentionally fudging when he observed that Legaré never spoke of Charleston but with "a sort of filial devotion," but shrewd to add, "He felt its rebukes as those of a parent." The Legaré who complained of Charleston was the same who, hearing of the great fire of 1838, wept. Toying with moving to New York, he hesitated and hedged that he might go, "if I did not see many reasons for *loving* Charleston."[39] He never did formally make a break, as William Drayton had done. There was much to hold him, the accumulated attachments of family and friends, however depleted. Molded by Charleston, he was never quite at ease elsewhere. Legaré was a marked victim of the truth that powerful cultures denote themselves by the capacity to make their citizens dislike them or love them, yet be held. Charleston society had a tone he had absorbed in youth, enjoyed in early manhood, and grieved for in maturity. Even in decline, it seemed sweeter than society elsewhere. And he had a taste for decline, a proneness to elegy. Hearing in Brussels in 1836 of the death of an old patron, he wrote, "You know some of our earliest childish recollections relate to Christmas holidays spent at St. Johns. They have been haunting me for some weeks past. The smallest incidents come back upon me with all that is sacred in the innocence & simplicity of childish thoughts and feelings. Mr. Rutledge & Richmond were so *very* characteristic of poor dear Carolina. Such a person and such a place could have existed no where else, & can't exist, even there, *long*. That is always the burthen of the song with me, you know." The bonds of Charleston snapped one by one, but there were many strands, and the thinning left still a formidable connection. For Legaré had that worst of loves: he did not love Charleston and South Carolina for themselves; he loved the idea of them. Commenting in 1833 upon the nullification convention, he shrewdly observed to himself, "For my own part, I do confess that the insolent & mad conduct of the convention has almost entirely alienated me from the state—which I do believe I loved more than any body in it."[40]

Much in this estrangement was personal, but much was social, the plight of his generation. His alienation had its intellectual sources, to which I shall turn, but its main rhythm was political. Here is an important general truth. Many of the Old South's intellectuals were engaged in politics; just as conversely and not often distinguishably, many of its politicians were interested in ideas. It has been argued that the necessary alienation of the intellectual life led to a self-conscious attempt to use the politics of slavery as a way to establish intellectual and social legitimacy.[41] This may be only half of the equation between politics and thought, and perhaps not the most important half. Politics could engender alienated intellect as much as alienated intellect engendered politics. In a small social world like Charleston and South Carolina, crowded with intelligent men ambitious for office and esteem, estrangement was intrinsic. In a culture that prized male friendship but faced politically divisive, volatile, and whirling tensions, alienation that cut to the marrow was everywhere. It was not just the politically dispossessed who felt it. William Campbell Preston, successful nullifier, senator, perhaps the most important man in South Carolina politics after Calhoun (the lid on this seething mass of self-consciousness), felt it too. In old age, Preston was to muse to his old ally, Waddy Thompson, on the cost: "Amidst the struggle of life while it was intense I met with many and most agreeable men at the bar[,] in the Senate, in the court, Scholars, orators, men of talents and of spirit, men with whom I thought I had contracted *friendship*. Where are they[?] It was seed sown by the wayside. I ask not of the dead but of the living, where are they? The fowls came and devoured them up. Where is Pettigrew and Butler, whom I met at the bar[,] Mangum and Crittenden whom I met in the Senate gone glimmering and off."[42]

*   *   *

Political change created the conditions for alienation, without comprehending it. If thought and politics danced together, one must pause to consider the intellectual presuppositions that Legaré brought to the vexations of his world. For thought mutated with society, with implications for our understanding of both Legaré and Charleston. Legaré had a poised sensibility, divided between the convictions of fixity and change; part of him believed in the stability of things, part in their mutability; part was classic, part romantic. This was a dilemma characteristic of his times, which gave him ample resources from which to ponder the tension. Legaré had been young in a South Carolina versed in the sensibility of the eighteenth century, but he was mature in a world that tampered, albeit gingerly, with that sensibility.

Romanticism was a new intellectual order of things, to which Legaré committed himself very gingerly, giving much, holding back much. One can, for exposition's sake, isolate five areas of his commitment—historicism, nationality, law, religion, and language—before making the caveats Legaré himself was careful to elaborate.

He possessed a marked historicist sensibility, caring how time and place varied, how context mattered. "There is not a more common error," he once observed of commentators upon Magna Carta, "than to ascribe our own notions to those who have gone before us, and to suppose that in politics, the same words always mean precisely the same thing."[43] The virtue of studying original texts lay not in asserting the similarities of ancient and modern but in measuring the distance. "Compare the knowledge," he asked, "which a scholar acquires, not only of the policy and the *res gestae* of the Roman emperors, but of the minutest shades and inmost recesses of their *character*, and that of the times in which they reigned, from the living pictures of Tacitus and Suetonius, with the cold, general, feeble, and what is worse, far

135

from just and precise idea of the same thing, communicated by modern authors. The difference is incalculable. It is that between the true Homeric Achilles, and the Monsieur or Monseigneur Achille of the Théâtre Français, at the beginning of the last century, with his bob wig and small sword. When we read of those times in English, we attach modern meanings to ancient words, and associate the ideas of our own age and country, with objects altogether foreign from them."[44]

So Legaré went to great pains to jar his reader, in essays for the *Southern Review*, out of a modern complacent understanding, instead to see the past without anachronism. "We are quite in a new world," he wrote of ancient Greece. "Manners and customs, education, religion, national character, every thing is original and peculiar. Consider the priest and the temple, the altar and the sacrifice, the chorus and the festal pomp, the gymnastic exercises, and those Olympic games, whither universal Greece repaired with all her wealth, her strength, her genius and taste— where the greatest cities and kings, and the other first men of their day, partook with an enthusiastic rivalry, scarcely conceivable to us." Here he dissented from those eighteenth-century Scots, influential upon Legaré both at South Carolina College and the University of Edinburgh, who, though they spoke of and wrote much history, were too absorbed in defining the principles of human sympathy to seek out and celebrate the discontinuities of time and cultures. On the other hand, it is not unsurprising that a man versed in the scholarship of the civil law should have had an instinct for historicism. The legal scholars of the French Renaissance, men such as Jacques Cujas and François Hotman, by meditating upon the mutations of Roman law in medieval France, by struggling with texts by ingenious philology, by adapting the traditions of Italian humanism, had arrived at an intimation of historicism, flawed less by theory than by weak technical accomplishment. With these, Legaré was very familiar, and he consistently paid tribute to their improvement and critical reinterpretation of a corrupted civilian tradition. The Abbé Terrasson, a later exponent, he had occasion to observe, had been among the first to attempt a reconstruction of the Law of the XII Tables, an attempt to be perfected by Barthold Niebuhr in the nineteenth century.[45]

Changing between time and place was national character, the spirit of culture, whether expressed in literature, jurisprudence, or politics. Literature, especially among the Greeks, "springing out of their most touching interests and associations—out of what would be called, by

136

German critics, their 'inward life'" was itself a social force, not the inert classical learning of bookworms, but interwoven into the very frame and constitution of society.[46] For Legaré the chief recommendation of recent scholarship was to transcend pedantic antiquarianism and come to terms with the "true genius and spirit of laws and institutions," in a way more satisfactory than "the random epigrams" of Montesquieu because more systematic and philosophical.[47] Political forms and systems were indeed influential and more than worthy of analysis, but they meant little beside the spirit that created meaning. For example, "Magna Charta was the means of bringing back the feudal aristocracy to its first principles—one of the worst governments upon the whole, as a practical system, that ever existed—yet, Selden and Coke and Hampden, regenerated the government of England by bringing it back to the principles of Magna Charta, as explained in an enlightened age. So pliable are all political forms—so absolutely do they depend upon the spirit which animates them, and the sense in which they are interpreted."[48]

So powerful was the spirit of national character that it could be expected to remold and reform political institutions, even after constitutional debacle. The civil compact should be distinguished from the constitutional compact.[49] Once, contemplating the possible breakup of the United States, he speculated that while the Union was perhaps "the cause of all our liberties" and "its dissolution would make their duration far more uncertain," all would not be lost. New England would retain its popular institutions; in other sections, given the "peculiarities in their situation," matters would be less clear. "But we have no reason to despair of any. The first, almost the only question in such matters is are the people prepared for free institutions. It is the national character that is to be looked to when we talk of constitutions—it is the national history that is to regulate our conjectures about the future."[50] So crucial was national spirit that patriotism amounted to a moral obligation. That Byron had been disloyal to England was one of the gravest charges Legaré could think to bring. "Except the admirable lines in Childe Harold, in which he describes England as the 'inviolate island of the sage and free,' we do not, at present, remember one syllable in all his works, from the *spirit* of which, it could be fairly inferred that he was even a citizen, much less a hereditary counsellor, lawgiver and judge—one of the privileged and honoured few—of that famous commonwealth." True to this, Legaré mistrusted his own plea-

137

sure in visiting Europe and reminded himself that expatriation was no virtue, and Byron's self-characterization as "citizen of the world" betrayed vice.[51]

Legaré was most distinguished as a lawyer for his interest in the civil law. He had studied it at Edinburgh, where the structure of Scottish jurisprudence had long mingled the civil with the common law. From Lord Stair to Dugald Stewart, law in Edinburgh had been construed in the spirit of the rational *philosophe*, a thing grounded in the logics of human nature and social necessity, largely independent of time and place. For Scottish law, like the Scottish Enlightenment, had sprung from the Latin cosmopolitanism of humanism, transmitted from Leyden to the Canongate, its elementary text for generations the works of the Halle scholar, Johann Heineccius.[52] Legaré had been aware even in 1818, sufficient to have planned to study at Göttingen, that such an approach was under challenge from German scholars, from Niebuhr, from Savigny, from a swarm resurrecting and editing Justinian, Gaius, Ulpian, the Salic Law, the niceties of the Witenagemot, just as another swarm were presenting new and surprising critical editions of the classics. In the 1830s, by learning German, by visits to Germany, by private reading, Legaré had measured the challenge and found it just. In 1837 he cited with sympathetic approval an observation by one of the older generation of German scholars: "Hugo quotes a letter from a friend . . . in which, congratulating the present generation upon the change, he declares, that he had taken his degree of Doctor, before he knew who Gaius or Ulpian was—writers now familiar to all his *hearers*; and Hugo confesses as much of himself, in regard to Ulpian and Theophilus. Our own experience, fortunately for us, is not quite so extensive, and yet it is difficult to imagine a greater contrast than that which presents itself to us, in comparing this *Lehr-Buch* of Göttingen lecturer [Legaré was reviewing Hugo's lectures], with what we remember was the *course* of professor of the Civil Law in the University of Edinburgh, just twenty years ago. One who was initiated into this study, as we happened to be, under the old plan of the eighteenth century, with Heineccius for a guide, will find himself in the schools of the present day, in almost another world—new doctrines, new history, new methods, new text-books, and, above all, new views and a new spirit." The import of the new doctrine was to make the law a historical and relativist study. "The great dogma . . . of the *historical school*, that, in the matter of government, 'whatever is, is right,' for the time being,

138

and nothing so for all times; that positive institutions are merely provisional; and that every people has, *ipso facto*, precisely those which are best adapted to its character and condition" was accepted by Legaré as a "great fundamental truth, without a distinct perception of which, history becomes a riddle, and government impossible."[53] Thus Heineccius, who had sought to import reason into the law by metaphysics, was displaced by Savigny, who sought reason through history. In turn, it became Legaré's mission and interest as a lawyer—as Joseph Story was to remark—to engraft on to the common-law roots of American jurisprudence the historical relativism of a reconsidered civilian tradition, to set up a dialectic between civil and common law within the delicate balance of English precedent and reasoned invention that was American constitutional law.[54]

Interwoven with the law was Legaré's view of the imagination and man's capacity for access to the sublime, which it was not the business of education to stunt by narrow concentration upon utility. Education was meant not mainly to produce "druggists and apothecaries, or navigators and mechanists" but "to form the *moral* character"; not to kill with "barren precepts" but to fashion the sensibility by "heroical models of excellence," warmly inspiriting. For what was the object of a liberal education but "to make accomplished, elegant and learned men—to chasten and to discipline genius, to refine the taste, to quicken the perceptions of decorum and propriety, to purify and exalt the moral sentiments, to fill the soul with a deep love of the beautiful both in moral and material nature, to lift up the aspirations of man to objects that are worthy of his noble faculties and his immortal destiny"? And what was poetry but "an abridged name for the sublime and beautiful, and for high wrought pathos[?] It is, as Coleridge quaintly, yet, we think, felicitously expresses it, 'the blossom and the fragrance of all human knowledge.'" Such poetry was pantheist, "spread over the whole face of nature." It lay in every human deed or passion that created "the deep, the strictly *moral* feeling, which, when it is affected by chance or change in human life, as at a tragedy, we call sympathy—but as it appears in the still more mysterious connection between the heart of man and the forms and beauties of inanimate nature, as if they were instinct with a soul and a sensibility like our own, has no appropriate appellation in our language, but is not the less real or the less familiar to our experience on that account."[55] These mysteries were important because moral, instructive by making man conscious of smallness in the scheme

139

of things: they taught resignation and submission; they expressed ambition and made failure tolerable; they served, in short, many of the usual purposes of religion.

Religion itself played a small part in Legaré's cosmogony, an offshoot of these mysteries rather than their cause. Religion was poetry, and so Legaré preferred Milton, whose verse he carried *vade mecum*, to the scriptures. The Bible was of use in discussing whether Hebrew poetry could be made to fit modern critical theories, but theology was Whiggishly useful if intellectually limited: "Take this very principle of utility for an example. In the hands of Paley, it is quite harmless—it is even, in one point of view, a beneficent and consoling principle. It presupposes the perfect goodness and wisdom of God; for the rule of moral conduct, according to that Divine, is His will, collected from expediency. This—whatever we may think of its philosophical correctness— is a truly christian doctrine, christian in its spirit and its influences, no less than its origin and theory." Thomas Grimké had insisted that Christianity, especially that of the Reformation, had rendered the ethics of the ancients supererogatory, but Legaré was cagey. He quoted Grimké with sly parenthesis: "'that in every department of knowledge, whether theoretical or practical, where thinking and reasoning are the means and the criterion of excellence, our country must, if there be truth and power in the principles of the Reformation, (and that there is, no man entertains so little doubt as Mr. Grimké) surpass every people that ever existed'"; and he could suggest that disquisitions on the Garden of Eden were less than riveting, though they were becoming the stock-in-trade for romantics for whom the Fall was a potent allegory of man's alienation. The Huguenot could not cry havoc on Christ, nor would he have wished to. Did he not politely note that revealed religion was "by far the most serious and engrossing concern of man"? So Legaré conceded the point, with irony sufficient to indicate that the concession was something to keep his mother and sister happy. "We have always been accustomed to think, that if those [ancient] refined ages have left us anything, in any department of knowledge, of which the excellence is beyond dispute, it is (after the Greek geometry, perhaps,) their moral philosophy. We presume it will not be considered as derogating from their merit in this particular, that they did not by mere dint of reasoning, *a priori*, make themselves partakers in the benefits of the Christian Revelation. Neither do we conceive ourselves responsible for certain strange customs and heathenish practices, into

which they occasionally fell, in their conduct and way of living. . . .
We concede, therefore, to save trouble, that their morality—that for
instance of Rome in the time of the first Punic war—would not be good
enough to stand the *severe* censure of London, of Paris, or of New-York."
"The grand idea of Religion," Alexander Everett was to marvel, "which
lies at the bottom of the whole, does not seem . . . to have made any
impression upon him."[56]

Yet religion hinted at mystery, as did poetry and the music of
Meyerbeer and Gothic cathedrals and great waterfalls, the more sublime for being inexplicit.[57] So Legaré found deism, the solution of the
eighteenth century to the inadequacies of Christianity, not intellectually mistaken but emotionally thin. He spoke partly of himself—
though only partly—when he wrote to the editor of the *Southern Literary Messenger* in 1838 and commented on a shared quality of modern
writers: "They almost all *feel* the want of *faith*, as they love to call it—
faith in religion, faith in morals—*faith* in political doctrine, faith in
men & women. There are proud blasphemies, there are wild ravings,
there is demoniac phrenzy & moonstruck madness, but they believe
& tremble—or what comes to nearly the same thing, they tremble that
they do not believe. There is a craving void left aching in the hearts
of the present generation. They are rebuilding the temple which the
'march of mind' had demolished, & putting away their proud philosophy to become as little children before their long desecrated altars. . . .
The age of sciolists, called Age of Reason, is past with them."[58]

This sense that reason merged emotion with rationality gave Legaré's social understanding an instability. Emotion, being mobilized,
could be wayward. Politics could not, as David Hume had hoped, be
reduced to a science. "The springs and causes which operate in human
events are so mysterious, so multifarious, so modified by the slightest
circumstances, the most subtile and shadowy influences, that nothing
is more unsafe than a political theory. The test of accurate knowledge
in matters of inductive science, is to be able to predict the effect of
any given cause. . . . But a politician should avoid prophecy as much
as possible. Hume exemplified this in the instance of Harrington, who
thought he had found out the secret of all government in the arrangements of property, and, on the strength of his discovery, ventured to
affirm most confidently that monarchy could never be re-established
in England. The words were scarcely written before the prediction was
falsified by the restoration." Little wonder that Legaré was fond of Ed-

mund Burke and, like so many of his contemporaries, used the French Revolution as a great fund, illustrating the dangers of speculation and the vagaries of life.[59]

Legaré's intellectual generation gave him a great controversy on which to make these perspectives turn: the dispute between classicism and romanticism. He followed the controversy with care and interest, noting both its origin and usefulness. He judged that its chief source was Germany, in those days when one could with justice say (August von Schlegel had immodestly made the claim himself), "The Germans are, of all nations that ever existed, the fairest in their criticism upon others. Their studies are too enlarged for bigotry, and excessive nationality has never, we believe, been numbered among their faults." And he judged correctly both the motive and the nature of these studies in a passage worth extensive quotation: "Since the beginning of that struggle, which resulted in the deliverance of German literature from the bondage of French authority and a servile imitation of foreign models, a new order of researches, and almost a new theory of criticism have been proposed by scholars. It has been discovered that there is no genuine, living beauty of composition which springs not spontaneously, if we may so express it, out of the very soil of a country; which is not connected with the history, animated by the spirit, and in perfect harmony with the character and opinions of its people. It has been found that all imitative or derivative literatures are in comparison of the truly primitive and national, tame, vapid and feeble – that Roman genius, for instance, did but dimly reflect the glories of the Attic muse, and that, even in the *chefs d'oeuvre* of the Augustan age of France, replete as they are in other respects with the highest graces of composition, the want of this native sweetness, this 'color of primeval beauty,' is universally complained of by foreigners. The German critics, therefore, and, after their example, many others have, within the present century, busily employed themselves in tracing the history of modern literature up to its sources, with a view to show its connection with national history and manners. The repositories of antiquarian lore have been ransacked for forgotten MSS. The oldest monuments – the most scattered and mutilated fragments have been brought to light, and collated and compared. The simplest traditions, the wildest fictions, the superstitions of the common people, the tales of the nursery and the fireside, legend and lay, and love-ditty and heroic ballad, have all been laid under contribution, to furnish forth such pictures of national manners, and 'to show the very age and body of the times' which produced them, 'its form and pressure.'" This was to discriminate against the not inconsiderable claim of the Scots to have been the progenitors of historicism.[60]

He read and pondered the latest literature and scholarship: Goethe, Herder, the Schlegels, Savigny, Niebuhr, Wordsworth, Coleridge—these and many others. He pondered as far as his taste would take him, which was short of the most abstruse of German metaphysics; Schelling, Fichte, and Hegel, even the precedent Kant, were too cloudy for him. "Nothing is more possible," he confessed, "than that we are ignorant of the understanding of these writers, instead of understanding their ignorance, according to the distinction of an ingenious admirer of the philosophy of Kant [Coleridge, in the *Biographia Literaria*]. Be it so. We do, however, for our own part, cheerfully resign these thorny and unprofitable studies to those who profess to comprehend and to read with edification such things as the Theaetetus of Plato or the cloudy transcendentalism of the German school." And he added, in rueful footnote, "We really debated with ourselves a long time whether we should venture to encounter those awful personages, the Metaphysicians," and, by way of commentary, quoted from the *Aeneid* about the Underworld, of "Gods whose dominion is over the Souls, Shades without sound, Void, and you, Burning River, and you, broad spaces, voiceless beneath the night." This indifference to epistemology extended even to Legaré's discrimination of the Scottish Enlightenment, for he was as uninterested in the formal psychology of common sense philosophy, exemplified by Thomas Reid, as he was absorbed by the social meditations of David Hume and Dugald Stewart. He was to react with irritation when the American legal commentator, David Hoffman, felt it necessary to preface law with metaphysics, a discipline "in the last degree unprofitable as a science." Yet this indifference, since it scanted an epistemology that struggled mightily with the problem of man's place in nature, meant also a neglect by Legaré of the racist anthropology that was sketched in the speculations of Lord Monboddo and Lord Kames and became so vital in Southern thought.[61]

The critic he heeded most was August von Schlegel, the accessible popularizer of German romanticism. The poet he wrestled with, as casting most light upon modern times and upon himself, Legaré, was Byron. It is in an essay upon Byron, with a digression upon Schlegel, that Legaré most considered the controversy.

"The distinction," he began, ". . . originated in Germany. It was seized by Madame de Staël with avidity, as well adapted to her purposes of metaphysical, mystical and ambitious declamation, and it has since been entertained, with more respect than we conceive it deserves, in the literary circles of Europe. A.W. Schlegel, in his valuable Lectures upon Dramatic Poetry, makes it the basis of all his comparisons between the ancients and the moderns in that art." Both accuracy of scholarship and the German philosophical temperament in Schlegel induced, by the comparison of the Greek and the modern drama, a belief that "in all the arts of taste, the genius of modern times is *essentially* different from that of the Greeks, and *requires*, for its gratification, works of a structure totally distinct from those which he admits to have been the best imaginable models of the classic style." Schlegel explained the distinction by religion. The "gay, sensual and elegant mythology" of the Greeks "addressed itself exclusively to the *senses*, exacted of the worshipper only forms and oblations, and confirmed him in the tranquil self-complacency or the joyous spirit which the face of nature and the circumstances of his own condition inspired." But in Christianity, to quote Schlegel, "every thing finite and mortal is lost in the contemplation of infinity; life has become shadow and darkness, and the first dawning of our real existence is beyond the grave. Such a religion must awaken the foreboding, which slumbers in every feeling heart, to the most thorough consciousness that the happiness after which we strive we can never here obtain. . . . Hence the poetry of the ancients was the poetry of enjoyment, and ours is that of desire; the former has its foundation in the scene which is present, while the latter hovers between recollection and hope. . . . The *feeling of the moderns is, upon the whole, more intense, their fancy more incorporeal, and their thoughts more contemplative.*"[62]

With much of this, Legaré was "disposed to assent. . . . We think that modern Literature does differ from that of the Greeks in its *complexion and spirit*—that it is more pensive, sombre and melancholy, perhaps, we may add, more abstract, and metaphysical—and it has, no doubt, been 'sickled o'er' with this sad hue, by the influence of a religious faith which connects morality with worship, and teaches men to consider every thought, word and action of their lives as involving, in some degree, the tremendous issues of eternity." But this was as far as Legaré was willing to go. "The *spirit* . . . is changed . . . but does this alter, in any essential degree, the *forms* of beauty? Does it affect the *proportions* which the parts of a work of art ought to bear to each other and to the whole? Does it so far modify the relations of things that what would be fit and proper in a poem, or oration, a colonnade, a picture, if it were ancient, is misplaced and incongruous now? In short, has the philosophy of literature and the arts, the reason, the logic . . . undergone any serious revolution?" Schlegel was convinced that it had, but Legaré was unsure.[63]

For one thing, Schlegel was inclined to compare like with unlike, ancient sculpture with modern painting, or ancient melody with modern harmony. In architecture, for instance, modern taste hinted at a preference for the Gothic. No doubt, Legaré admitted, "A Gothic cathedral has its beauties. . . . The origin of the style was in a dark age; but it has taken root, nor is it at all probable that, so long as Christianity shall endure, the modern world will ever be brought to think as meanly of these huge piles, as a Greek architect (if one were suddenly revived) possibly might. Still, there are very few builders of the present age who do not prefer the orders of Greece—and, even if they did not, how would that prove that future ages would not?" In so arguing, Legaré was disdaining to accept a central point of Schlegel, that the classic had separated genres, while the romantic had mingled them.[64]

One needed to distinguish between essential and accidental, form and associations: "Suppose the object described to be twilight. If the pictures were confined to the *sensible phenomena*, it is obvious there *could not be* any variety in them, as any one who doubts what is obvious to reason, may convince himself by comparing parallel passages in the ancient and modern classics—e.g., Milton's lines, 'Now came still evening on, and twilight gray', Virgil's beautiful verses on midnight, in the fourth Aeneid, Homer's on moonlight in the eighth Iliad. The exquisite sketches . . . are all in precisely the same style, and if they were in the same language, might easily be ascribed to the same age of poetry." This was essence. There were, to be sure, contingent associations of ideas or circumstances that would make a very material difference. "For instance, Dante's famous lines on the evening describe it, not as the period of the day when nature exhibits such or such phenomena . . . but by certain casual circumstances, which may or may not accompany that hour—the vesper bell, tolling the knell of the dying day, the lonely traveller looking back, with a heart oppressed with fond regrets, to the home which he has just left—very touching circumstances no doubt to those who have a home or have lived in Catholic countries, but still extraneous, and it may be, transitory circumstances." Thus spirit and associations could vary, but "ideal beauty, with which human nature, that never changes, will rest forever satisfied," could not.[65]

Yet it was a historical fact that the ancient and classical differed from the modern and romantic. The classical had unity of purpose, simplicity of style and ease of execution. The romantic was the less as art for not having these qualities. "The superiority in their exquisite *logic* of literature and the arts . . . is, we fear, a lamentable truth, nor will it help us much to call our deformities, peculiarities, and to dignify what is only *not* art with the specious title of the 'romantic.'" In short, Legaré conceded the historical point to Schlegel but bridled at the implication that classic and romantic might be coequal, or the romantic superior.[66]

This discussion Legaré applied to Byron. For "Lord Byron's speculative opinions in literature, were . . . all in favour of the classical models. His preference to Pope is owing to this. . . . But," and this was a crucial *but*, for Legaré as for Byron, "theory and practice are unfortunately not more inseparable in literature than in other matters, and of this truth there is no more striking example than the author of Childe Harold." Nothing more exemplified the conflict between theory and practice, classic and romantic, than Byron's *Manfred*, which Legaré deemed to be the poet's flawed masterpiece. Manfred's situation was classic, the lone hero struggling with the Fates. Yet the treatment was romantic, for the burden of Manfred's anguish was the internal demons of his moral imagination. "The *spirit* of Manfred is strictly modern or romantic. The air of abstract reflection, the moral musing, the pensive woe, which pervade it, are a contrast to the sensible imagery and the lively personifications of the Greek play [the *Eumenides* of Aeschylus]. Yet its *frame and structure* are strictly 'classical.'"[67]

As he confessed, *Manfred's* special interest, for Legaré as for Goethe, lay in Byron's "conception of Manfred's character and situation." The effect was religious: "We never take it up but with some such feeling as we conceive to have possessed of old the pilgrims of Delphi and Dodona, or those anxious mortals, who, like Count Manfred himself, have sought to learn the secrets of their own destiny, by dealing with evil spirits. The book contains a spell for us, and we lay our hands upon it with awe." What satisfied Legaré's aesthetic ambitions about *Manfred* was classical. Yet what drew him to the poem was romantic: the internal monologue, the tangle of remorse, "not self-condemnation for a mere crime or sin committed," but the exemplification of Byron's ruling idea. "That idea is that, without a deep and engrossing *passion*, without *love*, in short, intense, devoted love, no power, nor influence in the world, nor genius, nor knowledge, nor Epicurean bliss, can 'bestead or fill the fixed mind with all their toys'; and that a man may be completely miserable for want of such a passion, though blessed, to all appearance, with whatever can make life desirable." In this definition lay much of Legaré's melancholy, his struggles with ennui, his dissatisfaction with his own ambition even when fulfilled, his sense of "that dreariest of all solitudes, the utter loneliness of the blighted heart." And why should *Manfred* be more evocative for Legaré than *Childe Harold?* "The style of Manfred is more sober and subdued . . . is, indeed, remarkable for a degree of austere and rugged force."[68] It embodied a spirit of resignation and submission to untoward forces, which Legaré felt himself to possess. For Byron usually lacked the morality of the disciplined and impartial spectator, that lauded by Adam Smith, which, "instead of consecrating the absurd conceits of vanity, the bitter moodiness of despite, the wild sallies of vengeance, the spirit of rebellion against restraint; the pride, envy, hatred, and all uncharitableness, which are the accursed brood of this concentrated *égoisme* . . . inculcates upon the aspirant that there can be neither happiness nor virtue where there is not resignation, and that it is not more the lot, than it is the duty and the interest of man, to acquiesce in the order of nature and of society."[69]

Lastly, even in his aesthetic of style did Legaré flirt with romanticism, particularly in the historicist typology that he adopted from Schlegel and Sismondi: "The first efforts of genius are . . . the spontaneous effusions of nature, uttered without any idea of rules, or pretensions to elegance, or fear of criticism. . . . This is the whole sum and substance of the rhetoric and poetry of rude ages." A little learning thereafter induces inhibition, formality, and pedantry. Later yet, "a still more advanced age generally brings back the simplicity of nature, because it restores the confidence of genius—the Ariostos and Macchiavellis take the place of the Dantes and Boccaccios, and, making allowance for improvement in minuter matters, extremes in literature —the perfection of discipline and the total absence of it—may be said to meet." This is the archetypal Romantic rhythm: simplicity, overrefinement, restored but complex simplicity. It is the rhythm that justified the Whiggish medieval romances of Walter Scott and Legaré's

147

own interest in the likes of Amadis of Gaul, El Cid, Geoffrey of Monmouth, the Troubadours, and the romances that surrounded Charlemagne, whose tomb Legaré never failed to visit when in Aix-la-Chapelle. It is the rhythm by which the Germans had medievalized the classics, making Homer the Beowulf of the antique, the Greeks primitive Germans who chanced to live in a warmer climate, the Romans pedantic imitators and militarists.[70]

Yet balanced with, and in tension against, Legaré's romanticism was his training in the suppositions of the eighteenth century. He admired not just Adam Smith's political economy but the *Theory of Moral Sentiments.* He echoed Hume in thinking human nature "the same in all ages." He owned of morality that "we are content to explain the phenomenon after the manner of the Scottish school of metaphysicians, in which we learned the little that we profess to know of that department of philosophy." He found the concept of "an original law of nature" appealing.[71] Hence, an attempt to explain Legaré by reference to Dugald Stewart, as Preston once hinted, would be almost as persuasive as a try by means of Schlegel.[72] Intellectual worlds collided in Legaré's mind, as is best exemplified in his straining attempts to come to grips with Byron. In this, he was a child of his times. Legaré was of that generation, occurring at different times in different countries, of first-footing romantics. Byron, Coleridge, the Schlegels gave such rapt attention to alienation, sketched it so laboriously in their verse and philosophy, because it was so fresh to them, astonished as they were by the French Revolution or the younger Pitt or Hume's cheerful explosion of rational belief. So it was for Legaré. To be born in Charleston in 1797 was to inherit a stately pleasure dome, or so it seemed. Did it seem likely that Legaré would find himself propelled towards exile? Did it then seem probable that the Charleston of the Pinckneys would grow little? Yet limbs were stunted, friends died, politics was deranged, and romanticism grew necessary and plausible.

*   *   *

Intellectual life often flourishes past the moment of power. The Charleston of the Pinckneys was powerful without being subtle. The Charleston of Hugh Legaré was subtle without being powerful, compelled by doubts into self-awareness. His city had grown paradoxical. It had come to build railroads and canals and to pronounce boldly upon the potentialities of a dizzy economic and political future. This

148

is Charles Fraser, Legaré's friend, writing in the early 1850s: "Amply has she [Charleston] realized the advantages to which her enterprize entitles her; for to the agency of steam is mainly attributable the prosperity she now enjoys. Since its introduction her local manufactures have been improved, her business relations have been extended, her educational, professional and charitable institutions enlarged, her municipal structures repaired or rebuilt with great architectural beauty, new streets opened and former ones improved, her limits enlarged, her banking and commercial capital increased, new business ventures established." And this is Henry Cruger, Legaré's friend, reviewing James Fenimore Cooper's Venetian novel, *The Bravo*, in the *Southern Review* twenty years earlier: "Beneath a southern climate and sunny skies, in a champain country, and with a choice harbour, the structures of . . . [Charleston], as you approach from the water of Sullivan's Island, corresponding to the Lido, forcibly induce a mutual recollection—and when the moon has thrown its light around, as the solitary passenger, through the deserted and sepulchral streets of Charleston, meditates upon her time-worn, rusty and mouldering edifices, he is gloomily reminded of the blank, icy and desolate aspect of that other city afar; now manifestly 'expiring into the slime of her own canals.'" Each of these voices taken singly, is unexceptional. Together, mingled as they often were in one mind, the texture was Charlestonian, later erected by William Gilmore Simms into a Social Principle, denoting "the vast importance to civilization of a community, at once stationary, yet susceptible of progress." This was robust elegy, energetic melancholy.[73]

No one better defined this ambivalent tone than Legaré. At the meeting place of politics and intellectual sensibility, he had fashioned an image of Charleston, interwoven with South Carolina. The image is best known from a letter of Legaré to Isaac Holmes in 1833, quoted by Paul Hamilton Hayne and Vernon Parrington later, and used by William Freehling as a motto.[74] Legaré wrote, "*We* are (I am quite sure) the *last* of the *race* of South-Carolina; I see nothing before us but decay and downfall,—but, on that account, I cherish its precious relics the more."[75] It is a famous sentiment, antediluvian in the midst of the freshet of nullification and before the flood of civil war. From the standpoint of 1865 and Hayne, it came to seem prophecy, its subtle unease transformed into the sentiment of the Lost Cause, the leitmotif of the city's history. Yet its pain was that of a special moment and a particular part of Charleston society, latterly annexed to a greater moment and wider

culture. Its original context, apart from the special tension of nullification, was a sense of declension from the Revolutionary generation.
As early as 1828, Legaré was writing to Jesse Burton Harrison, "You
complain of the downfall of Virginian prosperity & reputation. Alas!
Sir, I know how to sympathize with you & have the very same sort
of objects to excite my feelings: decaying *chateauxs*, once magnificent
gardens & groves dilapidated & grown up in weeds & festive old elegance & hospitality departing. We have just this morning committed
to the grave the most delightful specimen of our old Carolina gentlemen—a scholar worthy of the name—the mirror of all social virtues
& accomplishments—Gen: Thomas Pinckney."[76] It was elegy drawn
not only from Goldsmith's "The Deserted Village" but from Wordsworth's sonnet, "London, 1802": "Milton! thou shouldst be living at
this hour: / England hath need of thee: she is a fen / Of stagnant wa-
ters: altar, sword, and pen, / Fireside, the heroic wealth of hall and
bower, / Have forfeited their ancient English dower / Of inward happiness. We are selfish men; / Oh! raise us up, return to us again; / And
give us manners, virtue, freedom, power." It was the cry of the romantic conservative.[77]

It is crucial to observe that whatever the standing of such elegy as
prophecy or social criticism, it was unquestionably the product of the
two themes, alienation and romanticism, the occasion and the formative language. The city had, after all, been beautiful and vexed by
politics and economics in the eighteenth century, without producing
such an image. But by the 1830s Charleston had an intoxicating chemistry: beauty, intimatable decline, rancorous dispute, and a generation
literate in the new language of alienation. Charleston became an education in moral awareness, the occasion for and example of the *Bildungs-
roman*, the embodiment of graced childhood evolving into pained self-
consciousness and migrant alienation. The city became the archetype
of the romantic spiral, though downwards not upwards.

That such an image was not idiosyncratic to Legaré is apparent from
others of his generation. This is Preston, writing in 1855, after the death
of his wife, in the same letter in which he had spoken to Waddy Thompson of the decay of friendships, the price of politics: "Things have much
changed here. Poor Carrington is in his grave. My sister is a widow.
There is an old dead tree in the field near which does not seem to have
changed since I saw the sun glinting on it last year. It is still naked
and lifeless but does not seem nearer to falling. The wind does not

shake it, the lightning does not strike it. There is no other limb to drop from it but near it is green grass and a few flowers."[78] It is the romantic language of organic change applied to society. And here is Legaré, in a letter which, when published in 1846, the Charleston *Courier* found especially evocative, "impossible to read without emotion." It is in a letter to Alfred Huger in 1834, after Legaré had heard of the death of Thomas Grimké and had paused to reflect, in his exile, upon the passing of Stephen Elliott and John Gadsden: "The worst of it is that, as such persons have never been produced any where else in America than in the low country of South-Carolina, so that soil is now worn out, and, instead of these oaks of the forest, its noble original growth, is sending up, like its old fields left to run to waste, thickets of stunted loblolly pine, half choked with broom grass and dog fennel. Take it all together, there are few spectacles so affecting as the decay of our poor parish country, which I often think of, even at this distance, with the fondness of disappointed love."[79]

5

James Louis Petigru in 1861. From James Petigru Carson, Life, Letters and Speeches of James Louis Petigru . . . (Washington, D.C., 1920), opposite p. 376. Courtesy of the South Carolina Historical Society.

James Louis Petigru: The Last South Carolina Federalist

LACY FORD

On 13 December 1861, a fire raged in the heart of Charleston, leaving one part of the city almost utterly destroyed and consuming such important landmarks as St. Andrews Hall, home of the St. Cecilia balls, St. Finbar's Cathedral, and the residence of James Louis Petigru, South Carolina's most distinguished Unionist. To a few observers the fire seemed an ominous portent, a sign that Providence might not wait on the Union army to avenge the sins of the birthplace of secession. Mary Boykin Chesnut, however, visiting in Charleston at the time of fire, took a somewhat different view of the tragedy. The entry in her diary on December 14 contained a touch of the wry sarcasm that has made Mrs. Chesnut the most quoted Southern woman of the Civil

War generation: "Carolina Institute, where secession was signed, burned down. From East Bay—along Broad St. down to the river—Mr. Petigru's house. So being anti-secessionist does not save. The fire, as the rain, falls on the just and the unjust."[1]

Mary Chesnut was fond of James Petigru: she found his wit charming and his honesty disarming; she admired his political courage. Undoubtedly the remark in her diary was meant as nothing more than a comment on fate's disregard for virtue and as a mild jab at the sometimes sanctimonious Petigru, whose own fondness for sarcasm was well known. Unwittingly, however, the famous diarist had written a fitting epitaph for Petigru. Petigru's real home was the Union, a house of many mansions built by patriots like his father and grandfather, Scotch-Irish immigrants who served the Whig cause in South Carolina during the Revolution. When South Carolina seceded from the Union in 1860, and other states joined her in a new Southern Confederacy shortly thereafter, Petigru felt that his political home had literally been destroyed by the fire-eating politicians of his native state.[2] Indeed, when the bells of Charleston began to peal in celebration of the passage of the secession ordinance, Petigru rushed out of his Broad Street office and asked his friend J.D. Pope the whereabouts of the fire. Pope answered, "Mr. Petigru, there is no fire; those are the joy bells ringing in honor of the passage of the Ordinance of Secession." Petigru, growing livid, retorted, "I tell you there is a fire; they have this day set a blazing torch to the temple of constitutional liberty and, please God, we shall have no more peace forever."[3] The Constitution was, for Petigru, the ark of the covenant where the cherished principles of liberty and order handed down by the Founding Fathers were preserved, and the Union was the political Holy of Holies built by the same men to protect liberty from its many enemies. Interpreted in light of this biblical metaphor, one suggested by Petigru's own words, the historian can see secession as Petigru saw it, as an act of sacrilege and parricide destined to bring suffering, bloodshed, and ultimately destruction to the South as well as to the Union.[4]

Petigru, who died in 1863, did not live to see his prophecies fulfilled, or to see his beloved Union reconstructed, yet his dogged Unionism, and the depth of the convictions behind his political stance, insured Petigru a reputation among the historians of sectional conflict. The search for indigenous Southern dissenters, for voices who urged the road not taken, has been one of the many staples of Civil War historiography for decades. Petigru, the intelligent and respected Unionist from the Hotspur state, has always received at least an obligatory mention in these studies, which usually declare that he was a brilliant but eccentric political maverick who had almost no following in South Carolina at the end of his career.[5] Indeed, it is difficult to quarrel with Carl Degler's assessment of Petigru as a Unionist whose views were "tolerated rather than influential."[6] After the nullification episode, Petigru held only one elective office, but he remained active in the campaigns of his allies, especially Charleston congressman Hugh Swinton Legaré. When the Compromise of 1850 precipitated an active secessionist movement in South Carolina, B.F. Perry, himself a long-time Unionist, advised Petigru that there were no more than five unconditional Unionists in the South Carolina legislature; in 1860, when South Carolina seceded, Petigru was the only well-known figure in the state who refused to shift his loyalty to the newly formed Confederacy. Try as he might, Petrigru was unable to win converts to Unionism or to slow the drift of the Palmetto State toward secession.[7]

Yet the most productive aspects of Petigru's life, and probably his most significant contributions to public life, came outside of the political arena. Throughout his adult life, Petigru was a busy and successful lawyer. After a brief stint as a teacher following his own education at Moses Waddell's log academy, Willington, and South Carolina College, Petigru devoted his entire professional life to the study and practice of law. First as a young attorney in the ramshackle rural village of Coosawhatchie and later as a distinguished leader of the venerable Charleston bar, Petigru earned a reputation as a tireless and skillful advocate and a painstaking legal scholar. A hard worker, Petigru usually carried one of the heaviest case loads in Charleston, did much of his own research, and frequently worked twelve-hour days. Early in his career Petigru served as state attorney-general for eight years before resigning in 1830 to take an active role in the fight against nullification, and late in his life, Petigru served for two years as United States District Attorney in Charleston, when President Fillmore could find no other South Carolinian willing to accept a federal appointment. Moreover, Petigru often handled controversial and politically sensitive cases. He defended a man accused of being a Negro trying to "pass" as white, and in the 1850s represented a Northern emigrant to Goose Creek who was accused of preaching abolitionist doctrines. In politically motivated litigation, Petigru challenged the "test oath" passed by

154

the nullifiers, and in 1861 he disputed the legal authority of the Confederate government to sequester the property of its domestic enemies. His legal career was also highlighted by active interest in legal reform, and at the age of seventy he was chosen by the South Carolina legislature, a body dominated by his political opponents, to codify the massive body of state laws.[8]

While attaining distinction as a lawyer, Petigru also enjoyed a productive career as something of a "professional Charlestonian," serving in a number of official and unofficial capacities to help promote the cultural, educational, and intellectual life of the city. Indeed, as Petigru grew less and less influential in politics, he seemed to loom larger and larger in the civic life of his adopted Charleston. Always a popular guest in the drawing rooms and at the dinner tables of Charleston's most prominent families, Petigru was an intimate of Legaré, William John Grayson, William Elliott, the Heyward family, the Huger family, and many other members of South Carolina's parish "aristocracy."[9] In his early years in the city, Petigru acquired a reputation as a poor dancer that he was never able to live down, but his other reputation, as a brilliant conversationalist, made him a central figure at most Charleston galas. Smart, well-informed, humorous, and capable of biting political satire, Petigru became the most quoted man in antebellum Charleston. Yet Petigru's public reputation grew not only out of his high standing in Charleston society but also out of a long record of service to the city. During his lifetime, Petigru served as an intendant for the city, as a vestryman for St. Michael's Episcopal Church, and as one of the agents officially appointed by the city to help negotiate loans to rebuild after the disastrous fire of 1838, in addition to his two terms in the state legislature. Petigru was also a strong supporter of groups and institutions that fostered the intellectual development of the city. He was a patron of the old and famous Charleston Library Society, one of the founders of the South Carolina Historical Society, and a regular at the semiofficial gatherings of Charleston's literati in the back room of John Russell's noted bookstore. All of this public service and work on behalf of civic improvement made Petigru one of Charleston's most respected public figures despite the unpopularity of his political views. Throughout most of his life, Petigru was a familiar figure on the streets of downtown Charleston, a man whose stature in the large urban community had somehow risen taller than the significance of his achievements would seem to have dictated. It is not surprising, then, but certainly ironic, that no public figure's memory was more cherished by postbellum Charleston, that cradle of the Confederacy, than that of James Louis Petigru, the diehard Unionist and devoted Charlestonian.[10]

For all his gifts, his learning, his industry, his wit, Petigru left—except for his legal briefs and private correspondence—no substantial corpus of work. He wrote no novels, no memorable proslavery or antislavery tracts, and no systematic statement of his political theory. Unlike many of his peers, he was not a prolific writer of political essays for the Charleston newspapers. As a result, it is difficult for the historian to assess Petigru's considerable intellectual gifts apart from his legal and political activities. Petigru once told his grandchildren that if history remembered him at all, it would be as a "good lawyer" and little more. Distinguished attorneys, no matter how lofty their reputation as jurists, seldom attract much attention from cultural or even intellectual historians, and Petigru has been no exception. Ultimately, therefore, it is his notoriety as a principled political maverick in a state known for its internal harmony that has made him a figure of enduring interest to students of the antebellum South.[11]

Petigru, I think, left historians a clue to understanding the intellectual and psychological underpinnings of his persistent Unionism in an anecdote he liked to tell about his early political career. While he was serving as a young attorney in Coosawhatchie, Petigru's political views were attacked by a rowdy young man outside the village courthouse. After hurling as many foul epithets as he could think of, the man finally called Petigru "a damned Federal"—at which point Petigru leveled his abuser with a hard punch to the jaw. Later, William Hutson, an old Federalist himself, asked why he had responded so violently to being called a Federalist while enduring being called "a rogue and a rascal" so calmly. "Certainly," Petigru replied, "I incurred no injury by being called a rogue, for nobody believes the charge; but when he said I was a Federalist he came too near the truth."[12] Well over thirty years later, after the South had seceded from the Union, Petigru admitted that he had never lost those sympathies, declaring that "anyone who thinks that it will help his argument may say that I was one [a Federalist]."[13] Thus, in a very real sense, Petigru's singular political views can be best understood as those of the last South Carolina Federalist, a man who tenaciously embraced Federalist principles long after the party was defunct in South Carolina and long after the dramatic social and economic changes of the so-called "Age of Jackson" had shattered neo-Federalist hopes of preserving the old order. Petigru was, to borrow a phrase from George Fredrickson's study of New England Federalists who survived their party's demise, a "conservative in a radical age."[14]

Petigru's devotion to Federalism was rather curious for reasons other than the political isolation that it was certain to produce. In the late eighteenth century, Federalism thrived in South Carolina, just as it did throughout the rest of the new nation; it was especially virulent among the wealthy rice and sea-island cotton planters of the coastal region and in the large and influential Charleston mercantile community. Both lowcountry planters and Charleston merchants were deeply integrated into the transatlantic economy and generally desired the continued security of trade under the British mercantile umbrella. Members of this Federalist elite helped ratify the Constitution despite active opposition in the backcountry and played important roles in the Federalist administrations of Washington and Adams. By the early 1800s, however, a series of political embarrassments, including the extremely unpopular Alien and Sedition Acts, and the rapidly growing population of the overwhelmingly Republican backcountry first placed South Carolina Federalists on the defensive and eventually routed them altogether. By 1810, Federalism was essentially confined to the city of Charleston and a few other tidewater strongholds, where it became the creed of an aging and embattled aristocracy that was losing power and influence to the burgeoning class of short-staple cotton planters in the upcountry.[15]

Petigru, of course, was a product of the upcountry, born on a modest farm in the Flatwood section of the Abbeville District, and educated by Waddell at Willington, an academy only ten miles from his home. Thus he spent his formative years in the upper Savannah River valley, an area that enjoyed great prosperity during the first short-staple cotton boom of the early 1800s and became a veritable Mesopotamia for the "country-republican" ideology which did so much to shape South Carolina's response to the political crises of the antebellum period. In the upper Savannah valley on the South Carolina side of the river were the homes of John C. Calhoun and his brothers, Patrick Noble (a South Carolina governor), and George McDuffie's plantation at Cherry Hill, as well as the birthplaces of Petigru and Langdon Cheves. On the Georgia side of the river, in the same general vicinity, were the homes of four prominent Old South politicians: William H. Crawford, Alexander H. Stephens, Robert A. Toombs, and Howell Cobb, Jr. In a very real sense, the Savannah River valley was a fertile breeding ground for Southern Rights politicians of varying stripes, and probably the ideological birthplace of the Confederacy.[16]

Despite his humble upcountry origins, however, a mature Petigru was impressed, indeed almost enthralled, by the rich and cultured plantation and mercantile aristocracy of the coastal parishes. At Willington, where he got his first taste of the world beyond his family's farm, Petigru met Hugh Swinton Legaré, William John Grayson, and other scions of the lowcountry elite. Their elegant attire and their breadth of interest intrigued him and made his own provincialism seem like a curse, until he proved that he could hold his own in Latin and Greek against the adolescent tidewater gentry. Petigru later remembered his education at Willington with great fondness, calling the day when "a Latin grammer as a substitute for the plough was placed in my hands" as "an important epoch in my life."[17]

The young upcountry prodigy excelled at Willington and was offered a position on the staff there when he graduated, but turned down the offer in order to continue his education at South Carolina College. In Columbia, Petigru studied the usual classical curriculum and was active in the Clariosophic Society, one of the college's two prestigious debate clubs. He graduated from South Carolina College in 1809 with the highest scholastic honors of his class. Upon returning to Abbeville after graduation, however, the young honor pupil's smoldering resentment of his father, William Pettigrew, exploded. James found the family farm deteriorating and family debt mounting, and blamed the problems on his father's laziness and legendary fondness for horseracing. Full of scorn for his father's earthiness and lack of ambition, James adopted the French spelling of the family name, in a considered effort to identify himself with the Huguenot tradition of his mother's family, and accepted a teaching position in the coastal district of Beaufort, near the home of his schoolmate, Grayson.[18]

Once settled in the lowcountry, Petigru's efforts to cloak himself with the desirable qualities, in particular the refinement and sophistication, of the lowcountry gentry surprised even his friends and sponsors within the gentry itself. When Grayson introduced Petigru to the Heyward family in Beaufort, the young upcountryman quickly threw himself into the orbit of the old, wealthy Federalist family and read law in

158

the magnificent library of the deceased Thomas Heyward, a signer of the Declaration of Independence.[19] Petigru compensated for his lack of wealth and social rank with intellect and ambition, and by the time he moved to Charleston in 1819, the young lawyer was already a favorite of the lowcountry gentry. Not only were they flattered by his eagerness to join their ranks but also genuinely impressed with the young up-countryman's genius, a trait that was too often lacking in the second, third, and fourth generation sons of the old tidewater chivalry. Young Tom Heyward acknowledged Petigru's ability and gave an air of legitimacy to the ambitious attorney's aristocratic pretensions when he told Petigru, "Whatever parties may exist in a country and under whatever name they may go, there are always two aristocracies—the aristocracy of talent and the aristocracy of wealth. You belong to the one and I belong to the other."[20]

If Petigru was an eager aristocrat, blessed with the energy of an *arriviste*, the lowcountry gentry were anxious to receive an infusion of new talent and industry. As George C. Rogers has noted, the coastal aristocrats "were not without fears." Aware of their own decline and frightened by the "democracy tending to rear its ugly head in the sphere of politics," the aristocrats, according to Rogers, were determined to find a refuge for order and authority.[21] Petigru, the newcomer, shared that determination and believed that the foundation of any such refuge had to be the preservation of the Union and the running of the government along Federalist lines. In New England, such views were common throughout the Jacksonian era. Francis Parkman, the Brahmin historian who believed that the American aristocracy had to first redeem itself and then redeem America, explored the Oregon trail in 1846 in order to find models of manliness among the frontiersmen to hold up as examples to the effete Boston aristocracy. In the South, Petigru, a self-styled aristocrat, simply brought the robust energy of rough-and-tumble rural Abbeville with him as he moved into the ranks of lowcountry elite.[22] Petigru loved his adopted Charleston more than his native Abbeville and threw himself behind the cause of declining Federalist chivalry with the zeal that only a convert can muster. It mattered little to him that the Federalist party was dead or that the citizens of the republic appeared to have repudiated Federalist policies; as long as the Union endured and as long as an aristocracy committed to the nurture of Federalist sympathies survived, the possibility remained that the nation might once again be guided by that elite and by its neo-Federalist vision.[23]

Like so many of his generation, Petigru saw the Founding Fathers as heroic and noble statesmen, men worthy of wearing the grand republican togas of the ancient Roman senators. Moreover, he believed that the Union, the fruit of the Founders' labor, would be the vehicle of national glory and greatness. Petigru's emphasis on the role of the Union as an instrument for preserving liberty and ensuring progress was reminiscent of Daniel Webster's emotional attachment and typical of neo-Federalist sentiment.[24] For all his ability as a legal scholar, Petigru always based his Unionism more on the psychological appeal of an ennobling and uplifting force than on closely reasoned constitutional principles. The logic behind his constitutional reasoning, when he did attempt it, was relatively straightforward and, again, relatively typical of conventional Federalist thinking. Petigru argued that sovereignty was divisible and that once they had ratified the Constitution, the states had irreversibly surrendered part of their sovereignty to the federal government. The Union was not, as Calhoun argued, a conditional compact among sovereign states, but a once-and-for-all contract binding all parties in perpetuity.[25] Nullification, Petigru contended, was unconstitutional because the Constitution guaranteed the general government the "power to execute its own laws," which were to have precedence over state laws."[26] Without the power to execute its own laws, Petigru argued, the Union would cease to exist.

These arguments were neither original nor, for the most part, particularly sophisticated. They were the garden-variety objections to state interposition and nothing more. Certainly Petigru's plenary statement on divisible sovereignty, "I am for . . . the semi-sovereignty of the U.S. and the quasi-sovereignty of the State," was hardly a satisfactory rebuttal to the carefully reasoned arguments of Calhoun, the consummate logician.[27] Petigru's most effective pleas for the Union were, like those of Webster, emotional appeals to the greater glory of the nation. "The glorious inheritance is at stake," Petigru asserted in one such appeal. "The same blow which destroys the Union, levels to the ground the defences of liberty. Under the Federal Constitution we have enjoyed all which the patriots of the American Revolution desired to see. Our country has increased in riches, in knowledge, and in honor." Growing even more eloquent, he continued:

And those who offered up their lives in the cause of America would have closed their eyes in peace if they could have been blessed with a vision of that future which we have enjoyed. The happiness of our citizens has formed the admiration of the wise and good; and now when the scene is changed, and discontents created by the acts of Government, have brought the Constitution itself into danger, it depends on the moderation and wisdom of the sons of liberty, to repay in some degree the debt of gratitude, by transmitting the same inheritance to their posterity.[28]

In private, Petigru seldom hesitated to admit his undeniable Federalist sympathies, opinions shared in South Carolina by only a small band of parish aristocrats. As a practical politician, Petigru championed the causes he believed in while remaining quiet about his latent Federalism. He praised the conservative Bank of the United States as a bastion of financial stability but eyed the proliferation of state and private banks in the 1830s with alarm, fearing that rapid expansion of the currency would fuel reckless speculation. Always a nationalist, Petigru favored internal improvements, especially canals and railroads, but detested the crass pork-barrel politics that always accompanied state aid to such projects.[29] As a Federalist, he endorsed the intentions of the Northwest Ordinance, which forbade the expansion of slavery into free territory, and opposed every Southern effort to promote the expansion of slavery westward. "So much am I a disciple of Locke and Montesquieu," he wrote, "that my mind does not balance between freedom and slavery."[30] Yet if Petigru was a precocious "free-soiler," he was no abolitionist. His respect for established institutions predisposed him to oppose radical attacks on slavery; more importantly, his own position as a slaveholder made him sensitive to the requirements of Christian stewardship. On the whole, Petigru found Southern planters lacking in the qualities needed by humane masters, but congratulated himself on the condition of the slaves at his own Savannah River plantation in 1835. "The only thing to flatter my vanity as a proprietor," he observed, "is the evidence and striking improvement in the moral and physical condition of the negroes since they have been under my administration. When I took them they were naked and destitute. Now there is hardly one that has not a pig, at least, and with few exceptions they can kill their own poultry when they please."[31] Apparently, nothing was so good for slaves as a little Federalism, or Tory paternalism, in their master.

By 1830, however, Petigru had little fear of being branded a Federalist in politics, because the political labels in vogue in South Carolina were "Nullifier" and "Unionist." As a Southerner, Petigru was opposed to high tariffs and freely admitted that "there is no tariff party in South Carolina; we agree on every side that the tariff should be resisted by all constitutional means."[32] Privately, however, Petigru was astonished at the radicalism of the antitariff leaders in the Palmetto State. In a letter to his close friend Grayson, who had reluctantly sided with the Nullifiers, Petigru revealed his scorn of the radicals and his amazement at the hyperbolic rhetoric of the nullification campaign:

> I am devilishly puzzled to know whether my friends are mad, or I beside myself. . . . That we are treated like slaves, that we are slaves in fact, that we are worse than slaves and made to go on all fours, are stories that seem to me very odd, and make me doubt whether I am not under some mental eclipse, since I can't see what is so plain to others. But I am not surprised that the people have been persuaded they are ill used by the government. Old Hooker says, "If any man will go about to persuade the people that they are badly governed, he will not fail to have plenty of followers." And I am inclined to think that the better the polity under which men live, the easier it is to persuade them they are cruelly oppressed.[33]

To his friend and fellow Unionist William Elliott, Petigru branded Beaufort planters who favored nullification as "Jacobins"—a term of opprobrium Federalists loved to use. "They are fond of two things together," Petigru argued, "power and liberty. In every strife we find them against the established order of things and it always must be so."[34]

The nullification crisis brought Petigru to the crowded center stage of South Carolina politics. In 1830 he ran as a Unionist candidate for the state legislature, touted by the anti-Nullifier Charleston *Courier* as "no Aristocrat" but a man "sprung from the body of the people, to a nobly earned distinction."[35] Petigru won a seat by polling about 55 percent of the votes cast, and proceeded to spend most of the next two and a half years working for the Union cause. Although there were many local cliques that opposed nullification loosely united under the Union banner, the bulk of Unionist support came essentially from two factions. The largest was that of the true Jackson Democrats, loyal followers of Old Hickory who would have felt quite at home among the wildly pro-Jackson majorities in other Southern states. In South Carolina, this faction was led in the upcountry by Benjamin F. Perry, the favorite of mountaineers and backwoodsmen, and in the lowcountry by Joel Poinsett, a former diplomat and loyal Jacksonian; it received most of its popular support from yeomen in the upcountry and Pee Dee who were only marginally involved with commercial agriculture. The second Unionist faction, though smaller, supplied most of the leaders, the bulk of the polemical talent, and almost all the wealth required by the Union cause. Its adherents were essentially conservative in the broadest sense of the term: great planters, bankers, powerful Charleston merchants, scholars—many of them members of prominent colonial families with lingering Federalist sympathies. As representatives of a refined, self-conscious, parish elite, these Unionists were cautious and cosmopolitan and turned to cautious and cosmopolitan men like Petigru, Legaré, the Hugers, the Draytons, and William Elliott for leadership.[36]

Petigru plunged into the campaign against nullification with a vigor and optimism that he would never again demonstrate in politics. Once the battle lines were drawn, however, the Unionists quickly proved no match for the Nullifiers in the art of rallying the voters to their cause. As polemicists, debaters, and authors of political tracts, the Unionists excelled, but on the stump and at the militia musters, only Perry could rival a score of leading Nullifiers in wooing the crowd. The endless stream of political rallies, public dinners, gala balls, and military exercises organized by the Nullifiers almost literally turned South Carolina, in Grayson's words, "into a great talking and eating machine," and won broad support for nullification from the state's citizens.[37] William Freehling has laid a large part of the blame for the failure of the Unionist party on the shoulders of the conservative lowcountry Unionists whose own scorn for democracy left them poorly equipped to take their case to the people.[38] Petigru, who was critical of the way the Nullifiers played on popular passions during the campaign, was frustrated by the disdain many of his Unionist allies showed for the electorate and viewed the tidewater gentry's attitude toward the campaign as hopelessly priggish. "If we had missionaries to traverse the country as they [the Nullifiers] do," Petigru observed during the heat of the campaign, "I believe we could dispute the ground with them successfully. But we have none."[39]

When the Unionists were crushed at the polls in the fall of 1832, Petigru was bitter. His complaint to the trusted Legaré was typical: "The majority of our folks are such citizens as Rome had in her worst days. No republic ever had worse as far as their duty to the United States is concerned. Here is one of the anomalies produced by our strange system: As citizens of the United States they are traitors, but as citizens of the State they are true men."[40]

Although the stigma of his support for a doomed Unionist cause probably ruined Petigru's political future in South Carolina, he remained reasonably active in politics for another dozen years. After the tariff question was temporarily compromised and nullification became moot, Petigru worked closely with his old law partner, James Hamilton, a leading Nullifier, to avert civil strife between Nullifiers and Unionists in South Carolina over the requirement that all militia officers swear a test oath promising paramount loyalty to the state.[41] During the period of relative calm that followed the compromise settlement of the test oath controversy, Petigru remained doggedly loyal to his neo-Federalist views. Virtually alone among South Carolinians, he eulogized John Marshall when the powerful Chief Justice died in 1836. Nevertheless, when Calhoun and his followers decided to oppose the incumbent congressman from Charleston, former Nullifier Henry L. Pinckney, for breaking with other Calhounites on the question of how Congress should dispose of incoming abolitionist petitions, Petigru agreed to make common cause with the despised Calhoun faction in support of the Unionist Legaré, a reconciliation candidate. With the help of a cadre of Calhoun lieutenants, Petigru engineered a narrow victory for the effete and foppish Legaré, while remaining skeptical of Calhoun's true interest in affecting a reconciliation with Unionists.[42]

In 1837, both Petigru and Legaré were again involved in a disagreement with Calhoun. Long a supporter of vigorous commercial activity and often a champion of Charleston's mercantile interests, Petigru favored a strong, stable, and conservative banking system. He also believed that the second Bank of the United States had provided the perfect foundation for such a system until Jackson began what Petigru felt were demagogic attacks on the national bank.[43] Thus when Calhoun announced his support for Martin Van Buren's Sub-Treasury scheme, a system designed to effect a separation of the government and the banks, Petigru tried to use the issue to undermine Calhoun's position in the state. Knowing the heavy commercial involvement of many South Carolina planters and the strong support of such prominent Nullifiers as George McDuffie, William Preston, and Waddy Thompson for a national bank of some type, Petigru thought the bank issue might prove to be Calhoun's undoing.[44] During a visit to Washington in September of 1837, Petigru commented, "I have just heard

Mr. Calhoun on the Divorce of Bank and State, but it is in reality a divorce of Calhoun from his little party."[45] Along with his old friend Legaré, Petigru joined a small band of South Carolina politicians, including the popular Nullifiers Preston and Thompson, who sought to build a strong Whig opposition in South Carolina while Calhoun returned to the Democratic fold. By December of 1837, however, Calhoun had pushed through the state legislature by decisive margins a series of resolutions endorsing his position on the Sub-Treasury. A disgusted Petigru offered a sarcastic summation of Calhoun's success: "The unanimity of the Legislature and of the people is unnatural. It is a forced and unsettled state of things. Mr. Calhoun's triumph is complete and even too great, for he has crushed his lieutenants."[46]

Despite Calhoun's victory, Petigru remained active in South Carolina's small Whig party and continued to be a loyal supporter of the party's national leader, Henry Clay. Petigru saw the Whigs as the best hope for orderly economic progress and social stability. Although they sought popularity by tailoring their rhetoric to fit the prevailing democratic distemper, they were, Petigru believed, comfortable with the idea of returning the mantle of leadership to a cohesive aristocracy, including men of talent as well as social rank.[47] Petigru admitted that members of the old South Carolina aristocracy had either abdicated their leadership roles to Calhoun and other upcountry parvenus, or attempted to rescue their old declining positions by joining the newcomers in ceaseless agitation against the national government. Before the South Carolina chivalry could reform the state, it had to rejuvenate itself and purge its ranks of pretenders. At a Whig political rally in the early 1840s, Petigru used a parable to describe his view of South Carolina's political dilemma. "This dear old State of ours," he observed, "reminds me of a refined, rich, fat, lazy old planter who took his wine at dinner and his nap in the afternoon. He employed an overseer of unsurpassed abilities and turned over the management of the large estates to him. One morning the planter woke up and found the overseer master of the plantation."[48] Petigru's story was but one more example of the satirical anecdotes for which he had become so widely noted; at the same time, it revealed his belief that a smug and self-satisfied coastal aristocracy had yielded the stewardship of South Carolina to a new generation of politicians, composed largely if not entirely of upcountry planters, whose ambition would ultimately bring the state to ruin.

After Henry Clay's failure in 1844, Petigru's hopes for a rebirth of the Whig party in South Carolina died, and he virtually abandoned politics. He did remain loyal to Whig principles and offered quiet but solid support for Whig presidential nominee Zachary Taylor in 1848, but he spurned overtures from prominent young Charleston politicos who were organizing a group of "Taylor Democrats" in the city because he believed that the faction was dominated by crass opportunists.[49] Petigru was convinced that nothing short of disunion would satisfy hot-headed Palmetto politicians. "Tired of New England," he complained, "they [S.C.] desire divorce and a second marriage."[50] By 1850, Petigru had essentially withdrawn from active politics and was content simply to sally forth on occasion and jab his opponents with wit and satire, to become what one foreign journalist would later call "a bumblebee in everyone's bonnet."[51] Ultimately, Petigru summarized his feelings about the state and its politics in a letter to his fellow Unionist B.F. Perry:

> If all our countrymen were as lost to respect for the difference between Right and Wrong as South Carolina, it would be time for Hell to enlarge its borders. . . . The truth is, my friend, I have contracted a disinclination to write or speak when truth is in question. For I look upon my countrymen with the despair of old Fontenelle who said that if he had the truth in his closed hand he would not open it. And why should one put himself to the pains of speaking to the insane if he has not the power of commanding a strait jacket for them?[52]

Unable to command a straitjacket for South Carolina, Petigru found politics futile. In his profession and in the active role he played in the civic life of his adopted Charleston, however, Petigru was better able to practice the stewardship demanded by his Federalist world view.

* * *

Wealth, political success, and literary fame all eluded Petigru. Either his ambition was insufficient (as in the case of moneymaking), his talent lacking (as with literary achievement), or the circumstances forbidding (as in politics). Fame and elevated reputation did, however, come his way in the field of law, his reluctantly chosen profession. The young upcountryman, fresh from the almost obligatory stint of duty in the rural courthouse village of Coosawhatchie, rose quickly to the top of the Charleston bar after beginning practice there in 1817. By 1822, Petigru's legal ability was so widely respected that the state legislature elected the young barrister to the office of attorney-general. By the 1850s

166

the office of attorney-general was frequently handed out by the legislature as a reward for a long record of public service, but earlier in the century the office was more often used as a proving ground for keen young legal minds who were perceived as future political chieftains of the state. At age thirty-three, Petigru had already earned the confidence of South Carolina's legal community and no doubt thought himself well-positioned for future political prominence.[53]

While serving as attorney-general, Petigru showed his first signs of interest in legal reform, a subject to which he would devote considerable time and attention for the rest of his life. As Charles M. Cook has pointed out, the spirit of legal reform was abroad throughout the nation during the 1820s, and it was only natural that Petigru, one of the preeminent gentlemen of the South Carolina bar, would play an active role in the reform movement in his native state. South Carolina participated vigorously, and with less than its usual idiosyncrasy, in the movement to "republicanize" American jurisprudence and stamp the legal system of the young republic with a distinctly American imprimatur. Since the founding of the republic, American thinkers had shown a desire to declare their intellectual as well as political independence from Great Britain. Legal reformers of the Jeffersonian era yearned to declare their own professional independence from Westminster Hall. American law—that bulwark of liberty in a young and dynamic republic still very self-conscious about its experimental nature—should not be burdened, legal reformers argued, by the dead weight of the British past, with all of its useless feudal precedents and flagrant accommodations to monarchy and aristocratic privilege. Instead, American jurisprudence should embody republican virtues, including simplicity and rationality, and as a group, legal reformers vowed to do whatever professional housekeeping was necessary to accomplish these goals.[54]

In South Carolina, Petigru was part of a small but extremely capable band of legal reformers who used their legal and polemical talents and their political influence to keep various reform proposals before the state legislature throughout the 1820s. A number of the foremost members of the South Carolina bar—Petigru, Legaré, Thomas Smith Grimké, Henry W. DeSaussure, and Benjamin F. Perry—joined noted scholar and jurist Thomas Cooper on behalf of legal reform. Legal reformers in South Carolina, however, frequently disagreed vehemently among themselves, and out of these disagreements came many of antebellum South Carolina's finest moments of legal discourse.[55] Some, such as Thomas Cooper and John Lyde Wilson, advocated a radical transformation of the state's legal system, centered on the elimination of equity courts and the codification of the massive body of laws. Others, like Petigru, were cautious reformers, desirous of changing only what was absolutely in need of refinement. Petigru was eager to remake the bloated and confused South Carolina legal system into a lean and rational one that could function effectively, efficiently, and quietly, and would smooth the path of the capable practicing attorney in his day-to-day endeavors. At the same time, however, Petigru maintained a deep and abiding respect for the law, with all its complexity and tradition. He had little use for legal panaceas and proffered a stern rebuke to all those inclined to prostrate the law before narrow and selfish purposes.[56]

Petigru's guarded endorsement of functional legal reform eventually drew him into a heated debate with other reformers over the future of equity courts in South Carolina. Attacks on the equity court system proceeded along three different but related lines. First, legal reformers criticized the tendency of equity courts to assume jurisdiction over matters that properly belonged in the common law courts. In South Carolina, a certain vagueness in the definition of equity jurisdiction was compounded by the existence, prior to 1824, of separate and parallel appellate courts for equity and common law. This parallel system allowed equity appellate courts to issue rulings contrary to common law decisions but failed to provide any mechanism, such as a single supreme court with final authority over all cases in both common law and equity, to resolve such conflicts.[57] The second complaint against the equity system was that it took far too long for cases to reach their final disposition. Thomas Cooper, a vocal opponent, compared its long delays and tedious proceedings to the convoluted operations of the British Chancery Court, which Charles Dickens caricatured in his novel *Bleak House*. A playwright, Cooper wrote, was once badgered by a critic who suggested that the "hero and heroine are in such profound distress in the fourth act, that you have left no misery to inflict in the fifth." The dramatist, according to Cooper, did not hesitate for even an instant before replying, "Pardon me, I will throw them into Chancery."[58] The third and most serious complaint against equity courts had nothing to do with jurisdictional ambiguities or agonizing slowness but with the danger posed to republican values by the very existence of equity courts. The primary evil, critics charged, was the broad discretionary power concentrated in the hands of individual equity chancellors, each of whom handed down dozens of decisions yearly without the benefit of juries and usually with but a small, uncertain, and poorly documented body of precedent to guide them. To good American republicans, dedicated to preserving the right of trial by jury and fearful of unchecked power, the evils of the "judge-made law" of the equity system were clear.[59] John Lyde Wilson, governor of South Carolina during the mid-1820s and a leading critic of equity jurisprudence, charged that "the Courts of Equity go on to legislate at will, and the citizen is wholly unable to say by what tenure he holds anything that is his." In an obvious overstatement designed for polemical impact, Wilson compared the excesses of the equity chancellors to those of the French Directory, and warned, "Their Prerogatives can not be defined by any one. They decide the same case, according to different rules, and no precedent governs them, when they choose to be untrammeled."[60] Thomas Cooper was equally harsh. The coexistence of common law courts and equity courts created he said, "a bungling intermixture" of "Saxon law, and feudal law, and Roman law, and anomalous bench-made law" that reduced South Carolina jurisprudence to "a system of ignorance and incongruity" and left the state with one set of courts (equity) for "quibbles" and another (common law) for "common sense."[61]

Petigru, well aware that the equity system in South Carolina was in need of a major overhaul, nevertheless responded to the criticism with a spirited defense of equity jurisprudence in an essay published in Legaré's *Southern Review* in 1829. In this closely reasoned essay, Petigru acknowledged that the distinction between common law and equity was "a great anomaly in English jurisprudence" but insisted that equity was nothing more than "a regular consequence of a still greater anomaly—Trial by Jury." According to Petigru, trial by jury, the chief virtue of Anglo-American jurisprudence and a cornerstone of the Bill of Rights, would remain practical only so long as the question before the courts could be resolved by "the simple affirmation or negative of the jury." "The whole procedure of the common law," Petigru pointed out, "has a reference to the functions of the jury; everything is done to bring the matter to such a state, that the jury may have nothing more to do, than to give a precise answer." In the equity courts, few matters lent themselves to such straightforward resolution. Equity jurisprudence had evolved, Petigru argued, to allow the legal system enough flexibility to handle complex business and commercial matters—including property settlements, partnership arrangements, and trusteeships—whose resolution often involved complicated directives from the bench. "If the courts of Common Law were opened to the subjects which require the long and minute decrees of a Court of Chancery," Petigru maintained, "the jury would be perplexed with duties for which they are not prepared by education or habit. In this state of things they would soon sink into neglect, and with the loss of their usefulness, they would lose popularity, and be gradually abolished."[62]

Thus Petigru linked the need for equity jurisprudence directly to the need to maintain the integrity of jury trials in common law. Equity courts prevented the common law courts from becoming cluttered, encumbered, and eventually overwhelmed with much of what might be referred as "lawyers' law," the endless tedium of trusts, estates, partnerships, and other property matters whose sheer complexity would have confused juries and placed a grave strain on the common law courts. "As we consider the trial by jury to be every way inestimable, and particularly as connected with the spirit of liberty," Petigru wrote, "we regard the Chancery as an admirable regulation for preserving that institution in its usefulness and vigour."[63] To Petigru's mind, equity jurisprudence had the residual benefit of fostering creativity in the area of business and property. The economy of the young republic was both expanding rapidly and becoming increasingly complex. Common law, based heavily on precedent, was by its very nature ill-equipped to deal with this economic expansion, and statutory law was far too rigid and difficult to change to accommodate a burgeoning economy. Particularly troublesome to South Carolinians was the natural silence of common law, with its British heritage, on a variety of legal questions surrounding the existence of slave property. Equity jurisprudence was far better suited for smooth accommodations to rapid economic change, and for the easy adjustment to peculiar forms of property, such as chattels personal. Indeed, in South Carolina, Petigru's close friend and political ally, Chancellor Henry William DeSaussure, headed one of the most creative and flexible equity systems in the United States, allowing equity jurisprudence to expand rapidly enough to handle the demands on the legal system made by the expansion of slavery and the sea-island and short-staple cotton booms that occurred in the state between 1790 and 1830.[64] "In the earlier stages of society, when personal property was of small account," Petigru noted, there was "little call" for the services of equity courts, but "in time, the great increase of personal property and new modes of industry gave rise to cases" that called for the sort of relief that could be provided only through equity.[65]

Having offered what he believed to be an irrefutable legal and practical justification of equity jurisprudence, Petigru went on to suggest sweeping reforms of the existing equity system in South Carolina. While he believed equity to be a necessary complement to the common law, he also agreed with its critics' charge that equity was expanding its scope at the expense of common law and to the detriment of republican values. Equity courts, Petigru warned, were becoming "like Aaron's rod, that swallowed up all the others." As a remedy, Petigru proposed that the General Assembly quickly enact legislation clearly defining the jurisdiction of equity and strictly limiting that jurisdiction to matters which common law was totally unprepared to handle. Moreover, once the number of questions handled by the equity courts was sharply reduced, Petigru argued, it would be possible to address the problems of confusion and delay that plagued the system. Limiting equity's jurisdiction would allow the number of equity chancellors in the state to be reduced from five to one. If a single chancellor presided over all equity cases in South Carolina, Petigru maintained, the discretion exercised by equity chancellors would then be bounded not only by the suggested new legislation but also by the judge's own personal requirements of consistency. It was hardly a firm restriction on judicial latitude, Petigru admitted, but it was better than none at all.[66]

On the whole, Petigru's ideas about equity jurisprudence and the equity system in South Carolina reflected his general attitude toward law and society. He was a lawyer talking about reforming the legal system for the sake of lawyers as well as for the benefit of society. He had the professional's respect for the utility, even the necessity, of equity jurisprudence. He knew that equity existed not to rival common law or, worse, to insult and threaten it, but to help preserve the integrity of common law by saving it from unbearable strains. At the same time, Petigru's later Whiggish procommercial proclivities were clearly evident in his "Court of Chancery" essay. He believed that the law should be a tool to foster business and encourage commercial activity, and to do so in an orderly fashion, rather than an intractable hindrance to an expanding economy. The reforms he suggested were to limit equity's excesses, to improve its efficiency, and to demand higher degrees of professionalism from lawyers and judges who practiced in the equity courts. There was no trace of iconoclasm or lack of reverence for legal tradition in his argument.

Despite Petigru's plea on behalf of equity, the cries against the system continued. Thomas Cooper still favored a radical solution to the problems besetting the equity system. "Abolish your Court of Chancery," he insisted. "Give chancery powers to common law courts, and make a court of law what it ought to be, a court of justice."[67] The South Carolina legislature, however, ignored both Petigru's plea for a restructuring of the state's equity system and Cooper's appeal for its elimination, and soon the nullification crisis diverted the legislature's attention away from such arcane matters as legal reform. Despite continued clamor, equity courts in South Carolina survived until 1868, when a new state constitution, written largely by Radical Republicans, eliminated the existing equity system and replaced it with a Court of Common Pleas, which had jurisdiction over civil and probate cases, including all matters of equity.[68]

On the codification of the law, the other major issue raised by legal reformers during the 1820s, Petigru had little to say in public, leaving the serious debate to others. Petigru's reticence on the issue is puzzling, since he was a lifelong supporter of codification and was seldom reluctant to make his views, even unpopular ones, public. Perhaps he felt his position as attorney-general required a public neutrality, or perhaps he was reluctant to make common cause with his persistent nemesis, Cooper, against his dearest friend, Legaré.[69] Aided by Thomas Smith Grimké, John Belton O'Neall, and others, Thomas Cooper waged a strong campaign in favor of codification. The existing body of laws, Cooper maintained, was so voluminous, wordy, and unintelligible that "they serve only to bring, not the law, but the lawyer home to every man's door."[70] Praising the Napoleonic Code, Cooper called for a codification of state law that would be simple enough for the average citizen to understand. Many in the state's legal community, however, opposed codification, and Hugh Swinton Legaré, a lawyer and the state's most versatile scholar, took up the cudgels against Cooper and his allies. Legaré perceived codification not as reform necessary to simplify matters for practicing attorneys but as a panacea. "In short," Legaré observed, "codification is to make every man his own counsellor and every judge infallible—or rather, it is to supersede, in a good degree, the necessity of both."[71] Legaré was quick to ridicule such visions, pointing out that no code, no matter how perfect, could ever make every man his own lawyer, and warning of the futility and even danger of trying to diminish the role played by professionals in the state's legal system.

Petigru's support of codification actually grew out of the latter half of Legaré's objection to it. The inadequacy of the various legal digests available in the early decades of the nineteenth century, and the inability of a simple compilation to provide the necessary clarification of apparent conflicts within the constantly expanding body of common and statute law, convinced Petigru that some sort of code was necessary to prevent the lawyer's task from becoming impossible or, differently phrased, to save the experts from drowning in the law's own quagmire. By the late 1820s, however, the codification movement had been infused with the fire of Jacksonian democracy; for Jacksonians like upcountry reformer B.F. Perry, codification was a means of demystifying the law and revealing its shrouded wisdom to the common man. Petigru, naturally, had little sympathy with such arguments, and undoubtedly shared Legaré's cynicism about reducing something so essentially complex to a form accessible to all citizens. Petigru's support of codification, like his advocacy of equity reform, was in the interest of procedural reform, smoothing the path for dedicated professionals rather than changing the role of law in society.[72]

The campaign for codification in the 1820s was defeated by the state legislature—largely, according to John Lyde Wilson, a proponent of codification, because "lawyers are averse to reform, and they have always had in our legislature a strong, if not prevailing, influence."[73] Yet the issue was revived frequently during the antebellum period, and in the late 1850s, more than thirty years after the first codification campaign, the legislature agreed to proceed with a codification of the state's statute law—and selected Petigru for the task. When appointed Commissioner for the new South Carolina Code in 1859, Petigru had already lived a full three score and ten, but despite his age and political isolation, he was the consensus choice. Undoubtedly, a few of his political adversaries thought of the assignment as a way of keeping the old Unionist too busy for politics, but most political leaders knew by 1859 that Petigru's following was small and his influence slight.[74] He was chosen because his qualifications were widely recognized and his ability widely respected. Given a salary of $5,000, a budget that allowed him to hire two assistants, and access to the needed libraries, archives, and court records, Petigru plunged into the work with a vigor that belied his years. Temperamentally unable to delegate anything other than clerical tasks to his aides, he labored day and night at his obligation for more than a year. In October of 1860, as talk of secession ebbed and flowed about him, even the industrious Petigru seemed exasperated by his work. "My task proceeds slowly," he complained to his sister. "It is extremely tedious to pick out the meaning of various Acts and weave them into something like a consistent discourse."[75]

In 1861, Petigru submitted a preliminary report on his work to the legislature, where the Judiciary Committees of both House and Senate failed to lodge any major objections. Late in 1862, therefore, after more than three years of arduous work, Petigru presented a completed three-volume draft to the General Assembly. He planned to appear before the select commission appointed to examine the code and was twice invited to do so, but his final illness prevented it. The commission did not formally review the code until after Petigru's death in 1863; when it did, a majority recommended that it be rejected and that a new task force be appointed to draft another. The majority report praised the brevity of Petigru's code but criticized its organization — which was patterned after that of Blackstone's *Commentaries* — contending that it did little "to make the law ready and accessible to the people." The commission minority, led by Henry D. Lesesne, a Charlestonian and former law partner of Petigru, recommended that the code be adopted as drafted by Petigru, claiming that a rejection was an affront to his memory. B.F. Perry, Petigru's old friend, added his endorsement to that of the minority, but the legislature found friendship and respect for the deceased author to be poor reasons for adopting a code of law, and the painstaking work of Petigru's last years never became official.[76]

Yet his labor was not entirely in vain. The Republican administrations of Reconstruction used the discarded Petigru code as a basis for drafting their own, which appeared in one volume in 1872. There was little or no political malice involved in the legislature's refusal to accept Petigru's version in 1863; indeed, there was genuine regret among Petigru's old foes, as well as among his friends, that his memory and his professional reputation could not be honored by the adoption of the code.[77] Still, it was somehow fitting that this final diligent labor, in which Petigru almost literally worked himself into the grave, was not rewarded by the elected representatives of Confederate South Carolina: by rejecting the code, the crowning achievement of a long and distinguished legal career, the state rejected Petigru posthumously just as it had rejected his counsel during his lifetime. His work on the code, like his earlier efforts to balance equity and the common law, was part of his lifelong desire to bring an elegant republican symmetry to American jurisprudence. The law, in Petigru's mind, was the very foundation of the American republic, and his faith in the efficacy and virtue of that republic never wavered, even as his opinion of his own state slowly soured.

*   *   *

Petigru's tireless work as a lawyer, legal reformer, and scholar was matched by his dedication to civic improvement and his determination that Charleston maintain and encourage vigorous cultural and intellectual life. It was the very urbanity of Charleston that had so attracted him to Charleston in the first place, and he was relentless in his effort to enrich the cultural aspects of the patrician society that had drawn him away from his plebeian upbringing among the stark red hills and sandy bottomlands of the upcountry. To say that Petigru, accepted by the gentry but not born to it, ultimately became a "professional Charlestonian" is not to raise disparaging images of the man as an insecure backcountry parvenu vigorously aping the refined habits of one of the Old South's most proud and self-conscious elites, but simply to note that although initially an outsider, he threw himself headlong into the cultural, intellectual, and institutional life of the city.

A pious man in many ways, though hardly willing to accept the personal asceticism required as proof of piety by the evangelicals who flourished in the upcountry, Petigru was a devoted Episcopalian and a regular supporter of St. Michael's Church in Charleston, where he served as a member of the vestry. He was never a supporter of the clergy's efforts to command "rigid obedience" among laity on such matters as the keeping of the Sabbath, but he did support the Charleston clergy's efforts to prevent a grand ball honoring Henry Clay, during his visit to the city in 1844, from being held on Maundy Thursday. Petigru himself was a Clay supporter and an arranger of the Whig presidential candidate's visit; when it became clear that plans for the Clay celebration would not be changed, however, Petigru "retired from connexion" with the festivities, since "there could be no greater contempt of the disci-

175

pline of the Church than the converting of a day of mourning into one of revelry and feasting."[78] Still, despite the occasions on which it was not possible to be both devout and popular, Petigru's standing as an Episcopalian expanded his influence in a city where the local elite was so predominantly Anglican.

Petigru was also an important and influential member of a number of local societies. He was an avid patron and prominent member of the Charleston Library Society. The Library Society, founded in 1748, provided those who supported it by fees and endowments with the best reading material available in antebellum South Carolina. Of all the institutions in the city, the Library Society was perhaps the most successful in enhancing local intellectual life and development, serving as a musty oasis for local scholars, theologians, and other assorted characters with academic and literary interests.[79] On the occasion of its first centennial anniversary in 1848, the Charleston Library Society asked Petigru to deliver the plenary oration, and he, though badly overworked by his practice, considered the honor too great to refuse. Petigru's oration was in large part a detailed sketch of the world political situation during the era in which the Library Society was founded, but his deep attachment to the society and his faith that cultivation of the intellect was one of the first duties of a progressive civilization dominated both the introduction and conclusion. Praising the founders, Petigru noted, "They planted the tree which invites our noon-day steps from the cares of business, to its cool, refreshing shade." The Library's collection of 25,000 volumes, he maintained, tended "to elevate the taste of the city," and placed the Library among Charleston's "flourishing institutions."[80]

Also, Petigru was one of the founders of the Charleston-based South Carolina Historical Society; he was chosen as its first president and served several terms. He and Frederick A. Porcher of the College of Charleston, Dr. James Moultrie, Mitchell King, and several others organized the society in 1855, and beginning in 1856 the state legislature made a small appropriation annually to defray part of the expenses. The Historical Society flourished under Petigru's leadership until its operations were interrupted by the Civil War. In 1875, it was reorganized chiefly through the efforts of Porcher, who became the society's first postbellum president.[81]

Perhaps the most famous among the "organizations" of which Petigru was a "member" was the so-called Russell's Bookstore Group, a

176

literary set that held informal gatherings in the back room of Russell's Bookstore and—along with the smaller coterie of mostly literary figures who gathered at "the Wigwam," the Charleston residence of William Gilmore Simms, for suppers and conversation—made up the inner circle of the Charleston intellectual community. At Russell's, Petigru enjoyed intellectual discourse not only with Simms and Porcher but also with Basil Gildersleeve, a young student back from Göttingen who was destined to become a famous classical scholar; James Warley Miles, the skeptical Episcopalian theologian; Dr. Samuel Henry Dickson, a noted pathologist at the Charleston Medical College; Father Patrick Lynch, the Roman Catholic bishop of Charleston and a classical scholar; and William R. Tabor, editor of the Charleston *Mercury*. Moreover, William John Grayson, author of *The Hireling and the Slave*; promising young poets Paul Hamilton Hayne and Henry Timrod; Presbyterian minister Thomas Smyth; miniaturist and scholar Charles Fraser; and many other prominent Charlestonians joined the others on occasion.[82] Little is known about the inner workings of the group, which was very active in the late 1840s and 1850s, and even less about exactly what role Petigru played in its discussions. In his postwar reminiscences of the bookstore meetings, however, Paul Hamilton Hayne ascribed a prominent place to Petigru. In 1856, Petigru and other members were instrumental in initiating *Russell's Magazine*, the last of the literary magazines in the Old South. Published by bookstore owner John Russell and edited by Hayne, *Russell's* first appeared in April of 1857 and included the work of William Elliott, Grayson, Simms, Henry Timrod, and Hayne himself among many others. The importance of the bookstore group to Petigru, however, was chiefly the opportunity it provided for intellectual exchange, for developing a sense of collegiality with like-minded men in his community. No place in South Carolina and few, if any, in the entire South offered as much in this regard as Charleston, and Petigru adored Charleston for it.[83]

Out of these efforts to maintain and enhance the role of the church, local institutions, and the intellectual elite in defining the tone of public discourse and the ambience of civic life in antebellum Charleston, Petigru earned a far-flung reputation as one of the principal stewards of civic virtue and proponents of improvement in the city. These concerns, of course, were part and parcel of his neo-Federalist outlook. In Petigru's view, the elite, the aristocracies of both wealth and talent, was responsible not only for the preservation of order and authority in society but also for the cultivation of the civilized passions—art, literature, music, and scholarship. It was the duty of the elite not only to rule and rule wisely but also to work for moral uplift and the public good. Like most good Federalists, Petigru wanted to accomplish his good works through institutions, as evidenced by his vigorous support of Charleston's major religious, educational, and cultural establishments. Moreover, he never spared the Charleston elite from the sting of his sharp criticism when he found it lacking; indeed, perhaps his position as a one-time outsider, a critical *arriviste*, sharpened his perception of flaccidity and decadence among the gentry.

The more than occasional barb directed to friend as well as foe heightened the awareness among those closest to Petigru of his many frustrations. That most of his political and literary ambitions were unfulfilled gave sustenance to what was probably Petigru's worst quality, a tendency toward pettiness in his assessment of other people's motives and a certain temperamental peevishness that surfaced in unflattering ways. The peevishness appeared even in his relationship with Legaré during the campaign of 1836. Petigru repeatedly rebuked Legaré for not returning quickly from Europe to begin the campaign, and also admonished him—wisely but still testily—to sport "no whiskers, no rings, no chain, no foppery, nothing but civility and common sense till the election is over."[84] Pettiness was even more blatant in Petigru's account of a visit with John C. Calhoun in 1848, when a mutual friend, Barnard Bee, arranged for Calhoun to invite him to dinner at Fort Hill. After enjoying, as did so many others, the Calhoun table and drawing room, Petigru did not emphasize Calhoun's hospitality but instead gloated over how he was able to dominate the great Carolinian in conversation.[85] Such playful denigration of peers and rivals, however, pales beside examples of real intolerance. Normally able to separate personal from political differences, Petigru worked behind the scenes to have Thomas Cooper ousted from South Carolina College in 1831 for his deism, probably as much because of Cooper's advocacy of nullification as for his religious heresy. Petigru was also given to speaking with considerable disdain of the Charleston Irish, or "Pat" as he preferred to call them.[86]

More often, however, an eye for the weaknesses of his fellowman transformed pettiness into stinging satire. Petigru's rapier wit was his finest weapon; much of the reputation he acquired beyond Charleston, certainly beyond South Carolina, he owed to that wit. Petigru, like his friend Grayson, was well-schooled in romanticism but never much taken by it; here, too, he was anachronistic, preferring—as a good Federalist should—the neoclassical idiom of Enlightenment rationalism. His own style was clearly and self-consciously patterned after that of the grand old Tory satirists, Pope, Dryden, and Swift, all of whom he admired. Undoubtedly, part of Petigru's attachment to these figures was simply a felt kinship with other satirists, but much of it arose as a result of his continued search for a lost Augustan age. Petigru was a child of the Enlightenment, imbued heavily with an Enlightenment faith in orderly and rational progress; small wonder that the contortions of South Carolina politics shook his faith. Yet Petigru remained convinced of the rightness of his own ideas, the clarity of his vision. Confident in the strength of his own armory of virtue, his loyalty to the Constitution, and his vast and growing stockpile of civic good deeds, he used his skill as a satirist to create an adversarial relationship between himself, speaking with the clear and sensible voice of reason and tradition, and the rest of the state, that ship of fools and lunatics demented by hyperbolic fears of enslavement and led by politicians crazed with ambition and vanity. In this conflict Petigru could use his wit as a rapier to keep his objectionable foe at a safe distance and, from time to time, even to draw blood. Much to his chagrin, however, the state seldom even noticed the wound.

Petigru's best piece of work was not satire. It was a serious, and quite diplomatic, oration given at the third annual meeting of the South Carolina Historical Society in 1858, while he was its president. Throughout his career, Petigru's reputation as an orator had grown so steadily that he was forced to refuse all but the most interesting offers to speak. Before 1858, he had delivered the Charleston 4th of July oration, given graduation speeches at Erskine College and the University of Georgia, spoken at the Semi-Centennial of South Carolina College, and addressed the Charleston Library Society, among many others.[88] His Historical Society oration, however, was the best summary and most elegant statement of his sentiments, his personal tour de force.

In the speech, Petigru turned to the twin guides, reason and history, that had influenced his thinking throughout his life, and heralded them as still the best hopes for the future of the republic. "It is the province of Reason to distinguish between right and wrong," he began, "and to deduce from that distinction rules for the conduct of life." Yet reason, Petigru admitted, "is not exempt from error." The "disturbing influence of interest and passion" force reason to "lean on the authority of Experience." "It is History that comes to the relief of conscience when perplexed by the conflict of opinion," he maintained, "and furnishes a guide for conduct and judgment when reason is at fault. It is to the human family what experience is to the individual." Aside from ascribing to the historian an almost sacred duty as keeper of the received wisdom, Petigru's argument was clearly an affirmation of the philosophical underpinnings of Federalism, a faith in the utility of reason and the necessity of tradition. In all societies, he declared, "the adherents of antiquity, under the name of Conservatives, and the partisans of progress, under the banner of Reform, wage an endless war." The lessons of History, however, allow free people a way of choosing the best from both parties and finding an Augustan golden mean in the equipoise of progress and tradition.[89]

The body of the speech was dominated by Petigru's skillful and imaginative sketch of the broad outlines of South Carolina's history, from the first voyages of Ribault through the American Revolution. It was from the Revolution that Petigru wished to make his point. The "bitterness of civil strife" that characterized the struggle between Whigs and Tories had left deep scars. With an obvious eye on the crisis of the 1850s, Petigru spoke about the Revolution: "Zeal in behalf of our country and our country's friends is commendable, and patriotism deservedly ranks among the highest virtues. But even virtue may be pushed to excess, and the narrow patriotism that fosters an overweening vanity and is blind to all merit except its own, stands in need of the correction of reason."[90]

The "correction of reason," of course, was what Petigru had long desired for South Carolina. Moreover, and again with an eye on the epithets hurled against him by the fire-eaters, he cautioned against a dangerous oversimplification of history. "It is not true," he said, "that all the virtue of the country was in the Whig camp, or that the Tories were a horde of ruffians." Then he leveled an overt warning to those who would taunt him as a "Tory" or "submissionist":

> And let it be remembered by those who are influenced by a name, and pin their faith upon party;—for the instruction of those writers who, like unskilful painters, daub their pictures with glaring colors; that it was after the epithet of Tory had become perfectly detestable that it was freely bestowed on the Federalists, their most redoubted enemies.[91]

Having sounded his cautionary notes, Petigru closed with an eloquent and heartfelt plea for peace and unity. South Carolina had, despite the civil strife of the Revolution, eventually "become the most united of all the political communities on this continent." Petigru urged that "that union be consecrated to peace, and the future history of the State contain the record of its steady advance in all the arts of life, and all the virtues that dignify humanity."[92]

The irony of his concluding remarks could hardly have escaped Petigru. Standing before a society he had helped found and in front of an audience which, on the whole, disapproved of his politics, he had taken to the defense of loyalists, or Tories, the hated enemies of the men he admired most, the Founding Fathers. It was ludicrous to Petigru that he could be branded a Tory by his opponents when he was so obviously an eighteenth-century Whig. He must also have noted the irony in the fact that he now placed his hopes for moderation on the state's peculiar unity, which was first and foremost the product of the labors of his arch-nemesis, the departed Calhoun. Yet the final irony, which Petigru noted in his later correspondence if he had not already sensed it by 1858, was the sad fate that lay ahead for Charleston. "Time, which is the destroyer of the works of men," he declared in his oration, "gives them History in return for what it takes away." Time seemed to be driving Petigru's beloved Charleston, and all that he had worked for there, inexorably towards secession and willful self-destruction. Out of the ruins would rise shared memories and shared grief colored by the blood of fallen Confederates. The History that time gave to Charleston in place of her antebellum glory was the inchoate myth of the Lost Cause, and enough true heroism and sacrifice to make that myth viable. Petigru would have considered it paltry compensation.[93]

*   *   *

Only once in his latter years did Petigru show any glimmer of optimism about South Carolina's political future, and that was in the immediate aftermath of Calhoun's death in 1850. Petigru agreed with B.F. Perry's assessment that the death of Calhoun "relieved South Carolina of political despotism." "Every man," Perry contended, "may now breathe more freely as England did after the death of Henry the Eighth. There will be divisions amongst us and I am glad of it."[94] Yet shortly after Calhoun's death, a strong secession campaign was waged in South Carolina, and Perry advised Petigru that "the whole legislature, with very few exceptions, are disunionists."[95] Petigru did, however, take some consolation from the fact that most legislators found Robert Barnwell Rhett, the leading fire-eater, "too radical." He was also hopeful that the efforts of Perry and James L. Orr to align South Carolina Democrats more closely with the national party would revive party politics in South Carolina.[96] On the whole, however, the political developments of the 1850s offered Petigru little reason for optimism. The demise of the Whig party, and the marriage of Northern antislavery sentiment with the democratic "free-soil" ethos of the rural Midwest in the new Republican party, convinced Petigru that the Union was in great peril. "The Constitution is only two months older than I," he wrote to his daughter Susan in 1860, and, "My life will probably be prolonged till I am older than it is."[97] In the final days of the secession crisis, Petigru was relatively quiet, perhaps recognizing his lack of influence among the citizens of Charleston. Nevertheless, he took occasion to pronounce one final malediction on the whole drama of disunion: addressing a body of secessionists, he warned that "South Carolina is too small to be a Republic, and too large to be an insane asylum."[98]

Bitter over the dissolution of his beloved Union, an aging and infirm Petigru became embroiled in one unexpected controversy that caused him as much embarrassment as any in his long and controversial career. William H. Russell of the London *Times*, visiting Charleston shortly after the fall of Fort Sumter, was guest of honor at a dinner party given by Petigru. More than a month later, R.B. Rhett, Jr., of the Charleston *Mercury*, penned an editorial strongly implying that Petigru had admitted to Russell that he was a monarchist. J. Johnston Pettigrew, James' cousin, attacked Rhett for dragging private conversations into the public realm with the sole intent of subjecting the old Unionist to public ridicule. Rhett defended his actions and claimed that Petigru's views on monarchy were well-known.[99] Petigru refused to respond to the charges in public, but privately observed that "Rhett, Jr. is fool enough to call me a monarchist because I am a Union man," and that his "attachment to popular government would outlast that of a whole brigade of Secessionists."[100] It is unlikely that Petigru was a monarchist; more likely, thoroughgoing distrust of the generation of demagogues which he believed had been bred by the democratic revolution in American politics convinced Russell that Petigru had given up on the American experiment in republicanism.[101]

As the Civil War began to rage around him, Petigru explained his disappointment and confusion in a long letter to J. Johnston Pettigrew, who was to command the division to Pickett's left during the ill-fated charge at Gettysburg:

> It is very well for the common soldier to despise his enemy, for probably he has no better reason for fighting than that he hates him. But why should we (you and I) despise the Yankees. Is it because they are below the people that we admit are fellow-citizens in civilization. . . . Your father was a Federalist and your grandfather, as well as I. They were churchmen, as well as I. Certainly there were ten Federalists at the North to one in the South, and, even including New England, we would find more brethren in the North than at home. I take it that we are fighting the Yankees, not from personal animosity, but an opinion that it is the true interest of the South to erect a separate Government. . . . Whether that opinion was the result of sound reason or passion, history will judge. Perhaps the regard which the North profess for the old flag is a superstition, but it is the same sort of sentiment which has led men to shed their blood for a fallen dynasty, and I don't think it is visited with contempt by posterity.[102]

A member of a fading aristocracy, Petigru lived just long enough to see his worst fears realized. With the Union dissolved, the North and South at war, and Charleston under seige by the Union army, Petigru died on 9 March 1863. His death was mourned in Charleston as if he had died a Confederate war hero rather than as a loyal Unionist.[103] In a real sense, though, Petigru's world was not destroyed by secession and Civil War but had vanished with the rise of Jacksonian democracy. Petigru was most at home in a political culture where cautious, conservative Federalist lions defended the republic from cunning Jeffersonian foxes.[104] Even Calhoun, in his later years, yearned, as Clyde Wilson has noted, to "lock horns" once again with his old Federalist adversaries, men who were at least willing to live up to the terms of the bargains they made.[105] Petigru was, in some ways, an unlikely Federalist, an upwardly mobile upcountryman who admired the refined coastal gentry and who lived to become as thorough an aristocrat and a more dogged Federalist than any of them. Clearly the most rewarding friendships of his life were those he made with Grayson, Legaré, William Elliott, and the Hugers, all like-minded men with persistent Federalist sympathies. To some observers, however, Petigru's aristocratic pretensions seemed to be essentially a deliberate, and somewhat superficial, posture. As Mary Chesnut noted, Petigru "Huguenotted his name but could not tie up his Irish."[106] There was no single moment of revelation, no "road to Damascus" experience, that called Petigru to Federalism. It was, instead, a decision made by an ambitious young man, temperamentally inclined to elitism, who was confronted with a hard choice. As George Fredrickson has argued, an intellectual of Petigru's era "could admit that he had no special claim to prominence and sink anonymously into the democratic ranks," or "he could wage an apparently hopeless battle against the new forces, attempting to shore up the collapsing institutions that formerly provided positions of prestige and authority."[107] Petigru, of course, chose the latter, at the price of eventual isolation. Why then is this man who lived in political exile among his own people significant? To what larger issues does the example of James Petigru speak?

In recent years, historians have increasingly come to view the Civil War as a product of the rapid economic expansion and social tensions associated with the process of modernization.[108] Modernization, however, also generated intellectual tensions, which are now beginning to garner some historiographical attention.[109] As Bertram Wyatt-Brown has noted, the rapidity of the social and economic change during the Jacksonian era first strained and ultimately exceeded the capacity of the republic's institutional structure to contain them. The nation, expanding economically and being revolutionized by the spirit of social and political democracy, was literally bursting at its seams in 1860.[110] In this turbulent and sometimes frightening world, intellectual and other elites looked for ways to avoid being displaced by democratic upheavals. Some Southern intellectuals, according to David Donald, developed the proslavery argument largely as an effort to prove their continued usefulness to Southern society.[111] Developing a related argument, Drew Faust has suggested that beleaguered Southern intellectuals saw themselves as stewards of virtue in a corrupt society and attempted to apply the principles of Tory paternalism to the wilds of the backwoods South.[112]

Like so many other intellectuals, Petigru recoiled from the uncontrolled fury of the Age of Jackson, yet he rejected the glorification of Southern society and the encouragement of Southern nationalism as romantic and visionary.[113] His own response to the crisis of the old order was to seek a restoration, and he turned to the security of a tested set of values, those of Federalism, to bring order to a chaotic world.

Petigru's response to crisis was not predetermined by social or economic factors, but was rather an intellectual choice, suggesting that perhaps the study of intellect, ideology, and (to borrow the term Henry Adams loved to use when referring to Southerners) temperament can still tell historians much about the coming of the Civil War.[114] For Petigru, however, the search for stability was futile. He ended his life convinced that he was the only sane man in a state gone crazy, affected in spite of himself with the paranoia and disorientation that became a collective phenomenon as the crisis of Jacksonian America reached its denouement.[115]

William Gilmore Simms, engraving, 1861, Johnson, Fry, & Co. Courtesy of the Library of Congress.

6

Poetry and the Practical: William Gilmore Simms

JOHN McCARDELL

> He look'd beyond
> His own horizon, bounded to a span,
> And long'd for other regions, unknown lands,
> Deeming imprisonment, the close confine,
> Of his first birth-place.
>
> (*The Vision of Cortes*, 60)

"IT WAS A LIFE affording few opportunities to talents that did not lie in certain beaten grooves. It was a life gaining its intellectual nourishment . . . largely from abroad,—a life that choked all thought and investigation that did not tend to conserve existing institutions and opinions." Such, according to William Peterfield Trent, was the nature of intellectual life in antebellum Charleston at the time that William Gilmore Simms reached maturity. Trent's judgment, published in 1892, has proved surprisingly durable. Young, brash, and overly reconstructed Trent may have been, yet to this day his is the only full-scale biography of antebellum South Carolina's leading man of letters. Vigorous, if occasionally tendentious, correctives have appeared, usually in obscure academic journals; but in the main, for almost a century, the most visible scholarship has deviated only slightly from the trail blazed by Trent. As a result, for far too long both antebellum Charleston and her greatest literary light have been misunderstood; most of Simms' work remains inaccessible because out of print; and such important recent studies as Larzer Ziff's *Literary Democracy*, which examines the emergence of American literature in the mid-nineteenth century (and which a New York *Times* reviewer claimed "deserves all the awards they give"), dismisses Simms in two paragraphs. "Simms . . . within a static frame was unable to start a resonant action because all human and social issues had been settled," writes Ziff, citing only a 1954 publication written by one of Trent's former graduate students. "Simms lacks," he continues, "the dynamic sense of social issues" possessed by such non-Southern contemporaries as James Fenimore Cooper. The spirit of Trent persists. After ninety years it is time to reconsider.[1]

Generations of scholars since Trent have been misled in part, perhaps, by a too literal reading of Simms' laments, expressed only in his private correspondence, that his native city did not appreciate him or his work. These complaints were echoed long after Simms' death in 1870 by both his family and his friends, upon whom the devastations of war and Reconstruction had fallen especially hard. Picked up by Trent on a visit to Charleston in December 1890, at the very moment when the "sanctity of Confederate grey" was being challenged by a new generation of politicians, these resentments, acutely perceived by the embattled remnant of the antebellum days, formed the basis of the 1892 biography.[2]

Such apparently impeccable sources doubtless account for Trent's interpretive durability and make the reality of Simms' relationship with Charleston far more difficult to penetrate. Nevertheless, there are angles of vision, some new, others not so new, that force a reassessment. "Life," wrote William Gilmore Simms in 1841, "is an ordeal, in which our powers of endurance, and our capacities of achievement are to be tested,

187

in order that our future rank may be determined."[3] For the author, who at that moment was thirty-five years old, this little maxim seemed especially appropriate. It stated what appeared to him to be the troublesome truths of the literary vocation in mid-nineteenth century America; it contained what for later readers would be a theme around which Simms' own life and achievement might profitably by organized and reconsidered; and it offered a plausible explanation of Simms' feelings about Charleston, the city of his birth. For much of the "ordeal" that was Simms' life took place in Charleston, and even more of what we today know—or think we know—about his "powers" and "capacities" and "rank" is rooted in our understanding of his lifelong and complex relationship with the city by the sea.

*   *   *

If ever a city can be said to have shaped a man, Charleston shaped Simms. It could hardly have begun any earlier than it did. Simms' mother died in childbirth when young William was but an infant. His father, emotionally prostrated by Mrs. Simms' death and financially bankrupted by the failure of his mercantile enterprise, decided to move west, to Mississippi, leaving his son in the care of a widowed maternal grandmother. The child was sickly and lonely, but he read omnivorously, and his fertile imagination, undoubtedly enriched by tales of Revolutionary Charleston told by his grandmother, more than made up for his lack of childhood friends.[4]

Just how close a tie had been established between the young boy and the only blood relative he ever truly knew became apparent in 1818. His father returned to Charleston in that year and demanded custody of his twelve-year-old son. After failing to remove the lad forcibly (such a scene was created on the streets of Charleston that the father had to resort to other means), the elder Simms took the matter to court. In what must have been an incredibly bizarre trial, a judge who was terribly hard of hearing and who had a reputation for being sympathetic to feminine entreaties (as well as for making wrong decisions) told the twelve-year-old boy to decide for himself. Charleston or Mississippi? Grandmother or father? In the biggest decision of his life, the child chose Charleston, as the man would again and again throughout his sixty-four years.[5]

Thus forced at an early age to choose between the known and the unknown, the maternal and the paternal, the venerable old city and the dynamic frontier, Simms ever after possessed – and expressed – strong feelings about Charleston. His native city he regarded perhaps as the mother he had never known, always seeking her approval, jealous of the claims of competitors for her affection, and at once protective and critical in that special way only a son may display. In a very literal sense, Simms saw in Charleston a maternal aspect. This concern was particularly evident when the subject was emigration. For example, in his *History of South Carolina*, written in 1840, Simms admonished: "One lesson, in chief, may be gleaned, among many others from this imperfect story of the past. It is that which teaches the citizen to cling to the soil of his birth in the day of its difficulty, with the resolution *of a son who stands above the grave of a mother* and protects it from violation" [emphasis added].[6]

If, in this particular formulation, Charleston was maternal, it also stood in contrast to the alternative – emigration elsewhere, most likely to the frontier, the "border," perhaps to Mississippi. Or so he seemed to think in 1836:

> Ought we then to emigrate? . . . No! No! To him, then, and to all, would we say, be content, and remain where you are. Remain amid old influences, and the strong and strengthening power of old associations. Remain where education, and all the comforts, conveniences, and circumstances of life, render life a blessing, and where no avaricious passion, no grasping spirit, no wild speculation, no selfish, sordid feeling touch and taint society.[7]

Charleston clearly represented the antithesis of what the emigrant would find in the western South, the South of Simms' father, the South of "avaricious passion" and "wild speculation." Much to be preferred were the "old associations," the refinement and security of maternal Charleston.

To so sensitive a man as Simms, Charleston was surely a symbol of his own experience of familial separation. Years later, in 1839, he recalled the custody trial and admitted, "Had I gone with my father, I should have shown less feeling, but more world wisdom." His father, he remembered, was "a discontented & forever wandering man . . . of great energy & enthusiasm of character, a lively & playful temper."[8] Two visits to see his father and tour the frontier South provided Simms ample evidence for the opinions he later ventured on the wisdom of emigration. Always curious about the road not taken, Simms naturally enough ascribed, to both that road and to the one more traveled, certain absolute qualities. Clearly, in his mind there was a frontier/paternal association that evoked a wide range of images. Equally clearly, there was a Charleston/maternal connection that offered a sharply contrasting alternative. Most important, as time went on, Simms saw these two roads diverging, in his own life and in that of his country. Repeatedly he addressed the need to reconcile what he identified in the title of a public lecture, frequently given, as "Poetry and the Practical." This notion, central to an understanding of both Simms and Charleston, lay at the heart of Simms' thought. Explored, it throws new light upon those "powers," "capacities," and "rank" to which he referred in 1841.[9]

*　　*　　*

Fully to understand the place of Charleston in Simms' thought, however, one must first probe more deeply the dynamic tension between "poetry" and "the practical" that shaped his world view. In sensing the interplay between the two, Simms was hardly unique. Indeed, the tension—variously defined as poetry/practical, head/heart, ideal/real—was central to the thinking of the best minds in this romantic era. The romantics felt themselves increasingly alienated from the mainstream of life in mid-nineteenth-century America. The rapid and accelerating pace of change both attracted and repelled, bringing with it both the promise of reform and the threat of upheaval. Not surprisingly, intellectuals responded ambivalently, simultaneously desiring to separate themselves from the coarse, leveling, often violent, and usually disorienting effects of "progress" and to play a guiding, usually restraining, role in managing and directing change. The result was frustration and seemingly inconsistent behavior: the pose and language of the isolated genius alongside a persistent belief that the man of mind had a central social and political function he must serve. One answer, a common answer, was that arrived at by Simms: namely, a wish to restore a sort of social equilibrium through the mediating agency of the intellectual, whose acute sense of "poetry," the sublime, the transcendent, might balance the dislocating tendencies of modern life.[10]

To be sure, this was an outlook more easily described than acted upon, as Simms and others, to their dismay, would discover. But it also afforded comfort and made sense of things otherwise incomprehensible. For Simms, "poetry" and "the practical" meant much more than the simple juxtaposition of Charleston and Mississippi, or even

190

seaboard and interior. The terms defined the boundaries of society's behavior and thus, offering succor to the romantic artist who often felt himself to be in the world though not of it, helped Simms to achieve a fuller understanding of himself. Moreover, they helped explain the patterns of daily life, and so they provided a model for the literary as well as the social critic. Finally, they represented a broad view of the nature and progress of civilization, and as such they informed Simms' comprehension of historical processes. All of these diverse intellectual strands would meet at a crucial moment in 1849, when Simms would reveal, in a series of penetrating essays, the extent to which "poetry" and "the practical," as they related explicitly to Charleston, figured in his thinking about his life and art. But it took time for those strands, originating in his earliest years, to become plaited into a fabric of thought, and each deserves a closer look.

Simms viewed himself as a poet. By this he meant not simply a composer of verse but rather a man of letters, whose purpose was to give "wingéd thought" to "present impulse."[11] The poet, Simms believed, must be "an original thinker . . . a seer . . . inspired."[12] Indeed, the best poetry should "denote a high order of thinking" by expressing "the profoundest of human philosophies." Poetry, he continued, was "the mysterious voice of the deeper nature lying in the heart."[13] Such a voice could find expression in verse—Simms himself composed some 1,800 such poems—but it might also find other outlets in prose, and these, too, Simms frequently sought. What mattered most to Simms was not the medium of poetic expression but the constant application of the poet to his craft. He loathed nothing so much as the "elegant trifles" produced by "amateur authorship" and revealing "*dilettantism*, affectation, pretence [*sic*], and the most miserable conceit."[14] In short, he despised most of what passed for serious poetry not only in Charleston but everywhere in America. Such work was the product of minds primarily engaged in other pursuits and of men to whom works of the mind were acceptable only to the extent that they did not penetrate very far below surface appearances or feelings.

The true poet, Simms believed, did not—could not—engage merely in "occasional dalliance" with the poetic muse.[15] The result of true poetry must be "not to tickle a fancy, but to penetrate a soul." And the role of the poet must therefore be "to *think & feel* . . . observe closely, think earnestly, & sing boldly, not wantonly or diffusely, but with resolute purpose."[16] Thus, he who would create "that sort of Poetry which

191

is the only sort that is ever transmitted through the ages," namely poetry of thought rather than fancy, must be a "professional author—
surrendering life to this one object."[17]

Not surprisingly, then, a subject in which Simms had a great interest (and the title of another of his frequently given public lectures)
was the choice of a profession and, more specifically, the role of the
professional man of letters. Simms believed that the profession in fact
chose the poet rather than the poet the profession. The poet "is called,
as Samuel was in the night-time, by a voice whose summons he does
not understand, but dares not disobey. It is the voice of his own nature—
of a special endowment, which tasks him wholly. It demands not only
all his obedience, but all his faculties." This inner voice promised no
earthly rewards or fame, as Simms well knew; the poet's work was a
labor of love alone. "He builds," Simms wrote, "not for the shelter, not
for the recompense, scarcely for the fame and the praise."[18] Poetry's
"cravings are of another sort. It asks for consideration. Possessed of great
truths, its first and only care is to procure a hearing. It demands an
audience, attention, appreciation—and, these accorded, there is no more
humble creature in all God's creation."[19]

Few, however, even of Simms' strongest admirers, then or now, would
choose the adjective "humble" to describe him; his personality was such
as to belie all claims of humility. No one realized this more clearly than
Simms himself. "I am a very unconventional sort of person," he confessed in 1841, "very ardent in my temperament, very earnest in my
object; express myself usually in the first words that come uppermost;
write usually as I talk; and as the world goes, am accounted a somewhat rude, blunt man. An unamiable character, enough, but one which,
perhaps, is not without its virtues."[20] Contemporaries as well as later
Simms scholars often overlooked the virtues because they misunderstood the "ardent temperament," not only of the man but also of his
work. Bandying such terms as "romantic" and "realistic," criticizing Simms
for producing too much too swiftly, and (justly, for the most part) regarding most of his work as second rate at best, they mostly missed
the larger point. They neglected the qualifying clause in Simms' shrewdly
accurate self-portrait: "I am a very unconventional sort of person."[21]

For Simms' time and place, this remark was perhaps an understatement, and Simms scholars ignore it at their peril. In this statement
lies an explanation of much that has for so long baffled the casual reader
as well as the specialist. It contains the key to Simms' own view of his

life and art. It suggests why he was so preoccupied with such matters as choosing a profession. It amplifies the interplay of "poetry" and the "practical." And, as a result, it goes to the heart of Simms' feelings about intellectual life in antebellum Charleston.

To attempt to be a professional man of letters in antebellum America —that is, to attempt to make one's living by the pen—was about as unconventional as one could be. No American author had successfully attempted the feat before Simms determined to try. The difficulties were many and, to a less energetic spirit, would have seemed insuperable. For one thing, there were certain economic realities. The professional writer could not count on a steady income. Nor could he depend upon a very widespread or sophisticated network for the marketing, promotion, and review of his work. The fledgling publishing industry in Jacksonian America was still taking shape, and its workings were, in Simms' time, primitive. Finally, the absence of an international copyright accord allowed overseas publishers to pirate American authors, reprint their works cheaply, and flood the market. Authors, competing with themselves, received not a cent in royalties from the pirated editions. Add to all these difficulties the uncertainty of the national economy, which only slowly recovered from the Panic of 1837, and the prospects for the professional author seemed bleak indeed.[22] That all these vicissitudes affected Simms at one time or another during his professional career is certain. He was chronically short of cash, frequently in debt, and forced to make ends meet with the equally uncertain profits of the dubiously managed plantation "Woodlands," which belonged to his father-in-law. He complained about the unavailability of many of his works, and continued these laments despite almost annual trips to New York to maintain his ties with publishers. He led the campaign for an international copyright law.

But very little changed. By December 1847, Simms was pouring out his troubles to James Henry Hammond, his closest friend: "Our planting interests barely pay expenses and my income from Literature which in 1835 was $6000 per annum, is scarce $1500 now, owing to the operation of cheap reprints which pay publishers & printers profits only & yield the author little or nothing. To earn this $1500 I have to labor constantly."[23] Such was the price of unconventionality, and such was Simms' response.

To these economic realities must be added the social consequences of professional authorship. Simms surely was aware of the self-imposed

193

isolation experienced by the man who answered the call of poetry. Indeed, he was obsessed by it, repeatedly explaining the hazards of genius. Society would not always fully appreciate the poet. "As he stands alone in his objects," Simms wrote, "he is soon isolated among his associates. . . . Directly, and upon the time in which he lives, the mere man of letters, whatever his degree of endowment, does not exercise much, if any, apparent influence."[24] This lack of attention in Jacksonian America was due in part to the widespread belief that a man should "do" something with his life. The man of letters had little to show for his efforts. What was a book measured against a canal or a turnpike or a factory or a plantation? The sense of isolation was deepened further by the general thinness of American literature at the time Simms made his crucial choice of a profession. Simms' indictment of the state of poetry was all too close to the mark.

The two problems—the dearth of professional writers and the concomitant dearth of American literature—were of course related, but few at the time recognized that fact. Thus to choose as Simms had chosen was to flout convention and to court hardship. This Simms knew. But for one "called" as he felt himself called, there was no other choice.

In mid-nineteenth-century America, it mattered little where one chose thus to be unconventional; such were the prevailing sentiments against professional writers and such was the general state of American letters. Charleston, South Carolina, was no different from Boston, Massachusetts.[25] But Simms, harboring another unconventional idea, believed that might be changed: the man of letters in antebellum America could also, in his own way, be a useful member of society. It is striking how often the term "useful" appears in Simms' writings in the 1840s. "Poetry" and the "practical" might be yoked.

In this belief Simms was not alone. In fact, the notion of the useful poet inspired in the mid-1840s a movement, based in New York and involving Simms' generation of writers, which called itself "Young America."[26] The creed of Young America was deceptively simple, and Simms subscribed to it wholly. Poetry, Young America believed, embraced all forms of literature, even the novel. The poet must pursue his art relentlessly, fully, and employ his imagination with vigor and virility, as befitted a rugged new nation. In this pursuit lay the artist's usefulness. In the magazines they founded to advance these unconventional ideas, Young America trumpeted the contention, as in the

Literary World in 1849, that American literature must be "practical as well as poetic."[27]

These allies and their ideas reinforced and strengthened Simms as he waged the campaign for them in the South. The battle was not easy, in Charleston or in Boston. "God *damn* them all," implored the Boston Brahmin George Sumner. To him the ideas of Young America were radical indeed, threatening as they did the sterile conventions of polite literature.[28] New York periodicals engaged in vicious editorial assaults upon one another. These literary wars, in which Simms at one time or another during the 1840s was both participant and victim, put the ideas of Young America repeatedly to the test. The result was a thorough, if seldom dispassionate, airing of a wide range of views concerning literature in America. An equally important byproduct was a honed critical sensibility on the part of editors and a remarkably diverse outpouring of works from increasingly daring publishers.[29]

The difficulties encountered by Simms in Charleston were no less serious but of a different sort. There is little evidence to suggest either the fearful negativism that characterized the reaction of provincial Boston or the stimulating engagement that punctuated the diatribes in the New York press. What evidence there is, however, rather forcefully indicates that rowdy New York, not sedate Boston, was the exception and, further, that whatever attitude the Charleston press may have exhibited, whether toward Simms or toward Northern authors, was more nearly in keeping with a national literary consensus than some scholars may have supposed. Returning to Charleston after a lively annual summer sojourn in New York may well have affected Simms' judgments about intellectual life in both places. The accuracy of such judgments, uncritically accepted by many Simms scholars, must be measured anew.

The vigor of "Young America," indeed its very name, bespoke a rising clamor among American intellectuals for the creation of a distinctive national literature. Simms, like most literary nationalists, would have found little fault with Edward Tyrrell Channing's call as early as 1818 for "a domestic literature [based] upon what is peculiarly our own—our scenery, our institutions, our modes of life, our history, and the antiquities of our country." Simms put it somewhat differently: "To be *national* in literature," he wrote, "one must needs be *sectional*"—but his impulse was the same. And it had its counterpart in other sections of the country. "New England," wrote Nathaniel Hawthorne, "is quite as large a lump of earth as my heart can take in." In Ohio, William Coggeshall added, "It is required of a nation which combines wide differences of characteristics, that each shall have its own representation. A Republic of letters may be a confederacy of individualities."[30]

With great enthusiasm, Simms and his intellectual peers waged their campaign. Only in New York did the campaign encounter serious intellectual challenge or debate. Almost everywhere else—Boston, Cincinnati, Charleston—a different pattern appeared, usually in the form of a total and uncritical embrace of native sons and their works by editors of chauvinistic and frequently short-lived sectional publications. Despite his incredible productivity during the first decade of his professional career—poetry, border tales, historical romances—and despite the controversy aroused in other quarters by his unconventional ideas and unconventional associates, Simms by the early 1840s found himself either ignored or, more often, superficially praised. This sort of puffery was typical of the numerous notices of his work in Southern literary periodicals. The Charleston-based *Southern Literary Journal*, to which Simms was a frequent contributor, regularly offered reviews of his latest efforts. It called *The Partisan* a "perfect picture of the revolutionary times in South Carolina." It did dare to criticize *Richard Hurdis*, which was published pseudonymously, because it believed the work inferior to that of Simms.[31] The *Southern Quarterly Review*, successor to the *Journal* and established in 1842, reviewed Simms' *History of South Carolina* and concluded that this was by far his most important contribution to his state.[32] The Charleston *Mercury*, meanwhile, daringly said of the *History*, "The work indeed seems to us to be in its kind perfect."[33]

Such uncritical praise likewise emanated from other aspiring literary centers outside New York. Accusations of puffery directed against Boston periodicals are familiar enough. Less well known are parallel developments in the Western states, where one scholar has discovered that "comments on books by local authors were so universally favorable as to become stereotyped."[34] In short, if writers such as Simms had a grievance, it pointed not toward a neglect of things literary (indeed most daily newspapers around the country had regular literary columns) but rather toward an unwillingness, easy enough to understand in a country still seeking its cultural definition, to indulge in serious literary criticism.

It was thus perhaps less than coincidental that Simms in the mid-

1840s pondered a new approach to poetic usefulness. The first decision was to abandon fiction, at least temporarily, for other fields. If Southern literary periodicals lacked critical backbone, then Simms himself would become an editor, a duty with which he was familiar but to which he now turned with new determination. If the Southern mind lacked a serious appreciation of the new national literature he was helping to create, then Simms would devote much of his time to literary and social criticism. And if Southern reviewers deemed works other than fiction or verse to be more useful, then Simms would develop new skills. If history was what they wanted, then history they would have, and it would be history that combined "poetry" and the "practical"—or as Simms, echoing Thucydides, put it, it would be "philosophy teaching by example."[35]

Thus Charleston, which had seemed to Simms in his early years the maternal embodiment of what he meant by the term "poetry" and which had provided a focus for his romantic formulation of the intellectual's dilemma, now took on a third trait, which was rooted in his literary nationalism. The city became for him in mid-career the target of unrelenting efforts to be useful. Nor was it conceivable that he could leave his native city, though he occasionally contemplated removal. The city generally, and this city in particular, was the only place where literature had a chance to flourish. "Literature, indeed, is the growth of the city only," Simms had written in 1837. "Types would never be made in the country, or in any other than a commercial city. The various classes of the mart afford more material for thought than all the mountains and woods and vallies put together that ever man saw or fancy dreamed of."[36] Simms the romantic literary nationalist would abide with mother Charleston while seeking to introduce more paternal practicality into its intellectual life. So long as that life was stimulated, as it was in New York, Simms would ask for no more.

*   *   *

The first step was to take stock of the state of Charleston's literary art. The result was the publication, in the autumn of 1844, of *The Charleston Book*, a compendium of Charleston literature from the pens of its most able minds. Simms wrote the preface to the volume in a tone at once explanatory, apologetic, and damning. A portion of that preface points both forward and backward at this pivotal moment in Simms' life:

The sources of the compilation are not those of professional authorship. The writers of the South are persons, generally, of other professions and pursuits. What is done among us, in a literary point of view,
is the work of the amateur, a labor of stealth or recreation, employed
as a relief from other tasks and duties. From this fact the reader will
be able to account for that air of didactic gravity, that absence of variety, and of the study of artistical attributes, which would not strike
him so obviously had the sources of the collection been found in the
more various fields of a national literature.[37]

Perhaps because this was a subscription volume, or perhaps because
it was a collection comprising wholly the work of amateurs (though
edited by a professional), or perhaps (more likely) because the book
was a none too subtle barb aimed at Charleston, it proved for Simms
to be another labor of love only. The Charleston press ignored the
volume; few of the literary magazines noticed it. The New York *Morning News*, however, gave a lukewarm recommendation, concluding, "No
one else could have been more courteous and liberal to his brethren
in making up the book than this gentleman [Simms]."[38]

But Simms' one-man literary reform movement continued to advance
on all fronts. "I am shortly to have a magazine of my own," he confided to
one of his Young America colleagues in New York.[39] The new journal,
officially titled the *Southern and Western Magazine and Review*, was based
in Charleston and quickly became known as "Simms's Magazine." To
his friend George Frederick Holmes, Simms explained, "My chief motive for consenting to this editorship is based upon the mutual desire
we entertain to establish a manly & proper organ of literature and
criticism in the South."[40] The first number appeared in January 1845,
and for the rest of the year Simms labored to make his magazine pros-
per. Often this meant, as in the case of the March, April, and May issues, supplying most of the copy himself: essays, reviews, and short
stories. The grueling pace was more than any man could sustain, and it
was not often mitigated by frequent notices in the local press. Only the
Southern Quarterly Review gave even the briefest mention. By year's end
Simms welcomed the decision to merge his magazine with the established
Southern Literary Messenger in Richmond. "The works thus blended,"
Simms announced in the December number, "will be eminently useful
in concentrating and forming public opinion among us, in all those
things, particularly, which belong to *Belles Lettres* and the Arts."[41] More
useful, it would appear, than editor Simms had managed to be.

Editing, however, was only one of Simms' occupations in 1845. In preparing so much of the copy that appeared in his magazine, Simms also found occasion to amplify many of his social and literary opinions. The ideas that constituted the essays did not of course originate in 1845. But in his desperation for publishable material, Simms was inspired to reconsider, refine, and develop them so that readers of such pieces as "Our Agricultural Condition," "Weems the Historian," and especially "Epochs and Events of American History" were treated to incisive analyses of life and letters.

Simms had three major criticisms of mid-nineteenth-century life in the South.[42] The first was that the South was intellectually lazy. This shortcoming was especially glaring, Simms believed, in Southerners' ignorance of their own history. "Satisfied, each man, with his individual supply of mental food, [the Southerner] gives himself no concern to ask whence it comes, and thus leaves it to strangers . . . to furnish the means of knowledge and of opinion to his neighbors and his children."[43] Thus Southerners permitted such falsehoods as their disloyalty during the American Revolution to be perpetrated by non-Southern historians. "For Heaven's sake," Simms pleaded, "let us no longer continue insensible. . . . Our responsibilities to the race and to the world, are in due proportion to the degree of civilization which we claim."[44] He left no doubt in his readers' minds as to the type of intellect he deplored. Though the specific context of the following statement was a criticism of New England, it was written for a Charleston audience, and Charlestonians might profit by the example:

> They are a people who suffer their tastes to get the better of their energies—who, in their solicitude to be nice, sometimes cease to be manly—who delight in neat little prettinesses of style and manner . . . and, in due degree as they are delighted with these, will revolt at the rude expression, the coarse or clumsy phrase—the slightest inelegancy making them heedless of the just claims of the work.[45]

Readers with long memories might, reading this indictment of effeteness in New England, have recalled Simms' likening of Boston to Charleston in an essay published in 1844. "The character may be found in Boston and in Charleston," he had written then, "individuals who would have been victim of the circumstances which they should have mastered —the victim to [*sic*] organization and education—to a temperament the energies of which are naturally feeble."[46]

This feebleness was attributable, in Charleston at least, to another feature of Southern life that Simms deplored. The South, he argued, was agriculturally backward, its chief weakness being its reliance upon a single staple crop. "Staple cultivation must always, in the end, be fatal," he declared. "A nation which makes but one thing, to exchange for everything else . . . will always be at the mercy of her neighbors." Dismissing the canard that soil exhaustion was to blame for Southern economic woes, Simms argued that "the paralysis of our fortune is not so much because of the inferior condition of our soil, as because of the peculiar fate of the commodity which we cultivate," namely, cotton.[47]

Worse, though, than economic retardation was the effect of agricultural backwardness upon intellectual life. Citizens in such circumstances lacked "most of those means of moral strength which are desirable" for removing "the provincial feeling of dependence [that] is too strong upon us."[48] Simms had long held the position, which he articulated as early as 1841, that "the Good Farmer feels the importance of knowledge for his children, to be far greater now than it was in his boyhood."[49] This was the more important because "agriculture, being expressly a divine institution, [has] the natural effect of subduing the passions of men, of regulating their appetites, promoting gentleness, harmony, and universal peace among them."[50] But the South seemed to possess fewer and fewer "Good Farmers."

And the result was not simply intellectual decline but economic weakness. Simms emphatically did not oppose economic diversification; indeed, he saw increased reliance upon industry as one of the keys to the South's survival. The "age of iron" was coming, he recognized, and the South, especially Charleston, must adapt. Adaptation included agricultural reform—moving away from staples, sharing agricultural information, adopting more scientific techniques—but it also included acceptance of the fact that "change naturally follows . . . even as the stronger appetites and desires of the man overgrow and absorb those, more gentle and limited, which prevail in the bosom of the child."[51] The South could accept this change, could encourage reform and progress simultaneously, and in so doing could restore that balance of "poetry" (agriculture, the "age of gold") and the "practical" (industry, the "age of iron") necessary for happiness and prosperity. Or it could continue along the path it seemed thus far to have followed, simultaneously suffering agricultural decline and general economic and intellectual stagnation.

Simms went on at such length and in such detail because of what his study of history revealed to him. He knew civilized Charleston; he knew equally well the less civilized frontier South. And from this knowledge he had derived what he termed the "Social Principle," which was in essence an explanation of history based upon the interplay of "poetry" and the "practical" or civilization and the frontier. On the one hand, Simms believed that "the first requisite to the civilization of any people is to make them stationary."[52] Emigration cost the settled regions "the resources of genius and talent which they might have commanded."[53] On the other hand, westward movement was inevitable and not entirely bad, since the frontier "tends to break down most of the barriers which a strict convention establishes for the protection . . . of its own tastes and prejudices."[54] The "Social Principle" represented the careful balance between permanence, stability, polish, and devotion to home, and innovation, exploration, and the crude, disorderly realities that accompany the progress of a people. The "Social Principle" envisioned a society that embraced both "poetry" and the "practical." The message for Charleston was clear, and Simms delivered it explicitly in the pages of the Charleston *Southern Patriot*: "There are others in your venerable city, who need but two things, enterprise and industry . . . to become famous and do credit to that which sends them forth. . . . Old established communities, whose population is stationary, thus always refine themselves at the expense of their energies; and, in the great improvement of their tastes, lose their virility."[55] Not surprisingly, this diatribe was written from New York.

Human and social issues, then, were far from settled for Simms. At the same time that he was refining his ideas about social and intellectual life in 1845, he was also beginning to publish those works deemed most useful by his Southern readership, works of American history. Simms believed strongly that history must be instructive and that the historian "must have a purpose." History "implies art, system, arrangement, grouping, great discrimination, [and] the severe judgment of the critic."[56] If philosophy were successfully to teach by example, then the most appropriate medium would be biography. Accordingly, between 1844 and 1849 Simms brought out four biographies of, respectively, Francis Marion (1844), Captain John Smith (1846), the Chevalier Bayard (1847), and Nathanael Greene (1849).

These biographical forays represented a response to matters both professional and personal. By the mid-1840s the reading public's in-

satiable desire for historical writing was quite clear. A long line of writers, Simms included, had touched the public's yearning in the age of
Jackson for heroic tales of the nation's past. As the last of the Revolutionary generation passed from the scene, a sense of cultural indirection, to which literary nationalism was one response, seemed to make
the imaginative re-creation of the country's short history an urgent priority. By the mid-1840s Simms recognized that the rendering of the
past through fiction might have reached the limits of profitability but
that biography would still sell.[57] The figures Simms chose to study had,
in almost every case, already been the subjects of earlier biographies,
so there was certainly a commercial dimension to his decision.[58]

Still, the specific choices seemed to have very little in common. Beyond romanticism, beyond nationalism, even beyond immediate financial prospects, a careful reading of these four biographies reveals the
way in which Simms again returned to his longstanding concerns about
poetry and the practical. Through these four works he reexamined the
role of the intellectual in society. What most united them, in other
words, was the way in which they allowed Simms to speak out in a
personal way about himself as a writer in Charleston.

The connections were subtle but undeniable. Bayard's grandfather,
like Simms' maternal grandfather Singleton, "acquired great credit in
the wars with the English." Greene's mother, like Simms', "died when he
was yet a child, and his father was something of a Spartan." Marion,
like Simms, had no formal schooling in his youth. Rather, he "drew
from the great mother-sources of nature . . . his want of education neither
lessened his energies, his confidence in himself, nor baffled any of his
natural endowments. On the contrary, it left his talents free to their
natural direction." Likewise, Greene's "natural ascendency [sic] of mind
was felt in spite of the deficiencies of education." Only after Greene's
"intimacy with a man named Giles" (Simms' first wife's maiden name)
did he "begin to direct his attention to the acquisition of books. The
shelves of his friends were ransacked with the view to the satiation of
this newly-aroused appetite." But "this habit was not grateful to his father. He regarded it as a form if idleness."[59]

Choosing a profession posed difficulties. Greene, reared in a "new
settlement" realized that "the distinguishing merit of the citizen must
be his usefulness." Bayard chose a profession at once poetic and useful.
"He obeyed an instinct. It was not that he chose war as his vocation—

the vocation had chosen him. His natural endowments required that he go and be a soldier."[60]

Perhaps the closest parallel lay in the life of Smith. Smith's "talents were all certainly of his own acquisition. They did not come from the free schools." Apprenticed at an early age, as Simms had been, Smith felt stifled. Travel to distant regions beckoned, and as a young man he "lived rapidly" and saw "so much of the world" that "there could have been no condition so well calculated to pall upon his tastes as the tame and monotonous movement of daily life." To one who was in no way "indebted to his parents," his remedy against the "apathy into which he was in danger of falling from his intercourse with a society which to him could afford no nourishment, was of a kind to denote the impatience and independence of his mind." Smith craved adventure; he also sought recognition. Yet, once placed in charge of the settlement in Jamestown, Smith ran up against "the vanity, the worthlessness, and the utter selfishness of those to whom much of the power had been intrusted." This natural man, confident, self-assured, gifted, able to grasp intuitively a situation, was also a man whose merits were frequently envied. "Thus indefatigable, our hero [was] yet doomed to discover that his toil consists in drawing water in a sieve. He toils for the worthless and the ungrateful."[61]

This last remark accurately portrays the state of Simms' mind by the end of the 1840s, for all his efforts seemed to have gone for naught in Charleston. Neither the *Mercury* nor the *Courier* reviewed any of the biographies, though the *Mercury* did at least note the publication of *Marion*. The *Southern Literary Messenger* was silent. The *Southern Quarterly Review* noticed only the life of Smith, which it praised.[62]

Personal difficulties further blackened Simms' mood. After serving a term in the South Carolina legislature in 1844–46, he failed to win reelection. He hoped for a political appointment by President James Polk but was passed over. His plantation continued to struggle financially. He was forced to borrow $1,000 from his friend Hammond with no promise that it would ever be repaid.[63] Gloomily, he composed a poem, suggestively entitled "The Struggle of Endowment with Fortune":

> When thou shalt put my name upon the tomb,
> Write under it, "here lies the weariest man
> That ever struggled with a wayward ban,

The victim from his birth-hour to a doom
That made all nature war against his will,
Made profitless his toil, its fruits denied
To patient courage and ambition still,
His tasks decreed, his industry decried,
And left him weary of the sun, whose flight,
Brought him the gloom without the peace of night.
His toilsome pathway ever was uphill,
A hill forever growing,—still his draught
Was *water in a sieve* that could not fill
And bitter was his cup, or drunk, or left unquaff'd."
                                    [italics added][64]

So bitter was Simms that he contemplated removal from Charleston to the North. Again, he expressed his longings in verse:

Hopeless of place, of chance, to try his strength,
He yields the field, and quits the soil at length,
Mournful retires, in Western woods to find,
That freedom for his spirit and his mind,
Which his own home, by cunning tribes o'errun,
Hath shown him there he never could have won!
And what remains, the native mind expell'd,
But vile debasement from the rank we held?[65]

Yet he could never quite bring himself to leave mother Charleston. Instead, he decided once again to attempt to reform the city he still found beautiful. Perhaps he inwardly believed what he would put into words in 1849: "What is hope itself but a happy sort of discontent? It tells us of unattained objects and conditions, and so paints their attractions to our mind, that we naturally yearn and strive for their acquisition; and hence our best performance." Discontented but yearning, hopeful and thus still striving despite many setbacks, Simms by 1849 had not yet surrendered his hope of poetic usefulness; it remained his ideal. "And the pursuit of [a man's] ideal," Simms wrote, "affords the clue to his existence. It is thus that he works out his deliverance. It is thus that he finds out and exercises his powers."[66]

*   *   *

"I am weary and weak," Simms confided to Hammond in September 1849. "My head is all in commotion and confusion." The preceding six months had been unusually grueling, even for a man of his robust constitution. In February he had assumed the editorship of the *Southern Quarterly Review* in Charleston, an assignment a practical poet could not refuse but also an obligation that, by September, was keeping him "scrawling and scribbling throughout the day, in vain seeking to lessen the pile before me."[67] Moreover, at one time or another during 1849, he had a volume of poetry and a colonial romance in press in Charleston, and his life of Greene in press in New York; he was putting the finishing touches on a Revolutionary romance for serialization in *Godey's* beginning in February 1850; and he was about to begin a series of articles for the Charleston *Mercury*. And as if these exertions weren't enough, Simms somehow managed to spend almost the entire month of August, as he was fond of putting it, "on the wing," touring the Georgia mountains and then visiting Sullivan's Island.

Simms' weariness was not simply physical; it was also pecuniary and psychological. Confronted on all sides by demands for yet more of his time, more of his energy, more of his resources, his thinking turned inward and homeward; and he focused his attention on Charleston, the city that had shaped him. His native city in 1849 afforded him a convenient target for all of the social, literary, and political ideas it had subtly influenced since his birth. In the articles for the *Mercury*, running between 18 September and 3 November 1849 under the revealing title "The Home Tourist," Simms reexamined himself, his home, and his art. For a brief moment the patterns of a lifetime were thrown into sharp relief. The result was a clear and complete statement by the Old South's leading man of letters on the condition and the prospects of intellectual life.

To a great extent the series was an intensely personal statement. "Father Abbot," from whose oracular lips most of the weightiest pronouncements fall, is meant to be Simms himself. Like Simms, Father Abbot had been orphaned at a young age. "The habits of my boyhood were the fruits of a neglect, which . . . it would not become me to deplore," Abbot explains. "I had no parents to be troubled at my absence, or to chide and chasten me at my return." Like Simms, Abbot knew not only Charleston society but also frontier life, "travelling . . . among the wildest regions of the South and West, at periods when they were a thousand time wilder than now." Like Simms, Abbot enjoyed the company of others. "I can enjoy no pleasure," Abbot states, "unless I share it."[68]

Finally, like Simms, Abbot had feelings about Charleston so strong that he could revel in its "thousand attractions" while yet remaining sensitive to its "thousand deficiencies." Among those attractions were "our graces of society, our frank hospitality; the elegance of our women, the high character of our gentlemen; [and] . . . the physical beauty of our home." But undue emphasis on these good qualities had produced, among the "thousand deficiencies," a type of "city-bred gentleman, full of his conventional laws and not able to overcome old habits," cherishing "his old strut and his new waistcoat."[69]

Thus, by 1849, there was not one Charleston but two, which, Simms believed, were in "deadly conflict." One community was practical, industrious, striving. It comprised "a people coerced by the necessities of life, devoted to toil and business, and bringing to their work the capital of fresh energies, eager hopes and sleepless enterprise." The other "had acquired a certain permanence of position." The former "had no acknowledged place in society"; the latter "had, in various ways, reached a very high distinction. . . . Its people could boast of a *past*. They could look back with pride to their ancestry."[70]

The results of this social division, Simms concluded, were unsatisfactory on every count. "Society's" polish was "of a sort that rendered it feeble and effeminate. . . . In the perfection of [its] tastes," Charleston had lost "some of [its] necessary energies," becoming at once "fashionable and foolish." The "man of manners and refinements," Simms argued,

> is apt to make them especial objects of pride; and in so doing, emasculates his mental energies. He perpetually contrasts his quiet, graceful manner, with the wide hurry of the working man; and in proportion as the rough energy of the other offends his tastes, will he then turn away equally disgusted with, or unobservant of, the vigor and power which are coupled with the roughness that offends him. In rejecting what is evil, or inferior, in the manners, he makes the mistake of rejecting also the virtues of that manhood which is the secret of safety in all communities.

In consequence, the community had lost "enthusiasm . . . one of the most sovereign of virtues. . . . Without this virtue, society languishes everywhere; the energies lie prostrate . . . the community lacks courage; trade and commerce wither . . . while cold-blooded and soulless self-conceit sniggers and sneers at every appeal to patriotism, and every sentiment which seeks to encourage the resurrection of the nobler virtues." Worst of all, "the arts abandon the soil in loathing, or bury themselves from sight."[71] Simms could hardly have made a more forceful statement of how he perceived his relationship with Charleston.

And yet this society's division and decline were not irreversible; the conflict was neither inevitable nor permanent:

> When society shall recognize the necessity of coupling manhood always with its refinements; not suffering taste to degenerate into fastidiousness, or good manners into feebleness; – but honoring these only as they are tributary to manly performance; – and when, on the other hand, the performing and the business men shall recognize the just claims of a social organization; – shall recognize what is due to good taste, social refinement, delicacy and propriety of manners . . . then shall the two branches of society work together.[72]

The agent of reconciliation was to be the literary artist, the professional writer, who was at once mediator and advocate, poet and prophet. "Art . . . tutors the sensibilities," wrote Simms, "and civilizes the rude humanity." The writer – or "poet," to use his term – "conducts us out of the present. That is something. He lifts us from the earth. That is something more. He thus weans us from the pleasures of the sense, and raises us up from the wallow into which the brutal part of our nature would constantly conduct us." In this very act lay the poet's "usefulness," which once again Simms thought the most appropriate word to explain the poet's role. A divided society, a society where poets and practical men seemed further apart than ever before, should pay heed to the literary man, who was in fact "the world's great benefactor."[73]

This assessment of Charleston was far more than a simple exercise in social criticism. Rooted in a tangle of emotions, experiences, and impulses that had marked Simms' personal and professional life from its earliest years, "The Home Tourist" represented Simms's fullest statement ever about his life and work in Charleston. For him, Charleston was symbolic of what was right with mid-nineteenth-century American and also of what was wrong. The city needed to reestablish that balance between "poetry" and the "practical" in order to advance. The lessons of history taught that civilization made its greatest progress when "poetry" and the "practical" were reconciled. This was the "Social Principle" for which Charleston must strive.

*   *   *

If the publication of "The Home Tourist" and its subsequent reissue, in December 1849, as *Father Abbot* was not in itself a cathartic exercise for Simms, it was at least part of a transformation that he must have considered salutary. To some extent, his own continued exertions were responsible for a renewed sense of self-esteem that paralleled his growing prominence in the South; perhaps to a greater extent, national political developments effected a change in attitude both in Simms and in the Southern mind. Whatever the case, during the 1850s Simms increasingly felt himself to be playing the role of the practical poet that he had for so long desired to play.

As the South's growing sense of alienation from national trends fostered an ever more acute consciousness of its minority status in the Union and an ever more widely expressed sense of a separate national destiny for itself, Simms found himself speaking to the condition of his fellow Southerners as never before. He resumed his series, interrupted in 1841, of Revolutionary romances with the publication of four new volumes between 1851 and 1856, and the reissue, in New York, of these and revised versions of earlier works that had been out of print. A central theme of the Revolutionary cycle was the conflict of loyalties, which surely was a preoccupation of many Southerners during the 1850s. A second theme concerned character; the heroes of these works, without exception, combined "poetry" and the "practical" in order to succeed. From Singleton in *The Partisan* through Porgy in *Woodcraft* and down to Colonel Sinclair in *Eutaw*, the "poetic" aristocratic hero possesses also a "practical" side—often in the form of a sidekick—that serves the patriot cause.

By the mid-1850s, moreover, there were hopeful signs of a dawning critical awareness in Charleston that owed much to the influence of Simms. A young coterie of aspiring writers began to hold regular meetings in the back rooms of Russell's bookstore in Charleston, there to discuss the latest currents in books and ideas. With Simms' encouragement, this group, led by the able young poet Paul Hamilton Hayne, established *Russell's Magazine* in 1857.

And as never before, Simms received extended treatment in the Southern press. The *Mercury* and the *Courier* devoted considerable space to reviews of his new romances; other Southern papers and magazines conferred long overdue recognition. "No other man," declared the *Mercury*, "has done so much to illustrate our own country, and to embody the elements of poetry in our present and past history."[74] By decade's end Simms even found himself in the midst of a "literary war," much like those that had raged in New York in the 1840s. During the summer of 1859, editors in New Orleans and Charleston debated the merits of his work in such detail and with such language as to suggest the dawning of a livelier critical age upon the field of Southern letters. Though Simms held his critics in low regard, and though he apparently complained in private about the severity of their attacks, by 1859 he had achieved recognition unmatched in the South by any other writer.[75]

Increasingly, too, Simms became a spokesman for the secession of the South. The practical poet carried the war into the North in the autumn of 1856 when he commenced a lecture tour in Buffalo, New York, on the subject of "South Carolina in the Revolution." So hostile were the reviews and so small was the turnout that he ended the tour abruptly, concluding, "Forgive me, my friends, if I have spoken warmly; but you would not, surely, have me speak coldly in the assertion of a Mother's honour!"[76]

To the very end of his life, Simms was ardent in his loyalty to that mother. After the war, homeless and penniless, Simms nevertheless continued to edit, to research, and to write. He died in 1870 in Charleston; as his body was laid to rest on a rainy June day in Magnolia Cemetery, Paul Hamilton Hayne—to whom Simms had given such encouragement and who now, at Simms' passing, was probably the South's leading poet—lovingly bade farewell to the fallen giant: "Gallant old man! whatever his faults I, for one, loved him with all my heart. . . . He had fought a good fight and kept the faith, at least the faith he had plighted to his own genius and will." Simms would have appreciated the tribute. Shaped by Charleston to view the world in a special way, Simms had devoted his life to becoming a practical poet and urging his fellow Charlestonians and Southerners to do likewise. At the end of the "ordeal" he considered his life to be, the "powers of endurance" to which he had referred thirty years before had revealed tremendous "capacities" and secured a high "rank." But at the bottom of his creative, romantic soul, Simms always knew that the true poet could never be satisfied; the struggle goes on:

It is the study of a life . . . and the end of it may leave us still in doubt whether we have pursued the true vocation. But there can be no doubt that the search is still decreed. . . . The genius which conceives the truth

209

passes on to other discoveries. The true worker never rests. The seeker is never satisfied with the found,—for the forms of truth are infinite, and the tasks of search are strictly set for each succeeding generation.[77]

In his pursuit of the "true vocation," William Gilmore Simms was relentless. To grasp that simple truth is to recalculate the liveliness and complexity of intellectual life in Simms' Charleston.

7

C.G. Memminger, Watercolor on ivory by Charles Fraser (1823). Collection of the Carolina Art Association–Gibbes Art Gallery.

Schemes of Usefulness: Christopher Gustavus Memminger

LAYLON W. JORDAN

H E WAS BORN in an age of revolution when America and Europe had begun to experience a profound unsettlement and alteration under the impact of the ideas and process of "modernization"—rationalism, urbanization, industrialism, mechanized agriculture, expansionist finance, vastly improved transportation systems, a more democratic politics, nationalism, socialism, "big" government—and, complicating all, a contagion of benevolence, moral perfectionism, and social activism.[1] "In all the history of the world," declared an acute observer from the perspective of Concord, Massachusetts, in 1841, "the doctrine of Reform had never such scope as at the present hour . . . all things . . . hear the trumpet, and must rush to judgment—Christianity, the laws, commerce, schools, the farm, the laboratory; and not a kingdom, town, statute, rite, calling, man, or woman" but feels "the new spirit."[2]

Students of American society and politics, faced with the necessity of explaining a seemingly aberrant Southern provincialism, racial prejudice, economic backwardness, and political conservatism in recent times, have generally assumed that an intrinsic antithesis between the South and the rest of the nation predated the Civil War and that the Southern experience of the new attitudes and practices of the early nineteenth century was expressed largely, or even entirely, in shrill tones of adamant opposition, a refusal to confront the present, and a dread of the future.[3] The Old South was fundamentally backward-looking, writes C. Vann Woodward. "The utopian schemes and the gospel of progress that flourished above the Mason and Dixon line never found very wide acceptance below the Potomac. . . . In that most optimistic of centuries in the most optimistic part of the world, the South remained basically pessimistic in its social outlook and its moral philosophy."[4] John Hope Franklin's judgment is still more severe. He insists that "there was no communal life, no civic responsibility, and no interest in various programs for the improvement of mankind" in all the antebellum South, and opines that the plantation system, by preserving primitive frontier individualism, was at fault.[5]

While the theme of Southern exceptionalism arose out of the real cultural differences that have divided Americans, it may be asked whether it pushes oversimplification beyond reasonable limits. There were, of course, social environments in the antebellum South rather far removed from the plantation. Charleston, while "premodern and largely preindustrial in both its economic and social configuration," was an urban center undergoing significant change: cotton factories along the Cooper riverfront, a multiplication of railroad tracks, and a rising crescendo of registrations in local Irish and German ethnic societies, were visible signs.[6] And if the city still existed primarily as a crossroads of maritime transport and commercial exchange, such urban centers predicted the future. Habitués of Southern towns, wrote Fanny Kemble (an Englishwoman who in the 1830s sojourned in coastal Georgia and South Carolina before offering the world her impressions of urban Southerners), were in terms of morality and vision and rhetoric much like urbanites in the world at large. They were "softened and enlightened by many influences—the action of city life itself, where human sympathy and human respect, stimulated by neighborhood, produce salutary social restraint."

> They travel to the Northern states and to Europe, and Europe and the Northern states travel to them, and, in spite of themselves, their peculiar conditions receive modifications from foreign intercourse. The influence, too, of commercial enterprise, which in these days is becoming the agent of civilization all over the earth, affects even the uncommercial residents of the Southern cities, and, however cordially they may dislike or despise the mercantile tendencies of [North] Atlantic Americans or trans-atlantic Englishmen, their frequent contact with them breaks down some of the barriers of difference between them.[7]

Kemble was making the point by hyperbole, but the point itself is valid enough to suggest a fundamental truth that historians are beginning to recognize. In cities and towns of the Old South, Clement Eaton has written, "could be discerned . . . signs of the breaking down of slavery, particularly as the result of the hiring system and the greater sophistication of town slaves. The introduction of factories and railroads was subtly modifying typical agrarian attitudes, even to the point of relaxing opposition to a protective tariff."[8] Southern municipalities were wavering opponents of extreme state action and precipitate secession in defense of the "Southern interest."[9] Some of their leading citizens were emphatic instances of the South's continuous involvement in a modernizing passion for rationalism, technology, humanitarian reform, and material success, which transcended political boundaries and regional tradition.[10]

In the 1840s and 1850s, a circle of business and professional men in Charleston, including William James Rivers, an academic historian, and John Bachman, a clergyman and scientist, spent occasional evenings together over dinner at Christopher Memminger's residence, discussing, among other things, the "social systems most conducive to human happiness." George C. Rogers, Jr., who relates this fact in his *Charleston in the Age of the Pinckneys*, goes on to say that the conclusion "they obviously reached was that their own was such."[11] No doubt this is true, to a point. On "matters of last importance," the great desiderata of Southern life, slavery and the staple crop–based economy, a general consensus of support (if not absolute unanimity) prevailed among white people of the city, the state of South Carolina, and the Southern region after, say, 1830.

The commitment was not necessarily exclusive, however. To be sure, historians have said that the fundamental choice confronting Southerners of this generation was clear-cut: "land and slaves or commercial diversification, Southern distinctiveness or Southern self-sufficiency," affluence, prestige, and power.[12] But for some Southerners, including Memminger and his friends, the decision was not easily made. Their special regional context did interpose barriers to modernization, but not, they believed, absolute barriers. Why not have the best of both worlds? Why not treat ideas and things in a purely expedient manner? Too astute not to perceive the elements of bravado in Southern patriotism and pride in culture, they understood that modernization had brought the Northern states a great new vigor; the South was outstripped in almost every measurable category—economic, social, demographic, and cultural. Charleston, which in the later eighteenth century was the fourth city and third seaport in the nation, had become, as a Northern editor acidly observed, a minor port and a "tenth-rate city in size."[13] In the circumstances, it seemed madness to these reasonable men to restate old truths and hold tightly to the status quo. Rather, the formative principle should be guided change, change carried on by established leaders and through means determined by their utility, change reconciled to continuity and order, change leading directly to specific goals: prosperity, political efficacy, social cohesion, self-identity, and cultural excellence.[14]

Memminger, at least, had reason to believe that persevering effort would result in achievement: his life was an American success story. An emigré from Würtemberg, Germany, he landed at Charleston in 1806, aged three years, and was orphaned and institutionalized soon after. But at the age of seven he was plucked from the Charleston Orphan House by Thomas Bennett, an industrial and mercantile entrepreneur newly sprung from artisans. From the time of his adoption, Memminger lived a life not much different from the lives of gentlefolk "of the best calibers" in Charleston and mixed familiarly in their society. He was educated at a private school for boys; took a degree from South Carolina College; studied law in the office of a foster uncle; married Mary Wilkinson, the daughter of a Georgetown physician of Virginia background and English descent; and was admitted to the practice of law in the same year he was naturalized an American citizen, 1824. His legal practice was large, intimately related to local and state business enterprise, and no doubt profitable, although he was never

214

a truly wealthy man: in 1860 at age 57 he had real property worth $25,000, personal property worth $150,000, and fifteen slaves. In his early thirties he gravitated into politics, his adoptive father—a Jeffersonian Democrat—having paved the way by rising to the office of state governor in 1820. Memminger served briefly in the Charleston city council and for twenty-five years in the state legislature, exerting some influence on many of the major public events of Southern and South Carolina history in the middle decades of the nineteenth century. He seldom looked back on his lowly origins, and indeed would be criticized by ethnic Germans for allegedly disowning them. But one of the major impulses that made him a reformer was the desire to harmonize differences between the class called "poor whites" from which he came and the upper class of merchants, great planters, and well-educated professional men into which he moved from the Orphan House.[15]

An able but not original intellect, Memminger left his attitudes and reflections scattered through a busy life without regard for system. However, deep continuities in his ideas disclose a mind at once intimately, if sometimes ambiguously, related to major Western and American traditions and main currents of the era of Jefferson and Jackson, as well as doubts and hopes peculiarly Southern, and encompassing fragments of an agenda for a new nation, a new world. In his pragmatism and ideological pluralism—motifs shared by a larger or smaller segment of, at least, the upper levels of Charleston society—he was in some ways a universal nineteenth-century type.[16]

"Memminger had five major interests in life," suggests an editorial of two decades ago in the *Advertiser-Journal* of Montgomery, Alabama, where he was Secretary of the Treasury of the Confederate States of America during the early days of the Civil War. These were "education, law, finance, children, and religion. Above all, came religion."[17] Although this dogmatic appraisal requires careful qualification, anyone who would understand Memminger might well begin with his piety.

By tradition, Würtembergers were Lutherans, and a church based on the Augsburg Confession had been formed in Charleston about 1750. But Memminger as easily adopted the church as the lifestyle of his foster family. The Bennetts were Protestant Episcopalians, and of a part of that denomination much affected by the Second Great Awakening which swept the United States in the early nineteenth century. This explosion of religious energy spawned Adventist sects, Mormonism, and John H. Noyes' perfectionism. It also inspired in more orthodox Christians a new moral intensity and a new commitment to social activism. The enthusiasm and contention it engendered may have influenced the splintering of St. Philip's Episcopal church and the creation of St. Paul's, the congregation to which the Bennetts adhered, in 1810. In any event, the new church in suburban Charleston was "evangelical" in that it laid powerful and equal stress on the idea of God's active sovereignty and the idea of personal responsibility; assumed that man's ability to be saved is, on one level, a matter of his own will, although actual conversion is the work of the Holy Spirit; and acted on the belief that a Christian is at once an agent in the prosecution of divine plans, a productive member of society, and a brother and servant of men.[18]

The household in which young Memminger found himself at age eleven felt an impelling impulse to just this sort of vital piety. "Around the fireside or in the councils of the nursery, at the dinner table, or in the drawing room, there were no associations but those of the Christian gentleman, the devoted Patriot, and the upright citizen."[19] After he left the Bennett hearth, Memminger did not deviate from the pattern. He read the Bible regularly and knew it well. Biblical allusions occupied an important place in his public and private utterances: in the pamphlet that may be said to have launched him into politics during 1832, he used biblical parody to lambast both the federal tariff and the doctrine of nullification.[20] And the momentousness of religion in his life did not diminish as he grew older. He was constantly involved in religious business, his name appearing frequently in the annals of St. Paul's as being in the forefront of those who gave their time and resources for the advancement of Christian work. He took a leading role in an extensive effort by lower-state churches to build and maintain churches for unchurched free Negroes and chapels for the religious instruction of black slaves. Two of his sons became clergymen; one of them would write and publish a number of theological treatises.[21]

On occasion, in middle and later life, Memminger professed a "feeling of disappointment" with the vanity of human wishes, and he made the public argument that the Bible, as the revelation of the mighty acts of the absolute Creator and master of history, is the most important study, and that true melioration in a fallen world is accomplished by divine Providence or not at all.[22] In this mood, he tended to see Christianity as a panacea, applicable and efficacious in all the ills of life, and to press the importance of moral training over education of the mind. As he said, "If superior intelligence be directed to evil ends, it becomes only a more efficient instrument of evil. . . . The same gifts and genius which have corrupted the moral sense of the world with a Don Juan . . . might, if directed by true moral principle, have blessed mankind with a fitting sequel to *Paradise Lost*, or [Locke's] *Essay on the Human Understanding*."[23] Yet he remained confident that "Physical Science, as well as mere Mental Philosophy," has its place. And he ever adhered to the doctrine that society, though ordained in principle, is man's own creation, sustained and alterable by human beings. "It has pleased the great Creater to place us in the midst of facts, and to leave us to build up systems from those facts, by the operations of inductive reasoning." "The Providence of God cares for the future; our business is with the present." "It is the law of God, that everything valuable must be attained by effort." "A great ancient poet has well said – 'For they can conquer, who but think they can.'"[24] These are not the expressions of an obsessively religious and passive man but one deeply involved in the physical, tangible world.[25]

Memminger's concern for salutary activism, deriving in part from evangelical Christianity, had further justification in doctrines of "civic idealism." Although not original to it, civic idealism was central to the liberal Whig tradition which, emerging first in seventeenth-century England, supplied potent ideological ammunition in the thirteen colonies' fight for independence and subsequent efforts at state-building. At the center was a conception of relationships among liberty, authority, and virtue. The relationships are delicate: wielders of authority, whether one or a few or a majority, forever menace liberty and right. The best safeguards are a written constitution and public virtue, which induces individuals to subordinate private desires to the good of the whole, or *res publica*.[26] These doctrines constituted the central motif in David Ramsay's pioneer account of the American Revolution, a standard schoolboy text in the years of Memminger's youth, and in *The Columbian Orator*, a widely used primer of rhetoric. The same themes were regular fare in courses in moral philosophy, the pivotal educational discipline at South Carolina College, with illustrations drawn from "great books" traced through two millennia to the Enlightenment.[27]

Enlightenment ideas – cognizance of cosmic design, of a world system directed by natural law and/or Nature's God; trust in the competence of men to plumb the meaning of those laws and of the human will to be guided by them; commitment to free inquiry; and assurance

217

that man is intended for happiness—balanced out the element of Christian pessimism in Memminger's thought, forming an enduring theme in his speeches and writings. One of his very first efforts as an orator, in 1819 when he was but sixteen, sounded the motif in a burst of flowery rhetoric. It described approvingly the efforts of the natural philosopher, applying the methods of inductive reasoning that Locke had hallowed, to discover new truths; it lauded the presumed concomitants of the growth of knowledge—the improvement of man in the mass, the decay of obtrusive superstition, the softening of manners, the progressive limitation of the tyranny of the strong over the weak, and the multiplication of material comforts—and truly became airborne while contemplating the philosopher's-eye view of atmosphere and heaven:

> And now the azure sky, decked with those countless myriads of constellations which stand like immortal lamps of effulgent splendor, round the throne of heaven, appears in full glory before him. Gliding on an embodied ray of light, he walks amid thousands of worlds which mark their regular orbits around the central sun and is astonished at the harmony and order which prevails throughout. Like the fallen Archangel, traversing the newly-created regions, illuminated by the lamp of day he gazes, admires and is compelled to reverence the Author of all.[28]

While these sentiments might have been drawn from any of a large and diverse company of eighteenth-century rationalist humanists, the particular turn of young Memminger's rhetoric was noteworthy. The suggestion that the findings of science, especially astronomy, are proof of a beneficent Creator illustrated a rationalism firmly harnessed to piety, as it usually was in the "moderate" Enlightenment—in London or in Charleston. And his conclusions, which touched briefly on the mortality of the human soul, intimated an important debt to the philosophy of Common Sense, a late phase of the Enlightenment that originated in Scotland about 1760 as a response to the antireligious and antirationalist skepticism of David Hume and finally, just before Memminger matriculated at South Carolina College, came to dominate academic philosophy in the United States as the last phase of the Enlightenment in America.[29] Wholly in the spirit of Common Sense philosophers like Thomas Reid, he proclaimed the practical demonstration of man's immortality by "intuitive reason": "the passions and sentiments of the soul." But as if reflecting that some of his auditors might doubt the conclusiveness of this proof, he ended, in a Common

218

Sense way, by disdaining intellectual quibbles and contending that, in any event, belief in life after death was a social necessity. In its absence, "that excellent system of ethics which is founded on a basis of a state of future rewards and punishments would immediately crumble and fall," and mankind would prey upon itself.[30]

But that was not the anticipated scenario. Whatever their differences in emphasis, votaries of the Enlightenment looked to the future with immense hope, not trepidation, and anticipated "a great liberation" of some sort, "not from this earth but upon it."[31] Man is part of a naturally harmonious order. Evil exists, but incident to greater good. The crucial test of all public measures — and public reputations — is whether and to what extent they further man's ascent. Memminger's standard of value was utilitarian, as he forecast in an address delivered in an exhibition of his collegiate senior class in 1819: "The labors of a Homer and a Milton have justly obtained from an admiring world the due tribute of immortal honor," he said. "But it is to actions which in their general tendency ameliorate the conditions of millions, that we are to ascribe the *greatest* praise."[32] Nothing is better calculated to elevate man than his enlightenment. "Ignorance is the foster parent of slavery; science the nurse of freedom . . . [and] universal happiness," declared young Memminger. "Knowledge is power and wealth," a mature Memminger echoed the youth more than three decades later in a document produced as justification for revolutionizing the common-school system in Charleston.[33]

The regnant historical model of the Old South posits a peculiar Southern propensity for romanticism, and perhaps Memminger did find reinforcement for a part of his cosmology in that movement in literature and the other arts begun in Europe toward the end of the eighteenth century, seemingly as a reaction to the Enlightenment emphasis on reason and proportion.[34] On a tour of Europe in 1854, he spent most of his time in the British Isles going through ancient abbeys and castles. On the mainland of Europe, he was repelled (as he confided to his wife) by evidence of social rigidity, political oppression, and opaque religious ritual. But he reacted as the English romantic Tory Samuel Taylor Coleridge had to Alpine mountains, ravines, and glaciers — "rushing cataracts" suddenly arrested in midplunge and "made solid." The Alpine tableau had for him, as analogous scenes had for Coleridge, a mystical effect, the capacity to open "new views of the almighty power and glory of God."[35] In fact, the romantic cult of

219

"sensibility"—the notion, associated with Rousseau, that all reality is ultimately spiritual, derivative from a living spirit, and so knowable by the processes of the "heart" rather than the mind—was not wildly unlike the Common Sense doctrine of "intuitive reason," which, as we have seen, Memminger absorbed as a youth.[36] On the other hand, Memminger was no romantic if romanticism is taken as sentimental or softheaded. That much is suggested by a favorite lyric which he included in an important address in 1860:

> Oh Freedom! thou art not, as poets dream,
> A fair young girl, with light and delicate limbs,
> And wavy tresses, gushing from her cap.
> A bearded man
> Armed to the teeth art thou; one mailed hand
> Grasps the broad shield; and one the sword;
> Thy brow,
> Glorious in beauty though it be, is scarred
> With tokens of old wars.[37]

And his concept of nationality, an important concept for him, was fundamentally at variance with the romantic conventions of certain Germans of great contemporary influence—Fichte, Schlegel, and others —for whom the nation stood over and above the people who composed it; in their view, members had common mental and spiritual characteristics that marked them off indelibly from other peoples, and thus the will of individuals was irrelevant.[38]

Memminger's college years were a time of ripened nationalism in the United States.[39] Upwardly mobile himself, the immigrant youth idealized American freedom and opportunity; he found his first patriotic center in identification with the world's most successful libertarian revolution, declared in 1776, and his political preceptors in the Founding Fathers, Patrick Henry, Washington, Jefferson, and Madison, "friends of freedom" and lawgivers whose resourcefulness and virtue were legend while the younger of them still lived, whose handiwork, the Union and federal constitution, were things of primary moral and practical value.[40] One of the strengths of the Founders, he believed, was their large vision, the fact that their "love of country," in contrast to the exclusivistic "theory of blood" of romantic nationalism, stressed rational choice and assumed the fundamental likeness of all nations and the possibility of international political aggregation, or at least cooperation, with the young United States, an "empire of liberty," serving as a new world model.[41] In 1817, a college sophomore, he gave salient expression to the primary distinction. "That attachment which mankind have in common to the place of their nativity," he said, "is nothing more than a mere natural regard arising from local circumstances and confirmed by habit, but which long absence and better advantages in a foreign country may eventually eradicate." The savage tribesman has a natural attachment to the unbounded woods where he was accustomed to roam. But the higher patriotism arises neither from the impulse of nature nor from local partialities, but is taught—"instilled into the mind"—and "comprehends in one vast view nations, dynasties, empires. It rageth in the breast an inextinguishable flame, and burns unceasingly and forever.[42]

For Memminger, native of a distant place and an urban man, patriotism could not have its roots solely, or even primarily, in memory or organic nationality or blood or the land; it must be an act of invention and will. His associations and interests were concentrated in Charleston and South Carolina, and he came to identify with, and hold real affection for, his adopted hearth and turf. But his associations and affections were not parochial, were never confined to the fragment of humanity and wedge of land situated between North Carolina and Georgia. He was well traveled as well as well read, and his interregional friends included Agassiz, the Swiss naturalist who in the 1840s settled at Harvard, and Henry Barnard, the Connecticut educator.[43] Until the very eve of the Civil War, he was a nationalist, devoted to the Union and loath to see it broken. He viewed the United States in essentially Madisonian terms, as a multiplicity of competing interests held together in harmony by economic as well as constitutional and ideological threads.[44] Thus his efforts in support of an intersectional railroad linking Charleston and towns of the Mississippi Valley were politically as much as economically motivated. In the increasingly bitter sectional conflict over slavery, the Western territories, and the Constitution, he was an inveterate peacemaker. Even when, "under the impulse of deep-felt wrongs," he ceased being an "unconditional" Unionist—about 1848, with the controversy over the organization of the Mexican Cession with respect to slavery—he still rejected hasty and separate action, most of all secession, by South Carolina. The liberal ideas that had "made" the American Revolution, especially the concept that a stable and just constitutional order depends upon

221

a nice balance of power within government as well as extraordinary public virtue,[45] now justified caution. "The great balance wheel in our system," he declared in a public address in 1851, "is the check of the State and Federal Governments."

> The great outcry in South-Carolina, against the Federal Government, for the last twenty years, has been its tendency to consolidation. . . . And [now] . . . we are advised by the Secessionists to set up an actual consolidated government. . . . If we secede alone, we can, of necessity, have but one Legislature, and one Executive. Domestic and foreign policy must be guided by the same hands. Patronage and power—the sword and the purse—must all be delivered to the same chief magistrate; and if, under these circumstances, liberty can be preserved in South-Carolina, it must be that every public man is an Aristides, and every citizen a Phocion.

If secession became the proper remedy, "a Southern Confederacy" was the "desirable mode," a union with all the elements of greatness and strength.[46]

Memminger constantly invoked principles of the American Revolution in political discourse. In a long and eventually successful campaign against the Bank of the State of South Carolina, he hammered away at that great fiscal institution's quasi-public character, long-term charter, and unregulated power over money as "at variance with the spirit of the Constitution" and an "unfit machine for a Republican Government," given the historical tendency of unchecked power to effect its own increase. To be sure, he also attacked the Bank as an unprogressive influence that utilized its hegemony over public money and investment capital to maintain an economic status quo.[47] On both grounds, the "bank war" in South Carolina had close kinship with President Andrew Jackson's struggle with the Bank of the United States a few years earlier. And Memminger, who was connected with local banking as a director of the People's Bank of Charleston, fits well the pattern, perceived by Bray Hammond in the greater struggle, of an aggressive and forward-looking individual whose attack on "monopolistic" banking was designed to open up enterprise as well as serve democracy.[48] For all his civic-mindedness, he was the product of a common experience in America—and the South—which put great store in individual aspiration and private economic opportunity.[49]

Until the very eve of the Civil War a member of the national political party of Jackson and Madison and Jefferson, Memminger differed from those great Democrats in that, while he had important planter associations, his direct experience was entirely outside farm and country life, and he was never attached to agrarianism or its key values, notably the principle of noninterference by government in economic or social affairs. On the contrary, although he liked a balanced polity and opposed some government initiatives as harmful, he recognized that the state, with unmatched fiscal resources and organizing power, could do things individuals could not; in fact, he tended to view the state in modern terms, as a positive and expanding force.[50] Still, the substance and style of his working political assumptions were largely subsumed in Jefferson's. He was capable of warm celebrations of "the people" and public opinion. If "popular opinion" is a "dread tribunal," as he declaimed as a young man, he would later decide that it is also discriminating and just at best, although subject to corruption, as in the case of Northerners whose minds were "poisoned" against the South by antislavery "fanatics."[51]

No more than Jefferson did Memminger accord blacks and black slaves—about one-half of the residents of Charleston but treated by law and custom as minors—a significant place in his political conceptualizations. Probably at one time he regarded slavery, as Jefferson had, as philosophically indefensible, a wrong but inveterate and even essential economic and social institution.[52] We know that Governor Bennett, Memminger's first mentor in politics, held this view; in 1822 he wrote:

> Slavery abstractly considered would perhaps lead every mind to the same conclusion; but the period has long since passed when a correction might have been applied. The treasures of learning, the gifts of ingenuity and the stores of experience have been exhausted, in the fruitless search for a practical remedy. The institution is established—the evil is entailed and we can do no more than steadily to pursue that course indicated by stern necessity.[53]

It is not clear whether Bennett believed that the South's "peculiar institution" would endure indefinitely or—somehow, some way, when the time was right—be transcended in the march of progress. However that may be, within two decades the spread of slavery southward and westward from South Carolina and Georgia made increasingly untenable the idea that slavery might imperceptibly pass out of existence;

223

Southerners came to admit that the only real social alternative to slavery, racial integration, was unacceptable. John C. Calhoun and others popularized, if they did not create, an elaborate justification: not only was black slavery not an unmitigated evil; it was "a good—a positive good" sanctioned by divine intentions, by ancient Hebrew and Greek usage, and by the scientific "fact" of Negro inferiority—as well as an integral part of the Southern way of life.[54] There is no evidence that Memminger, an owner of black men and women, did not adopt this orthodoxy. But as a local politician in a period after its almost universal acceptance in South Carolina, he was not called upon to defend slavery. It was a part of the air he breathed. The most interesting thing he said about slavery was addressed to an outside audience—the governor and assembly of Virginia, in 1860—and suggests a contrast between the vehemence of Northern clergymen in berating the South's "peculiar institution" as a sin, and the tolerance of the apostle Paul: "The great apostle of the Gentiles," he said, "could encompass the Roman world, and preach to the thousands and tens of thousands of slaveholders without one word of reproach."[55] Slavery was Memminger's moral blind-spot.

Nevertheless, he was a "democrat." Like Jefferson, he assumed some sort of hierarchy of accomplishment and prestige but demanded that status come, for white men at least, not from ascription but from ability and effort. Moreover, like the Virginian, he supported the proposition that the power of government emanates from "the people" and should serve the general interest, and he was disposed to define "the people" and the general interest broadly. If his thinking about blacks and black slaves was rote and apparently unconcerned about anything except their religious instruction (and continued enslavement), he was creative in his thinking about the role and condition of common white people, non-slaveholders who lived by their own labor. In Charleston, this class was made up of mechanics, stevedores, porters, draymen, and the like, and included a large proportion of Irish and German immigrants. That it was beginning to develop a sense of class consciousness was suggested at midcentury by sporadic strikes and, most important, by a formal and informal movement to exclude black slaves from competing with whites for general urban employments. In 1849, when Memminger first took a real interest in these matters, it was in the context of exploding revolutionary crises and class and ethnic clashes abroad, and in Charleston the emergence of a vibrant public debate over the relative expense and economic and social impact of free and slave labor.[56]

Initially, Memminger assumed what was for him an uncharacteristically doctrinaire and conservative position. In a letter to James Henry Hammond, who was a strong advocate of white labor in an urban context because he feared that city employment permitted slaves a dangerous measure of freedom, Memminger expressed a strong contrary fear of a white proletariat, especially one foreign-born and unassimilated. This was "the only party from which danger to our institutions is to be apprehended among us," he wrote. "Drive out negro mechanics and all sorts of operatives from our Cities, and who must take their place [?] The same men who make the cry in the Northern Cities against the tyranny of Capital . . . and would soon raise the hue and cry against the Negro, and be hot abolitionists—and every one of those men would have a vote."[57]

If Memminger's assessment were true, it would follow that Charleston and other Southern cities had two possible courses of action. An assortment of nativists, radical secessionists, and proslavery extremists suggested that the better course was to suppress further immigration of white people, reopen the slave trade, and create city codes that favored slave over free labor.[58] The conclusions Memminger came around to after further reflection was that the fate of the city, state, and region was inseparable from that of the common white people; that free labor should be encouraged as more efficient than slave labor (though not to the exclusion of the latter); and above all that the common white people, including the worthy among the immigrants, should be given reason to identify themselves as part of a social establishment, members of a genuine, not merely theoretical, "peerage of white men."[59] And he came to believe that—important as were railroads and steam engines—the innovation of singular importance, if Charleston and the South aspired to corporate unity, "strength and consideration," would be to build up the system of education, the means by which standards of feeling and thinking and skills of living in amenity and affluence may be compounded and disseminated.[60]

On the small stage of Charleston, Memminger and other men of pragmatic temperament and "liberal" ideas eventually gathered the requisite power and resources to determine public decisions and attempt to translate their thinking into policies and programs. In 1854, Memminger and his adoptive brother, W. Jefferson Bennett, were appointed by the state legislature Commissioners of Free Schools for Charleston, with Memminger assuming the chairmanship. In 1855, William P. Miles, lately a professor of mathematics at the College of Charleston, captured the mayoralty, joining the great merchant Robert N. Gourdin and other progressive spirits on a city council (momentarily) united in the intention "to sweep away the remains of old fogyism" and get on with a new order of things.[61] They launched a remarkable reform effort based on what was in that time and place a radical allocation of power to government.[62]

Using ideas, administrators, and even teachers drawn from Northern cities like Boston and New York, Memminger and Bennett made over the old free schools (which in reality had been inadequate schools for the poor) into modern public schools, well funded by local taxes and designed to serve as a great cementing influence in society, the support for culture, morality, and productivity. Although children of color were carefully excluded, girls were for the first time admitted on an equality with boys, and children of rich and poor without distinction; thus the new system, which by 1860 had experienced a fourfold increase in enrollment, represented a significant, if limited, democratization of opportunity and association.[63] At the same time, Memminger pressed a renewed effort, based on private subscription in Charleston and state-subscribed bonds, to "scale" the Blue Ridge Mountains with a railroad hookup that might bring the produce of the Ohio and Mississippi valleys through Charleston port.[64] And Miles and the city council enacted laws and undertook measures to deepen the Charleston harbor, promote direct trade between Charleston and ports in Europe, enhance public sanitation and drainage, improve streets and park grounds, provide separate correction for juvenile delinquents, and — adopting an innovation of the English — create a full-time metropolitan police department (which in terms of organization, function, routine, and even dress, would endure).[65]

Despite concrete achievements, the gap between the reformers' hopes and their accomplishments was great. The Blue Ridge Railway never reached its western terminus, Cincinnati; intercity and interstate rivalries, combined with conservative opposition and the disruption of the Civil War, prevented its completion even within South Carolina.[66] A company chartered with a grant of state funds to build two steamships to ply between Charleston and Liverpool, England, produced one packet, built in New York; when it was discovered that the boat could not traverse the Charleston bar under load, it was sold and the enterprise abandoned.[67] The project into which Memminger put the greatest effort, the new system of public schools—symbol of a corporate commitment to moral uplift, efficiency, opportunity, enlightenment, and white unity—was never effective outside the Charleston parishes and even there did not survive the Civil War.[68] The judgment of historians has most often been that the result was inevitable, that the reformers' ends and means were hopelessly confused, and that their opponents—radical conservatives like Robert B. Rhett of the Charleston *Mercury*—were right after all: trains and steamers and free labor and public schools do not integrate well with slaves and plantation agriculture, "moonlight and magnolias."[69] Yet the mixed regime of free enterprise and welfare state under which the majority of Europeans and Americans live in the last quarter of the twentieth century shows very well that human society may embrace apparent opposites. Of deeper significance than their several failures were the reformers' analysis of their situation, their methods, and their program. Unable to bequeath the postbellum South a legacy of solid achievement, they left as a legacy the essence of the "New South Creed."

Sometime between 1850 and 1860, Memminger became estranged from the United States. "Nobody on God's earth has loved this Union more than I," he asserted with deep regret at the time of the Wilmot Proviso controversy in 1850.[70] He came by degrees to accept the necessity of secession as the lesser of evils; the alternative was the acceptance of a federal leviathan dominated by interests deemed to have become increasingly hostile.[71] He was forced to admit the failure of a policy, the main weapons of which had been Southern unity and "progress," that would enable the South to demand equality with the North in the Union. He was called upon to draft a "declaration of immediate causes" for the South Carolina convention that made the final decision. The document paralleled Jefferson's great declaration of 1776 in form if not in eloquence and idealism. First stating the compact theory of the federal constitution, it proceeded to enumerate violations by Northern states and the federal government that justified the breaking of ties. The tariff was not mentioned. Secession was put before the world upon the simple matter of formal and informal sanctions against Southern property in slaves.[72]

The trial of arms precipitated by the events of 1860 and 1861, which left the city of Charleston, the state of South Carolina, and the South

227

as a whole desperately poor and alternately ridiculed and pitied abroad, produced a new generation of leaders, largely urban, who groped for some kind of salvation. They seemed to find it in the "New South Creed," a cluster of ideas whose time was come, an avowed program of modernization the necessity of which could no longer be doubted, the "product of a subtle interaction between national ideals and achievements on the one hand and regional aspirations and failures on the other" and between past and present.[73] They issued a challenge to the South to finally achieve parity with the North and to build a superior society in which the people were elevated to higher consideration and greater usefulness through general education erected upon the best and most liberal footing; a regional economic order in which modern transportation networks by land and sea and diversified industry would importantly supplement diversified and scientific agriculture for the fullest possible utilization of natural and human resources; and a national reconciliation in which erstwhile enemies would write a finish to the great political, racial, and economic issues of the Civil War and Reconstruction and find peace and happiness in magnificent progress, a new burst of national patriotism, and a formal segregation of blacks and whites in a context of black subordination.[74] The design for action was familiar to those who recalled antebellum times in Charleston, for they fully anticipated it.[75]

Memminger remained close to the center of affairs in Charleston for two decades after Appomattox and helped give direction to the new era. He served again, briefly, in the state assembly. But his most important efforts were spent outside politics, as a booster of business enterprise and as chairman of the Charleston school commissioners. In the first role, he led by example. As chief executive and a major stockholder in the Spartanburg-Asheville Railroad, he took up an old dream: the bringing together of South and West, Charleston and the Carolinas, "a commodious seaport, a country abounding in capacity for improvement," and, beyond "a narrow belt of mountains," a rich continental heartland in "a lasting union of friendship and profit." This time the dream was not denied; ribbons of steel connected Charleston and Chicago in the last three decades of the nineteenth century.[76] He was a founder of a fertilizer works upon an immense bed of phosphate rock about a mile above Charleston on the Cooper River, "the pioneer of a grand industry" that elicited encomia from New South publicists.[77] He resumed his efforts in the cause of public education, now not excluding blacks from its benefits. He resisted racial integration in schools as in society, for he harbored a profound prejudice that while education was necessary to fit blacks for citizenship, it was "best for both races that this training should be conducted at separate institutions." As reestablished in Charleston in the 1870s and 1880s, "his" schools fixed the late pattern for South Carolina.[78]

In 1885, aged eighty-two years, Memminger retired to his grandchildren, his garden, and his Bible. A typical Southerner? Indubitably not. But if we may accept as valid Carlo Ginzburg's assertion that a determinate historical environment "offers to the individual a horizon of latent possibilities—a flexible and invisible cage in which he can exercise his . . . conditional liberty, physical, moral, and ideological,"[79] we must conclude that the forms and accepted principles of antebellum Charleston had more in common with America and the Occident of Memminger's day as well as ours than has sometimes been supposed; that there was another South besides the stereotype, Southerners who grappled with some of the complexities of a post-Revolutionary, increasingly urban world and who on some issues and in some ways made peace with modern America before the Civil War.

Townhouse of Charles Pinckney III. Collection of the Carolina Art Association–Gibbes Art Gallery.

III: Sensibilities

8

Friends and Amateurs in Musik, *drawing by Thomas Middleton, ca. 1827. Collection of the Carolina Art Association–Gibbes Art Gallery.*

Intellectual Life in the 1830s: The Institutional Framework and the Charleston Style

JANE H. PEASE *and* WILLIAM H. PEASE

To ASSESS the institutional framework of a city's intellectual life is not necessarily to premise that without the former the latter could not exist. Nonetheless, the life of the mind is not disembodied abstraction.

It is shaped by, as it also shapes, the society of which it is a part. Just as time and place help define the subjects that intellectuals address, the boundaries within which they work, and the audiences whom they reach, so too particular societies either thwart or encourage creativity by the institutions they foster. Because this is so, those cultural and educational institutions that serve intellectuals provide a means of understanding the society of which they are part. They become, in short, lenses to magnify and clarify those underlying ideals and values that shape the minds and attitudes of its citizens.[1]

Charleston is a case in point. Not surprisingly, in the strife-filled but economically challenging years of the 1830s, the city's cultural institutions reflected those issues that shaped the lives of Charlestonians and the style with which they met and addressed them. Twice within a single decade, their city had been threatened by revolutionary upheaval in crises fostered by the Vesey revolt and nullification. Moreover, after 1833, increasing antislavery propaganda from England and the North pressed citizens to make their extant institutions yet more inclusive to assure social stability. And while they sought thereby to knit their community still more closely in an all-encompassing network, they also cultivated a smooth style to keep those ties binding.[2]

Confined geographically to a small peninsula, this people of diverse origins, interests, and positions opted for rounded edges. Fearful of acrimonious debate as the prelude to blunt confrontation, Charlestonians of power and influence perfected a language and a bearing that dulled sharp differences; when those devices failed, they resorted to behind-the-scenes mediation to reduce and obscure difference or, at the very least, to muffle fractious public debate until passions had cooled. Familiar as the ritual to keep gentlemen from dueling, this technique was pervasive in a community that offered few alternatives to explosive violence other than the soft style.[3]

There was, however, more to the Charleston style than rounded edges. As its citizens preferred the gentleman to the Gradgrind, so they valued amateurism over expertise. Reflecting the demands of both patrician and democratic politics, they insisted that city government remain a bastion of volunteer public service, where civic dedication was more important than specialized training.[4] The choice was a conscious rejection of a modernization already setting new scientific and professional standards, as it was also a reflection that no clear distinction should exist between public and private life.[5] Thus it nourished the expectation that as citizens gave of themselves to city governance, so the public purse should fund projects designed to enhance the city's cultural amenities. Reinforced by the compulsions of a capital-short urban economy whose profits were regularly siphoned off to buy rural land and the slaves to farm it, the city council as readily subsidized libraries and colleges as it did railroads and hotels, all of which elsewhere were more often left to private investment.

Well aware and even proud that their practices differed markedly from those of more prosperous Northern cities, Charlestonians nonetheless suffered a quasi-colonial self-doubt. It was not only that they shared the national sense of cultural inferiority. To the burden of being American in a European-dominated literary and scientific world was added that of being Southern in a Northern-dominated America. This pervasive lack of self-confidence both fed and fed upon the peculiar amalgam of broad inclusiveness and civic involvement, gentlemanly amateurism and rounded edges. And it was their interaction that created the Charleston style, that special matrix within which the institutional framework of the city's intellectual life took on shape and meaning.

*   *   *

Of major importance were those associations that aspired to be learned societies—first and foremost the Literary and Philosophical, the Horticultural, and the Agricultural. The South Carolina Agricultural Society was organized in the fall of 1825. Responding, perhaps, to the sharp fall in cotton prices that year, the society initially launched a vigorously innovative program. Sponsoring competitive exhibitions of stock and produce, planning an agricultural library, organizing its members to experiment with new seeds, equipment, and cultivation patterns, it addressed fundamental questions in a manner consonant with scientific progress. Yet before long, society members betrayed the attitudes of the upper-class planters who spent much of their time in Charleston. Resolutely rejecting the cash incentives that were encouraging mechanic inventors elsewhere, the Agricultural Society voted in 1828 to oppose patenting farm machinery. While no immediate causal connection can be made, their action did nothing to encourage technological innovation or alter South Carolina's thirteenth place among American states in the number of patents awarded.[6]

Equally clear was the superficiality of the society's interest in scientific farming. By 1836 its experimental farm was primarily the locale

235

for elaborate monthly dinners, and its annual meetings heard more about laying down the society's madeira than about cattle shows, flint corn, or caterpillars.[7] Gentlemanly amateurism had clearly defeated scientific endeavor even where economic self-interest seemed to demand the latter. Virtually all the club's officers owned plantations. Three-quarters of them listed planting as their primary occupation, and over half of them either ranked among the city's wealthiest men or exerted marked economic power in a city whose economy rested on agricultural commodities.[8] If, as Yankees were fond of saying, "knowledge is power," this segment of Charleston's economic elite did precious little to increase the city's potential either to create or to disseminate valuable practical information. The Agricultural Society was, in the judgment of planter-member Frederick Porcher, merely a "social club," and so it remained at least until the mid-1840s.[9]

The Horticultural Society, chartered in 1830, might have been expected to address similar concerns. It had, however, a very different membership and quite different interests. In its early years the city's undisputed center for natural history, the society's scientifically inclined members collected and classified local specimens. John Bachman, Lutheran cleric by profession and competent zoologist by avocation, drew to it visiting notables like John Audubon and eager novices like Moses Curtis of North Carolina. There they encountered a natural history circle composed largely of physicians but including as well such men as farmer Philip Noisette and statesman-politician Joel Poinsett—amateur botanists all. After he was introduced to their ranks, German-born and Tübingen-trained Edward Leitner excitedly reported that there were "more men in Charleston who were favorably inclined towards natural sciences than in New York or Philadelphia." Captivated by the city's exceptional "spirit . . . for natural history," Leitner stayed on, organizing scientific expeditions into the countryside and adding significantly to the classification of Southern flora and fauna.[10]

More dedicated to serious science than the members of the Agricultural Society, the horticulturists were also more attuned to cultivating broad public interest. They regularly arranged exhibits where amateur gardeners displayed their flowers, fruits, and vegetables and where, year in and year out, a redoubtable Miss Muckenfuss won prizes for her superior productions. Nor did society members' links to national and even international natural science circles divert their attention from their local power bases. As young Curtis observed, sometime society president Dr. Joseph Johnson—former bank president and Unionist politician—fumbled badly on botanizing ventures: he "seemed . . . to pretend to more than he really knew, but hid his ignorance under a bad memory, never or rarely being able to give the name of a plant." No matter. The society valued Johnson and its other officers, who were more likely to be merchants and factors than practical farmers or dedicated scientists.[11] For them, natural history and gardening were no more than hobbies; nonetheless, their amateurism and their public prestige strengthened the society, which in its early years provided an active forum for scientific discourse. On the other hand, their dedication and their resources were too limited to generate the long-term institutional support needed to sustain professional scientists or even to make the Horticultural Society a center for diffusing practical knowledge.

Of all Charleston's intellectual organizations, none outshone the Literary and Philosophical Society. The *Courier*, attesting to its local reputation, compared it to the French Institute, the British Royal Society, and the American Philosophical Society.[12] Like them, the Literary and Philosophical Society had, since its 1813 founding, embraced all areas of knowledge—from mathematics and mechanics to literature and the fine arts. After a period of decline in the 1820s, it was revived by men active in the Unionist cause—Thomas Grimké, James Petigru, Joseph Johnson, and William Gilmore Simms among them. But quickly demonstrating a determination to transcend partisanship, it forthwith admitted those arch-nullifiers, James Hamilton, Jr., and Robert Y. Hayne.[13]

The society's determination to be inclusive did not stop at bridging political differences; like the Horticultural Society, it also tried to close the gap between a self-conscious intellectual elite and the public at large. Although it attracted its membership primarily from the learned professions and those of high social standing, it earnestly disseminated the substance of its meetings to the general public. It opened its museum of natural history to the community at large, having first rearranged its displays and then having moved them at mid-decade to larger and better-located quarters in the Charleston Library Society building on Broad Street; it published selected papers which its members had read to each other in the society's rooms at the Depository on Chalmers Street; and finally, perceiving the limited impact of these devices, it transformed its meetings into a public lecture series to which all were invited—but few came. The outcome was predictable. Essaying a universalism that neither attracted the general public nor stimulated individual effort, the society became by the 1840s just another "literary and social club" meeting in private homes for conversation.[14]

Taken together, the Agricultural, Horticultural, and Literary and Philosophical Societies reflected the city's dominant values. The Agricultural Society excepted, they were self-consciously inclusive in membership and programs. Reluctant to offend any part of their constituencies, they skirted controversial issues and rarely provided a forum for the discussion of unsettling new ideas. Rounded edges set unspoken limits on the territory into which they ventured. Only the Literary and Philosophical Society entertained social questions. And even there the most controversial topics—such as D.K. Whitaker's essay on the right of all to free public education, and John B. White's proposal to curtail capital punishment—were presented tentatively as explorations from which their authors could withdraw gracefully.[15]

The gentlemanly amateurism that such a milieu fostered exacted a price. If rounded edges reduced controversy, and inclusivity brought diverse groups together, so also they frustrated those who, like William Gilmore Simms, Samuel Gilman, and Charles Fraser, sought excellence in matters cultural and intellectual. Simms, lamenting the demise of the Academy of Fine Arts in 1830, saw in it evidence of Charleston's narrow aesthetic commitment. If the state of civilization was to be "determined by taking what the arts are, which are permitted to live on and are encouraged," the city gave "but one melancholy answer." And that answer fell hard on painter Charles Fraser, who concluded he must find recognition "any where but in Charleston." Unitarian minister Samuel Gilman's talent was, as his biographer put it, "enervated by a stifling environment" of which Gilman complained when he wrote Harvard professor Benjamin Peirce that he despaired of finding a single person in the city "to whom I c[ould] apply with any hope of assistance" to deal with errors he had discovered in a mathematics text. Thwarted by unspoken limits, they all chafed bitterly at their inability to pursue a creative life in Charleston—doubting their own resources and carping at their city's backwardness.[16]

*   *   *

Twice during the 1830s the tranquil course of Charleston's intellectual institutions was disrupted in a manner that threatened the very premises governing city life. Acrimonious debate, sharp dealing, and

238

overt hostility exposed the omnipresent tensions and contradictions underlying the ostensibly unified and unchanging city.

The College of Charleston, like similar institutions elsewhere in America, was expected to serve a variety of goals. Educating, as they always had, classicists, clerics, and gentlemen, the nation's colleges increasingly employed the country's professional scientists to teach both the theory and the practical applications of their fields. In major cities they offered professional education in law and medicine as well. Thus America's colleges remained the resort of those for whom collegiate education was a cultural accomplishment and token of status, while they attracted also those who sought the requisite credentials to rise economically as lawyers, doctors, and engineers.

But expectations for the College of Charleston were still more complex. Local citizens insisted that it be a haven of moral purity. If local youth could attend school near the junction of St. Philips and Boundary Streets and live at home under parental supervision, they might escape the riotous dissipation associated with college life elsewhere, especially at South Carolina College.[17] Moreover, the lower costs inherent in such an arrangement enhanced opportunities for the upward-aspiring sons of modest families—an especially important consideration in Charleston. In this city whose population was static at best, the alternative of encouraging her sons to go west or north to improve their position was simply unacceptable. Faced in fact with a diminishing population and a lagging economy, Charleston needed to keep all the native talent she had. The city could ill afford the risk that young men sent away to study would stay away, but she could not promise them, as did Yankees their sons, that hard work would open the way to property and prestige if they stayed at home. To do so where labor was associated with black slavery would threaten the very foundations of the social structure. Providing the education to satisfy youthful aspirations was thus a sine qua non of civic well-being.

When Stephen Elliott, planter, bank president, and naturalist, addressed the first class of the South Carolina Medical College back in 1825, he put the issue into sharp focus. Colleges, whether publicly aided or privately supported, he said, opened "opportunities by which even the poor and the humble might attain instruction." By cultivating their "intellectual powers," they could rise "into life and [might] have the power of guiding public opinion, not only as professional but as public men." But if, as lawyer-painter Charles Fraser warned three years later, higher education were not available locally, those young men who could would continue to go north to be educated. They would lose their regional identity and be lost forever to the city. Charleston's peculiar interests and particular culture demanded, he concluded, that her citizens keep their children—and their tuition—at home.[18]

Committed to reenforcing clearly formulated social values—hometown prosperity, moral soundness, upward socioeconomic mobility, and regional identity—Charlestonians revived their local college in the mid-1820s. Originally chartered as a private collegiate institution in 1785, the College of Charleston had in fact been mostly a grammar school. But by 1829 it had acquired a new building and an endowed professorship, and thereby the ability to lure back to its presidency Episcopal clergyman Jasper Adams, who, only three years earlier, had left to become president of Geneva College in New York. Still, even with a staff of three other professors, two tutors, and an instructor, Adams could not make the college flourish.[19] While he struggled with limited finances, suspicious faculty, and unprepared students, his dour personality and abrasive style—utterly lacking in rounded edges—made enemies among gown and town alike.

It was bad enough that the college continued to function primarily as a grammar school, seldom having more than thirty advanced students among the two hundred pupils it enrolled each year. In addition, its trustees, except for a few like Elias Horry and Charles Fraser, were only minimally dedicated to the institution over which they presided or to the goals their fellow Charlestonians set for it. Many had been educated in the North; others sent their children to schools outside Charleston; most showed, by deed if not word, a limited commitment to strengthening the college, even refusing on one occasion to support faculty discipline against rebellious students. For their part, the faculty were increasingly alienated. They watched college funds diminish and student numbers dwindle until at last they were driven to moonlighting to augment their meager salaries. As things grew ever worse, they vented their frustration on the president, who, so one instructor claimed, was primarily concerned "to get as much money as he could, and do as little labour as [he] could." An isolated and bookish man, Jasper Adams saw the college fall apart until he and three students were all that was left.[20]

Thus by the summer of 1836, faced with either reorganizing the college or closing it, the trustees chose the latter course.[21] In so doing, they avoided the acrimonious debate that confronting personality clashes and incompatible values would have produced. Ironically, the most endemic problem, shaky finances, was the most easily managed. As a private institution, it is true, the college depended for its income on student fees; but they had been supplemented by the gifts of public-spirited Charlestonians who had contributed generously to its revitalization. Lawyers John Potter, Thomas Grimké, and Mitchell King had given substantially, while others had contributed more modestly for the new building. English-born merchant Thomas Hanscome had, from his $300,000 fortune, bequeathed the college over $12,000 for its general endowment, and planter-entrepreneur Elias Horry had pledged $20,000 for endowed professorships. Nonetheless, by 1834 what remained of the college's endowment, no more than $12,000, was sold to pay operating costs.[22]

The college's financial plight reflected the problems inherent in an agrarian society where philanthropy was circumscribed by a scarcity of liquid capital.[23] Horry's gift is a case in point. The owner of nine plantations and nearly six hundred slaves, he could in 1829 honor only half his $20,000 pledge to the college. The 1834 inventory of his estate illuminates the college's as well as his own financial problems. Valued at over $400,000, his holdings included only $10,000 in negotiable personalty, while the whole was burdened with debts of over $100,000.[24]

On the other hand, it is not surprising, given such constraints and the well-established practice of mingling public funds in private endeavors, that the city had already contributed significantly to the college. In 1829 the city council had voted $1,000 for a library.[25] At other times they had appropriated funds for the college building. So in 1835, faced with financial crisis, the trustees asserted that the city was "bound not to suffer [the college] to go down." Apparently agreeing with them, the city fathers voted another $2,000 for the salaries of one or more professors.[26]

Yet even with that promise of continued support, the trustees suspended college operations before the next term began. Clearly, access to the public purse was not the determining factor either in the 1836 decision to close the college or the 1838 decision to reopen it as a municipal institution. Far more critical was the still pressing need to reshape college policy consonant with the societal role Charlestonians expected education to play. The college, it was obvious, had to become dedicated less to improving the community's intellectual life than to

241

providing social and economic opportunity for Charleston youth. Once again, city council, trustees, and press rang the changes on the merits of keeping boys under parental control and of keeping money spent on education at home.[27]

That the college must reinforce an inclusive society was also clear. "All classes of our citizens," the city council argued, should have access to the classical education that promised transgenerational economic mobility.[28] The seriousness of that commitment had already surfaced in the 1831 tiff between trustees and faculty, representing conflicting interests of town and gown: as a quid pro quo for the support it had already given the college, the council requested that boys from the orphan asylum be admitted to the school free of charge, and in the spirit of good public relations, the trustees had agreed. But the faculty balked, arguing that the arrangement not only infringed on their prerogatives to admit students but reduced their incomes by the amount of fees not paid.[29] When, however, the college became a municipal institution in 1838, the city promptly imposed the arrangement and the broader policy it represented. "This College belongs to Charleston," averred a trustee anticipating the change; only if it is "established on a proper basis" will "its advantages to our citizens . . . be inestimable."[30] Constantly pressing the concept of broad inclusiveness, the city council also forced a reduction of tuition for all students after the first year of municipal operation.[31] Finally, chastened by reality, even the faculty joined the democratizing process. Believing, as at least one of their number did, that declining enrollment in the private college had been a response to high academic standards, they agreed in 1840 not to fail students who had attended classes and recited regularly during the year just because they did poorly on their examinations.[32]

Certainly as obvious, though never openly discussed, was the city council's determination to make the board of trustees more representative of Charleston's diversity. From the onset of municipal control, three aldermen had joined the sixteen trustees remaining from the old board, and though the latter had rejected proposals for more extensive change, within five years the council had quietly used its power to fill other vacancies as they occurred to achieve its goal. With but two known exceptions—Unitarian judge Thomas Lee and Lutheran cleric John Bachman—only Episcopalians or the unaffiliated had sat on the old board. The new board, on the other hand, included between 1838 and 1843 not only a Presbyterian, a Unitarian, two Congregationalists, and three Lutherans (two of whom were German ethnics) but also a Methodist, two Baptists, and a Catholic. Where ten years earlier Baptist minister Basil Manly had thought the college an unbreachable enclave where none but an Episcopalian could be president, in 1838 the president was Baptist cleric William Brantley.[33]

That the change was more than denominational, Caroline Gilman could attest. Writer and bluestocking as well as wife of Unitarian minister Samuel Gilman, she well understood the connection between church and social position. "Episcopacy," she had complained when she first arrived from Boston, "takes the lead" in "fashions and aristocracy." Despite her husband's mild demurral, she insisted that in Charleston "there [was] unquestionably a light feeling of contempt . . . among [Episcopalians] for all Presbyterians & Congregationalists."[34] Even if Gilman was overresponding to the Episcopalians' aristocratic tendencies, too much cannot be made of the social change that the religious mix of the new trustees betokened. Its intellectual life sacrificed to more immediate goals, the College of Charleston had become a bulwark for the city's social process, reinforcing its inclusive network and easing strains by reconciling diversity.

* * *

The upheavals that beset the college pale before those which, during the 1830s, gave Charleston two medical schools. Like the politics of the nullification crisis and unlike those that finally rebuilt the College of Charleston, the conflict between the South Carolina Medical Society and the faculty of its medical school barred no holds. That the controversy was so singular an exception to Charleston's style of conflict resolution was no accident. Climate, location, and—as we now know—mosquitoes were so life-threatening that the community accepted among physicians a professional style it welcomed nowhere else. Displaying an expertise carefully cultivated because it was highly valued, Charleston's doctors were disproportionately its intellectual leaders, ready to assert their professional standards against conflicting social values.[35]

Charleston was not unique, of course, in experiencing strains between the concepts of equal opportunity and an aristocracy of talent. South Carolina only acted like most other American states when it repealed its laws governing professional licensing. What made Charleston distinctive, however, was her preoccupation with high-quality medical training at a time when neither doctors nor medical schools were held to any recognized standards. Since 1822, when Thomas Cooper, president of South Carolina College, had proposed that the state charter a medical school, a small group of Charleston physicians had pressed hard to make good medical training available locally. First petitioning for a state-supported college, they were turned down by the legislature. Then they went to the College of Charleston, requesting that it shelter a medical school under its degree-granting power, but the board of trustees rejected their plea. Finally they turned to the South Carolina Medical Society, to whom, ultimately, the legislature granted the authority to award doctorates in medicine.[36]

Other than that, the Medical Society took little responsibility for creating the school. It did appoint the first faculty, and its honorary members were the school's first trustees, but the school was actually operated by its faculty, who had contributed their own funds and garnered city subsidies to build and equip the institution. The board of trustees, though it was reconstituted in 1829, never met from 1825 to 1832.[37]

Despite the school's autonomy, however, tensions developed between the faculty and other society members. They were brought into the open in 1829 by the alcoholism of James Ramsay, professor of surgery. His teaching colleagues, believing he had become incompetent from "great physical and mental debility," voted to dismiss him. Counterpoising the etiquette of rounded edges and collegiality, the society disagreed, refusing to offend one of its members. Two years later, when Ramsay finally resigned of his own accord, the society further angered the faculty by acting unilaterally to appoint his successor.[38]

This time professional competence per se was not at stake; the society's choice had fallen on John Wagner, who was already a demonstrator of anatomy at the medical school. But the faculty insisted that their particular qualifications entitled them to a special voice if not to full power in making academic appointments. At first the customary soft style blurred the issue. Wagner, cognizant of faculty views, quickly resigned his new appointment. The society then appointed the faculty's choice, Eli Geddings. But Geddings, alert to the internal strife, also resigned, joining instead the staff of the University of Maryland Medical School. Only then did both faculty and society agree to reappoint John Wagner in a ritual designed to smooth ruffled feathers.[39]

244

Ad hoc resolutions, however, were no way to run a professional school, and the faculty remained dissatisfied. As long as the society claimed full power to make appointments and refused to recognize the faculty as a body both separate from the society and enjoying special competence to select their colleagues, professional standards remained at stake. Samuel Dickson's stand dramatized the faculty's position. A Yale graduate with a medical degree from the University of Pennsylvania, Dickson resigned his professorship of the institutes of medicine in 1832. "The Faculty . . . have literally no share whatever" in the college's governance, he charged. They are "absolutely and without appeal under the control of the Medical Society," which has "refused even to recognize the existence of the Faculty as a body."[40]

But even before Dickson resigned, the faculty had approached the legislature for a change in the college charter. They sought a board of trustees composed equally of faculty members and laymen. Faculty would furnish professional expertise; laymen would ensure that the school met its social obligations. Conflicting self-interest disqualified current board members, the faculty claimed, because as nonacademic physicians they competed with those they governed for patients and professional prestige. Such trustees, they implied, served neither the college's nor the community's best interests.

Stung by the challenge, the Medical Society took the offensive. Claiming credit for having founded the college, it asserted that its right to award medical diplomas gave it full authority to run the school and appoint its trustees. Returning the faculty's charges, it accused them of being "high handed," self-serving, and committed to creating "an oligarchy in the Medical profession in [the] State." By challenging the society's stewardship over South Carolina medicine, the faculty were trying to seize "the power of controlling the whole Medical Community; to shut the door against competition, and to monopolize office."[41]

As the language was Jacksonian, so also were the fears and the interests it clothed. If the faculty had the exclusive or even principal power to appoint its own members, a self-perpetuating "two-class" structure would develop within the profession. While the faculty for their part admitted the distinction but argued that it reflected only expertise, other society members chafed at the differences in emoluments. Like similar institutions throughout the country, the Medical College of South Carolina was a proprietary establishment. Its fees supplemented the income of its faculty, whose private practice was further enhanced by their positions in the college. Nor were the faculty unaware of these financial implications. They constantly reiterated their economic investment in the college's building and equipment. And their insistence on controlling appointments and strengthening the school's reputation was at least partly to guarantee their personal investment of more than $11,000 in the physical plant on Queen Street.[42]

As society members mistrusted faculty motivation, so faculty suspected that society and trustee decisions were also tainted by economic self-interest. Since 1829, when the society began electing trustees from both its regular and honorary members, candidates previously defeated for faculty appointments had had singular success in gaining appointment to the board. Among them was the politically inclined Thomas Y. Simons, who had sought the professorship awarded to scientist-physician Edmund Ravenel in 1825. As trustee, Simons led the campaign against the faculty. Then in 1832, when Samuel Dickson resigned his chair, Thomas Simons was appointed in his stead.

By that time, no one was in a mood to compromise. Drawn into the maelstrom in December 1831 by the faculty request for charter revision, Charleston legislators intervened to mollify both factions. Following their lead, the state legislature passed an act to reconstitute the board of trustees, making it half society members and half laymen. But even though Simons, acting as lobbyist for the society, agreed to the bill, the full membership rejected it out of hand and took their case to court. There, in short order, Judge John Belton O'Neall, relying heavily on John Marshall's decision in the Dartmouth College case, ruled that the society's charter to operate the medical school was sheltered by constitutional guarantees of the sanctity of contract.[43] Armed with that decision and heady with victory, the society further stiffened its position. Its demand that the faculty produce an exact accounting of all college finances from 1825 onward was so unusual and so strident that the society's own attorneys urged restraint. "An enlarged and liberal confidence," they warned, "ought to subsist between the Society and the faculty of the College."[44]

The personal insult implicit in the society's refusal to display such confidence became overt in December 1834: in a massive blackballing of prospective members, the society rejected nine applicants who were known friends of the dissident faculty, who had by this time established a rival school. In the past, "gentlemen of merit in the Medical profession" who met the general requirements for practice in the state had been almost automatically admitted.[45] Never in recent history had the society excluded anyone except on grounds of race. Here surely was a slap with the back of the hand—an insult not assuaged by assurances that no personal slur was intended.

Once the society had turned to the courts, the dispute degenerated into farce. Fearing eviction from their Queen Street building after O'Neall's decision, the faculty instructed the janitor to exclude anyone who lacked the dean's permission to enter. The society solemnly responded that the faculty lacked the power to "appoint a Janitor or Person to take charge and custody of the College Building" and once again went to court to validate its claims.[46]

With that the faculty hired the old Broad Street theater and established there a medical school about whose control there was no doubt. Chartered as the Medical College of the State of South Carolina under politically appointed lay trustees, the new school overshadowed the society's institution from its inception. Yet from 1833 until 1839 the society's college struggled on, seldom mustering more than two dozen students. In its first year under a new faculty, when Queen Street had hired outsiders, they were inexperienced young Northerners. After 1834, half the faculty were former trustees of the institution, each of whom had resigned from the board shortly before his appointment as a professor. Meanwhile, the Broad Street school was thriving, attracting over one hundred students each year and graduating between thirty and fifty young doctors annually. In 1836, Queen Street graduated just two.[47]

The success of the new school only exacerbated the original rancor. Refusing to give up its 1825 contract with the city, the society's college co-opted use of the Alms House and the Marine Hospital for clinical training—and incidentally gained for its members the city salaries attached to the physician's post in each of them.[48] Cut off in this way from their former clinical facilities, the Broad Street faculty established their own infirmary, only to run afoul of the Medical Society once again. By advertising low rates to ensure a sufficient clientele for clinical demonstration, they violated the society's fee schedule and, as members, were ordered to stand trial before their peers, who swiftly convicted them. Then, ironically, the society received a request from its own school for a similar facility. With clear loss of face, it had to rescind its condemnation of the State Medical College faculty and vote that "the establishment of an Infirmary by either or both of the Medical Colleges during the term of Lecturing, is not a violation of the obligation of the Members to support the Fee Bill."[49]

Appalled by this comic opera, James Moultrie, recently appointed professor of physiology at the Broad Street college, struggled to recapture the original concern for professional expertise and to stop wasting resources on two schools. Arguing that neither school was maintaining high enough standards, Moultrie urged their merger as the first step towards improving a system that now professed to produce qualified doctors after only two four-month terms of training; he also called for better clinical facilities and a faculty more specialist than generalist. Even so, he asserted—challenging Charlestonians' proclivity to give in to a quasi-colonial mentality—the city's medical education was already as good as if not better than that offered elsewhere in the United States; in some respects it even compared favorably with training offered in Europe. If only it would give up the duplication of effort that two schools involved, Charleston's medical education could be made still more competitive.[50]

Moultrie's enthusiasm doubtless encompassed brash aspiration and local boosterism; nonetheless, it unmistakably challenged the practice of excusing intellectual flaccidity as the product of place. His contentions, if not in themselves demonstrable, bespoke an intellectual self-confidence rare to the city and reflected the assumptions that had allowed the old medical faculty to break with local style, spurn inclusivity, exalt professionalism, and squarely face controversial issues of substance. Their strength also enabled the Broad Street faculty in 1839 to accept merger with their Queen Street rivals without compromising those commitments.[51]

That reunion did of course involve changes—among them a return to the Charleston style of conflict resolution. When, for instance, the general medical fraternity insisted on a new, binding fee schedule to curb competition in an overcrowded field, the medical school closed its low-fee infirmary for a year and then reopened it under a new name suggesting more limited functions. Still, the return to rounded edges did not render the decade's warfare meaningless, as Samuel Dickson, stalwart leader of the faculty revolt, made clear. Addressing the 1841 graduating class of the reconstituted medical school, Dickson, like Moultrie, attacked regional defensiveness and insisted that Charleston's medical training could be brought up to European standards.[52]

248

That Charlestonians tolerated a decade of medical warfare at a time when all other institutional life was hostage to a felt need for social cohesion was a tribute to the perceived "usefulness" of medical knowledge. So immediately connected to individual survival, its substance could not safely be treated as an adornment to cultivated leisure or left to those who would use it primarily as a force for upward mobility. The city endured both sharp controversy and threats to inclusivity because, in this case, applied knowledge promised greater public utility than did maintaining a conservative equilibrium.

*　　*　　*

All other institutions shaping Charleston's intellectual life were generalist in nature and unlikely to challenge the city's prevailing style. A number of small libraries—those of the Washington, the Franklin, the Young Men's, and the Mercantile societies among them—existed during the 1830s to serve particular readerships. They were, however, overshadowed by two major libraries, operated respectively by the Charleston Library Society and the Apprentices Library Society. The former, established in 1748 and from 1835 occupying the old Bank of South Carolina building at Broad and Church, was more a gentlemen's preserve than a bibliophiles' retreat. Its officers were commonly men of high social status, some of whom also exerted political and economic power in the city, others of whom had gained distinction by professional accomplishments. In the Library Society, however, they joined together to cultivate that learning which enriched leisure. Increasing steadily, their library grew from about 5,000 volumes in 1830 to 25,000 in 1848, strong in collections of literary and historical works and well stocked with volumes on political theory, philosophy, and natural science. During the 1830s the Library Society also turned special attention to city and state history, seeking the primary records of the colonial and revolutionary past. Although it thus acquired the libraries of David Ramsay and C.C. Pinckney, William Wragg Smith's collection of diplomatic correspondence, Francis Marion's orderly books, and a number of early city plats and land grant papers, it remained first and foremost a gentlemen's club. There resident planters and other men of leisure gathered to read, discuss politics, and pass their morning hours. There neither knowledge nor books were judged by utility.[53]

In marked contrast, the Apprentices Library Society, organized in 1824 explicitly to benefit young mechanics, was self-consciously utilitarian, and its officers as a group were neither upper class nor visibly wealthy, although a fifth of them were economic and political leaders. Representing many occupations, they were intent on retaining and enlarging the pool of skilled craftsmen indispensable to the city's prosperity. Like the College of Charleston, the Apprentices Library Society praised education as the instrument of upward mobility for the artisan as well as the professional. Taking Ben Franklin as its model, it sought "to encourage genius, industry, and good conduct in Mechanics and their Apprentices, and to facilitate and extend the knowledge of Mechanism, and the improvements daily made in the Arts."[54] During the 1830s the society not only enlarged its library, already strong in works on agriculture and technology, but also established a Mechanics Institute, which offered instruction in subjects ranging from arithmetic and mensuration to architecture, chemistry, and natural philosophy.[55] In 1837, it extended its audience by inaugurating public lectures on similar topics, attempting to popularize science, which even then had grown too specialized for an untutored general public. Like lyceums elsewhere, these lectures considered subject matter from magnetism to mesmerism, archaeology to astronomy. More popular than the similar series offered by the Literary and Philosophical Society, they were also a recruiting device, attracting an older and more diverse membership than the young mechanics the library was intended to serve.[56]

The society did not, however, lose its original purpose, as Dr. Samuel Dickson once again made clear in his persistent exploration of Charleston's cultural life. Important as it was, the task of providing the useful knowledge necessary for socioeconomic mobility among mechanics was not enough. The library must also disseminate books and lectures that would turn artisans into public-spirited citizens committed to upholding prevailing civil values. Thus the society's collection of over 600 volumes of religion and practical ethics, in addition to its textbooks and books of science and technology, spoke to the molding of community values; its 500 volumes of history and biography and 600 novels provided uplifting examples and healthful diversion for leisure moments. Indeed, the library was fully justified if it did no more than provide socially acceptable amusement. From this perspective books were valued as an antidote to booze, education as a restraint on uncontrolled emotion. Innocent pastimes were essential where "the nature of . . . [Southern] domestic arrangements" demanded "the absolute extinction of *the mob*, so much and so justly dreaded wherever it is found."[57] Whether to cultivate, to civilize, or just to control, libraries – like Sunday Schools and free public education – met social as well as intellectual needs.

*　　*　　*

Samuel Dickson was only one of the many Americans who saw education as a means of social control and praised it accordingly. Yankee proponents of free public schools made the point repeatedly. It is therefore ironic that the questions of who should be educated and who should be educated at public expense were answered so differently North and South. What separated those responses was less the ideal structure of a school system or the public value of literacy than the awareness that education, however much it was an instrument of social control, could also become an instrument of revolution if extended universally in a slave society. Nevertheless, in failing to support the broad-based free school system necessary for universal literacy, Charlestonians served social restraint at the cost of literary accomplishment. Lacking neither talent nor printing presses, the city's authors and editors did lack the market that only a broad readership could provide. Raw young Cincinnati published more magazines and newspapers in 1839 than all of South Carolina. At a time when 1,000 to 2,000 subscribers were needed to keep a periodical alive, 400 to 500 seemed the maximum that Charleston could generate, with only a few hundred more obtainable elsewhere in the state. Of the many journals that Charlestonians planned and proposed, few ever saw the light of day, fewer still lasted beyond one or two issues, and almost none survived for more than a year or two.[58] The ability to produce far exceeded the ability to consume.

How much this was a function of illiteracy can only be guessed. But sure it is that state law prohibited anyone's teaching nearly half the city's population either to write or to read. And free state-supported public education for the rest was confined to five schools – the exact minimum required and funded by law – and served only orphans and children of the poor. If they attended primary school at all, others paid fees to proprietary institutions. At the secondary level, profitmaking schools were supplemented by the academies that some churches and the German Friendly and the South Carolina Societies sponsored. The only schools for which city funds were expended were the Orphan Asylum school and the city high school, the latter not established until 1839 and then charging $40 a year tuition.[59]

Despite this record, Charlestonians valued education. In its pursuit they supported at least seventy-two local proprietary schools,[60] paid fees to eleemosynary academies, or sent their children to distant boarding schools.[61] But their very practice betrayed ambivalence. In a community where citizens looked to the public purse for so much, why did they exclude elementary schooling from their calculations? And why did the city fund both a classical high school and a college while it ignored its abecedarians? Underlying the answers to these questions was a limited belief in the proposition that "useful knowledge" and the functional literacy needed to diffuse it were essential to Charleston's economic prosperity. For the children of the wealthy, education was valued primarily as a means to enrich their leisure and adorn their lives. For children of the middling and aspiring ranks, education was the vehicle for individual upward social and economic mobility. But for the children of the poor and humble, the state and do-good societies provided the rudiments of education only as they provided other charity. No clarion call for universal free public education echoed through the city—for the same reason that there was no paean of praise for hard work as a universal social and economic escalator.[62]

In the end, even those who benefited most from that social structure and the values it promoted paid dearly for their benefits. Welcoming students to the medical school in 1826 and celebrating therein a new beginning for higher education in the South, Stephen Elliott analyzed the psychological impediment to intellectual growth that faced Southerners sent north to study. No one "who is brought up amidst scenes of luxury, amidst the constant exhibitions of wealth," Elliott reflected, believes "that he in time will have to labour for his future maintenance. . . . [At most] he will feel it a remote, perhaps uncertain and improbable contingency. And it is under such circumstances," he warned, "that the habits of many of our youth have been formed." Their lassitude, he noted, was most often attributed to the warm climate. But Elliott rejected that excuse and pointed accusingly at "our own manners and state of society." "To form and establish habits of severe and laborious industry in youth," he concluded, "it is, perhaps, an indispensable condition, that they should from infancy, believe labour their inevitable allotment."[63]

Like Elliott, Jasper Adams, Yankee president of the College of Charleston, knew that the imperative to display leisure burdened the life of the mind. In a culture "where our peculiar institutions free most of our young men from the necessities of personal labour," he said to

252

the collegians of the Euphradian Society, "the love of ease, the appetite for frivolous amusements, the seductions of pleasure, and the impulses of false honour, constitute obstacles . . . [most] formidable" to intellectual achievement.[64]

William Gilmore Simms, a product of that society, seemingly agreed when he found in the fertility of Southern soil and the presence of slavery the "true source[s]" of Southern "enervation."[65] Even for those who disciplined their minds, the impedance to intellectual exertion remained. Simms, as a producing writer, felt isolated in his native place. Hugh Legaré and Frederick Porcher both complained that the Charleston style had killed the intellectual drive which foreign study had stimulated in them. Edmund Ravenel, who had made a mark nationally and internationally as a conchologist, succumbed to the irresistible lure of conspicuous leisure. Resigning his professorship at the state medical college in 1835, he saddled himself with a lifelong debt to become a planter and to live the life of a gentleman amateur in the land of rounded edges.[66]

It is true that Ravenel did only what Charleston's successful professionals and merchants customarily did. It is also true that as Charleston lost population or at least failed to grow, it offered fewer attractions to professionals, little employment to scientists, and less readership for writers. The city lacked the critical mass to sustain those institutions that elsewhere promoted intellectual life. It had no equivalents for Boston's Harvard and American Academy of Arts and Sciences, or Philadelphia's University of Pennsylvania and American Philosophical Society.[67]

But to stop there is to overlook the degree to which Charlestonians' perceptions inhibited even their quest for such institutions. Their inclusive democracy, as physician Samuel Dickson lamented, blurred "the distinctions which divide the wise from the foolish . . . the well-informed from the ignorant."[68] Their preference for rounded edges and gentlemanly amateurism diverted those who might otherwise have been driven to discover and excel. Their agricultural economy and their labor system not only made them fear the consequences of new ideas vigorously pursued but left them short of the resources with which to endow an institutional framework for a diversely creative intellectual life.

Finally, all these factors contributed to a quasi-colonial mentality, to unsettling doubts about the quality of the culture. Yankees too were stung by unfavorable comparisons with Europe, by that scornfully asked question, "Who reads an American book?" Yet viewed from the perspective of Boston, the price of self-doubt that Charleston paid for its soft style becomes even clearer. Citizens of the hub city did not send their children south to be educated; nor did its writers send their manuscripts to Charleston or New Orleans to be published. When Boston's youth or books and magazines went south, it was to teach rather than to learn, to proffer expertise rather than to seek recognition. This very self-confidence was what made Northerners simultaneously welcome and unwelcome in Charleston. At issue was a pervasive unease. Though Charlestonians valued education, pursued science, and admired the arts, they doubted their own ability to excel and their society's commitment to intellectual achievement.

9

Slave cottages west of Charleston, from Hall, B. MSS no. 65, Manuscripts Department, Lilly Library, Indiana University, Bloomington, Indiana. Capt. Basil Hall (1788–1844) was the British author of Travels in North America in the Years 1827 and 1828 (London and Edinburgh, 1829).

"If You Ain't Got Education": Slave Language and Slave Thought in Antebellum Charleston

CHARLES JOYNER

H‍E BEGAN softly, conversationally, almost like a white man. His voice was cool and level. Slowly and gradually at first, in a carefully measured way, he built toward a more rhythmic, more powerful progression.

> O Gawd,
> I know de time ain' long

> When my room gwine be lak a public hall,
> My face gwine be lak a lookin' glass
> An' my teet'll be shet 'gainst a silence.

The slaves in the congregation did not receive his words passively. As the rhythm rose and fell, they became participants as well. "Amen!" "Yes, Lord!" "Yes, Jesus!" "Yes! Yes!" They fanned themselves rhythmically; a few feet began to pat. Under the influence of congregational response, the preacher built steadily.

> No mo' breat'll heave een my breas';
> My han's'll be col' an' empty,
> An' be layin folded pun-top 'em.
> Dese ol' feet'll be tu'n todes de wes'.
> Tain' no use den fo' my eyes to crack dey-se'f open.

"Preach the sermon!" someone shouted. "Yes, Lord!" "Yes, Jesus!" "Yes!" The preacher began to pace back and forth, raising his hands. Relying heavily on tone, on gesture, on rhythm, he preached a sermon defiant enough to release pent-up frustrations among the slave community, although not so incendiary as to stir hopeless revolts or so obvious as to bring down the wrath of the masters upon their heads.

> De life ob a man is same lak de pat' ob de sun.
> Een de mawnin' 'e rise up bright een de east—
> Ebyting look shine an' beautiful.
> 'E soon sta't plowin' 'e furrow 'cross de element ob de sky.

As he moved his congregation towards a crescendo of exaltation, he broke into a chant. The response was no longer confined to antiphonal amens but included shouts and cries, the clapping of hands and the stamping of feet, and the indescribable sounds of religious transcendence. The congregation worshipped with soul and body in unison.

> 'E strong, 'e brabe—
> When de cloud come stan' een 'e way, 'e fight 'em.
> 'E knock (e,—'e ain' faid);
> De lightnin' flash een 'e han'
> Tell de cloud fall down een rain.

Someone started humming a mournful air. The humming spread throughout the congregation. The slaves' bodies rocked, their heads nodded, their hands clapped, and their feet stamped a steady rhythm, pushing the preacher onward.

> But de time haffer come w'en 'e strengt' gwine fail.
> 'E ceasted f'om climbin higher.
> 'E sta't fo' drap todes de wes'.
> 'E moan tell de sky tu'n red.
> But 'e haffer go to 'e res'.
> 'E sink.
> 'E gone.
> 'E gone down behime de hill.
> De hill whe' de pine trees is t'ick,
> De hill whe' de night be's black.

The congregational response was essential to worship, a religious requirement. Just as in Africa, such antiphony exemplified the solidarity of the community while the sermon called forth the profoundest expression of the individual, neither I-Thou nor I-you, but the sacred link between the individual and the social body. The slaves *had* to talk back to the sermon. The preacher had not come to give his own opinions; he had come to preach the word of God to a people who refused to be passive and uncritical receptors.

> Dey's pine trees a waitin yonder now
> Fo drap pine needles ober my grabe.
> Oh, Lawd! dat's de time!
> My hea't git weak w'en I t'ink on 'em—
> Dat how-come I down on my knees!
> Fader, stan' by me den!
> Be a light on da da'k crooked pat';
> Be a shade f'om da' hot bunnin' sun;
> Be a bridge fo' me ober deep water;
> Hol' my han' tell I git across,
> Till I git Home![1]

A white who might have witnessed such a religious service in antebellum Charleston, or on one of the nearby plantations, would undoubtedly have found it difficult to conceive of intellectual life among the slaves. How could there be intellectual life among illiterates who could not even *speak* proper English? Both law and custom in antebellum South Carolina conspired to keep slaves illiterate. Former slave

257

Elijah Green testified in the 1930s, "An' do for God's sake don' let a slave be catch with pencil an' paper. That was a major crime. You might as well had kill your master or missus." Henry Brown, another Charleston exslave, added that for such an offense "in slavery he would be whip' 'til not a skin was lef' on his body."[2]

But not only were the slaves mostly illiterate; few of them even spoke what the whites regarded as "proper" English. Visitors like Edward King reported that "the lowland negro of South Carolina has a barbaric dialect. The English words seem to tumble all at once from his mouth and to get sadly mixed whenever he endeavors to speak." Most Charlestonians believed that such speech represented the deterioration of eighteenth-century English through the mental indolence of the slaves, the imperfect result of what John Bennett called "a savage and primitive people's endeavor to acquire for themselves the highly organized language of a very highly civilized race."[3]

It was not easy for commonsensical Charlestonians, untrained in phenomenology, biased toward empiricism, to imagine intellectual life among a people unable to read, write, or speak "proper" English. Written language was presumed to be the indispensable common denominator in all human thought. But oral language may also serve the intellect; contemporary sociolinguists have discovered that vernacular speech in oral exchanges can serve purposes of high seriousness. Literacy has not always been considered a defining criterion for intellectual activity. The discourses of Socrates were communicated to posterity by means of writing, but Socrates' thought was developed in oral dialogue. In the present age of growing centralization of newspapers, magazines, and publishing houses, it is at least arguable that literacy has as much potential for trivializing intellectual life as for enriching it. Intellectual life is not, after all, a matter of accumulated information but a matter of thought. The intellectual life of Charleston's slaves should be seen not as a canon of shared information but as a pattern of shared meanings. To understand their consciousness and reflection, one should begin with the distinctively human element, should see human beings as symbolizing, conceptualizing, meaning-seeking animals. Inquiry should be redirected from an exclusive preoccupation with erudition and the means of its dissemination. It should also include analysis of the organization and capabilities of human faculties and the services they afford—through language—to the knowledge of ordinary people in everyday contexts. As one black Carolinian, whose mother was born

a slave on a lowcountry rice plantation, told me, "If you ain't got education, you have to use your brain."[4]

*   *   *

It is now understood by linguists that the language of Charleston's
slaves resulted from the convergence of a number of African languages
with English. The intricate process by which a language based on the
convergence of other languages undergoes expansion in both use and
form is called creolization. Creole languages became widespread among
slaves in the New World. Afro-Portuguese creoles developed in Brazil
and Curaçao; Afro-Spanish creoles in Cuba, Puerto Rico, and Colombia; Afro-French creoles in Louisiana, French Guiana, Haiti, Guadaloupe, and Grenada; an Afro-Dutch creole in the Virgin Islands; and
Afro-English creoles in Barbados, Antigua, Guyana, Jamaica, Surinam,
Georgia, and South Carolina. By various devices of sound and syntax,
semantics and lexicon, gesture and intonation, Charleston's slaves—
like their counterparts of the lowcountry plantations—combined elements of their various African languages to create a new creole language. The South Carolina creole was, and is, called Gullah. The slaves
of Charleston belonged to a distinctive speech community that stretched
southward from Georgetown District through Charleston to Beaufort
District and on into coastal Georgia.[5]

While the vocabulary of Gullah was largely (but not exclusively)
English, as a language Gullah did not behave like English. Its grammatical rules were different. Gullah pronouns in antebellum Charleston were no respecters of person, using an all-purpose pronoun for
masculine, feminine, and neuter forms. In this behavior Gullah retained
a grammatical structure common to several African languages, notably Ibo, Ga, and Yoruba. The initial all-purpose Gullah pronoun was
e, as in the following:

"Any time any one say *e* hab fish it wus understood *e* mean cow meat."
(Any time anyone said he had fish it was understood he meant cow meat.)

"Ole hag, '*e* does come in de house, en peeps et yuh, gits on yuh en
rides yuh." (Old hag, she comes in the house and peeps at you, gets
on you, and rides you [gives you nightmares].)

"My master house been beautiful—'*e* dey yet!" (My master's house was
beautiful—it is there yet!)

E was also used to indicate possession.

"One time man tek *e* gun gone out huntin'." (One time a man took his gun and went out hunting.)[6]

Later, under the ever-present influence of English, *he* replaced *e* as the all-purpose Gullah pronoun (although *e* was not completely replaced during the slavery period, when the last generation of slaves was learning to speak the language). The Gullah pronoun *he* was not the same, however, as the English pronoun. *He* served in Gullah as the form for masculine, feminine, or neuter gender. Interchangeable with *e*, *he* could serve as subject or indicate possession:

"I going to keep dis. *He* jest fit me." (I am going to keep this [coat]. It just fits me.)

"Yes, Ma'am, *he* name Rachel, and *he* lick we." (Yes, Ma'am, her name was Rachel, and she licked us.)

"When Mosser call fer *he* fine likker to hand 'round, John came back and tell him all gone." (When the master called for his fine liquor to hand around, John came back and told him it was all gone.)

Occasionally, both the older form *e* and the newer form *he* would occur in the same sentence:

"*He* say '*e* tired see colored mans wuk hard an' git nuttin'." (He said he was tired of seeing colored men work hard and get nothing.)

Him was also sometimes used interchangeably with *e* and *he*:

"*Him* ain't no man, *him* my grand daughter, Ellen Jenkins." (She is not a man, she is my granddaughter, Ellen Jenkins.)[7]

The Gullah pronoun form for the objective case in Charleston—and throughout the lowcountry—was *um* (or '*em*), which served for masculine, feminine, and neuter gender, whether singular or plural:

"Mausa t'ink uh lot of *um*, 'cause he been uh good field hand." (The master thought a lot of him, because he was a good field hand.)

"De Mausa would come and say 'Where Jennie,' tell *um* to put clothes on dat baby, I want *um*. He sell de baby and de ma scream and holler." (The master would come and say, "Where is Jennie?" He would tell her to put clothes on that baby, I want it. He sold the baby. . . .)

"I keep muh co'n and grain nuts in yuh so mah eye can sta' on '*em*." (I keep my corn and grain nuts in here so my eye can stay on them.)

"Him duh hide een de bus en see de b'ar eat *um* up, hide, huf, en haiah." (He is hiding in the bushes and sees the bear eat it up, hide, hoof, and hair.)[8]

We was the all-purpose first person plural pronoun, serving as subject, object, or possessive:

"*We* put um in *we* pan.

"Dey give *we* clabba and cow peas and ting out de garden." (They gave us clabber and cow peas and things from the garden.)[9]

Gullah pronouns of the period were more complex than English pronouns in one respect, however: they included a form for second person plural—*yinneh* or *oona*:

"I say, 'Come on *yinneh* boy, less we git um out ob de groun' for bukra riscober we." (I said, "Come on you boys, let us get it out of the ground before the whites discover us.)

"If *oona* duh dey de dee duh no de dey; ef *oona* no duh dey de dee dey dey." (If [all of] you are there, the deer will not be there; if [all of] you are not there, the deer will be there.)

"Mausa come and he say: '*Who-na* nigger take care of yourself, I must leab to take my fambly away.'" (The master came and he said: [All of] you Negroes take care of yourselves, I must leave to take my family away.)[10]

The slaves of Charleston and the lowcountry had two other distinctive features in their nominal system. One was that they marked possession by juxtaposition:

"I stayin here with my youngest *sister chile*—youngest son." (I am staying here with my youngest sister's child—her youngest son.)

"I go up to *Mausa house* ebery day for de milk for we." (I go up to the master's house every day for our milk.)[11]

The other distinctive feature was the slave's practice of nonredundant pluralization, which stood in sharp contrast to the English requirement that determiners and the nouns they modify should agree in number:

"Old nigger been live on de place cut *all dem tree* down." (An old Negro who lived on the place cut all those trees down.)

"What been more old John play fer *all de dance* on the plantation." (What is more, old John played for all the dances on the plantation.)

"Old John den gather up *five ax*, and go to de *five tree* layin down on de ground." (Old John then gathered up five axes and went to the five trees lying down on the ground.)

"Dat bery same hag ride me fuh *thirty-t'ree night*." (That very same hag rode me for thirty-three nights.)

"My wife, she 'bout *sickty-fibe year* ole." (My wife is about sixty-five years old.)[12]

The prepositions of Gullah speech in the lowcountry used the same forms for approach prepositions (for going somewhere) and for static-locative prepositions (for already being there):

"W'en Fort Sumter was fired on mossa carried seventy of us *to* Greenville, South Ca'lina." (When Fort Sumter was fired on, master carried seventy of us to Greenville, South Carolina.)

"De fust year after freedom I gone to school on Mr. John Townsend place, down *to* Rockville." (The first year after freedom I went to school on Mr. John Townsend's place, down at Rockville.)[13]

If the slaves' nominal system was somewhat simpler, their verbal system was considerably more complex than that of English, from which it differed in several ways. First of all, equating verbs occurred in past tense but were usually omitted in present tense:

"*It been* a cold *day*." (It was a cold day.)

"Dem *Yankee* wicked *kind* a people, drive me from my home." (Those Yankees were a wicked kind of people, to drive me from my home.)

The slaves of Charleston also used zero copula (the omission of an equating verb) for verbal adjectives:

"*I old* now but I ain't forgit what my missus larn me." (I am old now, but I have not forgotten what my mistress taught me.)

"T'aint many people left now kin tell 'bout dat time. *Eberybody dead*." (There are not many people left now who can tell about that time. Everybody is dead.)

In this regard, Gullah retained the verbal adjective construction of several West African languages, including Ewe, Fante, Kikongo, and Yoruba.[14]

Another Gullah construction that retained West African linguistic forms was the combination of verbs both to take an object and to serve as a connective:

> "One gentman at de gate *tell me say* he Messus broder, is Messus dare in? (A gentleman at the gate told me that he is the mistress's brother. Is the mistress therein?)
>
> "I *hear tell* my boy William been marry to a w'ite 'ooman in England and hab t'ree chillen." (I heard that my boy William was married to a white woman in England and had three children.)

This usage retained both form and function of the construction in Ibo and Twi.[15]

The most distinctive feature of the verbal system of Charleston's slaves was its sophisticated time sense. Rather than specifying the relative time of action (*tense* in English), the slaves distinguished between continuing actions and momentary or completed actions (or *aspect*), reflecting a deeper distinction between time as duration and time as sequence. The slaves rarely marked past tense in Gullah; when they did they used the verb-form *been*:

> "When dem boat come up de ribber . . . dat *been* de awful time." (When those boats came up the river, that was the awful time.)
>
> "I *been* right here when de Yankees come through." (I was right here when the Yankees came through.)

Past completed actions the slaves marked with *done* plus the verb.

> "De time *done pass* when dis generation hold with any'ting but de debbul." (The time has already passed when this generation holds with anything but the devil.)
>
> "But John *done promise* some nigger on Fenwick Island to play fer uh dance." (But John had already promised some Negro on Fenwick Island to play for a dance.)

If the slaves only occasionally marked past tense, they typically marked aspect, whether ongoing, completed, or habitual. They indicated continuing actions by using the old creole form *duh* preceding the verb or the newer, somewhat decreolized form-*ing* following the verb.

> "Him *duh hide* een de bus en see de b'ar eat um up, hide, huf, en haiah." (He is hiding in the bushes and sees the bear eat it up, hide, hoof, and hair.)

263

"You *getting* this beating not for you task—for you flesh!" (You are getting this beating not for [failing to finish] your task, [but] for your flesh!)

The slaves of Charleston indicated continuing actions in the past by using *been* plus the action verb:

"I *been livin'* in Beaufort when de war fust break out." (I was living in Beaufort when the war first broke out.)

"T'ing *bin goin'* too good." (Things were going very well.)

Habitual actions, past or present, the slaves marked with *be* plus the action verb:

"You orter *be carry* money with you." (You ought [habitually] to carry money with you.)

In their emphasis on aspect over tense, the slaves of Charleston retained the grammatical rules of such West African languages as Ewe, Kimbundu, Mandinka, and Yoruba.[16]

Gullah speakers also distinguished between ongoing and momentary negation in their verbal system. Momentary negation was indicated by *ain't*:

"I *ain't know* cause dem as could fly flew home." (I do not know, because those who could fly flew home.)

Charleston slaves marked ongoing negation by *didn't* (for past ongoing negation) or by *don't* (for present ongoing negation):

"I *didn't hab* nothing to boder my mind and mek me remember dose days." (I didn't have anything to bother my mind and make me remember those days.)

"I ain't know whut uh ghos' want wid obercoat cause dey *don'* wear no clothes." (I don't know what a ghost wants with an overcoat because they don't wear any clothes.)

Multiple negation was often used by the slaves for additional emphasis:

"I *ain't scarcely* know w'at fuh do." (I scarcely knew what to do.)

"She say she *never couldn't* refuse when the old people ask for a drink." (She said she could never refuse when the old people asked for a drink.)[17]

Thus the slaves of Charleston spoke a language that differed from English in a number of fundamental features but did not lack a regular

264

structure of its own. Gullah speakers distinguished neither among genders in their pronouns nor between location and approach in their prepositions. They indicated pluralization only once in a sentence, not redundantly, but they used distinctive forms of the second person pronoun to distinguish between singular and plural. They designated possession by juxtaposition. Their use of equating verbs was varied, but they combined other verbs in distinctive ways. Both verbs and negators distinguished between ongoing and momentary actions rather than when those actions might have taken place. And negation could be intensified by using multiple negators. These linguistic features were quite regular.

Not only did Gullah follow a different set of grammatical rules; it also manifested different intonation patterns, defined eloquence differently, and placed a different valuation on the role of the "man-of-words," all of which manifested continuities with African linguistic patterns creatively adapted to a new social and linguistic environment. Those white Charlestonians and their guests who considered Gullah to be an imperfect imitation of English were mistaken. While English and Gullah may have shared much of the same vocabulary, grammatically and sociolinguistically they were not the same language at all.[18]

It is now clear that the slaves — a people of diverse linguistic backgrounds and limited opportunities — did not "fail" to adopt the language of their masters; rather they "succeeded" in creating a creole language. Gullah represents not divergence from English but convergence of various African and European linguistic features. A speech community, even more than a political community, implies shared culture and shared world view. To understand Gullah within the context of its functioning social relations, one must recognize that shared categories of thought are not only a function of but also a prerequisite for intellectual activity. Gullah, the shared property of everyone in the speech community, was loaded with the symbols of that community's cultural values. The slaves of Charleston could not communicate with one another without using the symbols held in common by the community and embodied in their language. Thus Gullah became the principle channel of intellectual activity.[19]

Language was, of course, only one aspect of the transformation of African culture into Afro-American culture, but the process of linguistic change provides a model for explaining other aspects of culture change. What might be called the "creolization of culture" involves the unconscious "grammatical" principles of culture—the "deep structure" that generates specific cultural patterns. Such "grammatical" principles survived the middle passage and governed the selective adaptation of elements of both African and European culture.

*   *   *

The ethos of Charleston's slaves—their ethical and aesthetic style, the quality and character of their intellectual lives—was perhaps best synthesized in the religion they created out of the creolization of African and European elements. Their religion shaped their world view as much as reflected it. The religion of the slaves reveals both their mental picture of the unalterable shape of reality and their deepest, most comprehensive concepts of cosmic order. For them religion functioned to portray their ethical and aesthetic preferences as normative—given the imposed conditions of reality—while at the same time it undergirded such preferences by invoking deeply felt ethical and aesthetic beliefs as evidence of their truth. The African contribution to Afro-Christianity was enormous. The slaves did not simply adopt the God and the faith of the white missionaries. In establishing a spiritual life for themselves, they reinterpreted the elements of Christianity that they learned from the whites in terms of deep-rooted African cognitive orientations. Africa was not culturally homogeneous, nor did it bequeath to its exiles in the African diaspora a legacy of static survivals. In fact, religious expression in Africa was diverse, and borrowings among ethnic groups were common. Rising above the variety of rites and practices, however, was a shared bond—a concept of the sacred cosmos in which virtually all experience, from the naming of children to beliefs about when to plant and how to hunt and fish, was religious. Underlying those African cultures were shared cognitive (or "grammatical") orientations—mental rules governing appropriate behavior—that profoundly affected the slaves' adoption, adaptation, and application of Christianity.[20] The fragmentation of a unified African religion into separate streams was especially marked among the slaves of Charleston and the lowcountry.

One stream of inherited African cosmology included ideas regarding polytheism, rebirth, and spirit possession in religious ritual. This stream converged with elements of Christianity to create an influential new religion. Afro-Christianity was the result of the creolization of African and European religious orientations. Examination of the Chris-

266

tianity evangelized to the slaves may thus provide some perspective on the process by which Charleston slaves mixed both elements and by which they adapted both to the realities of slave life. The originality of Afro-Christianity, then, lies neither in its African elements nor in its Christian elements, but in its unique and creative synthesis of both.

Early lowcountry planters had reluctantly tolerated missionary efforts among their slaves. A former slave described the attitudes of South Carolina planters at the dawn of the nineteenth century: "There has always been a strong repugnance amongst the planters, against their slaves becoming members of any religious society," he wrote. "They fear the slaves, by attending the meetings, and listening to the preachers may imbibe the morality they teach, the notions of equality and liberty, maintained in the gospel." Some planters doubted that the Charleston ministry could be depended upon to defend slavery. "The abolition measures have excited such a spirit of jealousy and suspicion that some planters will not listen to the introduction of religion on their places," wrote one Charleston clergyman in 1836. Gradually, however, at least some ministers won the trust of the slaveholders and began missionary work among the slaves. Charleston ex-slave Henry Brown recalled that his master's slaves "went to meeting two nights a week and on Sunday they went to Church, where they had a white preacher Dr. Rose hired to preach to them." Increasingly, slave church-going began to meet with the approval of the masters, many of whom believed that slavery was sustained rather than threatened by religion. On his deathbed one Charleston master beseeched his children, "I wish you also to give all the indulgence you possibly can to the negroes in going to Church, and making them repeat their questions, for this reason that if neglected we will have to answer for the loss of their souls." In late antebellum Charleston, increased attention was given to slave religion, especially to its *content*.[21]

Slaveholders supported religious instruction partly out of sincere Christian concern for the salvation of the slaves. The Christianity they disseminated, however, was very selective, emphasizing obedience in the here and now as much as salvation in the hereafter. Many felt that the slaves were going to get religion whether their masters liked it or not, so making that religion safe for slavery became a matter of high priority. Robert F.W. Allston, from his palatial residence at 51 Meeting Street, described his slaves as "attentive to religious instruction, and greatly improved in intelligence and morals, in domestic relations, etc.

267

. . . Indeed, the degree of intelligence which as a class they are acquiring is worthy of deep consideration." If the planters evidenced a genuine concern for their slaves' spiritual welfare, they also recognized that religion was a more subtle, more humane, and more effective means of control than the whip.[22]

It would be untrue to suggest that Charleston slaveholders cynically reduced Christianity to patience, humility, and the fear of sin, or that they were more concerned with the discipline of slaves than with the salvation of souls. As James Henley Thornwell insisted, "In our philosophy, right is the highest expediency, and obedience to God the firmest security of communities as well as individuals. We have not sought the protection of our property in the debasement of our species; we have not maintained our own interests in this world, by the deliberate sacrifice of the eternal interests of the thousands who look to us for the way to salvation." Slaveholders were convinced, however, that preaching had a significant effect on slave discipline, and ministers went out of their way to appease the slaveholders by approaching slave religion with the utmost discretion. The masters knew that so long as the slaves were listening to a trusted white preacher, they could not (at least for the moment) be listening to a subversive black one.[23]

White preachers had to face the dilemma that their Christianity was—at least potentially—subversive of slavery. During the 1834 legislative debate over the prohibition on teaching slaves to read and write, Whitemarsh Seabrook noted that anyone who wanted slaves to read the *entire* Bible belonged in "a room in the Lunatic Asylum." To be fair, the ministers were not mere sycophants of cynical slaveholders. They did not select only the texts that promoted order and discipline among the slaves. But they could hardly help realizing that if religion promoted order among the slaves, it also contained the seeds of disorder. They certainly would not preach to their congregations that Pharoah had enslaved the children of Israel and held them in bondage in Egypt, that the Lord then visited plagues on the slaveholders, or that Moses led the slaves in a mass escape out of bondage in Egypt to the Promised Land.[24]

If the white ministers shied away from scriptural passages with clear analogies to the condition of the slaves, they did preach the equality of all in the sight of God and the equality of universal sinfulness. The Rev. James Henley Thornwell put it thus:

> It is a publick testimony to our faith, that the Negro is of one blood with ourselves — that he has sinned as we have, and that he has an equal interest with us in the great redemption. Science, falsely so-called, may attempt to exclude him from the brotherhood of humanity. Men may be seeking eminence and distinction by arguments which link them with the brute; but the instinctive impulses of our nature, combined with the plainest declarations of the word of God, lead us to recognize in his form and lineaments — in his moral, religious, and intellectual nature — the same humanity in which we glory as the image of God. We are not ashamed to call him our brother.

Christianity, such ministers preached, imposed obligations not just on the slaves but on their earthly masters as well. Both master and slave on this earth would be held to the same account before the heavenly master. As the Bible taught servants to obey their masters, they preached, so it required masters to rule their servants wisely, and it required the rich to use their riches to do good.[25]

Thus was the dilemma posed: as Christians, slaveholders were committed to the religious instruction of their slaves, but the religion preached to the slaves also called the masters to account. Masters were as subject as slaves to the requirements of Christianity. That created a problem of role boundaries and emphasized tensions and anomalies within the institution that could not easily be ignored. Governor Robert F.W. Allston believed that the "best inducement to keep the slaves both Christian and quiescent" was "example on our own part; next a just, consistent, systematic administration of domestic government."[26]

In Charleston, far from the African context of their sacred cosmos, the slaves worshipped their new Christian God with the kind of expressive behavior their African heritage taught them was appropriate for an important deity. African expressive behavior persisting in slave religion manifested itself in a high degree of emotionalism in worship, especially the use of dances and chants to rhythmic accompaniment, leading to trances and spirit possession. The phenomenon of spirit possession, one of the most significant features in African religion (especially pronounced among the Bantu, the Yoruba, and the Fante-Ashanti), was reinterpreted in Christian terms to become a central feature of expressive behavior in Afro-Christianity, a necessary part of the conversion experience. Conversion was the climax of a spiritual journey called "seeking." The seeker's prolonged praying and meditating induced an ecstatic trance without which conversion was not considered authentic. Not until one had experienced spirit possession was one accepted as a church member; others were still regarded as sinners.[27]

Slave families often went to one another's houses at night to hold prayer meetings, to sing, and to "shout." The shout was often described as a dance by white observers. Frederika Bremer, a Swedish visitor to Charleston and the lowcountry, reported having heard that "the Methodist missionaries, who are the most influential and effective teachers and preachers among the negroes, are very angry with them for their love of dancing and music, and declare them to be sinful." Such hostility seemed to her "a very unwise proceeding on the part of the preachers. Are not all God's gifts good, and may they not be made use of in His honor? And why should not this people, by nature joyous and childlike, worship God in gladness? I would, instead, let them have sacred dances, and let them sing to them joyful songs of praise in the beautiful air, beneath the blossoming trees. Did not King David dance and sing in pious rapture before the ark of God?" Exemplifying the creative Afro-Carolinian adaptation of the West African ring "dance," which was performed to complex drum rhythms, the shout—after the African *saut*, meaning to walk or run around—consisted of body motions performed to the accompaniment of spirituals. The drums, upon which Africans articulated their spiritual life, were mostly lost in antebellum Charleston, but slaves improvised a substitute with polyrhythmic handclapping and foot-stamping. Such expressive behavior was widespread among blacks in the Caribbean as well as in the South Carolina lowcountry. While slave Christians typically deprecated dancing itself, they "shouted" with great enthusiasm.[28]

When slave Christians gathered for praise meetings at one another's quarters, the soaring rhetoric of the prayers, the antiphonal singing, and the ecstatic shouts provided a release for pent-up emotions. The praise-meeting style of worship led some whites to lament that slave congregations could be moved only by black ministers. That was not entirely true, but the Rev. Paul Trapier admitted that "with the present tastes of our city congregations, it would be no easy matter for any pastor so to minister from the pulpit as to instruct and move the servant at once and the master; and we agree that, until that is done, the wishes and wants of the superior must be chiefly regarded, and the inferior left, in consequence, with little to attract him to a Gospel which, however congenial essentially to the yearnings of his soul, is, in the form of its presentation, not adapted to his comprehension." For the slaves, religious services constituted not a relationship between a performer and an audience but a mutual performance. Just as the spirituals were marked by the strong call-and-response antiphony of African music, so prayers and sermons were punctuated by congregational responses.[29]

A second stream of African cosmology, the ancient African distinction between hags and haunts, proved less compatible with Afro-Christianity. Haunts were spirits of the dead who had returned to harass the living: a modified Afro-Carolinian version of the Congo *zumbi* or the Haitian *zombi*. Hags, or "boo hags," were the disembodied spirits of witches or conjure men, who were said to release their astral bodies at night and send them about the earth to "ride" (give nightmares to) people who had aroused their ire. Even more horrible were those malevolent, shape-changing spirits called "plat-eyes." Such beliefs were neither abandoned by slave Christians nor quite incorporated into Afro-Christianity. Hags, haunts, and plat-eyes persisted in a parallel stream of belief.[30]

Hags—or boo hags—were especially bothersome creatures; they were believed able to fly through the air to midnight rendezvous, and to sail through keyholes by placing a black cat bone in their mouths. It was said that a hag could bewitch a person merely by looking at the victim. Slaves could take precautions, however, to keep hags from riding them: conjure balls (hair balls filled with roots, herbs, and other substances) were sometimes successful in keeping them at bay. But the only certain preventive was to eliminate the hag. That could best be done by the traditional African method of salting and peppering her skin while she had left it behind to go out "hagging."[31]

Slave opinion was divided as to whether haunts were more fearsome creatures than hags. The slaves of Charleston seemed to agree that no haunts ever helped people and that they returned to earth for malevolent purposes, frightening the good and bad alike. Still, haunts did not physically assault humans or do them bodily harm (although they sometimes caused humans to do themselves bodily harm). Some slaves were said to be able to hear and feel haunts but not see them; others could see but not hear them; still others could see, feel and converse with the spirits. "Ghosts? I'se met plenty of um!" recalled ex-slave Solbert Butler.

271

When I wuz courtin' I met many a one—One got me in de water, once. And another time when I wuz crossing a stream, I wuz on de butt end of de log, an' dey wuz on de blossom end, an' we met jes' as close as I is to you now. I say to him, same as to anybody, "I sure ain't goin' to turn back and fall off dis log. Now de bets t'ing for you to do is to turn 'round and let me come atter you. You jes' got to talk to 'em same as to anybody. It don't pay to be 'fraid of 'em. So he wheel 'round. (Spirits can wheel, you know.) And when he gets to de end of de log, I say, "now you off and I off. You kin go on cross now."

Slaves who reported having seen haunts described them as similar in appearance. "An' when you see 'em you see a sight," Solbert Butler affirmed. "Dey all favors, Dey all looks alike." Haunts were most likely to appear at certain times, such as a full moon, or on Friday nights when the moon was young, although they were believed also to show themselves in broad daylight at certain places. Others believed that haunts rose up in every graveyard on the stroke of twelve; one haunt—the spirit of the oldest dead—would stay behind to guard the vacated graves while the others roamed the roads, entered houses, and haunted various spots. Baby ghosts, however, were considered too small to be seen: "De speerit od dem too weak to show -em self." At "fust fowl crow" the spirits returned to their graves. At slave funerals efforts were made to contain the spirits of the ancestors; the living sought to prevent the dead from remaining behind as malign spirits.[32]

The most hideous and the most malevolent of the occult spirits of this stream of African cosmology was the plat-eye, who changed shapes at will in order to lure victims into danger and drive them out of their minds. An exslave recalled one rainy night journey on Edisto Island. Just as he reached a swamp, a little white kitten ran out in front of him. Then, to his amazement, it grew in size until it was tall as a pine tree, whereupon it began to tumble and roll over so rapidly that he could scarcely follow its movements: "De t'ing fair der pitch in front ob my eye like 'e crazy," he testified. Suddenly, the gigantic creature rolled into a nearby pond with an enormous splash, which drenched the onlooking slave; "den 'e tu'n in lee back kitney and staa't in run 'tween my leg and holler me-ow. [Then it turned into a little black kitten and started in running between by legs and hollering meow.] I contend wid dat cat 'most four hour and cuss 'um good, but it 'most been day break when 'e t'un me loose and I git home. Dat been de wust night I eber spend on dis earth."[33]

Many features of African religion either converged or coexisted with Christianity, but voodoo or hoodoo (as African conjuration was called in the New World) maintained a subterranean existence outside of and inimical to Afro-Christianity. Documentation is inevitably scanty, as such magical shamanism was practiced clandestinely. This aspect of slave religion continues to be both largely unknown and at least partly unknowable. Still, sufficient evidence remains to testify to the existence of an underground stream of magical shamanism not only throughout the slavery period but beyond.[34]

Slave conjuration involved certain rituals in which voodoo priests summoned up the spirits of the dead to offer advice or to perform cures. The process of dying, according to West African belief, was incomplete for up to five years. The spirits of the ancestors—the living dead—were considered to be the closest link between the world of the living and the world of the spirits: they were considered to straddle both worlds. Illness was regarded as supernatural in origin; thus it was necessary, through sorcery, to summon the spirits for protection. Voodoo, or hoodoo, could be used for either protective or malevolent purposes: it could cure an illness, kill an enemy, or secure someone's love. All misfortune was regarded as the result of magical shamanism, including (presumably) slavery. The only way a slave could gain protection from sorcery was by stronger countersorcery. With some variation, voodoo was known throughout the slave societies—including Charleston's—of the New World.[35]

The survival of African sorcery in South Carolina seems to have been most pronounced in the lowcountry, where slaves were concentrated in significant numbers. Voodoo grew with the arrival of slaves from the West Indies, or directly from Africa, who adapted African snake cults to a new environment. High in the African pantheon, the snake god of the Ewe, Fon, Bantu, Dahomey, Whydah, and Yoruba symbolized the cosmic energy of nature, the dealer of fortune or misfortune. The African names for the voodoo gods were lost; their personalities converged with those of Judeo-Christian prophets and saints, demons and devils. They continued to comfort believers and to wreak havoc on the wicked. Only the snake god's sorcerers could invoke his protective power. Snakeskins were prominent in initiation rituals; snake-charming was featured in some rites; and all sorts of supernatural might was attributed to serpents in the snake lore of Charleston's slaves. One of them recalled a boy's having been shown a sorcerer's bestiary of familiars as part of his initiation rites: "When de ole man lif' up de trap door de boy look down and 'e eye fair pop out 'e haid. Dere been big snake all quoll [coiled] up and big red-cow wid horn shaap sekker [shaped like a] needle. Dey all mix up monx [among] lizzard and toady frog. De snake heabe up and down conder der spit, de cow moan low. De boy nerve give way and 'e broke loose run. Ole man cuss 'um fer coward, but de boy ain' cum back. 'E tak[e] strong man tuh follow dem kind of trade, yas suh."[36]

Voodoo in Charleston never approached the complexities of Haitian Vodun; nevertheless, it would appear to have achieved a distinctive character above the level of simple, unorganized sorcery. More of Charleston's slaves took their physical or personal problems to local conjurers—the priests of the old religion—than to their masters. Such conjurers often enjoyed considerable power within the slave community, even among some of the Christians. They were spoken of with great awe; some were considered invulnerable; and no feat of black magic was considered beyond their ability to perform. As one exslave commented, "Ain't so positive 'bout now, but de old Rebel time been awful cunning." Conjurers gained and held their influence over the slaves by various methods, especially by fear. Their patrons relied upon them for both protection and relief from spells and for casting spells upon their enemies.[37]

The status of sorcerers was occasionally inherited; parents liked to pass on their arcane powers to their offspring, whom they would train to take their place. More typically, however, a sorcerer's powers resulted from some peculiar circumstance of birth, such as being born with a caul. Babies born with a caul over the face were considered to be "gifted" with second sight. Such children, for better or worse, would always be able to see spirits and other supernatural phenomena. "You have to be born to see 'em," an exslave testified. "If'n you be born wrapped in de caul, you kin see 'em. But if you ain't, you can't see 'em." Thus "gifted" sorcerers were reputed to have known in advance who was coming to them, and to be able to read a question in the visitor's mind and reply before it was asked.[38]

The sorcerers made use of various combinations of common and uncommon substances believed to have magical powers, such as "conjer balls," "green bush" (to be placed under a residence), snakeskin, crab claws, graveyard dirt, and black cat bones. An African-born slave conjurer was said to have carried a little black bag containing bat wings, frog livers, and human bones on his person at all times. He swore that he could fly back to Africa any time he wished. A striking defensive charm was the use of "logfire" (phosphorus) as protection against "conjer horses." As one story has it, just as a conjure-horse was bearing down upon a slave, ready to pound him into the earth, the slave reached into his pocket and drew forth a piece of logfire. The horse stood still in the air, then wheeled around and galloped off in the opposite direction.[39]

Not all of the sorcerer's spells were malign. If conjurers were considered the source of most misfortunes, they were also held in high esteem as healers. So long as the white man's medicine was regarded with suspicion, the sorcerers were assured of patients; moreover, the positive role played by the sorcerers in treating slave illnesses demonstrates the role religion played in every aspect of life among the slaves. Voodoo allowed slaves the exalted feeling of direct contact with the supernatural in attempting to cope with their ailments. Depending upon their diagnosis, the conjurers might take a pharmaceutical approach to treatment: their highly esteemed African pharmacopoeia had accompanied slaves to Charleston as part of their oral traditions. There they had found the semitropical environment sufficiently similar to that of West Africa that their pharmaceutical knowledge was easily adapted to somewhat new flora. But other ailments might call for a sort of psychotherapy, as expressed in divination. An exslave recalled his father's experience with a sorcerer:

> Pa axed me to go long wid him, 'cause he been bery weak and so I go. We gits to dis here man's house, and find him setting down by de fire stirring he pot. Pa and him talk and talk, and by-by he axed Pa if he got any silver. . . . He make Pa stand up straight and place saucer by he foot . . . and de man go to de next room and bring out one of dem big cow horn, and place um under Pa's arm. Den he put whiskey in de saucer and stir um round wid stick, and put some in he own mout'. He press de horn close and tell Pa to look down at de saucer. Yes, suh, I been watching him close. He say something or todder, might be prays, and please God a rat jump out of Pa body and run roun de room!
> De man pray 'gain and den a lizzard run out from Pa leg. Pa been scare I tell you and I been scared too. "You tru," Pa holler. "No," say de man. . . . De man take de horn and place um on Pa belly, and great God a toad frog hop out! I git scared den sure 'nough and run home. . . . When Pa does come home, he say he feel some better and next morn-

ing he just as spry as me, and I been young man den. Rebel time people
—no use for talk. Dey sure know dere business all right, all right.

If a sickness had been caused by sorcery, the evil spell could be removed
by countersorcery. Conjurers sometimes turned spells back upon their
perpetrators, and occasionally they even attempted to "lay a trick" on
the master or overseer.[40]

Not all of Charleston's slaves believed in magical shamanism; the
sorcerers neither commanded universal adherence nor approached the
political power of the priests of Obeah, Myalism, or Vodun in the West
Indies. Most Christian slaves—if they did not summarily reject the appeal of sorcery—considered the shaman's powers to be evil, hostile to
the spirit of Christianity. Nevertheless conjurors exercised an extraordinary influence over the lives of other slaves that they could neither
have gained nor maintained if they had not fulfilled a real function.
Even if considered frauds and extortionists, sorcerers served their fellow slaves in time of suffering. They were interpreters of those unob-
servable spirits whose activities directed everyday life; they were awesome beings whose supernatural powers could be enlisted in the redress
of grievances. Gullah Jack, one of the organizers of the Denmark Vesey
plot, enlisted his occult powers in the cause of the slave revolt. One
of the rebels testified: "He gave me some dry food, consisting of parched
corn and ground nuts, and said eat that and nothing else on the morning it breaks out, and when you join us as we pass put into your mouth
this crab claw and you can't then be wounded, and said he, I give the
same to the rest of my troops—if you drop the large crab-claw out of
your mouth, then put in the small one." For the slaves of Charleston
and the surrounding lowcountry, their sorcerers bridged the precari-
ous life of servitude in this world and the mysteries of the spirit world.
They tuned human behavior to a perceived cosmic order and projected
images of that order onto the plane of the slaves' everyday experience.
They created a buffer against mental and emotional submission to the
slave system for even the most credulous slaves. Many—perhaps most—of
the slaves abandoned shamanistic traditions, but those who held tenaciously to their beliefs, by helping to preserve and extend an
autonomous African heritage, made an important contribution to community and survival.[41]

Thus was a once-unified religious cosmology fragmented into various, and sometimes divergent, streams. As one might expect, adher-

276

ence to the various components was by no means uniform. Some Charleston slaves abandoned belief in all forms of non-Christian supernaturalism; many selectively adhered to some beliefs and abandoned others.[42]

To Charleston's Christian slaves, the slave preachers were men of status. "My pa was a preacher why I become a Christian so early," testified one. "He used to tell us of hell an' how hot it is. I was so afraid of hell 'till I was always tryin' to do the right thing so I couldn't go to that terrible place." The slave preachers' continuing importance as men-of-words exemplified another adaptation of African traditions to Afro-Christianity. Utilizing ritualized language and behavior as symbolic action, they transformed religious ritual through transcendental ecstasy into structured meaning, renewing and recycling the energies of the slave community. Such "gifted" men, straddling the sacred and secular worlds, were believed to exercise sacred powers within the secular domain. They often mediated between the slaves' Christian beliefs and the workaday world of Charleston. The role they played as arbiters in settling disputes among the slaves was itself a product of their African heritage of religion's involvement in everyday life. Through such mediation they not only promoted social order (one of the motives of white missionaries) but also played a major role in solidifying a sense of community among the slaves. In addition, as strong cultural personalities whose identities did not depend upon their positions as slaves, they served younger slaves as important role models.[43]

Yet slave preachers also tended to sow seeds of discontent. The spiritual life of slaves was largely hidden from white observation; their preachers often held religious services apart from the whites and without their knowledge. It was under cover of such religious associations that the antebellum South's major slave insurrections—those of Gabriel Prosser, Nat Turner, and (in Charleston itself) Denmark Vesey—were planned. According to Charleston's official account of the Vesey plot, "among the conspirators a majority of them belonged to the African church," a recently formed Methodist church described as "composed wholly of persons of color and almost entirely of blacks." The importance of the slaves' religion thus rested upon its capacity to serve them as a source not only of cultural values, but also of an understanding of themselves, of their world, and of the relations between them. It served them, in other words, both as a model *for* behavior and as a model *of* behavior. The power of Afro-Christianity in supporting the social values of Charleston's slaves rested upon its ability to make plain a world in which those values, as well as the forces opposing them, were primal elements.[44]

Not all of Charleston's slaves embraced Afro-Christianity. African-born slaves often maintained their traditional religions. "At the time I first went to Carolina, there were a great many African slaves in the country," recalled fugitive slave Charles Ball. "Many of them believed there were several gods; some of whom were good, and others evil." Other African-born slaves continued to embrace Islam. "I knew several who must have been, from what I have since learned, Mohamedans [sic]" Ball noted. "There was one man on this plantation who prayed five times every day, always turning his face to the east." On some lowcountry plantations Muslim slaves were given a ration of beef instead of pork.[45] But Afro-Christianity played a critical role in the intellectual lives of most slaves. In their praise meetings, in their ecstatic prayers and exuberant shouts, and especially in their transcendent spirituals (no less than in their masters' sermons, essays, and poetry), the slaves of Charleston gave eloquent voice to their deepest values.

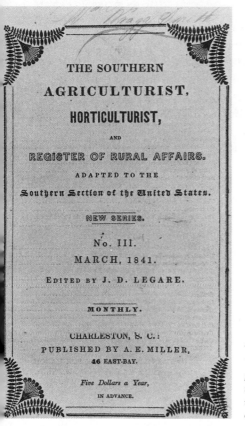

THE SOUTHERN
AGRICULTURIST,
HORTICULTURIST,
AND
REGISTER OF RURAL AFFAIRS.
ADAPTED TO THE
Southern Section of the United States.

NEW SERIES.

No. III.
MARCH, 1841.
EDITED BY J. D. LEGARE.

MONTHLY.

CHARLESTON, S. C.:
PUBLISHED BY A. E. MILLER,
46 EAST-BAY.

Five Dollars a Year,
IN ADVANCE.

Title page of the Southern Agriculturist. (William Wragg Smith (1808–75) was a planter-botanist, poet, and short story writer who helped found the Elliott Natural History Society and contributed to the Southern Literary Journal). Courtesy of the South Carolina Historical Society.

The Southern Agriculturist
in an Age of Reform

THEODORE ROSENGARTEN

IN 1819, the bottom fell out of the cotton market. When it became clear to planters of long-staple cotton that the abrupt and calamitous drop in prices was "not due to temporary conditions but to fundamental changes,"[1] they began reducing their cotton acreage and looking for solutions to the problem of diminished profits. Leading growers called for reform, not only of the cotton market but of the planting class. Sensing that something was wrong with their traditional agricultural practices, and desiring to strengthen the bonds of rural life, which were strained by the depression, several members of South Carolina's State Agricultural Society proposed publishing a journal. The society investigated the idea and rejected it on the grounds that such a publication could not be self-supporting. But the society's librarian, John D. Legaré, determined to try it himself. In January 1828, the inaugural issue of *The Southern Agriculturist* appeared in Charleston.

Legaré announced ambitious goals for the journal. He aimed "to establish the science of agriculture on a surer foundation" by encouraging experimentation and providing a forum for testing and reporting innovations. He wanted to elevate the status of planting in an era of uncertain monetary rewards by painting the charms and satisfactions of the countryside, so that men with money might once again regard the country as a good place in which to live as well as to invest. He sought to build a sentiment of common interest among individual planters who were used to conducting their business in isolation. Legaré believed his journal had the potential to become "the medium of communication" for gathering "a most useful Agricultural knowledge which would be . . . the commencement of a new era among us."[2]

The Southern Agriculturist was the first journal south of Baltimore devoted to farming. It lasted eighteen years, during which time some two dozen agricultural journals flourished and failed—mostly failed— in the United States. Thus, while Legaré's publication originated in a local economic and cultural crisis, it partook of a general movement of knowledge. Eighteen years was well above the life expectancy for a periodical of any kind; most agricultural journals of the 1820s to 1840s flickered out by the age of three. The *Tennessee Farmer* quit after six years. The *New York Farmer* stuck it out for nine. The *Maine Farmer* was a significant exception; it started up in the mid-1830s and published continuously for more than a century.

* * *

"We never thought of changes or improvement," confessed a sea-island cotton planter, recalling the prevailing self-contentment before 1819. "These happy times are changed and we must change with them,"[3] he counseled, shaken but determined to take his fate into his own hands. But which customs needed to be cast off and which preserved? Not all old practices were bad, and some of the inefficient customs had a hidden efficiency. Breaking land with hoes instead of the plow, for example, required a vast expenditure of labor, but the extra hands employed to plant in winter and pick in the fall were available in other seasons to pamper their masters on fishing, hunting, and pleasure excursions.

The call for rural revival and the plans to carry it out came from the city but not necessarily from city men. Many reformers who wrote for *The Southern Agriculturist* were wealthy planters who maintained second homes in Charleston or smaller lowcountry towns such as Beaufort and Walterboro. They were joined in their attacks on agricultural ignorance by urban merchants and cotton factors, lawyers, and other professionals whose standard of living was threatened by the regional decline in cotton income. Commerce was withering away, and Charleston's port facilities were falling apart from neglect. Exports of sea-island cotton from Charleston fell by 60 percent between 1821 and 1842, while the city's share of the South's uplands cotton crop declined steadily. New Orleans, which as late as 1824 handled fewer bales of uplands cotton than Charleston, was exporting more than three and a half times as many bales by 1842. Business was so bad in Charleston, it was reported, that grass grew "uninterruptedly in some of her chief business streets."[4]

Because plantations produced nearly all the wealth of society, every class of people had a stake in the profitability of agriculture. *The Southern Agriculturist* persistently addressed the question: how can planting be made more profitable? The journal encouraged two courses of action simultaneously. First, it urged planters to restrict the supply of cotton by taking land out of production and to improve the quality of the remaining crop by developing better seeds and applying more efficient agricultural techniques; in consequence, argued Legaré and his friends, a small quantity of fine long-staple would fetch more money than a large supply of inferior lint. Second, the journal exhorted planters to diversify their operations, to branch out from cotton to other crops and break their dependency on a single staple.

Many growers refused to believe that their problems were due to overproduction. Every last bale of every long-staple crop found a buyer, they pointed out. Some men insisted that the cry of overproduction was a hoax perpetrated by cotton buyers to keep prices down. Even those who agreed that the crop should be curtailed were not enthusiastic about cutting it. William Elliott, of Beaufort and Hilton Head Island, grandson of the William Elliott who produced South Carolina's first successful sea-island crop, suggested in 1828 that if long-staple acreage were reduced by a third, the remaining two-thirds would be worth as much as the original whole.[5] Ten years later, however, he endorsed the opinion that the planter's object "is to make a full crop—six hundred pounds of clear cotton to the hand."[6] Had he changed his mind? Or was he consistent insofar as he had always looked forward to growing more cotton on fewer acres? Whitemarsh B. Seabrook, a prosperous, enlightened planter and governor of South Carolina from 1850 to 1852, attributed the failures of sea-island planters to overplanting and poor management. But a careful reading of his addresses and essays in *The Southern Agriculturist* reveals that he chastised planters not for producing too much cotton, but for planting more than they had the manpower to prepare correctly for market and for ignoring methods that could increase their yields.

The disagreement over something so fundamental as the meaning of overproduction should caution us not to think of reform as a unified movement. The will to change generated conflicting ideas, though reformers agreed on the basic goals—increased profits and security. We should not imagine all the progressives on one side, pushing for reform in accordance with scientific principles, and all the philistines on the other, setting fire to plow stocks and dumping manure in the woods. The actual contenders for the mantle of reform were those who believed that planters erred in planting too much cotton, and those who believed they did not plant enough. The cotton-minded men urged a greater use of the plow, more acres to the hand, and the use of new manures. They fussed at their brethren for underworking their slaves and keeping "a floating capital of labor unemployment—a boat's crew for pleasure excursions."[7] And they pressed to open some hunting grounds to cultivation. The diversifiers, represented by Legaré and his allies, instructed planters to grow cereals, vegetables, and fruits, and to revive the ancient livestock industry.

In each monthly issue through the first two years, *The Southern Agriculturist* featured some new crop and offered detailed instructions for cultivating it. "Anything but cotton," Legaré seemed to be saying. Grapes, sugar cane, indigo, silk, and sheep were all put forward as alternatives, with no acknowledgment that all had been tried before and had been either abandoned or kept up as secondary crops only. Indigo, an herb in the pea family whose leaves yield a brilliant blue dye, preceded long-staple cotton as the major money crop on the Sea Islands of South Carolina and Georgia; it was given up during the American Revolution, when Britain revoked a bounty on it and turned to the East Indies to meet its needs. Wine grapes, tried by every generation, mature too quickly near the coast, and the Sea Island and seaboard soils were not hospitable to the large-scale production of sugar cane. By 1830, *The Southern Agriculturist* was promoting Irish potatoes, sugar beets, orchards, and dairy cattle, all of which were being raised in more suitable soils and climates outside the South, and none of which needed, or was readily adaptable to, the intensive labor system of plantations. As substitutes for cotton they were unrealistic; that they were proposed with vigor suggests the depth of discontent with the old staple. Meanwhile the world was hungering for cotton, and the economies of western Europe, particularly of England, which alone consumed the entire crop of sea-island, could not survive without it.

Legaré's principal weapon in his campaign against cotton was the gentle science of horticulture. He regularly published the proceedings of the Charleston Horticultural Society, using them as an instrument of criticism and a curriculum of reform. Horticulture, the cultivation of fruits, vegetables, flowers, and ornamental shrubs, had become a pastime of urban gardeners. Gone from the country-side were the rich and varied orchards established in the late colonial era. Cotton planted right up to the doors of the slave cabins had the effect of "starving" everything else. In the pursuit of extensive yields, planters had neglected the perfection of individual plants. The horticultural mode of "constant attention and special protective guardian-ship"[8] was a reproach to plantation thinking. Horticulture held a special gift for agriculture: the view that plants were good for more than food, fuel, or commodities. They were good, too, for shade, fragrance, and beauty—qualities that "refine . . . and purify the mind."[9] By bringing planters into contact with horticulturists, Legaré hoped to temper utility with idealism, custom with learning, and the craving for profits with an appreciation of beauty. Horticulturists were not modest in their claims. We have it in our power, wrote the Reverend John Bachman, one of antebellum Charleston's great men of science, "to create a love for natural pursuits and the beauties of nature." Horticulturists might "do much for the sunny south," he prophesied in 1833. "We may form a population fitted to its beauty."[10]

Legaré knew better than to appeal primarily to aesthetics. In his journal, spokesmen for horticultural science argued that their methods could mean money for large-scale growers. For example, melons raised early in the season in South Carolina, using hothouse techniques, could be sold in New York and Boston six weeks before Northern melons matured. Corn, improved by seed selection procedures refined by horticulturists, could be grown for export, as it once had been. In truth, many cotton growers would have been pleased to grow enough corn simply to feed their labor force. Saddled with debt and needing to plant cotton in order to secure credit, they were forced to buy provisions to get through the year. They bought locally, in a pinch, but they came to prefer sweeter and softer varieties of corn from Pennsylvania and Maryland. Even if they had produced surplus corn for a cash crop, they would have faced stiff competition from the mid-Atlantic states.

By the late 1830s, Sea Island planters had adopted many horticultural techniques without diversifying their crops. Toward cotton and corn they showed a more scientific approach, while the output of other goods for market actually declined. In 1841, even though the tendency in cotton prices was steadily downward, Sea Island growers began planting more acres in cotton. Legaré could never demonstrate the superiority of any other crop. Nor had *The Southern Agriculturist* addressed the practical difficulties of supplanting the old staple, such as building a network of brokers, buyers, and processors for cotton's replacement. Reports of phenomenal individual success in the midst of the depression kindled memories of the great fortunes founded on cotton in the past and encouraged dreams of spectacular wealth in the future.[11] Resistance to change was more than economic. White people identified cotton with a life of privilege and power, a sentiment felt strongly in both country and city.

More and more, plantations on the seaboard turned into great cotton fields devoid of other significant agricultural uses. "Oranges are rare," observed Beaufort's William J. Grayson (author of *The Hireling and the Slave*, the South's answer, in verse, to *Uncle Tom's Cabin*). "Pomegranates formerly seen everywhere are seldom met with, figs are scarce and small. Few planters have a good peach or strawberry."[12] While the intensification of cotton occurred in the 1840s and 1850s, any alternative, barring the complete collapse of the cotton market, had been precluded in the stagnant 1820s and 1830s by the inability of any food or other fiber to seriously challenge cotton's hold on the land. The point of view of *The Southern Agriculturist* did not prevail—not in regard to cotton; Legaré's readers were devoted to the staple of their fathers. Legaré, an entrepreneur who had never raised a crop himself, diverted his attack from cotton per se; after 1832, he and his journal turned to the problem of modernizing the countryside.

*   *   *

Legaré supported the work of local agricultural societies, which he viewed as agencies for disseminating new ideas. He urged them to send him copies of lectures delivered at meetings by guest speakers, and to use *The Southern Agriculturist* as a means for corresponding with one another. Once, two societies debated in print whether to pack sea-island cotton in round bales or square bales. Two others argued the merits of using crushed lime to sanitize the floors of Negro cabins.

Legaré also invited local societies to publish the results of crop competition in his journal, but the published reports often obscured what was going on in the field. In 1829 the St. Helena Agricultural Society reported that Benjamin Chaplin had won the premium for corn with a yield of 53½ bushels to the acre; he won again in 1830 with a yield of 73 bushels to the acre. The problem was that a sensational output on a single acre concealed the miserly average yield over a whole field. Twenty bushels to the acre was considered a good *average*, and 12 to 15 bushels was normal. A 73-bushel yield could be achieved only by taking hands off other jobs to work the corn or having the extra hands to work it, by unusually heavy manuring, by planting a cover crop the winter before, and by close supervision throughout the growing season— all desirable practices, perhaps, but not within the capacity of most planters. A 73-bushel yield of corn was analogous to a four-pound tomato—mouthwatering and sensational, but also freakish and wasteful. By the mid-1840s, the St. Helena Society had changed the standard of its corn premium to the best average yield.

Just as reports of huge outputs did not tell the whole story about production, so the charters of these rural clubs did not describe adequately what went on at meetings. Planters visited their clubhouses to find camaraderie and to escape the boredom of the plantation. Several societies had formed out of older hunting and dining clubs, modeled on clubs of the English gentry, and eating and drinking remained their chief activities. "As the hour for dinner comes on," wrote Joseph E. Jenkins, a prominent cotton planter from Colleton District, "the countenances which before were heavy and dull, become bright and radiant with expectation." When many planters rejected this regime and stayed out of the clubs altogether, the membership crisis inspired Jenkins to write a polemic on "Some of the Causes of the Decline and Fall of Most of the Agricultural Societies of South Carolina" for the May 1835 issue of *The Southern Agriculturist*. Jenkins picked up a line of attack begun the year before by Whitemarsh B. Seabrook.[13] With militant candor and not a trace of humor, both men blamed the troubles of agriculture on planters who had grown intellectually lazy and incurious from a life of wealth obtained without effort. Seabrook called the loss of intellectual enterprise in farming "a great public calamity."[14] Jenkins, writing under the nom de plume "Colleton," charged that a man who publicized his experiments was censured by his neighbors: either he had "some uncharitable motive imputed to him," or else he came "under the ban . . . 'a writing Planter is a bad Planter.'"[15] This sounds suspiciously like a personal grievance, and it is true that Jenkins tested his friends with his penchant for exactness and an enthusiasm for his own theories. Yet his remark suggests that Colleton District planters shared the familiar rural distrust of a person who seeks prestige outside of his own social circle. It hints at the difficulty *The Southern Agriculturist* had in soliciting articles. Social pressure against standing out from the pack and against writing was, in fact, a chronic prejudice that became a stock theme in urban critiques of the countryside.

All that planters might themselves improve—their conduct and attitudes, their agricultural techniques and appreciation of rural pleasures—constituted fair subjects for *The Southern Agriculturist* during Legaré's tenure. Politics was an exception; Legaré, Seabrook, and William Elliott agreed that political factions were turning men's minds away from their fields and destroying the morale of the agricultural societies. Seabrook took to task "men of enlarged and cultivated minds" who devoted "their time and talents to the preservation of the rights of property, the security of our civil institutions, and the promotion of the arts and ornaments of life," but closed their minds to "the science which forms the foundation of our private wealth and public prosperity."[16] First, last, and always, *The Southern Agriculturist* was an agricultural magazine. Legaré took pride that it never became a sounding board for politics. Even in the mid-1830s, during the nullification crisis and after Nat Turner's rebellion in Virginia, when planters became acutely aware of belonging to a cultural entity called the South, and agricultural societies assumed greater policing functions, the primary motive of the journal remained to broadcast new agricultural ideas and to combat the isolation and pessimism of the planting community. A reader today must marvel at how broadly men of that time conceived the interests of the planter. Medicine, astronomy, architecture, ancient languages were all part of a useful education; but politics, which produced nothing useful or beautiful, was shunned.

Legaré also steered clear of the slavery controversy. Many issues of *The Southern Agriculturist* contain not a single reference to the system of forced labor responsible for producing the crops of the South. If planters had a quarrel with their slaves, it concerned nothing more fundamental than the theft of sweet potatoes or the ill-treatment of horses. If slaves had any quarrel with their masters, it could not be discerned in the pages of *The Southern Agriculturist*. The journal gave the impression that master and slave "always pull the same end of the rope."[17] Every other domain in life was governed by the principle of change, but the relationship of whites to blacks was fixed and beyond discussion. Still, since methods of managing slaves might be improved and the workers' efficiency could be increased at virtually every task, about once a year Legaré would publish some planter's scheme for governing Negroes: a list of rules and aphorisms covering diet, hygiene, work loads, and personal relations. Planters were advised to make their slaves wash themselves every day and to keep them from eating green fruit, to allow them half of each Saturday to cultivate their own gardens, and to flatter the women by giving them something pretty to wear.

But peace and security were threatened by the faltering economy. Not that the slaves would grow restless and revolt (though that was always an unspoken possibility): in the view of successful cotton planters like Whitemarsh B. Seabrook and William Wigg Hazzard, the slaves, not the masters, had the most to lose. The danger of declining profits and rising food costs was that masters might come to feel their slaves were a burden.[18] Poor harvests could force a planter to sell some of his "people" to meet his creditors' demands, or take some more drastic action to cut his losses. He might even sell them all and get out of planting entirely, thus severing them from their families and community and subjecting them, perhaps, to a harsher life should they be sent to the Western states and territories. Or he might swallow his losses and emancipate them—not likely, but not unheard of, either. What

287

was the fulfillment of a dream for the greater part of the slave population was the equivalent of a death sentence in the minds of whites who believed that black people in America were doomed without the protection of white masters.

Agricultural writers worried more about urban conspiracies led by free people of color than about rural uprisings. Free blacks, they contended, posed the greater threat to the continuance of slavery. In an address to the State Agricultural Society in 1832 — ten years after the trial and hanging of Denmark Vesey, the free black leader of a failed rebellion in Charleston — Edward R. Laurens, grandson of the Revolutionary statesman Henry Laurens, called for harsh measures to police the free black population and to ensure that no more slaves would be set free. Free blacks were an insurrectionary class, he warned, because they had so tenuous a hold on the necessities of life. (Not all of them, certainly: Denmark Vesey himself had amassed a fortune of several thousand dollars.) Because no one was compelled to feed them, and hard times made it difficult for them to feed themselves, they had to be closely watched. Laurens doubted that a black revolt could succeed; but he feared that if the source of trouble were not eliminated, periodic conflicts would turn a majority of whites in the state against all blacks, slave and free, and could lead in time to a movement to expel them all. He urged slaveholders like himself to move against free blacks before the antiblack feelings of non-slaveholders, particularly in the Western districts, could be catalyzed. And he appealed to the pride, if not the pocketbook, of planters who lived within the cultural and commercial orbit of Charleston by suggesting that Charleston would never take its place among the great modern cities of the world so long as its proletariat was black. Free blacks discouraged white working people from living in Charleston, he alleged, referring indirectly to the provocative immigration problem: Europeans arriving in America were not settling in South Carolina, and the state's native-born whites were leaving at a terrific rate. Laurens did not support colonization society schemes to remove free blacks to Africa, however, because he suspected that colonization was a foil for abolition.[19]

Agricultural writers distrusted city workers of any color; blacks simply posed the most immediate danger. At the top as well as the bottom of society, observed William Wigg Hazzard, who had recently moved from well-mannered Beaufort to remote St. Simons Island, Georgia, city life had "failed to strengthen social virtue."[20] The upper classes seemed to be more polished, but they had coarsened underneath their fine manners. Yet, planters who could afford to do so flocked to the city—to get a dab of that polish, to see new sights, and to hear new voices. Instead of investing their profits in their plantations, complained Francis D. Quash, planter and legislator from St. Thomas Parish, Charleston District, they spent their money in the city and had nothing to show for it but "the ghost of departed city joys."[21] Values were changing: the pleasures of old, savored at home in the bosom of one's family and calculated to nourish affections (however actual this scene might have been) now were less sought after than ephemeral treats consumed with strangers. Hazzard, whose West Point Plantation was one of the fourteen "patriarchal" plantations on St. Simons, worried that old bonds of sympathy were giving way to new social arrangements. Where this would lead, and how it would resound in the countryside, no one could say. But the example of Europe was not consoling.

Even writers who lamented country dullness worried that planters might find the city too stimulating. "I would not desire that a planter should exchange his physical duties for mental toil," declared Seabrook in 1832, softening his earlier judgment and assuring his friends of where he stood. "In the first alone solid profit exists. The other is only an important auxilliary to his labors."[22] The writer who signed himself "A Practical Planter" distinguished between urban science—which had become overrefined and "committed to paper"—and the science practiced by planters who learned through their own experiments. He ended an article on the benefits of plowing with an anecdote about a slave who explained his master's lack of success: "Ah massa, massa plant too much from the book."[23]

The country's distrust of the city is a very old tradition. Juvenal, the Roman satirist, could have been speaking for the cotton planter when he had a small farmer say, "What can I do in Rome? I never learnt how to lie."[24] Charleston was the planters' Rome. There they sold their cotton and bought almost everything they did not produce on their plantations. Rarely were they pleased with the prices their cotton received, and frequently they griped that city measures did not come up to their own: that cotton bales weighing 350 pounds when they left the plantation weighed twenty pounds less on the cotton factor's scales, that corn purchased from the factor lacked several quarts to the bushel. Planters felt cheated, poorer planters especially, and ones who did not grow the finer grades of cotton. Their factors complained in

289

turn: the cotton was late, or wet, or dirty, or the planter was living beyond his means.

Though factors and merchants were acid-tongued critics of planters and country living, and though nearly all of the plantation output not consumed at home went through their hands, they played a small part in the public discussion of agricultural reform. They kept account books and wrote letters, but they submitted very few articles to *The Southern Agriculturist*. In a rare appearance in print, "A Merchant" exhorted planters to sample their cotton before sending it to market, to compare samples picked from different fields, and to learn what buyers were looking for[25] – good advice, if the object were to help planters feel more at home at the marketplace. But the advice was given insolently, as if by someone who was unsure of his social position and wanted to impress upon his readers that he did not regard them as his equals. It was one thing for planters to criticize themselves but quite another to take criticism from men to whom the plantations were merely a means of employing capital and producing goods for market, and who would no sooner live on a plantation themselves than they would live in Africa.

*   *   *

The Southern Agriculturist can be read as a guide to farming in the coastal region, with an emphasis on the evolution of agricultural knowledge. Many of the methods of tillage, of cultivating and harvesting crops, and of increasing the efficiency of hand labor that were introduced to readers of the journal are still valid today. Only the crops are gone, and the land is planted in pine. The journal documents the first phase in the effort to modernize a sector of Southern agriculture; it anticipated the struggle that was postponed by the return of high cotton prices in the 1850s, partially accomplished by the Civil War in the 1860s, and set back by the social adjustments of the 1870s. People read the journal in its own time because they found it entertaining. News about agricultural experiments in their own and nearby parishes was news about neighbors, and greedily consumed. Anecdotes about extravagant harvests of honey in France or new ways of packing butter in New York state – culled from other agricultural publications – gave glimpses into the mysterious world beyond the limits of the lowcountry. While the journal criticized some customs and habits of its readers, it always respected their intelligence. And it spoke their language – shared a vocabulary, figures of speech, and a store of allusions influenced by classical education and a common way of life. To quote Greek and Roman literature in an article about a contemporary subject was to send a fraternal greeting to men assumed to share a code of behavior, a sense of breeding, and a certain moral outlook toward agriculture. Vergil's *Georgics* seemed a favorite source of quotations. "Denique apertos—Bacchus amat colles," repeated N. Hebremont, at the beginning of an essay on grapes, the very first piece in the first issue of *The Southern Agriculturist*: "The Vine delights in an airy, hilly country." Was this practical advice to would-be vintners? Not likely, for there are no hills to speak of in the lowcountry, home of most of the journal's readers. Nor is the line merely decorative; it is placed too strategically for that. Rather, the quotation invokes the authority of an idealism sadly wanting in the depressed climate of the late 1820s. The *Georgics* condemns petty political bickering, overeating and overdrinking, the gentlemanly distaste for work, superstition, intellectual inertia, and other human failings that contribute—in different times and different societies—to the langor of country life. The *Georgics* had a quickening effect on enlightened planters in times of distress, something like the appeal of Sophocles to Europeans in the middle years of the twentieth century. Planters' concerns found striking parallels in the themes of the old Roman poet: resting and replenishing tired soil; tolerance for new methods and crops; agricultural education and the importance of hard thinking in husbandry.

Vergil was a true friend of the reform-minded planter. He himself had been the son of a small landowner who faced eviction by authorities wanting to confiscate his land to resettle soldiers of the Roman Army. There was enough land to go around—just not enough fertile land. Vergil advocated mixed farming and gave advice on plowing, rotating crops, selecting seeds, building fences. Some of his advice was bad, and some of it merely transmitted conventional mythology, such as the notion that bees reproduce without copulating. But the wisdom of his critique outlived the errors of his natural science.

Horace was another ancient poet whose name was invoked in the cause of reform. William Elliott concluded an essay on the use of tufted cotton seeds with a greeting "to each intelligent planter . . . in the language of Horace—'Si quid novisti, rectius istis, candidus, imperti— Si non, his utere mecum'" (If you know anything more correct than this advice, be so kind as to share it—If not, then use this along with me.)[26] Dr. Samuel H. Dickson, founder in 1833 of the Medical College of South Carolina, informed the Horticultural Society of Charleston that the reader of Horace who travels from Rome to Naples "to inquire for the Falernian [wine] once so esteemed" will not find it. Instead, he will find what a traveler in the lowcountry would find—that the land had weakened and soured and was no longer capable of producing the fine crops of old.[27] Dr. Dickson, who loved wine and hated distilled liquors, established the first temperance society in the South. A versatile thinker and a specialist on febrile diseases, Dickson was also one of the early writers on racial anthropometry. He had no agricultural experience, but he conceived it his duty to communicate the lesson of his broad learning and methodical observation—that the fortunes of civilization are bound to the fertility of the soil.

*   *   *

In the spring of 1834, shortly before he gave up the editorship of *The Southern Agriculturist*, Legaré went on an extended tour of plantations in the coastal plain. His aims were to study the state of agriculture in different locales, to measure the reach and impact of his journal, and to find new subscribers and writers. He made his report in a series of articles that compared crops, yields, field practices, cultural activities, and living conditions from place to place. Much of what he saw astonished him, particularly the almost universal ignorance of elementary science and the hold of habit on the minds of intelligent men. He visited plantations where slaves carried corn from the fields to the storehouse in their arms while horses and wagons stood idle. He listened to planters swear that Negroes could not be taught to work a plow, and he watched other planters direct slaves to open more land than they could ever cultivate. He met more progressive planters, too, educated experimenters who never had to buy an ear of corn; they manured their fields heavily, carefully selected their seeds, and made a profit in the worst of times. Their slaves ate good meat, slept in tightly built, whitewashed cabins, and wore adequate clothing in all seasons. In turn, the blacks performed a great variety of tasks; some even operated machines.

Legaré paid close attention to the condition of plantation buildings, which indicated to him the morale of the people, white and black. With a city man's appreciation for landscape, or "rural scenery," Legaré preferred hedged gardens, sculptured shrubs, regular walkways, tree-lined avenues, and spaces designed for distinctive uses rather than sprawling, promiscuous yards. He admired planters who set aside places for nonremunerative purposes such as promenading and bird-watching. If his tour had a unifying theme, it was the search for the ideal planter, a man who could do many things well and was equally proficient in his fields, study, and drawing room; a conservationist who exploited his land and slaves without destroying them; a consumer who valued the things money could buy more than the money itself.

The progressive planter was the hero of *The Southern Agriculturist*. Legaré searched hard for him, and created him in the image of the contributors of his journal. Following his tour, Legaré left Charleston and bought a health spa in Virginia called "the Gray Sulphur." At first he was "pretty well patronized" by the many friends he had made as an editor, but "the water of his Spring had so little of the Sulphur about it that people could not be persuaded that it had any tonic or healing values";[28] his business fell off as customers looked for more odiferous water. The spa failed, and Legaré returned to Charleston in 1840, where he found his old journal being published as *The Southern Cabinet*. When the editor's job was offered to him, he took it, and the first thing he did was change the name of the journal to *The Southern Agriculturist, Horticulturist, and Register of Rural Affairs*. With characteristic zeal, Legaré confronted old problems: the general backwardness of agricultural practices that impoverished the people and the land, and the departure of white farmers from the state. Manuring, he insisted, was the key to rejuvenating the land and stemming the tide of emigration. He proposed banking and draining the lowlands to make new fertile farms for industrious people who otherwise would leave. Existing farmland could be improved, he suggested, by improving the farmers through some sort of public agricultural education. He published the results of numerous field experiments, particularly those involving cover crops and grasses—thinking to raise fodder for plow beasts and to enrich the land between plantings of food and cotton crops. He ran serialized histories of cotton and rice, the resilient old staples, and he borrowed articles from a host of other agricultural journals—a sign, perhaps, that it was difficult to obtain local writing.

Although contributors were less willing or able than before to suppress their political feelings, talk of Southern rights and states' rights was subdued. Under Legaré, *The Southern Agriculturist* defended the South by promoting its economic well-being through a program of healing and nourishing the land and expanding its yield.

Legaré left the journal for good in 1842 and went into the seed and farm supply business. For the second time, he was succeeded as editor by Bartholomew R. Carroll, who stayed at the post until the journal ceased publishing in 1846. What can we say *The Southern Agriculturist* accomplished in eighteen years of publication?

In an address to the state Agricultural Society in 1831, Francis D. Quash, who had studied ancient languages at Cambridge University, told how Vergil's *Georgics* had revolutionized Rome. Men who had heaped up wealth and honors in the city "suddenly grew enamored with rural life . . . the Roman villas became not seats of opulence but of refinement in manners and elegance in literature."[29]

We could not begin to claim as much for *The Southern Agriculturist*. The journal did not transform the countryside; its achievements were more modest. It opened lines of communication among men engaged in common economic activities who were facing common problems. It kept up an energetic discussion of ideas in an era of economic stagnation. It fought the prevailing pessimism with a plan for personal and occupational reform. It helped to secure, in the circles it influenced, a conception of progress as a norm in agriculture, although reform in this time and place did not challenge slavery. Technological advances, in both agriculture and manufacturing, favored the modern or industrial aim of raising a single large staple crop, while the history and organization of the plantations, and the established commercial apparatus, determined that that crop would be cotton.

11

Elizabeth Washington Burnet Rhett (d. 1852), wife of U.S. Senator Robert Barnwell Rhett, Sr., and their daughter, Elizabeth (b. 1841). Charcoal on paper by unknown hand. Courtesy of the South Carolina Historical Society.

City, Country, and the Feminine Voice

STEVEN M. STOWE

In a book as fine-grained and agreeable as the Charleston she depicts, Harriott Ravenel remarks that the South Carolina planters were "as much town folk as country gentlemen."[1] It is a useful reminder. As planters themselves frequently explained to their wives and families, a successful man could not afford for too long a time the tucked-away pleasures of the country. So men came to the city offices of their lawyers and factors, to the business and political life of Meeting Street, and to the intellectual and social pursuits of Library Society and club. Agreements were reached, problems solved, political arguments asserted and countered, friendships established and recalled. Much of this activity was practical and contingent; some of it was aesthetic and self-contained. But all of it, formal and informal, made sojourns to Charleston a time of social encounter and perhaps renewal.

If the lives of planter-class men must be thought of in terms of city as well as country, what of the lives of women? In particular, what of the intellectual experience of planter-class women; in what sense did it, too, combine city and country? What meaning did each place hold for women and how did it change in the antebellum years? I was led to these questions by studying what the planters meant when they ascribed social and intellectual "spheres" to each sex. I discovered that when writing about the "woman's sphere," women themselves often linked it to distinct experiences of city and country, tying locale to feminine sensibility. In diaries, novels, and memoirs written and read by antebellum women, the sense of their own sphere often was expressed in terms that sharply contrasted urban life to life on the plantation. This contrast, I hope to show, reveals important intellectual realities characteristic of their class and sex. In exploring this theme, I wish to suggest further that the general intellectual life of planter-class women was much occupied with portrayals of themselves and their world, and that the meaning they made is revealed in the shared terms and usages they employed in their writing. The relationship between city and country became an important conventional way for women to explain themselves to themselves. More than an entertaining rhetorical device, though it was also that, the theme of contrast between city and country helped define the values, routines, and common sense concepts that lent substance to the woman's sphere and made it habitable.

In recent years historians have begun to take seriously the nineteenth-century belief in sexual spheres, realizing how deep and complicated the differences between the sexes were understood to be. Education, courtship, marriage, child-rearing all were shaped by the belief—the conviction—that temperamental differences between the sexes were as profound as biological ones. Indeed, the perceived distinctions between male and female character and feeling were understood as being part of the natural world. Culture appeared as nature; thus the social arrangements based on the belief in separate spheres—the division of labor, intense same-sex friendships, political activity for men, domestic authority for women—seemed not only orderly and rich but also unlikely to be altered.[2]

Flowering in the antebellum South, though elsewhere as well, this culture had roots in the changed market economy that produced different patterns of consumption and leisure between men and women, in the organization of slavery that required a visible, hierarchial control, in the romanticism that exalted individual struggle and transcendence, and in the evangelism that contained loss and focused the spirit. Each penetrated the woman's sphere, and women made each their own to the degree they could. In doing so, they encountered the restrictions of their sphere as well as its entitlements, tempering their femininity accordingly. Caricatures are readily at hand today: the swooning city belle, the all-competent plantation mistress. But beneath these, the texture of women's lives still is traceable in the intellectual themes that explained it, in their memories and stories.

This essay will examine the city-and-country theme from three perspectives. First, it will look at some of the experiences of planter-class women that introduced them to the differences between city and country. The main body of the essay will then explore the contrast between city and country in the writings of three women connected to Charleston and acutely aware of their sphere. Finally, I will suggest—hazard might be the word—some aspects of social change revealed in the shifting use of the city-and-country theme from the 1830s to the late 1850s.

In their memories of childhood, Charleston women recalled city and country in terms of an annual migration from one to the other. The two places were spliced together by scenes of packing, of black people in the yard listening to departing directions, and of hours spent riding through miles of resinous pine broken by tilled fields at some stage of the cycle of sowing and harvest. Plantation and city fit into the rhythms of season and family custom. Christmastime is especially bright in the memories of women as a time when life in the country was at its fullest and the yearly pattern of movement began. The pattern was this: the family came to the plantation a month before Christmas, after the frost had killed the fever. They took stock of domestic and farm necessities and then prepared for the year end celebration. Here they remained until January, when older brothers and sisters went off to Charleston, perhaps with one parent or an older sibling, for the "gay season" of parties and courtship. Young girls who heard talk of the "St. Cecelias, the Dancing Assemblies, the Philharmonic Concerts, the races, and above all the Jockey Ball" could only guess at what wonders there were in the winter city. In late February or early March, the family came together again in the country, where the children usually remained until May or June. For many families during these months, the plantation became a world of children and women as the men went away in pursuit of business or political election. The onset of the sickly season, signaled more precisely than anyone knew by June rains and mosquito netting, sent everyone packing again for the shore or the upcountry springs. Occasionally they returned to the country in the early fall, but not in a settled way until the frost finished the fever and anticipated Christmas again.[3]

This movement from country to city and back again as the climate and social events required became part of reality itself for young girls. In their memories, and in the images of childhood they created in their writings, women's feeling for the plantation often seems foremost. The fragrant quiet, the abundance of food and space, the comings and goings of servants and parents doubtless seemed to many children to be at the fulcrum of everything else in the world. It should not be surprising; the rounds of visiting neighbors and return visits, the cycle of the crops, the absence of the father punctuated by his letters, the lines of slaves moving to and from the quarters all fed orderly anticipation and a sense of dependable permanence. Charleston, when it appears at all in women's early childhood memories, is more a source of delightful supply than a place of its own. At Wyndam plantation, in Mary Howard Schoolcraft's idealized vision, there are many scenes of horsemen arriving with news, or schooners "bringing some two hundred blankets, groces of large needles, pounds of skeins of flax thread, brass thimbles, firey red, white, and blue bandanas . . . for the women."[4] If Charleston is magically near at these times it is because it almost seems to glide upriver itself to the center of life, the country.

This pattern changed for most young women when they became boarding students at one of Charleston's female academies or, as often was the case before 1835, roomed with a family friend or a relative and took lessons with a tutor. Now for the first time, at age thirteen or fourteen, a girl encountered city life each day, understanding that its quick, cobblestone rhythms existed independent of the plantation. A girl came to the academy to learn her academic subjects, of course. Like Susan Petigru King's character Lily, an academy girl "studied her lessons and recited them; she kept her things in order; she read improving books, and practiced music and drawing."[5] She certainly did not range freely through the streets. Institutions like Madame Togno's school, with its cascade of gracefully curved balconies on Meeting Street, or Madame Talvande's, surrounded by a high wall topped with cut glass, did not establish themselves with planter families by being lax. But in her daily walks to the Battery, in rain or sun, dressed like her com-

panions and walking in file with Miss Mary, Miss Louisa, or Miss Eliza
at the head, a girl also became an urban phenomenon herself. She
was changed into an "academy girl," as familiar a city sight as slaves
at the market or lawyers at the court. She was there both to become
educated and to grow into womanhood, purposes for which the city
was indispensable. Charleston was Society, and a young woman's self-
display was all the more meaningful for being part of a group of sister
students. No matter what her singular qualities, or how much she was
the pet of her country home, a girl became a young lady by emerging
from the walls of the academy in the modest company of her sisters,
moving into some part of Charleston on an outing or for the air, and
then returning to the safety of the walls. It was a preeminently urban
style in its structured variety and self-consciousness.

Now the plantation was distant. Its childhood solitudes were replaced by the constant companionship of young women. Like the urban setting of the academy, the daily intimacy of the students and their
teachers was a key to growing up—to being "finished off," a term uttered without irony. For most girls, it seems, the initial homesickness
and annoyance with close quarters usually gave way after the first term
to feelings of warmth and caring that were as much of the essence of
academy life as its recitations. Girls who complained about sleeping
two to a bed in their first term (two terms lasted four months each,
with breaks in the winter and summer) often eagerly chose their "dearest" companion by the second term. Close friendships lasting many
years sometimes grew from academy days, rooted in trust and familiarity. And most women recalled with pride the security of a wholly
feminine world. Academy hierarchy and daily routine supported this
sense of collective identity. "We boasted three beauties," Elizabeth Allston Pringle remembered of her school, "who were always put in the
first rank when we went to concerts or to the theater."[6]

Teachers, many only a few years older than their charges, were friends
and also models of a lady's accomplishments. When jealousy or conflict arose, there was the headmistress or principal who restored order
and at least the appearance of good feeling. As Mary Boykin Chesnut
recalled of the "small, but beautifully formed" Madame Talvande: "She
had the faculty of inspiring terror, and by that power she ruled us absolutely." She could quite literally control a social gathering by entering the room in a certain manner; she spoke subtle French and chose
favorites at will. Yet in Chesnut's recollections, Madame's private life

was not inaccessible. Or, rather, she apparently wished her girls to see her as a woman as well as obey her as a headmistress. Chesnut recalled that "different rooms in the house looked down upon her dressing room. So in warm weather, when open windows were a necessity, we saw her in absolute dishabille—her head tied up in a red bandana, and her torn and soiled dressing gown flying in the breeze. Slippers down at the heel, or kicked off."[7] This was intimacy in another form. Student and headmistress alike were women, and in the woman's world femininity was seen in all its guises.

A young woman's country life was not abandoned, of course, and there still were times to be a girl. Sullivan's Island was not far away, and there academy students found a place "free from conventional rules, where you are not forced to remember 'behavior,' nor to conduct yourself with . . . stiff propriety and full-dress customs."[8] But never again would freedom and solitude be without a counterpull of the intimate sisterhood and urban style found in the Charleston academy. For most women, it was the first time they were conscious not only of their sexuality and the duties of their sex but also of the link between these and their elite social class. When this link was forged as the academy intended it to be, a planter-class woman lived ever after with that bond. "Why did I think—and why do I now prefer [Charlestonians] to the whole world," Chesnut asked rhetorically. "One always likes the best of its kind. . . . The fine flavor still lingers."[9]

After three or four years at the academy, a young woman might return to the country for a brief time. Here she took long walks, made handkerchiefs, played the piano for her father, and wrote longing letters to academy friends that held the feeling of their city days together in a blend of playfully arch allusion and warm phrases of love. Charleston entered her life again at her first "gay season," a time when young men and women measured their social standing by the number of small embossed party invitations that collected on their parlor tables. Charleston became another kind of stage, one on which young men appeared for the first time in great numbers and at close range. The gay season was a time that again mixed sexuality with social class, self-display with strict convention. The finished lady emerged from the closeness of academy life and the quiet of the plantation to an exhausting and exhilarating time when her accomplishments in conversation, music, dancing, and personal beauty led her through flirtation (it was hoped) to the serious attentions of two or more men.[10] The city be-

300

came theater, with its illusions and realities aimed at ending the un-attached glory a young woman brought with her to town. Charleston became charged with a brilliance and meaning that must have dimmed many a young woman's memory of the city as only a distant dream of a plantation child or a territory of adventure to be shared with school sisters. But all three times in a woman's life combined to give her a sense of what the city held and how it differed from the country. This emotional terrain remained for women to explore intellectually in adulthood.

The changing experience of city and country in a woman's life was a context for thinking about herself and her social place, but not an exact vocabulary. The precise terms were formulated by women who wrote about the woman's sphere in one way or another, drawing upon common knowledge of both city and country and raising it to thematic significance. In looking closely at the writings of the three women to whom we now turn, it is possible to see how a city-and-country theme was a means of sharpening exactly what a woman could say about her-self. Changes in feminine discourse in the antebellum South, and what they reveal about the woman's sphere, are signaled by changes in this and other themes. Such themes, I have suggested, stemmed from a woman's youth, but their greater meaning lay in the way they en-abled her to make sense of her life long after. Taken together, the three writers—Caroline Howard Gilman, Susan Petigru King, Mary Boykin Chesnut—suggest variations in a feminine voice: that is, a kind of ex-pression that characterized women's predicament and organized the cultural resources they commanded. Gilman, King, and Chesnut are a useful trio to consider because each woman developed the city-and-country theme in a distinct way, in part reflecting the change that took place over a generation of antebellum writing. These distinctions were not only in the content of their plots and memories but also, I hope to show, in the literary form chosen to express them. More-over, each woman had a direct tie to Charleston as a specific city. For each of them, as for the other women already briefly quoted, Charles-ton was a place, a sensibility, and a time in their lives as a woman and as a writer.

Before looking at their writing in detail, however, it is worthwhile to recall the tack taken in this essay. I am most concerned with explor-ing the relationship between the social experience of women and the intellectual activity of writing. It was here that the woman's sphere was

301

constructed. Of course, Chesnut, Gilman, and King all were well read in the literature of their time, but the import of their own writing did not primarily derive from this fact. Gilman, for example, was well acquainted with literary convention, ranging from the Bible to the stories of Catherine Sedgwick and Sarah Hale. King clearly read widely in the popular fiction of the 1840s and 1850s, including the stories of E.D.E.N. Southworth (which managed to be both hardheaded and breathless), Caroline Lee Hentz, Susan Warner, and Lydia Sigourney. King especially admired William Makepeace Thackeray, whom she considered a consummate social observer. Chesnut read popular "women's authors" as well as Thackeray, Dickens, Hugo, Trollope, Kingsley, and Stowe. In the gallery of writers from Sedgwick to Madame de Staël, and from Walter Scott to Jane Austen, thematic use of the differences between city and country can be found; no doubt Gilman, King, and Chesnut drew upon what they read. But it is a premise of this essay that their reading played only a supporting part in their activity as writers. Their intellectual lives are most importantly seen as efforts to make meaning in the full pattern of their experience, not as mere linear transactions between their mature reading and their writing. The theme of city-and-country had its deepest meaning, in this view, wherever it was found – in the words they read or in the words they wrote – because it was implanted in their past and present; it was not simply a device absorbed from their reading.[11]

In the fiction of Caroline Howard Gilman, the woman's sphere plainly coincided with domestic life, but not without the sort of difficulty that made a story morally appropriate. Gilman's *Recollections of a Southern Matron*, published in 1838, tells a story that makes domesticity seem all that a woman should desire, even though she may need many other qualities as the story unfolds. Gilman considered herself a Southerner, though she was born in Boston in 1794, and lived there with kin after the death of her mother when Caroline was ten years old (her father had died when she was three). She moved to Charleston in 1819 upon her marriage to the Rev. Samuel Gilman, and lived there until her death in 1888. She bore seven children, managed her household, and had an energetic literary career that included editing, founding a children's newspaper (the *Rose-Bud*, which developed into an occasional magazine for young women), and writing verse, stories, and travel sketches. Her first novel, *Recollections of a Housekeeper* (written in 1834 and later titled *Recollections of a New-England Housekeeper*) is attributed on the title page to "Mrs. Clarissa Packard" and has but a slight plot over-shadowed by an engaging exposition of Mrs. Packard's daily routine. Gilman's last novel, *Love's Progress* (1840), is a heated melodrama of madness and family strife, often affecting but somewhat improbable even by the standards of the day.[12]

Southern Matron falls between these works, both in time and in lit-erary style and intent. Though obviously a fictional story, neatly paced and carefully symbolic, *Southern Matron* has passages devoted to a woman's social routines and awareness. Gilman wrote that she intended *Southern Matron* to be a window into "the habits of a Southern do-mestic life," and in fact it can be considered the first novel of Southern womanhood that goes beyond stereotype and caricature. Gilman told John S. Hart's readers that she never intended to write a novel that was not "a mere hinge for facts," and although *Southern Matron* is much more than this—and was popular for many years—Gilman certainly saw herself as a social observer as well as a teller of stories.[13] Because of this, there is a tension in the novel between her delight in fictional invention, which was appropriate, and a desire to reflect on Southern society, which might seem either unladylike or foolish. Fictional in-vention more often dominates in *Southern Matron*. Gilman entertained her readers with versions of the finest sentimental and romantic con-ventions (the death of a child, the triumph of pure love), while her effort at social commentary slipped into imperative moral scenes meant to improve rather than report.

The story of *Southern Matron* concerns the coming of age of a coun-try maiden, Cornelia Wilton. The course of the novel follows a chan-nel well-worn by domestic ideals and romantic convention: Cornelia, a beautiful, mild, yet resourceful young woman, at first suffers and then transcends loss and peril as she grows from maiden to matron. It is most importantly a moral journey with three different male characters serving as milestones of Cornelia's progress. Her Christian tutor Charles Duncan, sensitive to a young woman's hopes yet fatally consumptive, is followed by the deceiving son of a neighboring planter who would master Cornelia's feelings as he masters his slaves. Appearing at just the times when he is most needed (but when Cornelia feels either com-promised or ridiculous) is the Stranger, whom we know to be the planter Arthur Marion, who ultimately triumphs over many conspiring events to declare his love and claim Cornelia. But the heroine's journey is also a geographical one; her moral pilgrimage is given structure as a move from the country to the city and back again. Cornelia becomes a moral woman, a true Southern matron, because she risks this transition just as she tests the fortunes of love. In Gilman, as in other novelists, city and country are fashioned into a theme showing the extreme moral contrast between the two places. Throughout, the plantation is Home and the city is the Other—not quite the same thing as a dichotomy between good and evil, but a sharp duality of values nonetheless. It gave Gilman the moral edge to her story, sharpening her values on a contrast that shapes Cornelia's understanding of a woman's place in the world.

The first place Gilman reveals to her readers—and she is always whisking away veils to reveal something—is Roseland Plantation, Cornelia's childhood home. Cornelia's life is centered in the rhythms that Gilman's elite readers knew well. Cornelia's girlhood is enriched by the "winters . . . passed at Roseland, with an occasional visit to Charleston; our summers at a Pine-land settlement."[14] Emotionally growing at the pace of the seasons, Cornelia becomes a young, golden-haired beauty, her admirably mild temperament implied by her faithfulness to the yearly routine. The plantation is a place of rinsing quiet. It is a place without extensive rules or competing interests, so that wherever Cornelia stands, she becomes the center: "A plantation is solitary; shut out from the noise of the world, surrounded by a vast amphitheatre of trees, its occupants see little but the wide fields around, the graduated foliage in the distance, and the over-arching sky."[15] It is a world apart, but somehow intimate. The images are deeply peaceful, yet complicated by a sense of anticipation. The plantation is like a stage, a setting spread before the watcher that might be awaiting a scene but might simply be all there is to know of life. The layers of trees, the bright punch bowl of the sky, the sounds of insects, the feel of sun—all this holds the young Cornelia and her story, while it absorbs the many possible stories she daydreams.

Although in a passage or two Gilman hints that loneliness may threaten ("There may be danger of the aristocracy of solitude"), she is quick to say that even loneliness is morally preferable to "the little irritations, the paltry rivalry" of city life. If the plantation was a place where Cornelia's far-reaching gaze created order and meaning, the city was a place where the blind intrusions of others threatened to destroy meaning. Atop a hill by her family's graves, Cornelia thanks God that all of her dead are with her there, "that stranger-dust mingles not with mine! The tumult of the city rolls not across this sanctuary; careless curiosity treads not on these secluded graves; nor does the idler cull the blossoms that affection has planted. . . . No rude sound disturbs the silence." The contrast is divisive and the images absolute: the peace of the countryside was the familiarity of Home, the quiet of eternal rest; the city was rudeness, idleness, curiosity. Everything there was movement.[16]

Expressions of this theme run throughout the novel and are somewhat abstracted from the early action of the story; they do not further Cornelia's fortunes as much as they define the structure of fortune itself. But the theme of contrast between city and country is deepened when the time comes for Cornelia, like all young women of her class, to go to Charleston for the gay season. Her first tour is no routine occasion, however; just before she is to leave, Roseland burns to the ground, and the handsome Stranger appears to make a rescue and then disappears in the first of several near encounters that mark Cornelia's romance. Thus, by the time Cornelia arrives in Charleston, readers have been prepared for deep changes in character and scene.

In a sense, Cornelia also has been prepared for the coming contrast between agreeable virtue and disquieting temptation. Thus far her rural sensibility has been enough to fill the female sphere; but now she is warned that in the city her place as a woman will be sharply redefined. As a disappointed country suitor tells her: "You will visit Charleston, and a thousand fools will linger near you, and catch your smile, and listen to your voice."[17] As a woman, Cornelia could no longer simply enjoy gazing upon the countryside and knowing the truths of her femininity; now, in the city, she must display truths about herself to the gaze of others. Here was a very different place with a demanding if yet unknown audience, a place of interiors instead of expanses. It was a place curiously scorned by the very persons who introduced a young woman to it. Cornelia's father, a shadowy figure before the tour of Charleston, now comes forward in the novel on a tide of moral aphorisms: "Follow fashion no further than fashion follows propriety," he tells Cornelia. "Never let your mantuamaker dictate to your morals." Cornelia, mimicking her father's values, says of the gay season: "Now came the realization of what is *termed* pleasure." It was a time "which shatters the constitution and confuses the brain. I was soon drawn into the vortex; and, when once entered, nothing but the voice of conscience or the sobering tie of matrimony brings us back."[18]

She speaks here for all the young women, not only for herself, who faced the distinction that the city demanded: something *like* pleasure was found there, but for a moral woman the matronly virtues of conscience and domesticity were preferred and strengthened. In its way, of course, this theme mirrors exactly the extensive literature that depicts urban life as a career of sin and overexcitement. But Gilman cannot dismiss the city outright. Despite its moral dangers, the city held a few experiences that were emblematic of what a wise woman should know. Early in her Charleston tour, for example, Cornelia attempts to stitch together the city and country with a social comparison, instead of a moral one. "The belle of the plantation is, in some sort, the same airy creature who treads the boards of the city ballroom," she reasons. "The respectable matron of the field has a similar range of influence with her who presides and dictates in polished circles." Perhaps the familiar sphere of country women could be superimposed over the beauty and power that city women displayed. Airiness and influence, two attributes prized by the finished lady, were not restricted to the social relations of Charleston but could be exported to the country like buttons or flax. In this and other brief reflections, Gilman suggests that the city, even the otherwise frivolous ballroom, tightened women's intellectual grasp on the culture of their sphere. Cornelia discovers at her first ball that "one gradually finds one's own relative importance. Mamma's plum-colored satin and feather no longer seemed to me the *ne plus ultra* of dress when I observed the row of brilliant-looking ladies who lined the room . . . and I shrivelled up into almost nothingness. . . . [I] saw the easy, graceful, practiced forms of the city belles."[19]

At these times, with these insights, the negative image of the city is not so seamless. Indeed, in looking at the structure of the novel it is clear that while the plantation scenes establish the moral standard, the events necessary to move Cornelia to her apotheosis as a Southern matron must take place in Charleston. The parties, the crowded streets, the races, and a visit to a fortuneteller give Cornelia more than a superficial polish: they bring her to a kind of knowledge—a knowledge of the link between society, the woman's sphere, and her own temperament. Without her tour of Charleston, she would not have learned how to compare and to judge. The city broke society into its parts but made them seem whole again. In a pivotal scene, Cornelia discovers the Stranger's identity as Arthur Marion, whom she has admired from afar, and they climb the spire of St. Michael's church, accompanied

by another young planter couple and a rustic upcountry girl. The view
of the city—its order and beauty apparent from a distance—is their
backdrop as they discover truths about love, aspiration, and even something about social class (Cornelia's lover first condescends to, then ad-
mires the rustic girl). Looking about, they discover *place* and find
themselves centered in it. Cornelia, for a moment, forgets even Arthur
as she looks down upon Charleston, for the first time calling it "my
own fair city," and sees it set *into* the countryside, not apart from it.
The Ashley and Cooper Rivers flow evenly from the woods; the ships
in the harbor are like eagles and Castle Pinckney like a swan: "I felt
like a being from another sphere."[20]

In a way she is, for even though she makes a certain sense of her
sphere in the city, she cannot stay there. She returns to the country
with Arthur, now her husband, and her life as a Southern matron
is sealed. The city taught its lessons, but had to be left behind. The
contrast between the plantation as Home and the city as Other remained intact, despite the scene in the spire when it nearly became
dialectical and the differences between the two places almost carried
Cornelia to a new social awareness. There is nothing in Gilman as a
storyteller to suggest that any other outcome would have been possible, given the satisfying conventions of domestic fiction. The accepted
moral values of the woman's sphere in the 1830s ultimately shaped her
storytelling, and Gilman's calm, rounded voice mirrors the vision of
the sphere that the story celebrates: though not without conflict and
risk, the experience of women led them to where they *belonged*. The
insight Cornelia discovered in the wide world of Charleston, and the
wisdom she showed in choosing Arthur as her mate, translated into
a domestic bond at the center of life: the plantation. Even when their
first son dies soon after birth, Cornelia and Arthur are not shaken
because they are at home, surrounded by comforting fields and shelter-
ing trees obscuring the road to Charleston.

Caroline Gilman allowed that some readers felt her stories had "too
much sunshine about them," but she believed that to write in any other
way would be unfaithful to "fact."[21] This may sound disingenuous to
modern ears because her novel so clearly depicts an idealized female
life. But in a sense we can take Gilman precisely: hers is, as she said,
a novel of domestic "habits," and its action and structure were meant
to bolster a typical female sensibility. Stories like Gilman's depicted
women's sphere as growing naturally from a woman's daily routine to

307

enclose her whole life's course; in other words, as habitual, inevitable, and inescapably factual. In the very act of reading such novels, women plumbed their subjectivity in order to find this meaning. The novels thus occupied an important intellectual borderland between subjective experience and wider social values. At every turn in a story at once conventional and moving, a woman could feel the sphere where she belonged. For Gilman, the country was an analogue to the female domain, and she left the reader there, gazing like Cornelia at the silent amphitheater of the trees.

In contrast, Susan Petigru King wrote as a woman familiar with the social intricacies of the city who more or less preferred them to the solitude of the plantation. Her preference for city life, however, was problematic; her difficulties with it represent another, different motif in the general city-and-country theme. From the first pages of her 1855 novel *Lily*, it is clear that Susan King was a woman whose voice took its tone from a showy and self-conscious region of the female sphere: from the dress and furnishings of the city drawing room, the gestures of the dance, the expressions of confessional conversation, and the many social obligations that accompanied ornamental womanhood. Instead of attempting to close the circle of morals and manners, as Gilman did, King spoke from the gap between them.

The youngest daughter of the prominent Charleston lawyer James Louis Petigru, Susan DuPont Petigru was born in the city in 1824. Set into the heart of elite society, she never left it; many of her detractors (and there were many) said she never stopped abusing it. She was a "lively" child, according to her father. She first attended Madame Talvande's school and then was sent by her father to Madame Giyou's in Philadelphia for the final finish. By her own account, the young Susan preferred conversation and reading romances to studying. Petigru noted his dissatisfaction with the fifteen-year-old girl, telling her aunt, "Sue I am afraid will after all of our pains turn out a wit. . . . She affects to be very unhappy, but it appears to me she is very unreasonable." Susan returned home to marry Henry C. King, an attorney in her father's office. She wrote four novels between 1854 and 1864, all of which contain long passages of commentary on the constrictions of an elite woman's life, the unhappiness of which seems neither affected nor unreasonable. In these years, she gained a reputation for being "fast," a term that might mean a number of mildly objectionable things but suggested that while she was more than "strong-minded"

in a purely intellectual way, she stopped short of being "loose." "Like
her father," one postwar critic remarked without irony, "she was famous
for her wit and cleverness at repartee," and another recalled her "always surrounded by a group." Susan King died in 1875, and her tomb-
stone proclaims her mind as "gifted with genius" and, what seems closer
to the mark, her soul as "bruised, but not crushed."[22]

In subject and style, Susan King's novels represent a kind of wom-
en's writing altogether different from the "sunshine" genre of Caroline
Gilman. King's expectations, if not all her prejudices, hardly ever coincided with dominant social values. *Lily* combines city life and country
life into a theme in which the woman's sphere encircles neither life
completely. The female sensibility in King is marked by a constant state
of suspension between city and country values—a suspension that mirrored women's physical journeyings between the two worlds and gave
a sharp edge even to King's entertaining moments.[23]

In *Lily*, King initially places her protagonist amid "the wide-spreading
lands in their Southern loveliness," but the early rural scenes serve mainly
as a foil for what is to come. King thought of herself as a social realist
(which may have had something to do with her being considered "fast")
and as having no interest in the "sudden surprises, mysterious secrets,
and dark horrors" dear to romantic convention. "Mine is simply a little tale which seeks neither to dazzle nor to terrify," she wrote in her
anonymous preface to *Lily*. "I try to write of human nature as it passes
daily beneath our windows." It is an urban image. Susan King took
up her pen in her Charleston townhouse, not in a country manor.
She hoped to pursue human nature itself, not chronicle the habits that
structured its morality. Her author's voice is not smooth but well-suited
to the drawingroom's barbed dialogue; she is restless, and one never
is sure where she is going.[24]

Lily Vere is a Charleston-born girl who is given over to the care
of a planter couple at the outset of the novel. In depicting Lily's girlhood on the banks of the Pee Dee River, King drew upon typical experiences—plantation childhood, Charleston schooling, summers at
the shore—to set her heroine firmly into the web of elite female experience. As the story unfolds, however, King implies that a country life,
whatever its beauties, might not be an unmixed blessing for Lily. Early
in the story, for example, King's description of the natural beauty of
the plantation is tempered by an ironic view of the planter couple. Lily's
guardian, Mrs. Clarendon, is "an excellent, worthy *Southern Matron*,"

309

singularly devoted to her domestic duties and to religion. She is so devoted, in fact, that she is something of a drudge. She is wrapped in the fabric of her domestic routine, and "though she had been quite a belle . . . no one would have believed it, she was so plain and fusty now." As for Mr. Clarendon, King verges on scorn when she describes him as "an admirable judge of a horse's points" but possessing little "discernment about an individual's qualities."[25]

Though made in passing, these observations openly challenge the value of country life by suggesting its severe limitations as a truly social world. Country people were profoundly ignorant of collective experience and its appearances; worse, they were complacent in their ignorance. Mrs. Clarendon, for example, "never saw deeper into her acquaintances than the outer cuticles of their skins," as King's narrator remarks. Yet Mrs. Clarendon goes about her duties as though they were the world. Distant from the human nature passing beneath the city's windows, the Southern matron becomes in King's novel someone to be pitied, almost ridiculed, for the self-satisfied morality tied to her apron strings.[26]

Midway into *Lily*, then, Susan King has developed a view of the plantation that implies the worth of living in a city among social relations because only they give an obvious shape to woman's sphere. Country life fills out a woman's realm, but in a deadening way that she neither fully sees nor grasps. Once Lily goes to the city, however, the entropy of the countryside is exchanged for an equally blind vanity.

Falseness and self-display replace rural dullness, and King's voice shifts from irony to anger. Charleston women, for instance, push their young daughters into the gay season, abandoning them to the temptations of society without so much as a warning. King's narrator is emphatic: a woman who refuses to take the trouble to explain the rituals of drawing room life "is casting away a privilege and disregarding an urgent necessity." What was this necessity? Being a "watchful guard" of one's charges as they "enter upon the stage of grown-up life" in the city. What many Southern matrons forget, King suggests, is that a young woman's entry into her sphere—a sphere that encompassed all that a lady could expect of power, satisfaction, and glory—could end in personal disaster if rural virtue were all that she possessed. Moralisms about the city as Other were not the point, in King's view, nor were paeans to the country. A young woman like Lily had to be *informed* about her sphere: its circumference, texture, and climate, so to say. She had to

310

be told of designing men, warned of women who betrayed confidences, and weaned from the youthful intimacy of the academy—or else she was in danger of falling victim to the only realm she was destined to occupy.[27]

Thus King's women cannot give outright allegiance to either city or country. The woman's sphere never coincides, morally speaking, with either locale. Even if properly warned, a young woman still might become a lovely shell of a sort well known in King's circles: "Nature gave her a straight, slight figure, and art added the 'fillings in' . . . but she was a lively, conversable girl, full of the smart phrases of society, who made a little talk wherever she went, looked interested in what was said, never dreaded to compromise her dignity by being seen with so-and-so, decidedly preferred her 'own set' but could chat just as gayly in someone else's."[28] A belle *manqué*, to be sure.

How might a woman save herself from such an end, from being the object of others' amused looks and the occasion for coyly lifted fans? By staying in the city but staying on guard. Compelling in this respect is the character of Angelica Purvis, Lily's older cousin. She is a figure of intensely felt longing for peace, yet she just as obviously thrives on the seething society of the drawing room. Angelica is beautiful, of course; she is also spiteful and world-weary. She toys with both men and women, in order to be desired enough to receive the attention she wants and feared enough to avoid what she does not want. But she also is the only one who warns Lily, in a burst of confessional candor, that every girl's sensibility is skewed by either the social ignorance or the social ambition of her parents. Her own mother, Angelica says, "brought me before the world early, because it was easier to do than to keep me in; and her pride and interest in me amble at an even pace with the admiration that I excite. Papa has grown to—what is the word? love me? yes, that is the comprehensible syllable—love me more after every rich offer for my hand.[29] An unhappy woman, Angelica nevertheless gives Lily a chance to see social reality. On display before the world, the ladies of city society felt true feeling subside under the hot gaze of all who sought them. And it seemed as though everyone did. Yet what was the alternative to the lady of the ornamental realm? The "plain and fusty" matron who attended to her duties and stifled the beating of her own heart. Susan King's female sphere, then, drifts between city and country, borne on longing and regret. Faced with the muteness of the plantation, King spoke in the bright, ironic voice of the bruised

311

city belle who nevertheless *knew*. Yet country life continued to promise her much-desired rest.

Interestingly, Charleston itself as a city did not necessarily embody all the damaging effects of a woman's place in an urban setting. At times, King almost seized upon Charleston to free her from her dilemma. The middle third of *Lily* is set not in Carolina but in New York and Philadelphia. Many of the scenes in which King spins out her sense of the drifting female sphere take place in these two cities, not in Charleston; the hardened belles and predatory rakes are more often than not New Yorkers. Lily confronts sectional antagonisms as they filter into New York drawing rooms: the condescension of Northern belles, the coldness and haste of the cities of Yankeeland. These scenes permit King to depict Charleston, despite its drawbacks, as "dear, drowsy Charleston." When Angelica says that Charleston is "the dearest place to love at a distance," Lily protests, "Oh, Angel! . . . it is a place to live and to die in. I like to visit other cities, but for a home, give me Charleston." Even allowing for the fact that Lily is still rather naive at this point, King seems to be reaching toward Charleston as a city in which a relatively slow pace, even its "irregular and peculiar construction," might be a refuge from the worst of Southern rural complacence and Northern urban malice and therefore become a home for female sensibility.[30]

Still, what ultimately is striking about Susan King's fiction is its homelessness; it seems to belong nowhere happily. Her many female characters who yearn for peace and trustworthy social relations nevertheless persist in following—even relishing—the ways of drawing room society. Both Angelica and Lily feel the emptiness of this glittering life, but neither escapes its risks nor fully repudiates its falseness. At just the point when Lily's perceptions might translate into a liberating judgment, or when the judgments of Angelica almost coalesce into feminist criticism, they succumb to either the ambitions or the attractions of drawing room femininity. In this hothouse realm, judgments were turned into repartee and true feelings dragged on stage with false ones.

In a sense, the novel as a literary form did the same thing to Susan King's intellect. The conventional usages of plot, character, and dialogue did not seem to attract her as much as the novel's imaginative "license" for revealing intimate detail. The novel as expressive form enabled King to re-create the subjective pain and reward of her sex's social life with almost seductive dexterity. But this often amounted to

312

self-indulgence, limiting her critical powers. In turning the drawing room inside out to her readers' view, King meant to expose its hazards; instead she folded herself—and the woman's sphere—inside the realm of fashionable nuance, word play, gesture, and lamplight where subjectivity reigned. She wrote of manners in order to puncture them; but she wrote a *novel*, and the devices of storytelling transformed her best insights into a work only too vulnerable itself to drawing room gossip. The novel as a form was too "fast." It was too much a part of the female sphere to rechart what that sphere might otherwise have included, and the novelist's voice was too close to that of the clever artist of the drawing room for a new tone to be heard.

The conclusion of *Lily* suggests how King finally confronted these limitations of the novel form. She simply rang down the curtain on the whole subjective display. With stunning, almost bathetic force, Lily returns to Carolina, marries, and is poisoned by her new husband's black mistress all in a few pages. There is an analogue in this sudden ending to the way an elite woman could dictate a conversation or cut off an admirer simply by choosing no longer to ornament the occasion. It is as though King closed down her protagonist's story because Lily's youth and urban experience had been used up, and with them the brilliance of King's own drawing room style.

Maiden, belle, matron: these were the milestones on a Southern woman's journey through her own womanhood. For each marker there was a set of conventional yet highly charged expectations and actions that gathered the singularities of her life into a pattern; the pattern made her, to that degree, typical of her sex and class. In this sense, the city-and-country theme traced the transition from girl to woman. Probably few women readers remained unmoved by the clean satisfactions of the woman's sphere in Gilman's fiction, just as they could not have failed to recognize King's troubled, bright-eyed heroines. In their passage from country to city to country, the women of these stories did what women ought: became accomplished in the ways of ornamental femininity, encountered men in their various guises, felt the boundary of their domain, and—in most of this fiction—triumphed by attending to it and beautifying it.

This style of femininity, this particular map that guided most elite women through their social and sexual lives, changed with the onset of war in 1861. The change was not sudden, and it surely was not complete; the elevated Lost Cause tributes to women would not have been

313

unfamiliar to Gilman and King, effusive though they would have seemed to both of them. The change was gradual, propelled by circumstances of war and resisted by elite tradition: women learned to do without; assumed even more of the management of plantation and household; saw their men dress as generals and die like anyone else; lived alone with the remaining slaves; discovered things about their husbands' financial affairs that they never had dreamed; knew grief and obligation; cursed fortune and prayed to God. In all these wartime particulars, women began to see certain reaches of their sphere for the first time.[31]

Mary Boykin Chesnut's postwar memoirs are interesting in this respect because they capture themes of antebellum femininity undergoing scrutiny and change. The Janus-faced character of her long manuscript is precisely its historical value; to read it is to understand that no sharp line divided "antebellum" from "postbellum" intellectual life. Its diary form, in contrast to the novel, is especially suggestive of a feminine voice in transition. This is not to imply, however, that Chesnut was more perceptive than novelists in some absolute sense. Chesnut herself tried writing novels, and it is not altogether clear what final shape her book would have taken had she lived to see it published. But the diary form of her book is significant here because its contrasts with the novel throw into different relief the city-and-country theme, deepening our sense of the theme's social roots and its explanatory power. What to call the form of Chesnut's book has been the subject of much discussion; it is not the simple diary it was once taken to be. But it was based on a wartime diary, and Chesnut chose to retain that literary form when she worked to recapture the denouement of the antebellum years. Whatever it is called (a memoir in diary form seems best, if cumbersome; at most, the document is a kind of palimpsest), it is important to consider what the form permitted Chesnut to do differently as a writer before looking at how she viewed the city and the country.[32]

More than any other woman writer of antebellum South Carolina, Mary Chesnut has had her words studied and her biography ably told.[33] Born in 1823 to Stephen and Mary Boykin Miller, Mary grew up in Carolina, lived briefly in Mississippi, and attended Madame Talvande's, where she was a schoolmate of Susan King. In 1840, Mary married James Chesnut, Jr., a Camden planter and aspiring politician who was to become a United States senator, a brigadier general in the Confederate Army, and an aide to Jefferson Davis. Her family had deep roots in South Carolina's economic and political life, though throughout most of her mature writing Chesnut had surprisingly little to say about them and not much more to say about the postwar years. Clearly, the war and the immediate antebellum decade focused her work. She tried her hand at autobiographical sketches, fiction, and biography (of her husband), and her prose reveals her as an intelligent, opinionated woman who loved entertaining, traveling, reading, telling stories to her advantage, and other satisfactions of elite life. A man who enjoyed her friendship once wrote to his wife, after dining at the Chesnuts': "Mrs. C. very talkative introducing great names in her discourse as if intimate with them & giving her husband sharp hits in a quite unprovoked way." It is a typical glimpse of this energetic woman. Her honed remarks often cut deep into the foibles of her class, but she just as keenly enjoyed its rewards. For all her criticism, she usually reined in her political sense enough to avoid being called "strong-minded," and was not sexual enough in company to be considered "fast." Even so, sufficiently strong was her will and quick enough her mind that she stayed socially visible.[34]

Her critical sense is immediately noticeable in her book. Mary Chesnut is present as *herself*, talking about what she is doing and how she is writing. In the diary form, she stumbled upon—seized upon—a means that permitted her to claim the foreground of her own literary expression. She could be conversational yet analytic, and here the contrast with fiction is illuminating. However deep the differences between Gilman and King, both women shared a genre that forever reminded the reader, "This is imaginary." Even though Gilman dressed her novel as a "recollection" and King often placed a critical narrator at the cutting edge of her story, these devices scarcely permitted them the freedom to speak directly to the reader as themselves. Though both devices served to sharpen fictional realism, both also severed the writer from her craft (as did the practice of omitting one's name from the title page, severing identity from voice). Thus Gilman and King burrowed further into the tunnels of conventional women's fiction even as they tried to say something about women's wider realities.

Aside from calling attention to its own limitations and excesses, novel-writing had no means of permitting a woman to make a plain judgment or a sustained self-scrutiny—two risky, strong-minded activities. What is so striking about Chesnut's writing is the way the diary form enabled her to give a running commentary on the act of writing even as she told her stories: it released her from the set of conventions that trapped King in the drawing room and made Gilman "sunshiny." Many times in Chesnut's book, and in the portions of the original diary left to us, she commented on the expressive freedom that the diary gave her simply to bear witness without elaborate art or artifice. Sometimes this freedom was heady: "I am reckless," she remarks at one point in her book. "Almost shameless about changing my mind." Yet at other times she was pleased with simple accuracy, satisfied that her writing "may some future day afford dates, facts, and prove useful to more important people than I am." She gained a sense of literary mastery over rapidly changing events that was more typical of the male sphere of journalism or historiography.[35]

Moreover, the diary form convinced Chesnut that in bearing witness she had to interpret events. A diary by its nature encourages an intellectually active, organizing voice, putting the diarist legitimately at the center of determining the meaning of things. There was no need to be either supinely ornamental or cleverly self-deprecating and allusive, as novel-writing encouraged women to be. Indeed, when Chesnut herself attempted a novel, she often slipped into a voice not unlike Susan King's: arch, witty, defensive. The diary allowed her to shed some of this drawing room style. As a form, in short, the diary was suited to interpreting instead of moralizing; Chesnut could make an effort to *know* rather than an effort to *appear*.[36]

Her adoption of the diary form, of course, had its most immediate impetus in the war, but I think her own reflections about the prewar years reveal antebellum roots of her diarist's voice—the voice of a knowing interpreter of events. These roots tapped her experience as the wife of a politician and U.S. senator, an experience that elaborated the contrast between city and country. The political life in Washington, D.C., allowed her to associate with a group of people whom she considered to be clear-headed and knowledgeable as well as polished and agreeable, urban as well as urbane. If they sometimes indulged in drawing room games, they were also unusually self-humorous and intellectually critical. In a comment reminiscent of her antebellum life, Chesnut noted that these people could be counted upon to gather in cities. "Our world collects here," she noted with satisfaction about wartime Richmond, "—gravitates [here] as it did to Charleston and Montgomery." With the war, she at first despaired of losing this life, and alluded in one of her

316

earliest journal entries to her fear of leaving Washington society upon her husband's resignation from the Senate, noting, "I am not at all resigned." But as the crisis at Fort Sumter grew in significance, so did the urban context she loved, and she saw that "all the agreeable people South seemed to have flocked to Charleston at the first gun." She took her stand, often seated, and "held a sofa against all comers" in order to be first to hear the news. There never was such a place in the country.[37]

Her enjoyment of political, city life was joined to specific reasons for disliking country life. Of course her dislike was not unmixed; indeed, the attractions of the plantation—the "luxurious bed linen" and the "delicious fresh cream"—made it all the more difficult for her to organize and express her discontent. Like King and Gilman, Mary Chesnut has passages where she invites the reader to see from her country window a vision of the "primeval forest" and to smell the nearness of "violets, jasmine, crab apple blossoms, roses." But almost always afterwards, Chesnut stirs uneasily; she judges, becomes wry: "A pleasant, empty, easygoing life," she remarks. "If one's heart is at ease." She did not find ease in the country; in fact, she needed ease beforehand in order to live there at all.[38]

In part, this was because of her unhappiness with her husband's family—a situation far too complicated to be more than touched upon here. Her unease seems to have stemmed less from any specific animosity between herself and her in-laws than from a more general dissatisfaction with the forced intimacy that country life imposed:

> My experience does not coincide with the general idea of public life. I mean the life of a politician or statesman. Peace, comfort, quiet, happiness I have found away from home. Only your own family, those nearest and dearest, can hurt you. Wrangling, rows, heart burnings, bitterness, envy, hatred and malice, unbrotherly love, family snarls, neighborhood strife, and ill blood.[39]

The contrast between public life and private life—city and country— is seen here as also a contrast between male and female spheres. Chesnut realized that for her, a woman, the typically male sphere of public life had been a release from the intrigues of intimate domesticity. This is an almost complete reversal of what is found in Gilman and other idealized fiction about the plantation, a reversal of what Chesnut began to think of as social ideology, or in her phrase a "general idea." Far from the harmony that a woman was supposed to cherish in the

317

country, Chesnut experienced the "alive and rampant" conflicts of family life, all the more exhausting because there was no one around other than family. Intimate personal life became the world; the subjectivity of family emotions spread itself across a woman's entire horizon. A woman who permitted herself to do so could become ignorant of all else. In Chesnut's portrait of her mother-in-law, for example, there is something of Susan King's socially oblivious matron. Though hardly fusty, the elder Mrs. Chesnut maintained an iron-clad sweetness of temper and a controlling fastidiousness, perfected by the end of the war into a "roseate-hued mist for her own private delusion." Mary could admire the older woman's competence and goodness, but she believed that her husband's mother had no warm friends and "is content to dwell in proprieties forever."[40]

Related to this theme of rural discontent is a second, even more extensive motif that deepens and in effect reverses the familiar depiction of country quietude in novels: the enforced personal isolation of plantation life, which Chesnut expressed a number of times in many ways. Country life placed women "miles away from the rest of the world." Despite visits, despite entertainments, despite even family quarrels, the isolation made "one day curiously like another" in a disturbing way. The plantation, Chesnut began to realize as she wrote and rewrote, had gutted her ability to define events and desires. It made her susceptible to preoccupations and to hours of useless daydreams at her window. Clean linen and perfumed air notwithstanding, "I could sleep upon bare boards if I could once more be amidst the stir and excitement of a live world." Saddened by the Southern landscape itself, Mary Chesnut left no doubt that the live world was to be found in the cities she knew. "I feel blue-black with melancholy," she wrote typically in a scene at Mulberry plantation. "But I hope to be in Richmond before long. . . . That is some comfort."[41]

As the war wound down, Chesnut struggled to keep from sinking back into feminine subjectivity. It was different for her husband, perhaps for most men. James grew disgusted with the misery and bickering that filled the last months of the Confederacy and suggested to Mary that they go home and think. "And go mad?" Mary responded. "Catch me at it!" In her diary, she had mounted the beginnings of an attack on subjectivity, and she was not about to open herself to it again. With dismay she must have read Varina Davis' letter from the country asking, "What do you do all day long? I dream. I do not even sew. I cannot read. I dream." Even in 1861, Chesnut had written to herself what might have served as a response to such seductive emptiness. The country had always been the place for women to dream and to drift. When novels did not directly recommend this life, as Gilman's did, they often came around to cultivating it by turning it over and over to view, as in King. "This journal is intended to be entirely *objective*," Chesnut wrote that day in 1861. "My subjective days are over. No more *silent* eating into my own heart."[42]

Holding to this resolution would prove difficult. In making it, Mary Chesnut cut close to the heart of the woman's sphere and confronted the profound subjectivity that pulled the intellectual life of women into its orbit. Change only just began with the sort of promise Chesnut made to herself in 1861. Similarly, our understanding of the intellectual lives of elite women in the antebellum South has barely begun. Much remains to be accomplished in linking what women wrote to the way they lived. It can be done, however, because the themes that saturated women's writing are at once specifically personal and broadly cultural; city and country entered into women's lives as exact places and also as a shared literary sensibility. And as they lived in both places, women also learned to think about both as having qualities important to their common moral and social experience.

In this sense, intellectual continuity, not change, is initially most striking in their writing. The women writers considered in this essay each took a different tack along the same course. Each came to appreciate the city and the country as basic to the woman's sphere and as orienting her temperament and thought. As a writer, each woman struggled with language, convention, and desire; each discovered her version of the classic dichotomies—the city as noise, movement, risk; the country as quiet, stasis, security—and her discovery animated them, inventing them anew. It is true that each woman possessed a different degree of self-consciousness in using the theme. Only Caroline Gilman can be said to have deliberately led her heroine to the city in order to bring her Home. Much less designedly, but no less certainly, Susan King thrust Lily onto the city's harsh stage so that death might come tellingly in the country. Least intentionally of all, Mary Chesnut seized upon the contrast between country and city as she chronicled and re-chronicled events, sorting through antebellum culture and finding autobiography. Yet for all three women, the locus of intellectual life was not in the city alone; it was in crossing the threshold between city and country. Each crossing invited a woman to take a stance in her sphere, to take a knowledge of its many parts and fashion a sense of what it meant to be both an individual and a lady. And so Gilman strode calmly into the countryside; King agonized in the gaze of others; Chesnut, not choosing a novelist's voice, stood in the gap between the past and what came after, describing over and over again the past, touching on polarities and subjectivities that all women would have recognized.

The continuities are important. But as Raymond Williams has observed, literary themes such as the contrast between city and country persist over long periods of time because they undergo many subtle changes in response to altered social circumstances. In the writings of the three women and, I believe, also in the social experience of the many other women who read and lived as they did, change is signaled. Like all cultural change, it was neither succinct nor linear, and there is no space here to do more than suggest its broad pattern.[43]

The observations of some of the men in Charleston's intellectual life in the late antebellum years will help to sharpen our understanding of the nature of this change in the woman's sphere. From the late 1820s to 1860, men who interested themselves in literary life increasingly acknowledged women's novels in their criticism, compelled to do so by the fiction's popularity if not by a conviction that it merited serious attention. Even the few friendly critics, usually from the North, scarcely did more than condescend to the "authoresses," often judging not the work's qualities but whether or not a woman "retained her place in [the public's] affections" through her writing.[44] Usually, Southern male critics managed an attitude somewhere between amusement and hostility. Reviewing Susan King's *Busy Moments of an Idle Woman*, Frederick A. Porcher followed up his wry understatement that the novel "appears intended to bear directly upon our Charleston society" with the double-edged judgment that the book was "clever." He became serious on the subject of marriage, pointing out that even if a woman married a brute, she should enjoy the happiness of knowing she had done her social duty.[45] Porcher may have been aiming at irony here, too, but the light-and-dark tone of his review is typical of male criticism and suggests that even hostile men had difficulty maintaining a critical balance bespeaking certainty. At any rate, hostile or not, most of the increasing number of male reviewers by the late 1850s were careful to place women's novels within the confines of the female sphere.

A novel was judged only in terms of this domain, not as freestanding amid the writings of men, implying that whatever their specific criticisms, men were more and more aware of a growing division between the sexes in this as in other pursuits. It was a division in the broad society beyond literary interests. In the face of a rising tide of conversation among women through their novels, the men of their city and class shored up the gender boundaries that contained it.

Further signs of change between the sexes add to the picture. In their own writings, men also explored the theme of city and country but in notably different directions. Male writing as such deserves its own study, but a single sharp contrast is illuminating here. Men, as well as women, esperienced country and city as they matured to their duties and pleasures; they, too, had childhoods in the country and their first gay season. But the experience that seems most often to have moved men to speak of the contrast between city and country was their immersion in the risky and speculative world of politics. It was a world of almost endless fascination, thick with the images of personal glory and mortification, memories of friends gained and lost, and strategies for success and reputation. The city was politics, and therefore preeminently male. Yet struggling to master the upsets of political life, men did not always enjoy one another's company; beneath the enjoyable surface, male company was known to breed intrigues complicated enough to be worthy of any woman's drawing room. A man needed a lull, nourishment, quiet; he needed the country—the "bosom" of the country as so many men tellingly phrased it.

Mary Chesnut saw the reversal in this when she took her stand against the "rampant" conflicts of intimate country life: men were comforted by the country, women confined by it. And James H. Hammond gave it characteristic words in 1846 when he pleaded exhaustion with the demands of political advancement: "Oh for a snug little farm where I could indulge my fondness for the country . . . without the anxiety created by the idea that the 'main chance' depends on having every screw tight & the whole machinery moving on clock-work principles." In the city, as Frederick A. Porcher remarked, a man "forms a very insignificant atom in the vast mass of humanity which surrounds him," while in the country he "feels he is a man of note . . . he can calculate the political value of his life." Much had changed since the 1830s, Porcher reflected, when, fifty miles from Charleston at Pineville, a family and friends might gather for the season and feel the satisfaction of people "who meet together on board ship for the purpose of making a long voyage." Faster roads and pressing social demands had brought Charleston too near for such enjoyments. The yearning for country harmony was strong among such men, and one did not have to push as far back into memory as Porcher did when he nostalgically depicted Craven County planters as possessing "the same interests, the same wishes, the same hopes, the same fears."[46]

Hammond, not a man to suffer nostalgia easily even in his youth, was able in a few miles of travel through the backcountry of Georgia to find, unexpectedly and against all his class bias, true feminine beauty in a rural homestead:

> [My] hostess is a most beautiful woman, clad in striped home-made homespun without a corset to correct the squareness of her figure – tall & rather gangling in her gait very careless in her manners. She has one of the sweetest of faces and softest of voices, while in everything she says and does is inhabited one of those mild, clear, chaste spirits so enchanting in a female. . . . She is about 22 years old and has three children. She is a flower in the wilderness.

He was impressed enough to note the woman again on his return trip three weeks later. This time her husband was with her, and Hammond thought they seemed completely happy tucked away on their farm.[47] Imaginings of this sort abound in men's writing, formal and informal, and unmistakably outline a part of the male sphere given over to a wish for relief from the tension of being a man of affairs. Also unmistakable is the sharp contrast with the sense of debilitating isolation these same country scenes held for women like Chesnut. If such men and women had been granted their respective wishes, it seems they would have passed each other on the Charleston road, women streaming into the city in search of company and conversation, men fleeing to the country in search of respite from the consequences of their own desire for power and position.

This division between men and women, expressed in the language of city and country, did not suddenly happen in the 1850s, but it clearly was heightened enough to attract notice and to enter more and more into public and private discourse. William Porcher Miles, writing of Charleston literature and manners in 1853, saw the terms of the change as clearly as anyone. Miles, whose "perfectly modulated voice" Chesnut admired, repeatedly came around to women as he characterized

Charleston society. Something had gone wrong in the past generation, he decided; a "social deterioration" had taken place, signaled by the increasing separation of the sexes. In contrast to previous generations, women by 1853 "no longer shared the amusements and pleasures of their lords. They moped at home . . . gradually sunk into mere house-keepers and nurses . . . for immediately upon marriage [women] seclude themselves." In this way "'Charleston Society' subsides into 'domestic bliss'" in the country home. But it was not only this matronly ideal that had sapped society; the proprieties of the city's drawing rooms had also become ever more destructive of relations between men and women. Fearing the grip of proprieties, women spoke either too shrilly or not at all. Fearing a precipitous slide into marriage, men kept their distance, sparring with the very ladies who should have enriched their lives. "This infrequent, stiff, constrained intercourse between the sexes, prevents their ever becoming acquainted with each others characters," Miles lamented.[48] Neither city nor country held the rewards it had seemed to promise. As city and country marked the division of sexual spheres, the sexes divided their social responsibilities. Something had gone wrong; what had been a harmonious transition between locales and sensibilities had become a ragged contradiction.

From his vantage point at the center of Charleston's political life, Miles saw what Susan King perceived from the interiors of drawing rooms and what Mary Chesnut understood from wartime upheaval: instead of being parts of a single intellectual and social domain, city and country had grown more distinct and distant; always represen-tative of different sensibilities, they represented by the 1850s a theme of disturbing polarity. For women, it became a strong motif in their description of their sphere and its new, problematic artificiality and constriction. The feminine voice of Caroline Gilman that so surely touched women's feelings and aspirations in the 1830s had become less audible, less convincing in its story of the smooth road Home. The older subjective truths locked away from the city's rush began to seem not simply deluded but fundamentally unreal. In her diary, and in her memoir shaped like the diary, Chesnut abandoned the moral scaffold-ing of the novel for a new set of conventions that seemed to better fit the new alienation of city from country. The war convinced her that a woman had to choose between what the two places had come to repre-sent; in war, as in the city, "life is so real, so utterly earnest."[49] Though never wholly free from the older feminine accents, Chesnut did not strive so much to touch readers with her art as to feel the very bound-aries of the woman's sphere itself. And here, along with others, she found another widening duality that paralleled the growing separation of city from country: the schism between men and women that, in some ways, the city-and-country theme always had been about. To say that the realms of men and women were becoming ever more alienated in the late antebellum years is not to say that the older cultural styles of the sexes had become empty of pleasure or meaning. Nor did every-one agree that a crisis was at hand; the war soon supplied the defini-tion of crisis. But the bonds of feeling and expression between women and men, as women's writing suggests, were stretching thinner and more precariously across a deep misgiving about social life. It was a misgiving about whether the separate realms of the sexes, in dividing up social reality, splintered personal happiness. And perhaps these Charlestonians began to doubt whether the separate duties and satis-factions of each sex truly strengthened the society they feared they might soon be losing.

12

Bust of Louisa Cheves McCord, by Hiram Powers. Collection of the Carolina Art Association–Gibbes Art Gallery.

Ludibria Rerum Mortalium: *Charlestonian Intellectuals and Their Classics*

RICHARD LOUNSBURY

While in Columbia we saw Cheves McCord at his mother's. He had been badly wounded at Second Manassas, in both the head and the leg.

Mrs. McCord went at once to Richmond and found he was still at or near Manassas Junction. She went to Mr. Miles to get her a passport to go down for him. He said the thing was impossible. Government had seized all trains, and no passports were given. "I let him talk," said

Mrs. McCord, "for he does it beautifully. That very night I chartered a special train. We ran down to Manassas and I brought back Cheves in triumph. You see he is nearly well, with our home nursing."

"Mother of the Gracchi," we cried.[1]

It was the opinion of Thomas Grimké that ancient literature was barren of female character. It seems an absurd opinion. From Helen to Hypatia the classical record abounded in remarkable women: to ignore a poet like Sappho, a tragic heroine like Antigone or Medea, an empress like Livia or Agrippina, appears not so much foolish as inexplicable. But Grimké was neither ignorant nor a fool, and his reasons find more explanation than only in a literary taste which pronounced that "the works of Scott, alone, exhibit a greater variety of the grand, the pathetic, the beautiful, in female character, than all the classic writers of antiquity." Grimké was making a moral argument. He had the highest hopes for woman. Already, "in the best virtues of Christian perfection she has always exceld man," nor was he disposed to deny her equality, when the chance was given her, in "arts and arms," in literature, philosophy, and politics. Antiquity could offer nothing: "The woman of ancient Greece, if virtuous, was the slave of her parents and the captiv of her husband", and if not—well, Grimké did not think it necessary to exclude the beauty of Thaïs and the acumen of Aspasia, in view of the path by which these excellences had been brought to fulfilment. There had been a momentous division, cutting off woman from her classical past, and woman herself had most accomplished it. Now that "the mightiest revolution which has been wrought in modern literature has resulted from the universality of female character and female influence throughout the whole of society, and from their transfusion into every department of literature," the literature of the ancients was exposed as an Eden without inhabitants, without any "sublime and touching character."[2]

It could afford no *exemplum*—neither (the Latin word comprehended both) a precedent by which present conduct might be judged, nor a model for conduct in the future. Louisa McCord gave much thought to the *exemplum*. Her catalyst was the feminist plundering of the past for convenient models and precedents. Opposing the arguments which the plunder was meant to support, Mrs. McCord was skeptical. Feminist models were, as she confronted them, not heroines from the store of antiquity but rather queens and regents from the Middle Ages and thereafter. These, she reasoned, were unsuitable to prove the political rights of modern women; on the contrary, hemmed about with chivalric codes and other "laws and habits of society" that conferred a special prestige upon their sex, or—in the case of Joan of Arc, "decidedly the most remarkable of heroines"—exalted above the "rights and habits of manhood" by community with God, such women but proved that only by men's permission, retractable at any time, were women able to rule. Nor were examples from literature at all persuasive: Portia and others of that kind "require all Shakspeare's genius to cause them to be tolerated even on the stage," and Louisa McCord indulged her grim glee in depicting her feminist opponents baffled "at the New-York bar" and hissed for their pains by boys in the street. "If ladies will borrow arguments from imaginary characters, why not take at once the powerful Minerva springing full-armed from the brow of Jove?" Why not, indeed? The classical world, as Grimké saw, was dubious and treacherous material, and not only goddesses would be improper models for Christian ladies. Caroline Dall's solution, to "retouch" historical portraiture, could not have satisfied any standard of Mrs. McCord's: her refurbished Aspasia, the alliance with Pericles scrubbed into respectability, was not less than Portia a fictional creation.[3]

But Louisa McCord's skepticism was of the instances, not the principle, of searching amid an instructive and encouraging past. Grimké's barriers troubled her as much as would William Porcher Miles' impossibilities in the summer of 1862. Such phantoms as Mrs. Dall's were imaginary without the benefit of, nor yet discrediting, the imaginative: when he declared that "the great end of the art is to strike the imagination," it was of the painting of history that Sir Joshua Reynolds spoke.[4] Not that the fanciful was to be excluded, when vividness came to the argument, when an affronted nature punished some reforming quack and "the hair-brained Phaeton, who would guide the chariot of the sun, must perish amid the suffering he has caused," or when affronted Southern apology, having "again and again . . . forced aside the foul load of slander and villainous aspersion," was doomed, like Sisyphus, to oppose again and again "the old refuted libels, vamped, remodelled, and lumbering down upon us with all the force, or at least impudent assumption, of new argument." Nor to be excluded were the lessons of a legendary past, decorated with Livian elegance: separate secession would be the sacrifice of Marcus Curtius without the rescue of the state for which the sacrifice had been made.[5] The Roman household gods and guardians, the Penates, were a metaphor of woman's role, of woman herself, who ought not to worship them but to be worshipped among them: a bold apotheosis, but proper and easy for Mrs. McCord, at home among the Romans.[6]

"The choice of this subject, the severe classic simplicity of the play, in plot and incident, and the author's disdain of the accompaniments which have opened the way of others to a brief popularity, will prevent its acquiring a sudden reputation; yet it evinces powers of a very high and uncommon order, and deserves special attention as a brilliant anomaly in our literature."[7] That *Caius Gracchus* was something unusual was agreed by one who, however, unlike the critic of *DeBow's Review*, did not like Mrs. McCord's play: "A tragedy by a Southron," concluded the *Southern Quarterly Review* grumpily, "and a lady, is surely no such ordinary event, that we should pass it with indifference."[8] Indifference was impossible, not for patriotic reasons only, or because the author was a woman, but also on account of the poetic tradition and the criteria of style (where the importance of the author's sex arose again) which the play embraced. Hence the *Quarterly*'s disapproval of the play: it offended against "grace and repose," against "one essential condition of poetry [which] is harmony, symmetry and exquisite arrangement." Force, rapidity, impressiveness there were in abundance; there were earnestness and eloquence. But these leaped from a mind the attributes of which, excellent in analytic and polemical prose, were deficient for poetry—were, indeed, "all masculine."[9]

DeBow's concurred—"she is wholly unlike any of her sisters of the lyre, and writes with a terseness, vigor, earnestness and masculine energy"—but *DeBow's* was delighted, not distraught. The modern Muse offered to the fancy "a store of sweets" in "an air full of delicate harmonies" diffuse and genial, murmurous with the sensuous luxuriance of contemporary English poetry and German philosophy, and her votaries were many and indistinguishable. But Mrs. McCord, schooled in the Greek and Latin poets, had imparted to her work "a purely classic tone which no unlearned writer could have given"; she had shunned "the attractions of the romantic school"; her versification demonstrated her "partiality to old models in English verse"; her principles were "of those days when there were giants of English literature." "A new era in our literature, indicating a returning of taste to the old and admirable standards," was promised in her.[10] *DeBow's* was applying a criterion proper to Mrs. McCord's intention and ambition, flattening the wall between poetry and eloquence built by the *Quarterly* even as it praised the "energy and force," the epigrams and emphasis, of that eloquence. For Shakespeare, Louisa McCord's "great master of the human mind,"[11] eloquence and poetry were one; him she followed in appealing, by a "sinewy strength of thought and expression," "to the intellect more than the fancy."[12]

The vigor and polemical accuracy that the *Quarterly* identified and admired in her prose, Mrs. McCord conveyed into her dramatic poetry, rushing upon the splendid occasions that periodical writing could but little (albeit she made the most of them) supply. The daughter of Langdon Cheves (his oratory earned praise, and some antique comparisons, from Washington Irving) and a connoisseur of eloquence,[13] she had chosen for her hero an orator whom, although he disliked his politics, Cicero could scarcely have esteemed more generously: *ecce in manibus vir et praestantissimo ingenio et flagranti studio et doctus a puero C. Gracchus*, and much more besides.[14] His character is introduced into the play by his worst enemy, the consul Opimius, who is compelled to weep where the Gracchan oratory directs him to weep, and to feel at command, against his will and hatred.[15] When she came to impersonate that oratory, Louisa McCord, working from hints and summaries in Plutarch, and placing the two speeches at the center of her play, spoke forth an eloquence not unworthy of Gracchus and of herself.[16]

Gaius Gracchus was not the only eminent orator whom Rome produced. The *Quarterly* had objections to this man who, of a great family and assured thereby of political and military preferment, in 123 B.C. yet followed his brother Tiberius, murdered when tribune ten years before, into the same office and into policies similar to his and even more outrageous to many of the most powerful of the Senate; more successful than his brother at first, after two years he met an end as terrible, ordering a slave to kill him amid the bodies of his slaughtered friends.[17] To the *Quarterly*, the politics was monotonous; the hero's own character was vacillating, his wife no Lady Macbeth to drive him to a suitably dramatic pitch, and his purposes—for the sake of a "capricious, selfish, timid and unworthy" people—incapable therefore of tragic dignity.[18]

Louisa McCord need not have been distressed by this, nor any of her predecessors with the theme. Marie-Joseph Chénier's *Caius Gracchus* opened in Paris in February 1792, a time untroubled by political

monotony: rival claques of aristocrats and "patriots" competed to interpret the contemporary allusions for their own purposes, a feat re-
quiring preponderant ingenuity from the aristocrats:

> J'épargne du sang. Dieux protecteurs du Tibre,
> Voici mon dernier voeu: que le peuple soit libre![19]

Such dying words were their own interpretation. Drawing from Chénier
(and Shakespeare), Vincenzo Monti composed his *Caio Gracco* in 1800,
and James Sheridan Knowles his *Caius Gracchus*, in two versions, in
1815 and 1823 – the latter deserving well, and better, the insults often
scattered upon Louisa McCord's play.[20] But certainly the theme is not
one immediately expected to have suited her taste. Whether for good
or ill, the Gracchi brothers were invariably known as promoters of social upheaval for the benefit, or at least by manipulating the desires,
of the common people: *quis tulerit Gracchos*, said Juvenal assailing hy-
pocrisy, *de seditione querentes?*[21] Comparing the hotheads of separate
secession to Robespierre and his friends – "God shield us from such self-
constituted guides and protectors" – Mrs. McCord showed herself no
friend to the French Revolution, the "bloody toy of the multitude,"
the intent of which, in 1792, Chénier had deemed Gaius Gracchus
excellent to promote. Scarcely less disdainful was her opinion of "Mr.
Jefferson's great humbug flourish," the free-and-equal doctrine of the
Declaration. For, at the time of writing her *Caius Gracchus*, there was
that confidence in the superiority of "those born in the purple, the
gentry," which was to be ratified by their behavior in her hospital during the war.[22]

   But the play is more about leadership than the led. Louisa McCord,
even when her enthusiasm for political economy had induced her to
hymn "man's nature, his soul, and instinct, alike lead[ing] him to the
light," had also been aware of the fanaticisms perverting his progress.
The masses must be taught "to think rightly."[23] Gracchus and his
lieutenant Fulvius are made to represent two opposing opinions of
this teaching task, explicitly debated between them[24] and enacted
throughout the play, as the audacious cynicism of Fulvius drags the
hero, cautious too late, to his doom. It is the theoretical counterpoint
to sectional passion. *DeBow's* discovered a political cause behind the
anomaly of *Caius Gracchus*: from Mrs. McCord's state a splendid poetry had been evoked by "the idea of external repression, exciting personal feeling, and turning the mind to the contemplation of heroic

resistance." Protesting against the insolent and indifferent depredations of the Senate, "at once aggressor proud, and vengeful tyrant," Gracchus was a son of Carolina.[25]

"Mrs. McCord is the clearest-headed, strongest-minded woman I know, and the best and the truest." Mrs. Chesnut was not the sort to admire a mind which she did not know: when she introduced Louisa McCord into her journal as "she who wrote *The Mother of the Gracchi*," that title was an accurate error.[26] In his catalogue of women, Juvenal addressed *te, Cornelia, mater Gracchorum*: chaste, noble, devoted, and intolerable.[27] The satirical edge cut as much into the pervasiveness of the *exemplum* as into its validity, for about the memory of Cornelia accumulated elevating and tenacious anecdotes, most illustrating her dedication to the education and eminence of her children. To a wealthy matron boasting of the jewels glittering about her person, Cornelia presented her two sons, saying, "These are *my* jewels": this tale, preserved in a Roman collection of memorable sayings and actions, stuck to the European imagination, blossoming into a theme for neoclassical art that was repeated in Italy, France, and England—by Benjamin West, for instance, and adapted to a contemporary portrait by Reynolds—and imitated for a salubrious witticism by Mrs. McCord herself.[28] In her *Caius Gracchus*, Gracchus himself seems most obvious as the hero, his wife and mother illustrating his tragedy as Virgilia and Volumnia that of the Shakespearean Coriolanus; but an Aristotelian argument backing Cornelia would be not unpersuasive, as Mrs. Chesnut suggests. Cornelia had much to recommend her to Louisa McCord, who for her *exemplum* of prudent courage standing against factional rashness (she was defending her father against the slanders lobbed by advocates of separate secession) chose Aemilius Paullus, Cornelia's grandfather. After the zealous folly of his colleague in the consulship had mired the Roman army in a hopeless position, Paullus, refusing to take an opportunity of flight, had consecrated his honor in the blood of Cannae.[29] That awesome disaster had been avenged at Zama by Cornelia's father, Scipio Africanus, and in the destruction of Carthage by her cousin and son-in-law, Scipio Aemilianus; her uncle, another Aemilius Paullus, had conquered the last king of Macedon; her husband in serving the republic had gained two triumphs, the consulship twice, and had been censor. Widowed young, Cornelia bore a magnificent tradition to her sons, but it lay not dormant in her: the excellence of her character and understanding was recognized by a proposal of

331

marriage from the king of Egypt (she refused it for the sake of her responsibility to her sons) and by the admiration of such judges as Cicero, Quintilian, and Tacitus; Juvenal's *quis feret uxorem cui constant omnia?* voiced very much a minority view.[30]

This was the mother whom Louisa McCord placed in the play dedicated to her own son. Cornelia speaks much that Mrs. McCord wrote in her articles on woman's place and nature; her words to her son Gaius recall exhortations to restraint and reason made in the essays on politics and economic theory. Cornelia, whose *doctissimus sermo*, perceived in her letters, Cicero and Quintilian had approved,[31] made surely a worthy mouthpiece, whether in conversation with Licinia, Gracchus' wife, or with Gracchus himself. But she was more, because there was more. As in Cornelia Mrs. McCord discovered a dramatic correlative to her idea of woman, so in a Gracchan world there was a dramatic correlative to her grim apprehension of the world wherein that idea must work its way. Woman, "the conservative power of the world," had to appeal to a world seeming to conserve nothing. Barred by her proper role from action, she "may counsel, she may teach, she may uphold the weary arm of manhood—of the husband, the brother, or the son—and rouse him to the struggle for which nature never designed her": these were anaphoras smooth in a periodical essay, disrupted in the confusion of a drama.[32] Granted that Cornelia is the orator of the home, of equal vigor to her son in the forum; granted that she is the "home-divinity" presiding over the scene as Licinia vainly attempts to keep her husband at home, safe from the death awaiting him abroad; granted that her admonitions and adjurations can appear to have the essayist's bland certainty: "Nay, stay within doors, daughter; 'tis the place / Most meet and fitting woman";[33] yet Cornelia is also the Louisa McCord of the essays liberated by the complexity and ambivalence with which her choice of dramatic form and tradition, and—this was no Portia—the Roman record itself, furnished her.

The reputation of Cornelia was not wholly excellent: fragments of a darker aspect survive. She was suspected of having goaded her sons into excesses of ambition by reminding them that she was famous thus far as the mother-in-law of Scipio Aemilianus, not yet as the mother of the Gracchi; and even to have procured, in conspiracy with her daughter, the death of Aemilianus in order to terminate his opposition to her son's reforms.[34] Chénier preferred something of this Cornelia, exhorting Gaius, albeit always nobly, toward zeal and boldness of purpose. Louisa McCord, whose Cornelia advocates prudence in aspiration, restraint in perseverance, chose not to use this Cornelia, nor to explore through the play the tensions between an ambitious mother and the son through whom the ambitions must make their way.[35] Rather, she explored the tensions within the mother, testing her role as a woman and struggling to evade its insufficiencies. Licinia, bold to break out of Cornelia's rigorous code, is the occasion of demonstrating the code's workings in its author. The more she advocates control, the more violent are shown the passions she would curb, even in her first exchange with her daughter-in-law on a woman's conduct:

> 'Tis meek endurance, quiet fortitude,
> That make her life and beauty. We may rear
> Heroes, whose dauntless will shall shake the world,
> Or like a moral Atlas, bear its burden,
> A universe of care, upon their shoulders.
> But in our bosoms, if too fierce the flame
> That feeds such spirit-struggles, we must check,
> Or drive it back, at least, to seeming quiet.
> If hard the effort, it is woman's task.
> Her passions, if not smothered, must be hid,
> Till in their faintly-beating pulse, herself
> Will scarcely know her blood the same which bounds
> Through manlier veins unchecked.[36]

But Cornelia knows indeed her blood the same; through the play, her knowledge breaks from her. As his doom closes around Gracchus, Licinia, her uselessness intolerable, bursts out:

> I would I were a man, with a man's soul,
> And not the coward nature modelled me.

Cornelia must pity her the prayers as useless as herself, but she does not rebuke her.[37] As husband parts the last time from wife, a scene piteously described by Plutarch and (Frederick Porcher noticed) a favorite with neoclassical sculpture,[38] Cornelia—whom Mrs. McCord inserts although Plutarch does not have her there—prays for, in her son, "strength to bear / This heavy trial; parting, worse than death, / From the heart-stricken loved ones," and, as he departs, harangues herself:

> Up! up! and work!
> Life yet has its duties, and my comfort is
> Yet to fulfil them.[39]

But her part is not complete, and the record of history is again revised. Gracchus, flying before the relentless Opimius, took brief refuge in the temple of Diana, in despair and thinking of suicide, until urged onward by his few surviving friends (the respite was equally brief). But Louisa McCord represents Cornelia — flouting her first admonition, that a woman should remain within doors — coming to Gracchus in the temple. Their conversation ends:

> Cor.   Rouse! For shame!
> Wake up your flagging energies; be bold
> To probe beneath these flutterings; you will find
> Your courage sound beneath them. For the right
> Man even in despair should ever strive.
> The very effort, howsoever vain,
> Is always something gained. To the great work
> It warms the blood of the world, which wrestles on
> Still against failure, like the strong man struggling,
> Until the end of truth at last is reached.
> We are the thews and sinews of the world,
> And in our efforts there is nothing lost;
> All work to good or ill. Go with these friends;
> For life and duty strive; nor be the coward
> Who, shrinking, dreads on his own heart to look,
> And dies, to shun responsibility.
> My son, I know, can never thus be brought
> By fear to shirk his manhood.
> Gr.   Mother, I go.
> May heaven so bless you, as your son shall strive
> To prove the honor and the love he bears you,
> By working out the noble thoughts you teach.
> Cor. Then once again farewell! These bursting tears
> Now come to show the woman's heart, whose boldness,
> Your sickly resolution to upbraid,
> Usurped the man. Oh! were they tears of blood,
> Feebly they'd speak my anguish.[40]

The whole of their exchange is not only without historical ground but also structurally disproportionate to the skillful rapidity of the tragedy's last scenes. But it is needed for Cornelia. She has performed throughout the play the part of the Greek chorus. Like the chorus, she supplies the moral context in which the action is to be understood; like the chorus, although the action is meaningless without her, she herself is powerless to act. It was a role that Mrs. McCord's idea of woman was most fitted to play, but for the mother of the Gracchi it was a role that impelled even as it forbade escape from itself and, finally, could be satisfied only within a radical ambiguity: she translates her manhood to her son.

It is easy, because it is often right, to be suspicious of the classical name, the classical precedent, sonorous enough, but replacing rather than promoting awareness and analysis, of oneself and of others. Voicing the voiceless grief which succeeded the death of an eminent classicist of Charleston, George Frederick Holmes cited Lucan—and not inappositely, until with some discomfort it is recalled that the recipient of Holmes' elegy had disliked Lucan's epic poem and had never been able to read it through.[41] For ceremonial productions could be especially vulnerable to the allurement of classical splendors. If James Henley Thornwell should mingle into the first paragraph of his memoir of Robert Henry a phrase from Cicero and the names of a couple of ancient historians, and thereafter scarcely mention antiquity, had he not but indulged in—as he himself said—that "richness of classical allusion" which is one of "the ornaments, but not the essence of thought"? Thornwell, however, knew what that essence was. Thucydides and Tacitus were the models for Henry's spirit of inquiry and the guides to Thornwell's appreciation of it: "He seized at once upon the principle which pervaded the details of a subject, and the conciseness with which he announced it, was but a reflection of the energy with which he conceived it." That assessment has its full meaning only when its audience knows the antique authors behind it, how their "brief and pregnant maxims" expose and empower their thought. Allusion is swift and introductory not because it is automatic but because, sufficient, it sets the cast of mind within which the whole memoir should find its meaning. And the cast is emotional, also: Thornwell evokes Cicero's meditation upon the death of Lucius Crassus, orator and mentor, upon the "melancholy interest" of his friends gazing upon the vacant place, where he had last spoken, of his excellence. That meditation had appealed to later students, wishing to embrace its authority as an emotional testament and to graft that authority into their own emotion. To Tacitus it had appealed, and now to Thornwell.[42]

The *exemplum* becomes Idea because time, through its instrument the imaginative tradition, has been its apotheosis. Easy in the classical adherence to Nature and Nature's God, and in the power of the intellectual conception (it is noteworthy that Gracchus deems "the popular majesty an enthroned thought," and that the poem dedicating the play "To My Son" closes in a prayer for God "to make thee stainless, pure, / Upright and true, e'en as my thought doth paint thee"),[43] Louisa McCord composed her Idea of womanhood out of the *exemplum* of Cornelia, and composed herself.

> Who ever hopes to see a woman Shakspeare? And yet a greater than Shakspeare may she be. It may be doubtful whether the brilliant intellect, which, inspiring noble thoughts, leaves still the great thinker grovelling in the lowest vices and slave of his passions, without the self-command to keep them in sway, is superior to that which, knowing good and evil, grasps almost instinctively at the first. Such, in its uncorrupted nature, is woman's intellect—such her inspiration. While man *writes*, she *does*; while he imagines the hero-soul, she is often performing its task.[44]

Caius Gracchus had attempted at once to imagine and to perform. Cornelia, memorialized in the record of antiquity and to the present in the imagination of art, transcended the opposition of duty to fame by reaching fame through duty.[45] Louisa McCord, contributing to the tradition of that fame, partakes of it—and would have need of it. That amused valor which, in the mother, rescued Cheves McCord after Second Manassas, in the son compelled him, over her protests, back to Richmond before his wounds were healed, where he died.

> Wolves breed not lambs, nor can the lioness
> Bear fawns among her litter. You but chide
> The spirit, mother, which is born from you.[46]

Plutarch concluded his life of Gaius Gracchus with praise of Cornelia, who bore her disasters "nobly and with greatness of heart." Mary Chesnut, knowing that her friend's anguish had been terrible, knew the courage that bent it to duty. It was proper that the inscription on the statue raised by the Romans in honor of Cornelia, Louisa McCord should adapt to her own epitaph.[47]

*   *   *

"He returned to the bar with an earnestness of purpose, enhanced by his short congressional career, and he came to it with surpassing brilliancy and power. Animated by a competition which tasked all his resources, he displayed so much learning, ability, and eloquence, that

336

the courts in which he appeared expanded into a forum, and became objects of public attraction, to which multitudes flocked as to a theatre, and from which opinions, principles and emotions were propagated through the community."[48] When William Campbell Preston spoke of a forum, it was not the dead metaphor of which such present phrases as "the forum of public opinion" are the withered remnants. When he thus spoke of Hugh Swinton Legaré returning to Charleston after the mission to Brussels and an interval in Congress, Preston affirmed a conscious effort by Legaré to transpose the Charlestonian courts of law into the forum at Rome where, as Cicero describes the scene in his dialogue the *Brutus* (a passage to which Preston is alluding), the courts met in the open air, many different ones at the same time, and the crowds, shifting and passing between one and another, were captured by the predominant orator and, clustered about the tribunal where he performed, knew that a Roscius, the David Garrick of the late Republic, was on stage; there the splendid trials of state criminals were held; there the nobility carried out their principles or their feuds; there Cicero made himself a senator and a consul.[49] Nor was Preston paying but an automatic, if allusive, compliment to Legaré by comparing him to Cicero; it was, rather, part—the eulogistic counterpart—of that Ciceronian edifice that Legaré sought to raise out of himself, learning and ambition his often indistinguishable materials. Legaré was a student of the classics after whom other students, in imitating their own classic models, ought to model themselves: thus recommended Bartholomew Carroll in his "Sketch of the Character of the Hon. Hugh S. Legaré," published in the *Southern Quarterly Review* four months after Legaré's death.

"He was a *classique*," the "Sketch" concluded, "in every sense of the word—in mind, in disposition, and he would have been, in person—with a model for everything he said or did derived from antiquity—from a heroic antiquity, with its fine ideal—its forms of beauty and magnificence—its graces and doric simplicity—its mighty and marvellous enthusiasm. When he accused, he felt like the Athenian; when he defended, it was with the ingenious audacity of the friend of Archias."[50] That friend was Cicero, of course; and "the Athenian" was designation enough of Demosthenes. Legaré, with Plutarch (and Hugh Blair) his precedent, was fond of comparing the two. Largely because he believed that "forensic eloquence . . . cannot rise to the sublimity of the deliberative, on such subjects and occasions as those which inspired the

337

genius of Demosthenes," upon Demosthenes he must confer the superiority (and hence supremacy) as an orator, the orator of that superlative eloquence which subordinates itself to a practical and a patriotic end.[51] As such, Demosthenes was the model for the Legaré who, as Preston put it, had eloquence as "the chief object of his ambition."[52] Chief, but not entire — or, rather, the orator comprehended "such a singular assemblage . . . of moral, intellectual and physical qualities" that "in the annals of the whole world, fewer men have been distinguished by true eloquence than by any other gift of nature."[53] This opinion Legaré derived directly from Cicero, and Cicero it was who might satisfy that insatiable taste for models which Legaré everywhere displays and his eulogists everywhere celebrate, a taste which Legaré obeyed in his every conception of himself. At the age of nineteen planning his future and discussing his plans with Francis Gilmer, an aspiring lawyer somewhat his senior, Legaré sought to resolve the division between "the *mere* scholar and the *mere* man of business" by recourse to ancient ideals of the "whole man," the "intellectually social and active being," and in particular by recourse to the learning of Cicero, which "can be instrumental in promoting the purposes of active life, in elevating the man of business into the sage, and the mere statement of wholesome truths, into sublime and touching eloquence." The youthful and Ciceronian aspiration, although he might later doubt the chances of its success, he never lost.[54] "In a word," he wrote twelve years later, "if one were called to name the man, in all history, who had made the most of great natural gifts — in whom [were] the effects of that perfect intellectual discipline, which brings out and developes and matures every talent and 'the mind through all her powers irradiates,' he could scarcely fail to ascribe that enviable distinction to Cicero." It is fitting that this period in its cadence and solemnity should itself be modelled on another, that whereby Edward Gibbon identified with the Antonine century the age of mankind "most happy and prosperous."[55]

The necessity of models, deeply rooted in Legaré, bespeaks a way of thinking which subsumes a relevant standard of comparison, and this standard is fecund because it unites the historical and the unhistorical. A man cannot understand himself or explore his capacities unless he understands the past and can use it, can absorb its lessons, its examples, its heroes and heroic texts; he must strive to know in order to make himself out of the knowledge. This was the attitude of the rhetorical theorist of antiquity. It was also the attitude of Thucydides, whom Legaré praised at length as the greatest of historians: the Greek wrote so that later students of men, learning from his work, might the better comprehend the causes and persons at the back of events in their own day.[56] The prescriptive and descriptive uses of antiquity were difficult to disentangle; it was incongruent to be anything but moral about *mores*; one might wish to understand a society, a man, or a text, but was it for the sake of, or in the way of, transposing the first, emulating the next, and worshipping the third?

Legaré, and not he alone, was aware of the difficulty. He was aware of it especially as an orator, not only because his whole ideal of conduct and glory was *ille perfectus et consummatus orator*, but also because an audience, a social audience, empowers an orator; but for it he must be nothing. Cicero lived in a Ciceronian society, and Legaré had long known what this meant. Already in his youthful discussion with Gilmer, he worried that "the quibbles of special pleading and the drudgery of an office seem to be the farthest things in the world from the 'immensum infinitumque etc' that Tully talked of." "Even Racine, with all his admirable talents" for tragic poetry, fell "far short of the Greeks," for "Greek tragedy was essentially and unchangeably Greek."[57] How much more must such a failure, for such a reason, beset the orator? Jacob Cardozo contributed to the *Southern Review* an article demonstrating that the orator must be empowered or enfeebled by his times; that "all the peculiarities in the eloquence of a people are reflected from its manners, habits, and institutions"; and how "these circumstances influence and modify the genius of the speakers." Thereupon, under numbered heads, with estimably methodical sobriety he carries out his task. Has eloquence, then, declined? Say, rather, that "there has been a revolution in its style and spirit."[58]

Most of Cardozo's arguments were anticipated and some expanded by Legaré; what is noticeable is the difference in tone and, in close relation to this, an absolute disagreement of conclusion. Everything that Legaré wrote on ancient oratory is steeped in a regret and a resentment unmistakable. The achievement of Demosthenes was not only glorious but also induplicable (even by Cicero), not on account of individual genius but because of a unique political environment, a particular audience, and rhetorical occasions "momentous and imposing almost beyond anything that can be imagined in these times." Deliberative speaking was the most splendid because it mattered the most: hence Legaré's admiration for that "immortal paper," that work of "true genius," the Declaration of Independence, at once called forth by, and matching, "an occasion destined to form one of the most important aeras in the history of nations."[59] And the achievements of forensic, too, were special: Cicero was possessed of an audience urgent and discriminating, rejoicing in their delicacy of ear, their demanding sensibility "that is not to be met with even in the most cultivated assemblies of modern times."[60]

Demonstrative eloquence remained, "which," he said, "circumstances have made far more common in the United States than anywhere else." And what did Legaré think of this? The critic must be indulgent, of course; rigor was out of place when transitory amusement was the only thing at issue; after all, "a fourth of July orator finds it hard enough, even with the assistance of a little poetry, and the whole artillery of tropes and figures, to say any thing that can be listened to, or deserves to be printed," and Legaré himself had turned his hand to that genre. But the indulgence of the critic, and of the audience, had been abused. "We do not suppose that it would be possible in any other country under the sun, or at least in Christendom—not even excepting Spain—to make such a collection of vapid bombast and rhodomantade, blended with every vice of style for which grammar or rhetoric furnishes a name, as might easily be got up in any single city in the United States under the title of 'American Eloquence.'" Legaré's is the passion not of a connoisseur but of a creator: it is not coincidental that his anger surfaces in his judgment of William Crafts, a fellow Charlestonian not unlike himself, a lawyer with a taste for belles-lettres and an aspiring orator, classically educated (though his Latinity was "execrable") and knowledgeable of ancient and modern eloquence. But Crafts was debauched by his vanity and by the wanton indulgence of his "extraordinary facility" for occasional effect.[61]

"We have no hesitation in repeating what Hume"—in his "excellent Essay on Eloquence"—"says about the eloquence of Demosthenes, viz. that could it be copied, its success would be infallible over a modern assembly."[62] But could it be copied? Hume, who had concluded ancient eloquence to be a worthy and a just model, judged that it could; Cardozo that it could not, in the same style and spirit. Legaré despised the new style and the new spirit. "The age of chivalry—the heroic age—of eloquence, as of everything else in this degenerate world, is gone." That heroic age was, of course, the age of the Revolution, which had constructed the reputation of Patrick Henry and the monument of the

Declaration of Independence.[63] Cardozo also, writing two years later, spoke of "heroic ages of eloquence" and among them that "season of general fermentation," the Revolution and the antecedent, usually forensic struggle for elucidated principle. But he was willing to extend, and so attenuate, the range of that heroic eloquence, demanding "a complete and comprehensive collection of American oratory" down to the present, and also allowing that even the Revolutionary Age had not been able to restore the glories of the ancient speakers: "the real grandeur of eloquence," its "vehemence and energy," were incompatible with the modern "spirit of generalization" which, philosophical and therefore abstract, and however respectable and praiseworthy the attendant cultural facts, must encumber even a Mirabeau or a Patrick Henry.[64] For Legaré, the incompatability had a different diagnosis, because the chronology was different: modernity was a portcullis dropped *after* the Revolutionary generation had advanced into the past. The eloquence of "that cultivated and heroic age" was a part, as it was a proof, of the civilization creating and equaling it, commemorated best in one man, "a venerable relic," "a union, in one accomplished character, of the patriot, the gentleman, and the scholar—of the loftiest virtue, exercised in all the important offices and trying conflicts of life, with whatever is most amiable and winning in social habitudes, in polished manners and elegant taste." Representing the Charleston that had been the home of such men, irreplaceable now that "our youth are . . . taught to form themselves upon other models," General Thomas Pinckney was most properly honored by a graceful echo from one of the texts of his tradition: a phrase from the *De Senectute* of Cicero, artfully condensed, placed him among the heroes acclaimed by Cato in that dialogue and elevated him above them.[65]

Chronology was a function of tone. It was not so much that Cardozo differed from Legaré as that the brisk analysis of Cardozo differed from the regretful melancholy of Legaré. George Frederick Holmes adjusted the chronology, and the tone, again. After nearly a generation, a debater had become evidence in the debate: if aspirants to American eloquence were foolish enough to ignore the example of the ancients, Legaré himself was the example arraigning their folly. Already, then, adjustment was necessary: praising Legaré, Holmes could scarcely intern him amid a degenerate eloquence. In fact, the praise was secondary to the scheme of modern oratory which Holmes subsumed within his discussion of the ancient. This scheme, in its beginning, concurs with Legaré's: since the development of oratory is contiguous upon that of democracy, American eloquence had been born with the birth of her free institutions. But now, with "every day the possession of popular eloquence growing to be the *sine qua non* of popular strength and public authority," the American orator was even better able to profit from the ancient models. Pericles and Patrick Henry were contemporaries, the American Demosthenes was still to come: Legaré's achievements, however splendid, had been of forensic art.[66] Yet there was a grim complication. Eloquence might develop in degrees of excellence; democracy in developing was transformed into something else: itself.

> A close examination into the phenomena of history will, we think, clearly evince that true oratory can exist only under a free government, and scarcely under any but a democracy; that the period of its use is exactly at that stage of democratic development when the power of the people is theoretically if not practically supreme: and that its growth and perfection advance with the progression from temperate democracy to turbulent mob-rule. It will, therefore, be a manifestation of intellectual ability, not so much desirable in itself, as necessary from its constituting the sole surviving check upon the rabid passions of the multitude become dissolute; and even in its best form dangerous from the uncertainty of the hands—whether those of Demosthenes or Demades—into which so potent an instrument of authority over the people may fall.

Reluctant to accept "oratory to be in some measure the instrument and the production of national decline"—it was true of Athens, yes, but must it be true as an axiom?—nevertheless, Holmes could see no more hopeful course than "while the State is yet sound and the people uncorrupted, [to] indulge and admire that oratory which is scarcely second to the best."[67]

Despite Holmes' adjustment of Legaré's scheme, it is easy to suppose the two chronologies to be of a kind. Tone, dividing Legaré from Cardozo, seems to join Holmes to Legaré. Is not Legaré's funereal resonance but little distant from Holmes' hurried savoring of oratorical displays before the expected corruption and collapse of the nation? Even these displays—a poor enough salvage—Holmes was very ready to despise. Just as Legaré damned a discourse for being "as long and stupid as a congressional speech" or the Belgian legislators for "their coarseness, *grossièreté* and personality [which] beat even our Congress—*c'est tout dire*," Holmes mocked "the sops thrown to Cerberus" during 4th of July orations; listed the progressive axioms of American demagogues which were but translations of Athenian catchwords; and, admitting the scandalous taste of the Athenians for vituperation, added, "The discussions in the Senate of the United States during its last session, were characterized by equal coarseness and vulgarity, but by less point, without the excuse of the example of either Comedy or Dionysia."[68] But the concordant tone, or the concordant ill temper, is delusive. Holmes had been concerned to postpone not the degeneracy of eloquence oppressing Legaré but the political degeneracy that would, quite the contrary, accompany and create "the most perfect triumphs of eloquence" still to come. His chronology is thus quite separate from Legaré's; their initial agreement is coincidental. More than, something other than, adjustment had occurred. Holmes founded his chronology upon the Athenian example from Pericles to Demosthenes; Legaré had turned elsewhere.

His assertion of degeneracy and loss was composed in 1828. In that year Legaré depicted the consequences of nullification "in a few glowing sentences—brother struggling with brother, parent with child, and the face of the land wrapt in conflagration and streaming with blood—while the slave, amidst the awful confusion, clanking his manacles, leaps up to join the dreadful revelry." William Campbell Preston the connoisseur was applying the correct context: so Cicero, in one of the two supreme deliberative occasions of his life, painted the destruction of Rome, should Catiline and his fellows have their way.[69] Surely now, when events were beginning towards, as Legaré said later, "the revolutionary pitch,"[70] there was the opportunity to emulate Cicero, not only the artist of oratory but likewise the leader of a polity in danger; to produce an achievement worthy of earlier revolutionary times, of Patrick Henry and the Declaration. The opportunity, if it was attractive as Preston testifies, was attractive very briefly. After his death Legaré's performance in 1828 was condemned as frigid, timorous, faltering; and when, having quit the field, he in letters home bewailed the folly of the Nullifiers, there was no mention of the stupendous oratory which that folly ought to produce out of its friends and foes both; and only impatience, now, with Revolutionary analogies, with Mirabeau, great orator, doomed, if he had lived, to die at the hands of "hair-brained metaphysicians and empirical demagogues."[71] Also in 1828, Legaré had transferred his energies to a new arena, the *Southern Review.* "I thought I could help to shew that people did not know what

343

our race was:—I *felt* that, in speaking its language, I should be thought eloquent,—and I have not been mistaken."[72] But that experiment, too, was brief: at its very beginning Legaré had identified the press as the destroyer of "true eloquence," as "a mighty leveller of all distinctions, and the means of advancing the mass at the expense of the individual."[73]

There was no escape. The distress and disillusionment of letters written from Brussels were there in the 1828 diagnosis of degeneracy. The diagnosis was prescient because it looked back, to the *Dialogus de Oratoribus* of Tacitus. Legaré preferred a less accurate title (in fact of a lost work by Quintilian), *De Causis Corruptae Eloquentiae*, and denied to Tacitus the "admirable piece of criticism."[74] The denial is puzzling, but the preference makes sense. Consciously invoked amid the melancholy of 1828,[75] the *Dialogus* supplied the chronology and the tone for Legaré's perception of modern eloquence. Like him, it looked back to a tumultuous and brilliant age, convulsed by revolution; like him, it allowed there were even now "good speakers, able and skilful debaters" but refused to name them eloquent; like him, it ironically praised current standards of speaking, "quite good enough for all practical purposes—at least under a government of laws, and in times of order and repose." What need of eloquence now (asked the former orator Maternus), *magna illa*—Legaré was fond of the phrase—*et notabilis eloquentia alumna licentiae*, when policy is decided not by messy liberty but by the emperor, *sapientissimus et unus?*[76] So, too, asked Legaré, contemplating Demus, that mass which ruled and to which the press pandered.[77] Preston affected to believe that the American advocate, and especially the advocate of Carolina, had his counterpart in the Roman Republic; that, as there, eloquence, office, and honors were a harmony.[78] Nullification, for Legaré, finished all that; and in the courts there prevailed a bald, professionalized, bullying litigation, what had been left to oratory under the Empire and now, as William Grayson observed, produced an advocate in keeping: formidable because relentless, without respect for opponents, without scruples in feeling or language, his only purpose "to gain his case at all hazards"—lineaments adapted from the character of Roman imperial prosecutors.[79] Legaré, commemorating elegantly and variously the "*last* of the *race* of South Carolina," was at home with the collocutors of the *Dialogus*, gathered, beneath the soaring indifference of Flavian architecture, some to inter, some to resurrect eloquence, and irrelevant to do either.[80]

But the ancients, even by appealing to one among them, could not be appeased, nor could conviction catch up with belief. As Legaré's eulogists knew, few who mourn decline desire to share in it. Acknowledging that Legaré was often charged with too great an artistry in his speaking, with—an old charge, troubling Legaré already in his letters to Gilmer—literary attainments pernicious to legal skill, William Campbell Preston, in support of Legaré's aspirations, went on to cite Hume, confident that "ancient eloquence—that is, the sublime and passionate —is of a much juster taste than the modern, or the argumentative and rational; and, if properly executed, will always have more command and authority over mankind."[81] Legaré, if he erred, erred nobly. By Bartholomew Carroll he was likened to Pericles, laboring "to make Athens the chief city of Greece, that he might become the most illustrious of her citizens"; and George Frederick Holmes averred that on account of Legaré's efforts and example, in South Carolina—the "Attica of America"—"there is infinitely more of classic culture than exists, to our knowledge, anywhere else on this side of the Atlantic."[82] Antique comparisons might expose modern collapse; antique models ordained modern ambition, and Legaré was compelled to worship even what he could not bring himself to approve. For who could approve "the deep and disgusting moral depravity of the ancient world"?[83]

Thomas Grimké could not, rejoiced that he could not, and pressed the indictment. His *Oration on the Comparativ Elements and Dutys of Grecian and American Eloquence*, delivered in 1834, promoted "the cause of Christian American eloquence," and that cause, it seemed, had better rely largely upon abuse. A political, religious, literary, cultural jingo, Grimké amalgamated his animosities—but little blurred by his zeal for orthographical reform—against an enemy outrageous everywhere. The Athenian orator had spoken out of the Athenian, and the Greek, experience, and this experience was detestable, irredeemable, its politics "stamped by fraud and violence, by rapin, ambition, and injustice"; its political institutions "monstrous compounds of aristocracy and democracy"; and its democracy itself "equaly unprincipled, degrading, and violent; equaly marked by insolence, tyranny, and ingratitude." As for its religion, only revulsion would be the proper response to "such a mass of the absurd and the immoral, of folly and indecency," "a scheme, as complete as ever was devis'd to brutalize the heart, darken the conscience, and degrade the mind."[84] Some respect might be allowed to the literature of the Greeks: their tragedians, at least, "must hav contributed much to the dignity, vigor, and pathos of the orator," and com-

345

edy supplied data about human nature. But any just verdict must condemn, and involve all of classical antiquity. Its descriptive poetry, for
instance, was but "still life" in comparison to that of the moderns "full
of moving, activ life." Its poetry of the passions was "absurd and trifling," "awkward and preposterous." "Let any one compare the unlaw-
ful passion of Rowena for Samor, in the Lord of the Bright City, or
that of the wife for her brother-in-law in Rimini, with the love of Dido
for Aeneas, and he will be struck by the vast superiority of Milman
and Leigh Hunt over 'the prince of Latin poets.'"[85] The spirit behind
such salubrious corrections to the ineptitudes of earlier taste was wor-
thily injected into a tract on American education, and there expanded
in assurance and accuracy. Milman remained, of course, and in fitting
and glorious company: "There is more of the sublime, the moral, and
the beautiful, of patriotism, in the penitent, self-sacrificing Roderic, of
Southey, and in the virtuous, magnanimous Samor of Milman, than
in all the character of the Iliad and Aeneid, put together." And Scott
—arithmetic was enough to prove it—overtopped them all: "I am strangely
mistaken, if there be not more power, fidelity, and beauty in Walter
Scott, than in a dozen Homers and Virgils."[86]

Nor did that "boldness" of discourse to which a disputant demurely
animadverted[87] conceal or discover in Grimké any discomposure before the foe. It was true that ancient poetry, not merely inferior, was
also injurious: the example of Milton, otherwise "the greatest of poets,"
but confirmed Grimké's "decided conviction of the degrading, pollut-
ing, deforming influence of the classics over modern poetry." It was
true, further, as Grimké confessed of himself for an example, that "it
has been my misfortune to hav spent so much time upon them that
my stock, deriv'd from other sources, is comparatively small," and that
therefore the schools must be cleansed of "a foreign and pagan influence," and the Christian American orator, "the noblest speaker man
has ever heard," be exhorted to advance Christianity; to strengthen
religious, benevolent, and literary associations; to recommend peace
and justice; to admire, guard, and champion woman as "matron and
virgin"; and to promote the Union, which is "a part of the divine scheme
for the moral government of the earth . . . that is destind . . . like the
ascending sun, to shed its glorious influence backward on the states
of Europe, and forward on the empires of Asia"—all in defiance and
repudiation of "the narrow-minded, narrow-hearted, and therefore selfish, eloquence of Greece and Rome."[88] But this was annoyance, albeit—

346

as ever with Grimké—strenuous annoyance, not alarm; the superiority of the moderns, especially in the United States—"richest gift of God to man . . . light and hope to the nations"—was so manifest that no claim in its interest could be excessive. For Grimké, assertion was evidence; he thumped his tub not only at length but also at ease.

Legaré was not easy. Complexity—ambivalence—was the solvent of ideas like Grimké's. "Plutarch has scarcely a hero who would pass muster as a gentleman now."[89] Yet Demosthenes and Cicero are numbered among those heroes. The former "was of that peculiar race—that chosen people—to whom the image of ideal beauty was first revealed, and who cherished it ever as the highest, and holiest, and divinest of things, with a devotion in which it is hard to tell whether deep love, or just and exquisite discernment predominated." But this chosen people—and Legaré explicitly draws the paradox—was also "a tumultuary and excitable mob, wayward, fitful, and refractory, alternately slave and tyrant" of the demagogues whom they obeyed and destroyed.[90] That Ciceronian education which Legaré chose as his ideal of excellence enabled the pleader to shine in a theater of dramatic extravagance, bared scars, weeping generals, mobs of mourners, and—as when Cicero was about to be impeached—thousands of admirers attending him to, from, and in the court. "What an earnest of a strict and impartial trial!" was Legaré's scandalized sarcasm. Edward W. Johnston tells of a case—one, in fact, during that very time when, as Preston said, Legaré created a forum out of Charleston courts—in which Legaré depicted the sister of his clients on the deck of a foundering ship. "She called upon the husband," Legaré is quoted, "upon whom she had never before called in vain—upon whose arm she had ever leaned in danger—her stay, her rescue! She called—but he never answered: no, sir, he was dead! he was dead!"[91] It was an appeal out of the antique tradition of the pathetic proof; it was an appeal to bring a tear, and a wink, to Cicero's eye.

Such opportunities were not frequent; even this triumph was a forensic, not a deliberative one. Nor were deliberative occasions much more promising. Bartholomew Carroll said bitterly: "He had modelled himself for a people such as Demosthenes and Cicero addressed, and for occasions such as they enjoyed, not for such audiences as are presented in a country court, or on such subjects as opening a street, or cleaning out a city drain."[92] But it would be hasty to suppose that for Legaré the experience of antiquity had been bitter, that it had lured him into combats doomed to be lost with weapons whose very beauty and dignity but aggravated the folly and shame of the defeat. George Frederick Holmes discovered Legaré's peculiar persuasiveness as a critic of ancient oratory, and of ancient literature in general, in his intimacy, his sympathy, his dwelling with them. "The Greeks and the Romans were to Legaré living men – as marked in their individuality and as real in their vitality as his own contemporaries, and as such they were ever exhibited to him."[93] From Brussels, Legaré wrote to Isaac Holmes: "When I was crossing the ocean I was in horribly low spirits, and I do not know what I might not have been driven to by my despair, had I not taken the precaution to buy in Philadelphia a collection of all the Greek dramatists. I read a tragedy every day, so that, in the course of a voyage of three weeks, I got through Aeschylus, Sophocles, and many of the plays of Euripides." Philological dinner parties described in the European journals manifest a literary understanding that might ingeniously and suggestively compare Cicero and Byron, Demosthenes and Rousseau, Manfred and the Aeschylean Orestes; but it was more than a literary understanding: there had been cholera on board that ship.[94] A warrior ought to be good for more than war, or more than one war, and Legaré never doubted, never supposed it was possible to doubt, that the experience of antiquity made him worthy of his mind.

*　　*　　*

It might seem a little thing that challenged the death of the past. "Humanity acknowledges no sympathy with the dead. We instinctively reject the past, and cannot consent to live over again the scenes through which we have acted. . . . Whether for good or ill, the past lies behind us, and we may seek in vain to find it in the future which lies before us." But Hiram Powers' statue of John C. Calhoun was no little thing: the statesman was represented dressed in a toga, and for Frederick Porcher, who did not doubt it was for good that the past lay behind him, that toga shouted the arrogance of a past which insisted on surviving, a classical past, alien not only in time but in race. A sculptor "may be capable of executing a work which Phidias would condescend to approve, but unfortunately, he dooms himself to live only in the approbation of the contemporaries of Phidias," and Phidias was not of the Northern Race. Although admitting of variations within it, this Northern Race, of which "the people of the United States are originally and essentially members," possessed for Porcher a unique "moral and mental constitution," which he defined by opposing to it the con-

John C. Calhoun statue, by Hiram Powers. Courtesy of the City of Charleston and the Charleston Museum.

stitution of the Southern Race. The arts provided his texts. For example, "the different genius of the North and the South is strikingly exemplified in the art of architecture," a difference which overwhelmed the fashion for classicism: "Now, when every one pretends to have imbibed the spirit of the classic taste, the mind involuntarily turns from the wonders of the Parthenon, and revels in the glorious beauty of the ministers and old abbeys of the North."[95]

Classical antiquity belonged to the Southern Race, but Porcher was no mindless jingo: the Parthenon was wonderful, and when, denying that Greece was the birthplace of art, he said that "Greece developed

349

art only as the illustrator of the sublime and beautiful," that did not mean that the sublime and beautiful met with his disapproval. If George Washington demonstrated a greatness "far superior to anything in the conception of the Gallic, Grecian, or Roman mind," that was more patriotism than criticism; Porcher was willing to recognize the superiority of the Southern Race in painting: "The great masters of Italy and Spain are the great masters of Europe, and none venture to contest the palm with them." Indeed, both judgments illustrated the same principle. Washington was great within the context and conception of the Northern Race: he could not have been "a great Frenchman, a great Roman, a great Grecian"; Southern painting was great, as Dutch painting, its nearest Northern rival, was great, because it followed Nature: this Nature was not realism—although the Dutch detailed domestic life, Southern art triumphed with the opulence and energy of Catholic legend and classical myth—but rather truth to itself.[96] Continuity of the race with its arts, its heroes, its morality, was in accordance with Nature. That was why, for Porcher, to plead for a *natural* was to plead for a *national* literature: such a literature would fulfill the nature of the American character. That was why Marlowe's Dr. Faustus demonstrated "truth to nature"; Goethe's Faust, "of the mystico-classical school," did not (except when "the Northern spirit" broke in). Compare poets as they perform in the regions of the imagination: "how infinitely does the genius of Shakspeare soar above that of Milton!" Spenser and Milton were, no doubt, men "of great learning, of high classical attainments"—but that was attempting to be Phidias. "Milton and Spenser drew on the classical model, and their works are consigned to the libraries of the learned; Shakspeare drew after the old Teutonic model of his countrymen, and finds a responsive chord vibrating in the heart of every man of Gothic blood."[97]

Discontinuity was unnatural. It was the result, and the essence, of classicism, of the imitation of classical antiquity, everywhere ruinous.[98] Like French poetry after "the mighty hand of Corneille stamped it with classicality," art that imitated was "incapable of uttering a word which finds a response in the great heart of humanity." Like Hiram Powers, the artist who imitated "strips himself of all personality. The man is lost in the art, and he renounces forever the hope of living in his work."[99] And what he imitates, too, is lost: he "follows antiquity without a knowledge of the key by which, alone, the true meaning of his model is to be deciphered. He imitates merely that which is obvious, but has

350

no conception of the *thought* which his model was designed to express. Hence his productions have no vitality. Like the daguerreotype impressions of the face of a corpse, they present an accurate likeness of the features, but they are images of death."[100] Death doomed all who would not let the classical past die. It was the doom of Powers' statue (the sack of Columbia had not yet executed, with sturdy literalness, Porcher's sentence):

> A great opportunity was afforded to Powers, of striking a blow in defence of modern art. . . . He might have made Mr. Calhoun the type of the great man of the nineteenth century; he has preferred to invest him with conventional greatness. He might have founded a school of art, Northern as well as American; he has neglected his opportunity. He might have made a name for himself, as enduring as we hope that of Calhoun will be; he has condescended to swell the long list of humble imitators of a school which is dead beyond the hope of resuscitation.[101]

It was not Hiram Powers whom Porcher was most concerned to condemn but rather the high priest of classical life "which is not life but death," of an art that prescribed for sculpture, as for everything, "the cold and formal regularities of classical taste," dead itself and murderous.[102] "Possessing unbounded sympathy with nature," Wordsworth had innovated, had exalted the humblest material to the loftiest poetry, victoriously had set up "the truth of nature . . . in opposition to artistic and conventional truth." Yet Sir Joshua Reynolds was a villain whom even Wordsworth could not be counted upon wholly to refute. Of course, there was the matter of the naked figure: "Modern European civilization revolts at it, and will, we hope, forever continue to do so." More than prudery, propriety had been offended. Jacques-Louis David, "an enthusiastic admirer, and a successful imitator of the ancients," had represented Themistocles naked. Porcher had been disgusted because "to a civilization formed under the influence of Christianity, nakedness is revolting and humiliating." However accurate to ancient taste and even to ancient custom, however obedient to Reynolds, who had cited the nakedness of Laocoon—priestly robes stripped from him as a sacrifice to a "higher sense" of art—David had excluded himself from the realities of his spectators, and from the spectators themselves. This was true even more of the English artists, upon whom Reynolds "has hung like an incubus"; of Benjamin West and his ambitious works in the grand style, "all great bores": "Who brings away with him a single sentiment which repays him for a visit?" Hogarth alone stood apart; Hogarth alone "had the genius to appreciate and embody the peculiar taste of his countrymen." Therefore, Reynolds was unwilling or unable to recognize Hogarth's claims to be an artist. At this there could be no surprise, nor at Porcher's vehemence to oppose him: powerfully and perniciously, Reynolds advocated what he was: "only an imitator [for whom] nature seems to have had no charms."[103]

This Reynolds is a caricature—perhaps, since Porcher was capable of clipping a quotation in order to amplify his enemy's presumed servility to earlier masters,[104] intentionally so. His reading of Reynolds' attitude toward Hogarth is, to say the best of it, imaginative, and to deny to Reynolds his vigilant grasp of Nature can make any sense only if the definition is cunningly contracted.[105] A representation rather than a representative of what Porcher called "classicality," his Joshua Reynolds stood for imitation obstructing Nature, a noxious cosmopolitanism that trespassed upon, and so falsified, frontiers of age and culture. Noxious not to Porcher alone: laboring to deliver their literature "from the bondage of French authority and a servile imitation of foreign models," German critics and scholars had sought authority in "a new order of researches, and almost a new theory of criticism." "Genuine, living beauty" resided only in a literature which was native and national, "in perfect harmony with the character and opinions of its people"; where this harmony was lacking, even "the highest graces of composition" could not prevent what was "tame, vapid, and feeble." There followed a craving to discover the sources of the nation and its literature, for theirs were common sources; and there was a rush to "ransack" all, however trivial, that antiquarianism could provide.[106] Whilst he might smile at the motive of the Germans in abusing the French, or at the zeal of antiquarian burrowing, nevertheless Hugh Legaré did not blame the motive and could commend the zeal. For German scholarship he had much admiration, and it was easy to attach "servile" to "imitation," to include "imitative" among a variety of slanders imputing sterility, weakness, and frigid discord. It was as easy to apply the slanders: "imitative mediocrity" designated the vacancy, barrenness, pedantry that were brief in Italy, tenacious in Spain; Philip Sidney's sonnets were lifeless and soulless, "all cold imitation and abortive effort"; and, confident in the example of August Wilhelm von Schlegel, Legaré scorned Roman literature, too, for being imitative, at

352

first with the utmost servility, even later starving in a "tame and prosaical" society and humiliated by an arrogant nobility considering the arts unworthy of their labor. It could not be a "national literature," pervading and quickening in artist and people alike the fabric of society, a literature such as the Greeks, without a peer, possessed; for despite a few exceptional cases, "Roman genius was stamped with a marked inferiority; it was tame, servile, and imitative, even to plagiarism—no depth, no pathos, no originality—nothing national, spontaneous, and awakening."[107]

Reverence for the Germans, contempt for the Romans, were bolder still when J.L. Reynolds surveyed both. "Germany is emphatically the land of scholars. . . . [Her] literary institutions . . . are the admiration of the world; their professors the instructors of all civilized lands." With "an admirable specimen of the profound and various learning which distinguishes the productions" of the Germans, Dr. Reynolds was not disposed to disagree: he recounted, and nowhere contested, the woeful tale told in Johann Christian Baehr's history of Roman literature.[108] Even in its heyday, the late Republic and the Augustan Age, that literature was but "a reflection, however inadequate, of the literature of Greece," and even such meager success was bought too dearly:

> The introduction of Grecian culture . . . was attended with at least this evil consequence; it eradicated the national element from [the Romans'] own literature, and introduced a false taste, which, particularly during the [post-Augustan] period, became more and more degenerate. . . . The ancient national traditions, which might have been wrought into forms of poetry stamped with the features of a truly Roman literature, were neglected and despised. The materials of poetry were taken, for the most part, from the Greek; its form was determined by Grecian models, and originality of conception was lost sight of, in the pursuit of a graceful and elaborate style. This proceeding was, of course, fatal to the existence of a national literature.[109]

But Reynolds drew back; no doubt he had read some of the literature to which he was attributing, "as its highest merit, a successful imitation" of the Greeks. For, shaking himself free of his German book, finally he recognized something else of the Romans: "The literature of this people possesses a character of its own. . . . It is pervaded, throughout, by a truly national spirit . . . [and] reflects, as in a mirror, the life and spirit of the Roman character."[110] How this character, this national spirit, could pervade a literature which was not national, Reynolds did not explain; still less did it occur to him that his definition of imitation might be faulty and deceptive, like the censure adopting it for ammunition.

"Genius may anticipate the season of maturity; but in the education of a people, as in that of an individual, memory must be exercised, before the powers of reason and fancy can be expanded; nor may the artist hope to equal or surpass, till he has learned to imitate, the works of his predecessors."[111] The cadence is seductive: for Legaré the orator and student of oratory, it did not need to be; the sentiment extracted compliance, an ineluctable compliance – not out of love for the home of imitation and its theories, however, the ancient rhetoric that judged, analyzed, and dictated the practice of the orators whom Legaré revered. His opinion of that rhetoric, indeed of any rhetoric, was not laudatory. Archbishop Richard Whately was apprehensive of the title of his own treatise on rhetoric, because "rhetoric" was part of the title; Edward Tyrell Channing shared his apprehensions, for the same reason: "Rhetoric has long had an ill name in the world," and now, stripped even of much of its villainy, was popularly but a label for tawdry deception or a list of tropes.[112] Tending towards the popular verdict, Legaré spoke of "babbling rhetoricians" incapable of deliberative excellence, and condemned William Crafts for sinking "the orator in the rhetorician"; Demosthenes, in whom "there is never the least prettiness or rhetoric – nothing fine, or showy, or theatrical," he imagined "would have scorned himself, if he had thought that people regarded him as a *rhetorician*." Quintilian, "of all critics, perhaps, the most enlightened and unerring," was nevertheless demoted to grammarian; rhetoric itself was banished into the grammar school; and for Aristotle's *Rhetoric*, for "all rhetorical and grammatical studies," there was but a scholium on Samuel Butler's couplet:

> All that one learns from them is *language* – the names of his tools – that what one speaks every day is *prose* – that this or that deviation from the *sermo pedestris*, is a trope or figure, with this or that sounding name. We do not deny that every scholar would do well to learn these names; but he will sadly deceive himself, if, after having done so, he mistake them for things, and set that down as an acquisition of science which is only the accomplishment of a linguist. In these studies, however, as in logic and metaphysics, great ingenuity and even originality and comprehensiveness of thought, may be, and have been displayed by cele-

brated writers—but it is all comparatively thrown away because the results of such inquiries never can be any substantial addition to the stock of human knowledge.[113]

Legaré spoke not from ignorance—he knew well enough that in the Athens of Demosthenes "Rhetoric and Statesmanship, indeed, were considered as synonymous terms"[114]—but his frequent citations from ancient rhetorics are critical, not prescriptive, and most frequent from the least (so it may seem) prescriptive of them. Dionysius and Longinus, identifying the qualities of Demosthenes, thus alert the student to the excellence of the model after whom their own sensibilities have been trained and accomplished: their experience of the text becomes part of the student's experience of it. For—in Dionysius' explicit declaration —the critic must seek to confront his text through a moment of instinctive and immediate perception, a critical inspiration, leaping reason, which comprehends the creative inspiration to which it is akin.[115] Legaré's Longinus was the Longinus whom Gibbon knew:

> Till now I was acquainted only with two ways of criticising a beautiful passage: the one, to shew by an exact anatomy of it the distinct beauties of it and whence they sprung; the other, an idle exclamation or a general encomium which leaves nothing behind it. Longinus has shown me that there is a third. He tells me his own feelings upon reading it, and tells them with such energy that he communicates them. I almost doubt which is most sublime, Homer's Battle of the Gods or Longinus' apostrophe to Terentianus upon it.[116]

When a critic's text is his model, the circuit of feeling is complete. "The *Treatise of the Sublime*, seems to have been as much formed upon the practice of Demosthenes, as the rules of the Epopee were drawn from the models presented by the Iliad and the Odyssey; and the emotion with which we read his orations, is an experimental proof to us, that, as that justly celebrated critic affirms, the effect of the highest order of speaking is not persuasion only, but rapture and ecstasy."[117] Homer and the "divine" Plato, too, the tragedians, Herodotus, Thucydides, Xenophon crowd the pages of Longinus; but Longinus and Demosthenes are united by Legaré, because the efficacy of the model is guaranteed by, as it guarantees, the experience of the critic. The circuit of feeling, though complete, is not rigid: it can expand, as it expanded for Legaré, to include a second critic within the communion; and it must expand, for its whole reason is to prescribe excellence not to the critic but to the student of the model. Identifying the inadequacy of an earlier writer on his subject, Longinus makes this clear at once:

> Two things are required of any textbook: first, that it should explain what its subject is; second, and more important, that it should explain how and by what methods we can achieve it. Caecilius tries at immense length to explain to us what sort of thing "the sublime" is, as though we did not know; but he has somehow passed over as unnecessary the question how we can develop our nature to some degree of greatness. . . . Let us then consider whether there is anything in my observations which may be thought useful to public men.[118]

Sublimity, for Legaré, was the touchstone of admiration. "'Whatever others do, I'll fight,' was, under the circumstances, as sublime as the *qu'il mourût* of the old Horace." Patrick Henry could be no better praised than by equating a glorious moment of his eloquence with a citation from Corneille made famous for its sublimity by Boileau and transferred by Hugh Blair to his definition of the "moral sublime."[119] It is in the sublime that Legaré located the supremacy of the deliberative over all other branches of oratory; "a severe and sublime simplicity" was the merit of the Declaration of Independence, immortal monument of that supremacy. Deliberative occasions created speakers "of the sublime and heroic stamp," and their object partook of their quality: to nullification must be opposed "the really sublime institutions of a federal jurisdiction." Supreme master of deliberative supremacy, Demosthenes was supreme master, thus, of Blair's "moral sublime," which "fill[s] the mind with admiration, and elevat[es] it above itself."[120] No wonder that he must be the supreme model, too.

> [There is] yet another road to sublimity. . . . This is the way of imitation and emulation of great writers of the past. Here too, my friend, is an aim to which we must hold fast. Many are possessed by a spirit not their own. It is like what we are told of the Pythia at Delphi: she is in contact with the tripod near the cleft in the ground which (so they say) exhales a divine vapour, and she is thereupon made pregnant by the supernatural power and forthwith prophesies as one inspired. Similarly, the genius of the ancients acts as a kind of oracular cavern, and effluences flow from it into the minds of their imitators. Even those previously not much inclined to prophesy become inspired and share the enthusiasm which comes from the greatness of others.[121]

So Winckelmann contemplated the Apollo Belvedere, his breast expanded and exalted like those filled with the spirit of prophecy. So Sir Joshua Reynolds instructed his students in the presence of the masters of their art: "The habit of contemplating and brooding over the ideas of great geniusses, till you find yourself warmed by the contact, is the true method of forming an Artist-like mind; it is impossible, in the presence of those great men, to think, or invent in a mean manner; a state of mind is acquired that receives those ideas only which relish of grandeur and simplicity." "When I pick up a speech by Demosthenes," wrote Dionysius, "I feel inspired; this way and that goes my mind, caught in the grip of a succession of emotions—incredulity, anxiety, fear, contempt, hatred, pity, favour, anger, jealousy, every passion that can dominate the human mind. I feel just like the initiates in the rites of the Great Mother or the Corybantes or some similar cult, who achieve all their varied visions by being affected by smells, if that is what it is, or sounds, or the spirit of the divinities." This was a testimony which was properly in Legaré's mind as he brought to a close his final meditation upon Demosthenes.[122]

Cicero the gentleman and the educator had molded the young man and was thanked with ample and fond honor; but the Greek possessed his votary. "Demosthenes: The Man, the Statesman, and the Orator" recorded Legaré's mature enthusiasm, his Pythian experience of his most revered master.

> Considering, as we do, the masterpieces of this great orator as the true and only models of popular eloquence—as its *beau idéal*—not Greek, not Attic, not ancient, not local or transitory or peculiar . . . but made like the Apollo or the Parthenon for all times and all nations, and worthy of study and imitation wherever genius shall be called to move masses of men by the power of the *living word*, we know not how we can do anything more profitable or more acceptible [sic] to our readers, than to fix their attention, for a few moments, upon the excellencies [sic] which distinguish him beyond every other orator that has ever appeared in any period of the world's history.[123]

"There can be but one form of ideal beauty, with which human nature, that never changes, will rest forever satisfied." Byron had tried to compete with the Apollo Belvedere to express "the most perfect image of beauty in the mind." But the statue was created of the ideal, as Winckelmann said; Legaré thought of Sophocles, no competitor but corollary.[124] So was Demosthenes, so his aspirations: this was his mas-

357

tery of the sublime. Unlike Frederick Porcher, Legaré was comfortable with Joshua Reynolds, who, by his description of Raphael's grand style (his frequent term for the ideal), had so described "the manner and the merit" of Demosthenes that no other critic, ancient or modern, could match him.[125] Reynolds knew that the sublime and the ideal were but different names for the same aspiration, toward a perfection of Nature which was Nature beheld by the inspired, because imitating, perceptions of the artist. The aspiration summoned his noblest period:

> The Art which we profess has beauty for its object; this it is our business to discover and to express; but the beauty of which we are in quest is general and intellectual; it is an idea that subsists only in the mind; the sight never beheld it, nor has the hand expressed it: it is an idea residing in the breast of the artist, which he is always labouring to impart, and which he dies at last without imparting; but which he is yet so far able to communicate, as to raise the thoughts, and extend the views of the spectator; and which, by a succession of art, may be so far diffused, that its effects may extend themselves imperceptibly into publick benefits, and be among the means of bestowing on whole nations refinement of taste; which, if it does not lead directly to purity of manners, obviates at least their greatest depravation, by disentangling the mind from appetite, and conducting the thoughts through successive stages of excellence, till that contemplation of universal rectitude and harmony which began by Taste, may, as it is exalted and refined, conclude in Virtue.[126]

"His standard was the *Ideal*. . . . His was that deep love of ideal beauty, that passionate pursuit of eloquence in the abstract, that insatiable thirst after perfection in art for its own sake, without which no man ever produced a master-piece of genius."[127] Present to the devout, to them Demosthenes communicated his idea of beauty; with the imitative union, he became what he would impart, "the most exquisite model of . . . the perfection of Greek art." In his presence all paradoxes were dissolved. Must a great orator be a good man? The intensity of Legaré's apprehension of his model, image of the Demosthenic intensity, was the goodness of the orator, who "must believe in the cause he pleads": Robespierre and Danton were thus good men.[128] There was the "shocking contrast," which Legaré had always recognized, between the glories of Athenian culture and the Athenians "steeped in profligacy to the very lips, and wholly without shame or sensibility in subjects of honor." How then did Demosthenes direct this multitude in the arena of Athenian eloquence, "where," as Grimké said, "the prince of orators was but the prince of demagogues"? How could the methods proper to such an audience satisfy the propriety of so glorious a model?

> But independently of [the] immediate relation between the author and his works, his eloquence, distinguished as it is by every excellence, is for nothing more remarkable, than for its *spirit*—its living spirit—it is full of soul, to use a familiar but expressive phrase. From its sublime character, therefore, we may be sure, that whatever may have been his practice and conduct, his natural impulses were all as high as his sensibility was deep and exquisite. . . . The character of Demosthenes [is] divined from his eloquence; and so the character of his eloquence was a mere emanation of his own. It was the life and soul of the man, the patriot, the statesman. . . . You see absolutely nothing of the artist; nay, you forget the speaker altogether: it is the statesman, or the man only, that is before you.[129]

For Legaré, intimacy with the ideal of eloquence was an exaltation that purified of all dross. There was no need of ancient rhetorics; there were only companions, like Longinus and Dionysius, in the Pythian moment. Apart from critics like Hume, who believed that "a few successful attempts [to reach the heights of ancient eloquence] might rouse the genius of the nation, excite the emulation of the youth, and accustom our ears to a more sublime and more pathetic elocution," there was no need of modern rhetorics which, with psychological, epistemological, historical, and religious argument, were for rejecting Hume's exhortation at all points.[130] Imitation was mandated by him who, even had his own models been denied him, would have composed monuments "infallibly hav[ing] formed an era in literature, and display[ing] very much the same excellences that now distinguish them." Apollo consults no oracle. "In seeking after the ideal, grand and sublime," Frederick Porcher warned, an artist "loses his own individuality."

> What wonder that the unprincipled though gifted Demades, the very personification of the witty and reckless libertinism of the age, should deride and scoff at this strange man, living as nobody else lived, thinking as nobody else thought; a prophet, crying from his solitude of great troubles at hand; the apostle of the past; the preacher of an impossible restoration; the witness to his contemporaries that their degeneracy was incorrigible and their doom hopeless, and that another seal in the book was broken, and a new era of calamity and downfall opened in the history of nations.[131]

Legaré might have bidden Porcher to recollect not only by whom but upon whom the Delphic rapture was bestowed. The model was also a mirror.

* * *

"Situations may recur, sayings may recur, but no characters come back. Nature always breaks her mould."[132] But some preferred the risky business of recalling men from their antiquity. Allowing that historical parallels were seductive and wayward, and promising to be on guard against the artistry, while he adopted the intent, of Plutarch, George Frederick Holmes conducted an ingenious comparison of Augustus Caesar with Louis Napoleon, "a character which has been either over-rated or underrated, according to the temper, the theories, the preju-dices or the partialities of the judge, rather than estimated with any intelligent reference to fixed data, recognized standard or predeter-mined landmarks." Landmarks, standard, data the history of Augus-tus could alone supply: of time and of error at once were the study and the student purged, even as they plunged deeply into the past.[133] When such a student, fixing upon the Jugurthine War, developed his "recurrence to the history of wars" in order to examine the war against Mexico, pressing utility and historical philosophy were served together. The country at war must know what it was up against: "this modern Jugurtha," General Santa Anna; the danger of collegial commanders falling out among themselves (look at Marius and Metellus); and "the tendency of popular suffrage and the inclination of the people, in all ages of the world, to elevate great military chieftains." Once General Jackson, now General Taylor, loomed behind the popular victor Marius. "The intellectual lights of the day are deemed but of use in the sub-ordinate offices: the Calhouns, Legarés and Clays, *veritably* do make most excellent secretaries and attorneys! But in this . . . *our day* is true to her mother, *antiquity*: for what, but spokesmen, were Cicero and Demosthenes? the mere equerries that held the stirrups of ambition." Philosophy teaches by examples, however rueful; the process is history: that is what "War and Its Incidents," while confessing the want of a Sallust, set out to do and to be, with a stern reminder in passing that the founding dictum sprang not from Bolingbroke but from Dionysius of Halicarnassus.[134]

More systematically, at greater length, but with essentially the same presumptions at his back, Hugh Legaré moved through the Roman civil law, the Athenian political economy, the Athenian democracy: yet as the description was more exhaustive, so the prescriptive impulse strengthened and swelled to make it so. Let Americans thank heaven, he stated at the conclusion of a long disquisition upon the Athenian democracy, that the turbulence of that polity cannot trouble their own land, so long as — and be warned! — the demagogue and the demagogue's arts are shunned. But this must be a trivial application of ancient example from one who had determined to complete a thorough analysis of Roman civil law in order to unite it, and its "immortal spirit" which had survived the wreck of empires, to the American inheritance of English common law.[135]

For antiquity was not something you received or enjoyed only; it was something you did. It took a classicist to understand that, and to fear it. Thomas Grimké could hardly, even with bluster, conceal his embarrassment when, laying siege to classical education, he was asked why in his argument and illustrations he everywhere betrayed that education within himself.[136] He need not have been embarrassed: Hugh Legaré did not remark unkindly upon the fact that Grimké could not have attacked so forcefully had not his adversary trained him for battle and supplied him his arms. That was a subtlety. Grimké was, to Legaré, a case alerting the physician to a "grievous malady rapidly growing epidemical," an antagonist who declared that the Greek and Latin languages, their literatures and civilization, "are absolutely good for nothing";[137] confronting him, Legaré could not be expected to observe in quiet that what he, too, feared was only what he understood, that Grimké was exposed to his assault only because of a bridge of understanding between them. The lethal foe was elsewhere, inaccessible.

Certainly the Grimkean thunder was tremendous, nor without thought. This was no mere essay in pedagogy; its capacious title promised no more than the effect.[138] If Grimké did not take all knowledge for his province, it was only because the spiritual knowledge of scripture and revelation was assumed, Christian and Protestant. His province was science, all knowledge which the scriptures did not teach, the "fellow-labourer, with religion, in advancing the glory of God."[139] Not in its nature (he admitted that it had existed before Calvin and Luther, even before Christ) but in excellence, this science also was Christian and Protestant, and it had to be both together. Until the Reformation "there had been no *focal* point in the regions of knowledge, no *centripetal* force to gather into a system around that point, the scattered orbs of Arts and Sciences; and constrain them by the bonds of a common destiny, to fulfil the prophecy of Scripture, and fit man to answer the ends of his being." Although "the true end" of science was to improve the moral and political nature of man, "to bless and not to adorn" the people, yet, until the Reformation, there had been "little or nothing" done for improvement; but for the Reformation, "the revival of learning, which had commenced, would have terminated as all others had, in public ostentation, princely patronage, and the dazzling homage of Genius and Taste." Without the Reformation—but Grimké noticed a difficulty, a point of etiquette. It was a delicate matter to speak, as Grimké with dubious delicacy went on to speak, of Catholic Christianity at the same time as of "the degraded condition of the whole circle of knowledge, at the close of the 15th century," and of the inferiority and stagnation of Catholic countries thereafter. There were Catholics in Charleston; there were Catholics in the audience; and an American citizen could not but remember that God had reserved for a Catholic the "enviable distinction" of having survived all others who had signed the Declaration of Independence.[140]

Cicero had not assisted at that occasion; Plato, unlike John England, was not a member of the Charleston Literary and Philosophical Society. Restraint imposed, however imperfectly, by rudimentary good manners need not apply to any treatment of the ancients. However great the glories of their arts and literature (Grimké had, to say the least, his doubts), they had produced no morally edifying polity or philosophy, no improvement for the individual man and the society of men. Hence their tradition was useless, its documents but clogging the minds of the young when not actively injuring and perverting them. This Grimké knew at first hand: educated in the classics, he had been seduced by what he fancied to be their nobility and their beauty until, coming to maturity as a Christian and an American, he had been compelled to recognize how ineradicably, how perniciously, the classics were un-Christian and un-American.[141] Rapidly there had succeeded the further recognition that the beauty and the nobility were, if not in themselves false, certainly but the meretricious cloak of falsehood. "The insolent and brutal Achilles," "the mean and treacherous Aeneas" exposed the perils of the works wherein they were described and warned the already apprehensive mind of wider perils. Grimké was properly disdainful of "a clergyman, the head of a college," who had ventured to claim that Cicero's De Officiis was essential to a moral education.

Did not a man of his profession, especially, understand that the New Testament was "a perfect code of moral duty," that Cicero, Epictetus, and Marcus Aurelius had no more value than—compared with modern astronomy—Aratus, Manilius, and Ptolemy? Since upon the Christian Testament "stand our civil and political, and all our literary, benevolent and social institutions," therefore, "so far as they breathe a Christian spirit, they are worthy of the Rock of Ages on which they rest: so far as they are unworthy, they must and will be reformd."[142] Grimké's logic was itself worthy of the syllogism of the caliph Omar. It participated in a frenzy gleaming with the flames of Alexandria:

> Whether in abstruse and comprehensive, or in refined and elegant speculation; in profound, energetic, logical reasoning; in powerful, commanding, persuasive eloquence; in the intellectual and imaginative poetry, in the descriptive and pathetic; in practical wisdom, moral, international, or political, civil, social or domestic; in those arts, which employ, while they improve and bless the people; in a word, in all that makes man industrious and useful, virtuous and happy, and prepares him for the service of God, of his fellow men and of posterity—if, with a view to these things, we contemplate the great men, who have arisen since the year 1500, we must acknowledge them, unrivalled by the Ancients. This is my creed, I glory in it: and this, I speak it with triumphant confidence, this, before the close of the 19th century, will be the creed of my country.[143]

Grimké's relentless confidence could be as wearisome as his unwearied, flat ferocity. From someone who judged himself a partaker of a Christian thought as devoted, and more venerable, than Grimké's, and of a classical heritage enriching that thought, propriety demanded a tolerant, amused sarcasm. Affrighted by antiquity, to it Grimké had opposed a chaste Christianity; he had not thought it worthwhile even to mention the *ratio studiorum* of the Catholic educators, the absorption into their faith of the classical legacy—except in passing to assert (copying an anti-Catholic tract) that the Jesuits, so that they might exclude "the moral and political branches of knowledge, which the Reformers were reviving," had developed an education founded on the classics and mathematics.[144] The mention of such bogeymen could scarcely delight the Catholic bishop of Charleston, already affronted by the presumptuous piety of those who affected to shrink from a depraved and molesting idolatry: "I trust," said John England, "that, with some few at least, I shall find credit for the declaration, that however imperfect my practice might be, there exists not an individual who holds [the Christian] dispensation in more high esteem than I do."[145] Nevertheless, Bishop England refused to be much troubled by all this fuss. How strange that "in the annals of eighteen centuries" no instance of apostasy could be found "fairly attributable" to the classics. Indeed, so shrilly to be menaced implied a poor opinion of the evidences of Christian belief. As for the "immoral tendency" of ancient texts, in part the accusation was unfounded; when not, the selection among them always customary in schools excluded anything more dangerous, and preserved what was much less objectionable, "than what is every day in our tongue within the reach of every schoolboy."[146]

And there was (shared by others) Grimké's remarkable taste. It was not necessary to be a heathen to balk at the assertion that the Old Testament included "a body of political and theological institutes, of historical, poetical, and moral literature, far beyond all that had been accomplishd by Greece"; that Greek literature had been ordained by God only to demonstrate, juxtaposed with that of the Hebrews, that merely secular literature "must be inferior to a literature descended from Heaven"; that, accordingly, the Bible must, with its concordances and commentaries, be the textbook "from the infant-school to the university," not only for moral instruction but for history, biography, philosophy, eloquence, and poetry.[147] Objections were practical, first of all: sectarian quarrels would be exacerbated because all reading must be in large part interpretation. They were aesthetic, next: although no doubt (the bishop of Charleston sounds, one supposes unintentionally, rather like Gibbon) the writers of the Scriptures had been inspired by God, yet they remained human, and so imperfect, instruments. Piety masked a fashionable philistinism; John England preferred not to be included among "a large class of our modern writers [who] cast obloquy upon the genius and acquirements of from twelve to fifteen centuries."[148] Who could comprehend, let alone stomach, a taste that affirmed "Mrs. Hemans has written a greater number of charming little pieces, than are to be found in Horace and Anacreon"?[149] Hugh Legaré did not command the bishop's authority or ordnance against pious effusions; but such a taste was impious.

"How far it is worth our while to study the writings of the ancients as models?"—that is the question at the base of Legaré's refutation of Thomas Grimké, a refutation thought deserving to be the first article in the first number of the new *Southern Review*.[150] For he had been offended as a scholar and as a public man, as a connoisseur of the tradition and a participant in it: how not, when all were combined in his perceptions? His ideal scholar would reconstruct the past "with all the force and impressiveness of a sober and ascertained, yet vivid and living reality"; this he would do "to make [the ancients] objects of sympathy, and examples of conduct to us"—conduct and sympathy in an active, public world.[151] As a connoisseur, Legaré shuddered at Grimké's apparent concession that the ancients had, at least, excelled in style: that, of course, was very true, and the orator Legaré expatiated happily upon the nicety of taste and delicacy of ear among even the lowest in society. But to award to the moderns, as an inevitable corollary, preeminence in thought was ridiculous: Legaré the emulator of the tradition pointed to Demosthenes as refutation, paradigm of that "naked simplicity of style, united with the highest degree of refinement," which possessed itself of the thought.[152] To divide style from thought was the same folly that divided art from practical effort, artist from the virtuous citizen: if that was necessary in order for Grimké to disregard America's want of poets, painters, sculptors, and architects, to Legaré—inspired rather than cowed by the examples of the past—it was a feeble and foolish necessity. "Sophocles held the rank of General along with Thucydides and Pericles—a matchless combination!"[153]

The division was everywhere destructive. It disemboweled Grimké's very conception of what education should do. Legaré did not endeavor to deny, he boldly and even delightfully denounced, the faults of the present instruction in the classics: the "stupid, unaspiring ignorance" of the teachers; the "wretched, vulgar, and worthless smattering of classical literature" which they taught, their manner of teaching but a butchery of the melodious and subtle text into "uncouth or nonsensical English" without any notion even of what was being butchered. But the German philology that he so admired, sensitive to the peculiarity and particularity of another culture yet vivifying it for the imitation and inspiration of the students, was shining ahead "the first flush of a kindling zeal and the dawn of a brighter hope." It was this which Grimké, with his "harsh and crabbed philosophy" of practicality, of useful knowledge, wished to obliterate.[154] What is truly useful knowledge, Legaré asked, and berated his enemy for a crude notion of the ideals of excellence: infecting all his arguments, it placed moral science, achieved in the individually excellent, on a level with practical science, which could be improved by an accumulation of hypothesis, experiment, and application.

Our youth are to be trained up as if they were all destined to be druggists and apothecaries, or navigators and mechanists—or, if it sounds
better, they are to be deeply versed in the economy of the universe,
and the most recondite and shadowy subtleties of transcendental geometry, or transcendent psychology—but what, after all, ought to be the
capital object of education, to form the *moral* character, not by teaching
what to think but persuading to act well; not by loading the memory
with cold and barren precepts, but forming the sensibility by the habitual, fervid and rapturous contemplation of high and heroical models
of excellence; not by definitions of virtue and speculations about the
principle of obligation, but by making us *love* the one and *feel* the sa-
credness of the other—would, in such a system of discipline, be sadly
neglected.[155]

For Legaré, education must be an individual experience, not the production of instruments for a use determined outside, even in opposition to, that education. Not only naturally but necessarily it followed
that liberty was at issue, was *the* issue: "Above all," he wrote, contemplating the education that is communion with the ancients, "our
American youth will learn, that liberty—which is sweet to all men, but
which is the *passion* of proud minds that cannot stoop to less—has been
the nurse of all that is sublime in character and genius." By that sublimity of character and genius, which classical learning represents and
supplies, is liberty known.[156]

Yet Thomas Grimké, too, had spoken much of freedom: it was the
great gift of the Reformation to science and human inquiry. It had accounted for the superiority of Greece to Rome, of Italy to Spain, of
Germany to France and Protestant to Catholic; it accounted for the
supremacy of Britain, and because of it America would soon surpass
even her.[157] Here, as so often, Grimké would reject the texts, while
he retained the spirit, of the classical tradition. In acknowledging literature and the arts to form the sensibility; in assuming the orator to
be the proper culmination, substituting the Christian American orator
for Demosthenes, of his system of instruction; in his emphasis upon
models, whether men or texts, moral and political, in the forming of
public man, Grimké showed himself the student of Ciceronian ideals.
His own education had won. Legaré's defense of classical learning was
hailed at once and long in the South (Grimké's own eulogist was apologetic); from the North in the same year—and with much the same frame
and, more, the same spirit of argument—the Yale Report in 1828 con-

firmed, against certain rebellious persons, the classical curriculum in its dominance.[158] "Mr. Grimké's speculative opinions we think utterly erroneous—his excellent example cannot be too closely imitated—but it is unfortunately easy for all to repeat the one, while few have the industry and perseverance to follow the other." Those few already included Grimké himself, who had pronounced this final boast for his nation: "We shall be the Greece of the Modern World, unrivalled by the Literature of three thousand years."[159] His opponent brought thus in submission to his own "excellent example," had not Legaré every reason to feel confident?

For Basil Gildersleeve, returning to Charleston in 1853, and from the perspective of a doctorate at Göttingen, confidence was radiant. Antiquity had lived through its successor ages of arts and literature, however much distorted to strange uses; now even that distortion was being corrected. "The dominant authority of the two classic nations cannot be shaken. . . . Classical machinery is worn out, but classic inspiration remains as fresh as ever." For as both natural and historic necessity demonstrated, "the classics are eternal norms and present facts." The quarrel between classicists and romanticists had been bombastic and absurd, a mock epic, but it had compelled scrutiny of the weapons and the ground; it had purified. Having done its duty of testing the mettle of its opponents, romanticism was falling away, "cherished only by a faction of modern obscurants." "A truer conception of the nature of classicism . . . has come forth triumphant," armed with the successes of German philology and criticism. "The science of textual criticism may now be regarded as complete," and other aspirations of the German school—in the collation of manuscripts, in hermeneutics, in the history of literature and the theory of history, in comparative and oriental philology—were being fulfilled and lifted yet higher.[160] To this ennobled and expansive study, transported into America, Gildersleeve foresaw and exhorted new contributions to be made, not in the North, prolific, commercial, and undiscriminating, but in the South:

> We must wake to higher efforts, for which we are well adapted by the quick conceptions, love of classic form and instinctive rejection of extravagance, which are our birthright. Here, the wild political, social and physical theories of our day, find no debateable ground between those who know too much and those who know too little. If united with vigorous action, this conscious self-possession would make us the arbiters of literary destiny. The sentences which we pass are confirmed

by time, but they lack the weight which power confers. If we make the South, where the materials abound, the centre of classical learning, we must hold the balance. To create and perpetuate such a classical school, we must have an enlarged and elevative system of education, and the rising generation must be trained in a domestic institution, of a higher type than the out-door schools, whither so many of youth go, seeking knowledge, and finding a miserable succedaneum.[161]

"In the American classical pantheon he sat enthroned as Zeus."[162] Basil Gildersleeve himself represents the fulfillment of his own exhortations. Yet he had dissolved a bond, a dissolution that was more than, as it was exemplified by, his departure from Charleston. From his post as professor of Greek at the Johns Hopkins University, to which he had been appointed at its establishment in 1876; from his work as founder and first editor of the *American Journal of Philology*, and as one of the founders and twice the president of the American Philological Association; from his direction of sixty-two doctorates which spread throughout the universities of the nation, Gildersleeve looked back upon Charleston with gratitude. It was the heart of his love, upon which were superimposed his affections for Carolina, then the South. However "wider and richer"—and it was wider and richer—the life of the scholar at Johns Hopkins, the grandeur and spaciousness "of my native city" endured, essential qualities, not measurements of degree. "No other names have ever made the same aristocratic music in my ear as the names of the old Huguenot families; and when courtliness of manner is mentioned, my memory at once recalls the ceremonious old gentlemen who were held up to us as models of politeness."[163]

But that was the thing. Gildersleeve held up no models of his own. His classics were "eternal norms and present facts," standards for interpretation, not models for conduct. Blockaded against new books during the war, "the Southerner, always conservative in his tastes and no great admirer of American literature, which had become largely alien to him, went back to his English classics, his ancient classics." So Gildersleeve, living "in an age when [classical] allusion is under the ban," blended his own past in that war—when, professor at the University of Virginia, he earned "the right to teach Southern youth for nine months . . . by sharing the fortunes of their fathers and brothers at the front for three"—that past he blended with his past in the Peloponnesian War, convertible pasts where Thucydides and Aristophanes were his comrades, his interpreters, but neither themselves nor the source

368

of "high and heroical models of excellence."[164] He accomplished much of what Legaré had desired, and accomplished it with imagination and intimacy that Legaré would have applauded, and had himself brought to his classics. But there had been a withdrawal; the urgency was gone. To the ancients Thomas Grimké had paid the honor of passionate hostility. Basil Gildersleeve looked to an innovated, a purified philology for the saving of the classics; in this he was right, but they were saved in no Periclean Carolina, no Charlestonian Forum, but in the new professional foundation of Johns Hopkins, in the *American Journal of Philology*, in doctoral dissertations, in multiplying academic departments of multiplying universities.

Surveying from Brussels the antics of nullification, Hugh Legaré was reminded, as he told Isaac Holmes, of Tacitus upon *ludibria rerum mortalium*, the ironies pervading human affairs; but then the Roman had meant a grievous derision, and "I really don't know whether I ought to laugh or cry at the picture you draw of our poor little community."[165] Irony itself ambivalent is for the connoisseur of detachment. There would be need of it, and of him. The *Southern Literary Messenger* was to judge Legaré's "immortal defence of the momentous cause of classical education" as "the most triumphant effort of his life."[166] It was worthy of Tacitus. For the *Messenger* had chosen to republish that ancient triumph, in the summer of 1862, in order that present aspirations might have their proper ground, "seeing we are henceforth to fill a new place among the nations of the earth."

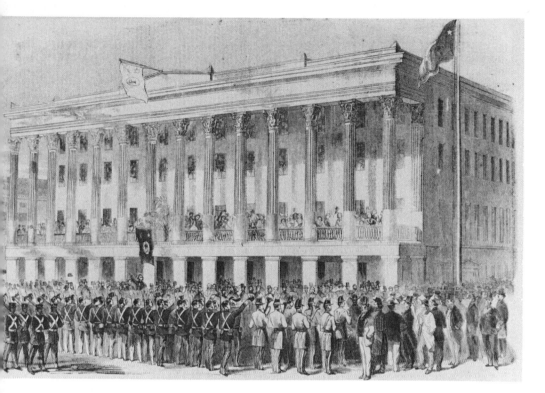

General M'Gowan Addressing the Abbeville Volunteers in Front of the Charleston Hotel, from Frank Leslie's Illustrated Newspaper, 23 February 1861, p. 218. *Courtesy of the South Carolina Historical Society.*

Abbreviations

All Clever Men: Michael O'Brien, ed., *All Clever Men, Who Make Their Way: Critical Discourse in the Old South* (Fayetteville, Ark., 1982)

AHR: *American Historical Review*

Calhoun Papers: Robert L. Meriwether et al., eds., *The Papers of John C. Calhoun*, 15 vols. to date (Columbia, S.C., 1959–83)

Chesnut: C. Vann Woodward, ed., *Mary Chesnut's Civil War* (New Haven, Conn., 1981)

Courier: Charleston *Courier*

Freehling: William W. Freehling, *Prelude to Civil War: The Nullification Controversy in South Carolina, 1816–1836* (New York, 1965)

JAH: *Journal of American History*

JSH: *Journal of Southern History*

LC: Library of Congress

Mercury: Charleston *Mercury*

Petigru: James Petigru Carson, *Life, Letters and Speeches of James Louis Petigru: The Union Man of South Carolina* (Washington, D.C., 1920)

PHS: Historical Society of Pennsylvania

Rogers I: George C. Rogers, Jr., *Charleston in the Age of the Pinckneys* (Norman, Okla., 1969)

Rogers II: George C. Rogers, Jr., *Evolution of a Federalist: William Loughton Smith of Charleston* (Columbia, S.C., 1962)

Simms Letters: Mary C. Simms Oliphant et al., eds., *The Letters of William Gilmore Simms*, 6 vols. (Columbia, S.C., 1952–82)

SCHM: *South Carolina Historical Magazine* (until 1940 the *South Carolina Historical and Genealogical Magazine*)

SCHS: South Carolina Historical Society, Charleston

SCSA: South Carolina Department of Archives and History, Columbia

SCL: South Caroliniana Library, University of South Carolina, Columbia

SHC: Southern Historical Collection, University of North Carolina, Chapel Hill

SQR: *Southern Quarterly Review*

SR: *Southern Review*

WMQ: *William and Mary Quarterly*

Notes

Preface: O'BRIEN

1. The bibliography for Charleston will be found everywhere in the following essays, but particularly in Moltke-Hansen, "The Expansion of Intellectual Life," *infra.*

2. Thomas Bender, "The Cultures of Intellectual Life: The City and the Professions," in John Higham and Paul K. Conkin, eds., *New Directions in American Intellectual History* (Baltimore, 1979), 181–95, and in an address, "The Place of Intellect," delivered to the Conference on Intellectual Life in Antebellum Charleston, March 1982.

3. William Gilmore Simms, *The Social Principle: The True Source of National Permanence* (Tuscaloosa, Ala., 1843), 7.

4. Henry James, "Charleston," in *The American Scene*, ed. Leon Edel (Bloomington, Ind., 1968), 403.

5. Simms, *Father Abbot, or, The Home Tourist* (Charleston, S.C., 1849), 101.

6. Rogers I, 141–66.

7. J.R. Pole, "The American Past: Is It Still Usable?" in *Paths to the American Past* (New York, 1979), 266.

1. The Expansion of Intellectual Life: MOLTKE-HANSEN

These notes do not record the debts owed the essays that follow; those will become apparent. For critical readings of earlier drafts, thanks go—in alphabetical order—to Mark Kaplanoff, James Meriwether, Michael O'Brien, Nicholas Olsberg, Jane Pease, William Pease, George Rogers, Theodore Rosengarten, Gene Waddell, and Clyde Wilson.

These notes are meant not only to document sources of quotation and specific information, but to introduce the historiography of antebellum Charleston's intellectuals and intellectual life and the changing contexts of that life. Such an introduction is desirable because existing bibliographic controls are inadequate and inconvenient. J.H. Easterby, *Guide to the Study and Reading of South Carolina History: A General Bibliography* (Columbia, S.C., 1950), is out of date, and Noel Polk's supplement, appended to the reprint (Spartanburg, S.C., 1975), notes only books and is itself now also dated. Richard N. Coté, *Local and Family History in South Carolina: A Bibliography* (Easley, 1981), is a splendid tool, but limited in scope. E.L. Inabinett, *A Dissertation Bibliography: South Carolina* (Ann Arbor, 1980), is updated by University Microfilms International, *U.S. History: A Catalog of Current Doctoral Dissertation Research* (Ann Arbor, 1983), and by periodic dissertation listings in the *JAH* and the *North Carolina Historical Review.* In turn, the *JSH* and *Mississippi Quarterly* annually list articles in Southern history and culture, respectively. Nevertheless, finding what has been written about antebellum Charleston, Charlestonians, and their intellectual products and pursuits has been time-consuming and difficult.

Scholars presently are little better served in their search for separate publications by ante-bellum Charlestonians. The bibliographies cited in n. 2 below can be supplemented by a series of Catholic University of America library science masters theses on Charleston and South Carolina imprints; by the *National Union Catalog of Pre-1956 Imprints*, 754 vols. (Chicago, 1968–81); by other relevant titles noted in G. Thomas Tanselle, *Guide to the Study of United States Imprints*, 2 vols. (Cambridge, Mass., 1971); and by Mary Dunlap et al., compilers, *A Catalog of the South Carolina Collection of J. Rion McKissick* (Columbia, S.C., 1977).

The major holdings of manuscripts of Charlestonians are described in the following: David Moltke-Hansen and Sallie Doscher, *South Carolina Historical Society Manuscript Guide* (Charleston, S.C., 1979), and updates to the *Guide* by Moltke-Hansen, Harlan Greene, and others in the *SCHM* (1980–present); Allen H. Stokes, Jr., *A Guide to the Manuscript Collection of the South Caroliniana Library* (Columbia, S.C., 1982); Susan S. Blosser and Clyde N. Wilson, Jr., *The Southern Historical Collection: A Guide to Manuscripts* (Chapel Hill, N.C., 1970), supplemented in a 1975 update of Everard H. Smith, Jr.; Richard C. Davis and Linda A. Miller, eds., *Guide to the Cataloged Collections in the Manuscript Department of the William R. Perkins Library, Duke University* (Santa Barbara, Calif., 1980); Ralph Melnick, "College of Charleston Special Collections: A Guide to Its Holdings," *SCHM* 81 (1980): 131–53; David Moltke-Hansen, "Charleston Library Society Microfiche Register," *SCHM* 83 (1982): 175–201, and the *National Union Catalog of Manuscript Collections* (Ann Arbor, Mich., 1962–).

Periodical contributions by antebellum Charlestonians are generally not accessible through bibliographies. More or less complete lists of contributors are available, however, for three of the city's principal intellectual journals: Michael O'Brien, *A Character of Hugh Legaré* (Knoxville, Tenn., 1985), for the *SR*; F.W. Simpson, "William Gilmore Simms and *The Southern Quarterly Review*" (M.A. thesis, Furman University, 1946), for the review during the years of Simms' editorship; and William Taylor Loftis, "A Study of *Russell's Magazine*, Antebellum Charleston's Last Literary Periodical" (Ph.D. diss., Duke University, 1973), for that journal. Several articles in James B. Meriwether, ed., *South Carolina Journals and Journalists* (Spartanburg, S.C., 1975), also should be consulted.

1. *Simms Letters*, V, 152–53. The articles appeared in six 1869 and 1870 issues of the *XIX Century* and have been gathered together and reprinted, with notes and an introduction by Jim Scafidel, as *Essays on the Literary and Intellectual History of South Carolina* (Columbia, S.C., 1977).

2. Charles Fraser, *Reminiscences of Charleston* (Charleston, S.C., 1854). For some sense of the scale and nature of Charleston's intellectual expansion, compare institutional and occupational listings in, e.g., Joseph Milligan, *The Charleston Directory and Revenue System* (Charleston, S.C., 1790); James Smith, *The Charleston Directory; and Register for 1835–6* (Charleston, S.C., 1835); and Means and Turnbull, *Charleston Directory* (Charleston, S.C., 1859). See also William S. Hoole, *A Check-List and Finding List of Charleston Periodicals, 1732–1864* (Durham, N.C., 1936); George A. Wauchope, *Literary South Carolina* (Columbia, S.C., 1923), and Joseph I. Waring, *A History of Medicine in South Carolina*, 3 vols. (Columbia, S.C., 1964–71); these works document incompletely but nevertheless tellingly the expansion of Charleston's press and Charlestonians' productivity.

3. See Arthur A. Ekirch, Jr., *The Idea of Progress in America, 1815–1860* (New York, 1944). Charlestonians' perceptions and definitions of progress are illustrated by Samuel Henry Dickson, *An Oration Delivered at New Haven, before the Phi Beta Kappa Society, August 17, 1842* (New Haven, Conn., 1842); Henry Laurens Pinckney, *"The Spirit of the Age": An Address Delivered before the Two Literary Societies of the University of North Carolina* (Raleigh, N.C., 1836); [Frederick A. Porcher], "Characteristics of Civilization," *Russell's Magazine* 2 (1857–58): 97–110. *All Clever Men*, 1–25, reviews and challenges the historiography of the South's intellectual poverty; the single most influential statement on the case of Charleston is Rogers I, which describes Charleston on the

eve of the Civil War as having become intellectually "The Closed City." William R. Taylor, *Cavalier and Yankee: The Old South and American National Character* (New York, 1961), anticipated Rogers. On more recent scholarship, see Michael O'Brien, "The Nineteenth-Century American South," *The Historical Journal* 24 (1981): 751–63, and Robert J. Brugger, "The Mind of the Old South: New Views," *Virginia Quarterly Review* 56 (1980): 277–95.

4. See David Donald, "Toward a Reconsideration of Abolitionists," in *Lincoln Reconsidered: Essays on the Civil War Era* (New York, 1956), 19–36; Robert Skotheim, "A Note on Historical Method: David Donald's 'Toward a Reconsideration of Abolitionists,'" *JSH* 25 (1959): 356–65; Ekirch, *Idea of Progress*, 225–51; Lewis Perry and Michael Fellman, eds., *Antislavery Reconsidered: New Perspectives on the Abolitionists* (Baton Rouge, La., 1979), esp. the essays by Ronald Walters, Jonathan Glickstein, and Bertram Wyatt-Brown; Bertram Wyatt-Brown, "Modernizing Southern Slavery: The Proslavery Argument Reinterpreted," in J. Morgan Kousser and James M. McPherson, eds., *Region, Race, and Reconstruction: Essays in Honor of C. Vann Woodward* (New York, 1982), 27–49; Drew Gilpin Faust, "A Southern Stewardship: The Intellectual and the Proslavery Argument," *American Quarterly* 31 (1979), 63–80. Cf. Jane H. Pease and William H. Pease, "Social Structure and the Potential for Urban Change: Boston and Charleston in the 1830s," *Journal of Urban History* 8 (1982): 171–95.

5. Illustrating the intricate networks of intellectual and personal friendships between Charleston and the North are Paul R. Weidner, ed., "The Journal of John Blake White," *SCHM* 43 (1942), 105ff; Arthur J. Roche III, "A Literary Gentlemen in New York: Evert A. Duyckinck's Relationship with Nathaniel Hawthorne, Herman Melville, Edgar Allan Poe, and William Gilmore Simms" (Ph.D. diss., Duke University, 1973); John H. Moore, ed., "Jared Sparks Visits South Carolina," *SCHM* 72 (1971): 150–60; the correspondence with William Cullen Bryant in the *Simms Letters*; Curtis Carroll Davis, *That Ambitious Mr. Legaré: The Life of James M. Legaré of South Carolina* (Columbia, S.C., 1971); Daniel M. McKeithen, ed., *A Collection of Hayne Letters* (Austin, Tex., 1944), which includes correspondence with, e.g., James Russell Lowell; also Alicia H. Middleton et al., *Life in South Carolina and New England during the Nineteenth Century* (Bristol, R.I., 1929). Fred J. Hood, *Reformed America: The Middle and Southern States, 1783–1837* (Tuscaloosa, Ala., 1980), 150–54, puts in comparative perspective the actions and philosophies of the Charleston Bible Society and the Charleston Female Domestic Missionary Society. The temperance movement in Charleston is illustrated by, e.g., Henry R. Frost, *An Address Delivered before the Young Men's Temperance Society* (Charleston, S.C., 1832), and James Tupper, *Introductory Address on the Principles and Progress of the Temperance Reformation. Delivered before the Charleston Total Abstinence Society, 31 March 1851* (Charleston, S.C., 1852). Ian R. Tyrrel, "Drink and Temperance in the Antebellum South: An Overview and Interpretation," *JSH* 48 (1982): 485–510, argues that temperance was relatively unimportant in the South, a much more rural region than New England, but this argument does not entirely fit Charleston, whose experience was more urban than Southern in this regard as in so many others. Cf. Stanley K. Schultz, "Temperance Reform in the Antebellum South: Social Control and Urban Order," *South Atlantic Quarterly* 83 (1984): 323–39. David Moltke-Hansen, "Why History Mattered: The Background of Ann Pamela Cunningham's Interest in the Preservation of Mount Vernon," *Furman Studies*, n.s., 26 (1980): 34–42, is only one of the more recent discussions of the origins and development of the Mount Vernon Ladies Association of the Union under the leadership of South Carolinian Ann Pamela Cunningham, one-time roommate of a daughter of John C. Calhoun; a leading supporter of her cause was Edward Everett of Massachusetts. See also Paul C. Nagel, *The Union in American Political Thought, 1776–1861* (New York, 1964).

6. On the historiography of American sectionalism, see David M. Potter, *The Impending Crisis, 1848–1861* (New York, 1976), 29–55, 448–84, and David M. Potter, *The South and the Sectional Conflict* (Baton Rouge, La., 1968), esp. 119–33. Michael O'Brien, *The Idea of the American South, 1920–1941* (Baltimore, Md., 1979), xiv, 3–5 and *passim*, introduces the question of the origins

in romanticism of nationalist as well as sectionalist ideology in the South, as elsewhere; his few pages are considerably more sophisticated and informed than Rollin G. Osterweis, *Romanticism and Nationalism in the Old South* (New Haven, Conn., 1942). For a third perspective, see Jay B. Hubbell, "Literary Nationalism in the Old South," in David K. Jackson, ed., *American Studies in Honor of William Kenneth Boyd* (Durham, N.C., 1940). Ulrich B. Phillips, *A History of Transportation in the Eastern Cotton Belt to 1860* (New York, 1908), remains a necessary point of departure for a subject since studied only in various details, but see also Max M. Schreiber, "The Development of the Southern United States: A Test for Regional Convergence and Homogeneity" (Ph.D. diss., University of South Carolina, 1978). The evolution of a regional culture more or less dominated by planter interests and ideology is assumed by most historians of the antebellum South but explored in J. Mills Thornton III, *Politics and Power in a Slave Society: Alabama, 1800–1860* (Baton Rouge, La., 1978), and Mark D. Kaplanoff, "Making the South Solid: Politics and the Structure of Society in South Carolina, 1790–1815" (Ph.D. diss., University of Cambridge, 1979); cf. Edward Pessen, "How Different from Each Other Were the Antebellum North and South?" *AHR* 85 (1980): 1119–49, and Lee Soltow, "Socioeconomic Classes in South Carolina and Massachusetts in the 1790s and the Observations of John Drayton," *SCHM* 81 (1980), 283–305.

7. See Jay B. Hubbell, *The South in American Literature, 1607–1900* (Durham, N.C., 1954), 568 and *passim*, the best informed, most judicious treatment of Charleston letters to date; Ronald L. Numbers and Janet S. Numbers, "Science in the Old South: A Reappraisal," *JSH* 48 (1982): 163–84, esp. 175.

8. George Frick, Introduction, *The Natural History of Carolina . . . by the late Mark Catesby* (London, 1771; rpt. Savannah, Ga., 1974); Thomas C. Johnson, Jr., *Scientific Interests in the Old South* (New York, 1936), 126–51; Horatio Hughes, "The Elliott Society," *Proceedings of the South Carolina Historical Association, 1938*, 25–31 (hereafter, *PSCHA*); William M. Smallwood, *Natural History and the American Mind* (New York, 1941), 102–19; G. Edmund Gifford, Jr., "The Charleston Physician-Naturalists," *Bulletin of the History of Medicine* 49 (1975): 556–74; Joseph Ewen, "The Growth of Learned and Scientific Societies in the Southeastern United States to 1860," in Alexandra Oleson and Sanborn C. Brown, eds., *The Pursuit of Knowledge in the Early American Republic: American Scientific and Learned Societies from Colonial Times to the Civil War* (Baltimore, Md., 1976), 208–18; William H. Longton, "Some Aspects of Intellectual Activity in Ante-Bellum South Carolina, 1830–1860: An Introductory Study" (Ph.D. diss., University of North Carolina, 1969) 63–84, 152–64, 230–45.

9. [John Beaufain Irving], "Contribution of Charleston to Natural Science," *Southern Literary Journal* 1 (1835–36): 447–48.

10. See Hans Kohn, *The Idea of Nationalism* (New York, 1944), and *The Age of Nationalism: The First Era of Global History* (New York, 1962); John McCardell, *The Idea of a Southern Nation: Southern Nationalists and Southern Nationalism, 1830–1860* (New York, 1979); A.V. Huff, Jr., "The Eagle and the Vulture: Changing Attitudes toward Nationalism in Fourth of July Orations in Charleston, 1778–1860," *South Atlantic Quarterly* 73 (1974): 10–22; William Gilmore Simms, *South-Carolina in the Revolutionary War* (Charleston, S.C., 1853); Kenneth S. Greenberg, "Revolutionary Ideology and the Proslavery Argument: The Abolition of Slavery in Antebellum South Carolina," *JSH* 42 (1976): 365–84; Jack P. Greene, "Slavery or Independence: Some Reflections on the Relationships among Liberty, Black Bondage, and Equality in Revolutionary South Carolina," *SCHM* 80 (1979): 193–214; George C. Rogers, Jr., "South Carolina Federalists and the Origins of the Nullification Movement," *SCHM* 71 (1970): 28–29.

11. *College [of Charleston] Magazine* 1 (1830–31): 25–27; Charles Fraser, "An Essay on the Condition and Prospects of the Art of Painting in the United States of America," *American Monthly Magazine* 6 (1835): 213; Joel Roberts Poinsett, *Discourse, on the Objects and Importance of the National Institution for the Promotion of Sciences, Established at Washington, 1840, Delivered at the First*

378

Anniversary (Washington, D.C., 1841), 44–47; William Gilmore Simms, "Southern Literature: Its Condition, Prospects, and History," *Magnolia* 3 (1841): 3. See also James W. Simmons, "American Literature," *Southern Literary Journal* 3 (1836–37): 68; McCardell, *Idea of a Southern Nation*, 19–20 and passim; John C. Guilds, Jr., "Simms's Views on National and Sectional Literature, 1825–1845," *North Carolina Historical Review* 34 (1957): 393–405.

12. [Daniel K. Whitaker], "The Periodical Press," *SQR* 1 (1842): 51–55; Guilds, "Simms's Views on National and Sectional Literature," 393–405.

13. See James L. MacLeod, "A Catalogue of References to Education in the 'South Carolina Gazette,' Charleston, South Carolina, 1731 to 1770, and Commentary" (Ed.D. diss., Mississippi State University, 1972). The quotations are in David Moltke-Hansen, "Newspapers in Colonial South Carolina Legal History," in Herbert A. Johnson, ed., *South Carolina Legal History* (Spartanburg, S.C., 1980), 261, and Fraser, *Reminiscences*, 110–11. See also J.N. Cardozo, *Reminiscences of Charleston* (Charleston, S.C., 1866), 14–22 and passim; John Furman Thomason, *The Foundations of the Public Schools of South Carolina* (Columbia, S.C., 1925), 64–175; and Laylon Wayne Jordan, "Education for Community: C.G. Memminger and the Origination of Common Schools in Antebellum Charleston," *SCHM* 83 (1982): 99–115, esp. 107ff, and J. Mills Thornton III, "Fiscal Policy and the Failure of Radical Reconstruction in the Lower South," in Kousser and McPherson, eds., *Region, Race, and Reconstruction*, 349–94.

14. J.H. Easterby, *A History of the College of Charleston* (Charleston, S.C., 1935), 27–36; Charles S. Vedder, "Centennial Oration," *Charleston Orphan House Celebration* (Charleston, S.C., 1891), 27ff; Thomason, *Foundations of the Public Schools*, 64ff; Nita K. Pyburn, "The Public School System of Charleston before 1860," *SCHM* 61 (1960): 86–98; Richard Walsh, "The South Carolina Academy–1800–1811," *PSCHA, 1955*, 5–14; Lowell Harrison, ed., "South Carolina's Educational System in 1822," *SCHM* 51 (1950): 1–9; Paul Staiti, "The 1823 Exhibition of the South Carolina Academy of Fine Arts: A Paradigm of Charleston Taste?" in David Moltke-Hansen, ed., *Art in the Lives of South Carolinians: Nineteenth-Century Chapters* (Charleston, S.C., 1979), essay XIV; J.H. Easterby, *The Rules of the South Carolina Society . . .* , 17th ed. (Charleston, S.C., 1937), 46–51; Samuel Henry Dickson, *Address, Delivered at the Opening of the New Edifice of the Charleston Apprentices Library Society on the Evening of 13 January 1841* (Charleston, S.C., 1841); *Southern Rose Bud* 2 (1833–34): 187; O.J. Bond, *The Story of the Citadel* (Richmond, Va., 1936), 17ff; *Constitution of the South-Carolina Institute: For the Promotion of Art, Mechanical Ingenuity, and Industry. Adopted January, 1849* (Charleston, S.C., 1849); Hughes, "The Elliott Society," *passim*; *Collections of the South-Carolina Historical Society* 1 (1857): v–vi.

15. Richard C. Wade, *Slavery in the Cities: The South, 1820–1860* (New York, 1964), 173–77; Marina Wikramanayake, *A World in Shadow: The Free Black in Antebellum South Carolina* (Columbia, S.C., 1973), 85–87, 167–68; Daniel A. Payne, *Recollections of Seventy Years* (New York, 1969), 64 and passim; Francis Asbury Mood, "Autobiography" (original MS dated 1875, typescript dated 1937, photocopy of the latter in SCHS), 14ff; Clionian Debating Society minutes (MS, 1847–51, Charleston Library Society).

16. Charles Pinckney, "Speech," in Max Farrand, ed., *The Records of the Federal Convention of 1787*, 4 vols. (Washington, D.C., 1911–37), I, 397–407, quoted in Greene, "Slavery or Independence," 205; Message of Governor Charles Pinckney, Charleston *City Gazette*, 6 December 1798, quoted in Thomason, *Foundations of the Public Schools*, 117; "A Friend of the People," Charleston *City Gazette*, 26 August 1812, quoted in Thomason, *Foundations of the Public Schools*, 118–19.

17. *College Magazine* 1 (1830–31): 27; [William Gilmore Simms], "Literary Prospects of the South," *Russell's Magazine* 3 (1858): 193. Cf. [Whitaker], "Periodical Press," 42. See also "Mental Development," *SR* 6 (1830): 1.

18. J.C[arr?]., Charleston *City Gazette*, 28 March 1810, cited in Thomason, *Foundations of the Public Schools*, 120; Sidney Charles Bolton, "The Anglican Church of Colonial South Caro-

lina, 1704–1754: A Study of Americanization" (Ph.D. diss., University of Wisconsin, 1973), 151–52, 193, 196–98; Frederick P. Bowes, *The Culture of Early Charleston* (Chapel Hill, N.C., 1942), 35–40; Edgar Legaré Pennington, "The Reverend Thomas Morritt and the Free School in Charles Town," *SCHM* 32 (1931): 34–45; J.H. Easterby, ed., "The South Carolina Education Bill of 1770," *SCHM* 48 (1947): 95–111; Henry S. Stroupe, *The Religious Press in the South Atlantic States, 1802–1865* (Durham, N.C., 1956); Hoole, *Charleston Periodicals*, 22; Hood, *Reformed America*, 77–81, 171–76, 180–83.

19. William D. Porter, "The Value of the Arts and Sciences to the Practical Mechanic," *Courier*, 12 April 1843; *Second Annual Report of the Board of Directors of the South-Carolina Institute, November, 1850* (Charleston, S.C., 1850); Sallie Doscher, "Art Exhibitions in Nineteenth-Century Charleston," in Moltke-Hansen, ed., *Art in the Lives*, essay X, esp. 7–10.

20. On aristocratic notions within the context of democratic ideology in the South, see George M. Fredrickson, "Aristocracy and Democracy in the Southern Tradition," in Walter J. Fraser, Jr., and Winfred B. Moore, Jr., *The Southern Enigma: Essays on Race, Class, and Folk Culture* (Westport, Conn., 1983), 97–104; Clement Eaton, *The Growth of Southern Civilization, 1790–1860* (New York, 1961), 21–24, 297; Raimondo Luraghi, *The Rise and Fall of the Plantation South* (New York, 1978), 75–80; also Raymond A. Mohl, ed., "'The Grand Fabric of Republicanism': A Scotsman Describes South Carolina, 1810–1811," *SCHM* 71 (1970): 170–88, esp. 183–84. The quotation is in Dickson, *Oration . . . before the Phi Beta Kappa Society*, 41. On southern intellectuals' ambition to be useful, see Drew Gilpin Faust, *A Sacred Circle: The Dilemma of the Intellectual in the Old South, 1840–1860* (Baltimore, Md., 1978), 45–111. On the assumed relationship between prosperity and cultural life, and between industrial and regional improvement, see the "Address" appended to the *Constitution of the South-Carolina Institute*, 11–22; Jos. H. Lumpkin, *An Address Delivered Before the South-Carolina Institute, at Its Second Annual Fair, on the 19th November, 1850* (Charleston, S.C., 1851); also Benjamin F. Perry, *Address . . . before the South Carolina Institute, at Their Annual Fair, November, 1856* (Charleston, S.C., 1857), 3–32.

21. [John McCrady], "A Few Thoughts on Southern Civilization," *Russell's Magazine* 1 (1857): 227; Dickson, *Oration . . . before the Phi Beta Kappa Society*, 47.

22. Merrill G. Christophersen, "The Earliest Law School in the South," *South Carolina Law Quarterly* 7 (1954–55): 375–78; Sarah Leverette, "The Carolina Law Journal of 1830," *ibid.* 12 (1959–60): 193–201; Waring, *History of Medicine*, II, 71–101, 354; Albert Sidney Thomas, *A Historical Account of the Prostestant Episcopal Church in South Carolina, 1820–1957* (Columbia, S.C., 1957), 691–92; Joe M. King, *A History of the South Carolina Baptists* (Columbia, S.C., 1964), 158, 163–69, 180–89, 208–9; Stephen S. Hahn, "Lexington's Theological Library, 1832–1859," *SCHM* 80 (1979): 36–49. According to a comparison of listings in city directories, there were twice as many teachers in Charleston in 1831 (53) as in 1790 (27); in the same period the city's white population had increased by two-thirds, but the school-age segment of that population (children ages five to twenty, inclusive) had increased by at most 60, (possibly only 50) percent, according to extrapolations from J.L. Dawson and H.W. DeSaussure, *Census of the City of Charleston, S.C. . . . 1848* (Charleston, S.C., 1849), 12–14. Between 1830 and 1861, the white population increased by just over 100 percent and its school-age segment about 90 percent. Over the same span of time, the number of pupils in the free schools increased about eightfold (from 533 in 1834 to 4,044 in 1861) and the teaching staff more than tenfold (from 5 in 1834 to 53 in 1860). See Jordan, "Education for Community," 108. On the quality of teachers, see Fraser, *Reminiscences*, 111, and Thomason, *Foundations of the Public Schools*, 164. On architecture and the arts, see Beatrice St. Julien Ravenel, *Architects of Charleston* (Charleston, S.C., 1945); Moltke-Hansen, ed., *Art in the Lives*; Anna Wells Rutledge, "Artists in the Life of Charleston," *Transactions of the American Philosophical Society*, n.s., 39 (1949): *passim*.

23. Numbers and Numbers, "Science in the Old South," 175; Keen Butterworth and James E. Kibler, Jr., *William Gilmore Simms: A Reference Guide* (Boston, 1980).

24. On the exceptional levels and concentrations of wealth in Charleston, see Soltow, "Socioeconomic Classes"; Gregory A. Greb, "Charleston, South Carolina Merchants, 1815–1860: Urban Leadership in the Antebellum South" (Ph.D. diss., University of California at San Diego, 1978); and Michael P. Johnson, "Wealth and Class in Charleston in 1860," in Walter J. Fraser, Jr., and Winfred B. Moore, Jr., eds., *From the Old South to the New: Essays on the Transitional South* (Westport, Conn.: 1981), 65–80. As Johnson notes (pp. 67–70), in 1860 "the mean wealth in the city was . . . three and a half times larger than the mean wealth in the North and almost twice as much as the mean wealth in the South. . . . A much larger fraction of the Charleston free population was rich by Northern standards; a much larger fraction of the free population of Northern cities was poor by Southern standards." For the abolitionist perspective and its influence on subsequent historiography and literary criticism, see, e.g., Edmund Quincy, "Where Will It End?" *Atlantic Monthly* 1 (1857): 244; Edmund S. Morgan, review of Richard Beale Davis' *Intellectual Life in the Colonial South* and Sacvan Bercovich's *American Jeremiad,* in *New York Review of Books* 26 (July 1979): 31–32; also Louis D. Rubin, *William Elliott Shoots a Bear* (Baton Rouge, La., 1975), 7–8, 16–27. For the views of Wells, Chesnut, Elliott, and Porcher, see respectively: David Moltke-Hansen, "A World Introduced: The Writings of Helena Wells of Charles Town, South Carolina's First Novelist," in James B. Meriwether, ed., *South Carolina Women Writers* (Spartanburg, S.C., 1979), 61–81, esp. 69; Michael P. Johnson, "Planters and Patriarchy: Charleston, 1800–1860," *JSH* 46 (1980): 45–72; William Elliott, *Carolina Sports by Land and Water* (New York, 1859), 193–213, and *passim*; Samuel G. Stoney, ed., "The Memoirs of Frederick Adolphus Porcher," *SCHM* 47 (1946): 94–95. For the evolution of the predominant views of slavery among white Southerners in general or Charleston intellectuals in particular, see William Sumner Jenkins, *Pro Slavery Thought in the Old South* (Chapel Hill, N.C., 1935), 65ff; Robert Shalhope, "Race, Class, Slavery and the Antebellum Southern Mind," *JSH* 37 (1971): 557–74; also Rosser H. Taylor, "The Mud-Sill Theory in South Carolina," *PSCHA, 1939,* 35–43. For a comparative perspective, see Peter Kolchin, "In Defense of Servitude: American Pro-Slavery and Russian Proserfdom Arguments, 1760–1860," *AHR* 85 (1980): 809–27; also Larry E. Tise, "The Interregional Appeal of Proslavery Thought: An Ideological Profile of the Antebellum American Clergy," *Plantation and Society in the Americas* 1 (1979): 58–72. For another discussion of the difficulties confronting southern intellectuals, see Faust, *Sacred Circle,* 7–14.

25. [William Gilmore Simms], "Southern Literature: Its Condition, Prospects and History," *Magnolia* 3 (1841): 1–6; [Bartholomew R. Carroll], "Valedictory," *Southern Literary Journal* 4 (1837–38): 474–75; Julian J. Petty, *The Growth and Distribution of Population in South Carolina* (Columbia, S.C., 1943).

26. Charleston *City Gazette,* 18 November 1830; Jane H. Pease and William H. Pease, "The Economics and Politics of Charleston's Nullification Crisis," *JSH* 47 (1981): 338–40. Pease and Pease indicate that in 1830, 27.1 percent of the electorate of white males over twenty were unskilled or semiskilled, while another 25 percent were "low-prestige, white collar workers." Frederick A. Ford, *Census of the City of Charleston . . . 1861* (Charleston, S.C., 1861), 8–9, shows a population increase of approximately 20 percent over the 1860 federal census. The discrepancy is apparently due not to a sudden flood of immigrants but to substantial undercounting in 1860. (See Ernest M. Lander, Jr., "Charleston: Manufacturing Center of the Old South," *JSH* 26 [1960]: 330n.) According to a private communication of George Terry, Director of McKissick Museums, University of South Carolina, even the 1861 census underrepresents blacks in the city; moreover, the total increase in housing between 1850 and 1860 (1,205 houses) suggests that either the 1860 population count is very low, or there was a quite dramatic, unnoticed, and unexplained drop in the average number of residents per dwelling. Earlier censuses were also prone to considerable error, as is made clear by Anne W. Chapman, "Inadequacies of the 1848 Charleston Census," *SCHM* 81 (1980): 24–34. Clearly, census figures should be taken *cum grano.* That said, here are the figures from 1790–1861:

	WHITE	BLACK	TOTAL
1790	8,089	8,270	16,359
1800	9,630	10,843	20,473
1810	11,568	13,143	24,711
1820	10,653	14,127	24,780
1830	12,828	17,461	30,289
1840	13,030	16,231	29,261
1850	20,012*	22,973**	42,985
1861	26,969+	21,440++	48,409

*Includes 4,570 from the Charleston Neck
**Includes 6,282 from the Charleston Neck
+ Includes 10,738 from the Charleston Neck
++ Includes 8,672 from the Charleston Neck

The Charleston Neck was incorporated into the Charleston City limits in 1849. Its population was still small in 1830, but increased rapidly thereafter. Had the Neck figures been included in the 1840 census, Charleston's population would have increased modestly rather than decreased between 1830 and 1840. Much of the increase in white population between 1840 and 1861 was due to immigration of Germans and Irish. See Christopher Silver, "A New Look at Old South Urbanization: The Irish Worker in Charleston, South Carolina, 1840–1860," *South Atlantic Urban Studies* 3 (1979): 141–72. According to Silver, in 1850 there were 779 unskilled, 489 skilled, and 852 white-collar workers from Ireland and Germany in Charleston. By 1860 the figures were respectively 1,225, 902, and 971—fully 25 percent of the white work force, according to Ira Berlin and Herbert G. Gutman, "Natives and Immigrants, Free Men and Slaves: Urban Workingmen in the Antebellum American South," *AHR* 88 (1983): 1187 and *passim*. On literacy among whites, see Soltow, "Socioeconomic Classes," 295–96.

27. Bureau of the Census, *A Century of Population Growth* (Washington, 1909); Samuel G. Stoney, ed., "The Autobiography of William John Grayson," *SCHM* 48 (1947): 127; Gilbert P. Voigt, "The 'Periclean Age' of Beaufort," *SCHM* 58 (1957): 218–23; [William Gilmore Simms], "Country Life Incompatible with Literary Labor," *Southern Literary Journal* 3 (1836–37): 297–99. See also Adrienne Koch, ed., "A Family Crisis: Letters from John Faucherand Grimké and Thomas Smith Grimké to Henry Grimké," *SCHM* 69 (1968): 171–93.

28. Stoney, ed., "The Memoirs of Frederick Adolphus Porcher," *SCHM* 45 (1944): 80; Elise Pinckney, ed., "Dr. Henry Ravenel of Poshee and Pineville," *SCHM* 81 (1980): 176–77. Helen R. Watson, "A Journalistic Medley: Newspapers and Periodicals in a Small North Carolina Community [Rocky Mount], 1859–1860," *North Carolina Historical Review* 40 (1983): 457–85, notes that "none of the South's important periodicals—*DeBow's Review, Southern Literary Messenger, Russell's Magazine*"—were subscribed to in Rocky Mount, although the postmaster distributed 194 subscriptions to 57 different journals in addition to 187 subscriptions to 36 different newspapers: "Out-of-state periodicals out-numbered North Carolina ones by 47, with one in doubt, but trailed North Carolina newspapers in popularity by 3." The only Charleston representation was one subscription to the *Mercury*, though 29 of the 97 out-of-state newspaper subscriptions were to Southern (including Washington and Maryland) papers. The ratio of Southern to Northern (and foreign) journals, exclusive of North Carolina ones, was comparable: 27 to 91. The Northern and foreign journals with the largest numbers of subscribers were of a religious cast, though *Harper's* and *Godey's* were also well represented, as were agricultural journals, such reviews as *Blackwood's*, and political papers. Clearly, if one adds the subscriptions to Northern religious papers and journals, then Stroupe's estimate (*Religious Press*, 27) that by 1859 there was "one subscriber to a religious periodical in every ninety-six persons" in the South is low. Presumably, if

one subtracts the largely illiterate black population, there was one subscriber in every fifty to sixty persons, or one for roughly every ten to twelve households. At least in Rocky Mount, many people must have subscribed only to a religious publication, for 123 of the 208 subscribers there in 1859 took only one newspaper or journal. As at Pineville, a small minority accounted for a large portion of total subscriptions, thirteen people (one-sixteenth) of the subscribers taking about 25 percent of the total number. The percentage of periodical subscribers among whites in the South Carolina lowcountry may have been considerably above the regional average. See Joseph W. Barnwell, ed., "Diary of Timothy Ford, 1785–1786," *SCHM* 13 (1912): 147n.

29. William Henry Trescot to James Henry Hammond, 4 April and 5 December 1858, Hammond Papers, LC; Clement Eaton, "The Land of the Country Gentleman," in Eaton, *Growth of Southern Civilization*, 1–24; Faust, *Sacred Circle*, 17–44; R. Nicholas Olsberg, "Desolate Places: The South Carolina Chivalry at the Time of the Civil War," (unpublished MS, SCHS), 137–38.

30. William Gilmore Simms, "The Conduct of a Magazine," *Magnolia* 4 (1842): 250; [Paul Hamilton Hayne], "Editor's Table," *Russell's Magazine* 1 (1857): 285.

31. [William Gilmore Simms], ed., *The Charleston Book* (Charleston, S.C., 1845), iii–iv; [Henry Timrod], "Literature in the South," *Russell's Magazine* 5 (1859): 285.

32. Frederic Cople Jaher, *The Urban Establishment: Upper Strata in Boston, New York, Charleston, Chicago, and Los Angeles* (Urbana, Ill., 1982), 336–99; A Charlestonian, *Statistics Which May be of Service to the People of South Carolina* (Charleston, S.C., 1860); Freehling, 26–36, 39–42; Greb, "Charleston, South Carolina Merchants"; David R. Goldfield, "Pursuing the American Dream," in *The City in Southern History: The Growth of Urban Civilization in the South* (Port Washington, N.Y., 1977), 23–51, and *Cottonfields and Skyscrapers: Southern City and Region, 1607 1980* (Baton Rouge, La., 1982), 28–79; Samuel M. Derrick, *Centennial History of South Carolina Railroad* (Columbia, S.C., 1930), 1–98; F.A. Porcher, *The History of the Santee Canal* (Charleston, S.C., 1903); Carl L. Epting, "Inland Navigation in South Carolina and the Columbia Canal," *PSCHA, 1936*, 18–28; Rogers II, 131–34; Phillips, *History of Transportation*, 132–66; Charles R. Schultz, "Hayne's Magnificent Dream: Factors Which Influenced Efforts to Join Cincinnati and Charleston by Railroad, 1835–1860" (Ph.D. diss., Ohio State University, 1966).

33. Kaplanoff, "Making the South Solid"; Jaher, *Urban Establishment*, 350–53; Donald A. Grinde, "Building the South Carolina Railroad," *SCHM* 77 (1976): 84–96.

34. Jaher, *Urban Establishment*, 353–59; John A. Eisterhold, "Charleston: Lumber and Trade in a Declining Southern Port," *SCHM* 74 (1973): 61–72. Because of fires and other factors, the 1860 figures are low, failing to show the growth in industrial investment and employment that had taken place over the preceding twenty years, according to Lander, "Charleston: Manufacturing Center of the Old South." For a review of southern perceptions of the region's colonial economic status, see McCardell, *Idea of a Southern Nation*, 91–140.

35. McKeithan, ed., *Collection of Hayne Letters*, 35.

36. [Simms], "Literary Prospects of the South," 199–200.

37. *Ibid.*

38. [William Gilmore Simms], "Griswold's American Poets," *Magnolia* 4 (1842): 120–21; [Timrod], "Literature in the South," 385–95; McKeithan, ed., *Collection of Hayne Letters*, 127 and *passim*; [Whitaker], "Periodical Press," 43.

39. [Timrod], "Literature in the South," 394. See also [Simms], "Griswold's American Poets," 120.

40. Louis Fitzgerald Tasistro, *Random Shots and Southern Breezes*, 2 vols. (New York, 1842), II, 119 24; [Timrod], "Literature in the South," 394.

41. *Simms Letters*, IV, 67–73.

42. Paul Hamilton Hayne, *Ante-Bellum Charleston*, rpt. from *Southern Bivouac* 1 (1885; Columbia, S.C., 1978): 11–31; Loftis, "A Study of *Russell's Magazine*"; Richard J. Calhoun, "The Ante-

Bellum Literary Twilight: *Russell's Magazine*," *Southern Literary Journal* 3 (1970): 102 and *passim*; Rayburn Moore, "Paul Hamilton Hayne as Editor, 1852–1860," in Meriwether, ed., *South Carolina Journals and Journalists*, 91–108.

43. Cardozo, *Reminiscences*, 73–74; Fraser, *Reminiscences*, 34, 50–51; Simms, *Essays on the Literary and Intellectual History of South Carolina*, 49. See also Woodrow W. Harris, Jr., "The Education of the Southern Urban Adult: Charleston, South Carolina and Savannah, Georgia, 1790–1812," (Ed.D. diss., University of Georgia, 1979), 225–93, 798–802.

44. Literary conservatism in Charleston is emphasized in Hubbell, "Literary Nationalism in the Old South," 209ff, and in Guy A. Cardwell, "The Influence of Addison on Charleston Periodicals," *Studies in Philology* 35 (1938): 456–70; it is a notion challenged in *All Clever Men*. The quotation is from Francis Hall, *Travels in Canada, and the United States, in 1816 and 1817* (London, 1818), 409–12. See also Fraser, *Reminiscences*, 39ff; Philip S. Foner, ed., *The Democratic-Republican Societies, 1790–1800* (Westport, Conn., 1976), 379–86; Rogers II, 245–50, 255–59; and Kaplanoff, "Making the South Solid," 140ff.

45. William Gilmore Simms, *The Social Principle: The True Source of National Permanence; An Oration, Delivered before the Erosophic Society of the University of Alabama, Dec. 13, 1842*, rpt. with preface by David Moltke-Hansen (Columbia, S.C., 1980); Tommy W. Rogers, "The Great Population Exodus from South Carolina, 1850–1860," *SCHM* 68 (1967): 14–21; [Mary S. Legaré, ed.], *Writings of Hugh Swinton Legaré*, 2 vols. (Charleston, S.C., 1845–46), I, 221–22. See also Alfred G. Smith, Jr., *Economic Readjustment of an Old Cotton State, South Carolina, 1820–1860* (Columbia, S.C., 1958). Cf. Robert M. Weir, "'The Harmony We Were Famous For': An Interpretation of Pre-Revolutionary South Carolina Politics," *WMQ* 26 (1969): 473–501; Jerome J. Nadelhaft, *The Disorders of War: The Revolution in South Carolina* (Orono, Maine, 1981); Larry Darnell Watson, "The Quest for Order: Enforcing Slave Codes in Revolutionary South Carolina, 1760–1800" (Ph.D. diss., University of South Carolina, 1980); Freehling; John Barnwell, *Love of Order: South Carolina's First Secession Crisis* (Chapel Hill, N.C., 1982); Steven A. Channing, *Crisis of Fear: Secession in South Carolina* (New York, 1970) – all works emphasizing Legaré's "blessed order" but, because of preoccupation with party politics and slavery, slighting the importance of the perceived threat to this order of the westward movement, an issue few have addressed in any detail. Important exceptions to this observation are Drew Gilpin Faust, "The Rhetoric and Ritual of Agriculture in Antebellum South Carolina," *JSH* 45 (1979): 541–68; Kaplanoff, "Making the South Solid," 28–49; and Smith, *Economic Readjustment*.

46. Stoney, ed., "Memoirs of Frederick Adolphus Porcher," *SCHM* 45 (1944): 95.

47. Fraser, *Reminiscences*, 51–52; Rogers II, 382–92. The "List of Members of the Literary and Philosophical Society, Charleston, February 8th – 1832" (typescript, SCHS) indicates that the overwhelming majority of participants in the most catholic intellectual organization in the city were professionals: thirty lawyers and judges, twenty ministers, nineteen doctors, three editors, two teachers, and a civil servant; there were also fifteen planters, twelve merchants, factors, and bankers, and one baker. This list is more or less representative of others (e.g., the membership rolls of the Charleston Library, Elliott Natural History, and South Carolina Historical Societies; see Loftis, "Study of *Russell's Magazine*," 60–62). A number of the Literary and Philosophical Society's members came from relatively poor circumstances (e.g., James L. Petigru and C.G. Memminger); many more came from long-established lowcountry families (e.g., Elliott, Gadsden, Grimké, Horry, Legaré, Manigault, Middleton, Pringle, Prioleau, Ravenel, Simons, and Smith). Ethnic community life in Charleston is suggested by the variety of ethnic organizations and institutions there: the German Friendly Society, the German Fusiliers, and the German Lutheran Church; the Hibernian Society; the Hebrew Synagogue and the Hebrew Benevolent Society. See George J. Congaware, *The History of the German Friendly Society of Charleston, S.C., 1766–1916* (Richmond, Va., 1935); Arthur Mitchell, *The History of the Hibernian Society of Charleston, S.C., 1799–1981* (Charleston, S.C., 1982); Charles Reznikoff, *The Jews of Charleston: A History of an American Jew-*

ish Community (Philadelphia, 1950); also Thomas J. Tobias, *The Hebrew Benevolent Society of Charleston, S.C., Founded 1784: The Oldest Jewish Charitable Society in the United States. An Historical Sketch* (Charleston, S.C., 1965). On shoulder-rubbing between classes, see, e.g., J. Franklin Jameson, ed., "Diary of Edward Hooker, 1805–1808," *Annual Report of the American Historical Association*. 1896, I, 900–901; Robert G. Gunderson, "The Southern Whig," in Waldo W. Braden, ed., *Oratory in the Old South* (Baton Rouge, La., 1970), 13 and *passim*; and Jane H. Pease and William H. Pease, "The Blood-Thirsty Tiger: Charleston and the Psychology of Fire," *SCHM* 79 (1978): 28 and *passim*. Kaplanoff, "Making the South Solid," 28–49, emphasizes the lack of personal contact between planters and other whites.

48. See, e.g., *South Carolina Genealogies*, 5 vols. (Spartanburg, S.C., 1983), a collection of articles culled from the pages of the *SCHM*. See also N. Louise Bailey and Elizabeth Ivey Cooper, *Biographical Directory of the South Carolina House of Representatives. Volume III: 1775–1790* (Columbia, S.C., 1981), and Bailey, *Biographical Directory . . . Volume IV: 1791–1815* (Columbia, S.C., 1984), where are intimated the Namierite dimensions of the vast cousinage shaping South Carolina politics in the Revolution and after. The origins and evolution of this cousinage are leitmotifs of M. Eugene Sirmans, *Colonial South Carolina: A Political History, 1663–1763* (Chapel Hill, N.C., 1966), a book drawing on Sirmans' 1959 Princeton dissertation, "Masters of Ashley Hall: A Biographical Study of the Bull Family of Colonial South Carolina"; and of Rogers II, 24–35, 124–29, and *passim*. Recent and judicious assessments are Robert M. Weir, *Colonial South Carolina: A History* (Millwood, N.Y., 1983), 229–36, and Kaplanoff, "Making the South Solid," 15–27. Essential as a reference is Coté, *Local and Family History in South Carolina*. The quotation is in Stoney, ed., "Memoirs of Frederick Adolphus Porcher," *SCHM* 47 (1946): 220–21. See also Cardozo, *Reminiscences*, 73–74; Tasistro, *Random Shots*, II, 119–24 and *passim*; Pease and Pease, "Social Structure and the Potential for Urban Change," *passim*.

49. *Simms Letters*, IV, 250–51; Charles Fraser to Simms, 27 June 1844 (MS, PHS; photocopy, SCHS).

50. Gerda Lerner, *The Grimké Sisters of South Carolina: Rebels against Slavery* (Boston, 1967); Katherine DuPré Lumpkin, *The Emancipation of Angelina Grimké* (Chapel Hill, N.C., 1974); Robert H. Abzug, *Passionate Liberator: Theodore Dwight Weld and the Dilemma of Reform* (New York, 1980); Adrienne Koch, "Two Charlestonians in Pursuit of Truth: The Grimké Brothers," *SCHM* 69 (1968): 159–70; James H. Smith, *Eulogium on the Life and Character of Thomas S. Grimké* (Charleston, S.C., 1835); Faust, *Sacred Circle*. Another lowcountry family split between abolitionism and slaveholding was the Brisbanes; the family deserves further study, but see E. Haviland Hillman, "The Brisbanes," *SCHM* 14 (1913): 115–33 and esp. 175–97; Blake McNulty, "William Henry Brisbane: South Carolina Slaveholder and Abolitionist," in Fraser and Moore, eds., *Southern Enigma*, 119–29; also *Speech of Rev. William Henry Brisbane . . . Delivered Before the Ladies' Anti-Slavery Society of Cincinnati, February 12, 1840* (Hartford, Conn., 1840).

51. George C. Rogers, Jr., "Preliminary Thoughts on Joseph Allen Smith as the United States' First Art Collector," in Moltke-Hansen, ed., *Art in the Lives*, essay XIII; Sarah Lytle, "Thomas Middleton [and His Family]: At Ease with the Arts in Charleston," *ibid.*, essay XVI; Gene Waddell, "The Introduction of Greek Revival Architecture to Charleston," *ibid.*, essay I; John R. Welsh, "Washington Allston: Expatriate South Carolinian," *SCHM* 67 (1966): 84–98; Diane J. Strazdes, "Washington Allston's Early Career, 1796–1811" (Ph.D. diss., Yale University, 1982); O'Brien, *A Character of Hugh Legaré*. See also Rogers II, 364 and *passim*, and Philip F. Wild, "South Carolina Politics, 1816–1833" (Ph.D. diss., University of Pennsylvania, 1949), 68.

52. The quotation is from the Introduction to Peter Charles Hoffer, *Revolution and Regeneration: Life Cycle and the Historical Vision of the Generation of 1776* (Athens, Ga., 1983). "Generation," in his usage and in the sense it is used in this essay, does not mean the time that sons take to become fathers, or the relationships between parents and children. Rather, emphasis rests on the collective experiences that create psychological cohorts. For comparable usage and its

theoretical bases, see Robert Wohl, *The Generation of 1914* (Cambridge, Mass., 1979), 5–35, 239–40, and *passim*; Stanley Elkins and Eric McKitrick, "The Founding Fathers: Young Men of the Revolution," *Political Science Quarterly* 76 (1961): 181–216; Morton Keller, "Reflections on Politics and Generations in America," *Daedalus* 107 (1978): 123–35; Karl Mannheim, "The Problem of Generations," in *Essays on the Sociology of Knowledge* (New York, 1952), 276–332, and Ortega y Gasset, "The Concept of a Generation," in *The Modern Theme* (New York, 1961), 50–84. By relating the concept of historical generations to the great events opening and closing antebellum Charleston's history, the Revolution and the Civil War, one finds that there were seven: (1) the fathers of the Revolution, those who achieved their power and formed their views before 1776, in the process bringing on the war; (2) the Revolutionary generation, those who fought the war and dominated the immediate postwar period, when state and national constitutions were ratified and the federal government formulated; (3) the children of the Revolution, those who were too young to participate in, yet grew up during, the war and its aftermath; (4) a transitional generation, too young to have experienced the Revolution or its consequences and too old to have much influenced secession; (5) the fathers of secession, those people who shaped the policies that led to the war fought by the next generation; (6) the Civil War generation, which fought the war and then reconstructed their world as best they could afterwards; (7) the children of the Civil War, those born in slavery times but too late to fight. From Bobby Gilmer Moss, *South Carolina Patriots in the American Revolution* (Baltimore, Md., 1983), it is clear that the Revolutionary generation was born between 1740 and 1763, for relatively few born earlier or later fought in the war. From John Amasa May and Joan Reynolds Faunt, *South Carolina Secedes* (Columbia, S.C., 1960), and Ralph Wooster, "Membership of the South Carolina Secession Convention," *SCHM* 55 (1954): 185–97, it is clear that the fathers of secession were mostly over forty and under sixty in 1860. Similarly, from Jon L. Wakelyn, *Biographical Dictionary of the Confederacy* (Westport, Conn., 1977), it appears that relatively few men, even in the ranks of senior officers, saw active service if they were born before 1820. By the same token, relatively few men who had not reached nineteen or twenty by the war's end would have been of an age to fight, though many youths and old men saw service in the home guard. It appears that each "historical generation" in Charleston was born over a fifteen- to twenty-five-year span: (1) the fathers of the Revolution between about 1720 and 1740; (2) the Revolutionary generation, 1740 and 1763; (3) the children of the Revolution, 1764 and 1780; (4) the next generation, 1780 and 1800; (5) the fathers of secession, 1800 and 1820; (6) the Civil War generation, 1820 and 1845; (7) the children of the war, 1845 and 1865. Of these generations, the first was too old and the last too young to figure significantly in antebellum Charleston's intellectual life.

53. See Edmund Berkeley and Dorothy S. Berkeley, *Dr. Alexander Garden of Charles Town* (Chapel Hill, N.C., 1969); David Moltke-Hansen, "The Empire of Scotsman Robert Wells, Loyalist South Carolina Printer-Publisher" (M.A. thesis, University of South Carolina, 1984); Ella P. Levett, "Loyalism in Charleston, 1761–1784," *PSCHA, 1936,* 3–17; Robert Barnwell, Jr., "The Migration of Loyalists from South Carolina," *PSCHA, 1937,* 34–42; Mary Beth Norton, *The British-Americans: The Loyalist Exiles in England, 1774–1789* (Boston, 1972). Rogers II, 355, dates the "snapping" of commercial ties with Britain at the end of the eighteenth century. C. Helen Brock, "Scotland and American Medicine," in William R. Brock, *Scotus Americanus* (Edinburgh, 1982), 118, shows that between 1765 and 1775 there were twelve Carolinians studying medicine in Edinburgh; between 1785 and 1795, fourteen; in the last five years of the century, thirteen. These figures do not serve as an index of Edinburgh's relative influence on Charleston medicine, however, as they fail to show what percentage of university-trained physicians practicing in South Carolina were Scottish-trained. The percentage was greater in the late colonial period than in 1800, despite the rise in the number of South Carolinians going to Edinburgh in the last fifteen years of the eighteenth century. See Waring, *History of Medicine,* I.

54. Turnbull, *Bibliography,* I; Richard P. Morgan, *A Preliminary Bibliography of South Carolina*

Imprints, 1731–1800 (Clemson, S.C., n.d.); Robert M. Weir, "The Role of the Newspaper Press in the Southern Colonies on the Eve of the Revolution: An Interpretation," in Bernard Bailyn and John B. Hench., eds., *The Press & and the American Revolution* (Worcester, Mass., 1980), 99–150; Jeffrey A. Smith, "Impartiality and Revolutionary Ideology: Editorial Policies in the *South-Carolina Gazette*," *JSH* 49 (1983): 517–22; Hennig Cohen, *The South Carolina Gazette, 1732–1775* (Columbia S.C., 1953), 12; Moltke-Hansen, "Newspapers in Colonial South Carolina Legal History," 262–63; Robert L. Brunhouse, "David Ramsay, 1749–1815: Selections from his Writings," *Transactions of the American Philosophical Society*, n.s., 55 (1965); William Charles Wells, *Two Essays . . . with a Memoir of His Life* (London, 1818).

55. Journal of the Proceedings of the Charleston Library Society, 1759–1790 (MS, Charleston Library Society); Cardozo, *Reminiscences*, 74–75; Simms, *Essays on the Literary and Intellectual History of South Carolina*, 8–20, 43–45; Fraser, *Reminiscences*, 20–21; Bowes, *Culture of Early Charleston*, 101–09; Robert J. Bagdon, "Musical Life in Charleston, South Carolina, from 1732 to 1776 as Recorded in Colonial Sources" (Ph.D. diss., University of Miami, 1978); John J. Hindman, "Concert Life in Antebellum Charleston" (Ph.D. diss., University of North Carolina, 1971); Mary J. Curtis, "The Early Charleston Stage: 1703–1798" (Ph.D. diss., Indiana University, 1968); Eola Willis, *The Charleston Stage in the XVIII Century: With Social Settings of the Time* (Columbia, S.C., 1924); Charleston Library Society Letterbook, 1758–1792 (MS, Charleston Library Society); Moltke-Hansen, "The Empire of Scotsman Robert Wells," chs. 3, 5.

56. Francis Asbury Mood, *Methodism in Charleston: A Narrative* (Nashville, Tenn., 1856); John O. Willson, *Sketch of the Methodist Church in Charleston, South Carolina, 1785–1887* (Charleston, S.C., 1888); Watson B. Duncan, *Trials and Triumphs of Charleston Methodism* (Charleston, S.C., 1910); Frederick Dalcho, *An Historical Account of the Protestant Episcopal Church in South-Carolina* (Charleston, S.C., 1820); George W. Williams, *St. Michael's, Charleston, 1751 1951* (Columbia, S.C., 1951), 46–49; Kaplanoff, "Making the South Solid," 76–94; Lewis P. Jones, "South Carolina," in Samuel S. Hill, ed., *Religion in the Southern States* (Macon, Ga., 1983), 267–69; Chalmers S. Murray, *This Our Land: The Story of the Agricultural Society of South Carolina* (Charleston, S.C., 1949), 15ff; Rogers II, 137–38, 151–52; Waring, *History of Medicine*, I, 118ff; Easterby, *History of the College of Charleston*, 20ff; Fraser, *Reminiscences*, 20–21.

57. Bailey and Cooper, *Biographical Directory . . . 1775–1790*; Bailey, *Biographical Directory . . . 1791–1815*; Francis Leigh Williams, *A Founding Family: The Pinckneys of South Carolina* (New York, 1978); Charles Cotesworth Pinckney, *The Life of General Thomas Pinckney* (Boston, 1895); Marvin R. Zahniser, *Charles Cotesworth Pinckney: Founding Father* (Chapel Hill, N.C., 1967); Anne Izard Deas, ed., *Correspondence of Mr. Ralph Izard of South Carolina* (New York, 1844); Felix Gilbert, ed., "Letters of Francis Kinloch to Thomas Boone, 1782–1788," *JSH* 8 (1942): 87–105; Rogers II; Lewis Leary, *That Rascal Freneau: A Study in Literary Failure* (New Brunswick, N.J., 1941); Harvey T. Cook, *Biography of Richard Furman* (Greenville, S.C., 1913); Isaac Stockton Keith, *Sermons, Addresses and Letters* (Charleston, S.C., 1819); Chalmers G. Davidson, *Friend of the People: The Life of Dr. Peter Fayssoux of Charleston, S.C.* (Columbia, S.C., 1950); George Logan, *A Biographical Sketch of Tucker Harris, M.D.* (Charleston, S.C., 1821); Tucker Harris, Reminiscences (typescript of 1818 MS, SCHS); John Blair Linn, "Matthew Irvine, M.D.," *Pennsylvania Magazine of History and Biography* 5 (1881): 418–24; R. Furman, *A Sketch of the Life and Character of Matthew Irvine, M.D.* (Charleston, S.C., 1827); Brunhouse, ed., "David Ramsay"; David H. Rembert, *Thomas Walter, Carolina Botanist* (Columbia, S.C., 1980); Barnwell, ed., "Diary of Timothy Ford," 132–47, 181–204; Julien Dwight Martin, ed., "The Letters of Charles Caleb Cotton," *SCHM* 52 (1951): 17–25, 132–44, 216–28; "Periodicals in the Charleston Library Society" (typescript, Charleston Library Society); *Catalogue of the Books Belonging to the Charleston Library Society* (Charleston, S.C., 1802); Cardwell, "Influence of Addison on Charleston Periodicals"; *All Clever Men*; Walter B. Edgar, "Some Popular Books in Colonial South Carolina," *SCHM* 72 (1971): 174–78. Principal sources of collected biographical information here and throughout this essay include the following: on

physicians and scientists, Waring, *History of Medicine,* and Johnson, *Scientific Interests in the Old South,* as well as Longton, "Some Aspects of Intellectual Activity"; on artists, Rutledge, "Artists in the Life of Charleston"; on lawyers, John Belton O'Neall, *Biographical Sketches of the Bench and Bar of South Carolina,* 2 vols. (Charleston, S.C., 1859); on planters, Chalmers G. Davidson, *The Last Foray: The South Carolina Planters in 1860* (Columbia, S.C., 1971); on architects, Ravenel, *Architects of Charleston;* on dramatists, Charles S. Watson, *Antebellum Charleston Dramatists* (Tuscaloosa, Ala., 1976); on Jews, Harry Simonhoff, *Jewish Notables in America, 1776–1865* (New York, 1956); on female writers, Caroline May, ed., *The American Female Poets* (Philadelphia, 1848); on writers generally, especially belletrists, George A. Wauchope, *The Writers of South Carolina* (Columbia, S.C., 1910): Hubbell, *The South in American Literature:* E.A. Alderman and J.C. Harris, eds., *Library of Southern Literature,* 16 vols., (New Orleans, La., 1907–13): Robert Bain et al., *Southern Writers: A Biographical Dictionary* (Baton Rouge, La., 1979): and David Moltke-Hansen and Harlan Greene, "Biographical and Bibliographical Notes," in Simms, ed., *The Charleston Book* (rpt., Spartanburg, S.C., 1983). Many of the people mentioned in this essay also figure in the *Dictionary of American Biography,* 21 vols. (New York, 1928–37), or in such predecessors as James G. Wilson and John Fiske, eds., *Appleton's Cyclopaedia of American Biography,* 6 vols. (New York, 1888–89). For less well-known figures, the notes to the *Simms Letters* are often useful. Biographical sources on churchmen are surveyed in a series of articles on South Carolina religious records in *SCHM* 84–86 (1983–85), but see also E. Brooks Holifield, *The Gentlemen Theologians: American Theology in Southern Culture, 1795–1860* (Durham, N.C., 1978).

58. Wild, "South Carolina Politics," 68–69; Rogers II, 355–74; Jaher, *Urban Establishment,* 336ff; *Catalogue of Books Belonging to the Charleston Library Society* (Charleston, 1826); J.D.B. DeBow, *The Industrial Resources . . . of the United States,* 3 vols. (New York, 1854), I, 243–54; Lewis C. Gray, *History of Agriculture in the Southern United States to 1860,* 2 vols. (Washington, 1932), II, 595–99, 610, 673–81; Marjorie S. Mendenhall, "A History of Agriculture in South Carolina, 1790 to 1860" (Ph.D. diss., University of North Carolina, 1940); John J. Winberry, "Reputation of Carolina Indigo," *SCHM* 80 (1979): 248–50.

59. N. 44 above; Hoole, *Check-List;* E. Milby Burton, *Charleston Furniture, 1700–1825* (Charleston, S.C., 1955), and *South Carolina Silversmiths, 1690–1860* (Charleston, S.C., 1942); Alston Deas, *The Early Ironwork of Charleston* (Columbia, S.C., 1941); Samuel G. Stoney, *This is Charleston: A Survey of the Architectural Heritage of a Unique American City* (Charleston, S.C., 1944); W. Stanley Hoole, *The Antebellum Charleston Theatre* (Tuscaloosa, Ala., 1946); and George C. Rogers, "Changes in Taste in the Eighteenth Century," *Journal of Early Southern Decorative Arts* 8 (1982): 1–24.

60. Cardwell, "Influence of Addison on Charleston Periodicals"; Cardozo, *Reminiscences,* 74–75; "Periodicals in the Charleston Library Society"; *Catalogue of Books Belonging to the Charleston Library Society* (Charleston, S.C., 1811); Harris, "Education of the Southern Urban Adult," 225, 293, 798–802.

61. Bailey, *Biographical Directory . . . 1791–1815;* James Moultrie, Jr., *An Eulogium on Stephen Elliott* (Charleston, S.C., 1830); George W. Williams, "Dr. Frederick Dalcho: First Diocesan Historian," *Historical Magazine of the Protestant Episcopal Church* 25 (1957), 310–58; Donald G. Morgan, *Justice William Johnson: The First Dissenter* (Columbia, S.C., 1954); Eola Willis, "Dr. J.L.E.W. Shecut," *Transactions of the Huguenot Society of South Carolina* 14 (1907): 44–48; Charles S. Watson, "Jeffersonian Republicanism in William Ioor's '*Independence,*' the First Play of South Carolina," *SCHM* 69 (1968): 194–203; A.V. Huff, Jr., *Langdon Cheves of South Carolina* (Columbia, S.C., 1977); William Harper, *Memoir of the Life, Character, and Public Services of the Late Hon. Henry William DeSaussure* (Charleston, S.C., 1841); Barnwell, ed., "Diary of Timothy Ford"; William Crafts, *Eulogium on Keating Simons* (Charleston, S.C., 1819); John Gadsden, *Eulogium on Keating Simons* (Charleston, S.C., 1819); James Hamilton, Jr., *An Eulogium on Public Services and Character of Robert Turnbull* (Charleston, S.C., 1834); Christopher E. Gadsden, *An Essay on the Life of . . . Theodore DeHon* (Charleston, S.C., 1833); Charles S. Watson, "Stephen Cullen Carpenter, First Drama

Critic of the *Charleston Courier*," *SCHM* 69 (1968): 242–52; Rogers II; J. Fred Rippy, *Joel R. Poinsett, Versatile American* (Durham, N.C., 1935); George A. Hruneni, Jr., "Palmetto Yankee: The Public Life and Times of Joel Roberts Poinsett, 1824–1851" (Ph.D. diss., University of California, Santa Barbara, 1972); Strazdes, "Washington Allston's Early Career"; on Brisbane, see Whitmarsh B. Seabrook, *Memoir on the Origin, Cultivation, and Uses of Cotton* (Charleston, S.C., 1844), 20; William Brisbane (1759–1821), Travel Account, 1801–ca. 1805 (MS, Charleston Library Society).

62. Charles Eliot Norton, "The First American Classical Archeologist [John Izard Middleton]," *American Journal of Archeology* 1 (1885): 4 and *passim*; Sarah Lytle, "Thomas Middleton"; Helen M. Gallagher, *Robert Mills, Architect of the Washington Monument* (New York, 1935); Blanche Marsh, *Robert Mills, Architect in South Carolina* (Columbia, S.C., 1970); Alexander Moore, "A Charleston Artist [Charles Fraser] and a National Art," in Moltke-Hansen, ed., *Art in the Lives*, essay XVII; Martha R. Severens and Charles L. Wyrick, Jr., eds., *Charles Fraser of Charleston: Essays on the Man, His Art and His Times* (Charleston, S.C., 1983); Anna Wells Rutledge, "Henry Bounetheau (1797–1877), Charleston, S.C. Miniaturist," *American Collector* 17 (1948): 12–18; Anna Wells Rutledge, "Cogdell and Mills, Charleston Sculptors," *Magazine Antiques* 41 (1942): 192–93; Weidner, ed., "Journal of John Blake White"; Paul W. Partridge, "John Blake White: Southern Romantic Painter and Playwright" (Ph.D. diss., University of Pennsylvania, 1951); Samuel Gilman, ed., *A Selection in Prose and Poetry from the Miscellaneous Writings of the Late William Crafts* (Charleston, S.C., 1828); [Hugh Swinton Legaré], "Crafts' Fugitive Writings," *SR* 1 (1828): 503–29; Theodore D. Jervey, *Robert Y. Hayne and His Times* (New York, 1909); George C. Rogers, Jr., "Henry Laurens Pinckney—Thoughts on His Career," in Meriwether, ed., *South Carolina Journals and Journalists*, 163–75; Louise V. Glenn, "James Hamilton, Jr., of South Carolina: A Biography" (Ph.D. diss., University of North Carolina, 1964); Carl Lewis Kell, "A Rhetorical History of James Hamilton, Jr.: The Nullification Era in South Carolina, 1816–1834" (Ph.D. diss., University of Kansas, 1971); O'Brien, *A Character of Hugh Legaré*; Julius G. Campbell, "James Louis Petigru: A Rhetorical Study" (Ph.D. diss., University of South Carolina, 1961); *Petigru*; Mrs. St. Julien [Harriott Horry Rutledge] Ravenel, *Life and Times of William Lowndes of South Carolina, 1782–1822* (Boston, 1901); Carl J. Viperman, "William Lowndes: South Carolina Nationalist, 1782–1822" (Ph.D. diss., University of Virginia, 1966). The quotations are in O'Neall, *Biographical Sketches*, II, 262, 402.

63. *In Memoriam. Hon Benjamin Faneuil Dunkin, Chief Justice of South Carolina* (Charleston, S.C., 1874), 15–16, 18.

64. Thomas J. Tobias, "The Many Sided Dr. De La Motte," *American Jewish Historical Quarterly* 52 (1963): 200–19; Joseph I. Waring, "Samuel Henry Dickson," *Journal of Medical Education* 35 (1960): 421–28; F.M. Robertson, *In Memoriam. Eli Geddings* (Charleston, S.C., 1878); Richard D. Worthington and Patricia H. Worthington, "John Edwards Holbrook, Father of American Herpetology," introduction to the Society for the Study of Amphibians and Reptiles' reprint of Holbrook's *North American Herpetology* (Athens, Ga., 1976); William T. Wragg, *Memoir of Dr. James Moultrie* (Charleston, S.C., 1869); A.S. Salley, Jr., *An Autobiographical Sketch of J.B. Whitridge* (Charleston, S.C., 1902); [A.O. Andrews], *Memoirs of Dr. Gilman* (Charleston, S.C., 1875); H.W. Foote, *Samuel Gilman: Author of "Fair Harvard"* (Charleston, S.C., 1916); Clarence Gohdes, "Some Notes on the Unitarian Church in the Ante-Bellum South: A Contribution to the History of Southern Liberalism," in Jackson, ed., *American Studies*, 337–44; Daniel W. Howe, "A Massachusetts Yankee in Senator Calhoun's Court: Samuel Gilman in South Carolina," *New England Quarterly* 44 (1971): 197–220; Claude H. Neuffer, ed., *Christopher Happoldt Journal. His European Tour with the Rev. John Bachman (June–Dec. 1838)* (Charleston, S.C., 1960); Catherine L. Bachman, *John Bachman, D.D., LL.D., Ph.D., The Pastor of St. John's Lutheran Church, Charleston* (Charleston, S.C., 1888); Raymond M. Bost, "The Reverend John Bachman and the Development of Southern Lutheranism" (Ph.D. diss., Yale University, 1963); W.W. Lord, *Life Crowned: A Discourse . . .*

after the Death of the Rev. Christian Hanckel (Charleston, S.C., 1870); Albert Sidney Thomas, "Christopher Edwards Gadsden, Fourth Bishop of South Carolina," *Historical Magazine of the Protestant Episcopal Church* 9 (1951): 294–324; Peter Guilday, *The Life and Times of John England, 1786–1842*, 2 vols. (New York, 1927); Peter Clarke, *A Free Church in a Free Society. The Ecclesiology of John England, Bishop of Charleston, 1820–1842* (Hartsville, S.C., 1982); Patrick Carey, *An Immigrant Bishop: John England's Adaption of Irish-Catholicism to American Republicanism* (Yonkers, N.Y., 1982); William M. Wightman, *Life of William Capers* (Nashville, Tenn., 1858); Harold Wilson, "Basil Manly, Apologist of Slavocracy," *Alabama Review* 15 (1962): 38–53; Joseph P. Cox, "A Study of the Life and Work of Basil Manly, Jr." (Ph.D. diss., Southern Baptist Theological Seminary, 1954); William S. Hoole, "The Gilmans and *The Southern Rose*," *North Carolina Historical Review* 11 (1934): 116–28; Janice J. Thompson, "Caroline Howard Gilman – Her Mind and Art" (Ph.D. Diss., University of North Carolina, 1975); Henry L. Pinckney, ed., *Miscellaneous Writings of the Late Isaac Harby, Esq.* (Charleston, S.C., 1829); Davis, *That Ambitious Mr. Legaré*, 6–12, 39–43 and *passim*; E.S. Thomas, *Reminiscences of the Last Sixty-Five Years*, 2 vols. (Hartford, Conn., 1840), esp. I, 30–41, 74–121, and II, 45–82; Cardozo, *Reminiscences*; Melvin M. Leiman, *Jacob N. Cardozo: Economic Thought in the Old South* (New York, 1966), and "The Economic Ideas of Jacob N. Cardozo," in B.F. Kiker and Robert J. Carlsson, eds., *South Carolina Economists: Essays on the Evolution of Antebellum Economic Thought* (Columbia, S.C., 1969), 10–43; Allen Kaufman, *Capitalism, Slavery, and Republican Values: Antebellum Political Economists, 1819–1848* (Austin, Tex., 1982); Beverley Scafidel, "The Author-Planter William Elliott (1788–1863)," *PSCHA, 1981*, 114–19, and "The Letters of William Elliott" (Ph.D. diss., University of South Carolina, 1978); B.A. Skardon, "William Elliott: Planter-Writer of Antebellum South Carolina" (Ph.D. diss., University of Georgia, 1964).

65. Thomas, *Reminiscences*, II, 45–82; Wild, "South Carolina Politics"; John H. Moore, ed., "The Abiel Abbot Journals: A Yankee Preacher in Charleston Society, 1818–1827," *SCHM* 68 (1967): 51–73, 115–39, 232–54; Samuel G. Stoney, ed., "The Poinsett-Campbell Correspondence," *SCHM* 42 (1941): 31–52, 122–36, 149–68 (esp. 35ff and 149ff), and 43 (1942): 27–35; "Le Debut," *Cosmopolitan* 1 (1833): 14–15; James F. Shearer, "Augustin de Letamendi [1795–1854]: A Spanish Expatriate in Charleston, S.C. (1825–1829)," *SCHM* 43 (1942): 18–26; Rogers I, 141ff; *Simms Letters*, I; [Legaré, ed.], *Writings of Hugh Swinton Legaré*; Greb, "Charleston, South Carolina, Merchants," 26ff; Doscher, "Art Exhibitions in Nineteenth-Century Charleston"; Christophersen, "Earliest Law School in the South"; Waring, *History of Medicine*, II, 71ff; Bertha-Monica Stearns, "Southern Magazines for Ladies (1819–1860)," *South Atlantic Quarterly* 31 (1932): 79 and *passim*.

66. Daniel W. Hollis, *South Carolina College* (Columbia, S.C., 1951), 255ff, notes that by 1835 "eight of South Carolina's nine representatives in the lower house of Congress were graduates" of South Carolina College. Hollis adds: "Within twenty years after the college had been established [in 1801] critics complained that its graduates dominated the [state] legislature." The Universities of Virginia and North Carolina as well as the College of Charleston and numerous other Southern schools were also drawing increasing numbers of Charleston's students. See Wild, "South Carolina Politics," 68.

67. Gertrude Himmelfarb, "The Victorian Ethos: Before and After Victoria," *Victorian Minds* (New York, 1968), 275–99; B.B. Thatcher, "Characteristics of Queen Victoria," *Southern Rose* 7 (1839): 264–69 (reprint from the "*Lady's Book*"); Fraser, *Reminiscences*, 55 and *passim*; Minnie C. Yarborough, ed., *The Reminiscences of William C. Preston* (Chapel Hill, N.C., 1933), 7–12 and *passim*; Tasistro, *Random Shots*, II, 119–24 and *passim*. On reform in Charleston, see citations in n. 5 above as well as Barbara Bellows, " 'Insanity Is the Disease of Civilization': The Founding of the South Carolina Lunatic Asylum," *SCHM* 82 (1981): 263–72; Gene Waddell and Rhodri Liscombe, *Robert Mills's Courthouses & Jails* (Easley, S.C., 1981); Barbara Ulmer, "Benevolence in Colonial Charleston," and Walter J. Fraser, Jr., "Controlling the Poor in Colonial Charles Town," *PSCHA, 1980*, 1–12 and 13–30, respectively, and commentaries by Theodore W. Cart and George B. Pruden,

Jr., which follow (pp. 31–35). Helpful in documenting the related interest in internal improvements is David Kohn, ed., *Internal Improvements in South Carolina, 1817–1828* (Washington, D.C., 1938).

68. Smith, *Economic Readjustment*; J.P. Ochenkowski, "The Origins of Nullification in South Carolina," *SCHM* 83 (1982): 121–53; Pease and Pease, "Economics and Politics of Charleston's Nullification Crisis"; Freehling; Jaher, *Urban Establishment*, 336–99; John G. Van Deusen, *Economic Bases of Dis-Union in South Carolina* (New York, 1928); Stoney, ed., "Memoirs of Frederick Adolphus Porcher"; Greb, "Charleston, South Carolina, Merchants"; Ralph A. Wooster, *The People in Power: Courthouse and Statehouse in the Lower South, 1850–1860* (Knoxville, Tenn., 1969); Cardwell, "Influence of Addison on Charleston Periodicals," 469; T.W. Heyck, *The Transformation of Intellectual Life in Victorian England* (New York, 1982); Moltke-Hansen, ed., *Art in the Lives*, esp. the essays by Kenneth Severens, Sarah Lytle, Marion Edmunds, Robert Stockton, Rodger Stroup, and William Douglas Smyth; *All Clever Men*; O'Brien, *A Character of Hugh Legaré*; Longton, "Some Aspects of Intellectual Activity," 237–40 and *passim*; Ann Fripp Hampton, ed., *A Divided Heart: Letters of Sally Baxter Hampton, 1853–1862* (Spartanburg, S.C., 1980); *Simms Letters*, esp. the correspondence with Forrest.

69. Joan Sturhahn, *Carvalho: Artist-Photographer-Patriot* (New York, 1976); Robert W. Gibbes, *A Memoir of James de Veaux of Charleston, S.C.* (Columbia, S.C., 1846); Barbara K. Nord, "George Whiting Flagg and His South Carolina Portraits," *SCHM* 83 (1982): 214–34; Samuel Gilman, ed., *The Poetical Remains of Mary Elizabeth Lee* (Charleston, S.C., 1851); "George S. Bryan, U.S. Judge for the District of South Carolina," *Year Book–1895. City of Charleston, S.C.*, 376–85; Juliet G. Sager, "Stephen A. Hurlbut, 1815–1882," *Journal of the Illinois Historical Society* 28 (1935): 53–80; William Gilmore Simms, ed., *The Remains of Maynard Davis Richardson, with a Memoir of His Life* (Charleston, S.C., 1833); Stoney, ed., "Memoirs of Frederick Adolphus Porcher"; John C. Ellen, Jr., "Richard Yeadon, Confederate Patriot," *PSCHA*, 1960, 32–43; Henry D. Capers, *The Life and Times of C.G. Memminger* (Richmond, Va., 1893); Laylon Wayne Jordan, "Between Two Worlds: Christopher G. Memminger of Charleston and the South in Mid-Passage, 1830–1861," *PSCHA*, 1981, 56–76; *Proceedings . . . on the Death of William D. Porter, 1883* (Charleston, S.C., 1883); Madeline B. Stern, "John Russell: 'Lord John' of Charleston," *North Carolina Historical Review* 26 (1949): 285–99.

70. *Tributes to Lewis R. Gibbes, 1810–1894* (Charleston, S.C., 1894); Charles S. Vedder, *In Memory of Colonel Gaillard* ([Charleston, S.C., 1889]); Arney R. Childs, ed., *The Private Journal of Henry William Ravenel, 1859–1887* (Columbia, S.C., 1947); Tamara A.M. Haygood, "Henry William Ravenel, 1814–1887: South Carolina Scientist in the Civil War Era" (Ph.D. diss., Rice University, 1983); South Carolina Agricultural Society, *Memorial to Dr. St. Julien Ravenel* (Charleston, S.C., 1882); J.B. Marvin, ed., *Original Researches in Mineralogy and Chemistry by J. Lawrence Smith* (Louisville, Ky., 1884); E.A. Hammond, ed., "Dr. Strobel Reports on Southeast Florida, 1836," *Tequesta* 21 (1961): 65ff; Ralph Luker, "God, Man and the World of James Warley Miles: Charleston's Transcendentalist," *Historical Magazine of the Protestant Episcopal Church* 39 (1970): 101–36; John B. Adger, *My Life and Times, 1810–1899* (Richmond, Va., 1899); John Johnson, *A Sermon, Commemorative of the Rt. Rev. Thomas Frederick Davis* (Charleston, S.C., 1872); Solomon Breibart, "The Rev. Mr. Gustavus Poznanski, First American Jewish Reform Minister" (typescript, SCHS); Thomas Smyth, *Autobiographical Notes, Letters and Reflections*, ed. L.C. Stoney (Charleston, S.C., 1914); J.F. Maclear, "Thomas Smyth, Frederick Douglass, and the Belfast Antislavery Campaign," *SCHM* 80 (1979): 286–97; Paul Trapier, *Incidents in My Life*, ed. George W. Williams (Charleston, S.C., 1954); *In Memoriam, Rev. Richard Shubrick Trapier, 1811–1895* (Charleston, S.C., 1895).

71. Simms has been the subject of more dissertations and scholarly articles than all the rest of his generation in Charleston put together. For a partial survey, see Butterworth and Kibler, *William Gilmore Simms*.

72. Hoole, *Check-List*; Carroll, "Valedictory," 474–75.

73. Potter, *Impending Crisis*, 14, discusses Young America in the South. David Donald, "The Proslavery Argument Reconsidered," *JSH* 37 (1971): 3–18, argues that Simms's generation was also backward-looking but is corrected by Faust, "Southern Stewardship." For civic improvements, see Laylon Wayne Jordan, "Police Power and Public Safety in Antebellum Charleston: The Emergence of a New Police, 1800–1860," *South Atlantic Urban Studies* 3 (1979): 122–40; [William A. Courtenay], "Centennial Address," *Year Book – 1883. City of Charleston, So. Ca.* (Charleston, S.C., 1883), 324–72 (a history of the city emphasizing the century following Charleston's incorporation in 1783); G.A. Gilmore, *Annual Report Upon the Improvement of Rivers and Harbors on the Coast of South Carolina* (Washington, D.C., 1885); Pease and Pease, "Blood-Thirsty Tiger"; Fraser, *Reminiscences*; Jordan, "Education for Community"; Ivan D. Steen, "Charleston in the 1850s: As Described by British Travelers," *SCHM* 71 (1970): 36–45.

74. Potter, *Impending Crisis*, 14ff; Rogers, "South Carolina Federalists," 19; James W. Gettys, Jr., "'To Conquer a Peace': South Carolina and the Mexican War" (Ph.D. diss., University of South Carolina, 1974); Ernest M. Lander, Jr., *Reluctant Imperialists: Calhoun, the South Carolinians, and the Mexican War* (Baton Rouge, La., 1980); McCardell, *Idea of a Southern Nation*, 227ff; Channing, *Crisis of Fear*, 141ff; Olsberg, "Desolate Places," 2–133.

75. Goldfield, "Pursuing the American Urban Dream"; Wooster, *People in Power*, 121–53.

76. James R. Loney, "The Poetry and Poetics of Henry Timrod, Paul Hamilton Hayne, and Sidney Lanier: An Essay on Art and Community in the Nineteenth-Century South" (Ph.D. diss., University of Georgia, 1977); Henry Timrod, "A Theory of Poetry," in E.W. Parks, ed., *The Essays of Henry Timrod* (Athens, Ga., 1942), 103–32; n. 8 above; Fraser, *Reminiscences*, 87ff; J.H. Easterby, ed., "Letters of James Warley Miles to David James McCord," *SCHM* 43 (1942): 185–93; Theodore D. Bratton, *An Apostle of Reality: The Life and Thought of the Reverend William Porcher DuBose* (London, 1936); David Moltke-Hansen, "William Henry Trescot," in Clyde N. Wilson, ed., *American Historians, 1607–1865* (Detroit, 1984), a volume of the *Dictionary of Literary Biography*.

77. Himmelfarb, *Victorian Minds*; Isaiah Berlin, *Russian Thinkers* (New York, 1978); George M. Fredrickson, *The Inner Civil War: Northern Intellectuals and the Crisis of the Union* (New York, 1965); Thornton, *Politics and Power*, 305–21; Brugger, "Mind of the Old South"; O'Brien, "The Nineteenth-Century South"; Wyatt-Brown, "Modernizing Southern Slavery"; Otis C. Skipper, *J.D.B. DeBow, Magazinist of the Old South* (Athens, Ga., 1958).

78. William Howard Russell, *My Diary North and South*, ed. Fletcher Pratt (New York, 1954), 72; *Chesnut*, 41, 42, 49.

79. Elizabeth Muhlenfeld, *Mary Boykin Chesnut: A Biography* (Baton Rouge, La., 1981); Paul Hamilton Hayne, ed., *The Poems of Henry Timrod* (New York, 1873); Edd W. Parks, *Henry Timrod* (New York, 1974); Rayburn S. Moore, "Paul Hamilton Hayne," *Georgia Review* 22 (1968): 106–24; Davis, *That Ambitious Mr. Legaré*; A.S. Salley, Jr., *William James Rivers* (Columbia, S.C., 1906); Clarence M. Smith, "William Porcher Miles, Progressive Mayor of Charleston, 1855–1857," *PSCHA, 1942*, 30–39; C.W.E. Miller, "Basil Lanneau Gildersleeve," *American Journal of Philology* 45 (1924): 97–100; Albert Sidney Thomas, *The Career and Character of Col. John Peyre Thomas* (n.p., 1964); Beverley Scafidel, "A Promoter of the Arts: Gabriel Edward Manigault," in Moltke-Hansen, ed., *Art in the Lives*, essay XI; Gail M. Morrison, "'I Shall Not Pass This Way Again': The Contributions of William Ashmead Courtenay," *ibid.*, essay XXI; Walter B. Capers, *The Soldier Bishop, Ellison Capers* (New York, 1912); "Memorial [to Wilmot Gibbes DeSaussure]," *Transactions of the Huguenot Society of South Carolina* 1 (1889): 26–40; Arthur Mazyck and Gene Waddell, *Charleston in 1883*, rev. ed. (Easley, S.C., 1983); Clyde N. Wilson, Jr., "Carolina Cavalier: The Life of James Johnston Pettigrew" (Ph.D. diss., University of North Carolina, 1971); Moltke-Hansen, "William Henry Trescot"; Louis deB. McCrady, *General Edward McCrady and Some of the Incidents of His Career* (Charleston, S.C., 1905).

80. Daniel E. Sutherland, "The Rise and Fall of Esther B. Cheesborough: The Battles of a Literary Lady," *SCHM* 84 (1983): 22–34; J.R. Scafidel, "Susan Petigru King: An Early South Caro-

lina Realist," in Meriwether, ed., *South Carolina Women Writers*, 101–15; correspondence of Ada Clare, Julian Mitchell Papers, SCHS; Skipper, *J.D.B. DeBow*; John A. Broadus, *Memoir of James Petigru Boyce* (New York, 1893); James H. Elliott, ed., *In Memoriam. Tributes to the Memory of the Rev. C.P. Gadsden* (Charleston, S.C., 1872); George A. Blackburn, *The Life Work of John L. Girardeau* (Columbia, S.C., 1916); A. Toomer Porter, *Led On! Step by Step* (New York, 1898); on Irving, see Smyth, "The Artistic Experience of South Carolinians Abroad in the 1850s"; August P. Trovaioli, *William Aiken Walker, Southern Genre Painter* (Baton Rouge, La., 1972); Margaret L. Coit, *Mr. Baruch* (Boston, 1957); James L. Carroll, *Julian John Chisolm, M.D.* (Baltimore, 1930); Neuffer, ed., *Christopher Happoldt Journal*; W.C. Coker, "Dr. Joseph Hinson Mellichamp," *Journal of the Elisha Mitchell Scientific Society* 27 (1911): 37–64; John F. Townsend, "Francis Peyre Porcher, M.D.," *Annals of Medical History*, 3d ser., 1 (1939): 177–88.

81. Anne King Gregorie, "The First Decade of the Charleston Library Society," *PSCHA, 1935*, 3–10. The College of William and Mary was at Williamsburg, Virginia; the College of Pennsylvania had a medical school in Philadelphia.

82. McCardell, *Idea of a Southern Nation*, 348–49, provides a convenient table of southern "Church colleges and State universities and Year of Founding."

83. By 1835 the *Southern Rose Bud*, for instance, had agents in, or received remittances from, Greensboro, Alabama; Athens, Augusta, Milledgeville, and Savannah, Georgia; Bangor, Maine; Boston, Dorchester, and Salem, Massachusetts (where the Gilmans had close connections); St. Louis, Missouri; Philadelphia, Pennsylvania; more than a dozen South Carolina post offices, and East Tennessee. See the *Southern Rose Bud* 2 (1834–35): *passim*. In the thirty years before 1860, Samuel Henry Dickson, Samuel Gilman, Thomas Smith Grimké, James Louis Petigru, Henry Laurens Pinckney, and William Gilmore Simms, among them, addressed Yale, Harvard, the Universities of Alabama, Georgia, Mississippi, North Carolina, and South Carolina, and numerous smaller schools, often more than once.

84. Harold S. Schultz, *Nationalism and Sectionalism in South Carolina,1852–1860* (Durham, N.C., 1950), 229–30.

85. Johnson, "Planters and Patriarchy," 52.

86. Greb, "Charleston, South Carolina, Merchants," 37, 39, 58–62, gives the figures on relative wealth and political activity; for further discussion of the political representation of different classes, see Pease and Pease, "Economics and Politics of Charleston's Nullification Crisis." John Radford, "The Charleston Planters in 1860," *SCHM* 77 (1976): 227–35, and Johnson, "Planters and Patriarchy," give the numbers and wealth of Charleston planters on the eve of the Civil War. Pease and Pease, "Economics and Politics of Charleston's Nullification Crisis," analyzes the figures for 1830: they note (p. 349) that in 1830 only 40 percent "of those in the most prestigious occupations (professions, wholesale commerce and banking, as well as planting) . . . owned plantations."

87. Pease and Pease, "Economics and Politics of Charleston's Nullification Crisis," 343, 349, and *passim*; Ochenkowski, "Origins of Nullification," 131–38, 148–53.

88. Robert Redfield and Milton Singer, "The Cultural Role of Cities," in Richard Sennett, ed., *Classic Essays on the Culture of Cities* (New York, 1969), 206–33, esp. 221.

89. The classic illustration is Simms' disastrous speaking tour of the North in 1856. See John Hope Franklin, "The North, the South, and the American Revolution," *JAH* 62 (1975): 5–23, esp. 11–16; cf. David Moltke-Hansen, "A Beaufort Planter's Rhetorical World: The Contexts and Contents of William Henry Trescot's Orations," *PSCHA, 1981*, 120–32. To say, however, that Southern writers became more sectional in their identities and writings is not to say that their writings were always, or even predominantly, sectional. However strident in tone, sectionally focused pieces never occupied more than a minority of the pages of the region's intellectual journals. See Loftis, "A Study of *Russell's Magazine*," 160; McCardell, *Idea of a Southern Nation*, 346–47.

2. *David Ramsay*: SHAFFER

1. Robert Y. Hayne, "Biographical Memoir of David Ramsay, M.D.," in David Ramsay, *History of the United States* (Philadelphia, 1816–17), I, xxvi–xxvii. For the details of Ramsay's life and career, see Robert L. Brunhouse, ed., introduction to "David Ramsay, 1749–1815: Selections From His Writings," *American Philosophical Society Transactions*, n.s., 55 (1965).

2. Ramsay to John Eliot, 11 August 1792, "Ramsay: Writings," 101.

3. Cited in Charles G. Sellers, Jr., "The American Revolution: Southern Founders of a National Tradition," *Writing Southern History: Essays In Historiography in Honor of Fletcher M. Green*, ed. Arthur S. Link and Rembert W. Patrick (Baton Rouge, La., 1965), 42.

4. David Moltke-Hansen, *supra*, 385–86.

5. Ramsay to Rush, 29 July 1774, "Ramsay: Writings," 51.

6. Diane Sydenham, "Practitioner and Patient: The Practice of Medicine in Eighteenth-Century South Carolina" (Ph.D. diss., Johns Hopkins University, 1979), 128–86; Rogers I, 94–95.

7. Brooke Hindle, *The Pursuit of Science in Revolutionary America, 1735–1789* (Chapel Hill, N.C., 1956), 17.

8. Rogers I, 95.

9. Moltke-Hansen, *supra*, 23–24.

10. Howard Miller, *The Revolutionary College: American Presbyterian Higher Education, 1707–1837* (New York, 1976): 49–102.

11. Ramsay to Benjamin Rush, 14 February 1776, "Ramsay: Writings," 53. For Philadelphia on the eve of independence, see Eric Foner, *Tom Paine and Revolutionary America* (New York, 1976), 19–70; Carl Bridenbaugh, *Rebels and Gentlemen: Philadelphia in the Age of Franklin* (New York, 1965), *passim*, and 294–95 for Ramsay's association with medical students throughout colonial America.

12. Ramsay's second wife, Frances, was the daughter of John Witherspoon. After her death in 1784, Ramsay and Witherspoon remained close friends.

13. For Ramsay's relationship with his many New England friends, see "Ramsay: Writings," *passim*.

14. Ramsay's many Philadelphia friends and contacts can be charted in his correspondence.

15. The quotations can be found in Arthur H. Shaffer, *The Politics of History: Writing the History of the American Revolution, 1783–1815* (Chicago, 1975), 10–11.

16. For discussions of American cultural nationalism see Joseph J. Ellis, *After the Revolution: Profiles of Early American Culture* (New York, 1979); Shaffer, *Politics of History*; and Lawrence Friedman, *Inventors of the Promised Land* (New York, 1975), *passim*.

17. Ramsay was present during the development of Rush's medical system: "In the autumn of 1789, I visited Dr. Rush. . . . He observed . . . that the system of Cullen was tottering . . . that he saw a gleam of light before him leading to a more simple and consistent system of medicine than the world had yet seen, and he pointed out some leading features." David Ramsay, *An Eulogium upon Benjamin Rush, M.D.* (Philadelphia, 1813), 23.

18. The names of the students Ramsay sent to Philadelphia can be found in "Ramsay: Writings," and Joseph I. Waring, *A History of Medicine in South Carolina, 1670–1825* (Columbia, S.C., 1964), *passim*.

19. David Ramsay, Fourth of July Oration (1794), "Ramsay: Writings," 191.

20. Moltke-Hansen, *supra*, 26.

21. Quoted in Gordon Wood, *The Creation of the American Republic, 1776–1787* (Chapel Hill, N.C., 1969), 71. For discussions of Country Whig ideology, see Robert M. Weir, "'The Harmony We Were Famous For': An Interpretation of Pre-Revolutionary South Carolina Politics," *WMQ* 26 (1969): 473–80; and Kaplanoff, *infra*, 85–122.

22. Moltke-Hansen, *supra*, 24.

23. Ramsay, Oration on the Advantages of American Independence (1778), "Ramsay: Writings," 189.

24. Rogers II, 135–58, and "South Carolina Federalists and the Origins of the Nullification Movement," SCHM 71 (1970): 17–32, deal with the unionist sentiments of leading South Carolinians and new ties with Northern politicians.

25. Quoted in Shaffer, Politics of History, 12; Ramsay to Benjamin Rush, 17 February 1788, "Ramsay: Writings," 19.

26. Ramsay's correspondence is filled with references to individuals he consulted about his histories. Even before it was published, the specific contents of his History of the American Revolution (1789) were common knowledge, for it was discussed during the congressional campaign of 1788.

27. Ramsay to John Eliot, 11 August 1792, "Ramsay: Writings," 133.

28. David Ramsay, The History of the American Revolution (London, 1793), I, 31. It was first published in Philadelphia in 1789, but the London edition will be hereafter cited.

29. Ramsay to Rush, 8 April 1777, "Ramsay: Writings," 54–55.

30. Ramsay to Rush, 18 August 1787, and Ramsay, An Oration, July 4, 1794, ibid., 113, 191; Ramsay, History of the Revolution, I, 32.

31. Ramsay, History of the Revolution, I, 29, 26–27.

32. Ibid., 33.

33. Ibid., 42.

34. Ramsay, Oration on the Advantages of American Independence (1778), "Ramsay: Writings," 189; Ellis, After the Revolution, 24–38.

35. Weir, "Harmony We Were Famous For," 485–86.

36. Richard Walsh, "Christopher Gadsden: Radical or Conservative Revolutionary?" SCHM 63 (1962): 198–99.

37. Oration on Independence (1778), "Ramsay: Writings," 185–86.

38. Throughout the 1780s Ramsay spoke frequently and intelligently in the legislature on commercial and fiscal matters. Jerome J. Nadelhaft, The Disorders of War: The Revolution in South Carolina (Orono, Maine, 1981), passim.

39. Oration on Independence, "Ramsay: Writings," 184.

40. Pauline Maier, The Old Revolutionaries: Political Lives in the Age of Samuel Adams (New York, 1980), 101–38, 273–74; Aleine Austin, Matthew Lyon: "New Man" of the Democratic Revolution, 1749–1822 (University Park, Pa., 1981), 1–7.

41. Maier, The Old Revolutionaries, 275; Wood, Creation of the Republic, 70–72.

42. Oration on Independence, "Ramsay: Writings," 186.

43. Ramsay, History of the Revolution, I, 355–56. For his views of the Pennsylvania Constitution of 1776 see ibid., 350–51, and Ramsay to Benjamin Rush, 3 February 1779, "Ramsay: Writings," 58–59. For views of Pinckney and Rutledge and Ramsay's relationship to them, see Marvin R. Zahniser, Charles Cotesworth Pinckney: Founding Father (Chapel Hill, N.C., 1967), 104–6, 123–24; and Rogers II, 148, 180–83, 268.

44. Henry F. May, The Enlightenment in America (New York, 1976), xiv–xvi, has defined the Enlightenment in terms of all those who believed two propositions: first, that the present age is more enlightened than the past; second, that we understand nature and man best through the use of our natural faculties. If this appears to be too inclusive a definition, it does exclude those who believed that the surest guide for human beings is revelation, tradition, or illumination, probably most people who lived in America in the eighteenth and nineteenth centuries. It does not, however, exclude most members of the Charleston intellectual community, those who belonged to the Library Society and the various other cultural organizations. Within this general framework, May has also made distinctions between such sharply different Enlightenment thinkers as Voltaire, Hume, Paine, Locke, Jefferson, and Rousseau. He has divided the

Enlightenment into four categories: (1) the Moderate or Rational Enlightenment, which preached balance, order, and religious compromise; (2) the Skeptical Enlightenment, whose grand master was Voltaire and which led either to the systematic epistemological skepticism of Hume or to the systematic materialism of Holbach; (3) the Revolutionary Enlightenment, the belief in the possibility of constructing a new heaven and earth out of the destruction of the old; (4) the Didactic Enlightenment, whose chief center was Scotland but which triumphed in America in the first quarter of the nineteenth century—opposed to skepticism and revolution, its aim was to save from what it regarded as the debacle of the Enlightenment an intelligible universe, clear and certain moral judgments, and progress. Among educated, intellectually articulate South Carolinians, each of these four categories was represented.

45. Ramsay to Thomas Jefferson, 6 August 1786, "Ramsay: Writings," 101.

46. May, *Enlightenment in America*, 245.

47. *Ibid.*, 72–73.

48. David Ramsay, *The History of South-Carolina*, 2 vols. (Charleston, S.C., 1809), I, 27.

49. May, *Enlightenment in America*, 147–49.

50. Ramsay, *History of South Carolina*, I, 27.

51. Donald H. Meyer, *The Democratic Enlightenment* (New York, 1976). xviii.

52. Ramsay, *History of the Revolution*, II, 324.

53. Before 1790, Ramsay's correspondence was filled with reflections, strategy, and gossip about national life and politics; after 1790, rarely so. Even state politics consumed less of his interest, although he continued in the legislature until 1799.

54. Ramsay to Jeremy Belknap, 11 March 1795, "Ramsay: Writings," 140.

55. Ramsay, *History of the Revolution*, I, 197.

56. Ramsay to Eliot, 6 August 1785, "Ramsay: Writings," 90.

57. Merrill Jensen and Robert A. Becker, eds., *The Documentary History of the First Federal Elections, 1788–1790* (Madison, Wis., 1976), I, 176–81.

58. Ramsay to Eliot, 26 November 1788, "Ramsay: Writings," 123.

59. See Ramsay, "An Address to the Freemen of South Carolina on the Federal Constitution," in Paul Leicester Ford, ed., *Pamphlets on the Constitution* (New York, 1968), 371–80.

60. Jane H. Pease and William H. Pease, *infra*, 234; James M. Banner, Jr., "The Problem of South Carolina," in *The Hofstadter Aegis: A Memorial*, ed. Stanley Elkins and Eric McKitrick (New York, 1974), 66–68.

61. "Ramsay: Writings," 51–123.

62. Ramsay to Rush, 3 February 1779, 29 July 1774, "Ramsay: Writings," 59, 51. For a thorough discussion of the slavery issue, see Arthur H. Shaffer, "Between Two Worlds: David Ramsay and the Politics of Slavery," *JSH* 50 (1984): 175–96.

63. Duncan J. MacLeod, *Slavery, Race and the American Revolution* (Cambridge, 1974), 31–32.

64. Ramsay to Rush, 20 June 1779, "Ramsay: Writings," 60.

65. Ramsay, *History of the Revolution*, I, 23–24.

66. *Ibid.*, 1–42.

67. Ramsay to Eliot, 26 November 1788, "Ramsay: Writings," 123.

68. Moltke-Hansen, *supra*, 25–26.

69. Ramsay, *History of South Carolina*, II, 217.

70. *Ibid.*, 213–15.

71. Oration, July 4, 1794, "Ramsay: Writings," 192.

72. Meyer, *Democratic Enlightenment*, 171–85.

73. Ramsay, *History of South Carolina*, II, 240.

74. Kaplanoff, *infra*, 104.

75. Ramsay, *History of South Carolina*, II, 251–77.

76. Hindle, *Science in Revolutionary America*, 279.

77. Ramsay, *A Review of the Improvements, Progress and State of Medicine in the XVIIITH Century* (1801), "Ramsay: Writings," 209–17.

78. *Ibid.*, 207; Ramsay, *A Sketch of the Soil, Climate, Weather, and Diseases of South Carolina* (Charleston, S.C., 1796), 21.

79. Ramsay to Rush, 11 February 1801, "Ramsay: Writings," 151; Ramsay, *History of South Carolina*, II, 36, 48, 49; *Medical Repository* 4 (1801): 100, 218; *ibid.*, 2d Hexade, 2 (1805): 365–66.

80. Martin S. Pernick, "Politics, Parties and Pestilence: Epidemic Yellow Fever in Philadelphia and the Rise of the First Party System," in *Sickness and Health in America: Readings in the History of Medicine and Public Health*, ed. Judith Walzer Leavitt and Ronald L. Numbers (Madison, Wis., 1978), 241–56.

81. Chris Holmes, "Benjamin Rush and the Yellow Fever," *Bulletin of the History of Medicine* 40 (1966): 246–50, 255.

82. *Medical Repository* 4 (1801): 101, 103; Ramsay, *Soil, Climate, Weather, and Diseases*, 26; Ramsay, *A Dissertation on the Means of Preserving Health in Charleston, and the Adjacent Low Country* (Charleston, S.C., 1790), 15–16. For an overview of the health issue, see Lawrence Friedman and Arthur Shaffer, "History, Politics and Health in Early American Thought," *Journal of American Studies* 13 (1979): 37–56.

83. Ramsay, *Dissertation on Preserving Health*, 7–8, 10, 12–13; *Medical Repository* 4 (1801): 219; *ibid.*, 2d Hexade, 2 (1805): 366.

84. Ramsay, *History of South Carolina*, I, 31–53: II, 241–49.

85. See Mark Kaplanoff, *infra*, 85–86.

86. O'Brien, *supra*, xi; Moltke-Hansen, *infra*, passim.

87. Shaffer, *Politics of History*, 175–78.

88. *Ibid.*, 178–80.

89. [Mary Legaré, ed.], *Writings of Hugh Swinton Legaré*, 2 vols. (Charleston, S.C., 1846), I, 257–69.

3. *Charles Pinckney:* KAPLANOFF

1. Pinckney's speech can be found in *The Debates and Proceedings in the Congress of the United States . . . 1789–1824*, 42 vols. (Washington, D.C., 1834–56), 16th Cong., 2d sess., 1310–29, 14 February 1820. (Hereafter cited as Missouri 1820.) The quotation is from p. 1328. For a contemporary comment on the speech, see *Niles' Weekly Register*, n.s., 5 (19 February 1820): 438.

2. *Niles' Weekly Register*, n.s., 6 (15 July 1820): 345, 349–57.

3. *Debates and Proceedings in Congress*, 16th Cong., 2d sess., 1129–45, 13 February 1821. (Hereafter cited as Missouri 1821.)

4. South Carolina's shift has been described in George C. Rogers, Jr., "The South Carolina Federalists and the Origins of the Nullification Movement," *SCHM* 71 (1970): 17–32, and Freehling, 90–133.

5. For a brief sketch of South Carolina's internal development in this period, see James M. Banner, "The Problem of South Carolina," in Stanley Elkins and Eric McKitrick, eds., *The Hofstadter Aegis: A Memorial* (New York, 1974), 60–93. I have discussed this development in detail in my unpublished dissertation, "Making the South Solid: Politics and the Structure of Society in South Carolina, 1790–1815" (Cambridge University, 1980), a copy of which is in SCL.

6. George Dangerfield, *The Era of Good Feelings* (New York, 1952), 220–21; Glover Moore, *The Missouri Controversy, 1819–1821* (Lexington, Ky., 1966), 125–26; and John McCardell, *The Idea of a Southern Nation: Southern Nationalists and Southern Nationalism, 1830–1860* (New York, 1979), 50.

7. Norman K. Risjord, *The Old Republicans: Southern Conservatism in the Age of Jefferson* (New York, 1965), 213. For similar comments see Moore, *Missouri Controversy*, 346, and McCardell, *Idea of a Southern Nation*, 49–50.

8. There is no full-scale biography of Pinckney, and it is doubtful that enough sources survive about his life for one ever to be written. The best and most detailed modern account of his career is in Frances L. Williams, *A Founding Family: The Pinckneys of South Carolina* (New York, 1978); the most useful short biographical piece is the very full and perceptive sketch by J. Harold Easterby in *Dictionary of American Biography*, 20 vols. (New York, 1928–36), XIV, 611–14. These can be supplemented by Pinckney's correspondence published in "South Carolina in the Presidential Election of 1800," *AHR* 4 (1898–99): 111–29, and the biographical information contained in John H. Wolfe, *Jeffersonian Democracy in South Carolina* (Chapel Hill, N.C., 1940), 42, 62–65, 84–86, 127–31, 138–39, 151–52, 154, 199–202, 221–23; Rogers II, 116–17, 146–47, 184, 278, 349–51, 380, 393, 399; Marvin R. Zahniser, *Charles Cotesworth Pinckney: Founding Father* (Chapel Hill, N.C., 1967), 111–12, 219, 222–28, 230–31, 255–56; and *The Biographical Directory of the South Carolina House of Representatives, Vol. III: 1775–1790*, ed. N. Louise Bailey and Elizabeth Ivey Cooper (Columbia, S.C., 1981), 555–60.

9. [Charleston] *City Gazette and Daily Advertiser*, 9 November 1824, and [W.S. Elliott], "Founders of the American Union–Charles Pinckney, of South Carolina," *DeBow's Review*, n.s., 1 (1866): 377.

10. See *Calhoun Papers*, X, xvi–xvii, and [W.S. Elliott], "Honorable Charles Pinckney, LL.D., of South Carolina," *DeBow's Review* 34 (1864): 63, 67.

11. Missouri 1820, 1318.

12. *Ibid.*, 1311.

13. *Ibid.*, 1310, 1311, 1313.

14. Missouri 1821, 1144.

15. Missouri 1820, 1316.

16. *Ibid.*, 1324.

17. *Ibid.*

18. Missouri 1821, 1136.

19. Missouri 1820, 1315, 1324–25.

20. *Ibid.*, 1326; Missouri 1821, 1134, 1140–41.

21. Missouri 1820, 1312.

22. Missouri 1821, 1138.

23. Missouri 1820, 1314, 1327, 1328; Missouri 1821, 1142.

24. Missouri 1820, 1327.

25. *Ibid.*, 1328.

26. *Ibid.*, 1327.

27. *Ibid.*, 1329; Missouri 1821, 1141, 1144–45.

28. On South Carolina's leadership of the South, see the sources cited in n. 6, above, and William Barney, *The Road to Secession: A New Perspective on the Old South* (New York, 1972), 193–94; McCardell, *Idea of a Southern Nation*, 28, 60; and Clement Eaton, *A History of the Old South* (New York, 1949), 384–85. On the South's hesitation to follow South Carolina's lead, see Freehling, 265; Charles S. Sydnor, *The Development of Southern Sectionalism, 1819–1848* (Baton Rouge, La., 1948), 208–9, 218–19; and Barney, *Road to Secession*, 115. On South Carolina's archaic political practices, see Banner, "Problem of South Carolina," 60–93; Barney, *Road to Secession*, 115; Eaton, *History of the Old South*, 315–16; Freehling, 89–91; Fletcher M. Green, *Constitutional Development in the South Atlantic States, 1776–1860: A Study in the Evolution of Democracy* (Chapel Hill, N.C., 1930), 248–51; Kenneth S. Greenberg, "Representation and the Isolation of South Carolina, 1776–1860," *JAH* 64 (1977–78): 723–41; McCardell, *Idea of a Southern Nation*, 28; and J.P. Ochenkowski, "The Origins of Nullification in South Carolina," *SCHM* 38 (1982): 121–53.

29. The development of American thought on the economic base for republicanism from the Revolution to the 1790s can be traced in Drew R. McCoy, *The Elusive Republic: Political Economy in Jeffersonian America* (Chapel Hill, N.C., 1980), 1–165.

30. The national debate can be followed in *ibid.*, 336–59. For the peculiarly Virginian point of view, see Robert Shalhope, *John Taylor of Caroline: Pastoral Republican* (Columbia, S.C., 1980), 43–50, 104–5, 129–39, 150–51, 185–88, and Duncan MacLeod, "The Triple Crisis," in Rhodri Jeffreys-Jones and Bruce Collins, eds., *The Growth of Federal Power in American History* (Edinburgh, 1983), 13–24.

31. Charles Pinckney, *Three Letters Addressed to the Public, on the Following Subjects: I. The Nature of a Foederal Union . . . II. The Civil and Military Powers . . . III. The Public Debt . . .* [signed, Tullius. Charles-Town, May 5th. 1783] (Philadelphia, 1783), 8, 26. (Hereafter cited as *Three Letters* 1783.)

32. *Mr. Charles Pinckney's Speech, In Answer to Mr. Jay . . . on the Question of a Treaty with Spain, Delivered in Congress, August 16, 1786* ([New York?], 1786). (Hereafter cited as *Speech* 1786.)

33. Pinckney made several speeches at the Philadelphia Convention in 1787, and reports of them (based on notes by James Madison and Robert Yates) are printed in Max Farrand, ed., *The Records of the Federal Convention of 1787*, rev. ed., 4 vols. (New Haven, Conn., 1937). (Hereafter cited as *Records* 1787.) For his comments on economic interests and trade regulation, see *ibid.*, II, 449.

34. *Ibid.*, 364–65.

35. See Pinckney's speeches to the legislature of South Carolina and in the South Carolina ratifying convention in Jonathan Elliot, ed., *The Debates in the Several State Conventions, on the Adoption of the Federal Constitution . . .* , 2d ed., 5 vols. (Philadelphia, 1861), V, 253–63, 318–32, 333–36. (Hereafter cited as *Debates* 1788.) For his comments on commerce, agriculture and trade policy, see *ibid.*, 253–54, 332–33, 330.

36. *Records* 1787, I, 398–400, 422–23, 431. For a comment on the exchange, see McCoy, *Elusive Republic*, 128–29.

37. *Debates* 1788, V, 321–22.

38. For later comments on the primacy of agriculture, see Governor's Message no. 1, South Carolina Senate journal, 23 November 1797, SCSA (Hereafter cited as Governor's Message 1797), and [Charles Pinckney] A Republican, "On the Election of the President of the United States," [Charleston] *City Gazette*, 3 October 1800, a series published on 28 August; 3, 4, 5, 6, 13, 16, 18, 19, 22, 25, 26, 29, 30 September; 1, 3, 6, 14 October 1800. (Hereafter cited as Republican 1800.)

39. *Three Letters, Addressed to the People of the United States, Which have Lately Appeared under the Signature of "A South-Carolina Planter" . . . On the Case of Jonathan Robbins . . . On the Recent Captures of the British Cruisers . . . On the Claims of the British Creditors . . .* (Charleston, S.C., 1799), 21, 28. (Hereafter cited as *Three Letters* 1799.)

40. For warnings about commerce and luxury, see *Debates* 1788, V, 321–22; [Charles Pinckney] A Republican, "To the Republican Citizens of South-Carolina, on the Election of Members of Congress and the State Legislature," *City Gazette*, 25 September 1810, a series on 18, 19, 20, 21, 22, 24, 25 September (hereafter cited as Republican 1810); and *Observations to Shew the Propriety of the Nomination of Colonel James Monroe, to the Presidency of the United States by the Caucus at Washington . . . by a South-Carolinian* (Charleston, S.C., 1816), 45–46 (hereafter cited as *Observations* 1816). Significantly, though, in each of these pieces Pinckney also mentioned the necessity of commerce; see *Debates* 1788, V, 322; Republican 1810, 18 September; and *Observations* 1816, 12–13. On the re-export trade, see Republican 1810, 18 September.

41. In 1791, Pinckney applauded the funding of state debts; see Governor's Message no. 1, South Carolina Senate journal, 13 January 1791, SCSA. (Hereafter cited as Governor's Message 1791.) In 1800, when he looked back at the political developments of the previous decade, he made no complaint about the Hamiltonian fiscal system; see *Speeches of Charles Pinckney, Esq. in Congress; On the subject of having Impartial Juries, by Lot, in all the Federal Courts. On the independence of the Judges in the same Courts. On the exclusive Right of the State Legislatures, and under their direction, of the People, to the Election of the President . . . On the defined Privileges of Congress,*

and the Liberty of the Press. And, On the Intercourse Bill with France ([Philadelphia?], 1800), 62–63. (Hereafter cited as *Speeches* 1800.) In 1816 he poked fun at Republican opponents of banks and funding; see *Observations* 1816, 31. His specific complaints about taxes under the Adams administration can be found in *Three Letters* 1799, 52; *Speeches* 1800, ii–iii; and Republican 1800, 5 September and 3 October.

42. On cities, see *Observations* 1816, 12–13; on immigrants, see *Speeches* 1800, 12–13; Republican 1800, 18, 22, 25, 26 September; *Observations* 1816, 50–51; and Missouri 1820, 1317. The quotation is from *Observations* 1816, 51.

43. On manufactures, see *Three Letters* 1783, 19, 26; Republican 1800, 18 September, 13 October; Governor's Message no. 1, Charleston *Times*, 7 December 1808 (hereafter cited as Governor's Message, 1808); Republican 1810, 19, 25 September; and *Observations* 1816, 51. (In none of these passages did Pinckney betray any of the common contemporary hesitations about manufactures as explained in McCoy, *Elusive Republic*, 63–66, 105–19, 157–59, and 223–31.) On protective duties, see Missouri 1821, 1143.

44. *Speech* 1786, 3–4; "Speech of Mr. Charles Pinckney . . . at a very numerous Meeting of the Citizens of Charleston, the 22nd July, 1795 . . . ," in Mathew Carey, ed., *The American Remembrancer; or, An Impartial Collection of Essays, Resolves, Speeches, &c. Relative, or Having Affinity, to the Treaty with Great Britain* (Philadelphia, 1795), I, 9 (hereafter cited as "Speech" 1795); *Observations* 1816, 22; Missouri 1820, 1142–24.

45. "Speech" 1795, 19; *Speeches* 1800, 96–98; and Republican 1810, 18, 19, 22 September.

46. "Speech" 1795, 19. For a similar comment, see also *Speech* 1786, 3.

47. Governor's Message 1797, and *Three Letters* 1799, 42.

48. Missouri 1820, 1311, 1314, 1328.

49. On the debate about economic development in Pinckney's lifetime, see McCoy, *Elusive Republic*.

50. *Three Letters* 1783, 26.

51. *Records* 1787, I, 398–400.

52. Madison's reply can be found in *Records* 1787, I, 422–23, 431. For a comment on it, see McCoy, *Elusive Republic*, 128–29.

53. Republican 1800, 14 October; *Observations* 1816, 45–46, 50.

54. *Records* 1787, I, 400.

55. *Three Letters* 1783, 8.

56. *Observations* 1816, 45–46. See also Missouri 1820, 1323, 1329.

57. There is a great deal of literature on Virginians and their reaction to slavery; see Robert McColley, *Slavery and Jeffersonian Virginia* (Urbana, Ill., 1964), 114–40; William Freehling, "The Founding Fathers and Slavery," *AHR* 77 (1972–73): 81–92; William Cohen, "Thomas Jefferson and the Problem of Slavery," *JAH* 56 (1969–70): 503–26; John P. Diggins, "Slavery, Race, and Equality: Jefferson and the Pathos of the Enlightenment," *American Quarterly* 28 (1976): 206–28; and Shalhope, *John Taylor of Caroline*, 40–45, 141–51. It is difficult to summarize such an extensive literature, but it does appear that articulate Virginians of Jefferson's time expressed qualms about slavery and that none defended it as a positive good in the way that South Carolinians did.

58. Governor's Message no. 1, South Carolina Senate journal, 29 November 1798, SCSA. (Hereafter cited as Governor's Message 1798.)

59. James Madison's notes; *Records* 1787, II, 371.

60. *Ibid.*

61. Missouri 1820, 1327.

62. For a detailed discussion of South Carolina's economic development, see Kaplanoff, "Making the South Solid," 1–14.

63. Missouri 1820, 1325.

64. *Ibid.*, 1310, 1315, and Missouri 1821, 1321, 1142.

65. Missouri 1820, 1311.

66. This tradition in the 1790s can be followed in Lance Banning, *The Jeffersonian Persuasion: Evolution of a Party Ideology* (Ithaca, N.Y., 1978). The literature on the development of American republican thought is extensive; for two good introductory essays, see Robert E. Shalhope, "Toward a Republican Synthesis: The Emergence of an Understanding of Republicanism in American Historiography," *WMQ* 29 (1972): 49–80, and Shalhope, "Republicanism and Early American Historiography," *WMQ* (1982): 334–56. The classic account of republican thought in the 1780s is Gordon S. Wood, *The Creation of the American Republic, 1776–1787* (Chapel Hill, N.C., 1969).

67. See Risjord, *Old Republicans*; Shalhope, *John Taylor of Caroline*; MacLeod, "Triple Crisis."

68. Richard Hofstadter, *The Idea of a Party System: The Rise of Legitimate Opposition in the United States, 1780–1840* (Berkeley, Calif., 1969).

69. Between his service in the Philadelphia convention and his election to the U.S. House of Representatives in 1816, Pinckney's only service in Congress was as a U.S. senator from 1798 to 1801, and during his Senate term he was much preoccupied with political affairs in South Carolina: see Charles Pinckney to Thomas Jefferson, 20 December 1800, Jefferson Papers, LC. The only other national office he held was that of Ambassador to Spain, 1801–05; however, this did not stop his alienation from the Jefferson administration: see Thomas Jefferson to James Monroe, 8 January 1804, Jefferson Papers, LC.

70. *Three Letters* 1783, 19–27.

71. See his speech before the legislature of New Jersey on 16 March 1786, which is given in "Account of a Deputation of Congress to the Assembly of New Jersey," *American Museum* 2 (1787): 153–60. (Hereafter cited as "Account" 1786.)

72. *Records* 1787, II, 390.

73. *Debates* 1788, V, 255–59, 261.

74. Governor's Messages 1797 and 1798; Governor's Message no. 1, *Courier*, 2 December 1807 (hereafter cited as Governor's Message 1807).

75. *Records*, 1787, I, 400; *Debates*, 1788, V, 322; and Republican, 1800, September 26.

76. Governor's Message 1797.

77. *Speeches* 1800, 76. For similar sentiments, see Republican 1800, 3 September; Republican 1810, 25 September; and *Observations* 1816, 45–46, 52.

78. *Three Letters* 1783, 5–7, 23; *Records* 1787, I, 404; *Debates* 1788, V, 326; Governor's Messages 1797 and 1798; *Speeches* 1800, i–ii, 5, 87, 92, 109; and Republican 1800, 13 October.

79. Governor's Message 1808.

80. Republican 1800, 16 September (italics in the original).

81. Governor's Message, 1798. For similar comments, see *Observations on the Plan of Government Submitted to the Federal Convention, in Philadelphia, on the 28th of May, 1787. By Mr. Charles Pinckney . . . Delivered at Different Times in the Course of their Discussions* (New York, [1787]), 3 (hereafter cited as *Observations* 1787); Governor's Message 1798; Republican 1800, 28 August; Republican 1810, 18 September; and Missouri 1821, 1130.

82. For conventional ideas about the problem of the large republic, see Wood, *Creation of the American Republic*, 499–506.

83. *Debates* 1788, V, 262.

84. *Observations* 1787, 22, and Missouri 1820, 1319.

85. *Three Letters* 1783, 9.

86. "Account" 1786, 154; *Observations* 1816, 47; and Missouri 1820, 1318–19.

87. On the fiscal system, see Governor's Message 1791; *Speeches* 1800, 62–63; and *Observations* 1816, 31. On war and the military, see *Three Letters* 1783, 22; "Account" 1786, 156; *Debates* 1788, V, 260–61; "Speech" 1795, 13; and Republican 1810, 21 September, 25.

88. Missouri 1820, 1313.

89. On New England's isolation, see *Speech* 1786, 3–4; *Debates* 1788, V, 323; and *Observations* 1816, 45, 49–50.

90. *Republican* 1800, 26, 29 September, 1 October; *Republican* 1810, 19, 21 September; *Missouri* 1820, 1310, 1313–14; and *Missouri* 1821, 1144.

91. *Missouri* 1820, 1319.

92. *Ibid.*

93. On Republican use of the concepts of influence and corruption, see Banning, *Jeffersonian Persuasion*, 128–29, 150–52, 158–59, 163–64, 171, 177, 186–207, 229–30, 248–50, and 286–87.

94. See MacLeod, "Triple Crisis."

95. *Observations* 1787, 15; and *Debates* 1788, V, 259. See also "Account" 1786, 158; and *Records* 1787, I, 400.

96. *Records* 1787, II, 490.

97. *Speeches* 1800, 87 (italics in the original).

98. *Speeches* 1800, 14, 20, 29, 73, 81, 87, 89, 91, 92, 101; *Republican* 1800, 28 August, 5, 16 September, 13 October.

99. *Speeches* 1800, 6–7, 13, 20, 29, 42, 72–73, 119; *Republican* 1800, 5–30 September.

100. *Republican* 1800, 28 August.

101. On the Virginian position generally, see Risjord, *Old Republicans.* For a precise analysis of the ways in which they continued to use the concepts of influence and corruption, see Shalhope, *John Taylor of Caroline*, 102–3, 125–27, 158–61, 164–71, 190–91, 193–202, 207–21; and Robert Dawidoff, *The Education of John Randolph* (New York, 1979), 174–83, 189–97, 233–38, 259–60. Pinckney's more relaxed view can be seen in *Republican* 1800, 5 September, and *Observations* 1816, 52.

102. *Missouri* 1820, 1314.

103. *Missouri* 1821, 1144.

104. "Speech" 1795, 17; and *Republican* 1810, 18, 24 September.

105. *Speeches* 1800 65–66; and *Observations* 1816, 47–48.

106. *Missouri* 1820, 1319–20.

107. See Hofstadter, *Idea of a Party System.*

108. For general comments on party, see "Account" 1786, 158; *Records* 1787, II, 298; *Observations* 1787, 16; and *Debates* 1788, V, 326–27. The quotation is from *Debates* 1788, V, 287.

109. *Speeches* 1800, 63.

110. On the necessity of a national Republican party, see *Observations* 1816, 3–4, 34–35, 41–44.

111. *Speeches* 1800, 14.

112. *Republican* 1810, 19 September.

113. *Observations* 1816, 20.

114. *Republican* 1810, 19 September.

115. *Missouri* 1820, 1132.

116. *Ibid.*

117. *Missouri* 1821, 1131.

118. *Ibid.*, 1131–32.

119. *Ibid.*, 1141.

120. See n. 28, above.

121. Freehling, 89.

122. See, e.g., Robert M. Weir, "The South Carolinian as Extremist," *South Atlantic Quarterly* 74 (1975): 92–93.

123. Much of the discussion of South Carolinian politics in the following paragraphs is based upon the detailed analysis in my "Making the South Solid." In giving citations for the following discussion, I have tried only to identify the sources of quotations and to cite published work that illustrates and confirms the points made.

124. For good accounts of Carolinian politics in the 1780s, see Jerome J. Nadelhaft, "The Revolutionary Era in South Carolina. 1775–1788" (Ph.D. diss., University of Wisconsin, 1965); and Rogers II, 97–158.

125. For the way that Federalists controlled office and patronage, see Rogers II, 180–92, 344–48. It is more difficult to document their illicit profits, but there are many hints. On the abuse of local office, see the reports in the *Acts and Resolutions of the General Assembly of the State of South Carolina . . .* (Charleston, S.C., published after each session of the legislature), 1796, 122; 1798, 53, 59; 1800, 56; 1801, 125–26. See also [Henry William DeSaussure], *Notes on the Finances of the State of South-Carolina, by a Member of the House of Representatives* (Charleston, S.C., 1799), ix; and the presentments of the Charleston District grand jury, February 1799, *City Gazette,* 4 February 1799. For complaints about corruption in the Charleston customhouse, see *State-Gazette,* 22 September 1798; *City Gazette,* 19 February 1800; Rogers II, 185–86; and Carl E. Prince, *The Federalists and the Origins of the U.S. Civil Service* (New York, 1977), 127–28. The comment about the "treasury squad" is from Henry S. Randall, *The Life of Jefferson,* rev. ed., 2 vols. (Philadelphia, 1871), II, 567.

126. Jacob Read to John F. Grimké, 24 January, 12 February 1791, Grimké Papers, SCHS; and Jacob Read to Ralph Izard, 30 September 1796, Izard Papers, SCL.

127. Robert Goodloe Harper speaking in the U.S. House of Representatives, *Debates and Proceedings in the Congress of the United States,* 5th Cong., 2d Sess., 1354 (29 March 1798), and 5th Cong., 3d Sess., 2511 (27 December 1798).

128. The term Jacobin seems not to have been used before 1797, but it came into common usage then. See William L. Smith to Alexander Hamilton, 4 May 1797, *The Papers of Alexander Hamilton,* ed. Harold C. Syrett 26 vols. (New York, 1961–79), XXI, 75–76; John Rutledge, Jr., to Edward Rutledge, 27 June 1797, Rutledge Family Papers, Dreer Collection, PHS; Richard Beresford, *Aristocracy the Bane of Liberty; Learning the Antidote . . .* (Charleston, S.C., 1797), 8–9; Robert G. Harper's remarks in *Debates and Proceedings in the Congress of the United States,* 5th Cong., 2d sess., 1178–89 (2 March 1798), and 5th Cong., 3d sess., 2506–10 (27 December 1798); *State-Gazette,* 10, 19 September 1798; Henry William DeSaussure to Jacob Read, 1 January 1799, miscellaneous MSS, New York Public Library; and Henry Dana Ward to Artemas Ward, 6 April 1799, Ward Family Papers, American Antiquarian Society, Worcester, Mass.

For Federalist references to Saint Domingue and the threat of black insurrection, see Robert G. Harper, *Debates and Proceedings in the Congress of the United States,* 5th Cong., 2d sess., 1176, 1530–31, 1646–47 (2 March, 24 April, 8 May, 1798); Thomas Pinckney, *ibid.,* 1663 (8 May 1798); John Rutledge, Jr., *ibid.,* 6th Cong., 1st sess., 242 (3 January 1800); Robert G. Harper's circular letter, 20 March 1799, "Papers of James A. Bayard, 1796–1815," Elizabeth Donnan, ed., American Historical Association, *Annual Report . . . 1913* (Washington, D.C., 1915), II, 90; and *State-Gazette,* 26 March, 10 September 1798.

129. For the use of these terms, see Pierce Butler letter book, 26 September 1793, SCL; Philip S. Foner, ed., *The Democratic-Republican Societies, 1790–1800: A Documentary Sourcebook of Constitutions, Declarations, Addresses, Resolutions, and Toasts* (Westport, Conn., 1976), 379, 380, 392; and *State-Gazette,* 11 June 1794, 8 January 1795, 9 November 1796.

130. Charleston *Times,* 8 October 1800. Similar comments can be found in virtually any issue of the *City Gazette* during the campaign before the election of 1800: see 21 July; 11, 18, 20, 23, 27 August; 15, 20, 27, 29, September; 1, 4 October 1800.

131. A good example of a prominent man who deserted the Federalists is Pierce Butler: see Rogers II, 184–85; and Lisle A. Rose, *Prologue to Democracy: The Federalists in the South, 1789–1800* (Lexington, Ky., 1968), 102.

132. The political activities of Charleston artisans can be traced in two works by Eugene P. Link: *The Democratic Republican Societies, 1790–1800* (New York, 1942); and "The Republican Society of Charleston," South Carolina Historical Association, *Proceedings . . . 1943* (Columbia, S.C.,

1943), 23–24. Their statements about their political grievances have been gathered in Foner, ed., *Democratic-Republican Societies*, 379–90. The background of the artisans' economic grievances has been analysed in Richard Walsh, *Charleston's Sons of Liberty: A Study of the Artisans, 1763–1789* (Columbia, S.C., 1959), 107–38. Similar grievances in the 1790s have not been studied in such detail, but they evidently continued. For complaints about competition from skilled slaves and free blacks, see Leonard P. Stavisky, "The Negro Artisans in the South Atlantic States, 1800–1860: A Study of Status and Economic Opportunity with Special Reference to Charleston" (Ph.D. diss., Columbia University, 1958), 100–1, 132–34, 141–42, 145–50, 171. For complaints about difficulties raising capital and credit, see *State-Gazette*, 7 July 1795, 7 January 1797, and *City Gazette*, 12 February, 9 April 1794; 2 March, 5 December 1796.

133. Western agitation has been described in William A. Schafer, "Sectionalism and Representation in South Carolina," American Historical Association, *Annual Report . . . 1900* (Washington, D.C., 1901), I, 400–26.

134. See the petition of the inhabitants of Winton County, House petitions, 18 January 1791, SCSA; petition of the inhabitants of Lancaster County, *ibid.*, 4 December 1797; presentments of the Edgefield grand jury, October 1798, Senate presentments, 3 December 1798, SCSA; and the presentments of the Charleston District grand jury, February 1799, *City Gazette*, 4 February 1799.

135. The best published account of the rise of the South Carolina Jeffersonians remains Wolfe, *Jeffersonian Democracy in South Carolina*, 1–165.

136. [W.S. Elliott], "Charles Pinckney," 377n.

137. *Ibid.*, 373–74.

138. Incidental information about Pinckney's financial affairs and difficulties can be found in the *City Gazette*, 30 September, 6 October 1800; 23 April 1803; 10 December 1807; *Courier*, 6 January 1808; D'Oyley, *Letter, Addressed to his Excellency Charles Pinckney*, and "Diary of Edward Hooker, 1805–1808," American Historical Association, *Annual Report . . . 1896* (Washington, D.C., 1897), I, 858–59. A discussion of charges about his dishonesty can be found in Ulrich B. Phillips, "The South Carolina Federalists," *AHR* 14 (1908–1909): 739; *Dictionary of American Biography*, XIV, 613; David D. Wallace, *History of South Carolina*, 4 vols. (New York, 1934), III, 358n; and Williams, *Founding Family*, 351, 483.

139. Williams, *Founding Family*, 311.

140. See the general comments in *ibid.*, 270–71, 294, 338, 346, 351, and the very pointed comments by George Washington in *Records* 1787, III, 131.

141. On Pinckney's break with the Federalists, see Rogers II, 184; and Rose, *Prologue to Democracy*, 102–3. On his relations with his family and friends generally, see Williams, *Founding Family*, 310–11, 328–29, 338, 346, 456.

142. For a good example of a vain and ambitious member of the Carolinian establishment, see the comments on Senator Jacob Read in Rogers II, 191–92, 347–48.

143. Charles Pinckney to Thomas Jefferson, 16 October 1800; 22 November, 3 December 1800, Jefferson Papers, LC; and Ralph Izard to Jacob Read, 12 October 1795, Izard Papers, SCL.

144. *State-Gazette*, 17 September 1798; 16 March 1799, 18 April, 2 August, 7 October 1800. The quotation is from 2 August 1800.

145. William Read to Jacob Read, 10 September 1795, Read Family Papers, SCHS.

146. Charles Pinckney to James Madison, 26 October 1800, Madison Papers, LC.

147. See Rogers II, 363–64; and Zahniser, *Charles Cotesworth Pinckney*, 238–39, 241–42, 244–46, 258.

148. There is a useful collective portrait of the great planters (those owning 100 slaves or more) in 1860 in Chalmers G. Davidson, *The Last Foray: The South Carolina Planters of 1860, a Sociological Study* (Columbia, S.C., 1971). Generalizations about changes are based on a comparison of Davidson's work with my own analysis of the great planters of 1790 and 1810, presented in "Making the South Solid," 15–27.

149. These conclusions are based upon my own analysis in "Making the South Solid," 120–29. For the best published discussion of great planters and political office, see Davidson, *Last Foray*, 54–82.

150. Freehling discusses the elitist structure of Carolinian politics and quotes some explicit statements of political elitism by Carolinian leaders; see Freehling, 89–91, 241. But these statements were now made privately; publicly, Carolinian leaders continued to affirm their faith in democracy. For a sensitive discussion of this point, see R. Nicholas Olsberg, "A Government of Class and Race: William Henry Trescot and the South Carolina Chivalry, 1860–1865," (Ph.D. diss., University of South Carolina, 1972), 101–07. Instead of attacking democracy directly, Carolinian leaders began to attack party.

151. There is no good study of local economic and social arrangements in antebellum South Carolina. These conclusions are based on my own studies of land use and plantation self-sufficiency in "Making the South Solid," 33–35.

152. See the very revealing comments in *Chesnut*, 193, 205, 830–32.

153. Before 1800 the average turnout in congressional elections had never exceeded 35 percent of adult white males; in the decade after 1810, it never dropped below 60 percent. For a detailed discussion of these figures and evidence generally about voting, see "Making the South Solid," 114–16.

154. See John Hunter to James Madison, 16 April 1801, Madison Papers, LC; Pierce Butler to Thomas Jefferson, 19 September 1801, Jefferson Papers, LC; Wade Hampton to Thomas Sumter, 20 December 1801, transcript, Draper MSS, Wisconsin Historical Society; and the general discussion in "Making the South Solid," 184–92.

155. This point has been noticed and commented upon by several historians; for the most perceptive discussion, see Banner, "Problem of South Carolina."

156. For discussions of popular excitements, see Freehling, 121; and Olsberg, "Government of Class and Race," 98–100. On contempt for politicians and the prestige of planters, see *ibid.*, 90, 240; George P. Germany, "The South Carolina Governing Elite, 1820–1860" (Ph.D. diss., University of California, Berkeley, 1972), 73–88, 222–24, 234–35, 239–46; Kenneth S. Greenberg, "The Second American Revolution: South Carolina Politics, Society, and Secession, 1776–1869" (Ph.D. diss., University of Wisconsin, 1976), 74–76, 96–103; and Olsberg, "Government of Class and Race," 74–76.

157. A good discussion of the style of leadership in antebellum South Carolina can be found in Weir, "South Carolinian as Extremist," 86–103.

158. *Observations* 1787, 3; Governor's Message 1798; Republican 1800, 28 August; Republican 1810, 18 September.

159. *Speeches* 1800, 106.

160. This point is made explicitly in Pauline Maier, "The Road Not Taken: Nullification, John C. Calhoun, and the Revolutionary Tradition in South Carolina," *SCHM* 82 (1981): 18–19, and implicitly in Weir, "South Carolinian as Extremist."

161. See William W. Freehling, "Spoilsmen and Interests in the Thought of John C. Calhoun," *JAH* 52 (1965–66): 25–42; Greenberg, "Second American Revolution," 123–213; Germany, "South Carolina Governing Elite," 236–41; Olsberg, "Government of Class and Race," 101–17; and Weir, "South Carolinian as Extremist," 89–95, 101–2.

162. John C. Calhoun to Samuel L. Gouverneur, 8 August 1831, in *Calhoun Papers*, XI, 453. For similar comments by Calhoun, see *ibid.*, X, 202, and XI, 466.

163. See Freehling, "Spoilsmen and Interests in the Thought of Calhoun," 25–42; Greenberg, "Second American Revolution," 123–213; Germany, "South Carolina Governing Elite," 236–41; Olsberg, "Government of Class and Race," 101–17; and Weir, "South Carolinian as Extremist," 89–95, 101–2.

164. [Elliott], "Charles Pinckney," 63, 67, 371.

165. Missouri 1820, 1328.

166. Hofstadter, *Idea of a Party System,* 212–71.

167. There is no general study of Republican rhetoric (including rhetoric in state and local politics) after 1800; one can, however, find much evidence of antiaristocratic rhetoric in various studies of local Republican politics in the North. See Alfred F. Young, *The Democratic-Republicans of New York: The Origins, 1763–1797* (Chapel Hill, N.C., 1967), 372, 382–84, 395, 405–12, 450–53, 458–59, 468–95; Howard B. Rock, *Artisans of the New Republic: The Tradesmen of New York City in the Age of Jefferson* (New York, 1979), 45–71, 80–81, 123–43, 279–83; Carl E. Prince, *New Jersey's Jeffersonian Republicans: The Genesis of an Early Party Machine, 1789–1817* (Chapel Hill, N.C., 1964), 19, 165–68; Paul Goodman, *The Democratic-Republicans of Massachusetts: Politics in a Young Republic* (Cambridge, Mass., 1964), 70–86, 154–81; Richard E. Ellis, *The Jeffersonian Crisis: Courts and Politics in the Young Republic* (New York, 1971), 171–81.

168. Banning, *Jeffersonian Persuasion,* 229–301.

169. On the Republican Party, see Eric Foner, *Free Soil, Free Labor, Free Men: The Ideology of the Republican Party before the Civil War* (New York, 1970).

170. See Shalhope, *John Taylor of Caroline,* 138–39, 157–71, 191–92, 193–202, 207–12; Dawidoff, *Education of John Randolph,* 233–38, 243–44; McCoy, *Elusive Republic,* 249–50; and Robert E. Shalhope, "Thomas Jefferson's Republicanism and Antebellum Southern Thought," *JSH* 42 (1976), 529–56.

171. See n. 57, above.

172. Shalhope, *John Taylor of Caroline,* 43–50, 104–5, 129–39, 150–51, 185–88.

173. Charles H. Ambler, *Sectionalism in Virginia from 1776 to 1861* (Chicago, 1909), 95–97, 137–74; Harry Ammon, "The Republican Party in Virginia 1789 to 1824" (Ph.D. diss., University of Virginia, 1948), 443–47; Harry Ammon, "The Richmond Junto, 1800–1824," *Virginia Magazine of History and Biography* 61 (1953): 397; and Dawidoff, *Education of John Randolph,* 225–29.

174. Rather little has been written about the thought of the newer areas of the Old South, but there are some suggestive hints. On proslavery, see McCardell, *Idea of a Southern Nation,* 71–84. On democracy, see J. Mills Thornton III, *Politics and Power in a Slave Society: Alabama, 1800–1860* (Baton Rouge, La., 1978), 43–44. On a general commitment to economic growth, see *ibid.,* 43. Certainly there were differences of opinion in these states about the sort of economic development desired; indeed, such differences lay beneath party political divisions (see n. 177 below), but both parties were arguing for growth—one for growth over space, the other for growth over time, in Major L. Wilson's formulation: "The Concept of Time and Political Dialogue in the United States, 1828–1848," *American Quarterly* 17 (1967): 662–63.

175. See Thornton, *Politics and Power in a Slave Society,* 53–58; Donald A. DeBats, "Elite and Masses: Political Structure, Communication and Behavior in Ante-Bellum Georgia" (Ph.D. diss., University of Wisconsin, 1973), 302–12; and Marc W. Kruman, "Politics and Parties in North Carolina, 1846–1865" (Ph.D. diss., Yale University, 1978), 19–22, 144–45.

176. Paul W. Brewer, "The Rise of the Second Party System: Missouri, 1815–1845" (Ph.D. diss., Washington University, 1974), 115–17, 141–209, 272–317, 464–95; DeBats, "Elite and Masses," 19–21, 27, 110–11, 478–503; Thomas E. Jeffrey, "The Second Party System in North Carolina, 1836–1860" (Ph.D. diss., Catholic University of America, 1976), 74, 119–46; Kruman, "Politics and Parties in North Carolina," 2–9, 18; Frank M. Lowrey, "Tennessee Voters during the Second Two-Party System, 1836–1860: A Study in Voter Constancy and in Socio-Economic and Demographic Distinctions" (Ph.D. diss., University of Alabama, 1973), 23–24, 28–39; Thornton, *Politics and Power in a Slave Society,* 117–62; and Henry L. Watson, "Bitter Combinations of the Neighborhood: The Second American Party System in Cumberland County, North Carolina" (Ph.D. diss., Northwestern University, 1976), 21–38, 319–27.

177. Thornton, *Politics and Power in a Slave Society,* 57; and Watson, "Bitter Combinations,"

266–68, Although other historians do not make this point explicitly, it seems consistent with the sort of voting patterns described in n. 179, below.

178. Thomas B. Alexander et al., "Who Were the Alabama Whigs?" *Alabama Review* 16 (1963): 6–11; Thomas B. Alexander et al., "The Basis of Alabama's Ante-Bellum Two-Party System," *Alabama Review* 19 (1966): 265–66; DeBats, "Elite and Masses," 372–474; Jeffrey, "Second Party System in North Carolina," 82; Kruman, "Politics and Parties in North Carolina," 35–36; Lowrey, "Tennessee Voters," 200–7; and Watson, "Bitter Combinations," 216–18, 251–56.

179. Alexander et al., "Basis of Alabama's Ante-Bellum Two-Party System," 266; Brewer, "Rise of the Second Party System in Missouri," 507–38; Michael F. Holt, *The Political Crisis of the 1850s* (New York, 1978), 245–46; Kruman, "Politics and Parties in North Carolina," 36; James R. Sharp, *The Jacksonians versus the Banks: Politics in the States after the Panic of 1837* (New York, 1970), 88–122; and Watson, "Bitter Combinations," 79–87, 133–36, 139–41, 310–12.

180. Brewer, "Rise of the Second Party System in Missouri," 210–71; DeBats, "Elite and Masses," 217–27; Jeffrey, "Second Party System in North Carolina," 154–57; Kruman, "Parties and Politics in North Carolina," 10–17; and Ralph A. Wooster, *The People in Power: Courthouse and Statehouse in the Lower South, 1850–1860* (Knoxville, Tenn., 1969).

181. Holt, *Political Crisis of the 1850s*, 245–46; and Watson, "Bitter Combinations," 152–62, 207–8, 220–25.

182. Brewer, "Rise of the Second Party System in Missouri," 126–38; Jeffrey, "Second Party System in North Carolina," 90; and Thornton, *Politics and Power in a Slave Society*, 98–100.

183. See particularly William J. Cooper, Jr., *The South and the Politics of Slavery, 1828–1856* (Baton Rouge, La., 1978), but also Kruman, "Parties and Politics in North Carolina," 41–75; and Watson, "Bitter Combinations," 48–50.

184. Holt, *Political Crisis of the 1850s*, 245–48.

185. *Ibid.*, 246; Kruman, "Parties and Politics in North Carolina," 13; and Thornton, *Politics and Power in a Slave Society*, 296–300.

186. Gene W. Boyett, "The Whigs of Arkansas, 1836–1856" (Ph.D. diss., Louisiana State University, 1972), 372–75; David R. Goldfield, "The Triumph of Politics over Society: Virginia, 1851–1861" (Ph.D. diss., University of Virginia, 1970), 11–14, 33, 138–65; Kruman, "Parties and Politics in North Carolina," 25–26, 76–115; and Thornton, *Politics and Power in a Slave Society*, 302–6, 308–12, 323–31.

187. For a sense of the way in which the rewards of prosperity were being distributed unequally, see Gavin Wright, "'Economic Democracy' and the Concentration of Agricultural Wealth in the Cotton South, 1850–1860," *Agricultural History* 44 (1970): 63–93; for a sense of the way in which people felt threatened by changes, see Thornton, *Politics and Power in a Slave Society*, 305–21.

188. Several Southern states had strong populist movements outside the existing party system; see James H. Broussard, "Some Determinants of Know-Nothing Electoral Strength in the South, 1856," *Louisiana History* 7 (1966): 5–20; Donald C. Butts, "A Challenge to Planter Rule: The Controversy over Ad Valorem Taxation of Slaves in North Carolina, 1858–1862" (Ph.D. diss., Duke University, 1978); and Marius M. Carriere, "The Know Nothing Movement in Louisiana" (Ph.D. diss., Louisiana State University, 1977). Likewise, there were many states in which populist leaders and populist issues emerged within one of the existing parties; see DeBats, "Elite and Masses," 175, 179–83; Jeffrey, "Second Party System in North Carolina," 337–54; Robert K. Peters, "Texas: Annexation to Secession" (Ph.D. diss., University of Texas, 1977), 228–29, 302–4; and Thornton, *Politics and Power in a Slave Society*, 323–31.

189. See Barney, *Road to Secession*, 49–84.

190. See Michael P. Johnson, *Toward a Patriarchal Republic: The Secession of Georgia* (Baton Rouge, La., 1977), 28–62, 143–78.

191. On the South's insistence on its own pure republicanism, see Holt, *Political Crisis of the 1850s*, 6, 37–38, 54–56, 238–40, 241–59; for massive documentation on the use of this sort of

argument, see Walter K. Wood, "The Union of the States: A Study of Radical Whig-Republican Ideology and its Influence upon the Nation and the South, 1776–1861" (Ph.D. diss., University of South Carolina, 1978).

192. For analyses of secessionist rhetoric, see Barney, *Road to Secession*, 112–22, 124–37; Steven A. Channing, *Crisis of Fear: Secession in South Carolina* (New York, 1970), 141–66, 229–85; and Johnson, *Toward a Patriarchal Republic*, 28–62.

193. [Elliott], "Charles Pinckney," 63, 67.

4. *Hugh Legaré*: O'BRIEN

1. So he is described in John D. Hart, *The Oxford Companion to American Literature*, 4th ed. (New York, 1965), 466–67; parallel is John R. Welsh's remark, "If Elliott was the city's Franklin, Legaré was its Samuel Johnson," in "An Early Pioneer: Legaré's *Southern Review*," *Southern Literary Journal* 3 (1971): 83: especially inapposite in view of Legaré's harsh opinion of Johnson, in *Writings of Hugh Swinton Legaré*, ed. Mary Legaré, 2 vols. (Charleston, S.C., 1845–46), I, 130.

2. William Campbell Preston, *Eulogy on Hugh Swinton Legaré* (Charleston, S.C., 1843), 31.

3. Legaré to Isaac E. Holmes, 8 April 1833, in *Writings*, I, 215.

4. Paul Hamilton Hayne, "Hugh Swinton Legaré," *SR* 7 (1870): 133; William P. Trent, *William Gilmore Simms* (Boston, 1892), 51. It is worth noting that the standard and very unsatisfactory biography of Legaré was first written as a dissertation at Vanderbilt University under John Donald Wade, who had studied with Trent at Columbia, and the book bears Trent's imprint: see Linda Rhea, *Hugh Swinton Legaré: A Charleston Intellectual* (Chapel Hill, N.C., 1934).

5. Hayne, "Legare," 134; cf. Hayne to James Russell Lowell, 11 August 1860, in Daniel M. McKeithan, ed., *A Collection of Hayne Letters* (Austin, Tex., 1944), 101: "But often–, how often! I think of the dear friends I have in Boston, & contrasting the society *there*, with the society of Charleston, (I mean of a *literary* kind),– it is impossible for me to feel otherwise than '*sad*.'"

6. Donald Davidson, "Introduction," in *Simms Letters*, I, xxxiv–xxxvi.

7. It is proper to observe that William R. Taylor, *Cavalier and Yankee: The Old South and American National Character* (New York, 1961), 53–57, though sometimes mistaken about Legaré, has an interesting discussion of Legaré's alienation.

8. Biographical information on Legaré can be found in Rhea, *Legaré*; [E.W. Johnston], "Biographical Notice," in *Writings*, I, v–lxxii; and, in many ways superior to Rhea, Merrill G. Christophersen, "A Rhetorical Study of Hugh Swinton Legaré: South Carolina Unionist," (Ph.D. diss., University of Florida, 1954), which has more than its title implies. See also Michael O'Brien, *A Character of Hugh Legaré* (Knoxville, Tenn., 1985), from which part of this essay is drawn.

9. I use the distinction, derived from E. Digby Baltzell, *Philadelphia Gentlemen: The Making of a National Upper Class* (Glencoe, 1958), cited by Jane H. Pease and William H. Pease, "The Economics and Politics of Charleston's Nullification Crisis," *JSH* 47 (1981), 348–49, which has influenced my understanding of both nullification and Legaré: as the Peases have it, "The elite are those with the power and skills to establish and carry out a community's values and goals; the upper class derives its influence from family, church, and club membership as well as form of wealth."

10. Legaré to Francis Walker Gilmer, 1 October 1816, Gilmer Papers, University of Virginia.

11. *Reminiscences of Public Men*, in *The Writings of Benjamin F. Perry*, ed. Stephen Meats and Edwin T. Arnold (Spartanburg, S.C., 1980), III, 38.

12. Legaré to his mother, 4 November 1832, Legaré Papers, SCL; all manuscripts not otherwise cited may be assumed to be in this collection.

13. For example, Legaré to Mary Legaré, 4 August 1833, and 19 August 1835; Legaré to his mother, 16 March 1835.

14. Legaré to Judith Rives, 19 October 1838, Rives Papers, LC; Legaré to William Cabell Rives, 3 December 1840, and 5 June 1840, Rives Papers, LC.

15. James Louis Petigru to Legaré, 17 February 1836, in *Petigru*, 181; Legaré to his mother, 24/25 November 1835; Stephen Elliott, Jr., to Legaré, 4 December 1839.

16. Legaré to Mary Legaré, 4 August 1833.

17. Legaré to Alfred Huger, 23 September 1838.

18. Legaré to his mother, 13 September 1841.

19. Legaré to Thomas White, 10 May 1838; Legaré to George Frederick Holmes, 10 December 1842, Holmes Papers, LC.

20. Legaré to his mother, 24 January 1829.

21. "Hall's Travels in North America," [1829], in *Writings*, II, 264, 288.

22. Legaré to Judith Rives, 5 April 1841, Rives Papers, LC.

23. Note his sorrowful condemnation of the insecurity of American judges in "Kent's Commentaries," [1828], in *Writings*, II, 141.

24. Legaré to Mary Legaré, 19 October 1835; Legaré to his mother, 2 September 1841.

25. Legaré to his mother, n.d. [Edinburgh, 1819], and 13 August 1832.

26. *Writings*, I, 123, 126; Legaré to his mother, 14 September 1840; "Spirit of the Sub-Treasury" [1837], in *Writings*, I, 284–85.

27. [Legare], "Stephen Elliott," *Courier*, 30 March 1840; [Samuel Prioleau], "Dyspepsia," *SR* 4 (1829): 208–41; Legaré to Mary Legaré, 25 January 1836; "Classical Learning," [1828], in *Writings*, II, 7; Legaré to Jesse Burton Harrison, 3 November 1828.

28. Legaré to his mother, 25 September 1838; Legaré to W.C. Rives, 5 October 1838, Rives Papers, LC; Legaré to Alfred Huger, 15 December 1834, in *Writings*, I, 216–19; Legaré to his mother, 4 November 1832; Legaré to Mary Legaré, 10 October 1839; Legaré to his mother, 27 September 1840.

29. Mitchell King to Legaré, 5 May 1833; Legaré to W.C. Rives, 5 October 1838, Rives Papers, LC.

30. Mary Legaré to Paul H. Hayne, 27 July 1878, Hayne Papers, Duke University: "I am gratified & well pleased with your own original remarks on my brother's career & character but deeply regret that so eloquent & beautiful a pen should have been betrayed by the *misrepresentations* of Wm. C. Preston & his creature Wm. Johnson (a little grammar master) whom the Hon Senator in a manner forced upon me as a proper person to write the Biography of Legaré. . . . Preston the appointed Eulogist of HSL opens his address with the remark that H S Legaré had been overpraised & he meant then and there to prove that he was so."

31. Legaré to W.C. Rives, 5 October 1838, Rives Papers, LC.

32. George Ticknor to Legaré, 29 December 1839, and 9 June 1842, in *Life, Letters and Journals of George Ticknor*, ed. George S. Hillard, 2 vols. (Boston, 1876), II, 191, 207; "Classical Learning," 7.

33. Joseph Cogswell to Legaré, 22 December 1838.

34. Nassau Senior to Legaré, 28 January 1840; Legaré to Mary Legaré, 12 October 1838; Legaré to Gouverneur Kemble, 9 June 1839, Charles L. Chandler Papers, SHC; Legaré to W.C. Rives, 29 October 1839, Rives Papers, LC.

35. Legaré to Judith Rives, 19 October 1838, Rives Papers, LC; Legaré to Mary Legaré, 10 September 1838, and 12 October 1838.

36. Joseph Cogswell to Legaré, 22 December 1838, and 24 April 1839; Legaré to Thomas C. Reynolds, 6 February 1841, in *Writings*, I, 236.

37. Legaré to Mary Legaré, 15 April 1835; Kemble to Poinsett, 29 June 1843, Gilpin/Poinsett Papers, PHS; Richard Lounsbury, on reading this characterization of Legaré the politician, observed that it reminded him of Cicero, Legaré's model: cf. Ronald Syme, *The Roman Revolution* (Oxford, 1939), 135–48, especially Syme's remark (p. 11), parallel to Kemble's judgment, "Cicero would have preserved both dignity and peace of mind had not ambition and vanity blinded him to the true causes of his own elevation."

38. Legaré to Stephen Elliott, Jr., 14 April 1839, Legaré Papers, Duke University.

39. Preston, *Eulogy*, 31; Legaré to his mother, 3 May 1838.

40. Legaré to Mary Legaré, 25 January 1836; Legaré to his mother, 10 May 1833.

41. Drew Gilpin Faust, *A Sacred Circle: The Dilemma of the Intellectual in the Old South, 1840–1860* (Baltimore, Md., 1977).

42. Preston to Waddy Thompson, 28 August 1855, Preston Papers, SCL.

43. "Law of Tenures," *SR* 3 (1829): 18.

44. "Classical Learning," 41–42; cf. Victor Hugo, "En trouvant fort ridicules les Néréides dont Camöeus obsède les compagnons de Gama, on désirerait, dans le célèbre *Passage du Rhin* de Boileau, voir autre chose que des naiades craintives fuir devant Louis, par la grace de Dieu, roi de France et de Navarre, accompagné de ses marechaux-des-camps et-armées": Preface, *Nouvelles Odes* [1824], quoted in Basil Gildersleeve, "Necessity of the Classics," *SQR* n.s., 10 (1854): 155.

45. "Classical Learning," 42; Gladys Bryson, *Man and Society: The Scottish Inquiry of the Eighteenth Century* (Princeton, N.J., 1945), 85–86, 106; Donald R. Kelley, *Foundations of Modern Historical Scholarship: Language, Law, and History in the French Renaissance* (New York, 1970); cf. "Roman Literature," [1828], in *Writings*, II, 67, with "The Origin, History and Influence of Roman Legislation," [1837], in *Writings*, I, 504–8.

46. "Roman Literature," 53–54.

47. "The Public Economy of Athens," [1832], in *Writings*, II, 503; "Cicero de Republica," [1829], in *Writings*, II, 242.

48. "Law of Tenures," 19.

49. "Hoffman's Legal Outlines," *SR* 3 (1829): 61–69, has a discussion of the social compact.

50. "Hall's Travels in North America," 268.

51. "Lord Byron's Character and Writings," [1830], in *Writings*, II, 390–91.

52. Jane Rendell, *The Origins of the Scottish Enlightenment* (New York, 1978), 1–27; cf. *Boswell in Holland, 1763–1764*, ed. Frederick A. Pottle (New York, 1952), 49; and Walter Scott to William Clerk, 6 August 1790, in *The Letters of Sir Walter Scott, 1787–1807*, ed. H.J.C. Grierson (London, 1932), 11: "I read *no* civil law. Heineccius and his fellow worthies have ample time to gather a venerable coat of dust"; Scott, *Redgauntlet: A Tale of the Eighteenth Century* (London, 1897), 11–12: "And what ill would the Scottish law do to him, though he had as much of it as either Stair or Bankton, sir? Is not the foundation of our municipal law the ancient code of the Roman Empire, devised at a time when it was so much renowned for its civil polity, sir, and wisdom?" There is a marked lack of writing about Heineccius, but see his *A Methodical System of Universal Law*, trans. George Turnbull (London, 1763), and articles in the *Encyclopedia Britannica* (11th ed.) and in the *Biographie universelle: ancienne et moderne* (Paris, 1856), XIX, 59–60, both of which are based upon his son's memoir, Johann Christian Heineccius, *Memoria Ioh. Gottl. Heineccii*, which prefaces the *Omnia Opera*.

53. "Roman Legislation," 509, 511.

54. "Sketch of the Character of Hugh S. Legaré," in *The Miscellaneous Writings of Joseph Story*, ed. William W. Story (Boston, 1852), 820–24.

55. "Classical Learning," 22, 24, 25.

56. *Ibid.*, 33–34, 8, 30–31; "Jeremy Bentham and the Utilitarians," [1831], in *Writings*, II, 469; Legaré to his mother, 9 September 1834, confesses a lack of religious instinct; Alexander Everett to wife, 25 June 1840, Everett Papers, Massachusetts Historical Society (I am grateful to Jane and William Pease for bringing this letter to my attention).

57. Legaré to Mary Legaré, 5 May 1833, in *Writings*, I, 225; Legaré to Judith Rives, 26 April 1833, Rives Papers, LC; "Classical Learning," 25.

58. Legaré to Thomas White, 10 May 1838.

59. "D'Aguesseau," [1832], in *Writings*, II, 591; "Cicero de Republica," 253.

60. August von Schlegel, "Abriss von den europäischen Verhältnissen der deutschen Litera-

tur," quoted in René Wellek, *A History of Modern Criticism: 1750–1950* (New Haven, Conn., 1955), II, 38; "Travels of the Duke of Saxe-Weimar," [1830] in *Writings*, II, 168; "Early Spanish Ballads," [1830] in *Writings*, II, 299–300; Bryson, *Man and Society*, 78–113.

61. "Classical Learning," 32, 48; "Hoffman's Legal Outlines," 49–58; Bryson, *Man and Society*, 53–77; cf. Josiah C. Nott, *Two Lectures on the Natural History of the Caucasian and Negro Races* (Mobile, Ala., 1844), with Legaré's amusement at Monboddo on the Etruscans in "Roman Literature," 61.

62. "Byron's Letters and Journals," [1831], in *Writings*, II, 426–28.

63. *Ibid.*, 428–29.

64. *Ibid.*, 430–31; Wellek, *History of Modern Criticism*, II, 59.

65. "Byron's Letters and Journals," 431–32.

66. *Ibid.*, 432–33.

67. *Ibid.*, 435, 440.

68. *Ibid.*, 439, 441–42, 443, 437.

69. "Lord Byron's Character and Writings," [1830], in *Writings*, II, 380; cf. Adam Smith, *The Theory of Moral Sentiments*, 10th ed. (London, 1804), I, 33.

70. "Early Spanish Ballads," [1830], in *Writings*, II, 320–21; M.H. Abrams, *Natural Supernaturalism: Tradition and Revolution in Romantic Literature* (New York, 1971), *passim*; Avrom Fleishman, *The English Historical Novel: Walter Scott to Virginia Woolf* (Baltimore, Md., 1971), 37–101.

71. "Classical Learning," 32, 40, 44–45.

72. Preston, *Eulogy*, 25.

73. "Charles Fraser, *Reminiscences of Charleston* (Charleston, S.C., 1854), 114–15; Henry Cruger, "Cooper's Bravo," *SR* 9 (1832): 398; William Gilmore Simms, *The Social Principle: The True Source of National Permanence* (Tuscaloosa, Ala., 1843), 7.

74. Hayne, "Legaré," 133–34; Vernon L. Parrington, *The Romantic Revolution in America, 1800–1860* (New York, 1927), 124, Freehling, 5.

75. Legaré to Holmes, 8 April 1833, in *Writings*, I, 215.

76. Legaré to Harrison, 3 November 1828.

77. For a persuasive case for Wordsworth as a transitional figure between the Enlightenment and romanticism, and as a social conservative, see Marilyn Butler, *Romantics, Rebels and Reactionaries: English Literature and Its Background, 1760–1830* (Oxford, 1982), 157–68; Butler has transferred from art history (p. 1–10) the term *neoclassical* to describe this sensibility, which itself may be applicable to Legaré.

78. Preston to Thompson, 28 August 1855, Preston Papers, SCL. For all its apparently artless simplicity, this passage, like much in Preston, is adapted from a literary source. Compare Fénelon's passage upon the grief of Idomeneus, in *Adventures of Telemachus*, trans., Hawksworth (New York, 1859), 531: "He withered like a stately tree which covers the earth with its shade, but is gnawed by a worm at the root: the winds in their fury may have attacked it in vain; the earth may have nourished it with delight; and it may have been spared, in reverence, by the axe; but if the latent mischief is not discovered, it will fade; its leaves, which are its honors, will be scattered in the dust; and the trunk and branches only, rifted and sapless, will remain. Such, in appearance, was Idomeneus, the victim of inconsolable grief." A more remote ancestor is Lucan, *Pharsalia*, I:129–43.

79. *Courier*, 3 April 1846; Legaré to Alfred Huger, 15 December 1834, in *Writings*, I, 218.

5. James L. Petigru: FORD

1. *Chesnut*, 262–63; Elisabeth Muhlenfeld, *Mary Boykin Chesnut: A Biography* (Baton Rouge, La., 1981), 96–130.

2. *Petigru*; William John Grayson, *James Louis Petigru: A Biographical Sketch* (New York, 1866).

3. *Petigru*, 364. The incident is also recounted, without documentation, in Sally Edwards, *The Man Who Said No* (New York, 1970), 65.

4. *Petigru*, 285–86, 361–64, 370–72. For a study of similar views of the Union held by men outside of South Carolina, see George M. Fredrickson, *The Inner Civil War: Northern Intellectuals and the Crisis of the Union* (New York, 1965), esp. 53–65. On support for the Union in South Carolina, see Lillian Kibler, "Unionist Sentiment in South Carolina in 1860," *JSH* 4 (1938): 346–66.

5. For examples of this search for Southern dissenters and the resulting interpretations of Petigru, see Clement Eaton, *The Mind of the Old South* (Baton Rouge, La., 1964), 22–42; Rollin G. Osterweis, *Romanticism and Nationalism in the Old South* (New Haven, Conn., 1949), 111–54; William R. Taylor, *Cavalier and Yankee: The Old South and the American National Character* (New York, 1961), 55–65; and Carl N. Degler, *The Other South: Southern Dissenters in the Nineteenth Century* (New York, 1974), 99–190.

6. Degler, *The Other South*, 129.

7. *Petigru*, 285; Linda Rhea, *Hugh Swinton Legaré: A Charleston Intellectual* (Chapel Hill, N.C., 1934), 156–77; J. Fred Rippy, *Joel R. Poinsett: Versatile American* (Durham, N.C., 1946), 253–59.

8. Julius Griffin Campbell, "James Louis Petigru: A Rhetorical Study" (Ph.D. diss., University of South Carolina, 1960), 27–42. For a more detailed account of Petigru's role as a legal champion for unpopular causes, see Lyon G. Tyler, "James Louis Petigru: Freedom's Champion in a Slave Society," *SCHM* 83 (1982): 272–86.

9. See *Petigru, passim*; Rhea, *Legaré*; Robert Duncan Bass, "The Autobiography of William John Grayson" (Ph.D. diss., University of South Carolina, 1933); Beverly R. Scafidel, "The Letters of William Elliott" (Ph.D. diss., University of South Carolina, 1978); Rogers II. The use of the term "aristocracy" as a label for Southern planters has itself sparked a good deal of controversy, and deservedly so. I use the term here, and throughout the rest of the paper, simply as a matter of convenience and not without recognition of the ambiguity involved. Rogers uses the term as a form of shorthand identification of the lowcountry plantation and mercantile elite, and I have adopted that practice here. Certainly if any group in the antebellum South was an aristocracy, it was the extraordinarily wealthy planters of the South Carolina parishes, where slaves outnumbered whites as much as ten to one, and where a mere handful of families controlled most of the land in the district.

10. *Petigru*, 28–58, 115–71, 395–409; Benjamin F. Perry, *Reminiscences of Public Men* (Philadelphia, 1833), 256–62; Grayson, *Petigru*, 149–60; Donald J. Senese, "Legal Thought in South Carolina, 1800–1860" (Ph.D. diss., University of South Carolina, 1970). John Belton O'Neall, *Biographical Sketches of the Bench and Bar of South Carolina* (Charleston, S.C., 1859), is dedicated to Petigru.

11. *Petigru*, 37–58. The case for internal homogeneity in South Carolina politics is made in James M. Banner, "The Problem of South Carolina," in Stanley Elkins and Eric McKitrick, eds., *The Hofstadter Aegis: A Memorial* (New York, 1974), 60–93; and Robert M. Weir, "The South Carolinian as Extremist," *South Atlantic Quarterly* 74 (1975), 86–103.

12. *Petigru*, 54–55.

13. *Ibid.*, 402.

14. On the demise of Federalism in South Carolina, see Rogers II, 342–400; and U.B. Phillips, "The South Carolina Federalists, Part II," *AHR* 14 (1909): 731–90; Fredrickson, *Inner Civil War*, 23–35.

15. Rogers II, 342–400; James Broussard, *The Southern Federalists, 1800–1816* (Baton Rouge, La., 1978); and Freehling, 7–48.

16. *Petigru*, 1–57. The case for the upper Savannah River as the cradle of Southern Rights ideology has been forcefully made by Clyde N. Wilson: See *Calhoun Papers*, XI, xxxii.

17. Campbell, "Petigru," 5–10; Petigru to Caroline Petigru, 14 October 1862, in *Petigru*, 458.

18. *Petigru*, 17–61.

19. *Ibid.*, 37–61.

20. Thomas Heyward to Petigru in Grayson, *Petigru*, 61; *Petigru*, 40.

21. Rogers II, 387–88.

22. Fredrickson, *Inner Civil War*, 33–35.

23. *Petigru, passim*. For a broader perspective on this issue see, Fredrickson, *The Inner Civil War*, 7–64; Linda K. Kerber, *Federalists in Dissent: Imagery and Ideology in Jeffersonian America* (Ithaca, N.Y., 1970); David Hackett Fischer, *The Revolution of American Conservatism: The Federalist Party in the Era of Jeffersonian Democracy* (New York, 1965); Shaw Livermore, *The Twilight of Federalism: The Disintegration of the Federalist Party, 1815–1830* (Princeton, N.J., 1962).

24. Major L. Wilson, "'Liberty and Union': An Analysis of Three Concepts Involved in the Nullification Controversy," *JSH* 33 (1967), 331–55; Irving Bartlett, *Daniel Webster* (New York, 1978).

25. For example, see *Petigru*, esp. 87–129; Wilson, "Liberty and Union"; Freehling, 159–73; and *Calhoun Papers* XI, xxxiii–xxxix.

26. *Petigru*, 92.

27. *Petigru*, 384–85; *Calhoun Papers*, X and XI *passim*. In his introductions to volumes X, XI, and XII of the *Calhoun Papers*, Clyde N. Wilson has produced a thorough and persuasive reassessment of the nullification crisis and of Calhoun's role in it. Wilson insists that nullification was part of an ongoing struggle to determine which of several strains of republicanism would control the American experiment in self-government and that state interposition should be interpreted as a response to ideological and constitutional debates dating back to at least 1798, rather than as a frightened, knee-jerk reaction of a guilt-ridden slaveocracy to the Denmark Vesey and Nat Turner slave insurrections.

28. *Petigru*, 91–96. Kenneth M. Stampp, "The Concept of a Perpetual Union," *JAH* 65 (1978): 5–33, has maintained that at the time of the nullification crisis, the arguments for a perpetual Union were far less sophisticated, and more reliant on emotion, than were the cases for nullification and peaceful secession. For a complete assessment of the varying responses of South Carolina Federalists to nullification, see George C. Rogers, Jr., "South Carolina Federalists and the Origins of the Nullification Movement," *SCHM* 71 (1970): 17–32; and William H. Denny, "South Carolina's Conception of the Union in 1832," *SCHM* 78 (1979): 171–83.

29. *Petigru, passim*.

30. *Ibid.*, 347.

31. *Ibid.*, 180.

32. Freehling, 137–76; *Petigru*, 91.

33. Petigru to William John Grayson, 1830, in *Petigru*, 79–80.

34. Petigru to William Elliott, 25 August 1831, in *Petigru*, 83–84; Lewis P. Jones, "William Elliott: South Carolina Non-conformist," *JSH* 17 (1951): 361–81.

35. Charleston *Courier*, 13 December 1830.

36. For a more complete analysis of factional alignments during the nullification crisis, see ch. 3 of my dissertation, now completed at the University of South Carolina. See also Clyde Wilson's summary in *Calhoun Papers*, XIV, xviii–xxiv; and Freehling, 219–60.

37. Bass, "William John Grayson," 168–69. On the superior talent of the Nullifiers in the area of campaign forensics, see James Brewer Stewart, "'A Great Talking and Eating Machine': Patriarchy, Mobilization and the Dynamics of Nullification in South Carolina," *Civil War History* 37 (1981): 197–200.

38. Freehling, 235–44.

39. Petigru to William Elliott, 20 September 1832, in *Petigru*, 96–97.

40. Petigru to Hugh Swinton Legaré, 15 July 1833, in *Petigru*, 123–25.

41. Freehling, 306–23; Petigru to Hugh Swinton Legaré, 15 December 1834, in *Petigru*, 167–71.

42. *Petigru*, 172–73; George C. Rogers, Jr., "Henry Laurens Pinckney—Thoughts on His Career," in James B. Meriwether, ed., *South Carolina Journals and Journalists* (Spartanburg, S.C., 1975), 163–76. For more on the campaign to oust Pinckney, see ch. 4 of my dissertation.

43. For a survey of Petigru's position on banks, see Campbell, "Petigru," 102–42.

44. George McDuffie to John C. Calhoun, 29 October 1837 in *Calhoun Papers*, XIII, 631–35; Charles M. Wiltse, *John C. Calhoun, Nullifier* (Indianapolis, Ind., 1949), 343–410; Ernest M. Lander, "The Calhoun-Preston Feud, 1836–1842," *SCHM* 59 (1958): 24–36; John S. Coussins, "Thirty Years with Rhett, Calhoun, and the Charleston *Mercury*: A Chapter in South Carolina Politics" (Ph.D. diss., Louisiana State University, 1971), 77–112.

45. *Petigru*, 191.

46. *Ibid.*, 193; *Calhoun Papers*, XIV, *passim*; Marvin R. Cain, "Return of Republicanism: A Reappraisal of Hugh Swinton Legaré and the Tyler Presidency," *SCHM* 79 (1978): 264–80.

47. For an excellent summary of Whig attitudes and intentions, see Daniel Walker Howe, *The Political Culture of the American Whigs* (Chicago, 1979).

48. *Petigru*, 237.

49. Petigru to Jane Petigru North, 12 June 1848, in *Petigru*, 265; Jon Wakelyn, "Party Issues and Political Strategy of the Charleston Taylor Democrats of 1848," *SCHM* 73 (1972): 72–86.

50. Petigru to Hugh S. Legaré, 31 May 1835, in *Petigru*, 173–76.

51. William H. Russell, *My Diary North and South* (New York, 1863), 56–58.

52. Petigru to Benjamin F. Perry, 8 December 1860, quoted in Campbell, "Petigru," 146.

53. Campbell, "Petigru," 27–42.

54. Charles M. Cook, *The American Codification Movement: A Study of Antebellum Legal Reform* (Westport, Conn., 1981), 23–68. For a broader survey of legal reform in nineteenth-century America, see Morton J. Horwitz, *The Transformation of American Law* (Cambridge, Mass., 1977); Roscoe Pound, *The Formative Era of American Law* (Boston, 1938); and Maxwell Bloomfield, "Lawyers and Public Criticism: Challenge and Response in Nineteenth Century America," *American Journal of Legal History* 15 (1971): 269–77.

55. For an excellent survey of antebellum legal thought in South Carolina, and an especially fine analysis of the legal reform movement, see Senese, "Legal Thought in South Carolina, 1800–1860."

56. Senese, "Legal Thought in South Carolina," 116–226.

57. Donald J. Senese, "Building the Pyramid: The Growth and Development of the State Court System in Antebellum South Carolina, 1800–1860," *South Carolina Law Review* 24 (1972): 357–79. The equity system did undergo a significant reorganization in 1824. One court of appeals, a three-judge panel, was established to handle all equity and common law appeals, and the number of equity chancellors was reduced. Legal reformers, however, were not satisfied and continued to call for thoroughgoing reforms.

58. William S. Holdsworth, *Charles Dickens as a Legal Historian* (New Haven, Conn., 1928), 79–112; Thomas Cooper, "Bentham's *Judicial Evidence*," *SR* 5 (1830): 381–426.

59. See Cook, *American Codification Movement*, 121–31; "The Judiciary System of South Carolina," *SQR* 2 (1850): 464–86.

60. Governor John Lyde Wilson, Message no. 1, 22 November 1824, SCSA.

61. Cooper, "Bentham's *Judicial Evidence*," 422.

62. Petigru, "Court of Chancery," *SR* 3 (1829): 63–77.

63. *Ibid.*, 66.

64. Between 1810 and 1830, DeSaussure wrote nearly half of the more than 2,000 decrees and opinions delivered by equity courts in South Carolina, and in the Charleston Court of Appeals, he delivered 185 out of 320 decisions: Senese, "Building the Pyramid," 363–64.

65. Petigru, "Court of Chancery," 64–65.

66. *Ibid.*, 68–77.

67. Cooper, "Bentham's *Judicial Evidence*," 425.

68. Senese, "Legal Thought in South Carolina," 164–66.

69. See Cook, *American Codification Movement*, 121–53; Senese, "Legal Thought in South Carolina," 167–226.

70. Thomas Cooper to William Sampson, 24 March 1824, Thomas Cooper Papers, SCL.

71. Hugh Swinton Legaré, "Codification," *SR* 8 (1831): 391–412.

72. Cook, *American Codification Movement*, 96–121.

73. John Lyde Wilson, *Codification* (New York, 1827), 25.

74. Senese, "Legal Thought in South Carolina," 398–400.

75. Petigru to Jane Petigru North, 29 October 1860, in *Petigru*, 360.

76. *Report of Certain Members of the Commission on Petigru's Code of the Statute Law of South Carolina* (Columbia, S.C., 1864).

77. Senese, "Legal Thought in South Carolina," 402–3.

78. Petigru to Jane Petigru North, 2 April 1844, in *Petigru*, 238.

79. Campbell, "Petigru," 175–81.

80. Petigru, "Oration Delivered before the Charleston Library Society," 13 June 1848, in *Petigru*, 266–73.

81. *Petigru*, 318; Campbell, "Petigru," 181–83; "Memoir of Professor F.A. Porcher," *Historical Society of South Carolina Papers* (Charleston, S.C., 1889), 1–6.

82. Fronde Kennedy, "Russell's Magazine," *South Atlantic Quarterly* 28 (1919): 125–44; Richard J. Calhoun, "The Antebellum Literary Twilight: *Russell's Magazine*," *Southern Literary Journal* 3 (1970): 89–110; Alton Taylor Loftis, "A Study of *Russell's Magazine*: Ante-Bellum Charleston's Last Literary Periodical" (Ph.D. diss., Duke University, 1973). For brief sketches of Miles, Porcher, and Gildersleeve, see *All Clever Men*, 263–66, 310–12, 398–400; and for reminiscences of Fraser, Dickson, Moultrie, Smyth, and Lynch, see Samuel G. Stoney, ed., "Memoirs of Frederick Adolphus Porcher," *SCHM* 47 (1946): 214–27.

83. Paul Hamilton Hayne, "Ante Bellum Charleston," *Southern Bivouac* 1 (1885): 327–36; Calhoun, "Antebellum Literary Twilight," 89–109.

84. Petigru to Hugh S. Legaré, 6 September 1836, in *Petigru*, 184–85.

85. Petigru to Susan Petigru King, 11 September 1848, *ibid.*, 274–75.

86. Petigru to William Elliott, 14 November 1831, *ibid.*, 85–86.

87. Campbell, "Petigru," 194–235; Bass, "William John Grayson," 249–64. For a study of romanticism among Petigru's contemporaries, see Michael O'Brien's essay on Legaré, *supra*.

88. Campbell, "Petigru," 143–93.

89. Petigru, "Oration Delivered on the Third Anniversary of the South Carolina Historical Society," 27 May 1858, in *Petigru*, 326–37.

90. *Ibid.*, 335–36.

91. *Ibid.*, 336.

92. *Ibid.*, 336–37.

93. *Ibid.*, 337. The most recent study of the Lost Cause is Charles Reagan Wilson, *Baptized in Blood: The Religion of the Lost Cause, 1865–1920* (Athens, Ga., 1980).

94. Quoted in Lillian Kibler, *Benjamin F. Perry: South Carolina Unionist* (Durham, N.C., 1946), 243.

95. *Petigru*, 284–86.

96. Harold S. Schultz, *Nationalism and Sectionalism in South Carolina 1852–1860* (Durham, N.C., 1950); Steven A. Channing, *Crisis of Fear: Secession in South Carolina* (New York, 1970).

97. *Petigru*, 361.

98. This famous statement was printed, in slightly different forms, in newspapers throughout South Carolina after the Civil War and has become part of the state's oral historical tradition. See also Edwards, *The Man Who Said No*, 164.

99. *Petigru*, 379–85; Clyde N. Wilson, Jr., "Carolina Cavalier: The Life of James Johnston Pettigrew" (Ph.D. diss., University of North Carolina, 1971). On the Rhett family, see Laura A. White, *Robert Barnwell Rhett: Father of Secession* (Gloucester, Mass., 1965).

100. *Petigru*, 384–85.

101. *Ibid.*, esp. 379–461.

102. Petigru to J. Johnston Pettigrew, *Petigru*, 459.

103. Grayson, *Petigru*, 256–62.

104. The use of the terms "lion" and "fox" to designate two different types of political leaders originated with the great economic theoretician, Vilfredo Pareto: See Pareto, *The Mind and Society*, trans. A. Livingston (New York, 1935), 1788–95.

105. See Wilson's introduction in *Calhoun Papers*, XIII, xvi–xviii.

106. *Chesnut*, 365–66.

107. Fredrickson, *The Inner Civil War*, 10–11.

108. The most complete, and properly qualified, statement of this position can be found in Eric Foner, *Politics and Ideology in the Age of Civil War* (New York, 1980), esp. 15–33. See also Richard D. Brown, *Modernization: The Transformation of American Life, 1600–1865* (New York, 1976). An excellent survey of the recent literature and evaluation of the usefulness of the modernization paradigm is Michael O'Brien, "The Nineteenth-Century American South," *The Historical Journal* 24 (1981): 751–63.

109. See especially Robert J. Brugger, "The Mind of the Old South: New Views," *Virginia Quarterly Review* 56 (1980): 277–95.

110. Bertram Wyatt-Brown, "Stanley Elkin's *Slavery*: The Anti-Slavery Interpretation Reexamined," *American Quarterly* 25 (1973): 154–76.

111. David Herbert Donald, "The Pro-Slavery Argument Reconsidered," *JSH* 37 (1971): 3–18.

112. Drew Faust, *A Sacred Circle: The Dilemma of the Intellectual in the Old South, 1840–1860* (Baltimore, Md., 1977); David Roberts, *Paternalism in Early Victorian England* (New Brunswick, N.J., 1979).

113. John McCardell, *The Idea of a Southern Nation: Southern Nationalists and Southern Nationalism, 1830–1860* (New York, 1979) provides a thorough survey of the emergence of Southern nationalism and a balanced assessment of its romantic and visionary aspects.

114. This suggestion has also been made in Foner, *Politics and Ideology*, 1–10; and Daniel Walker Howe, "Virtue and Commerce in Jeffersonian America," *Reviews in American History* 9 (1981): 347–53.

115. The standard account of the tensions arising from the rapid social and economic changes of the Jacksonian era is Marvin Meyers, *The Jacksonian Persuasion: Politics and Belief* (Stanford, Calif., 1968). The idea that the Civil War was a product of the imperatives of Jacksonian ideology and of the frantic pace of change during that era is one of the many provocative insights in J. Mills Thorton III, *Politics and Power in a Slave Society: Alabama, 1800–1860* (Baton Rouge, La., 1978), 365–461.

6. *William Gilmore Simms:* McCARDELL

1. William Peterfield Trent, *William Gilmore Simms* (Boston, 1892), 37, relentlessly stresses the debilitating influence of Charleston (and South Carolina) upon intellectual life. Variations on this theme appear in most subsequent major treatments of Simms, including Vernon L. Parrington, *The Romantic Revolution in America, 1800–1860* (New York, 1927), 119–30; Jay B. Hubbell, *The South in American Literature, 1607–1900* (Durham, N.C., 1954), 572–601; William R. Taylor, *Cavalier and Yankee: The Old South and American National Character* (New York, 1957), 268–97; more subtly in J.V. Ridgely, *William Gilmore Simms* (New York, 1962), cf. 45; and with an emphasis on Simms' political ambitions and frustrations in Jon L. Wakelyn, *The Politics of a Literary Man* (Westport, Conn., 1973). See also Larzer Ziff, *Literary Democracy: The Declaration of Cultural Independence in America* (New York, 1981), 181–82, whose judgment is based on Hubbell. The laudatory review of Ziff appeared in the New York *Times*, 23 August 1981. For modest revisionism on Trent, see A.S. Salley, "Biographical Sketch," in *Simms Letters*, I, lix–lxxxix; Thomas L. Mc-

Haney, "William Gilmore Simms," in Matthew J. Bruccoli, ed., *The Chief Glory of Every People* (Carbondale, Ill., 1973), 173–90; Keen Butterworth, "William Gilmore Simms," in Joel Myerson, ed., *Antebellum Writers in New York and the South* (Detroit, 1979), 306–18.

2. The story of the writing of Trent's *Simms* has never been fully told. The best unpublished account is Franklin T. Walker, "W.P. Trent: A Critical Biography" (Ph.D. diss., George Peabody College, 1943), ch. 6.

3. William Gilmore Simms, "Skeleton Essays," *Snowden's Ladies' Companion* 15 (1841): 110.

4. Trent, *Simms*, 1–11; Simms to James Lawson, 29 December 1839, in *Simms Letters*, I, 159–67.

5. Trent, *Simms*; Mary C. Simms Oliphant, "William Gilmore Simms – Historical Artist," *University of South Carolina South Caroliniana Society: Report of the Secretary and Treasurer for 1942* (Columbia, S.C., 1943), 16–29.

6. Simms, *History of South Carolina* (Charleston, S.C., 1840), 319.

7. Simms, "The Spirit of Emigration," *Southern Literary Journal* 1 (1835–36): 269.

8. Simms to Lawson, *Simms Letters*, I, 161.

9. *Simms Letters*, III, 73, 79–81, 86, 276–84.

10. The best recent treatment of Simms' romanticism and his relationship with other Southern intellectuals is Drew Gilpin Faust, *A Sacred Circle: The Dilemma of the Intellectual in the Old South, 1840–1860* (Baltimore, Md., 1977).

11. James E. Kibler, comp., *The Poetry of William Gilmore Simms: An Introduction and Bibliography* (Columbia, S.C., 1979), 33–34; Simms to Charles Stoddard, 24 October 1866, *Simms Letters*, IV, 616.

12. Simms, "The Writings of Washington Allston," *SQR* 4 (1843): 381.

13. Simms to George Frederick Holmes, 27 October 1843, *Simms Letters*, I, 378; Simms to Robert Shelton MacKenzie, 8 January 1854, *Simms Letters*, III, 275.

14. Simms, "Writings of Allston," *SQR* 4 (1843): 390.

15. *Ibid.*

16. Simms to Stoddard, *Simms Letters*, IV, 616.

17. Simms, "Writings of Allston," 390.

18. Simms, "Modern Prose Fiction," *SQR* 15 (1849): 48, 57.

19. Simms, "A New Spirit of the Age," *SQR* 7 (1845): 314.

20. Simms to Sarah Lawrence Drew Griffin, 8 June 1841, *Simms Letters*, VI, 27.

21. See, for example, Parrington, *Romantic Revolution*, 119–30. Simms criticism is helpfully catalogued in Keen Butterworth and James E. Kibler, Jr., eds., *William Gilmore Simms: A Reference Guide* (Boston, 1980).

22. William Charvat, *Literary Publishing in America, 1790–1850* (Philadelphia, 1959), 23–35.

23. Simms to James Henry Hammond, 24 December 1847, *Simms Letters*, II, 385–86.

24. Simms, "A New Spirit of the Age," 321.

25. John Paul Pritchard, *Literary Wise Men of Gotham: Criticism in New York, 1815–1860* (Baton Rouge, La., 1963), 14ff.

26. John Stafford, *The Literary Criticism of "Young America": A Study in the Relationship of Politics and Literature, 1837–1850* (Berkeley, Calif., 1952), 9–10. See also Perry Miller, *The Raven and the Whale: The War of Words and Wits in the Era of Poe and Melville* (New York, 1956), passim.

27. Quoted in Pritchard, *Literary Wise Men*, 21.

28. Stafford, *Criticism of "Young America"*, 10.

29. Miller, *The Raven and the Whale*, 105–7, 180–81.

30. Simms, *The Wigwam and the Cabin*, Redfield ed. (New York, 1882), 4; Hubbell, *South in Literature*, 450; David Donald, *Lincoln Reconsidered* (New York, 1956), 174.

31. *Southern Literary Journal* 1 (1835–36): 347–58; ibid., n.s., 4 (1838): 332–49.

32. *SQR* 4 (1843): 247–49.

33. *Mercury*, 18 July 1840.

34. Donald, *Lincoln Reconsidered*, 175–76.

35. Simms, "The Southern Convention," *SQR* 17 (1850): 195.

36. *Southern Literary Journal*, n.s., 4 (1838): 297.

37. Simms, *The Charleston Book: A Miscellany in Prose and Verse* (Charleston, 1845), iii.

38. New York *Morning News*, 14 November 1844. The Charleston *Southern Patriot*, 2 January 1845, noted briefly, however: "This elegant work reflects the highest credit upon the intellectual talent of our City."

39. Simms to Evert Augustus Duyckinck, 15 November 1844, *Simms Letters*, I, 439.

40. Simms to Holmes, 18 November 1844, *ibid.*, I, 442.

41. *Southern Literary Messenger* 11 (1845): 761–62.

42. John R. Welsh, "William Gilmore Simms, Critic of the South," *JSH* 26 (1960): 201–14.

43. Simms, "A Passage with the Veteran Quarterly," *Southern and Western Magazine* 1 (1845): 309.

44. [Simms], "Editorial Bureau," *ibid.* 2 (1845): 61.

45. Simms, "A Passage," *ibid.* 1 (1845): 300.

46. Simms, "The Moral Character of Hamlet," *Orion* 4 (1844): 45.

47. Simms, "Our Agricultural Condition," *Southern and Western Magazine* 1 (1845): 74, 83–84.

48. Simms, "A Passage," *ibid.* 1 (1845): 309.

49. Simms, "The Good Farmer," *Snowden's* 15 (1841): 156.

50. Simms, "The Ages of Gold and Iron; From an Agricultural Oration," *ibid.*, 12.

51. *Ibid.*, 13.

52. Simms, *The Social Principle: The True Source of National Permanence* (Tuscaloosa, Ala., 1843), 36.

53. [Simms], "Editorial Bureau," *Southern and Western Magazine* 2 (1845): 344.

54. Simms, *The Social Principle*, 36.

55. Charleston *Southern Patriot*, 10 October 1845.

56. Simms, "The Epochs and Events of American History, as Suited to the Purposes of Art in Fiction," *Southern and Western Magazine* 1 (1845): 183.

57. Simms to George Frederick Holmes, 27 October 1843, *Simms Letters*, I, 379. For discussions of trends and genres in American historical writing, see Michael Kammen, *A Season of Youth: The American Revolution and the Historical Imagination* (New York, 1978), *passim*, but esp. chs. 4 and 5. For a discussion of these issues in Charleston, see Rogers I, 150–55.

58. Greene, Marion, and Smith had all been the subjects of biographies before Simms' offerings appeared. See Kammen, *Season of Youth*, 42, 52, 81–82.

59. Simms, *Life of the Chevalier Bayard* (New York, 1847), 6; Simms, *Life of Nathanael Greene* (New York, 1849), 12–15; Simms, *Life of Francis Marion* (New York, 1844), 30–31.

60. Simms, *Life of Bayard*, 8.

61. Simms, *Life of Captain John Smith* (New York, 1846), 14, 19, 21, 123, 127.

62. Butterworth and Kibler, eds., *Simms*, 71.

63. Hammond to Simms, 20 June 1848, James Henry Hammond Papers, LC.

64. [Simms], "The Struggle of Endowment with Fortune," *Democratic Review* 20 (1847): 535.

65. Simms, *Charleston and Her Satirists* (Charleston, S.C., 1848), 11.

66. Simms, *Father Abbot, or, The Home Tourist* (Charleston, S.C., 1849), 101.

67. Simms to Hammond, 5 September 1849, *Simms Letters*, II, 548–49.

68. Simms, *Father Abbot*, 160, 48, 22.

69. *Ibid.*, 25–26, 48.

70. *Ibid.*, 182.

71. *Ibid.*, 145–47, 183.

72. *Ibid.*, 186.

73. *Ibid.*, 97, 102–3, 186.

74. *Mercury*, 12 January 1854.

75. *Simms Letters*, IV, 186n.

76. *Ibid.*, III, 549.

77. Trent, *Simms*, 321; Simms, *Father Abbot*, 169–71.

7. *Christopher G. Memminger:* JORDAN

1. See Robert R. Palmer, *The Age of Democratic Revolution* (New York, 1959); E.J. Hobsbawm, *The Age of Revolution, 1789–1848* (New York, 1962); C.E. Black, *The Dynamics of Modernization* (New York, 1967).

2. Ralph Waldo Emerson, quoted in C.S. Griffin, *The Ferment of Reform* (Arlington Heights, Ill., 1967), 1–2.

3. It was a syndrome embodied in acts of the South Carolina legislature in 1822 and subsequent years, which, as a hedge against servile insurrection, provided for the confinement of black sailors while their vessels were in the state's ports. A federal judge and attorney-general declared the acts illegal, and in 1844 Judge Samuel Hoar debarked at Charleston with a commission from Massachusetts to bring suit in federal court in Columbia on behalf of several Negro citizens of Massachusetts. After spirited debate, the state legislature resolved that Hoar had come "with the sole purpose of subverting our internal peace" and authorized his expulsion. A single member of the House of Delegates, C.G. Memminger, cast against the resolution. Matched by a single "nay" in the Senate, Memminger's negative was due to a personal sense of justice and constitutional scruple – the expulsion resolution was a legislative usurpation of judicial powers – but must be viewed as well in the context of his longtime opposition to the Negro Seamen Acts as unnecessarily severe and tending to bring South Carolina into disrepute abroad, to heap coals on the fires of abolitionism, and to discourage the sea commerce that was his home district's lifeblood. The episode is treated in Henry D. Capers, *Life and Times of C.G. Memminger* (Richmond, Va., 1893), 188–91.

4. C. Vann Woodward, *The Burden of Southern History* (New York, 1961), 21.

5. John Hope Franklin, *From Slavery to Freedom*, quoted in Griffin, *Ferment of Reform*, 27. See also W.R. Taylor, *Cavalier and Yankee: The Old South and American National Character* (New York, 1961).

6. Quotation, Christopher Silver, "A New Look at Old South Urbanization: The Irish Worker in Charleston, South Carolina, 1840–1860," *South Atlantic Urban Studies* 3 (1979): 152–53. See also Ernest M. Lander, Jr., "Charleston: Manufacturing Center of the Old South," *JSH* 26 (1960): 330–51; Raimondo Luraghi, "The Civil War and Modernization of American Society: Social Structure and Industrial Revolution in the Old South before and during the Civil War," *Civil War History* 18 (1972): 230–50.

7. Frances Ann Kemble, *Journal of a Residence on a Georgia Plantation in 1838–1839* (Chicago, 1969 [1864]), 302.

8. Clement Eaton, *The Growth of Southern Civilization* (New York, 1961), 247.

9. See *Mercury*, 13 May 1858. Cf. Michael P. Johnson, *Toward a Patriarchal Republic: The Secession of Georgia* (Baton Rouge, La., 1977), 40.

10. David Potter, *The South and the Sectional Conflict* (Baton Rouge, La., 1968), 30. Cf. Raymond Aron, *Progress and Illusion: The Dialectics of Modern Society* (New York, 1968); Daniel Boorstin, *The Republic of Technology* (New York, 1970).

11. Rogers I, 158–59.

12. John McCardell, *The Idea of a Southern Nation: Southern Nationalists and Southern Nationalism, 1830–1860* (New York, 1979), 103.

13. New York *Tribune*, 1854, quoted in Herbert Wender, *Southern Commercial Connections, 1837–1859* (Baltimore, Md., 1930), 116.

14. See, e.g., Allan McFarlane to William P. Miles, 4 February 1858, Miles Papers, SHC. Clin-

ton Rossiter recently identified political efficacy, social cohesion, self-identity, affluence, and cultural achievement as the "classic" goals of modern state-builders: see Rossiter, *The American Quest, 1790–1860* (New York, 1971). Cf. Chinese reformers of the late nineteenth century who tried to revitalize ancient China—so that it might thrive in a world dominated by socially, economically, and politically evolved Western nations—by adapting certain aspects of materially superior Occidental culture such as machine technology, to the end of enriching and yet conserving Chinese traditional culture according to the formula "Chinese learning for the basis; western learning for practical use." See Joseph R. Levenson, *Liang Ch'i-chao and the Mind of Modern China* (Cambridge, Mass., 1953); Mary S. Wright, *The Last Stand of Chinese Conservativism* (New York, 1966), 1 and *passim*.

15. Capers, *Memminger*, ch. 1 and *passim*; Ralph Wooster, "Membership of the South Carolina Secession Convention," *SCHM* 55 (1954): 189–92; Samuel G. Stoney, ed., "Memoirs of Frederick Adolphus Porcher," *SCHM* 47 (1946), 214 (quotation); John A. Wagener, "Christopher Gustav Memminger," *Der Deutsche Pionier* 7 (1875).

16. Since the final proof of belief is practice, what follows has almost as much to do with Memminger's actions as his ideas. I have not tried to weigh precisely the influence of interest and ambition on attitudes. I assume that personal and class interests and convictions mutually influence one another, but also that mind is never a simple deduction from social life, that "no sure correlation exists between condition and attitude": Edwin M. Yoder, Jr., Foreword, in John Shelton Reed, *The Enduring South* (Chapel Hill, N.C., 1972), xvi. Cf. Michael O'Brien, "The Nineteenth-Century American South," *The Historical Journal* 24 (1981): 751–63.

17. Montgomery (Ala.) *Advertiser-Journal*, 19 February 1961, clipping in Memminger Papers, SHC.

18. J. Douglas Holladay, "Nineteenth Century Evangelical Activism: From Private Charity to State Intervention, 1830–1850," *Historical Magazine of the Protestant Episcopal Church* 51 (1982): 53–79; Albert S. Thomas, *A Historical Account of the Protestant Episcopal Church in South Carolina* (Columbia, S.C., 1957), 241–42 and *passim*; Harriott Horry Rutledge Ravenel, *Charleston: The Place and the People* (New York, 1912), 440–42. Cf. Paul E. Johnson, *A Shopkeeper's Millennium: Society and Revivals in Rochester, New York, 1815–1837* (New York, 1978); R. Langbaum, ed., *The Victorian Age* (Greenwich, Conn., 1967).

19. Capers, *Memminger*, 18.

20. "The Book of Nullification" (1832), appendix in Capers, *Memminger*.

21. R.W. Memminger, *What Is Religion?* (Philadelphia, 1872); Capers, *Memminger*, 25, 33, 405, 508, 546–47; Thomas, *Protestant Episcopal Church*, 440–42.

22. Memminger, *An Oration on the Bible as a Key to the Events of Sacred and Profane History* (Columbia, S.C., 1842).

23. Memminger address on the opening of Girls' High and Normal School, Charleston *Daily Courier*, 24 May 1859. See also *The Duty of Combining Religious Instruction with Every System of Education—A Sermon Preached before the Convention of the Protestant Episcopal Church in the Diocese of South Carolina February 11, 1841 by Thomas J. Young* (Charleston, S.C., 1841): C.G. Memminger was listed among lay subscribers to the costs of publication.

24. *An Oration on the Bible*, 23–25; *An Address before the Assembled Authorities of the State of Virginia* (Richmond, Va., 1860), 42; *A Speech on the Bill to Afford Aid to the Blue Ridge Railroad* (Charleston, S.C., 1859), 26.

25. This effort to reconcile spiritualism and materialism, religion and science, this stance of fatalistic optimism, this belief in God's omnipotence combined with hope in human striving, was not at all unusual and indeed was a common mode of thought throughout the nineteenth-century West. For the United States, see Sacvan Bercovitch, *The American Jeremiad* (Madison, Wis., 1978); Rush Welter, *The Mind of America, 1820–1860* (New York, 1975); and Michael Kammen, *People of Paradox* (New York, 1972). Compare Agassiz, who described his classification of

animals as an effort to understand an order in the universe which is already there, the work of "the Almighty Intellect," or God: Guy Davenport, ed., *The Intelligence of Louis Agassiz* (Boston, 1963), ix.

26. Bernard Bailyn, *The Ideological Origins of the American Revolution* (Cambridge, Mass., 1967); Gordon S. Wood, *The Creation of the American Republic, 1776–1787* (Chapel Hill, N.C., 1969).

27. Fred Somkin, *Unquiet Eagle: Memory and Desire in the Idea of America, 1820–1860* (Ithaca, N.Y., 1967), 137 and ch. 4; Fletcher M. Green, *The Role of the Yankee in the Old South* (Athens, Ga., 1972), 42; R. Nicholas Olsberg, "William Henry Trescot: The Crisis of 1860" (M.A. thesis, University of South Carolina, 1967), 18 and *passim*; Capers, *Memminger*, 493–500.

28. "On Immortality of the Soul," an oration before the Clariosophic Society, South Carolina College (1819), appendix in Capers, *Memminger*, 497–98. For a discussion of the Enlightenment, see Henry Steele Commager, *The Empire of Reason* (Garden City, N.Y., 1978), xi, xii, 16–42, 256–66.

29. For a discussion of Common Sense in America, see Henry F. May, *The Enlightenment in America* (New York, 1976), 121 (quotation), 337–62; Cynthia E. Russett, *Darwin in America* (San Francisco, 1976), 2–4. Cf. Drew Gilpin Faust, *A Sacred Circle: The Dilemma of the Intellectual in the Old South, 1840–1860* (Baltimore, Md., 1977), 51–52 and *passim*.

30. "Immortality of the Soul," in Capers, *Memminger*, 498–99.

31. Pauline Maier, *The Old Revolutionaries: Political Lives in the Age of Samuel Adams* (New York, 1982), 50.

32. "On the Influence of Public Opinion" (1819), appendix in Capers, *Memminger*, 503. Cf. Memminger as follows: "Posterity ask not what a man was. . . . They demand what hath he done?" "Eulogy on President [Jonathan] Maxcy [of South Carolina College]" (1819), appendix in Capers, *Memminger*, 506.

33. "The Art of Printing" (1818), appendix in Capers, *Memminger*, 493; *Minutes of the Commissioners of Free Schools for the Parishes of St. Philip's and St. Michael's*, 22 January 1855 (MS in the City of Charleston Archives).

34. See Rollin G. Osterweis, *Romanticism and Nationalism in the Old South* (New Haven, Conn., 1949); Raimondo Luraghi, *The Rise and Fall of the Plantation South* (New York, 1978); and the more discriminating Faust, *A Sacred Circle*, 19–50.

35. Memminger to Mary Wilkinson Memminger, 21 and 23 August, 5 and 25 September, 2 and 5 October 1854, Memminger Papers, SHC.

36. Iredell Jenkins, "Romanticism," in Dagobert D. Runes, ed., *Dictionary of Philosophy* (New York, 1960), 272.

37. Poem included in Memminger's *Address before the Assembled Authorities of the State of Virginia*, 43. Memminger's associates agreed: he was neither idealistic nor sentimental. Rather, he exhibited prudential values that could have come from the lexicon of Benjamin Franklin, or Jeremy Bentham: he took "a practical view of Life"; had a mind "eminently logical"; indeed, was thought by some to be "devoid of sentiment." Capers, *Memminger*, 25, 183–85; M.C. Kneece, *The Contributions of C.G. Memminger to the Cause of Education* (Columbia, S.C., 1956), 10.

38. See Anthony D. Smith, *Theories of Nationalism* (New York, 1971), 15–20, esp. 16.

39. See George Dangerfield, *The Awakening of American Nationalism, 1815–1828* (New York, 1965), 1–4 and *passim*.

40. For the general context, see James Oakes, *The Ruling Race: A History of American Slaveholders* (New York, 1982), 28–33, 225, 226, 239–42. For expressions of Memminger's personal feelings, see his *Address before the Assembled Authorities of the State of Virginia*, *passim*, esp. 43; and his earlier *Speech at a Public Meeting of the Friends of Cooperation in the Cause of Southern Rights* (Charleston, S.C., 1851), 18, 21.

41. The nationalism of the Founders corresponds rather well with what Anthony Smith has isolated as the core doctrine of nationalism, the nationalism of the Enlightenment. The nation

is "a brotherhood born of those who have grown and suffered together." There is little presumption of indelibility—the sense of community, derived from immediate circumstances, might unravel if circumstances change. The relationship of general and particular wills is presumed to be direct and the relationship among nations to be supportive and complementary, a larger brotherhood. Smith, *Theories of Nationalism*, 15, 23, and *passim*.

42. "On the 'Love of Country'" (1817), appendix in Capers, *Memminger*, 491–92. See also the fragment of another essay written in July 1815, in Memminger Papers, SHC; and Memminger's *Speech upon the Bill and Resolutions Relating to Bank Issues and Suspensions* (Charleston, S.C., 1858), 30.

43. Some of Memminger's closest associates and fellow spirits among Charlestonians were born in the Northeast: the Reverend John Bachman was a native of New York; merchant Henry Gourdin and lawyer James B. Campbell were natives of New England. "Memoirs of Frederick Adolphus Porcher," 219; Merle Curti, *The Social Ideas of American Educators* (New York, 1935), 141n, 148–49; Virginius Dabney, *Liberalism in the South* (New York, 1970), 231.

44. Cf. Pauline Maier, "The Road Not Taken: Nullification, John C. Calhoun and the Revolutionary Tradition in South Carolina," *SCHM* 82 (1981): 1–19.

45. Wood, *Creation of the American Republic*, esp. ch. 2.

46. *Speech at a Public Meeting of the Friends of Cooperation*, 11, 21–22; also see Memminger's *Speech on the Bill to Afford Aid to the Blue Ridge Railroad* (Charleston, S.C., 1859); Letter to the Editor (D.K. Whitaker), *Mercury*, 8 March 1850; and *Courier*, 8 December 1854.

47. *Speech on the Question of Rechartering the Bank of the State of South Carolina* (Columbia, S.C., 1849), 4, 7–10, 13–14, 19, 22–25.

48. Bray Hammond, *Banks and Politics in America: From the Revolution to the Civil War* (Princeton, N.J., 1957), 328–29 and *passim*. Also see James R. Sharp, *The Jacksonians versus the Banks* (New York, 1970), viii, 277–79; Ernest R. Lander, Jr., "The Calhoun-Preston Feud, 1836–1842," *SCHM* 59 (1958): 28–29, 37.

49. See Oakes, *The Ruling Race*, 6–7.

50. This "modern" view of the state is implicit in his political career. See Kneece, *Memminger*, 15–17; and Memminger's *Speech on the Blue Ridge Railroad* (1859), 3–4.

51. "The Influence of Public Opinion" (1819), appendix in Capers, *Memminger*, 502; "The Art of Printing" (1818), *ibid.*, 493–97; "Oration on the Bible" (1842), *ibid.*, 533; *Courier*, 24 May 1859; and *Address before the State of Virginia* (1860), 24, 38–39.

52. Merrill D. Peterson, *Thomas Jefferson and the New Nation* (New York, 1970), 259–64.

53. David Duncan Wallace, *South Carolina: A Short History* (Columbia, S.C., 1961), 385.

54. See Richard N. Current, *John C. Calhoun* (New York, 1963), 19–20; George M. Fredrickson, *The Black Image in the White Mind* (New York, 1971), 47. Cf. John E. Fisher, "'On Slavery': The Congressional Debate of 1790," *The Annual Collection of Essays in History* 12 (1966–67) [University of Virginia]: 26–41.

55. *Address before the State of Virginia* (1860), 24.

56. Silver, "A New Look at Old South Urbanization," 146; L.W. Jordan, "Police Power and Public Safety in Antebellum Charleston: The Emergence of a New Police 1800–1860," *South Atlantic Urban Studies* 3 (1979): 123–25, 135n; Leonard P. Curry, *The Free Black in Urban America, 1800–1850* (Chicago, 1981), 34–35, 47, 59–60.

57. Quoted in Robert Starobin, *Industrial Slavery in the Old South* (New York, 1970), 9, 193, 199.

58. Eugene Genovese, *The Political Economy of Slavery* (New York, 1967), 232–34; William L. Barney, *The Road to Secession* (New York, 1972), 37–39. The particular approach anticipates the reactionary position of postbellum Southern advocates of what Barrington Moore and Jonathan A. Wiener have called the "Prussian Road" to economic social development: the achievement of wealth and power, individual and collective, by maintaining traditional technologies and social relations—master and slave, "aristocrat" and "poor white"—particularly squeezing more pro-

ductivity out of unfree blacks, chattel and tenant, and repressing "poor whites" into a marginal and subordinate economic, social, and political niche. The more progressive approach outlined in the next paragraph would also have advocates later, in the ideology of the New South Creed. Moore, *Social Origins of Dictatorship and Democracy* (Boston, 1966), 111–55; Wiener, *Social Origins of the New South: Alabama, 1860–1885* (Baton Rouge, La., 1978), 3–4, 71–73, 108, 146, 182–85, 202, 220–21, 227.

59. See *Report of the Board of Commissioners of Free Schools to the Citizens of Charleston* (Charleston, S.C., 1858), 5–6. See also William P. Miles, notes for a speech, 1855, in Miles Papers, SHC; Irving H. Bartlett, *The American Mind in the Mid-Nineteenth Century* (Northbrook, Ill., 1967), 74; Genovese, *Political Economy of Slavery*, 228–31, 234–35.

60. *Minutes of the Commissioners of Free Schools for the Parishes of St. Philip's and St. Michael's*, 22 January 1855, MS in the City of Charleston Archives; Capers, *Memminger*, 531. Cf. Curti, *Social Ideas of American Educators*, ch. 4.

61. Alfred Huger to W.P. Miles, 8 September 1855; Miles to Huger, 10 November 1857; Robert Gourdin to Miles, 29 August and 7 November 1856; and G. Bailey to Miles, 10 October 1856; all in the Miles Papers, SHC; also *Courier*, 29 November 1855; L.W. Jordan, "Education for Community: Christopher G. Memminger and the Origination of Common Schools in Antebellum Charleston," *SCHM* 83 (1982): 100–11.

62. Emory Thomas, in *The Confederate Nation, 1861–1865* (New York, 1979), suggests that the Confederate state, which was born, lived fitfully, and died during the Civil War, was forced by the demands of total war to become a different society and polity than the Old South had been; that ends and means were transformed and the localist, individualist, and agrarian South denied much of its heritage in an effort to assure national survival that introduced universal military conscription, substantial taxation at the national level, and significant national social and economic guidance and regulation, including public incentives for industrialization. But the public life and thought of Memminger suggests that the schism between what the Confederacy was supposed to be and what it became existed even before secession came.

63. Jordan, "Education for Community," 99–100, 109–13.

64. *Courier*, 8 December 1854; Memminger, *Speech on the Blue Ridge Railroad*, 11–15.

65. *Mayor's Report on City Affairs 1857* (Charleston, S.C., 1857); Jordan, "Police Power and Public Safety in Antebellum Charleston," 131–33.

66. McCardell, *Idea of a Southern Nation*, 126–27.

67. Barney, *Road to Secession*, 30.

68. Jordan, "Education for Community," 113n, 114.

69. Barney, *Road to Secession*, 31; McCardell, *Idea of a Southern Nation*, chs. 2, 3.

70. *Mercury*, 4 April 1850.

71. *Ibid.*; Capers, *Memminger*, 187–300.

72. Robert R. Russel, *Economic Aspects of Southern Sectionalism, 1840–1861* (Urbana, Ill., 1924), 243–45.

73. Paul M. Gaston, *The New South Creed* (New York, 1970), 13.

74. *Ibid.*, passim; George B. Tindall, *South Carolina Negroes, 1877–1900* (Columbia, S.C., 1952); Jack T. Kirby, *Darkness at the Dawning: Race and Reform in the Progressive South* (Philadelphia, 1972).

75. See David R. Goldfield, "Pursuing the American Dream: Cities in the Old South," in Blaine A. Brownell and Goldfield, eds., *The City in Southern History* (Port Washington, N.Y., 1977), 52–92.

76. Memminger, Address to the National Grange, Charleston *News and Courier*, 4 February 1875; Robert G. Rhett, *Charleston: An Epic of Carolina* (Richmond, Va., 1940), 322–24.

77. Capers, *Memminger*, 385–86; N.A. Pratt, *The Ashley River Phosphates* (Charleston, S.C., 1868); Charles V. Shepard, *South Carolina Phosphates* (Charleston, S.C., 1880); J.V. Nielson, "Post-

Confederate Finance in South Carolina," *SCHM* 56 (1955): 85–91; John E. Land, *Charleston: Her Trade, Commerce, and Industries, 1883–1884* (Charleston, S.C., 1884), 137–38.

78. Capers, *Memminger*, 389; Kneece, *Memminger*, 54–55, 70; *Courier*, 7 November 1885.

79. Carlo Ginzburg, *The Cheese and the Worms: The Cosmology of a Sixteenth Century Miller* (Baltimore, Md., 1980 [1976]), xxi.

8. The Charleston Style: PEASES

This essay started simply as an examination of those institutions which, in the 1830s, served—or disserved—Charlestonians aspiring to intellectual and cultural activity. But, informed by a larger study of Charleston's economic, political, and social life in the Jacksonian era, it expanded its scope to place those institutions within a framework presented here somewhat speculatively as the Charleston style. We would not argue that intellectual life is necessarily confined to an institutional framework or that individual Charlestonians could not escape the city's distinctive social style. But if we are to understand Charleston as a place distinguished, *inter alia*, by a cultural life unusual in so small and isolated a city, we must attempt a synthesis of its social institutions and values, to which some gave unquestioning loyalty, against which others rebelled, and by which still others generated a distinctive urbanity.

The authors wish to thank the following agencies and institutions whose assistance has helped make possible this essay: the American Philosophical Society; the University of Maine Faculty Research Fund; the National Endowment for the Humanities, Grant No. RS-1454-80; and the National Science Foundation, Grant No. SES-8023796.

1. For discussions of the relationship between ideas and their social context, see Thomas Kuhn, *The Structure of Scientific Revolutions* (Chicago, 1962); for the question of Jacksonian science and American culture, George Daniels, *American Science in the Age of Jackson* (New York, 1968), esp. 7–8, 11–15.

2. On class structure, see Daniel W. Rossides, *The American Class System: An Introduction to Social Stratification* (Boston, 1976), esp. 17–18; the question of constraints on Carolina intellectual life is discussed in William R. Taylor, *Cavalier and Yankee: The Old South and American National Character* (New York, 1961), 240–41; for a discussion of the general question of social structure and its relationship to urban development, see William H. Pease and Jane H. Pease, "Social Structure and the Potential for Urban Change: Boston and Charleston in the 1830s," *Journal of Urban History* 8 (1982): 171–96; a specific crisis in social stability, as it related to Charleston, is treated in Jane H. Pease and William H. Pease, "The Blood-Thirsty Tiger: Charleston and the Psychology of Fire," *SCHM* 79 (1978): 281–95; for a full elaboration of Charleston's experiences of the 1830s, Charlestonians' responses to them, and the Charleston style, see William H. Pease and Jane H. Pease, *The Web of Progress: Private Values and Public Styles in Boston and Charleston, 1828–1843* (New York, 1985).

3. The idea of rounded edges was suggested in part by Bernard Barber's discussion of similar issues in his *Social Stratification: A Comparative Analysis of Structure and Process* (New York, 1957).

4. The theme has been variously explored by Eugene D. Genovese, *The Political Economy of Slavery: Studies in the Economy and Society of the Slave South* (New York, 1967), and *The World the Slaveholders Made* (New York, 1969); by Raimondo Luraghi, *The Rise and Fall of the Plantation South* (New York, 1978); and in Taylor's *Cavalier and Yankee*.

5. Nathan Reingold, "Definitions and Speculations: The Professionalization of Science in America in the Nineteenth Century," in Alexandra Oleson and Sanborn C. Brown, eds., *The Pursuit of Knowledge in the Early American Republic: American Scientific and Learned Societies from Colonial Times to the Civil War* (Baltimore, Md., 1976), 33–69; Reingold (p. 39) uses the term "cultivators" for the gentlemen amateurs who encouraged interest in science and included it as part of "polite learning."

6. South Carolina Agricultural Society, Minutes (MS) 1825–60, SCHS; entries for the first few years of the society's life show considerable interest in various aspects of progressive farming: see, e.g., 23 February, 20 September, and 22 October 1825, and 20 February 1826; opposition to patenting appears in the minutes for 21 October 1828; for the count on patents issued, see *Courier*, 20 January 1830, copying the *National Intelligencer*, 14 January 1830. Although the *Southern Agriculturist and Register of Rural Affairs*, 1828–39, was edited by the society's librarian, the journal was not an organ of the society.

7. South Carolina Agricultural Society, Minutes, 18 July and 19 September 1837.

8. This and other statistical analyses used in this paper were drawn from a computerized data base of 2,292 Charlestonians who may be said to have exerted power or influence in the city in the 1830s. The attributes of economic power include holding office in the Chamber of Commerce or the bar and medical societies; acting as director of any bank, railroad, or insurance company; owning one hundred or more plantation slaves. The attributes by which wealth was established included owning twenty urban or fifty rural slaves; owning more than ten pieces of urban real estate or three pieces of farmland; owning stock in five or more corporations; leaving an estate valued at $20,000 or more. Upper-class status was attributed to those who had at least two of the following characteristics: service on an Episcopal Church vestry; owning two or more plantations, or fifty or more rural slaves; having a bachelor's degree; having studied abroad or earned professional degrees; holding office in the Hibernian Society, the South Carolina Society, or the Charleston Library Society, or simply being a member of the Academy of Fine Arts, the Jockey Club, the Literary and Philosophical Society, the Strawberry Club, and the South Carolina Agricultural Society. Exerting political power entailed holding office in city council, the state legislature, or the federal congress, or holding ten or more minor but prestigious city appointive offices. Where attributes overlap substance—e.g., giving upper-class status to Agricultural Society members when belonging to that society is itself one of the indicators—that overlap has been discounted. Of twenty-one Agricultural Society officers, 71–78 percent were planters; 62 percent were wealthy; 57 percent exerted some economic power. The data and programming for this analysis is available from the University of Maine Social Science Research Institute.

9. Samuel G. Stoney, ed., "Memoirs of Frederick Adolphus Porcher," *SCHM* 47 (1946): 48. So far as the minutes of the society indicate, it did not resume its regular exhibits and awarding of prizes after the late 1820s until the fall of 1843, when a fair and exhibition were scheduled for October 24: South Carolina Agricultural Society, Minutes, 18 July 1843.

10. *South Carolina Statutes at Large . . .* , Vol. 8, *Acts of Incorporation* (Columbia, S.C., 1841), 369; Catherine L. Bachman, *John Bachman, D.D., LL.D., Ph.D.: The Pastor of St. John's Lutheran Church, Charleston* (Charleston, S.C., 1888), 110; William Blanding to Rachel Blanding, 11 and 16 April 1832, William Blanding Papers, SCL, comments on Bachman's friendship with John Audubon; Moses Ashley Curtis Diary, 7 May 1832, Moses Ashley Curtis Papers, SHC. The material about Edward Leitner, including the quotations from Leitner to Lewis David Schweinitz, 1 July 1832, and to Benjamin Silliman, 14 July 1832, is in George E. Gifford, Jr., "Edward Frederick Leitner (1818–1838), Physician-Botanist," *Bulletin of the History of Medicine* 46 (1972): 568–90.

11. Curtis Diary, 8 May 1832; the general material on the activities of the Horticultural Society contained in this paragraph was gleaned from the pages of the *Courier* and the *Mercury*, *passim*; between 1828 and 1843, 63 percent of nineteen known officers were in commerce and the professions, while 24–28 percent were planters or farmers.

12. *Courier*, 9 March 1832.

13. T.C. Johnson, *Scientific Interests in the Old South* (New York, 1936), 128–36; *Mercury*, 6 February 1832.

14. Samuel Gilman attributed the major effort at reviving the society to Thomas Grimké, who was seeking "an ample infusion of new members": Samuel Gilman to M.L. Hurlbut, 26 January 1832, Manuscripts and Church Records, Unitarian Church, Archdale Street, Charleston.

The activities of the Literary and Philosophical Society are mentioned frequently in the pages of the *Courier* and *Mercury*, *passim*; for the reorganizing of the museum see, in particular, *City Gazette*, 17 May 1830, and issues of the *Mercury* for 2 and 9 April and 16 May 1836, 2 May 1837, and 30 May 1839; a second revival was planned in 1840, when the society tried unsuccessfully to buy land at Queen and Mazyck Streets for more commodious headquarters: Charleston, Commissioners of the Poor House, 1 April 1840 Minutes 1834–40, SCHS. Among the reported and sometimes published subjects of the society's meetings were essays on the "moral excellence of painting," the "pursuit of literature," the "objects of natural history," the "migration of the birds of North America," and Spurzheim's work on education: *Courier*, 17 July 1832 and 22 March 1833, and *Mercury*, 14 March 1840; John B. White's essay on the "moral excellence of painting" is in manuscript in John Blake White Papers, SCHS. The comment on the demise of the society is in Samuel Gilman to William Porcher Miles, 18 May 1842, William Porcher Miles Papers, SHC; two somewhat more sanguine assessments can be found in "Agriculture in South Carolina," *Magnolia*, n.s., 2 (1843), 200–3, and Frederick von Raumer, *America, and the American People*, trans. (New York, 1846), 422; 66 to 75 percent of its known seventy-five officers and members between 1828 and 1843 were physicians, lawyers, attorneys, or academics; 55 percent enjoyed moderately or very high social standing.

15. *Mercury*, 14 March 1840; *Courier*, 1 March 1834. Daniel W. Howe, "A Massachusetts Yankee in Senator Calhoun's Court: Samuel Gilman in South Carolina," *New England Quarterly* 44 (1971): 197–220, esp. 214–15, explores for one of the society's most intellectually active members the "debilitating inner tension between a desire to exercise moral leadership and the hyperconventional, placatory role thrust upon him in Charleston."

16. *City Gazette*, 22 and 29 July 1830; Charles Fraser to James Bowdoin, November 1831, Winthrop Papers, Microfilm Reel 22, Massachusetts Historical Society; Howe, "Massachusetts Yankee," 209; Samuel Gilman to Benjamin Peirce, 7 August 1937, Miscellaneous Manuscripts, SCL; Simms' letters lament the absence of a literary fellowship, although they also respond to local hostility to literary effort per se: see, e.g., Simms to James Lawson, 11 September 1830, in *Simms Letters*, I, 4–5.

17. Daniel W. Hollis, *South Carolina College* (Columbia, S.C., 1951), 90–92, 116.

18. Stephen Elliott, *An Address Delivered at the Opening of the Medical College, in Charleston, S.C. . . . the 18th of November, 1826* (Charleston, S.C., 1826); Charles Fraser, *An Address Delivered before the Citizens of Charleston, and the Grand Lodge of South-Carolina, at the Laying of the Corner Stone of a New College Edifice, with Masonic Ceremonies, on the 12th January, 1828* (Charleston, S.C., 1828), 17–18. Elliott (p. 7) also emphasized the moral dangers facing children sent away to school: "Children were sent abroad to learn industry by lessons that did not reach them; habits of control and self-government, by being liberated from all restraint; virtue and wisdom, and honor from exemplars selected at their own discretion."

19. [Jasper Adams], *An Historical Sketch of the College of Charleston, South Carolina. First Published in the American Quarterly Register* (n.p., [1837]), *passim*; College of Charleston, *Catalogue of Charleston College, February 1829* (Charleston, S.C., 1829).

20. For the evolution of the college, see James H. Easterby, *A History of the College of Charleston* (Charleston, S.C., 1935), 1–89; for factors impeding the growth of the college as well as for commentary on the inadequacy of the trustees, see Adams' *Historical Sketch*, 15–16, and the observations of "H.R." in the *Courier*, 27 August 1835. The lack of trustee interest is suggested by the fact that of the graduates of the earlier grammar school, only one is known to have served as trustee, and that incumbent trustees Mitchell King and James Hamilton sent their children north or to Europe for advanced schooling; see Virginia L. Glenn, "James Hamilton, Jr., of South Carolina: A Biography" (Ph.D. diss., University of North Carolina, 1964), 202; Mitchell King to Hugh Swinton Legaré, 5 May 1833, Mitchell King Papers, SCL. On the problem of student discipline, Adams observed (in a letter to Eliza Francis, 8 November 1834, Jasper Adams Manu-

scripts, SCL): "I have had a 'bit of a rebellion' in the college, which ended in dismissing three of the junior class, & which gave me much trouble." The disgruntled faculty member was Henry M. Bruns, who later became head of the city's high school: Bruns to Joseph Milligan, 20 June 1833, Milligan Papers, SHC. In addition to meager pay, part of Bruns' disaffection may have been attributable to Adams' difficult personality, about which a number of observations are made in the letters of Alicia H. Middleton to Nathaniel R. Middleton, 1827, *passim*, Nathaniel Russell Middleton Papers, SHC; see also "An Enquirer" in *Mercury*, 27 March 1837, and the comment of William H. Spear, assistant pastor at St. Michael's Church: "Our College here in Charleston has been for some time at a low ebb, dependent entirely on the personal labours of Dr Adams', who has been President, Professors & tutors in himself" (Spear to John DeB. Hooper, 1 July 1836, John DeBerniere Hooper Papers, SHC). On the day-by-day running of the college, see College of Charleston, Board of Trustees, Minutes, 1817–41, *passim*, typescript in College of Charleston library. Although during the early 1830s the press stressed the flourishing condition of the college with its enrollment of nearly 200 students (*Courier*, 20 March 1830), graduating classes never numbered over 14 (*Courier*, 25 March 1831, 2 November 1833, and 1 November 1834), including, amusingly, John C. Frémont, who was awarded both a B.A. and an M.A. degree in 1836 (*Mercury*, 31 March 1836).

21. College of Charleston, Board of Trustees, Minutes, 4 August 1836.

22. *Courier*, 1 January 1829; Alicia H. Middleton to Nathaniel R. Middleton, 15 November 1827, Middleton Papers; College of Charleston, Board of Trustees, Minutes, 9 April 1833; *Courier*, 7 January 1832; College of Charleston, Board of Trustees, Minutes, 2 October 1833, 15 October 1832, 19 July 1833, and 17 October 1834. Other contributions received by the college included nearly $7,000 from the estate of Col. Skivring and a legacy of about $1,200 from Sol Nathans: College of Charleston, Board of Trustees, Minutes, 15 October 1832.

23. In his *Lectures on the Elements of Political Economy* (Columbia, S.C., 1829), 353, president Thomas Cooper of South Carolina College struck at the heart of the problem of available wealth for cultural and intellectual development: "Without wealth there can be no pursuit of knowledge, no domestic libraries, no apparatus for scientific investigation, no expensive experiments, no public improvements by means of the voluntary pursuits of individuals who dedicate themselves to knowledge."

24. Estate papers, estate of Elias Horry, in Edward Frost Papers, Box 2, LC.

25. This donation brought irate responses from some citizens who argued that such a public contribution to a private cause, no matter how worthy, constituted a breach of public trust: *City Gazette*, late August 1829, *passim*, and particularly "Caroliniensis" in *Courier*, 12 August 1829.

26. College of Charleston, Board of Trustees, Minutes, 3 November 1835; *Ordinances of the City of Charleston; From the 15th February, 1833 to the 9th May, 1837* (Charleston, S.C., 1837), 71–72.

27. The city's decision to make the college a municipal institution can be followed in the *Mercury*, 18 August 1837, which printed the council's report on the college; see also the trustees' minutes for 25 August 1837. The virtues of having a local college were set forth from time to time in the public press: see, e.g., *Mercury*, 9 August 1837, 8 March 1838, and 28 December 1838; for notices of the college's success see *Mercury*, 27 February 1840, and the comments in "Science and Literature in South Carolina," *Magnolia*, n.s., 2 (1843): 272, which noted that although the college was still not well endowed, it provided a good education. Indicative of its success were the fourteen B.A.s awarded in February 1842, together with one M.A. How important the question of professional credentials was is suggested by the fact that between 1825 and 1840, forty of the sixty-eight graduates of the college went into the learned professions (medicine 15, clergy 14, law 11): *Names of the Graduates of the College of Charleston, South Carolina, from the Year 1825 to 1870, Inclusive* (Charleston, S.C., 1870).

28. The council position was stated in a resolution offered by Dr. Thomas Y. Simons and adopted by council, 18 July 1837: printed in *Mercury*, 21 July 1837.

29. College of Charleston, Board of Trustees, Minutes, 18 October 1830 through 5 March 1831, esp. 24 February and 5 March 1831.

30. *Mercury*, 9 August 1837.

31. *Mercury*, 20 August, 17 September, and 15 October 1838.

32. Henry M. Bruns to Joseph Milligan, 7 April 1835, Milligan Papers; R.P. Johnson to William Porcher Miles, 30 July 1840, Miles Papers.

33. The evolution of the board of trustees from its premunicipal to its municipal form can be followed in the minutes of the board of trustees from 1838 onward: see esp. 26 July, 15 and 19 September 1837, 12 January, 5 March, and 26 September 1838, and 14 and 19 October 1840; also *Mercury*, 12 January 1838, 11 October 1839, and 7 October 1840, and *Courier*, 20 October 1841. Basil Manly's observation occurs in a copy of his letter to the Rev. Dr. Staughton, 7 April 1827, in his "Diaries and Letter Books," Manly Family Papers, Microfilm, SCL, from originals at the University of Alabama. When Brantley made his annual report in October 1843, there were fifty-five students enrolled in the college, and graduates for the year numbered ten: College of Charleston, Board of Trustees, Minutes, January–March 1838, *passim*; *Mercury*, 8 March 1838; *Courier*, 20 October 1843.

34. Caroline H. Gilman to Harriet Fay, 4 March 1821, in Mary Scott Saint-Amand, ed., *A Balcony in Charleston* (Richmond, Va., 1941), 16. Jasper Adams, himself an Episcopal clergyman, had strong views about the importance of a close relationship between state and church, a point of view easily transferable to the college: "If the community shall ever become convinced, that Christianity is not entitled to the sustaining aid of the civil Constitutions and law of the country, the outposts of the citadel will have been taken. . . . We must be a Christian nation, if we wish to continue a free nation": *The Relation of Christianity to Civil Government in the United States. A Sermon . . . February 13th 1833 . . .* (Charleston, S.C., 1833), 17, 20.

35. In their self-conscious pursuit of professional standards and institutions, Charleston's physicians had little real competition from other professions. Although Unitarian Samuel Gilman, Lutheran John Bachman, and Presbyterian Thomas Smyth were nationally recognized for their acumen, and Episcopal Jasper Adams and Baptist Basil Manly, Sr., were offered college presidencies, there were no ministerial associations other than denominational meetings or informal social circles. Nor was it much different with lawyers; some had been systematically educated to their calling in Northern or European schools, but most had done little more than read law in local offices. Efforts to found a law school in Charleston failed, and the Charleston Bar Association played a minimally visible role in the city.

For general background on the issue of health and medicine in Charleston, see Wilson G. Smillie, *Public Health: Its Promise for the Future: A Chronicle of the Development of Public Health in the United States, 1607–1914* (New York, 1945), 34–35, 79, 85; and Joseph Ioor Waring, *A History of Medicine in South Carolina*, esp. Vol. II, 1825–1900 (Columbia, S.C., 1967). All during the 1820s and 1830s, a tremendous interest in yellow fever occupied Charlestonians' minds: see, e.g., James De La Motta, *An Oration on the Causes of Mortality among Strangers, during the Late Summer and Fall . . .* (Savannah, Ga., [1820]), delivered before a Savannah audience; and the debate in the *Mercury*, April–May 1840, growing out of a review of B. Strobel's study of whether yellow fever was transmissible or not, and how. The debate involved a number of the city's medical community.

36. [Adams], *Historical Sketch*, 9; Samuel H. Dickson, *Statements in Reply to Certain Publications from the Medical Society of South Carolina* (Charleston, S.C., 1834).

37. Dickson, *Statements*, 14–15.

38. Medical Society of South Carolina, Minutes 1823–58, Waring Historical Library, Medical University of South Carolina, 18 May–1 June 1829, and July–December 1831.

39. This game of musical chairs can be followed in the *Courier*, 4 July, 2 August, and 3 September 1831, and in the *Mercury*, 17 October 1831; Geddings' resignation is recorded in the minutes of the Medical Society, 1 November 1831.

40. Dickson, *Statements*, 18–19.

41. *Ibid.*, 15–16; Medical Society of South Carolina, Minutes, 5 December 1831.

42. Richard H. Shryock, *Medicine and Society in America* (New York, 1960), 141; Medical College of South Carolina, Broadside, Petition "To the President and Members of the Senate . . . from . . . Professors of the Medical College," November 1831, SCHS. The story of the ensuing struggle is compiled from several sources: Dickson, *Statements*; Medical Society Minutes; Medical Society of South Carolina, *An Exposition of the Affairs of the Medical Society . . . So Far as They Appertain to the Establishment of a Medical College in Charleston, and the Subsequent Division of the Latter . . .* (Charleston, S.C., 1833): *Courier*, esp. 4 June 1833, and *Mercury*, esp. 24 March 1832. Quotations and central points are noted separately.

43. *Mercury*, 23 March 1832, contains the statements of three Charleston legislators that they had understood that the bill did represent a compromise agreed to by both factions; "Decision of the Appeal Court. The State of South Carolina v. A. Heyward et al; in the Appeal Court, February Term. O'Neall, Judge," in *Courier*, 4 June 1833.

44. Medical Society of South Carolina, Minutes, 23 August 1832; the attorneys for the Society were Randall Hunt and Benjamin F. Hunt.

45. Medical Society of South Carolina, Minutes, 2 February 1835; Medical Society of South Carolina, *Report of a Committee . . . in Reply to a Protest Signed by a Minority of the Members Concerning the Rejection of Several Applicants for Membership . . .* (Charleston, S.C., 1835).

46. Medical Society of South Carolina, Minutes, 8 April 1833.

47. For the charter terms of the state school, see Medical College of the State of South Carolina, *Catalogue . . .* (Charleston, S.C., 1832), 5–8. Former trustees who became faculty members of the Queen Street school included T.Y. Simons, B.B. Simons, F.Y. Porcher, and Andrew Hazel. The number of graduates noted in the city press indicates the schools' differing success. In the three years prior to the split, 1829–31, the society's college graduated 39, 54, and 47. In 1836–38, the numbers were 2, 6, and 10. The Broad Street school, however, for the years 1834–38 graduated 39, 39, 46, 43, and 52.

48. Medical Society of South Carolina, Minutes, 1 July 1833.

49. *Ibid.*, 5 November 1834.

50. James Moultrie, *Memorial on the State of Medical Education in South Carolina* (Charleston, S.C., 1836).

51. The society's college had so declined that on 10 December 1838 its entire faculty resigned; thereupon, the society moved to open negotiations with the Broad Street college to reunite the medical forces of the city and create a single medical school: Medical Society of South Carolina, Minutes, 7 January 1839.

52. Samuel H. Dickson, *Annual Report to the President and Board of Trustees of the Medical College of the State of South Carolina with the Valedictory Address to the Class* (Charleston, S.C., 1841): the address is excerpted in an article in *Mercury*, 7 June 1841. Moultrie's and Dickson's enthusiasm was echoed by a doctor originally trained in Charleston who had gone to Alabama. Returning for a "refresher" course at the college, he noted the excellence of the faculty, the good facilities, and the availability of the library to students; he did, however, point out the need for a good teaching hospital: "Alabama" in *Mercury*, 29 January 1841. That the victory of the state college was not an unalloyed one for high standards, however, is suggested by the fact that almost simultaneously the state dropped its standards for licensing physicians. The issue between those who had merely a license to practice and those who had a thorough medical training became sharper than ever. Dickson pointed out in his *Annual Report and Valedictory* that therefore the Medical College had begun to give not only a diploma, but an "Introductory Document" to each graduate, attesting that he was a "well taught and disciplined physician." It was imperative that a state medical society be organized to police medical training and practice, Dickson argued, since at the moment no one did so except the United States Army and Navy and of course the Medi-

cal College of the State of South Carolina. In an observation made a decade earlier, Daniel Drake had damned the licentiate in words that Dickson would have approved: "What is a license but a certificate of inferiority? A licentiate may be a good physician, and become a great man, but still there is an original technical difference between him and a graduate, which everybody recognizes; and, as far as testimonials are concerned, his is one, who has not made the attainments, which entitled him to a doctorate": Daniel Drake in *Practical Essays on Medical Education* (1832), quoted in William G. Rothstein, *American Physicians in the Nineteenth Century: From Sects to Science* (Baltimore, Md., 1972), 106.

53. From 1828 to 1843, 60 percent of the Charleston Library Society's officers were men of high or moderately high social standing; between 39 and 52 percent came from the learned professions; 44 percent wielded some political power, while only 24 percent exerted economic power in the city. In 1826 the approximately 4,500 books in the library contained over 1,300 volumes of literature (half of them novels and romances), nearly 700 volumes of science and technology, 1,300 in history, and about 450 of religion and ethics; the library also received 93 periodicals; by 1831 another 500 volumes had been added to its collections: Charleston Library Society, *Catalogue of the Books . . .* (Charleston, S.C., 1826) and *A Supplemental Catalogue . . .* (Charleston, S.C., 1831); the 1848 figure is from James L. Petigru, *Oration Delivered before the Charleston Library Society . . . 1848* (Charleston, S.C., 1848). The drive to build a collection of primary historical material was headed by a committee whose members in 1834 included Mitchell King, Henry A. Middleton, Benjamin F. Pepoon, Lionel Kennedy, and Benjamin Elliott: *Courier*, 2 July 1834, and Benjamin Elliott, *Reports of the Historical Committee of the Charleston Library Society . . .* (Charleston, S.C., 1835). The very select, clublike nature of the society's membership is detailed in its rules and regulations; see Charleston Library Society, *Rules and By-Laws . . .* (Charleston, S.C., 1840). Frederick Porcher has a delightful description of the amiable, conversational, and not too intellectual social life of the "habitués" in the library during the middle 1830s: "Memoirs," *SCHM* 47 (1946): 44–47.

54. *Courier*, 3 July 1829. In his address to the society in 1843, W.D. Porter, himself the son of a grocer who had become a lawyer after attending the College of Charleston, asserted that education as well as technical skill was essential for success in the world. Citing Ben Franklin as an appropriate model, he urged young artisans, "If you would become a native workman, in the noblest sense of the word, you must first serve an apprenticeship to books as well as tools, to science as well as art": *Courier*, 12 April 1843.

55. The meaning of the varied fare offered by the Apprentices Library Society is reflected in Article II of its new constitution, adopted in 1829: "The instruction to be furnished by this Society shall be conveyed by means of a Library, of Lectureships, and hereafter, if practicable, of a Preparatory School; and emulation shall be excited, and skill and industry encouraged by premiums, by public recommendation and by private patronage": *Courier*, 2 October 1829. When he addressed the young apprentices at the annual awarding of premiums for "the neatness, taste, and elegance . . . [of] the several models" of their craftsmanship and skill, Dr. Joseph Johnson set forth the central purpose of the society in a nutshell. "The great object . . . is, to encourage a laudable spirit of emulation and rivalry, among the young Mechanics of Charleston—to afford them an opportunity of hearing and learning from the Lectures of those, who have had better means of acquiring knowledge, and to encourage all of them in visiting this Library daily and nightly if they think proper, for the purposes of mental improvement": *Courier*, 10 April 1843.

56. The extended fare offered the general public through its various lyceum lectures and courses is covered regularly in the *Courier* and *Mercury* during the late 1830s and early 1840s: see, e.g., the series of lectures for 1843, *Courier*, 23 February 1843; and the series, which was rendered less than effectual by fire and yellow fever, planned for 1838, *Mercury*, 13 March 1839. For the role that highly specialized knowledge must assume through popularization and the demonstration of utility in a democratic society, see Daniels, *Science in the Age of Jackson*, 41; thus Dr. Charles

Davis' twenty lectures on chemistry (with experiments) in the winter of 1837–38 consisted of subjects "judiciously selected as the most useful and essential to the objects of our association, the improvement of apprentices and others, who have no opportunities of acquiring such knowledge": *Mercury*, 16 March 1838.

57. Samuel H. Dickson, *Address Delivered at the Opening of the New Edifice of the Charleston Apprentices' Library Society . . . 1841* (Charleston, S.C., 1841), the quotation is on p. 26; Apprentices Library Society, *Catalogue of the Books . . .* (Charleston, S.C., 1840).

58. Boston *Post*, 17 July 1839, reported twenty extant publications in South Carolina, twenty-seven in Cincinnati, and 164 for Ohio as a whole. In the *American Quarterly Observer* 3 (1834): 135–49, the editor considered what city was likely to become America's publishing center; making no mention at all of Charleston, he did consider both Cincinnati and St. Louis.

Among the various printing establishments in Charleston during the 1830s, identified in the catalogue of Charleston imprints at the Charleston Library Society, were A.E. Miller, W. Riley, Sebring and Burges, E.J. Van Brunt, William S. Blain, William Estill, J.J. M'Carter, Dan J. Dowling, and Jenkins and Hussey. The plethora of printed matter in Charleston during the 1830s is matched only by the rapidity with which various periodicals failed. The *City Gazette*, 6 February 1830, listed an even dozen periodicals published in the city: nine newspapers, two monthlies, and one quarterly. Numerous others were begun or proposed during the next dozen years—including the *Southern Agriculturist*, the *Pleiades & Southern Literary Gazette*, the *Southern Rose*, the *Southern Planter*, the *Southern Baptist and General Intelligencer*, and the *Southern Quarterly Review*—but the high rate of mortality of such publications (not unique to Charleston) compromised the city's efforts to become a southern literary center. While William Elliott was hopeful that the prospects for the proposed *Southern Review* must "increase, when the honest prejudices of the South shall be enlisted in its support" (Elliott to Thomas Rhett Smith, 8 February 1827, Elliott-Gonzales Papers, SHC), the prospects were fulfilled for very few. William Gilmore Simms noted how much better his novels sold in the North, and James Elford commented on the relative cheapness of printing in Boston as compared to the cost in Charleston: James L. Elford to John R. Parker, 18 February 1833, James L. Elford Papers, SCL. For Simms, see John McCardell, *The Idea of a Southern Nation: Southern Nationalists and Southern Nationalism, 1830–1860* (New York, 1979), 147–56.

The difficulties of assembling a sustaining readership also beset Charleston writers and publishers (though here again they had no monopoly on the problem). Simms, writing to the founders of *Magnolia*, had bitter advice: "You have run up to five hundred [subscribers] so fast that you'll almost wish you had made three thousand the minimum—from five hundred to seven hundred you'll begin to think the prospectus has not been half circulated, from seven hundred to a thousand you'll begin to fret about the lack of public spirit in the South, and between a thousand and fifteen hundred it will gradually ease out of notice": McCardell, 157. Caroline Gilman also suffered doubts about her ability to make the *Rose Bud*, a children's periodical, successful in the face of rising costs and limited subscriptions: Caroline H. Gilman to Ann Maria White, Harriet Fay, and Louisa Loring, 1832–33, *passim*, Caroline H. Gilman Letters, SCHS.

Despite pleas such as that of the *Courier*, 4 June 1835, that it was "high time that the latent talent of our City and State should be called forth into vigorous and continued action," the *Mercury* lamented, 12 December 1840, that Charleston was still without a literary journal, depending upon the North for such fare. The situation was not different for nationally visible scientific publications: of those published between 1835 and 1839 in the United States, Massachusetts and Pennsylvania boasted eleven each, New York had eight, and South Carolina had but one: Daniels, *American Science*, 229. Yet there was, for those who could and would take advantage of it, considerable reading material available in the city. Roorbach's on King Street, one of the city's biggest booksellers, maintained a circulating library (*City Gazette*, 14 January 1831), and the advertising columns of the *Courier* and *Mercury* regularly carried extended notices of new books available at the several bookstores in town.

59. Reports of the Commissioners of Free Schools, St. Philip's and St. Michael's Parishes, 1836, Green File, Education, SCSA; J.L. Dawson and H.W. DeSaussure, *Census of the City of Charleston, South Carolina, for the Year 1848 . . .* (Charleston, S.C., 1849), 54–55. The Fellowship Society also offered orphans and children of the poor free primary education in its school. For the German Friendly Society, see Morris Goldsmith, *Directory and Strangers' Guide, for the City of Charleston and Its Vicinity . . .* (Charleston, S.C., 1831); also *Courier*, 8 February and 6 April 1843. For the South Carolina Society, see its *Rules . . . Eighth Edition Revised and Altered. Ratified 1827* (Charleston, S.C., 1827), and *General Plan of Education Appointed for the South Carolina Society's Male Academy, July 1827* (Charleston, S.C., 1827); see also *Mercury*, 12 April 1837. For the high school, see *Mercury*, 24 June 1839; *Courier*, 14 December 1843; and Jacob Newton Cardozo, *Reminiscences of Charleston* (Charleston, S.C., 1866), 20.

60. This figure is based on a survey of notices in the *Mercury* and *Courier* between 1828 and 1843.

61. Among the schools that Charlestonians of means chose to educate their sons and daughters were the Catholic Classical and Philosophical Academy and, late in the decade, the school operated by St. Peter's Episcopal Church. Some parents, of course, sent their children away to school: Moses Waddell's famous Willington Academy in the upcountry, or—following the common pattern of Northern education—Dr. Muhlenberg's Episcopal boarding school on Long Island. For the more educationally adventurous there was, until early in the 1830s, Round Hill school in Northampton, Massachusetts. For girls there were St. Mary's Hall in Burlington, New Jersey, and Miss Binsse's academy in New York City. It is thus clear that Charlestonians paid more, on average, to educate their children—reckoning both transportation and fees—than did families of similar standing in Boston.

62. In a society in which conspicuous leisure was a principal premise and the ennobling of physical labor taboo, the meaning of "knowledge is power" was quite different from what it was in Yankee New England. Bostonians harped vigorously on that theme in tracts and private letters, in sermons and admonitions to their young, identifying the benefits of a sound education in thoroughly pragmatic terms; for some of the implications of this theme see William H. Pease and Jane H. Pease, "Paternal Dilemmas: Education, Property, and Patrician Persistence in Jacksonian Boston," *New England Quarterly* 53 (1980): 147–67. In Charleston, on the other hand, while there was a keen recognition of the utility of education in preparing the young for suitable occupations, the emphasis lay rather on providing suitable adornment for an adult life centered in a richly textured leisure.

Indeed, the strongest recognition that a commitment to universal literacy would inevitably mean knowledge as power to blacks as well as whites was perhaps sounded by the *Courier*, 27 July 1830: "Let our City and State authorities look to the evil which is growing—or it will come upon the community like a thief, *in the night*." Although Henry Middleton's instructions to his son's teacher—to eschew drawing and art, except as training for a possible engineering career, and to emphasize science and subjects more practical—sounded utilitarian enough, his desire to have his son well versed in the arts of dancing and fencing for the grace, alertness, "elasticity of carriage," and "self possession" they developed betrayed his concern that education should be the making of a gentleman in "the most finished society of modern times": Henry A. Middleton to Rufus F. Stebbins, January 1842, Langdon Cheves Papers, SCHS.

63. Stephen Elliott, *An Address Delivered at the Opening of the Medical College . . . 1826* (Charleston, S.C., 1826), 5–6.

64. Jasper Adams, *Laws of Success and Failure in Life; An Address Delivered 30th October 1833 . . . before the Euphradian Society* (Charleston, S.C., 1833), 14.

65. William Gilmore Simms, *Slavery in America; Being a Brief Review of Miss Martineau on That Subject* (Richmond, Va., 1838), 79.

66. Taylor, *Cavalier and Yankee*, 29–31; Porcher, "Memoirs" (April 1946), 95–96; Edmund Ravenel to Messrs King and Durant, 20 November 1835, and (for the financial arrangements) the Negro and Land folders, all in Edmund Ravenel Papers, Ford-Ravenel Collection, SCHS.

67. The number of individuals in professional occupations in the city declined between 1830 and 1840 by about 15 percent.

68. Dickson, *Annual Report to the President*, 8.

9. *Charleston Slaves:* JOYNER

1. This is a composite of descriptions of slave religious services in Frederika Bremer, *Homes in the New World: Impressions of America* (New York, 1853), I, 289–90; William Wyndham Malet, *An Errand to the South in the Summer of 1862* (London, 1863), 49–50, 74; Laurence Oliphant, *Patriots and Filibusters; or Incidents of Political and Exploratory Travel* (Edinburgh, 1860), 140–41; Sir Charles Lyell, *A Second Visit to the United States of America* (New York, 1849), I, 269–70, II, 213–14; A.M.H. Christensen, "Spirituals and Shouts of the Southern Negroes," *Journal of American Folk-Lore* 7 (1894): 154–55; H.G. Spaulding, "Under the Palmetto," *Continental Monthly* 4 (1863): 196–200; Daniel E. Huger Smith, "A Plantation Boyhood," in Alice R. Huger Smith and Herbert Ravenel Sass, eds., *A Carolina Rice Plantation of the Fifties* (New York, 1936), 75; *Chesnut*, 213–14; John G. Williams, *De Ole Plantation: Elder Cotenay's Sermons* (Charleston, S.C., 1895), 2–11. The text is quoted from Julia Peterkin, *Green Thursday* (New York, 1924), 188–89. I recorded a similar black religious service at New Bethel Baptist Church on Sandy Island, S.C., 16 January 1972. William Faulkner includes a literary description of such a service in the "Dilsey" section of *The Sound and the Fury* (New York, 1929). See also W.E.B. Du Bois, "Religion of the Southern Negro," *New World* 9 (1900); Grace Sims Holt, "Stylin' Outta the Black Pulpit," in Thomas Kochman, ed., *Rappin' and Stylin' Out* (Urbana, Ill., 1972), 189–95; Le Roi Jones, *Blues People: Negro Music in White America* (New York, 1963), 45–46; Henry H. Mitchell, *Black Preaching* (Philadelphia, 1970); Bruce A. Rosenberg, *The Art of the American Folk Preacher* (New York, 1970), 7, 10, 14, 17, 40, 47, 51, 115–16; W.D. Weatherford, *American Churches and the Negro: An Historical Study from Early Slave Days to the Present* (Boton, 1957), 114–15; Carter G. Woodson, *History of the Negro Church* (Washington, D.C., 1921), 41; Clarence E. Walker, *A Rock in a Weary Land: The African Methodist Episcopal Church during the Civil War and Reconstruction* (Baton Rouge, La., 1982), 61. On the status of the slave preachers in the slave community, see John W. Blassingame, "Status and Social Structure in the Slave Community," in Randall M. Miller, ed., *The Afro-American Slaves: Community or Chaos* (Malabar, Fla., 1981), 114, 120–21.

2. David J. McCord, ed., *Statutes at Large of South Carolina* (Columbia, S.C., 1840), VII, 468; Elijah Green, Charleston, interviewed by Augustus Ladson, in "Slave Narratives: A Folk History of Slavery," typewritten records of interviews with former slaves; prepared by the Federal Writers Project, 1936–38, microfilm 14, part ii, 197 (hereafter cited as, e.g., SN 14, ii, 197); Henry Brown, Charleston, interviewed by Augustus Ladson, SN 14, i, 125. Cf. Lucretia Heyward, Beaufort County, interviewed by Chlotilde R. Martin, SN 14, ii, 279. Some slaveholders, however, defied the law and taught their slaves to read and write. For example, Thomas Goodwater, an exslave in Mt. Pleasant, told interviewer Augustus Ladson, "My pa cound read an' write cus he live' in the city here. His missus teach him" (SN 14, ii, 166). A facsimile edition of the "Slave Narratives," edited by George P. Rawick as *The American Slave: A Composite Autobiography* (Westport, Conn., 1972), includes parts i and ii of the South Carolina interviews in vol. II, and parts iii and iv in vol. IV; pagination is the same.

3. Edward King, *The Great South: A Record of Journeys* (Hartford, Conn., 1875), 429; John Bennett, "Gullah: A Negro Patois," *South Atlantic Quarterly* 7 (1908): 340. For similar sentiments, see Reed Smith, *Gullah* (Columbia, S.C., 1926), 22–23; and Ambrose E. Gonzales, *The Black Border: Gullah Stories of the Carolina Coast* (Columbia, S.C., 1922), 10–17.

4. Richard Hoggart, *The Uses of Literacy* (New York, 1970), esp. 27–32, 270–82. Hoggart emphasizes the negative effects of literacy on twentieth-century English working-class culture as a result of the growing consolidation of the publishing industry, with its increasing centralization of control of available reading matter and the trivialization of mass publications. On the other hand, sociolinguist William Labov stresses the vibrancy of oral nonstandard English in the inner city in dealing with subjects of high seriousness and at a high level of abstraction. See his "Logic of Nonstandard English," in Pier Paolo Giglioli, ed., *Language and Social Context* (Harmondsworth, 1968), 191–97, and his *Social Stratification of English in New York City* (Washington, D.C., 1966). Personal interview with Walter Geathers, Sandy Island, 16 January 1972. Cf. Roger D. Abrahams and Richard A. Bauman, "Sense and Nonsense in St. Vincent: Speech Behavior and Decorum in a Caribbean Community," in Roger D. Abrahams, *The Man-of-Words in the West Indies: Performance and the Emergence of Creole Culture* (Baltimore, Md., 1983), 88–97; Mary Douglas, *In the Active Voice* (Boston, 1982), and *Edward Evans-Pritchard* (New York, 1980), 2, 4, 11, 111, 129.

5. On creole languages, see Robert A. Hall, *Pidgin and Creole Languages* (Ithaca, N.Y., 1965), 15; William A. Stewart, "Sociolinguistic Factors in the History of American Negro Dialects," *Florida FL Reporter* 5 (1967): 12–13; Loreto Todd, *Pidgins and Creoles* (London, 1974), 5–6, 54, 67; J.L. Dillard, *Black English: Its History and Usage in the United States* (New York, 1972), 76. On the definition of creolization, see Dell Hymes, introduction to pt. 3 of Dell Hymes, ed., *Pidginization and Creolization of Languages* (Cambridge, England, 1971), 84. That volume also contains useful essays on the complexity of the relationships involved in the creolization process: see esp. Sidney W. Mintz, "The Sociohistorical Background of Pidginization and Creolization," 153–68; Mervyn C. Alleyne, "Acculturation and the Cultural Matrix of Creolization," 169–86; and David DeCamp, "Introduction: The Study of Pidgin and Creole Languages," 13–39. See also William A. Stewart, "Nonstandard Speech Patterns," *Baltimore Bulletin of Education* 43 (1967): 52–65; J.L. Dillard, "Non-Standard Negro Dialects: Convergence or Divergence," in Norman E. Whitten and John F. Szwed, eds., *Afro-American Anthropology: Contemporary Perspectives* (New York, 1970), 119–26; and Ralph W. Fasold, "Decreolization and Autonomous Language Change," *Florida FL Reporter* 10 (1972): 9. On other New World creole languages, see Ian F. Hancock, "A Survey of Pidgins and Creoles of the World," in Hymes, ed., *Pidginization and Creolization*, 512–15. On the special case of the development of an African-English creole in Dutch Surinam, see Charles R. Boxer, *The Dutch Seaborne Empire, 1600–1800* (New York, 1965), 241. A speech community is defined linguistically as "a community sharing knowledge of rules for the conduct and interpretation of speech. Such sharing comprises knowledge of at least one form of speech, and knowledge also of its patterns of use. Both conditions are necessary": see Dell Hymes, *Foundations in Sociolinguistics: An Ethnographic Approach* (Philadelphia, 1974), 51; and John Gumperz, "The Speech Community," in Pier Paolo Giglioli, ed., *Language and Social Context* (Harmondsworth, 1972), 219–31. On the development of the Gullah speech community in the South Carolina lowcountry, see Peter H. Wood, *Black Majority: Negroes in Colonial South Carolina from 1670 through the Stono Rebellion* (New York, 1974), 167–91; and Charles Joyner, *Down by the Riverside: a South Carolina Slave Community* (Urbana, Ill., 1984), 196–224.

6. Thomas Goodwater, Mt. Pleasant, interviewed by Augustus Ladson, SN 14, ii, 166; "Boo-Hag," collected by Dromgoole Ham, in *South Carolina Folk Tales: Stories of Animals and Supernatural Beings* (Columbia, S.C., 1941), 47; Jane Hollins, Charleston, interviewed by Martha S. Pinckney, SN 14, ii, 291; "Buh Rabbit and Buh B'ar," collected by John Bennett, in John Bennett Papers, SCHS. On interchangeable pronouns in creole languages, see Todd, *Pidgins and Creoles*, 17; William A. Stewart, "Continuity and Change in American Negro Dialects," *Florida FL Reporter* 6 (1968): 3; Irma Cunningham, "A Syntactic Analysis of Sea Island Creole ('Gullah')" (Ph.D. diss., University of Michigan, 1970), 21–22, 200–1; Patricia C. Nichols, "Linguistic Change in Gullah: Sex, Age, and Mobility" (Ph.D. diss., Stanford University, 1976), 86–111, esp. 104–7.

7. Ephraim (Mike) Lawrence, Edisto Island, interviewed by Chalmers S. Murray, SN 14, iii,

96; Maria Jenkins, Charleston, interviewed by Martha S. Pinckney, SN 14, iii, 27; Ephraim (Mike) Lawrence, SN 14, iii, 95; John Hamilton, Charleston, interviewed by Gyland H. Hamlin, SN 14, ii, 221; Maria Jenkins, SN 14, iii, 28.

8. Ephraim (Mike) Lawrence, SN 14, iii, 97; Susan Hamlin, Charleston, interviewed by Jesse A. Butler, SN 14, ii, 231; David White, Charleston, interviewed by Laura L. Middleton, SN 14, iv, 194; Jackie ——, Charleston, "Buh Rabbit, Buh Pa'tridge, en de B'ar," collected by John Bennett, in Bennett Papers, SCHS.

9. Both examples are from Maria Jenkins, SN 14, ii, 27.

10. Sam Samuel, Edisto Island, collected by Chalmers S. Murray, in "Memories of an Island," 115, MS, Chalmers S. Murray Papers, SCHS; "Why the American Negro Speaks No African," MS, Bennett Papers, SCHS; Maria Jenkins, SN 14, iii, 28.

11. Tena White, Mt. Pleasant, interviewed by Martha S. Pinckney, SN 14, iv, 196; Maria Jenkins, SN 14, iii, 27.

12. Ephraim (Mike) Lawrence, SN 14, iii, 94–95, 97; Sam Samuel, in "Memories of an Island," 116, Murray Papers, SCHS; Ephraim (Mike) Lawrence, SN 14, iii, 99; Anon., Edisto Island, collected by Chalmers S. Murray, in South Carolina Folk Tales, 94; John Hamilton, SN 14, ii, 221.

13. Prince Smith, Wadmalaw Island, interviewed by Augustus Ladson, SN 14, iv, 116; Amy Perry, Charleston, interviewed by Jessie A. Butler, SN 14, iii, 253. See Patricia C. Nichols, "To and From in Gullah: An Evolutionary View," paper presented at Linguistic Society of America, San Diego, Calif., December 1973; Nichols, "Linguistic Change in Gullah," 65–82.

14. Ephraim (Mike) Lawrence, SN 14, iii, 95–96; Elizabeth Collins, Memories of the Southern States (Taunton, Eng., 1865), 17; Mary Frances Brown, Mt. Pleasant, interviewed by Cassels R. Tiedman, SN 14, i, 134; Susan Hamlin, SN 14, ii, 223. See also Charles A. Ferguson, "Aspects of Copula and the Notion of Simplicity," in Hymes, ed., Pidginization and Creolization, 141–50; Ralph W. Fasold, "One Hundred Years from Syntax to Phonology," in Sanford Steever et al., eds., Diachronic Syntax (Chicago, 1976), 79–87; Dillard, Black English, 49; Stewart, "Continuity and Change," 3; Lorenzo Dow Turner, Africanisms in the Gullah Dialect, 216.

15. Collins, Memories of the Southern States, 19; Sam Polite, Beaufort County, interviewed by Chlotilde R. Martin, SN 14, iii, 275. See also Turner, Africanisms in the Gullah Dialect, 209–13.

16. Maria Jenkins, SN 14, iii, 28; Daphney Wright, Hampton County, interviewed by Phoebe Faucette, SN 14, iv, 267; Mary Frances Brown, SN 14, i, 134; Ephraim (Mike) Lawrence, SN 14, iii, 98; Jackie ——, "Buh Rabbit, Buh Pa'tridge, en de B'ar," in Bennett Papers SCHS; Ben Horry, Murrells Inlet, interviewed by Genevieve Willcox Chandler, SN 14, ii, 312; Daphney Wright, SN 14, iv, 266; Simon McClair, Edisto Island, in "Memories of an Island," Murray Papers, SCHS; Ben Horry, SN 14, ii, 300. See also Turner, Africanisms in the Gullah Dialect, 225–27; Todd, Pidgins and Creoles, 67; Joseph H. Greenburg, "Africa as a Linguistic Area," in William R. Bascom and Melville J. Herskovits, eds., Continuity and Change in African Cultures (Chicago, 1959), 23; William A. Stewart, "Foreign Language Teaching Methods in Quasi-Foreign Language Situations," in Stewart, ed., Non-Standard Speech and the Teaching of English (Washington, D.C., 1964), 18; Ralph W. Fasold, Tense Marking in Black English: A Linguistic and Social Analysis (Arlington, Va., 1972); John Rickford, "The Insights of the Mesolect," in David DeCamp and Ian F. Hancock, eds., Pidgins and Creoles: Current Trends and Prospects (Washington, D.C., 1974). On the analytical distinction between time as duration and time as sequence, see Robert F. Berkhofer, A Behavioral Approach to Historical Analysis (New York, 1969), 243–69.

17. Phyllis Green, James Island, interviewed by Cassels R. Tiedeman, SN 14, i, 134; Abbey Mishow, Charleston, interviewed by Jessie A. Butler, SN 14, iii, 198; Anon., Edisto Island, collected by Chalmers S. Murray, in South Carolina Folk Tales, 63, 62; Mariah Heywood, "Grandma Kit and Aunt Mariah Heywood," collected by Genevieve Willcox Chandler, Murrells Inlet, in WPA MSS, SCL. See also Cunningham, "Syntactic Analysis of Sea Island Creole," 84.

18. For a detailed analysis of Gullah's distinctive intonation patterns, definitions of eloquence, and the role of the man-of-words, see Joyner, *Down by the Riverside*, 209–24, 169–70.

19. On language as a symbol of shared culture, see David G. Mandelbaum, ed., *Selected Writings of Edward Sapir in Culture, Language, and Personality* (Berkeley, Calif., 1949), 15; William C. Spengemann and L.R. Lundquist, "Autobiography and the American Myth," in Hennig Cohen, ed., *The American Culture: Approaches to the Study of the United States* (Boston, 1968), 495–96; C. Wright Mills, "Language, Logic, and Culture," *American Sociological Review* 4 (1939): 677. On the impact of language on culture (rather than language as a "reflector" of culture), see Michael Silverstein, "Language as a Part of Culture," in Sol Tax and Leslie G. Freeman, eds., *Horizons of Anthropology*, 2d ed. (Chicago, 1977), 130. This interpretation may be taken to deterministic extremes, as it has been by Benjamin Lee Whorf, "Science and Linguistics," in Eleanor Maccoby, ed., *Readings in Social Psychology* (New York, 1958), 5; and Basil L. Bernstein, "Social Class and Linguistic Development: A Theory of Social Learning," in A.H. Halsey et al., eds., *Education, Economy, and Society* (New York, 1961). See also the critique by Gary J. Miller, "Linguistic Constructions of Reality," in Howard Shapiro, ed., *Human Perspectives* (New York, 1972), 84–93.

20. Cf. Clifford Geertz, *The Interpretation of Cultures* (New York, 1973), 89–90, 119; Darryl Forde, ed., *African Worlds: Studies in the Cosmological Ideas and Social Values of African Peoples* (London, 1954); Meyer Fortes, *Oedipus and Job in West African Religion* (Cambridge, 1959); Geoffrey Parrinder, *African Traditional Religion* (London, 1962); William R. Bascom, *Ifa Divination: Communication between Gods and Men in West Africa* (Bloomington, Ind., 1969); E.E. Evans-Pritchard, *Nuer Religion* (Oxford, 1956), and *Witchcraft, Oracles, and Magic among the Azande* (Oxford, 1936); W.E. Abraham, *The Mind of Africa* (London, 1962), ch. 2; R.S. Rattray, *Religion and Art in Ashanti* (Oxford, 1927); John Mbiti, *African Religions and Philosophy* (Garden City, N.Y., 1969), ch. 3; Melville J. and Frances S. Herskovits, *An Outline of Dahomean Religious Belief* (New York, 1933); Martha Warren Beckwith, *Black Roadways: A Study of Jamaican Folk Life* (Chapel Hill, N.C., 1929), chs. 2, 6; Dominique Zahan, *The Religion, Spirituality, and Thought of Traditional Africa*, trans. Kate E. Martin and Lawrence M. Martin (Chicago, 1979); Mechal Sobel, *Trabelin' On: The Slave Journey to an Afro-Baptist Faith* (Westport, Conn., 1979). The importance of a continuing Yoruba and Ashanti influence and declining Bantu religious influence in Afro-American religion, despite Bantu demographic dominance in the New World, is discussed in Roger Bastide, *African Civilizations in the New World*, trans. Peter Green (New York, 1971), 104–15.

21. Charles Ball, *Slavery in the United States: A Narrative of the Life and Adventures of Charles Ball, A Black Man, Who Lived Forty Years in Maryland, South Carolina and Georgia, as a Slave* (New York, 1937), 164–65, 201–3; Rev. Edward Thomas to the Rt. Rev. R.W. Whittingham, 10 March 1836, quoted in Eugene D. Genovese, *Roll, Jordan, Roll: The World the Slaves Made* (New York, 1974), 187; Paul Trapier, *The Religious Instruction of the Black Population: The Gospel to Be Given to Our Servants* (Charleston, S.C., 1847), 14; Henry Brown, Charleston, interviewed by Jessie A. Butler, SN 14, i, 120; John Rogers to "My Dear Children," 5 April 1842, quoted in Genovese, *Roll, Jordan, Roll*, 190. Cf. Freehling, 336–37; Luther P. Jackson, "Religious Instruction of Negroes, 1830–1860, with Special Reference to South Carolina," *Journal of Negro History* 15 (1930): 72–114.

22. Robert F.W. Allston, quoted in Ulrich B. Phillips, "Racial Problems, Adjustments, and Disturbances," in Julian A.C. Chandler et al., *The South in the Building of the Nation* (Richmond, Va., 1909–10), IV, 210.

23. James Henley Thornwell, *The Rights and Duties of the Masters: A Sermon Preached at the Dedication of a Church Erected in Charleston, S.C. for the Benefit and Instruction of the Coloured Population* (Charleston, S.C., 1850), 11; *Public Proceedings Relating to Calvary Church and the Religious Instruction of Slaves* (Charleston, S.C., 1850), 19.

24. Whitemarsh Seabrook, quoted in Freehling, 335; Seabrook, *Essay on the Management of Slaves* (Charleston, S.C. 1834), 15, 28–30.

436

25. Thornwell, *Rights and Duties of Masters*, 11; Alexander Glennie, *Sermons Preached on Plantations to Congregations of Slaves* (Charleston, S.C., 1844), 1–5, 21–27. Cf. John Blassingame, *The Slave Community: Plantation Life in the Ante-Bellum South* (New York, 1972), 170.

26. R.F.W. Allston, *Essay on Sea Coast Crops* (Charleston, S.C., 1854), 41. On the problem of role boundaries in cultures, see Mary Douglas, *Purity and Danger: An Analysis of Concepts of Pollution* (London, 1966), 143.

27. "Edisto's Ghosts Fond of Whiskey," in Murray Papers, SCHS. Cf. Peterkin, "Finding Peace," in *Green Thursday*, 94–101; Roland Steiner, "Seeking Jesus," *Journal of American Folk-Lore* 14 (1901): 672. For comparative examples of the convergence of African spirit possession with Christianity in Afro-American cultures, see Erika Bourguignon, "Spirit Possession and Altered States of Consciousness: The Evolution of an Enquiry," in George D. Spindler, ed., *The Making of Psychological Anthropology* (Berkeley, Calif., 1978), 479–515, and Bourguignon's "Ritual Dissociation and Possession Belief in Caribbean Negro Religion," in Norman E. Whitten, Jr., and John F. Szwed, eds., *Afro-American Anthropology: Contemporary Perspectives* (New York, 1970), 87–101; Elsa Goveia, *Slave Society in the British Leeward Islands at the End of the Eighteenth Century* (New Haven, Conn., 1965), 247–48; Edward Braithwaite, *The Development of Creole Society in Jamaica, 1770–1820* (Oxford, 1971), 219; George E. Simpson, "'Baptismal,' 'Mourning,' and 'Building' Ceremonies of the Shouters of Trinidad," *Journal of American Folk-Lore* 79 (1965): 537–50, and *The Shango Cult in Trinidad* (San Juan, P.R., 1965), 155.

28. Bremer, *Homes in the New World*, I, 290; "Tom-toms Sound for Edisto Rites," in Murray Papers, SCHS; Smith, "A Plantation Boyhood," 75–76; Charlotte Forten, "Life on the Sea Islands," *Atlantic Monthly* 13 (1864): 593–94, and *The Journal of Charlotte L. Forten*, ed. Ray L. Billington (New York, 1953), 153, 184, 190, 205; William Francis Allen, Charles P. Ware, and Lucy McKim Garrison, eds., *Slave Songs of the United States* (New York, 1867), xiv; Thomas Wentworth Higginson, "Negro Spirituals," *Atlantic Monthly* 19 (1867): 685–94, and *Army Life in a Black Regiment* (Boston, 1870), 197–98; Elizabeth Ware Pearson, ed., *Letters from Port Royal* (Boston, 1906), 22–28; Rupert S. Holland, ed., *Letters and Diary of Laura M. Towne: Written from the Sea Islands of South Carolina, 1862–1884* (Cambridge, Mass., 1912), 20–23; Society for the Preservation of Spirituals, *The Carolina Low Country* (New York, 1931), 198–201; Zora Neale Hurston, "Shouting," in Nancy Cunard, ed., *Negro: An Anthology* (London, 1934), 49–50; Willie Lee Rose, *Rehearsal for Reconstruction: The Port Royal Experiment* (Indianapolis, Ind., 1964), 91. The symbolic significance of drums, to both blacks and whites, is illustrated in Edward G. Mason, "A Visit to South Carolina in 1860," *Atlantic Monthly* 53 (1884): 244.

29. Trapier, *Religious Instruction of the Black Population*, 4; Almira Coffin to Mrs. J.G. Osgood, 10 May 1851, in J. Harold Easterby, ed., "South Carolina through New England Eyes: Almira Coffin's Visit to the Low Country in 1851," *SCHM* 45 (1944): 131.

30. MS vol., 10–17, 61–76, 103–4, 112, in Bennett Papers, SCHS; "Boo-Hags," "Conjer-Horses," "Edisto Reveres Old Time Magic," in Murray Papers, SCHS. Cf. Davis, "Negro Folk-Lore," 247; Newbell Niles Puckett, *Folk Beliefs of the Southern Negro* (Chapel Hill, N.C., 1926), 147; Bascom, "Acculturation among the Gullah Negroes," *American Anthropologist* 43 (1941): 49. In Josephine Pinckney's novel *Great Mischief* (New York, 1948), a retelling of the Faust legend, a nineteenth-century Charleston apothecary becomes enmeshed in black magic and is lured to his doom by a charming hag. For a comparative perspective, see Bastide, *African Civilizations in the New World*, 108–10; for an African derivation, E.E. Evans-Pritchard, *Theories of Primitive Religion* (London, 1965), 17.

31. MS vol., 10–17, 61, 76, 103, 112, in Bennett Papers, SCHS; "Conjer Horses Have Passed," "Edisto's Ghosts Fond of Whiskey," and "Edisto Reveres Old Time Magic," in Murray Papers, SCHS. Cf. Bascom, "Acculturation among the Gullah Negroes," 49; F.C. Bartlett, *Psychology and Primitive Culture* (Cambridge, 1923), 63, 110, 117–18.

32. Solbert Butler, Hampton County, interviewed by Phoebe Faucette, SN 14, i, 161–65; Isaiah

Butler, Hampton County, interviewed by Phoebe Faucette, SN 14, i, 160; MS vol., 45–50, in Bennett Papers, SCHS; "Gullahs Nearer to Spirit World," "Edisto Negroes Close to Spirits," and "Voodoo Gods Yet Alive on Islands," in Murray Papers, SCHS. Cf. Bastide, *African Civilizations in the New World*, 108–10.

33. "Memories of an Island," 90–94; "Conjure Horses Have Passed," "Edisto Treasure Tales Unfruitful," and "Negroes Plagued by Edisto Ghosts," in Murray Papers, SCHS. The quotations are from "Negroes Plagued by Edisto Ghosts." See also MS vol., 60, 63–64, in Bennett Papers, SCHS; Peterkin, *Green Thursday*, 77–78. Cf. Henry C. Davis, "Negro Folk-Lore in South Carolina," *Journal of American Folk-Lore* 27 (1914): 248; Puckett, *Folk Beliefs*, 130; Gonzales, *The Black Border*, 33.

34. "Voodoo Survivals Traced on Edisto," "Tom-toms Sound for Edisto Rites," and "Edisto Reveres Old Time Magic," in Murray Papers, SCHS; James R. Sparkman, "The Negro," in Sparkman Family Papers, SCL. For a similar fragmentation of African religion in Jamaica, see Bastide, *African Civilizations in the New World*, 103. That all three streams should be considered aspects of slave religion is suggested by Anthony F.C. Wallace's definition of religion as "that kind of behavior which can be classified as belief and ritual concerned with supernatural beings, powers, and forces" in his *Religion: An Anthropological View* (New York, 1966), 5, and by Mary Douglas, in her *Edward Evans-Pritchard*, 25–26.

35. MS vol., 18–24, 39A, 81–87, 158, in Bennett Papers, SCHS; "Voodoo Gods Yet Alive on Island," "Voodoo Survivals Traced on Edisto," and "Memories of an Island," 193–96, in Murray Papers, SCHS. Cf. George Eaton Simpson, "The Shango Cult in Nigeria and Trinidad," *American Anthropologist* 54 (1962): 1204–29, and *Shango Cult in Trinidad*; Harold Courlander, *The Dream and the Hoe: The Life and Lore of the Haitian People* (Berkeley, Calif., 1960); Alfred Metraux, *Voodoo in Haiti*, trans. Hugo Charteris (New York, 1959); Melville J. Herskovits, *Life in a Haitian Village* (New York, 1937); Mbiti, *African Religions and Philosophy*, 83; Bastide, *African Civilizations in the New World*, 59–60, 101–3; Martha Beckwith, "Some Religious Cults in Jamaica," *American Journal of Psychology* 34 (1923): 32–45; Donald Hogg, "The Convince Cult in Jamaica," in Sidney Mintz, ed., *Papers in Caribbean Anthropology* (New Haven, Conn., 1960); George Eaton Simpson, "Jamaican Revivalist Cults," *Social and Economic Studies* 5 (1956): 321–42: Puckett, *Folk Beliefs*, 167–310; E. Horace Fitchett, "Superstitions in South Carolina," *Crisis* 43 (1936): 360–71; Monica Shuler, "Afro-American Slave Culture," in Michael Craton, ed., *Roots and Branches: Current Directions in Slave Studies* (Willowdale, Ontario, 1979), 129–37.

36. "Voodoo Gods Yet Alive on Islands," "Edisto Overrun by Rattlesnakes," "Voodoo Survivals Traced on Edisto," and "Conjer-Men Keep Den of Reptiles," in Murray Papers, SCHS; *An Account of the Late Intended Insurrection among a Portion of the Blacks of This City*, 3d ed. (Charleston, S.C., 1822), 23. Cf. Davis, "Negro Folk-Lore in South Carolina," 245; Benjamin A. Botkin, "'Folk-Say' and Folk-Lore," in William T. Couch, ed., *Culture in the South* (Chapel Hill, N.C., 1934), 590; Bastide, *African Civilizations in the New World*, 134–47; Paul D. Escott, *Slavery Remembered: A Record of Twentieth-Century Slave Narratives* (Chapel Hill, N.C., 1979), 105; Genovese, *Roll, Jordan, Roll*, 220; Blassingame, *The Slave Community: Plantation Life in the Ante-Bellum South*, 2d ed. (New York, 1979), 41; Zora Neale Hurston, *Mules and Men* (Philadelphia, 1935), 247, and "Hoodoo in America," *Journal of American Folk-Lore* 44 (1931): 317–417; Leonora Herron and Alice M. Bacon, "Conjuring and Conjure-Doctors," *Southern Workman* 24 (1895): 118. Julia Peterkin's novels of Afro-American folklife in the South Carolina lowcountry are veritable catalogs of such folk beliefs: see, e.g., *Black April* (Indianapolis, Ind., 1927), 147–48, 245, and *Bright Skin* (Indianapolis, Ind., 1932), 59.

37. Lionel H. Kennedy and Thomas Parker, *An Official Report of the Trials of Sundry Negroes Charged with an Attempt to Raise an Insurrection in the State of South Carolina* (Charleston, S.C., 1822), 15–16, 78; "Memories of an Island," 108, 193–97, "Edisto Reveres Old Time Magic," in Murray Papers, SCHS; MS vol., 18–24, and "Edisto Negroes Close to Spirits," in Bennett Papers,

SCHS. Cf. Davis, "Negro Folk-Lore," 245–48; Fitchett, "Superstitions," 360–71; Puckett, *Folk Beliefs*, 200; Herron and Bacon, "Conjuring and Conjure-Doctors," 193–94; Blassingame, *Slave Community*, 109; Gilbert Osofsky, ed., *Puttin' on Ole Massa* (New York, 1969), 37; W.E.B. Du Bois, "Religion of the Southern Negro," *New World* 9 (1900): 618, and *The Souls of Black Folk* (Chicago, 1903), 144; "Lizard in the Head," collected by Genevieve Willcox Chandler, WPA MSS, SCL; Peterkin, *Green Thursday*, 158–63: *Black April*, 123, and *Bright Skin*, 114.

38. *An Account of the Late Intended Insurrection*, 23; Solbert Butler, SN 14, i, 165; Thomas Goodwater, SN 14, ii, 169; MS vol., 98–99, Bennett Papers, SCHS. Cf. Peterkin, *Black April*, 26; Bascom, "Acculturation among the Gullah Negroes," 48; J.E. McTeer, *High Sheriff of the Low Country* (Beaufort, S.C., 1970), 22; Elsie Clews Parsons, *Folk-Lore of the Sea Islands, S.C.* (Cambridge, Mass., 1923), 197; Roland Steiner, "Braziel Robinson Possessed of Two Spirits," *Journal of American Folk-Lore* 13 (1900): 226–28; Puckett, *Folk Beliefs*, 137; Herron and Bacon, "Conjuring and Conjure-Doctors," 117. On the African derivation of these beliefs, see Melville J. Herskovits, *The Myth of the Negro Past* (New York, 1941), 190.

39. "Memories of an Island," 196–97, "Edisto Man Has Come-back Boat," "Edisto Negroes Close to Spirits," and "Conjer-Horses Have Passed," in Murray Papers, SCHS; MS vol., 92, in Bennett Papers, SCHS; Kennedy and Parker, *Official Report*, 76–78. Cf. Davis, "Negro Folk-Lore," 247; Herron and Bacon, "Conjuring and Conjure-Doctors," 193–94. On the African provenience of using graveyard dirt, see Bascom, "Acculturation among the Gullah Negroes," 49.

40. "Edisto Reveres Old Time Magic," in Murray Papers, SCHS. Cf. Peterkin, *Black April*, 7; Julia F. Morton, *Folk Remedies of the Low Country* (Miami, Fla., 1974); Davis, "Negro Folk Lore," 246; Wayland D. Hand, *Popular Beliefs and Superstitions from North Carolina* (Durham, N.C., 1961), 858–62; Steiner, "Braziel Robinson," 226–28; Charles W. Chestnutt, "Superstitions and Folklore of the South," *Modern Culture* 13 (1901): 231 35; Herron and Bacon, "Conjuring and Conjure-Doctors," 210–11. The distrust of white medicine is well portrayed in Peterkin, *Black April*, 71, 275, 281–83. For a comparative perspective, see Metraux, *Voodoo in Haiti*.

41. Isaiah Butler, Hampton County, interviewed by Phoebe Faucette, SN 14, i, 160; "Edisto Negroes Close to Spirits," in Murray Papers, SCHS; Kennedy and Parker, *Official Report*, 76.

42. Cf. Peterkin, *Bright Skin*, 51.

43. Henry Brown, SN 14, i, 126. Cf. Albert J. Raboteau, *Slave Religion: The "Invisible Institution" in the Antebellum South* (New York, 1978), 136–37; Bastide, *African Civilizations in the New World*, 92. On the social position of the slave preacher in the slave community, see Blassingame, "Status and Social Structure," 114, 120–21. On the social position of the man-of-words elsewhere in the African diaspora, see Abrahams, *The Man-of-Words in the West Indies*. On the social position of the man-of words in African societies, see S.A. Bababola, *The Content and Form of Yoruba Ijala* (Oxford, 1966), 40–55; Dan Ben-Amos, *Sweet Words: Storytelling Events in Benin* (Philadelphia, 1975), and "Two Benin Storytellers," in Richard M. Dorson, ed., *American Folklore* (Garden City, N.Y., 1972), 103–14; Ruth Finnegan, *Limba Stories and Storytelling* (Oxford, 1966), 64–85; and Judith Irvine, "Caste and Communication in a Woloj Village" (Ph. D. diss., University of Pennsylvania, 1973). For a discussion of the "phenomenon of mid-transition"–those who straddle sacred and secular worlds–see Victor W. Turner, *The Forest of Symbols: Aspects of Ndembu Ritual* (Ithaca, N.Y., 1967), 110, and *Celebration: Studies in Festivity and Ritual* (Washington, D.C., 1982). See also Kenneth Burke, *Language as Symbolic Action: Essays in Life, Literature, and Method* (Berkeley, Calif., 1971), 391; and Peter Berger and Thomas Luckmann, *The Social Construction of Reality: A Treatise in the Sociology of Knowledge* (New York, 1966), 47–49.

44. *An Account of the Late Intended Insurrection*, 22–23, 30; Kennedy and Parker, *Official Report*, 14–15, 50, 54, 61. Other contemporary accounts include Edwin C. Holland, *A Refutation of the Calumnies against Southern and Western States: An Account of the Late Intended Insurrection among Blacks* (Charleston, S.C., 1822); [James Hamilton, Jr.], *Narrative of the Conspiracy and Intended Insurrection among a Portion of the Blacks in the State of South Carolina in the Year 1822* (Bos-

439

ton, 1822); and [Thomas Pinckney], *Reflections, Occasioned by the Late Disturbances in Charleston* (Charleston, S.C., 1822). There is a manuscript trial transcript in [Thomas Bennett] Governor's Message No. 2, 2 November 1822, Governor's Papers, SCSA. Book-length secondary accounts of the Vesey plot include John Lofton, *Denmark Vesey's Revolt: The Slave Plot That Lit a Fuse to Fort Sumter* (Kent, Ohio, 1983); and Robert S. Starobin, ed., *Insurrection in South Carolina: The Slave Controversy of 1822* (Englewood Cliffs, N.J., 1970). Cf. Geertz, *The Interpretation of Cultures,* 123–31.

45. Ball, *Slavery in the United States,* 164–65, Ball Family Papers SCL.

10. Southern Agriculturist: ROSENGARTEN

1. Alfred Glaze Smith, Jr., *Economic Readjustment of an Old Cotton State: South Carolina, 1820–1860* (Columbia, S.C., 1958), 7. For opinions on what caused the cotton depression, see E.J. Donnell, *History of Cotton* (New York, 1872), 79; Smith, *Economic Readjustment,* 7–11; Lewis Cecil Gray, *History of Agriculture in the Southern United States to 1860* (Gloucester, Mass., 1958), II, 737–39; John D. Legaré, "Introduction," *Southern Agriculturist* 1 (1828): iv (hereafter cited as SA).

2. Legaré, "Introduction," SA 1 (1828): i–iv.

3. Quoted from a special report of the South Carolina Agricultural Society, in Smith, *Economic Readjustment,* 9–10.

4. *Ibid.,* from a report of a special committee of the Charleston Chamber of Commerce.

5. William Elliott, "Reflections on Agriculture," SA 1 (1828): 61–66.

6. William Elliott, "An Address Delivered before the Beaufort (S.C.) Agricultural Society," SA 11 (1838): 346–60.

7. Beaufort, "Answers to 'Edisto-Island,'" SA 9 (1836): 346.

8. Dr. Samuel H. Dickson, "Address to the Charleston Horticultural Society," SA 5 (1832): 450.

9. Rev. John Bachman, "Address to the Charleston Horticultural Society," SA 6 (1833): 394.

10. *Ibid.*

11. In 1826, a year of deep pessimism, when prices for sea-island cotton hovered around the break-even point of 18 cents a pound, the fine variety grown by Kinsey Burden of St. John's Parish, Colleton District, brought $1.10; in 1827, $1.25. And in 1828, Burden sold two bags of cotton—about seven hundred pounds—for $2 a pound, a price never matched at the market.

12. Samuel G. Stoney, ed., "The Autobiography of William John Grayson," *SCHM* 50 (1949): 131.

13. Whitemarsh B. Seabrook, "On the Causes of the General Unsuccessfulness of the Sea-Island Planters," SA 7 (1834): 177.

14. Seabrook, "A Report Accompanied with Sundry Letters," SA 1 (1828): 26.

15. Colleton [Joseph E. Jenkins], "Some of the Causes of the Decline and Fall of most of the Agricultural Societies of South-Carolina," SA 8 (1835): 113–15.

16. Seabrook, "A Report," 26.

17. H.C., "On the Management of Negroes—Addressed to the Farmers and Planters of Virginia," SA 7 (1834): 369.

18. W.W. Hazzard, "Hints, at some of the causes of those evils Young Planters complain of, and a remedy proposed," SA 1 (1828): 252.

19. For an example of hostility toward colonization societies, see Legaré, "Editorial Remarks," SA 2 (1829): 575.

20. Hazzard, "Hints," 252.

21. Francis D. Quash, "An Address delivered in Charleston, before the Agricultural Society of South-Carolina," SA 4 (1831): 510.

22. Seabrook, "Reflections on the Theory and Practice of Agriculture," SA 5 (1832): 230.

23. A Practical Planter, "Further Observations on the more general use of the Plough on the Seaboard," SA 5 (1832): 69.

24. Quoted in Raymond Williams, *The Country and the City* (New York, 1973), 46.

25. A Merchant, "On Ginning Cotton, for a late Market," *SA* 9 (1836): 525.

26. Elliott, "On the Cultivation and High Prices of Sea-Island Cotton," *SA* 1 (1828): 162–63; he is quoting Horace, *First Book of Epistles*, 6th Epistle, lines 67–68.

27. Dickson, "Address," 456.

28. Samuel G. Stoney, ed., "Memoirs of Frederick Adolphus Porcher," *SCHM* 47 (1946): 85.

29. Quash, "Address," 505.

11. *City, Country, and the Feminine Voice:* STOWE

1. Harriott Horry Ravenel, *Charleston: The Place and the People* (New York, 1906), 385.

2. The literature on the historical meaning of the woman's sphere is ever-growing. Among the now almost classic studies are Carroll Smith-Rosenberg, "The Female World of Love and Ritual: Relations between Women in Nineteenth–Century America," *Signs* 1 (1975): 1–29; Nancy Cott, *The Bonds of Womanhood* (New Haven, Conn., 1977), esp. 197–206; Mary Beth Norton, "The Paradox of Women's Sphere," in Carol Berkin and Mary Beth Norton, eds., *Women in America: A History* (Boston, 1979), 139–49; Rayna Reiter, ed., *Toward an Anthropology of Women* (New York, 1975). More recent are Barbara Leslie Epstein, *The Politics of Domesticity: Women, Evangelism, and Temperance in Nineteenth-Century America* (Middletown, Conn., 1981); Mary P. Ryan, *Cradle of the Middle Class: The Family in Oneida County, New York, 1790–1865* (Cambridge, Mass., 1981), esp. chs. 4, 5; John Mack Faragher, *Women and Men on the Overland Trail* (New Haven, Conn., 1979), esp. chs. 4, 5. Interesting for the late nineteenth century and generally suggestive is Elizabeth Hampsten, *Read This Only to Yourself: The Private Writings of Midwestern Women, 1880–1910* (Bloomington, Ind., 1982).

3. Ravenel, *Charleston*, 385–86. See also Lawrence Fay Brewster, *The Summer Migrations and Resorts of South Carolina Lowcountry Planters* (Durham, N.C., 1947), *passim*.

4. Mary Howard Schoolcraft, *The Black Gauntlet: A Tale of Plantation Life in South Carolina* (1860), reprinted as *Plantation Life: The Narratives of Mrs. Henry Rowe Schoolcraft* (New York, 1969), 114–15.

5. Susan Petigru King, *Lily* (New York, 1855), 104.

6. Elizabeth Allston Pringle, *Chronicles of Chicora Wood* (New York, 1922), 129.

7. Mary Boykin Chesnut, "Two Years—Or the Way We Lived Then" (MS ca. 1875), 305, Williams-Chesnut-Manning collection, SCL.

8. King, *Lily*, 107 08.

9. Chesnut, "Two Years," 260–61.

10. For a typical description of the gay season, see Pringle, *Chronicles*, 160ff.

11. General reference works for reading and writing in this period are Lyle Wright, *American Fiction, 1774–1850* (San Marino, Calif., 1969); Louis D. Rubin, ed., *A Bibliographical Guide to the Study of Southern Literature* (Baton Rouge, La., 1969); Matthew J. Bruccoli, *The Profession of Authorship in America, 1800–1870* (n.p., 1968); Mary Kelley, *Private Woman, Public Stage: Literary Domesticity in Nineteenth-Century America* (New York, 1984); Nina Baym, *Woman's Fiction: A Guide to Novels By and About Women in America, 1820–1870* (Ithaca, N.Y., 1978); Helen Papashvily, *All the Happy Endings* (New York, 1956). Anne Goodwyn Jones, *Tomorrow Is Another Day: The Woman Writer in the South, 1859–1936* (Baton Rouge, La., 1982), has intriguing suggestions about the antebellum period as well. Helpful in placing women writers in a large cultural context are Ann Douglas, *The Feminization of American Culture* (New York, 1977), and Susan P. Conrad, *Perish the Thought: Intellectual Women in Romantic America, 1830–1860* (New York, 1976). Older views of Southern women writers, including selections from their work, are John S. Hart, *The Female Prose Writers of America* (Philadelphia, 1857); Julia Deane Freeman, *Women of the South Distinguished in Literature* (New York, 1861); Mary T. Tardy, *Southland Writers: Biographical and Critical*

Sketches of the Living Female Writers of the South, 2 vols. (Philadelphia, 1870); George A. Wauchope, *Writers of South Carolina* (Columbia, S.C., 1910). A critical study of the city-and-country theme in its many forms in English literature from the eighteenth century is Raymond Williams, *The Country and the City* (New York, 1973).

12. For Caroline Gilman's self-assessment, see her sketch in Hart, *Female Prose Writers*, 49–57; Freeman, *Women of the South*, 48–50; Wauchope, *Writers of South Carolina*, 165; Baym, *Woman's Fiction*, 67–71.

13. Caroline Gilman, *Recollections of a Southern Matron* (New York, 1838), 201; Hart, *Female Prose Writers*, 56.

14. Gilman, *Southern Matron*, 31.

15. *Ibid.*, 110.

16. *Ibid.*, 57, 10. Interesting parallels are seen in the diary of Mary Moragné, a young woman in the Abbeville District of South Carolina. See Delle Mullen Craven, ed., *The Neglected Thread: A Journal from the Calhoun Community, 1836–1842* (Columbia, S.C., 1951).

17. Gilman, *Southern Matron*, 78.

18. *Ibid.*, 11, 110.

19. *Ibid.*, 108, 118.

20. *Ibid.*, 138–39.

21. *Ibid.*, vii.

22. J.L. Petigru to Jane P. North, 21 May 1839, in *Petigru*, 204; Wauchope, *Writers of South Carolina*, 223; Tardy, *Southland Writers*, II, 861. There are biographical notes on King in *Petigru*, 204n, and in J.R. Scafidel, "Susan Petigru King: An Early South Carolina Realist," in James B. Meriwether, ed., *South Carolina Women Writers* (Spartanburg, S.C., 1979), 101–15. Petigru, perhaps to his surprise, came to appreciate and even admire his daughter's literary efforts, even to the point of once referring to her as a "great writer." Though hardly a reader of women's fiction, Petigru occasionally advised his daughter as to style and effort, and in suggesting Jane Austen as a writer to be emulated, he approved of novelists' attempts to "attain to the delineation of the passions." See Scafidel, "Susan Petigru King," 102.

23. In another novel, King has a character remark, upon hearing from her fiancé that he wished to take up planting: "I never engaged myself to a planter. . . . I vow you shall never have me vibrating between rice-fields and pine-lands": *Sylvia's World* (New York, 1859), 74.

24. King, *Lily*, 19, 187. The title page notes only "By the Author of 'The Busy Moments of an Idle Woman.'" The author's voice frequently breaks into the story, as in ch. 15, where she justifies the story's verisimilitude as a higher aesthetic.

25. *Ibid.*, 21, 28.

26. *Ibid.*, 28.

27. *Ibid.*, 24. King wrote a volume, *Crimes Which the Law Does Not Reach* (New York, 1859), every sketch in which unmasks a drawing room "crime" (flirtation, arranged marriage, false conversation) that imperiled women.

28. King, *Lily*, 86.

29. *Ibid.*, 24.

30. *Ibid.*, 191–92, 248. King could be critical of Charlestonians, however; see, e.g., *ibid.*, 95, 116–17, 193.

31. Illusion and reality in the lives of planter-class women is a theme that deserves more attention. See, for glimpses, Ann F. Scott, *The Southern Lady: From Pedestal to Politics, 1830–1930* (Chicago, 1970); Harriet E. Amos, "'City Belles': Images and Realities of the Lives of White Women in Antebellum Mobile," *Alabama Review* 34 (1981): 3–19; Harland D. Hagler, "The Ideal Woman in the Antebellum South: Lady or Farmwife?" *JSH* 44 (1980): 405–18; Steven M. Stowe, "'The Thing Not Its Vision': A Woman's Courtship and Her Sphere in the Southern Planter Class," *Feminist Studies* 9 (1983): 113–30.

32. This is not the place to give the discussion of the Chesnut manuscripts the full attention it merits. Changes in the way the manuscripts have been viewed by historians, and in the manuscripts themselves, are an interesting cautionary story of historical fashion and judgment. C. Vann Woodward has an excellent discussion of the manuscripts and their publishing saga in *Chesnut*, xv–xxix. Some of the important issues were confronted, if not resolved, at the Second Reynolds Conference at the University of South Carolina in 1975; see Meriwether, ed., *South Carolina Women Writers*, sessions V and VI. In the citations of Chesnut's manuscripts that follow, I rely on my own work with them in the Williams-Chesnut-Manning collection, SCL. Since then, Professor Woodward's definitive volume has appeared, so I include page references to it for convenience. In my citations, "1880s MS" refers to the memoir in diary form; "1860s MS" refers to the actual diary that survives.

Diarists receive little treatment in the literary criticism directed to the form and style of women writers. Female novelists command the most attention, and among the most generally useful works of criticism are Mary Ellman, *Thinking About Women* (New York, 1968); Elaine Showalter, *A Literature of Their Own* (Princeton, N.J., 1977), and Vineta Colby, *The Singular Anomaly: Women Novelists of the Nineteenth Century* (New York, 1970), which raise important questions of literary style and femininity. Joan Kennard, *Victims of Convention* (Hamden, Conn., 1978), and Nina Auerbach, *Woman and the Demon* (Cambridge, Mass., 1982), are two interestingly different studies of the thematic content of femininity in nineteenth-century fiction. Also suggestive in a more general way are Helene Roberts, "The Inside, the Surface, the Mass: Some recurring Images of Women," *Women's Studies* 2 (1974): 289–308; Ann Wood, "Mrs. Sigourney and the Sensibility of Inner Space," *New England Quarterly* 45 (1972): 163–81; Janice A. Radway, "Women Read the Romance: The Interaction of Text and Context," *Feminist Studies* 9 (1983): 53–78.

33. For a full biography see Elisabeth Muhlenfeld, *Mary Boykin Chesnut* (Baton Rouge, La., 1981). See also *Chesnut*, xxx–liii.

34. John Manning to "Dearest Wife" [1860], typed copy, Williams-Chesnut-Manning collection, SCL. Mary Chesnut sometimes traded "plain talk" with Susan King but was wary of King's public acerbity and wit, writing "I am as afraid of her as death": *Chesnut*, 692–93.

35. Chesnut, 1880s MS, 26 February 1865 (*Chesnut*, 740); 10 March 1862 (*Chesnut*, 301). Chesnut admired the writing of William Russell, the British journalist, who may have been a model for her new "public" voice. Eileen Gregory notes that the conventions of the diary permitted Chesnut to achieve intimacy with her readers, but it seems to me that the integrative power of a diary is even more important. See Gregory's interesting paper, "The Formality of Memory: A Study of the Literary Manuscripts of Mary Boykin Chesnut," in Meriwether, ed., *South Carolina Women Writers*, 229–40.

36. This is not to suggest that Chesnut did not want her book to be entertaining or that she did not polish her writing; she did both. I am suggesting that the diary form allowed her to do this while liberating her from the "feminine" conventions of fiction, daybooks, and commonplace books. In this regard, see C. Vann Woodward, "Mary Chesnut in Search of Her Genre," *Yale Review* 73 (1984): 199–209.

37. Chesnut, 1880s MS, ca. 24 July 1861 (*Chesnut*, 114); 1860s MS, bound book with entries February–August 1861; 1880s MS, ca. 23 April 1861 (*Chesnut*, 51). One woman in Chesnut's circle whom she both liked and admired was Louisa S. McCord, whose own literary work contrasted interestingly with the efforts of the women in this essay. McCord was unique among female authors with connections to Charleston in that she spoke from inside the male sphere of political discourse and, more particularly, literary criticism. Also a poet and dramatist, McCord was the exceptional woman whose strong critical voice neither betrayed femininity in the eyes of men nor critically extended woman's sphere beyond existing conventions. In this sense she might be seen as joining a tradition of women who, for different reasons, became accepted in the larger (that is, male) intellectual world. In intellectual Charleston this tradition ranged from the dar-

ing wit and good offices of Madame de Staël to the somber, densely argued ethics of Hannah More. McCord, too, was learned, incisive, often engaging, but finally orthodox in her world view and in her support of elite interests. She was proslavery, pro-South, aristocratic, and wholly accepting of the separate, long-suffering position of women. And though she was respected by intellectual men for her formulations of these concerns, periodicals did not resist noting "the female hand" behind her essays, thus calling attention to a femininity she herself neither emphasized nor explored; see, e.g., the editor's note in *SQR*, n.s., 7 (1853): 233, and Lounsbury, *infra*, 325–36.

38. Chesnut, 1880s MS, 19 March 1861 (*Chesnut*, 31); 30 November 1861 (*Chesnut*, 250–51). See also 11 November 1861 (*Chesnut*, 238).

39. Chesnut, 1880s MS, 29 August 1861 (*Chesnut*, 176).

40. *Ibid.*, 1880s MS, March 1865 (*Chesnut*, 762); 30 November 1861 (*Chesnut*, 248). See also, e.g., both 1880s and 1860s MSS in *Chesnut*, 72.

41. Chesnut, 1880s MS, October 1861 (*Chesnut*, 220); 24 May 1862 (*Chesnut*, 349); 30 November 1861 (*Chesnut*, 250); 10 June 1861 (*Chesnut*, 69).

42. Chesnut, 1880s MS, 5 January 1864 (*Chesnut*, 528); Varina Davis to Mary Chesnut, 20 September 1865, Chesnut letter book, Williams-Chesnut-Manning collection, SCL; Chesnut, 1860s MS, 11 March 1861 (*Chesnut*, 23).

43. See Williams, *Country and City*, 288–90.

44. John S. Hart's assessment of Caroline Gilman is in Hart, *Female Prose Writers*, 49.

45. F.A. Porcher, in *SQR* 9 (1854): 212–13.

46. James H. Hammond to W.G. Hodgson, 1 January 1846, James H. Hammond papers, Duke University; F.A. Porcher, "Historical and Social Sketch of Craven County," *SQR* 9 (1854): 378, 403–4.

47. James H. Hammond diary, 17 April 1838; see also entry for 6 May 1838, James H. Hammond papers, LC.

48. William Porcher Miles, "American Literature and Charleston Society," *SQR* 7 (1853): 405, 418. Mary Chesnut liked Miles himself, as well as his voice; see Chesnut, 1880s MS, September 1863 (*Chesnut*, 444, 447–49).

49. Chesnut, 1880s MS, 3 June 1862 (*Chesnut*, 359).

12. Ludibria Rerum Mortalium: LOUNSBURY

1. *Chesnut*, 428.

2. Thomas Grimké, *Oration on the Comparativ Elements and Dutys of Grecian and American Eloquence . . .* (Cincinnati, Ohio, 1834), 20–21, 23, 53–54. Orthographical oddities are Grimké's.

3. Louisa McCord, "Enfranchisement of Woman" [*SQR*, n.s., 5 (1852)], in *All Clever Men*, 349–50; "Woman and Her Needs," *DeBow's Review* 13 (1852): 280–82; Caroline Healey Dall, *Historical Pictures Retouched. A Volume of Miscellanies* (Boston, 1860), 3, cited in Susan P. Conrad, *Perish the Thought: Intellectual Women in Romantic America, 1830–1860* (New York, 1976), 167.

4. *Discourses on Art*, ed. Robert R. Wark (New Haven, Conn., 1975), 59.

5. Louisa McCord, "Woman and Her Needs," 268; "Uncle Tom's Cabin," *SQR*, n.s., 7 (1853): 81; "Separate Secession," *SQR*, n.s., 4 (1851): 307; Livy 7.6.1–5.

6. "Woman and Her Needs," 288. Cf. James Wood Davidson, *Living Writers of the South* (New York, 1869): "Her mind is Roman in its cast and heroic in its mould—she was Roman, always Roman, and not even Corinthian, always Doric" (cited by Susan S. Bennett, "The Cheves Family of South Carolina," *SCHM* 35 [1934]: 91). Reference to the orders narrows the Roman nature to its most austere.

7. "Mrs. M'Cord's Caius Gracchus," *DeBow's Review*, n.s., 1 (1852): 428.

8. Louisa S. McCord, *Caius Gracchus. A Tragedy in Five Acts* (New York, 1851); "Caius Gracchus," *SQR*, n.s., 4 (1851): 68. As it has turned out lately, *Caius Gracchus* has attracted a very ready indifference. The standard account of Southern literature mentions it only in passing, as a closet drama; to a history of Charleston dramatists, it is but a title: Jay B. Hubbell, *The South in American Literature, 1607–1900* (Durham, N.C., 1954), 607; Charles S. Watson, *Antebellum Charleston Dramatists* (Tuscaloosa, Ala., 1976), 48. In the biographical introduction to a recent edition of one of her essays, Mrs. McCord's play is explained in an impulse toward "sentimental verse and fiction," and is consigned to the level of a Beerbohm parody, but with "the disadvantage of seriousness" (a stage direction is usefully provided as evidence): *All Clever Men*, 337. An exception is Margaret F. Thorp, *Female Persuasion: Six Strong-Minded Women* (New Haven, Conn., 1949), 199–201; her whole chapter on Mrs. McCord, although published more than thirty years ago, remains valuable and without company. (Susan Conrad's discussion is little more than a paraphrase of Thorp: since she locates the subject of *Caius Gracchus* in "the early days of the Roman Republic" and believes the hostile *SQR* critique of the play to "ignore its artistic failings," one may wonder about her familiarity with reviewer or reviewed, wonder increased when she labels a "romance" what both *DeBow's* and the *SQR*, who had troubled themselves to read the play beforehand, explicitly judged nothing of the kind: Conrad, *Perish the Thought*, 194, 221. Calling the work "ponderous" is similarly automatic, and similarly to be diagnosed: *ibid.*, 221.)

9. "Caius Gracchus," 62–63.

10. "Mrs. M'Cord's Caius Gracchus," 428–29. Her own opinion of modern taste was not high: cf. "Uncle Tom's Cabin," 83 (on romantic novels); "Woman and Her Needs," 273 (on the "nauseous filth" of Sand, Sue, and Dumas). An edition of her poems, *My Dreams*, collected and printed by her husband as a surprise (Philadelphia, 1848), was a most unpleasant one, which she tried to correct by suppressing the book: Bennett, "Cheves Family," 91. Enjoying a Johnsonian hatred of cant, she also thought little of the virtuous queen who would lend her name to the new age: "The Right to Labor," *SQR* 16 (1849): 143–44; "Woman and Her Needs," 281.

11. Louisa McCord, "Uncle Tom's Cabin," 86–87.

12. "Mrs. M'Cord's Caius Gracchus," 428.

13. S.v. "Langdon Cheves," *Dictionary of American Biography*, IV, 63: "He was described by Washington Irving as the first orator he ever heard who satisfied his idea of Demosthenes." Thorp, *Female Persuasion*, 182, adds Cicero to the comparison. A discussion of Cheves' oratory, though without an antique reference, occurs in a letter to James Renwick, 8 December 1812: Irving, *Letters, Volume 1, 1802–1823*, ed. Ralph M. Aderman et al. (Boston, 1978), 346. Notice Mrs. McCord's judgment of the oratory of separate secession: "Separate Secession," 305–6.

14. Cicero *Brutus* 125–26: "But now we have before us a man of outstanding native intellect, of dedicated application, and rigorously trained from childhood, Gaius Gracchus."

15. *Caius Gracchus*, 14–15.

16. *Ibid.*, 51–57 (commencing with a reminiscence of the first line of Antony's funeral speech in Shakespeare's *Julius Caesar*), 61–71. Cf. Plutarch *Gaius Gracchus* 3.2–4; 5.2–3.

17. For Tiberius and Gaius Gracchus, see, most recently, David Stockton, *The Gracchi* (Oxford, 1979).

18. "Caius Gracchus," 63.

19. *Caius Gracchus. Tragédie en trois Actes*, in *Oeuvres de M.J. Chénier* (Paris, 1827), II, 167–220, 219. Cf. Eugène Jouffret, *Le Théâtre révolutionnaire (1788–1799)* (1869; rpt., Geneva, 1970), 155–60.

20. V. Monti, *Caio Gracco*, in *Opera*, ed. M. Valgimigli and C. Muscetta, "La letteratura italiana. Storia e testi" (Milan, n.d.), LIV, 820–922; J.S. Knowles, *Caius Gracchus: A Tragedy*, in *The Dramatic Works of James Sheridan Knowles* (London, n.d.), I, 1–58.

21. *Satire* 2.24: "Who would tolerate the Gracchi complaining about sedition?"

22. "Separate Secession," 300–2, 311; "Woman and Her Needs," 279; "Uncle Tom's Cabin," 89–90, 119; "Carey on the Slave Trade," *SQR*, n.s., 9 (1854): 167; *Chesnut*, 377.

23. "Justice and Fraternity," *SQR* 15 (1849): 356–57, 370–71; "The Right to Labor," 138–40, 143.

24. *Caius Gracchus*, 41–43.

25. "Mrs. M'Cord's Caius Gracchus," 428; *Caius Gracchus*, 68. Cf. Thorp, *Female Persuasion*, 200: "She makes no attempt to force parallels between the Roman and the contemporary political situation but all the characters [except, surely, Opimius and his friends] speak the word 'Senator' with such bitterness that one inevitably hears beside it the adjective 'Yankee.'"

26. *Chesnut*, 328, 304.

27. *Satire* 6.161–71: "You, Cornelia, mother of the Gracchi."

28. Valerius Maximus *Facta et Dicta Memorabilia* 4.4 *praef*; R. Rosenblum, *Transformations in Late Eighteenth-Century Art* (Princeton, N.J., 1967), 61–62; A. Pigler, *Barockthemen*, II (Budapest, 1956), 367; Bennett, "Cheves Family," 91: "As mistress of a plantation . . . when asked once why she wore no jewelry, she replied that a woman with two hundred children could hardly afford diamonds."

29. Livy 22.49; "Separate Secession," 311.

30. See Stockton, *Gracchi*, 23–26, and references there; Juvenal *Satire* 6.166: "Who can bear a wife who has everything?"

31. Cicero *Brutus* 211; Quintilian 1.1.6.

32. "Woman and Her Needs," 289–90.

33. *Caius Gracchus*, 20.

34. Plutarch *Tiberius Gracchus* 8.5; Appian *Bella Civilia* 1.20.

35. Chénier, *Caius Gracchus*, 181–82, 197–99; contrast McCord, *Caius Gracchus*, 24–25, 58–61, 75–77, 88–91.

36. *Caius Gracchus*, 21.

37. *Ibid.*, 106–08.

38. Plutarch *Gaius Gracchus* 15; Frederick Porcher, "Modern Art" [*SQR*, n.s., 5 (1852)], in *All Clever Men*, 319–20.

39. *Caius Gracchus*, 112–13.

40. *Ibid.*, 120–21; contrast Plutarch *Gaius Gracchus* 16.4–5.

41. George Frederick Holmes, "Writings of Hugh Swinton Legaré," *SQR* 9 (1846): 324; Mary Legaré, ed., *Writings of Hugh Swinton Legaré*, 2 vols. (Charleston, S.C., 1845–46), II, 408 (henceforth cited as *Writings*). Oddities of classical allusion can yet be of interest, quite against the author's intention. Legaré, observing "with a sensation of horror" Byron's animosity towards his mother, thinks "involuntarily" of Nero and Agrippina: rather a shrill shudder, illuminating Legaré's difficult sympathy with that poet (*Writings*, II, 394).

42. James Henley Thornwell, "Memoir of Dr. Henry" [*SQR* 2, n.s., 1 (1856)], in *All Clever Men*, 423; Cicero *De Oratore* 3.1–8; Tacitus *Agricola* 43–46.

43. *Caius Gracchus*, 42, 7.

44. "Enfranchisement of Woman," in *All Clever Men*, 353–54 (italics in original). Appearing a year after her play, these words may hint at her sense of its failure.

45. Cf. Louisa McCord, "Woman and Her Needs," 272: The feminists "forget the woman's duty-fulfilling ambition, to covet man's fame-grasping ambition. Woman was made for *duty*, not for *fame*; and so soon as she forgets this great law of her being, which consigns her to a life of heroism if she will—but quiet, unobtrusive heroism—she throws herself from her position, and thus, of necessity, degrades herself" (italics in original).

46. *Caius Gracchus*, 58. Cf. Shakespeare, *Coriolanus*, III, ii, 125–30.

47. Plutarch *Gaius Gracchus* 19; *Chesnut*, 429, 628, 787–88. The statue: Pliny *Naturalis Historia* 34.31; Plutarch *Gaius Gracchus* 4.3. The inscription read: *Cornelia Africani F. Gracchorum*

("daughter of Africanus, [mother] of the Gracchi"). Cf. Louisa S. McCord / Daughter of Langdon Cheves / Wife of David James McCord / Born Dec. 3, 1810 / Died Nov. 23, 1879 / At Rest (cited by Bennett, "Cheves Family," 92). The echo tells the model, the omission the ruin, of her hopes.

48. William Campbell Preston, *Eulogy on Hugh Swinton Legaré* (Charleston, S.C., 1843), 20.

49. Cicero *Brutus* 290; cf. *De Oratore* 1.30–34; Tacitus *Dialogus de Oratoribus* 6.4; Hugh Swinton Legaré, "The Roman Orators," SR 2 (1828): 504–7.

50. Bartholomew Rivers Carroll, Jr., "Sketch of the Character of the Hon. Hugh S. Legaré," SQR 4 (1843): 356, 360.

51. Legaré, "Roman Orators," 519–39; Plutarch *Comparison of Demosthenes and Cicero*; Hugh Blair, *Lectures on Rhetoric and Belles Lettres*, ed. Harold F. Harding, 2 vols. (Carbondale, Ill., 1965), II, 30–34.

52. William Campbell Preston, *Eulogy on Legaré*, 26.

53. Legaré, "Roman Orators," 492.

54. Legaré to Francis Walker Gilmer, 1 October 1816; the letter is given in Richard Beale Davis, *Literature and Society in Early Virginia, 1608–1840* (Baton Rouge, La., 1973), 298–302.

55. Legaré, "Roman Orators," 539; Edward Gibbon, *History of the Decline and Fall of the Roman Empire*, ed. J.B. Bury, 7 vols. (London, 1909–14), I, 85–86. Legaré also quotes Milton, *Paradise Lost*, III, lines 52–53.

56. Legaré, *Writings*, I, 385–88.

57. Legaré to Francis Walker Gilmer, 24 August 1816, in Davis, *Literature and Society*, 297; *Writings* II, 84.

58. Jacob N. Cardozo, "Ancient and Modern Oratory," SR 5 (1830): 319–37, esp. 321, 336.

59. Legaré, "Roman Orators," 513, 532–38.

60. *Ibid.*, 512.

61. Legaré, "Crafts' Fugitive Writings" [SR 1 (1828)], in *Writings*, II, 157–58, 144, 146. Legaré's speech of 4 July 1823 is in *Writings*, I, 257–69. Begun by invoking the exordium of a "celebrated" deliberative speech, Cicero's *De Imperio Cn. Pompei*, it soon returns to its own generic opportunities, lavish of *exempla*, allusions, exclamations, tremendous periods, questions indignant and triumphant, and poetic diction and devices assisted by the contribution of Gray's "Bard" and Byron's "Ode on Venice."

62. Legaré, "Roman Orators," 508, 527; David Hume, "Of Eloquence," in *Of the Standard of Taste and Other Essays*, ed. John W. Lenz (Indianapolis, Ind., 1965), 67. Cf. Hugh Blair, *Lectures*, II, 32.

63. Legaré, "Roman Orators," 514, 533, 538.

64. Cardozo, "Ancient and Modern Oratory," 319, 323–24.

65. Legaré, "Classical Learning" [SR (1828)], in *Writings*, II, 7n: "To add that he is now crowning the honors of his useful and blameless life, with a blessed and venerated old age, is only to say, that he has received the sure reward *pure et eleganter actae aetatis.*" Not all men, says Cato, can be great martial leaders like Fabius Maximus; as Plato and Isocrates testify, *est etiam quiete et pure et eleganter actae aetatis placida ac lenis senectus* (*De Sen.* 5.13): "There is also the peaceful and gentle old age of a life lived quietly, virtuously, and with civility." *Quiete* omitted, Legaré dissolves Cato's distinction and unites Pinckney to Fabius, Plato, and Isocrates together, as Pinckney unites their qualities in himself.

66. George Frederick Holmes, "The Athenian Orators," SQR, n.s., 4 (1851): 352–89; 354.

67. *Ibid.*, 373–75. Charles Fraser was similarly troubled. As a painter, he directed his attention to the correlation between the fine arts and political and moral decline. Precedents were not cheerful. In Athens, "amidst the vicissitudes and agitations of a turbulent and corrupt democracy, painting and sculpture attained to their greatest perfection," and so, too, in Rome they "spread the gorgeous drapery of luxury and refinement over her decaying form." Venice and Flor-

ence, more recently, confirmed the conclusion: the fine arts "are rather associated with the old age than the manhood of a country, and destined to be most exuberant and flourishing upon the very boundary line which separates national prosperity from decay." Defender of the arts, Fraser was obliged to prove his own country exempt from the laws illustrated by his precedents: fundamental differences between American and the ancient societies, and the example of Great Britain, he believed satisfactory to establish his case. See Charles Fraser, "The Fine Arts," *SR* 4 (1829): 70–76.

68. *Writings*, I, 218, 77; Holmes, "Athenian Orators," 386, 388.

69. Preston, *Eulogy on Legaré*, 28–29. Such description is frequent in Cicero's Catilinarian orations: e.g., *Videor enim mihi videre hanc urbem, lucem orbis terrarum atque arcem omnium gentium, subito uno incendio concidentem. Cerno animo sepulta in patria miseros atque insepultos acervos civium, versatur mihi ante oculos aspectus Cethegi et furor in vestra caede bacchantis*, and so on (*In Catilinam* 4.6.11–13): "For I seem to see this city, the light of the world and the citadel of all the nations, collapsing in one sudden conflagration. With my mind, I perceive in my buried fatherland heaps of citizens wretched and unburied; before my eyes loom the vision of Cethegus [one of Catiline's chief henchmen] and his madness, as he revels in your slaughter."

70. Legaré to Isaac Holmes, 2 October 1832, in *Writings*, I, 206.

71. Carroll, "Sketch of Legaré," 354; Legaré to Alfred Huger, 15 December 1834, in *Writings*, I, 216.

72. Legaré to Alfred Huger, 21 November 1835, in *Writings*, I, 224.

73. Legaré, "Roman Orators," 514. To Thomas Grimké, the press was "that master-piece of modern genius, that master-workman in the cause of the people," which helped to assure the superiority of the modern over the ancient orator: *Grecian and American Eloquence*, 29–32. Grimké was of the alien camp, but neither did Holmes share Legaré's alarm, merely noting that the great numbers of Athenian speakers presented "a striking analogy to the innumerable herd of authors . . . characteristic of our own days, when, as Macaulay justly observes, the press has in great measure supplanted the Bema" ("Athenian Orators," 375). Cf. Macaulay, "On the Athenian Orators" (1824), in *Miscellaneous Writings of Lord Macaulay*, 2 vols. (London, 1860), I, 135.

74. Legaré, "Diary of Brussels," entry for 8 May 1833, in *Writings*, I, 5.

75. Legaré, "Roman Orators," 514. Legaré notifies the reader at once: his separation of "eloquence" from "speakers" and "debaters" is a paraphrase of the first sentence of the *Dialogus*: *saepe ex me requiris, Iuste Fabi, cur, cum priora saecula tot eminentium oratorum ingeniis gloriaque floruerint, nostra potissimum aetas deserta et laude eloquentiae orbata vix nomen ipsum oratoris retineat; neque enim ita appellamus nisi antiquos, horum autem temporum diserti causidici et advocati et patroni et quidvis potius quam oratores vocantur* (1.1): "You often ask me, Fabius Justus, why, when former ages have flourished with the talents and fame of so many eminent orators, our own age lies deserted and deprived of the reputation for eloquence; it scarcely retains the very name of orator. For we never use this word except for the ancients; skilled speakers of our own times are called 'pleaders' and 'advocates' and 'counsel' and whatever you like rather than 'orators.'"

76. *Dialogus* 40.2, 41.4: "That great and famous eloquence which is the foster-child of license"; [the emperor] "wisest and by himself." Legaré's fondness: *Writings*, I, 5, 461.

77. Hence his dislike of Jefferson, whom, however much he praised the Declaration, he dubbed "the Arminius of our institutions" (referring to the barbarian leader under Tiberius) and "the holy Father in democracy—the servant of the servants of Demus (whose nose of wax he knew better than any body how to shape to his own convenience)": *Writings*, I, 43, 208. See also his admiration for the great antidemocrat, Aristophanes (I, 40), and the jibes at I, 204.

78. Preston, *Eulogy on Legaré*, 14.

79. William Grayson, *James Louis Petigru* (New York, 1866), 89–90; cited in William R. Taylor, *Cavalier and Yankee: The Old South and American National Character* (New York, 1961), 58. Cf.

e.g., *Dialogus* 19, 26.1–5; M. Winterbottom, "Quintilian and the *Vir Bonus*," *Journal of Roman Studies* 54 (1964): 90–97; George Kennedy, *The Art of Rhetoric in the Roman World, 300 B.C.– A.D. 300* (Princeton, N.J., 1972), 440–42.

80. Legaré to Isaac Holmes, 8 April 1833, in *Writings*, I, 215. Cf. similar remarks at I, 43, 203, 208, 211, 218, 221–23; also Charles Fraser to Legaré, 30 January 1833, in David Moltke-Hansen, ed., *Art in the Lives of South Carolinians: Nineteenth-Century Chapters* (Charleston, S.C., 1979), AM-6. Fraser prefers Ciceronian language: for his *respublica est afflicta*, see, e.g., *Epistulae ad Atticum* 1.18.3. Contrast the sanguine expectations for American oratory expressed by Thomas Roderick Dew, "Republicanism and Literature" [*Southern Literary Messenger* 2 (1836)], in *All Clever Men*, 149–51. Later, at the national level, Legaré too professed some hope for democratic eloquence: "Demosthenes: The Man, the Statesman, and the Orator" [*New York Review* 9 (1841)] in *Writings*, I, 443–44. But Bartholomew Carroll deemed his evidence, certain recent exhibitions of oratory and the discriminating response of their audiences, to have been misinterpreted by a secluded and scholarly temperament insufficiently aware of "all the tricks of party" that had whipped those audiences into a suitable mood beforehand: "Sketch of Legaré," 353–54.

81. Preston, *Eulogy on Legaré*, 29; Hume, "Of Eloquence," 69.

82. Carroll, "Sketch of Legaré," 358–59; Holmes, "Writings of Legaré," 351–52.

83. *Writings*, I, 439.

84. Grimké, *Grecian and American Eloquence*, 12, 7, 11.

85. *Ibid.*, 12, 45, 50–51.

86. Grimké, *Oration on American Education . . .* (Cincinnati, Ohio, 1835), 16–17.

87. Legaré, "Classical Learning," in *Writings*, II, 30.

88. Grimké, *Grecian and American Eloquence*, 17–18, 45, 19, 21, 40–41.

89. *Writings*, I, 439.

90. Legaré, "Roman Orators," 526, 530.

91. *Ibid.*, 507; [Johnston] "Biographical Notice," in *Writings*, I, lxvi.

92. "Sketch of Legaré," 350; cf. Juvenal *Satire* 3.29–33.

93. Holmes, "Writings of Legaré," 347.

94. Legaré to Isaac Holmes, 2 October 1832, in *Writings*, I, 205–06. See also II, 412, 419 (Cicero and Byron); I, 500 (Demosthenes and Rousseau); II, 440–41 (Manfred and Orestes). There are many more comparisons of this kind.

95. Porcher, "Modern Art," 325, 330, 313, 315.

96. *Ibid.*, 314, 332, 319.

97. *Ibid.*, 327, 317–18.

98. This imitation must be distinguished carefully from imitation in the sense of representing, in whatever way, Nature directly (Greek *mimesis* and Latin *imitatio* comprehend both senses): when Porcher calls "purely imitative" the arts of sculpture and architectural decoration, he means no opprobrium, only a contrast with literature (*ibid.*, 317, 328). See D.A. Russell, "*De Imitatione*," in D. West and A. Woodman, eds., *Creative Imitation and Latin Literature* (Cambridge, 1979), 1–16.

99. Porcher, "Modern Art," 319, 327.

100. *Ibid.*, 333.

101. *Ibid.*, 335.

102. *Ibid.*, 333–34.

103. *Ibid.*, 325–26, 324–25, 320–21.

104. *Ibid.*, 322 and O'Brien's note *ad loc.*

105. For Reynolds' attitude toward Hogarth, see *Discourses on Art*, 254–55. Nature is a continuous theme through the *Discourses*: e.g., "My notion of nature comprehends not only the forms which nature produces, but also the nature and internal fabrick and organization, as I may call it, of the human mind and imagination. The terms beauty, or nature, which are general ideas, are but different modes of expressing the same thing, whether we apply these terms to statues,

poetry, or picture. . . . This general idea therefore ought to be called Nature, and nothing else, correctly speaking, has a right to that name" (p. 124).

106. Legaré, "Early Spanish Ballads – Charlemagne and His Peers" [SR 5 (1830)], in *Writings*, II, 299–300.

107. *Writings*, II, 321, 350, 52–58; I, 529–30. On Legaré's admiration for the Germans, see, e.g., *Writings*, I, 444, and II, 168; cf. Jesse Burton Harrison, "English Civilization" [SR 8 (1832)], in *All Clever Men*, 80–81. On Schlegel's attitude to the classical literatures, see René Wellek, *A History of Modern Criticism, 1750–1950*: II, *The Romantic Age* (New Haven, Conn., 1955), 61–62; on Schlegel and Legaré, in particular their definitions of classicism and romanticism, see O'Brien, *supra*, 142–48; for Legaré's meeting with Schlegel, Legaré, "German Diaries," in *All Clever Men*, 98–104.

108. J.L. Reynolds, "Roman Literature," *SQR* 10 (1846): 352–76; 352, 355.

109. *Ibid.*, 358–59.

110. *Ibid.*, 375.

111. Gibbon, *Decline and Fall*, VII, 136–37.

112. Richard Whately, *Elements of Rhetoric*, ed. Douglas Ehninger (Carbondale, Ill., 1963), xxxiii–xxxiv; Edward T. Channing, *Lectures Read to the Seniors in Harvard College*, ed. Dorothy I. Anderson and Waldo W. Braden (Carbondale, Ill., 1968), 26–28.

113. Legaré, "Roman Orators," 533; *Writings*, II, 149, I, 497; "Roman Orators," 521; *Writings*, II, 70, 33, 464; Samuel Butler, *Hudibras*, First Part, Canto I, lines 89–90: "For all a Rhetoricians Rules / Teach nothing but to name his tools."

114. *Writings*, I, 463.

115. Dionysius of Halicarnassus *Lysias* 11.

116. Gibbon, *Journal* for 3 September 1762, quoted in D.A. Russell, ed., *'Longinus' On the Sublime* (Oxford, 1964), 89. Notice also "the sublime Longinus" in *Decline and Fall*, I, 63, 326; and Pope, *Essay on Criticism*, lines 675–80, ending "And is himself that great Sublime he draws." The *sententia* goes back to Boileau and beyond: see Russell, xlii, n. 2. The authorship of Longinus is very doubtful nowadays, but such expedients as 'Longinus' or pseudo-Longinus or "the author *On the Sublime*" are cumbersome and scarcely necessary.

117. Legaré, "Roman Orators," 522.

118. Longinus *De Sublimitate* 1.1–2. The translation is that of D.A. Russell in *Ancient Literary Criticism*, ed. D.A. Russell and M. Winterbottom (Oxford, 1972).

119. Legaré, "Roman Orators," 533; Corneille, *Horace*, line 1021; Hugh Blair, *Lectures*, I, 52–53.

120. Legaré, "Roman Orators," 532–38; *Writings*, I, 210; "Roman Orators," 521; Blair, *Lectures*, I, 52.

121. Longinus *De Sublimitate* 13.2.

122. Johann Joachim Winckelmann, *Geschichte der Kunst des Altertums* (Darmstadt, 1982), 365; Reynolds, *Discourses on Art*, 219, also 98–99; Dionysius *Demosthenes* 22 (trans. Russell); *Writings*, I, 501.

123. *Writings*, I, 444.

124. *Ibid.*, II. 432, 424–25; Winckelmann, *Geschichte der Kunst*, 364.

125. Legaré, "Roman Orators," 525–26, and citing Reynolds, *Discourses on Art*, 58–59, 61.

126. Reynolds, *Discourses on Art*, 171.

127. *Writings*, I, 489, 494.

128. *Ibid.*, I, 498, 483–85.

129. *Ibid.*, I, 476, 492, 494; Grimké, *Grecian and American Eloquence*, 39. On Demosthenic eloquence "full of soul," cf. Legaré, "Roman Orators," 523, referring to Quintilian 10.7.15.

130. Hume, "Of Eloquence," 68. Hugh Blair (for Legaré on Blair, see *Writings*, I, 457, 474, 496, 499) tried unsuccessfully to straddle the conflict. See Wilbur Samuel Howell, *Eighteenth-Century British Logic and Rhetoric* (Princeton, N.J., 1971), 614–16, 658–60.

131. *Writings*, I, 498, 494; Porcher, "Modern Art," 327; cf. Reynolds, *Discourses on Art*, 100.

132. Basil Gildersleeve, *The Creed of the Old South, 1865–1915* (Baltimore, Md., 1915), 77.

133. George Frederick Holmes, "Louis Napoleon and Augustus Caesar," *SQR*, n.s., 10 (1854): 1–37; 2–4.

134. "War and Its Incidents," *SQR* 13 (1848): 1–54; 2, 20, 5, 39, 53, 6.

135. Legaré, "Constitutional History of Greece–The Democracy of Athens" [*New York Review* 7 (1840)], in *Writings*, I, 367–442, esp. 441–42; "The Public Economy of Athens" [*SR* 8 (1832)], in *Writings*, II, 502–58; "The Origin, History and Influence of Roman Legislation" [*NYR* 5 (1839)], in *Writings*, I, 502–58, esp. 522–23. On Legaré and Roman civil law, see O'Brien, *supra*, 138–39.

136. Grimké, *Grecian and American Eloquence*, 45.

137. Legaré, "Classical Learning," in *Writings*, II, 7–8.

138. Grimké, *An Address on the Character and Objects of Science and Especially the Influence of the Reformation on the Science and Literature, Past, Present and Future, of Protestant Nations: Delivered . . . on . . . the Anniversary of the Literary and Philosophical Society of South-Carolina* (Charleston, S.C., 1827).

139. *Ibid.*, 11–12.

140. *Ibid.*, 29–30, 11–12, 34, 31–32.

141. *Ibid.*, 76–79.

142. Grimké, *Oration on American Education*, 16–18; *Grecian and American Eloquence*, 18.

143. Grimké, *Character and Objects of Science*, 62–63; cf. Legaré, "Classical Learning," 21.

144. Grimké, *Oration on American Education*, 11.

145. England, *Oration, Delivered on the Anniversary of the Literary and Philosophical Society of South Carolina, on Wednesday the Ninth of May, 1832 . . .* , in *The Works of the Right Rev. John England . . .* , 5 vols. (Baltimore, Md., 1849), V, 21.

146. *Ibid.*, 21–22.

147. Grimké, *Grecian and American Eloquence*, 18; *Oration on American Education*, 30.

148. England, *Oration*, 23–24, 19.

149. Grimké, *Oration on American Education*, 39.

150. Legaré, "Classical Learning," 38.

151. Legaré, "Public Economy of Athens," in *Writings*, II, 504.

152. Legaré, "Classical Learning," 47.

153. Grimké, *Character and Objects of Science*, 70; Legaré, "Classical Learning," 20–21; "Roman Literature" [*SR* 1 (1828)], in *Writings*, II, 57.

154. Legaré, "Classical Learning," 15–16, 21.

155. *Ibid.*, 22.

156. *Ibid.*, 50.

157. Grimké, *Character and Objects of Science*, 31, 66–73.

158. James H. Smith, *Eulogium on the Life and Character of Thomas S. Grimké . . .* (Charleston, S.C., 1835), 17–18. For the text of the Yale Report (with small omissions) see "Original Papers in Relation to a Course of Liberal Education," *American Journal of Science and Arts* 15 (1829): 297–351; extracts are given in Richard Hofstadter and Wilson Smith, eds., *American Higher Education: A Documentary History*, 2 vols. (Chicago, 1962), I, 275–91.

159. Legaré, "Classical Learning," 51; Grimké, *Character and Objects of Science*, 73.

160. Basil Gildersleeve, "The Necessity of the Classics" [*SQR*, n.s., 10 (1854)], in *All Clever Men*, 404, 408–11, 416.

161. *Ibid.*, 417–18.

162. C.W.E. Miller, "Basil Lanneau Gildersleeve," *American Journal of Philology* 45 (1924): 100. See also George A. Kennedy, "Gildersleeve, The Journal, and Philology in America," *American Journal of Philology* 101 (1980): 1–11.

163. Gildersleeve, "Formative Influences," *Forum* 10 (1891): 607–8, 617.

164. Gildersleeve, *The Creed of the Old South*, 85–87, 124, 8; Legaré, "Classical Learning," 22. See also George A. Kennedy, "A Southerner in the Peloponnesian War," *Southern Humanities Review, Special Issue: "The Classical Tradition in the South"* (Auburn, Ala., 1977), 21–25.

165. Legaré to Isaac Holmes, 8 April 1833, in *Writings*, I, 208; Tacitus *Annales* 3.18.4 (Legaré, quoting from memory, has *ludibrium rerum humanarum*).

166. "Classical Learning. Hugh Swinton Legaré *versus* Thomas S. Grimké," *Southern Literary Messenger* 34 (1862): 368–75, 368, 372.

452

Acknowledgments

THIS BOOK was planned in Columbia, when Michael O'Brien held a visiting research professorship and David Moltke-Hansen a graduate research assistantship at the former Southern Studies Program of the University of South Carolina. James B. Meriwether, that program's director, thus must assume an oblique responsibility for the volume's inception, though none for its shape and contents.

In order to concentrate minds, a conference was held in March 1982. The South Carolina Historical Society's director, Gene Waddell, agreed to ask the Society's board for permission to sponsor various grant applications. The Waring Medical History Library Society of the Medical University of South Carolina and the College of Charleston cosponsored these applications, themselves contributed funds, and offered conference facilities. The American Council of Learned Societies and the South Carolina Committee for the Humanities, an agent of the federal National Endowment for the Humanities, generously funded grant requests, as did the Foundation for American Education, whose president is Charles Scott Hamel. WSCI Radio of Charleston cosponsored as well as taped the conference and prepared eight programs, subsequently aired on South Carolina's public radio stations; John Dozier was the station's executive producer, and Timothy Bull its producer.

For the contributors to this volume, much was gained from the other invited participants in the Charleston conference: Thomas Bender, Carol Bleser, John C. Guilds, A.V. Huff, George A. Kennedy, E. Christian Kopff, James B. Meriwether, R. Nicholas Olsberg, George C. Rogers, Diane Sydenham, Mills Thornton, Jon L. Wakelyn, Clyde N. Wilson, and Peter H. Wood. As conference organizers and as editors, we have drawn upon the counsels of Mavis Bryant, Ann Donato, Curtis Worthington, the members of the Robert Wilson Medical History Club,

George Heltai, John Bevan, John Dressler, John Duffy, Henry Tom, Martha Fisher, and David Sloan. Some of the thoughts in the Preface were aired to the British Association of American Studies in Edinburgh in April 1983. For typing, we wish to thank Suzanne Stoner, Kim Cummings, Lori Sletten, and Suzanne Maberry. But the editors are most indebted to the essayists themselves, who have borne with fortitude a protracted gestation.

M. O'B
    Fayetteville, Arkansas

D. M-H
    Charleston, South Carolina

The Contributors

LACY FORD is Assistant Professor of History at the University of South Carolina. He served in 1982–83 as a Research Fellow at the Institute for Southern Studies, University of South Carolina, and in 1983–84 as a visiting Assistant Professor of Civil War and Reconstruction History at the University of California, Berkeley.

LAYLON WAYNE JORDAN is Professor of History at the College of Charleston. A North Carolinian, he received his Ph.D. from the University of Virginia. His publications include several essays on the evolution of Charleston as an urban center.

CHARLES JOYNER, who holds Ph.D. degrees in both history and folklore, is the author of *Folk Song in South Carolina* (1971) and *Down by the Riverside: A South Carolina Slave Community* (1984), which focuses on All Saints Parish in the South Carolina lowcountry.

MARK D. KAPLANOFF is a Californian who was educated at Exeter and at Yale, where he won the Henry Fellowship to study in England. He took his Ph.D. at Cambridge, where he is now University Lecturer in History and a Fellow of Pembroke College.

RICHARD LOUNSBURY teaches Classics and Comparative Literature at Brigham Young University. He is at work on a book dealing with classical antiquity in the intellectual history of the antebellum South.

JOHN MCCARDELL is Associate Professor of History at Middlebury College in Vermont. He received his Ph.D. from Harvard in 1976. His *The Idea of a Southern Nation* (1979) was awarded the Allen Nevins Prize.

He is now working on both a biography of William Gilmore Simms and a short interpretive history of the Old South, 1820–60.

DAVID MOLTKE-HANSEN, though born in Norway, is maternally a Charlestonian. He is a graduate of the College of Charleston and the University of South Carolina, and director of the South Carolina Historical Society. He is the editor of *Art in the Lives of South Carolinians: Nineteenth-Century Chapters* (1979), annotator of *The Charleston Book* (1983), and coauthor of *The South Carolina Historical Society Manuscript Guide.*

MICHAEL O'BRIEN is Professor of History at the University of Arkansas and a graduate of the University of Cambridge. He is the author of *The Idea of the American South, 1920–1941* (1979) and the editor of *All Clever Men, Who Make Their Way: Critical Discourse in the Old South* (1982). His *A Character of Hugh Legaré* is published with this volume.

JANE H. PEASE and WILLIAM H. PEASE are both Professors of History at the University of Maine at Orono. Their comparison of Boston and Charleston has been published as *The Web of Progress* (1985).

THEODORE ROSENGARTEN lives in McClellanville, South Carolina. He received his Ph.D. from Harvard in 1975. His first book, *All God's Dangers: The Life of Nate Shaw*, won a National Book Award in 1974. The recipient of a Lyndhurst Prize in 1983–85, he has just edited an antebellum plantation diary and written a biography of the diarist, Thomas B. Chaplin of Saint Helena Island, South Carolina.

ARTHUR H. SHAFFER is Professor of History at the University of Missouri, St. Louis. He is the author of *The Politics of History*, and the editor of *Edmund Randolph's History of Virginia* and (with James D. Norris) of *Politics and Patronage in the Gilded Age: The Garfield-Henry Correspondence.*

STEVEN M. STOWE is Assistant Professor of History at Pennsylvania State University. He received his Ph.D. in 1979 from the State University of New York, Stony Brook, working with William R. Taylor, and is completing a study of the family life and social values of the antebellum Southern elite.

Index

Abbeville District, 157, 159
Aberdeen, 50
Abolitionism, 182, 225
Achilles, 362
Adams, Henry, 37, 185
Adams, Jasper, 29, 240, 252, 428
Adams, John, 55, 94, 107, 108, 157
Adams, Samuel, 65
Addison, Joseph, 26
Adventists, 215
Aemilius Paullus, 331
Aeneas, 346, 362
Aeschylus, 146, 348
Agassiz, Louis, 33, 221
Agrippina, 326, 446
Aix-la-Chapelle, 129, 148
Alabama, 36
Alabama, University of, 30
Alexandria, 363
Alien and Sedition Acts, 106, 157
Allston, Joseph Blyth, 38
Allston, Robert F.W., 267, 269
Allston, Washington, 22, 27, 28
Alps, 219
Amadis of Gaul, 148
American Academy of Arts and Sciences, 253
American Journal of Philology, 368, 369
American Lyceum, 7
American Monthly Magazine, 7
American Philological Association, 368
American Philosophical Society, 4, 55, 237, 253
American Revolution, xii, 7, 8, 23, 24, 25, 48, 57–68, 86, 89, 90, 121, 150, 160, 199, 209, 217, 221, 222, 283, 340
American System, 91
Anacreon, 364
Anglicanism, 67, 176
Antigone, 326

Antigua, 259
Apollo, 359
Apollo Belvedere, 356–57
Apprentices Library Society, 9, 10, 249, 250, 430
Aratus, 363
Archias, 337
Ariosto, 147
Aristides, 222
Aristotle, 351
Arminius, 448
Arnold, Thomas, 33
Aspasia, 326, 327
Athens, x, 342, 345
Atlas, 333
Audubon, John James, 6, 236
Augsburg Confession, 215
Augustus Caesar, 360
Austen, Jane, 302
Austrian Empire, 129

Bachman, John, 6, 20, 29, 40, 82, 213, 236, 242, 283, 428
Baehr, Johann Christian, 353
Bailey, Nathan, 24
Ball, Caroline Augusta Rutledge, 38
Ball, Charles, 278
Baltimore, 16, 41, 128, 131
Bancroft, George, 33, 84
Bank of the United States, First, 27
Bank of the United States, Second, 161, 164, 222
Bantu, 269, 273
Baptists, 243
Barbados, 259
Barbot, Louis, 39
Barnard, Henry, 221
Baron, Alexander, 24
Bartram, William, 6
Baruch, Simon, 39

Baudelaire, Charles, 37
Bavaria, 129
Bay, Elihu Hall, 24, 56
Bayard, Chevalier, 201, 202
Beaufort, S.C., 13, 158, 162, 259, 281, 284, 288
Beaufort College, 30
Bee, Barnard, 178
Bee, Thomas, 24, 56
Beerbohm, Max, 445
Belgium, 129, 132, 342
Belknap, Jeremy, 52, 53, 57, 69
Bender, Thomas, ix
Bennett, John, 258
Bennett, Thomas, 216, 223
Bennett, W. Jefferson, 225
Beowulf, 148
Beresford, Richard, 24
Bermuda, 67
Bible, 88, 216, 229, 268, 269
Blackstone, William, 174
Blackwood's Magazine, 33
Blain, William S., 431
Blair, Hugh, 337, 356
Blue Ridge Railway, 16, 226
Boccaccio, Giovanni, 147
Boileau, Nicholas, 356, 450
Bolingbroke, Henry Saint-John, 1st Viscount, 360
Boston, x, 4, 12, 16, 17, 22, 25, 35, 40, 127, 128, 131, 159, 194, 195, 196, 199, 226, 254, 284
Bounetheau, Henry, 28
Bowen, Nathaniel, 27, 30
Boyce, James P., 39
Boyer, Abel, 24
Brackenridge, Hugh Henry, 53
Brantley, William, 243
Brantly, William T. Sr., 30
Brazil, 259
Breckinridge, John, 121
Bremer, Frederika, 270
Brisbane, Abbot Hall, 34
Brisbane, William, 27
Brown, Henry, 258, 267
Brown, Joseph Brownlee, 38
Browning, Robert, 33
Bruns, John Dickson, 38
Brussels, 22, 124, 127, 129, 134, 348, 369
Bryan, Edward Benjamin, 39
Bryan, George S., 34
Buffalo, N.Y., 209
Buist, George, 24, 30
Buist, John Somers, 39
Bull, William, 23
Burke, Edmund, xi, 18, 141–42

Butler, Pierce, 135
Butler, Samuel, 354
Butler, Solbert, 271, 272
Byron, Lord, 26, 33, 35, 137, 138, 143–47, 148, 348, 446, 447

Caecilius, 356
Cain, D.J.C., 34
Calhoun, John C., 37, 116, 130, 132, 134, 157, 160, 164, 165, 178, 181, 183, 224, 348, 351, 360
Calvin, John, 361
Cambridge, University of, 294
Cape Cod, 131
Capers, Ellison, 39
Capers, F.W., 34
Capers, William, 29
Cardozo, Jacob, 18, 19, 30, 339, 340, 341
Carey and Hart, 4
Carey, Matthew, 53
Carlyle, Thomas, 33
Carpenter, Stephen, 27
Carrington, 150
Carroll, Bartholomew, 34, 294, 337, 345, 347
Carroll, Charles, 34
Carroll family, 131
Carthage, 331
Carvalho, Solomon, 34
Castle Pinckney, 307
Cataline, 343, 448
Catesby, Mark, 50
Cato's Letters, 63
Cerberus, 342
Cethegus, 448
Chalmers, Lionel, 50
Channing, Edward Tyrrell, 195, 354
Chaplin, Benjamin, 285
Charlemagne, 148
Charleston, College of, xii, 7, 8, 9, 17, 24, 29, 30, 34, 38, 125, 226, 239, 240–43, 250, 252
Charleston, People's Bank of, 222
Charleston Bar Association, 428
Charleston *City Gazette*, 9
Charleston *Courier*, 30, 151, 162, 203, 208, 237
Charleston Democratic Club, 66–67
Charleston Forensic Club, 126
Charleston Horticultural Society, 283
Charleston Library Society, 23, 27, 41, 53, 57, 63, 126, 155, 179, 237, 249, 295, 430
Charleston Literary and Philosophical Society, 4, 18, 21, 26, 28, 237, 250, 362
Charleston *Mercury*, 30, 177, 182, 196, 203, 205, 208, 227

Charleston Neck, 382
Charleston *Observer*, 29
Charleston Orphan House, 8, 214, 215
Charleston *Spectator and Ladies Literary
   Folio*, 30
Cheesborough, Essie, 39
Chénier, Marie-Joseph, 329, 330, 332
Chesapeake, 5
Chesnut, James Jr., 38, 314–15, 318
Chesnut, Mary Boykin, 12, 38, 39, 152, 153,
   184, 299, 300, 301, 302, 314–23, 325–26,
   331, 336, 443
Cheves, Langdon, 18, 27, 38, 40, 157, 329
Chicago, 228
Chicora, 35
Childe Harold, 137
China, 420
Chisolm, Julian John, 39
Christ, Jesus, 140, 361
Christianity, 144
Cicero, 112, 125, 329, 332, 335, 337, 338,
   339, 340, 341, 343, 347, 348, 360, 362,
   363, 366, 409, 447
Cid, El, 148
Cincinnati, 196, 226
Civic humanism, ix, 217
Civil War, 87, 89, 90, 111, 116, 117, 187,
   226, 227, 228, 229, 290, 416
Clapp, John Milton, 34
Clare, Ada (McElhenney), 39
Clariosophic Society, 158
Classical and Philosophical Academy, 432
Clay, Henry, 91, 92, 94, 95, 165, 175, 360
Clitheral, James, 23
Cobb, Howell Jr., 158
Codification, 172–75
Cogdell, John Stevens, 28
Coggeshall, William, 196
Cogswell, Joseph, 131
Coke, Sir Edward, 137
Colden, Cadwallader, 50
Coleridge, Samuel Taylor, 26, 139, 143, 148,
   219
College of Pennsylvania, 25, 27
Colleton District, 285
Collinson, Peter, 50–51
Colombia, 259
Columbia, S.C., 38, 40, 82, 129, 158, 351
Columbia University, 4
Columbian Orator, 217
Commercial Review of the South & Southwest, 10
Committee of Public Safety, 64
Common sense philosophy, 148, 218, 220
Confederate States of America, 158, 215,
   318, 423
Congregationalism, 52, 54, 242, 243

Connecticut, 221
Conservatives, 127, 180
Constitution of 1787, 62, 89, 90, 92, 93,
   153, 157, 160, 179, 221
Continental Congress, 52, 64, 86, 102
Cook, Charles M., 167
Cooper, James Fenimore, 33, 35, 149, 187
Cooper, Thomas, 167, 168, 172, 178, 244
Coosawhatchie, S.C., 154, 156, 166
Coriolanus, 331
Corneille, Pierre, 350, 356
Cornelia, 331–34, 336
Cortes, Hernando, 186
Cosmopolitan, 35
Courtenay, William Ashmead, 39
Crafts, William, 28, 32, 340, 354
Crawford, William H., 158
Crittenden, John J., 135
Cruger, Henry, 149
Cuba, 259
Cujas, Jacques, 136
Cullen, William, 394
Curacao, 259
Curtis, Moses, 236
Cuvier, Georges L.C.F., 7

Dahomey, 273
Dalcho, Frederick, 26
Dall, Caroline, 327
Dana, Mary, 34
Dana, W.C., 34
Dante, 145, 147
Danton, Georges-Jacques, 358
Dartmouth College v Woodward, 246
Darwin, Charles, 37
David, Jacques Louis, 351
David, King, 270
Davies, Samuel, 79
Davis, Charles, 430–31
Davis, Jefferson, 315
Davis, Thomas Frederick, 34
De Leon, Edwin, 35
Deas, Elias Horry, 34
Deas, John, 55
DeBow, J.D.B., xii, 22, 37, 39
DeBow's Review, 121, 328, 330
Declaration of Independence, 227, 330, 340–
   41, 343, 356
Degler, Carl, 154
DeHon, Theodore, 27
Deism, 67
Delphi, 146, 356
Demades, 342, 359
Democrats, 120, 165, 166
Demosthenes, 337–40, 342–43, 345, 347–48,
   354–60

DeSaussure, Henry William, 27, 34, 167, 170
DeSaussure, Wilmot Gibbes, 39
DeVeaux, James, 34
Diana, 334
Dickens, Charles, 33, 168, 302
Dickson, Samuel Henry, 11, 29, 32, 177,
    245, 246, 248, 250, 253, 291–92, 429
Dido, 346
Dinnies, Anna, 34
Dionysius, 355, 357, 359
Dionysius of Halicarnassus, 360
Dodona, 146
Don Juan, 217
Donald, David, 184
Dostoevski, Fyodor, 37
Dowling, Dan J., 431
Drayton, John, 6, 25, 27
Drayton, William, 130, 133
Drayton family, 163
Dryden, John, 124, 179
Dueling, 77
Dukes, Joseph, 21, 34
Dukes, William Christopher, 31
Dunkin, Benjamin F., 29
Dunlap, William, 53
Dusseldorf, 33

East Indies, 283
Eaton, Clement, 213
Edinburgh, x, xi, xiii, 5, 17, 25, 27, 40, 50,
    129, 130, 131
Edinburgh, University of, 54, 125, 136, 386
Edinburgh Review, 26, 33
Egypt, 268
Eliot, John, 52, 70, 75
Elliott, Benjamin, 28
Elliott, Stephen (elder), 6, 26, 28, 41, 126,
    130, 151, 239, 252
Elliott, Stephen (younger), 127
Elliott, William, 12, 31, 155, 162, 163, 177,
    183, 282, 286, 291, 431
Elliott Natural History Society, 9
Embargo of 1807, 94, 110
Emerson, Ralph Waldo, ix, 33, 211–12
England, John, 20, 29, 362, 363–64
Enlightenment, 11, 48, 54, 59, 66–68, 84,
    179, 217, 218, 219, 395–96
Epictetus, 363
Episcopalians, 20, 175, 177, 242, 243
Equity law, 168–72
Erskine College, 179
Estill, William, 431
Euripides, 348
Evening Spy, 30
Everett, Alexander, 141
Ewe, 262, 264, 273

Fabius, 447, 448
Fante, 262
Fante-Ashanti, 269
Farmer, Henry Tudor, 29
Faust, Drew Gilpin, 184
Faustus, Dr., 350
Fayssoux, Peter, 24
Federalism, 78, 80, 101, 102–5, 109, 111, 112,
    114, 116, 156ff
Fénelon, Francois de Salignac de La
    Mothe-, 411
Fenwick Island, 263
Ferguson, Adam, 60
Ffirth, Stubbins, 27
Fichte, J.G., 143, 220
Fielding, Henry, 26
Fillmore, Millard, 154
Finley, Samuel, 79
Flagg, George Whiting, 34
Flinn, Andrew, 27
Floral Wreath, 35
Florence, 447–48
Fon, 273
Ford, Timothy, 27
Forrest, Edwin, 33
Fort Sumter, 262, 317
Founding Fathers, 160, 181, 220
France, 39, 50, 94, 98, 107, 129, 366
Franklin, Benjamin, 50, 55, 430
Franklin, John Hope, 212
Franklin Society, 249
Fraser, Charles, 4, 7, 8, 18, 20, 21, 28, 149,
    177, 211, 238, 239, 240, 447–48
Frederickson, George, 157, 184
Free blacks, ix
Freehling, William, 149, 163
French Directory, 169
French Guiana, 259
French Institute, 237
French Revolution, 19, 25–26, 66, 76, 142,
    329–30
Freneau, Peter, 24, 30
Frost, Henry Rutledge, 29
Fuller, Richard, 34
Furman, Richard, 24

Ga, 259
Gadsden, C.P., 39
Gadsden, Christopher, 18, 29, 56, 63, 64,
    65, 69, 78
Gadsden, John, 130, 151
Gaillard, P.C., 34
Gaius, 138
Gallagher, S.F., 18
Garden, Alexander, 23, 24, 50, 52
Garrick, David, 337

Gates, Mrs., 188
Geathers, Walter, 258–59
Geddes, John, 27
Geddings, Eli, 29, 244
Generations (concept of), 386
Geneva College, 240
Gentleman's Magazine, 24
Geoffrey of Monmouth, 148
Georgetown, S.C., 13, 214, 259
Georgetown, Va., 128
Georgia, 125, 205, 212, 221, 223, 259, 283, 288, 322
Georgia, University of, 179
German Friendly Society, 251
Germany (and Germans), 27, 39, 50, 142, 144, 212, 214, 215, 224, 243, 328, 352, 353, 365, 366, 367
Gibbes, Lewis R., 34
Gibbon, Edward, 67, 338, 355, 363
Gildersleeve, Basil Lanneau, 38, 177, 367–69
Gildersleeve, Benjamin, 29
Gilman, Caroline, 30, 40, 82, 243, 301, 302–8, 313, 314, 315, 316, 317, 319, 320, 323, 431
Gilman, Samuel, 29, 40, 82, 238, 243, 302, 428
Gilmer, Francis Walker, 126, 338, 339
Ginzburg, Carlo, 229
Girardeau, John L., 39
Giyou, Madame, 308
Glover, Francis, 34
Glover, Joseph, 27
Godey's Lady Book, 205
Goethe, J.W. von, 26, 33, 143
Goldsmith, Oliver, 18, 150
Goose Creek, 154
Gordon, Thomas, 63
Gospel Messenger, 29
Gothicism, 145
Göttingen, 27, 138, 177, 367
Gourdin, Robert N., 226
Gracchi, 326–36
Gray, Thomas, 26, 447
Gray Sulphur Springs, 293
Grayson, William J., 13, 28, 155, 158, 177, 179, 183, 284, 344
Greece (and Greeks), 98, 130, 136, 144–48, 291, 328
Green, Elijah, 258
Greene, Nathaniel, 201, 202, 205
Greenville, S.C., 262
Grenada, 259
Grimké, Angelina, 21, 22
Grimké, John Faucherand, 24, 56
Grimké, Sarah, 21, 22

Grimké, Thomas Smith, 21, 22, 28, 32, 130, 140, 151, 167, 172, 237, 241, 326, 327, 345–47, 359, 361, 362, 363, 365, 366, 367, 369, 448
Guadaloupe, 259
Guizot, François, 33
Gullah, 259–66
Gullah Jack, 276
Guyana, 259

Haiti, xii, 259, 274
Hale, Sarah, 302
Hall, Basil, 255
Hall, Francis, 19
Halle, 138
Hamburg Railroad, 15
Hamilton, Alexander, 78, 91, 95, 107
Hamilton, James, 28, 164, 237
Hammond, Bray, 222
Hammond, James Henry, 18, 193, 204, 225, 321, 322
Hampden, John, 137
Hanckel, Christian, 29
Hanckel, Thomas Middleton, 39
Hanscombe, Thomas, 241
Happoldt, Christopher, 39
Harby, Isaac, 18, 20, 22, 30, 35
Harper, William, 28
Harper Brothers, 4
Harrington, James, 141
Harris, Tucker, 24
Harrison, Jesse Burton, 150
Harrison, William Primrose, 24
Hart, John S., 303
Hart, Samuel, 32
Hart, Samuel Jr., 34
Harvard, 4, 17, 25, 221, 253
Harvey, James, 24
Hasell, Andrew, 34
Hasell, William Soranzo, 21
Hawthorne, Nathaniel, 33, 195
Hayne, Paul Hamilton, 14, 16, 17, 21, 22, 28, 36, 38, 124, 125, 149, 177, 208, 209
Hayne, Robert Y., 28, 38, 48, 130, 237
Hazzard, William Wigg, 287, 288, 289
Hebremont, N., 291
Heeren, Arnold, 11
Hegel, G.W.F., 33, 143
Heineccius, Johann, 138, 139, 410
Helen of Troy, 326
Hemans, Felicia Dorothea, 364
Henry, Patrick, 220, 340, 341, 342, 343
Henry, Robert, 335
Henry VIII, 181
Hentz, Caroline Lee, 302

Herder, J.G. von, 143
Herodotus, 355
Hewat, Alexander, 23
Heyward, Thomas (elder), 159
Heyward, Thomas (younger), 159
Heyward family, 155, 158
Hindle, Brooke, 50
Historicism, 135–36
Hoar, Samuel, 419
Hoffman, David, 143
Hogarth, William, 352, 449
Holbach, Paul-Henri Thiry, baron d', 396
Holbrook, John, 6, 7, 29
Holland, 50, 98, 129
Holland, Edwin C., 30
Hollinshead, William, 24
Holmes, Francis S., 6, 34
Holmes, George Frederick, 335, 341, 342, 343, 345, 348, 360, 448
Holmes, Isaac, 28, 129, 130, 149, 348, 369
Homer, 145, 148, 219, 346, 355
Hooker, Richard, 162
Horace, 24, 291, 356, 364
Horry, Elias, 240, 241
Hortensius, 112
Horticultural Society, 235–37
Hotman, François, 136
Huger, Alfred, 20, 151
Huger, Daniel Elliott, 27
Huger family, 155, 163, 183
Hugo, Ritter, 138
Hugo, Victor, 302, 410
Huguenots, 20, 125
Hume, David, 33, 60, 67, 141, 143, 148, 218, 340, 345, 359, 395
Hunt, Benjamin F., 29
Hunt, James Henry Leigh, 346
Hurlbut, Stephen Augustus, 34
Hutcheson, Francis, 60
Hutson, Richard, 54, 56
Hutson, William, 156
Hypatia, 326

Ibo, 259
Ibsen, Henrik, 37
Idomeneus, 411
Interpreter, 35
Ioor, William, 27
Irish, 212, 224
Irvine, Matthew, 24
Irving, John Beaufain, 34
Irving, John Beaufain, Jr., 39
Irving, Washington, 33, 35, 329
Isocrates, 447
Italy, 350, 366
Izard, Ralph, 24, 55, 56

Jackson, Andrew, 132, 162, 164, 202, 215, 222, 223, 360
Jackson, Henry, 24
Jacksonianism, 183, 184, 193, 245, 416
Jacobins, 67, 112
Jamaica, 259
James, Henry, x, 37
Jamestown, 203
Jamison, David Flavel, 34
Jay, John, 52
Jay Treaty, 94
Jay-Gardoqui Treaty, 92, 94
Jefferson, Thomas, 52, 55, 78, 79, 96, 97, 215, 220, 223, 227, 330, 395, 400, 448
Jeffersonianism, 86, 87, 89, 95, 101, 102, 107, 109, 110, 111, 112, 114, 116, 183, 215
Jenkins, Ellen, 260
Jenkins, Joseph E., 31, 285–86
Jenkins and Hussey, 431
Jervey, Caroline Howard Gilman, 39
Jervey, Francis Postell, 34
Joan of Arc, 327
Jockey Ball, 297
Johns Hopkins University, 368, 369
John's Island, 127
Johnson, John, 39
Johnson, Joseph, 6, 26, 237
Johnson, Samuel, 18, 24, 408
Johnson, William, 26, 27
Johnston, Edward W., 347
Johnston, William, 409
Jones, Edward C., 34
Jove, 327
Judaism, 20, 30, 31
Jugurthine War, 360
Justinian, 138
Juvenal, 289, 331, 332

Kames, Henry Home, Lord, 60, 143
Kant, Immanuel, 33, 143
Keith, Isaac, 24
Kemble, Fanny, 212, 213
Kemble, Gouverneur, 133
Kennedy, John Pendleton, 131
Kentucky and Virginia Resolutions, 116
Kikongo, 262
Kimbundu, 264
King, Edward, 258
King, Henry C., 308
King, Mitchell, 18, 28, 176, 241
King, Susan Petigru, 39, 182, 298, 301, 308–14
Kingsley, Charles, 302
Kinloch, Alexander, 39
Kinloch, Francis, 24, 67
Knowles, James Sheridan, 330

Ladd, Joseph Brown, 27
Lamartine, Alphonse de, 33
Laocoon, 351
Laurens, Edward R., 288
Laurens, Henry, 24, 55, 56, 67, 68, 73, 78, 288
Laurens, John, 55, 73
Laurens, Martha, 73
Lee, Francis D., 39
Lee, Mary Elizabeth, 34
Lee, Thomas, 242
Legaré, Eliza, 128
Legaré, Hugh Swinton, xii, 19, 20, 22, 28, 29, 35, 36, 38, 40, 41, 55, 84, 123–51, 154, 155, 163, 164, 165, 167, 169, 172, 173, 178, 183, 253, 337–48, 354–61, 364–67, 369, 448
Legaré, James M., 38
Legaré, John D., 30, 280–94
Legaré, Mary (mother of Hugh), 127, 128, 140
Legaré, Mary (sister of Hugh), 124, 125, 128, 130, 140
Legaré, Thomas, 125
Leitner, Edward, 236
Lesesne, Henry D., 174
Leutze, Emanuel, 33
Leyden, 50, 138
Licinia, 333
Lining, John, 50
Linnaeus, Carolus, xi, 23, 51
Linnen, William, 47, 48
Literary World, 195
Liverpool, 40, 226
Livia, 326
Locke, John, 60, 161, 217, 218, 395
Logan, George, 24, 27
Logan, Samuel, 39
London, xi, 5, 17, 22, 25, 40, 54, 83, 128, 141
London Magazine, 24
Longinus, 355, 356, 359
Lost Cause, 149, 313
Louisiana, 36, 258
Louisiana Purchase, 36, 97, 99
Louisville, Cincinnati & Charleston Railroad, 16
Lowndes, William, 18, 28
Lucan, 335
Lucifer, 218
Lucius Crassus, 335
Luther, Martin, 361
Lutherans, 20, 215, 243
Lyell, Sir Charles, 33
Lynch, Patrick, 177

Macadam, John Loudon, 129
Macaulay, Thomas Babington, 33, 448

McBride, James, 29
McCord, Cheves, 325, 326, 336
McCord, Louisa S., xiii, 325–36, 443–44
McCrady, Edward, 28, 39
McCrady, John, 39
McDuffie, George, 126, 157, 164
Machiavelli, Niccolo, 147
Mackey, John, 27
McKie, Thomas Jefferson, 39
Madison, James, 55, 90, 91, 93, 95, 96, 97, 98, 220, 221, 223
Magna Carta, 135, 137
Magnolia, 35, 431
Magnolia Cemetery, 128, 209
Maine Farmer, 280
Manassas, 325, 326, 336
Mandinka, 264
Manfred, 127, 146–47
Mangum, Willie P., 135
Manigault, Gabriel, 24
Manigault, Gabriel E., 39
Manilius, 363
Manly, Basil Sr., 30, 243, 428
Manzoni, Alessandro, 33
Marcus Aurelius, 363
Marcus Curtius, 377
Marion, Francis, 201, 202, 249
Marius, 360
Marlowe, Christopher, 350
Marshall, John, 57, 164, 246
Marx, Karl, 37
Maryland, 110, 284
Maryland Medical School, University of, 244
Massachusetts, 419
Massachusetts Historical Society, 53
Maternus, 344
Mazyck, Arthur, 39
M'Carter, J.J., 431
Medea, 326
Medicine, 79–82
Mellichamp, Joseph Hinson, 39
Memminger, Christopher, 34, 211–29
Memphis, 15
Metellus, 360
Methodists, 23, 30, 243, 270
Mexican War, 33, 36, 221
Meyerbeer, Giacomo, 141
Michel, Richard, 39
Michel, William, 39
Michaux, André, 50
Michelet, Jules, 33
Middleton, Henry, 432
Middleton, John Izard, 22, 28
Middleton, Nathaniel Russell, 34
Middleton, Thomas, 233

Miles, Francis Turquand, 39
Miles, James Warley, 34, 177
Miles, William Porcher, 38, 226, 322, 323, 325, 327
Military College of South Carolina, 9
Mill, James, 33
Miller, A.E., 431
Miller, Mary Boykin, 314
Miller, Stephen, 314
Milligen, George, 23
Mills, Robert, 6, 22, 28, 32
Milman, Henry Hart, 346
Milton, John, 24, 140, 145, 217, 219, 346, 350
Minerva, 327
Mirabeau, Victor Riqueti, 341, 343
Mississippi, 36, 189, 190, 314
Mississippi River, 92
Missouri Compromise, 33, 49, 85, 86, 87, 95, 97, 99, 100, 102, 108, 110, 119
Mitchell, Julian, 39
Mobile, Ala., 15, 16
Moise, Penina, 20, 31
Moltke-Hansen, David, 49, 55, 69, 83
Mommsen, Theodore, 37
Monboddo, James Burnett, Lord, 143
Montesquieu, 60, 137, 161
Montgomery, Ala., 316
Montgomery *Advertiser-Journal*, 215
Monti, Vincenzo, 330
Mood, Francis Asbury, 9
Morford, Edmund, 30
Mormonism, 215
Morse, Jedidiah, 52
Moses, 268
Motte, Jacob De La, 29
Moultrie, James, 29, 176, 248, 429
Muckenfuss, Miss, 236
Muhlenberg, Dr., 432
Muller, Albert, 29
Murden, Eliza, 30
Myalism, 276

Naples, 292
Napoleon, Louis, 360
National Institute, 7
Nationalism, 58–60, 136–38
Navigation Acts, 64
Negro Seamen Acts, 419
Nero, 446
New England, 94, 127, 137, 159, 166, 183, 195, 199
New Orleans, xii, 15, 16, 22, 38, 41, 209, 254, 281
New South, xii, 228

New York, x, xi, xii, 4, 5, 12, 15, 16, 17, 30, 35, 40, 41, 50, 110, 127, 129, 131, 133, 141, 195, 196, 198, 205, 209, 226, 236, 240, 284, 312, 327
New York Farmer, 280
New York *Morning News*, 198
New York *Review*, 128, 131
New York *Times*, 187
Newport, R.I., 127
Niebuhr, Barthold, 136, 138, 143
Nietzsche, Friedrich, 37
Niles' *Weekly Register*, 85
Noble, Patrick, 157
Noisette, Philip, 236
North American Review, 26
North Carolina, 221, 236
Northeastern Railroad, 16
Northwest Ordinance, 161
Norton, Charles Eliot, 37
Nott, Henry Junius, 130
Noyes, John H., 215
Nullification, xii, 13, 33, 87, 116, 131, 132, 160, 162–64, 178, 234, 243, 286, 343, 344, 413

Obeah, 276
O'Brien, Michael (reproved), 445
Ogilvie, George, 23
Ohio, 196
Olympics, 136
Omar, 363
O'Neall, John Belton, 172, 246
Opimius, 329, 334
Orion, 35
Orr, James L., 182

Paine, Thomas, 66, 395
Paley, William, 140
Palmer, Rev. Mr., 48
Paris, 17, 22, 83, 128, 130, 141, 329
Parker, Francis LeJau, 39
Parkman, Francis, 159
Parrington, Vernon, 149
Paul, Saint, 224
Peale, Charles Willson, 53, 72
Pease, Jane, 71
Pease, William, 71
Peirce, Benjamin, 238
Pennsylvania, 65–66, 110, 284
Pennsylvania Academy of Fine Arts, 27
Pennsylvania, University of, 54, 245, 253
Percy, William, 24
Pericles, 327, 342, 343, 345, 365
Perry, Benjamin F., 126, 154, 166, 167, 173, 174, 181, 182

Petrigru, James Louis, 18, 28, 40, 127, 152–85, 237, 308
Pettigrew, J. Johnson, 39, 135, 182, 183
Pettigrew, William, 158
Phaeton, 327
Phidias, 348, 350
Philadelphia, 4, 5, 12, 16, 17, 40, 50, 51, 52, 81, 92, 96, 98, 107, 131, 236, 308, 312, 348
Philadelphia, College of, 49
Phillips, Edward, 34
Philomathean Society, 18
Phocion, 222
Pinckney, Charles III, xii, 9, 24, 55, 56, 78, 83, 85-122
Pinckney, Charles C., 24, 25, 27, 55, 56, 66, 67
Pinckney, Eliza, 67
Pinckney, Henry, 132, 164
Pinckney, Henry Laurens, 28, 30, 39
Pinckney, Henry Laurens Jr., 39
Pinckney, Maria, 27
Pinckney, Thomas, 24, 55, 56, 130, 150, 341
Pineville, S.C., 26, 321
Pitt, William (younger), 148
Plato, 143, 355, 362, 447
Pleiades & Southern Literary Gazette, 431
Plutarch, 329, 333, 337, 347, 360
Poinsett, Joel Roberts, 7, 27, 37, 130, 133, 163, 236
Polk, James K., 48, 203
Pope, Alexander, 26, 146, 179
Pope, J.D., 153
Porcher, Francis Peyre, 39
Porcher, Frederick A., 12, 13, 14, 20, 21, 34, 176, 177, 236, 253, 320, 321, 322, 333, 348-52, 358, 359
Porter, A. Toomer, 39
Porter, William D., 10, 29, 34, 430
Portia, 327
Potter, John, 241
Powers, Hiram, 325, 348, 351
Poyas, Catherine, 34
Poyas, Elizabeth, 30
Poznanski, Gustavus, 34
Presbyterians, 20, 30, 243
Prescott, William, 131
Preston, William Campbell, 124, 125, 126, 128, 134, 148, 150-51, 164, 165, 337, 338, 343, 344, 345, 347, 409, 411
Princeton, 25, 49, 51, 52, 54, 78, 79
Pringle, Edward, 130
Pringle, Elizabeth, 130, 299
Pringle, John Julius, 24, 25, 56
Prioleau, Jacob Ford, 39
Prioleau, Philip, 27
Prioleau, Samuel, 130

Prioleau, Thomas Grimball, 29
Prosser, Gabriel, 277
Prussia, 129
Ptolemy, 363
Puerto Rico, 259
Punic War, First, 141
Pythia, 356

Quakers, 21
Quash, Francis D., 31, 289, 294
Quintilian, 332, 344, 354

Racine, Jean, 339
Rambler, 35
Ramsay, David, xi, xiii, 6, 18, 22, 23, 24, 26, 38, 47-84, 217, 249
Ramsay, James, 244
Randolph, John, 96
Ranke, Leopold von, 33
Raphael, 358
Ravenel, Edmund, 6, 7, 29, 246, 253
Ravenel, Harriott Horry, 39, 295
Ravenel, Henry William, 6
Reconstruction, 174, 187, 228
Redfield, Robert, 42
Reformation, 140, 362
Reid, Thomas, 60, 143, 218
Renan, Ernest, 37
Republicans, 182
Republicans, Radical, 172, 174
Reynolds, James L., 34, 353, 354
Reynolds, Joshua, 18, 327, 351, 352, 357, 358, 449
Reynolds, Thomas Caute, 39
Rhett, Elizabeth, 295
Rhett, Elizabeth Washington Burnet, 295
Rhett, Robert Barnwell, 182, 227
Ribault, Jean, 180
Richardson, Maynard Davis, 34
Richmond, Va., 16, 198, 316, 318, 325
Riga, 50
Riley, W., 431
Rivers, William James, 38, 39, 130, 132, 213
Robertson, William, 60
Robespierre, Maximilien de, 358
Rockville, S.C., 262
Rogers, George C. Jr., xii, 159, 213
Roman Catholicism, 20, 243, 366
Romanticism, 5, 33, 84, 143-48, 190, 219, 297
Rome, 17, 98, 142, 163, 289, 292, 294
Roscius, 337
Rose, Hugh, 23
Rose Bud, 30
Round Hill School, 432
Rousseau, Jean-Jacques, 220, 348, 395

Royal Society, 23, 50, 237
Rush, Benjamin, 49, 51, 53, 54, 65, 72, 73, 78, 79, 80, 81, 394
Ruskin, John, 37
Russell, John, 18, 34, 155, 176–77, 208
Russell, William Howard, 38, 182
Russell's Magazine, 10, 14, 18, 38, 177, 208
Rutledge, Edward, 25, 130, 134
Rutledge, John, 25, 56, 66

St. Andrews Hall, 152
St. Andrews University, 50
St. Cecilia Ball, 152, 297
St. Finbar's Cathedral, 152
St. Helena Agricultural Society, 285
St. John's Colleton, 126
St. Louis, Mo., 41
St. Michael's Church, 30, 155, 175, 306–7
St. Paul's Church, 29, 216
St. Peter's Church, 432
St. Philip's Church, 30, 216
St. Simons Island, 288, 289
St. Thomas Parish, 289
Saint-Domingue, 112
Salic Law, 138
Sallust, 360
Samuel, 192
Santa Anna, Antonio Lopez de, 360
Santee Canal, 15
Sappho, 326
Saratoga Springs, 127, 129
Savannah, Ga., 15
Savannah River, 157–58, 161
Savigny, Friedrich Karl von, 138, 139, 143
Schelling, Friedrich, 143
Schiller, Friedrich, 33
Schlegel, August von, 33, 142, 143, 144–48, 220, 352
Schlegel, Friedrich von, 33, 143, 148
Schoolcraft, Mary Howard, 298
Scipio Aemilianus, 331, 332
Scipio Africanus, 331
Scotland, 50, 129
Scott, Walter, 26, 33, 35, 147, 302, 326, 410
Scottish Enlightenment, 136, 138
Seabrook, Whitemarsh B., 268, 282, 286, 287
Sebring and Burges, 431
Sedgwick, Catherine, 302
Segregation, 229
Selden, John, 137
Self-Instructor, 10
Senior, Nassau, 131
Shakespeare, William, 24, 327, 329, 330, 331, 336, 350
Shecut, J.L.E.W., 6, 27

Shephard, Charles Upham, 34
Shephard, Thomas R., 27, 30
Shippen, William, 79
Sidney, Sir Philip, 352
Sigourney, Lydia, 302
Simmons, James Wright, 22, 30, 35
Simmons, William Hayne, 29, 30
Simms, Harriet, 188
Simms, William Gilmore, x, xii, xiii, 3, 4, 7, 8, 10, 13, 14, 15, 16, 17, 18, 19, 21, 22, 34, 36, 43, 55, 124, 149, 177, 186–210, 237, 238, 253
Simms, William Gilmore (father), 188
Simms's Magazine, 198
Simons, Benjamin, 47
Simons, Benjamin Bonneau, 27
Simons, Keating, 27
Simons, Thomas Y., 29, 246
Singer, Milton, 42
Sismondi, J.C.L., 33, 147
Sisyphus, 327
Slavery, ix, xi, 7, 8, 12, 70–78, 85–86, 87, 88, 90, 97–99, 100, 108, 161, 223–24, 255–78, 287, 292
Smallpox, 79
Smith, Adam, 147, 148
Smith, J. Lawrence, 34
Smith, John, 201, 203
Smith, Joseph Allen, 22, 27
Smith, Robert, 30
Smith, Samuel Stanhope, 52
Smith, William, 126
Smith, William Wragg, 34, 249
Smollett, Tobias, 26
Smyth, Thomas, 34, 177, 428
Snowden, Charles, 18
Society for Political Inquiries, 53
Society for the Propagation of the Gospel, 10
Socrates, 258
Sophocles, 291, 348, 357, 365
South Carolina, Bank of, 126, 222, 249
South Carolina, Medical College of, 239, 291–92
South Carolina Academy of Fine Arts, 7, 9, 238
South Carolina Agricultural Society, 235–37, 280, 288
South Carolina College, 29, 124, 125, 127, 136, 154, 158, 178, 179, 214, 217, 218, 239, 244
South Carolina *Gazette,* 30, 63
South Carolina Historical Society, 9, 155, 176, 179
South Carolina Institute, 9, 10, 153
South Carolina Medical Society, 243–49
South Carolina Society, 251

South Carolina Society Academy, 9
Southern Agriculturist, 10, 30, 279–94, 431
Southern Baptist and General Intelligencer, 431
Southern Cabinet, 293
Southern Christian Advocate, 29, 34
Southern Christian Intelligencer, 29
Southern Christian Sentinel, 34
Southern Literary Gazette, 35
Southern Literary Journal, 6, 35, 196
Southern Literary Messenger, 141, 198, 203, 369
Southern Patriot, 30, 201
Southern Planter, 431
Southern Quarterly Review, 8, 30, 35, 38, 196, 198, 203, 209, 328, 329, 337, 431
Southern Review, xii, 28, 30, 41, 126, 127, 128, 131, 169, 343, 364, 431
Southern Rose, 431
Southey, Robert, 26
Southworth, E.D.E.N., 302
Spa, 129
Spain, 92, 340, 350, 366
Sparks, Jared, 131
Spartanburg-Asheville Railroad, 228
Spenser, Edmund, 350
Staël, Madame de, 144, 302
Stair, Lord, 138
Steele, Richard, 26
Stephens, Alexander H., 158
Stevens, Charles, 14
Stewart, Dugald, 138, 143, 148
Story, Joseph, 139
Stowe, Harriet Beecher, 302
Strobel, Benjamin R., 34
Strobel, William Daniel, 34
Stuart, John A., 34
Sub-Treasury, 130, 132, 164, 165
Sue, Eugéne, 33
Suetonius, 135
Sullivan, James, 52
Sullivan's Island, 26, 149, 205, 300
Sumner, George, 195
Supreme Court, 128
Surinam, 259
Sweden, 50
Swift, Jonathan, 26, 179

Tabor, William R., 177
Tacitus, 48, 135, 332, 335, 344, 369
Talvande, Madame, 298, 299, 300, 308, 314
Tasistro, Louis, 18, 19
Taylor, John, 96
Taylor, Zachary, 166, 360
Tchaikovski, Peter I., 37
Tennent, William, III, 54
Tennessee, 36

Tennessee Farmer, 280
Tennyson, Alfred Lord, 33
Terentianus, 355
Terrasson, Abbé, 136
Texas, 30
Thackeray, William Makepeace, 33, 302
Thais, 326
Tharin, Robert, 24
Théâtre Français, 136
Themistocles, 351
Theophilus, 138
Thomas, Ebenezer Smith, 30
Thomas, John Peyre, 39
Thomas, Theodore, 39
Thompson, Waddy, 134, 150, 164, 165
Thomson, James Hampden, 54
Thornwell, James Henley, 268, 335
Thucydides, 197, 335, 339, 355, 365
Ticknor, George, 131
Ticknor and Fields, 4
Tidyman, Philip, 6, 27
Tillotson, John, 24
Timrod, Henry, 15, 17, 18, 19, 38, 177
Timrod, William Henry, 20, 30
Togno, Madame, 298
Tolstoy, Leo, 37
Toombs, Robert A., 158
Toomer, Joshua, 130
Townsend, John, 31
Trapier, Paul, 34, 270
Trapier, Richard, 34
Trenchard, John, 63
Trent, William P., 124, 125, 187, 408
Trescot, William Henry, 14, 22, 39
Trollope, Anthony, 33, 302
Troubadours, 148
Tübingen, 236
Tucker, Thomas Tudor, 24, 67
Tuomey, Michael, 6
Tupper, Henry Allen, 39
Turnbull, Robert, 27
Turner, Frederick Jackson, 5
Turner, Nat, 277, 286
Twain, Mark, 37
Tyler, John, 127, 132

Ulpian, 138
Unionists, 132, 162, 163
Unitarians, 242, 243
United States Catholic Miscellany, 29
Universal Magazine, 24

Valenciennes, Achille, 7
Van Brunt, E.J., 431
Van Burne, Martin, 130, 132, 164
Vaux Hall, 26

Venice, 149, 447
Verdi, Giuseppe, 37
Vergil, 24, 143, 145, 291, 294, 346
Vesey, Denmark, 33, 234, 276, 277, 288
Victoria, Queen, 32
Victorianism, xii, 4
Virgilia, 331
Virgin Islands, 259
Virginia, 36, 91, 94, 95, 97, 107, 108, 119, 127, 132, 224, 286, 293
Virginia, University of, 368
Vodun, 276
Voltaire, 26, 395, 396
Volumnia, 331
Voodoo, 274

Waddell, Moses, 154, 157, 432
Wade, John Donald, 408
Wagner, John, 29, 244
Wagner, Richard, 37
Walker, William Aiken, 39
Walter, Thomas, 6, 24
Walterboro, S.C., 281
War of 1812, 91, 96
Waring, Jennings, 130
Warner, Susan, 302
Warren, John, 79
Warren, Mercy Otis, 57
Washington, George, 10, 157, 220, 350
Washington, D.C., 22, 127, 128, 129, 316, 317
Washington Race Course, 26
Washington Society, 249
Webster, Daniel, 160
Webster, Noah, 52, 53, 56
Weems, Parson, 199
Wells, Helena, 12
Wells, Robert, 23
Wells, William Charles, 23
Wesleyan Journal, 29
West, Benjamin, 331, 351
West, American, 15, 19, 32, 36, 92, 94, 95, 97, 99, 100, 189, 196, 201, 221
West Indies, 74, 273, 276
Weston, Plowden, 34
Whately, Richard, 354
Whigs, 51, 52, 55, 63, 66, 67, 78, 79, 119, 127, 165, 166, 175, 180, 182, 217

Whitaker, Daniel K., 8, 17, 22, 34, 38, 238
Whitaker, Mary, 38
Whitaker's Magazine, 35
White, Edward Brickell, 34
White, John Blake, 28, 32, 238
White, Octavius Augustus, 39
White, Thomas W., 141
White Sulphur Springs, 127
Whitefield, George, 67
Whitman, Walt, 37
Whitridge, Joshua, 29
Whydah, 273
Wightman, William, 34
Wilkinson, Mary, 214
Williams, Raymond, 320
Williamson, Hugh, 52
Willington Academy, 125, 154, 157, 158, 432
Wilmot Proviso, 227
Wilson, Clyde, 183
Wilson, John Lyde, 28, 168, 169, 173
Wilson, Robert, 27
Wilson, Samuel, 27
Winckelmann, Johann J., 356–57
Winkler, Edwin T., 39
Witenagemot, 138
Witherspoon, John, 52
Women, ix, 8, 295–324
Woodward, C. Vann, 212
Wordsworth, William, 26, 33, 143, 150, 351, 411
Wurdeman, J.G.F., 34
Wurtemberg, 214, 215
Wyatt-Brown, Bertram, 184

Xenophon, 355

Yale College, 17, 21, 25, 245
Yale Report of 1828, 366–67
Yellow fever, 80, 81, 82
Yoruba, 259, 262, 264, 269, 273
Young, Edward, 34
Young America, 35, 194, 195, 198

Zama, 331
Zeus, 368
Ziff, Larzer, 187

Intellectual Life in Antebellum Charleston was set into type on the Compu-graphic digital phototypesetter in eleven point Goudy Old Style with two points of spacing between the lines. Goudy Old Style Italic was selected for display. The book was designed by Frank O. Williams, com-posed by Metricomp, Inc., printed offset by Thomson-Shore, Inc., and bound by John H. Dekker & Sons. The paper on which the book is printed bears acid-free characteristics for an effective life of at least three hundred years.

The University of Tennessee Press : Knoxville

DATE DUE